LET'S GO:
PACIFIC NORTHWEST, WESTERN CANADA & ALASKA

is the best book for anyone traveling on a budget. Here's why:

No other guidebook has as many budget listings.

We list 44 restaurants in Seattle; at most of these you can eat a filling meal for around $4. We tell you how to get there the cheapest way, whether by bus, plane, or thumb, and where to get an inexpensive and satisfying meal once you've arrived. There are hundreds of money-saving tips for everyone plus lots of information on student discounts.

LET'S GO researchers have to make it on their own.

Our Harvard-Radcliffe researchers travel on budgets as tight as your own—no expense accounts, no free hotel rooms.

LET'S GO is completely revised every year.

We don't just update the prices, we go back to the places. If a charming restaurant has become an overpriced tourist trap, we'll replace the listing with a new and better one.

No other budget guidebook includes all this:

Coverage of both the cities and the countryside; directions, addresses, phone numbers, and hours to get you there and back; in-depth information on culture, history, and the people; transportation between and within regions and cities; tips on work, study, sights, nightlife, and special splurges; city and regional maps; and much, much more.

LET'S GO is for anyone who wants to see The Pacific Northwest, Western Canada & Alaska on a budget.

About Let's Go

In 1960, Harvard Student Agencies, a three-year-old nonprofit corporation established to provide employment opportunities to Harvard and Radcliffe students, was doing a booming business selling charter flights to Europe. One of the extras HSA offered passengers on these flights was a 20-page mimeographed pamphlet entitled *1960 European Guide,* a collection of tips on continental travel compiled by the staff at HSA. The following year, students traveling to Europe researched the first full-fledged edition of *Let's Go: Europe,* a pocket-sized book with a smattering of tips on budget accommodations, irreverent write-ups of sights, and a decidedly youthful slant. The first editions proclaimed themselves to be the helpmates of the "adventurous and often impecunious student."

Throughout the 60s, the series reflected its era: a section of the 1968 *Let's Go: Europe* was entitled "Street Singing in Europe on No Dollars a Day"; the 1969 guide to America led off with a feature on drug-ridden Haight-Ashbury. During the 70s, *Let's Go* gradually became a large-scale operation, adding regional European guides and expanding coverage into North Africa and Asia. In 1981, *Let's Go: USA* returned after an eight-year hiatus, and in the next year HSA joined forces with its current publisher, St. Martin's Press. Now in its 30th year, *Let's Go* publishes 11 titles covering more than 40 countries.

Each spring, over 150 Harvard/Radcliffe students compete for some 70 positions as *Let's Go* researcher/writers. Those hired possess a rare combination of budget travel sense, writing ability, stamina, and courage. Each researcher/writer travels on a shoestring budget for seven weeks, researching seven days per week, and overcoming countless obstacles in the endless quest for better bargains.

Back in a basement in Harvard Yard, an editorial staff of 28 and countless typists and proofreaders spend four months poring over more than 50,000 pages of manuscript as they push the copy through 12 stages of intensive editing. In September the efforts of summer are converted from computer diskettes to nine-track tapes and delivered to Com Com in Allentown, Pennsylvania, where their computerized typesetting equipment turns them into books in record time. And even before the books hit the stands, next year's editions are well underway.

LET'S GO:

The Budget Guide to

PACIFIC NORTHWEST, WESTERN CANADA, and ALASKA

(INCLUDING ALBERTA and BRITISH COLUMBIA)

1990

Alexander B. Star
Editor

Jonathan Savett
Assistant Editor

Written by Harvard Student Agencies, Inc.

**ST. MARTIN'S PRESS
NEW YORK**

Helping Let's Go

If you have suggestions or corrections, or just want to share your discoveries, drop us a line. We read every piece of correspondence, whether a 10-page letter, a postcard, or, as in one case, a collage. All suggestions are passed along to our researcher/writers. Please note that mail received after June 1, 1990 will probably be too late for the 1991 book, but will be retained for the following edition. Address mail to: Let's Go: Pacific Northwest, Western Canada, and Alaska; Harvard Student Agencies, Inc.; Thayer Hall-B; Harvard University; Cambridge, MA 02138; USA.

In addition to the invaluable travel advice our readers share with us, many are kind enough to offer their services as researchers. Unfortunately, the charter of Harvard Student Agencies, Inc. enables us to employ only currently enrolled Harvard students both as researchers and editorial staff.

Maps by David Lindroth, copyright © 1990, 1988 by St. Martin's Press, Inc.

Distributed outside the U.S. and Canada by Pan Books Ltd.

ISBN: 0-312-03383-4

First Edition
10 9 8 7 6 5 4 3 2 1

Let's Go: Pacific Northwest, Western Canada & Alaska is written by Harvard Student Agencies, Inc., Harvard University, Thayer Hall-B, Cambridge, Mass. 02138.

Editor	Alexander B. Star
Assistant Editor	Jonathan Savett
Publishing Manager	Nathanael Joe Hayashi
Managing Editors	Allen R. Barton
	Helen McCracken Gould
	Alex MacC. Ross
Production/Communication Coordinator	Karen L. Thompson

Researcher/Writers

Portland & Salem, OR; Mt. Rainier, Olympic Peninsula, Puget Sound (except Olympia and Tacoma), Skagit Valley & Northern Cascades, WA; Vancouver Island, Vancouver, and Northern British Columbia and the Yukon, BC — Chris Cowell

Alberta; Okanagan Valley & Revelstoke, BC; Leavenworth, Wenatchee, and Eastern Washington (except Walla Walla and Pullman), WA — Jamie Rosen

Oregon (except Portland and Salem); Seattle, Olympia, Tacoma, Southwest Washington, Cowlitz Valley, Mt. St. Helens, Pullman, and Walla Walla, WA — Elijah Siegler

Alaska — David Schisgall

Advertising Manager	David A. Kopp
Advertising Representatives	Kathryn L. Cahir
	Anthony P. Denninger
	Suzanne J. Kohl
Legal Counsel	Posternak, Blankstein, and Lund

ACKNOWLEDGMENTS

I'll never know what benevolent spirit allowed me to edit this book with two people as talented and interesting as Jon Savett and Alex Ross. Jon's excellent General Introduction and terrifyingly flawless proofreading would have made him a superlative assistant editor by themselves; as it was, he did much more. Jon turned carefully over every page of the book, detecting hidden inconsistencies and misleading implications. Best of all, he always had a fresh metaphor or word available when the writing seemed awkward or stale. Jon's good conversation and high standards kept me alert. More than anyone else, the merits of this book owe to his perseverance and creativity.

"Managing Decorator" Alex Ross splashed his eloquence and humor all over the place. Not a single dull description or insipid introduction was safe from his verbal designs. An amazing number of the verbs in these pages sprang fully conjugated from his mind. Like Lord Tennyson, Alex seemed to know the exact value of every combination of sounds in the English language except "scissors." Unlike Tennyson, Alex had a taste for the absurd and a precise knowledge of human history from the slingshot to the atom bomb. Besides being a good friend, Alex was an ideal editor—Maxwell Perkins, William Shawn, and Tristan Tzara rolled into one.

Of course, none of this editorial assistance would have meant anything were it not for the work of the researchers themselves. While riding Greyhound buses through Oregon and Washington, Elijah Siegler found time to shoot a movie, impersonate John Lurie, and sell hot dogs. The weekly installments of his serial novel will be missed. Chris Cowell traveled to the farthest ends of the *Let's Go* universe, sending back meticulous research, perverse fish photos, and a coconut or two as he went. Jamie Rosen made his way through two provinces and one state without ever falling behind his itinerary. He was so taken with his trip that when it was over he decided to head back to Alberta, perhaps to begin it again. David Schisgall invaded Alaska with high spirits and enthusiasm. His pungent writing and aggressive curiosity improved the section immensely.

Back in Cambridge, many people made life in the *Let's Go* basement more bearable. Travel titan Joe Hayashi made us feel confident and comfortable with his warmth and good humor. Helen Gould added a lot of insight to the Portland section, and generally helped me tell one end of the Pacific Northwest from the other. Emily Mieras and Alex Tyler were great to have nearby; partly because they let me ramble on about the glories of Greece whenever I so chose. Debbie Benor was also excellent company; only together could we keep the Perry Como and De La Soul emanating from the other side of the office to a low volume when we needed to concentrate. Mallay Charters was always involved in making wise decisions on the size and shape of the North American coverage. All of the other editors deserve thanks as well: Vladimir Perlovich for his 100-proof brownies and a few odd rhymes, Ravi Desai for the tea and the books cluttered on his desk; also Pete Deemer, Jeff Richter, Erika Forbes, and Greg Schmergel. Former editor Jay Dickson was a readily available source of advice and calm.

Several friends put up with me during the summer, despite my inability to understand them when they spoke sentences that weren't in *Let's Go* format. Among them were Jesse Peretz, John Plotz, Johnathan Bolton, Ivan Krielkamp, and Paul Stein. Although he was on the other side of the world, Nicholas Butterworth, the greatest traveler I know, was usually in my mind.

When I think back a little while, I remember a few things that sparked my interest in the Pacific Northwest: Jack Nicholson's performance in *Five Easy Pieces,* John McPhee's book *Coming into the Country,* and the humble music of the band Beat Happening. Without these somewhat arbitrary reference points, I wouldn't have known where I was.

Finally, I'd like to thank my brother Anthony, my mother, and most of all, my father for their friendship and support and for showing me how to deal courageously and gracefully with challenges compared to which no travel guide is worth anything at all.

—Alexander

So I got this job because Minnesota is closer to Alaska than Boston, New York, and the other places most Harvard students come from, but the story begins much earlier. Somewhere in the depths of my very first memories there are two pictures, one of a house in Seattle where my cousins lived and one of my great-aunt in Vancouver—the only visuals left from my only visit to the Pacific Northwest, back when I was about five. During the three summers before this one, I worked appropriately enough at the Northwest Area Foundation at home, and the region began to take shape in my mind as a collection of economies and governments, universities and social service providers. Now, even though I still have to look at maps to get my bearings, I feel as though I've been to the Northwest—met the people, seen the waters, heard what they're proud of.

During my armchair journey through an area that would snarf down the first Hellenistic empire and still have room for dessert, I had the honor to tag along with two literary Alexanders the Great. Alex Star skillfully erased the line between world travel and world-view, awing me with his command of literature and cultural analysis and somehow making it ever so reasonable to find such heady things in fields and atop mountains. Alex was also the perfect boss, one who knew that working relationships can be friendships as well; I enjoyed just sitting and talking with him a great deal. If the English speakers of the world were a bestiary, Alex Ross would most certainly be an otter—his humor and mind-thesaurus made this book a pleasure for me to read so many times over. By the time it was done, we could each think the others' verbal thoughts—and thus if Paul Simon, Lionel Trilling, and Kirby Puckett were ever to form a book club, the first thing they'd read together would be *Let's Go: Pacific Northwest.* My hat is tipped as well to the researchers, to Joe and Helen for their kind manner and cool heads, and to Salil for his friendly chatter.

This was my most wonderful summer yet, and several of the people who made it so mean more to me than I can possibly tell them in words. I treasured the time I got to spend together and individually with my "crowd": Jon Kolodny, Michael Goldhaber, and Mia Diamond. There were a couple others whom I regret not spending more time with, Kevin Malisani and Tova Perlmutter; and one who was always just a phone call away, Danny Nevins. Mom and Dad, though we must spend so much time apart you are always deep inside of me and in all the good I do, and your friendship is my most precious treasure. I dedicate my part in this book to Grandma; though you didn't live to see what I'm becoming, I somehow think you know and are proud. Which brings me finally to the love and admiration I cannot possibly express for the three most important people of my summer. For my sister Ellen, whose talents and caring have already begun to touch the world. For my roommate Josh Lee, whose life of right, goodness, honesty, and friendship I hope to emulate. And more than anyone else, for Laurie Spira—you are all things beautiful and true, and your presence lights my every step and warms my every moment.

—Jon

Get Away From It All
The Pacific Northwest

American Youth Hostels has a network of hostels near scenic beaches, majestic mountains, raging rivers, unspoiled forests and friendly cities throughout the Pacific Northwest. For more information on AYH hostels, contact the AYH Councils listed below:

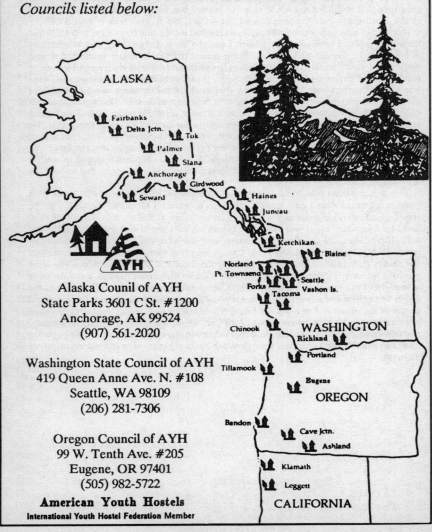

ALASKA

Fairbanks
Delta Jctn.
Tok
Palmer
Slana
Anchorage
Girdwood
Seward
Haines
Juneau
Ketchikan
Blaine
Norland
Pt. Townsend
Seattle
Forks
Tacoma
Vashon Is.
Chinook
WASHINGTON
Richland
Portland
Tillamook
Eugene
OREGON
Bandon
Cave Jctn.
Ashland
Klamath
Leggett
CALIFORNIA

Alaska Counil of AYH
State Parks 3601 C St. #1200
Anchorage, AK 99524
(907) 561-2020

Washington State Council of AYH
419 Queen Anne Ave. N. #108
Seattle, WA 98109
(206) 281-7306

Oregon Council of AYH
99 W. Tenth Ave. #205
Eugene, OR 97401
(505) 982-5722

American Youth Hostels
International Youth Hostel Federation Member

CONTENTS

x   **Contents**

LET'S GO: PACIFIC NORTHWEST, WESTERN CANADA, AND ALASKA

GENERAL INTRODUCTION

To travel through the continent's Great Northwest is to see the story of the world's history unfolding before you in living color. Primeval splendor, small-town community, and modern technology present themselves in turn. They nuzzle right up to one another: the mountains keep a watchful eye on the skyscrapers, the apple orchards view the freeways with suspicion, the technopolis stares back with confidence. Far from national centers of power, these representatives of the earth's ages jostle on even terms.

Climb the mountains of Alaska and hike through the majestic parks of Alberta, where time is still measured in eras and epochs. Stop over in the small towns of Washington and Oregon, where the frontier spirit still holds on in the face of commercial revolution. Live it up in the cities of Seattle, Portland, and Vancouver, whose faces look toward the Pacific and to the future. In this living chronicle of the earth, there is inscribed a wide range of culture and activity. Journey to the tiny town of Ashland, Oregon, and see the months-long Shakespeare Festival in progress. Listen to a festival of jazz in Portland as Mt. Hood arches over, approvingly. If you like your fun a little rough, go to Pendleton, Oregon, for the annual Round-Up, or to Calgary for the Stampede. Lose yourself in the largest shopping mall in the world—nay, the universe—in Edmonton. And don't forget to sample the fresh fruits, fish, and vegetables at every point along your way.

You can experience the pages of the picturebook and make it your own without decimating your bank account. *Let's Go: The Pacific Northwest, Western Canada, and Alaska* is written especially for the budget traveler. Researchers travel on a shoestring budget, and their concerns are the same as yours: how to get from place to place, fill their stomachs, drink in the sights, enjoy the evenings, and get some sleep, all in the most economical way possible. Their numerous tips on how to experience more while spending less, and their honest appraisals of everything from hostels to hamburgers, will give you the freedom to experience the Northwest without getting bogged down in humdrum logisitics.

The **General Introduction** provides useful and vital information that you will need to know before you leave. **Planning Your Trip** contains a slew of details organized as a checklist: where to write for information about the region, how and what to pack, how to maintain your supply of money, and how to stay safe and healthy. **Getting There and Getting Around** sorts out the various modes of transportation to and around the region. **Accommodations** covers everything from cheap motels to youth hostels to bed and breakfasts. **Camping and the Outdoors** discusses the various systems of parks in the region, and provides detailed information for those interested in camping, hiking, and biking. **Life in the Northwest** details the history of the area and its culture, art, and climate. **For International Visitors** is a guide to visas, customs, inexpensive transportation to the Northwest from around the world, foreign exchange, and the postal and telephone systems in the U.S. and Canada.

1

State, provincial, regional and city introductions acquaint you with both the layout and the ambience of the area. Following these introductions are sections on **Practical Information**, listing such crucial resources and information as tourist centers, emergency numbers and crisis hotlines, local and intercity transport, post offices, and telephone area codes. Sections on Getting There and Getting Around, Accommodations, and Food help you get oriented, moved around, settled, and fed. *Let's Go* lets you in on the most affordable entertainment and restaurants, and we point you toward the unique, the characteristic, the splendid, and the awe-inspiring wherever you go.

Keep in mind, though, that although the last explorers trekked this way years ago, not all has been discovered in the Great Northwest. Always keep an eye out for attractions and options that *Let's Go* doesn't list, and follow your spirit and your imagination. Despite our efforts to provide up-to-date and accurate information, things may have changed since we researched them—prices may have gone up, a business may have closed or opened, or public hours may have changed. Be sure to check other sources; the tourist bureaus of states, provinces, and regions can always provide detailed, updated information. And remember to call ahead!

If you intend to travel to other parts of North America as well, consult *Let's Go: USA* (which includes substantial coverage of Canada), *Let's Go: California and Hawaii,* and *Let's Go: Mexico.*

Enjoy your trip!

Planning Your Trip

Planning ahead is one of the keys to an enjoyable, neurosis-free vacation. Spend the time now rather than later getting in touch with travel resources in the region and figuring out how to handle the basic issues: when to go, how to have enough money on hand, how to stay in good health, and a variety of other concerns small or large. Set aside a few hours well before your trip to make calls and write letters to organizations with useful information, and to compile lists of things to consider and bring along. It'll save you time once you hit the road and will help you take the more unusual situations in stride.

One general resource worth writing to is the **U.S. Government Printing Office.** Among the government's many publications are a wide variety concerning travel and recreation. *Let's Go* lists many of the most useful, but you can call or write for complete bibliographies. Bibliography #17 deals with outdoor activities in general, and #302 with travel to particular regions. To receive free bibliographies or to order a specific publication, write or call the Superintendent of Documents, U.S. Government Printing Office, Washington, DC 20402 (202-783-3238).

When To Go

Traveling is like comedy—timing is everything. In the Pacific Northwest, your twin concerns will be the tourist season and the weather. In general, summer (June-Aug.) is high season; during those months, you can expect to share the warm weather with crowds of fellow tourists. If you prefer to experience the region as its human and animal residents do, go during the off-season, when crowds are smaller and rates are lower. Beware the disadvantages of winter travel in certain parts, however: slush, icy roads, and miserably cold weather will constrain your movement and outdoorsmanship. All things considered, May and September may be the best times to travel in the Northwest. See Climate below for details about the weather in different regions.Official Holidays

Keep in mind the following dates when you plan your vacation. Government agencies, post offices, and banks are closed on certain holidays, and businesses may have special (shorter) hours. Many holidays are the occasions for parades and public celebrations. These are the dates for 1990:

New Year's Day: Mon., Jan. 1

Martin Luther King Jr.'s Birthday: Mon., Jan. 15 (U.S. only)

Presidents' Day: Mon., Feb. 19 (U.S. only)

Good Friday: Fri., Apr. 13

Easter: Sun., Apr. 15 (next day also a holiday in Canada)

Victoria Day: Mon., May 21 (Canada only)

Memorial Day: Mon., May 28 (U.S. only)

Canada Day: Sun., July 1 (Canada only)

Independence Day: Wed., July 4 (U.S. only)

British Columbia Day: Mon., Aug. 6 (BC only)

Civic Day: Mon., Aug. 6 (Alberta only)

Discovery Day: Fri., Aug. 17 (Yukon only)

Labor Day: Mon., Sept. 3

Thanksgiving Day: Mon., Oct. 8 (Canada only)

Columbus Day: Mon., Oct. 8 (U.S. only)

Alaska Day: Thurs., Oct. 18 (Alaska only)

Veterans Day (U.S.)/Remembrance Day (Canada): Sun., Nov. 11

Thanksgiving Day: Thurs., Nov. 22 (U.S. only)

Christmas Day: Tues., Dec. 25

Boxing Day: Wed., Dec. 26 (Canada except Yukon)

Tourism Bureaus

Each state and province has its own travel bureau, which can refer you to other useful organizations, send you travel brochures, and answer your specific questions about the region.

Travel Alberta, Box 2500, Edmonton, AB T5J 2Z4 (800-661-8888; within AB, 800-222-6501).

Alaska Division of Tourism, P.O. Box E, Juneau, AK 99811 (907-465-2010).

Tourism British Columbia,, 1117 Wharf St., Victoria, BC V8W 2Z2 (604-387-1642).

Oregon Tourism Division, Dept. of Economic Development, 595 Cottage St. NE, Salem, OR 97310 (800-547-7842; in OR, 800-543-8838).

Washington Tourism Division, Dept. of Trade and Economic Development, 101 General Administration Bldg., Olympia, WA 98504-0613 (800-544-1800 for free travel booklet; 206-586-2088 for general information).

Tourism Yukon, P.O. Box 2703, Whitehorse, YT Y1A 2C6 (403-667-5340).

Student Travel

Students are often entitled to special discounts on admission prices, hotel and car rental rates, and airfares. Most places accept a current university ID or an **International Student Identity Card (ISIC)** as sufficient proof of student status. You can obtain an ISIC card from the student travel office of your university (if it has one) or else from one of the organizations listed below. When you apply for an ISIC, be sure to have up-to-date proof of full-time student status, a vending-machine photograph with your name printed in pencil on the back, and proof of your birthdate and nationality. In some places a university ID is enough to demonstrate student status, while in others an official school document is necessary. The ISIC card is good until the end of the calendar year in which it is issued. Students must be at least 12 years old to be eligible. Non-students of student age should look into the **Federation of International Youth Travel Organizations (FIYTO)** card, which may help you take advantage of discounts on the basis of age.

The following agencies specialize in travel for high school and university students. They sell ISIC cards and have tips on transportation discounts. For listings of similar organizations that serve foreign travelers, see For International Visitors.

> **Council on International Educational Exchange (CIEE) Travel Services:** Advice on questions ranging from package tours and low-cost travel to work opportunities and long-distance hiking. Special academic and employment exchange programs (see Work, Study, and Information Organizations). ISIC and FIYTO cards. Ask for the annual *Student Travel Catalog.* For more information, contact any one of these offices:
>
> **Atlanta:**12 Park Pl. S., #12, GA 30303 (404-577-1678)
> **Boston:** 729 Boylston St., #210, MA 02116 (617-266-1926).
> **Chicago:** 29 E. Delaware Place, IL 60611 (312-951-0585).
> **Dallas:** 3300 W. Mockingbird Lane, #101, TX 75235 (214-350-6166).
> **Los Angeles:** 1093 Broxton Ave., #220, CA 90024 (213-208-3551).
> **Minneapolis:** 1501 University Ave. SE, #300, MN 55414 (612-379-2323).
> **New York:** 205 E. 42nd St., New York, NY 10017 (800-223-7402 or 212-661-1450). One of 3 offices in NYC.
> **Portland:** 715 SW Morrison, #600, OR 97205 (503-228-1900).
> **San Francisco:** 919 Irving St., CA 94122 (415-566-6222). One of 2 offices in SF.
> **Seattle:** 1314 NE 43rd St., #210, Seattle, WA 98105 (206-632-2448).
>
> Write or call the NY office for general information and for the address and phone of an office closer to you; there are several in California and Massachusetts as well as branches in Austin, TX, and Providence, RI.
>
> **Let's Go Travel Services,** Harvard Student Agencies, Inc., Thayer Hall-B, Harvard University, Cambridge, MA 02138 (tel. (617) 495-9649 or (800) 5-LETS-GO). Managed by the same Harvard students who wrote these books. Sells Railpasses, American Youth Hostel memberships (valid at all IYHF youth hostels), International Student and Teacher I.D. cards, YIEE cards for nonstudents, travel guides and maps (including the *Let's Go* series), discount airfares and a complete line of budget travel gear. All items are available by mail.
>
> **Educational Travel Center (ETC):** 438 N. Frances St., Madison, WI 53703 (608-256-5551). AYH membership cards, flight information. Write or call for their free travel pamphlet, *Taking Off.*
>
> **Travel CUTS (Canadian Universities Travel Service, Ltd.):** 44 George St., Toronto, Ont. M5S 2E4 (416-979-2406). Canadian distributor of the ISIC, FIYTO, and IYHF cards. Discounts on domestic and international flights. Canadian Wilderness trips. Write for address and phone of branches in Burnaby, Calgary, Edmonton, Halifax, Montreal, Ottawa, Quebec, Saskatoon, Sudbury, Victoria, Waterloo, Winnipeg, and London.

Money

The best things in life are free. Inferior things abound, of course, and they all cost money. Your budget will be just that: a plan and a projection of how much you will spend. Overruns are to be expected. (This may be the only thing the budget traveler and the Federal government have in common.)

No matter how low your budget, if you plan to travel for more than a couple of days you will need to keep handy a much larger amount of cash than usual. Carrying it around, even in a money belt, is risky; personal checks from home may not be acceptable no matter how many forms of ID you carry (even banks may shy away). Inevitably you will have to rely on some combination of the innovations of the modern financial world. In addition, if you will be traveling between the U.S. and Canada, remember that a Canadian dollar and a U.S. dollar are identical in name only, and you will have to convert between them.

Traveler's Checks

Traveler's checks are the safest way to carry large sums of money. Most tourist establishments will accept them and most any bank will cash them. Usually banks sell traveler's checks for a 1% commission, although your own bank may waive the surcharge if you have a large enough balance or a certain type of account. In addition, certain travel organizations, such as the American Auto Association (AAA), offer commission-free traveler's checks to their members. Try to purchase traveler's checks in small denominations ($20 is best, never larger than $50)—otherwise, a small-to-medium purchase and you're back to carrying a large amount of cash. If the bank doesn't have small denominations available, try a larger institution or come back another day.

Always keep the receipts from the purchase of your traveler's checks, a list of their serial numbers, and a record of which ones you've cashed. Keep these in a separate pocket or pouch from the checks themselves, since they contain the information you will need to replace your checks if they are stolen.

American Express traveler's checks are perhaps the most widely recognized in the world, and the easiest to replace if lost or stolen. Other well-known banks also market traveler's checks. Call any of the toll-free numbers below to find out the advantages of a particular type of check and the name of a bank near you that sells them.

American Express: 800-221-7282 in U.S and Canada. From abroad, call their office in Brighton, Great Britain at (44) 273 57 16 00; from most countries this is toll-free, otherwise call collect.

Bank of America: 800-227-3460 in U.S.; from Canada and abroad, call collect 415-624-5400. Checks in US$ only. Free in CA. Checkholders may use the Travel Assistance hotline (800-368-7878 from U.S., 202-347-7113 collect from Canada), which provides free legal assistance, urgent message relay, lost document services, and up to $1000 advance for prompt medical treatment.

Barclay's: 800-221-2426 in U.S.; from Canada and abroad, call collect 415-574-7111. Connected with Visa. Checks issued in US$ in Canada and U.S., CDN$ as well in Canada. Any branch will cash Barclay's checks free Mon.-Fri.; surcharge on Sat.

Citicorp: 800-645-6556 in U.S and Canada; from abroad, call collect 813-623-1709. Checks in US$. Checkholders enrolled automatically in Travel Assist Hotline (800-523-1199) for 45 days after purchase.

Thomas Cook: 800-223-7373; from Canada and abroad, call collect 212-974-5696. Available at any bank displaying a Mastercard sign.

Visa: 800-227-6811 in U.S. and Canada; from abroad, call collect 415-574-7111 (San Franisco) or (01) 937 80 91 (London). No commission if purchased at Barclay's.

Credit Cards

Most places mentioned in *Let's Go* will not honor major credit cards. This is just as well—rely on them too much and your trip will soon no longer deserve the label "budget travel." However, credit cards have a variety of other uses for the budget traveler. Use them for large purchases to avoid depleting your cash on hand. Credit cards also make renting a car easier, and can be used often in lieu of a cash deposit. In addition, you can use credit cards to get a cash advance from a bank or electronic teller.

Visa and **MasterCard** can be used in more establishments than other credit cards, and they are also the most useful for getting an instant cash advance. Visa holders can generally obtain an advance up to the amount of the credit line remaining on the card, while Mastercard imposes a daily limit. Be sure to consult the bank that issues your card, however, since it may impose its own rules and restrictions. At a bank, you should be able to obtain cash from a teller, who will essentially "charge" you as if you had made a purchase. Not all ATMs will honor your credit card; those that do require you to enter your personal code number; there will also be a service charge.

American Express offers a number of services to cardholders. Local AmEx offices will cash personal checks up to $1000 for Green Card holders ($200 in cash, $800 in traveler's checks) and $5000 for Gold Card holders. You can do this once every seven days—note that the money is drawn from your personal checking account, not your AmEx account. Cash advances are available in certain places to Gold Card holders. At certain major airports, American Express also operates machines from which you can purchase traveler's checks with your card. Cardholders can take advantage of the American Express Travel Service. Benefits include assistance in changing airline, hotel, and car rental reservations, as well as Global Assist (800-554-2639), a 24-hour helpline that provides legal and medical assistance. At any American Express Travel Service office you can pick up a copy of the *Traveler's Companion,* a list of full-service offices throughout the world. For more information, contact the American Express Travel Service office or affilate nearest you.

If you're a student or your income level is low, you may have difficulty acquiring a recognized credit card. Some of the larger, national banks have credit card offers geared especially toward students, even those who bank elsewhere. Otherwise, you may have to find someone older and more established (such as a parent) to co-sign your application. If someone in your family already has a card, they can usually ask for another card in your name. When using your credit card, remember that there is no free lunch—in addition to the annual fee that AmEx and many Visa and Mastercard accounts charge, beware the hefty interest rate if you do not pay your balance each month.

Sending Money

If you run out of money on the road and have no credit card, you have several options. Most inexpensive is to have a **certified check** or a **postal money order** mailed to you. Certified checks are redeemable at any bank, while postal money orders can be cashed at any post office upon presentation of two forms of ID (one with photo). All you lose is a miniscule fee (in all likelihood, whoever sends you the check will forget they paid it and you'll be off the hook) and the time the money takes to arrive in the mail.

Another alternative is cabling money. Through **Bank of America's** Global Seller Services (800-227-3333), money can be sent to any affiliated bank. Have someone bring cash, a credit card, or a cashier's check to the sending bank—you need not have an account. You can pick up the money three working days later with ID. To send $1000, someone will have to pay 1% plus a $15 telex charge. Those who

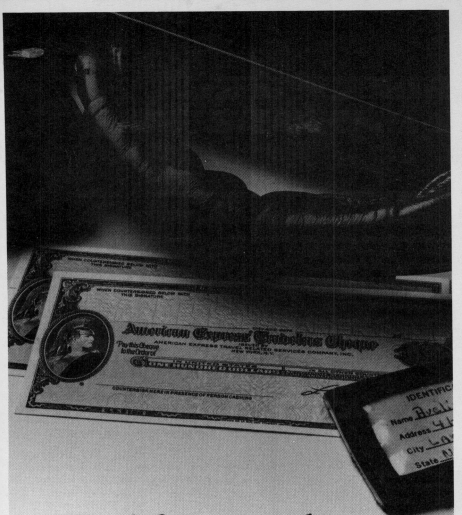

Don't forget to pack your peace of mind.

With American Express® Travelers Cheques you can be sure your vacation won't end sooner than planned. If lost or stolen, American Express can hand-deliver your refund wherever you travel, virtually anywhere in the world. And American Express Travelers Cheques are accepted by more merchants around the world than any other cheque.* Not all travelers cheques are the same. Insist on American Express Travelers Cheques. And enjoy your trip.

 **Travelers Cheques**

bank at **Barclay's** can receive their money within two to four working days. Again, have someone bring cash or a cashier's check to the sending location. You must present a driver's license or passport to pick up the dough. The fee is $15 for sums under $3000 within the U.S.; otherwise, the fee may be as high as $35-40. To take advantage of a classic, time-honored, and expensive service, use **Western Union** (800-325-6000). You or someone else can phone in a credit card number, or else someone can bring cash to a Western Union office. As always, you need ID to pick up your money. Their charge is $47 per $1000.

If time is of the essence, you can have money wired directly, bank to bank. Contact your bank by telegram or phone and state the amount of money you need, whether you need American or Canadian dollars, and the name and address of the bank to which the money should be sent. You should receive your money in about a day, although it will take longer to reach smaller and more out-of-the-way locales, and the cost will be at least $25 for amounts under $1000.

Currency

Keep in mind that your travels may take you through two countries, the United States and Canada. At this writing, US$1 is worth CDN$1.18 and thus CDN$1 is worth US$.85. This rate of exchange tends to be one of the most stable in the world. In Canada, U.S. coins will often be accepted at their face value. That is, Canadian shops will take a U.S. quarter as 25 Canadian cents—this is a small financial loss for you. Consult your conscience once you realize that Canadian coins can be used in many American pop machines with impunity, earning you a nice discount. If you will be using both currencies during your travels, try to exchange as much of it as possible at once and at a major bank, to avoid large fees.

Miscellaneous Information

Don't get your hopes up about the electronic banking revolution. Automatic teller machine (ATM) networks are continually expanding across the continent, but you'll need to find out whether or not your bank belongs to a network with machines in the region. Don't rely on ATMs too much—service charges are steep, and there is generally a limit on how much you can withdraw on any given day ($250 for most banks). If a machine tells you that "your bank cannot process this transaction at this time," give up—that's just the machine's polite way of saying your card won't work on that network.

Prices in stores and restaurants (and thus in *Let's Go*) do not include a state or provincial **sales tax** of up to 8%, which will be added before you pay. Waiters, taxi drivers, and many others will expect you to add a **tip** to the bill: 15% is the general rule. Bellboys and airport porters expect about a dollar per piece of luggage.

In the U.S., banks are usually open weekdays 9am to 5pm, and some are open Saturdays 9am to noon or 1pm. Canadian banks are open Monday through Thursday 10am to 3pm, Friday until 6pm, and some banks are open Saturdays 10am to 3pm. In northern Alaska, banks are scarce and may operate only a few days per week. All banks, government agencies, and post offices are closed on legal holidays (see Official Holidays above for a list). When you arrive in a major city, or if in a smaller town you know you will need to use a bank, find out the hours of the major bank(s); they may vary somewhat from place to place.

Safety, Security, and Insurance

Even the minimal wares of the low-cost traveler have their allure to theives. With an appropriate amount of caution and common sense, you can reduce the risk of theft. After protecting yourself, protecting your money should be your first concern. First the don'ts: don't carry your money in your back pocket, don't take out your money and count it on the street or in front of strangers, don't leave your money dangling from a bag or pouch that can easily be grabbed off your shoulder. You should always keep your important documents—ID, passport, traveler's check numbers and receipts—separate from the bulk of your belongings, along with a small amount of emergency cash and a credit card. What you need at your fingertips you should carry in a well-protected fashion. Most impervious to theft are **necklace pouches** that stay under your shirt; they are not easily accessible, though, and large ones can be quite uncomfortable. **Money belts** can be worn around your waist and buried under one or all your layers of clothing—these are more convenient and nearly theft-proof.

Wherever you stow your stuff, either for the day or for the evening, try to keep your valuables on your person and leave little other than clothing in your room. In the dorm-style rooms of some hostels, consider this rule ironclad. In general you may as well err on the side of caution and carry around a small daypack with your documents, credit cards, and camera. Lockers at bus and train stations are safe, and very useful if you want to sleep outside without most of your bulk. Label as many of your belongings as feasible with your name, address, and home phone. Label your luggage inside and out, including easy-to-drop items such as sleeping bags and tents. Try to memorize as many of your important numbers as possible in case they disappear (a good pretravel exercise): passport, ID, driver's license, health insurance policy, traveler's checks, credit cards.

More important than your belongings is yourself. Avoid bus and train stations and public parks after dark. Walk on busy, well-lit streets, especially in the larger cities. When you're walking alone, walk as though you know where you're going, even if you don't; avoid passing too close to dark alleyways or doorways and stay in the light. Don't walk though parking lots at night. When you get to a place where you'll be spending some time, find out about its unsafe areas from tourist information, from the manager of your hotel or hostel, or from a local person you meet whom you trust. Both men and women may want to carry a small whistle to scare off attackers or attract attention, and it's not a bad idea to jot down the number of the police if you'll be in town for a couple days. In addition, you may feel safer sleeping in places with either a curfew or a night attendant.

Purchasing insurance against accident, sickness, or theft may make sense, although you will have to weigh the costs, benefits, and conditions carefully. Beware of unnecessary coverage. Check whether your own or your family's homeowners' insurance covers theft or accident during travel. Homeowners' insurance often covers the loss of travel documents such as passports, airplane tickets, and rail passes up to $500. If you are a student, your university's term-time medical plan may include insurance for summer travel. Before an insurance company will reimburse you for theft, you will have to provide a copy of the police report filed at the time of the theft. To be reimbursed for medical expenses, you will have to submit a doctor's statement and evidence that you actually paid the charges for which you are asking to be reimbursed. When you file for any kind of insurance reimbursement, make sure that you are filing within the time limit specified by the policy and that either you or someone at home can be in touch with your insurer if necessary. Leave important numbers—passport, traveler's checks, etc.—with someone at home.

If you are an ISIC cardholder, you automatically receive US$2000 of accident-related coverage and US$100 per day of in-patient health coverage, up to 60 days. These benefits do not cover the continental U.S. and Alaska, however. CIEE also offers the **Trip-Safe** plan, which *does* cover the entire U.S., to ISIC holders and non-holders alike. Trip-Safe includes the above package as well as insurance for medical treatment and hospitalization, accidents, baggage loss, trip cancellation, emergency evacuation and repatriation, and coverage for charter flights missed due to illness. Cost of the package varies with the length of your trip. Call or write CIEE (see Student Travel above) for information.

The following firms also specialize in travel insurance. You can buy a policy either directly from them or through an agent operating on their behalf:

Carefree Travel Insurance, P.O. Box 310, Mineola, NY 11501 (800-645-2424). Package includes coverage for baggage loss, accidents, medical treatment, and trip cancellation or interruption (which can also be purchased separately). 24-hour hotline.

Edmund A. Cocco Agency, 220 Broadway, #201, P.O. Box 780, Lynnfield, MA 01940 (800-821-2488; in MA, 617-595-0262). Coverage against accident, sickness, baggage loss, and trip cancellation or interruption. Emergency medical evacuation covered as well. Payment of medical expenses "on-the-spot" anywhere in the world. Protection against bankruptcy or default of airlines, cruise lines, or charter companies. Trip cancellation/interruption coverage US$5.50 per $100 of coverage. Group rates available. 24-hour hotline.

The Traveler's Insurance Co., 1 Tower Sq., Hartford, CT 06183-5040 (800-243-3174; in CT, HI, or AK 203-277-2318). Insurance against accident, baggage loss, sickness, trip cancellation or interruption, and company default. Covers emergency medical evacuation as well. Available through most travel agencies.

Travel Guard International, P.O. Box 1200, Stevens Point, WI 54481 (800-782-5151). Basic (US$19), deluxe (US$39), and comprehensive "Travel Guard Gold" (8% of total trip cost) packages cover baggage delay, car rental, accidental death, and trip cancellation or interruption. 24-hour hotline for policyholders.

WorldCare Travel Assistance Association, Inc., 6505 Market St., #1300, San Francisco, CA 94105 (800-666-4993). Annual membership US$162 covers all trips under 90 days. Coverage for 1-8 day trips US$86; longer trips less per day. Free repatriation and medical evacuation. Trip cancellation/interruption coverage additional.

Alcohol and Drugs

In Oregon, Washington, and Alaska, the drinking age is 21 years of age and is strictly enforced. British Columbia and the Yukon Territory prohibit drinking below the age of 19, while in Alberta you can drink at 18.

Drugs and traveling, however, are mutually incompatible. Even where possession of marijuana no longer constitutes a felony, if you are caught with any amount of a "controlled substance" you will be fined. At the Canadian border, if you are found in possession of drugs, you will be subject to an automatic seven-year jail term, regardless of how small an amount you are found with. Police attitudes towards drugs vary widely across the region. In some cities, police tend to ignore pot smokers who mind their own business. But don't be fooled by their seeming lack of interest; arrests are not uncommon. In Alaska, possession and use of marijuana is legal only on private property.

Health

Common sense is the simplest prescription for health while you travel: eat well, drink enough, get enough sleep, and don't overexert yourself. You will need plenty of protein (for sustained energy) and fluids (to prevent dehydration and constipation, two of the most common health problems for travelers). Carry a canteen or water bottle and make sure to drink frequently. Sunscreen is a must—sunburned skin will make both your clothes and your luggage feel prickly, and more importantly, dry skin doesn't keep the body as cool or retain moisture as well. Wear a hat. And lavish your feet with attention; make sure your shoes are appropriate for extended walking, do not wear the same pair of socks for too long, use talcum powder frequently, and have some moleskin on hand to pad your shoes if they become uncomfortable. If possible, bring an extra pair of good walking shoes and alternate between the two pairs.

For minor health hazards, a compact self-assembled **first-aid kit** should suffice. For car travelers, an excellent one is the **American Red Cross Automobile First Aid Kit,** which local chapters sell for $26.20. Each kit contains a roll of gauze, gauze pads, band-aids, a triangular bandage, a rescue blanket, safety scissors, and instructions. Your own kit should include those items plus any or all of the following, depending on your plans: aspirin, soap (both mild and antiseptic), antibiotic, thermometer in a sturdy case, multiple vitamins, decongestant (particularly important for clearing your ears if you fly with a cold), antihistamine, motion sickness medicine (such as Dramamine), medicine for stomach problems and diarrhea, burn ointment, lip balm, elastic bandage, and Swiss Army knife (with tweezers). If you anticipate sexual activity during your travels, be aware of safe sex procedures and carry your own condoms. If you're taking oral contraceptives, remember to take time zone changes into account. If you wear glasses or contact lenses, bring a prescription and/or an extra pair along with you. Lens wearers can avoid dried-out contacts by drinking sufficient fluids and switching to glasses where the air is dry or dirty.

Unforeseen health emergencies are always disconcerting, and they are even more harrowing away from home. Before you leave, check and see whether your insurance policy (if you have one) covers medical costs incurred while traveling. If you're Canadian, the health insurance plan of your home province will cover you, but coverage varies from province to province. Contact your provincial Ministry of Health or Health Plan Headquarters for details. Regardless of how you plan to be covered, always have both proof of insurance and policy numbers on hand. See Safety, Security, and Insurance above.

If you choose to risk traveling without insurance, you still have avenues for health care that bypass hospitals and private practice. In an emergency, call the local hotline or crisis center listed in *Let's Go* under Practical Information. These operators have numbers for public health organizations and clinics that treat patients without demanding proof of solvency. Such centers charge low fees. University teaching hospitals usually run inexpensive clinics as well.

If you have a chronic medical condition that requires medication on a regular basis, consult your physician before you leave. Carry copies of your prescriptions and an ample supply of all medications; it might be difficult to find pharmacies in rural areas. Always distribute medication and/or syringes among all your carry-on and checked baggage in case any of your bags is lost. If you are traveling with a medical condition that cannot be easily recognized—such as diabetes, an allergy to antibiotics or other drugs, epilepsy, or a heart condition— you should obtain a **Medic Alert identification tag** ($25) to alert both passersby and medical personnel of your condition in case of emergency. Your tag is engraved with the name of your ailment, and you receive a wallet card with personal and medical information. Fee includes access to an emergency phone number as well. Contact Medic Alert Foundation International, Turlock, CA 95381-1009 (800-432-5378).

While you travel, pay attention to the signals of pain and discomfort that your body may send you. Expect some adjustment to a new climate, diet, water quality, or pace when you first arrive or after a couple of weeks—often this is nothing, but keep an eye on it. Once you get going, some of the milder symptoms that you can safely ignore at home may be signs of something more serious on the road, and your increased exertion may wear you out and make you more susceptible to illness.

Airplane travelers are often plagued by **jet lag.** Jet lag sufferers are generally uncomfortable and tired, but unable to sleep normally. To avoid or cure jet lag, the best thing to do is to adopt the new region's time as soon as you arrive and to try to sleep during the appropriate hours. Some studies caution sufferers against excessive eating and alcoholic drinking as well.

Be on the alert for **heatstroke.** This term is often misapplied to all forms of heat exhaustion, but in fact it refers to a specific ailment that can cause death within a few hours if it is not treated. Heatstroke can begin without direct exposure to the sun; it results from continuous heat stress, lack of fitness, or overactivity following heat exhaustion. In the early stages of heatstroke, sweating stops, body temperature rises, and an intense headache develops, soon followed by mental confusion. To treat heatstroke, cool the victim off immediately with water and shade. Then rush the victim to the hospital.

In the Pacific Northwest, be on the lookout for **poison oak,** which grows plentifully in forested areas along the Pacific Coast. Skin that comes in contact with poison oak becomes inflamed and fiercely itchy. If you do develop a poison oak rash, do not wash or scratch it; these actions will spread the rash. Instead, find a doctor who can tell you what kind of medication to apply. And be careful—the rash spreads on contact, so stay at (more than) arm's length from your loved ones and fellow travelers. To recognize poison oak, remember the Girl Scout rule: Leaves of three, let it be. Each stalk of the plant has three dark green leaves with serrated edges. In the fall, poison oak may turn red as well.

Those exploring very cold areas need to be able to detect and treat **frostbite**. A frostbitten part of the body will turn white then waxy and numb. Victims should drink warm beverages, stay dry, and warm the frostbitten area slowly and gently with a dry blanket, a piece of clothing, or steady body contact. Never rub the frostbitten area. Serious frostbite must be treated by a doctor or medic.

Before you venture out into the wilderness to hike or camp in any weather, familiarize yourself with the dangers of **hypothermia**. Hypothermia can strike in cold, windy, or wet conditions—and this can include temperatures well above freezing—when body temperature drops rapidly, resulting in a failure to produce body heat. Symptoms are easy to detect: uncontrollable shivering, poor coordination, and exhaustion followed by slurred speech, sleepiness, hallucinations, and amnesia. You can often save victims of hypothermia by keeping them warm and dry. *Do not* let victims fall asleep if they are in the advanced stages—if they lose consciousness, they might die. To avoid hypothermia, always keep dry. Wear wool, even in wet weather—it retains its insulating ability even when wet. Dress in layers, and stay out of the wind, which carries heat away from the body. Remember that most loss of body heat is through your head, so always carry a wool hat with you.

For more information, consult *The Pocket Medical Encyclopedia and First-Aid Guide* (Simon and Schuster, $5; write to Mail Order Dept., 200 Old Tappan Rd., Old Tappan, NJ 07675, or call 800-223-2348). Both **The Mountaineers Books** and **Wilderness Press** publish several books about travel medicine and mountaineering medicine in particular. Write or call for free catalogs—for their addresses and phone numbers, see Camping and the Outdoors below. In addition, the **International Association for Medical Assistance to Travelers (IAMAT)** provides members with free pamphlets and a directory of fixed-rate physicians throughout the world. Membership is free, although donations are encouraged. Contact IAMAT in the U.S. at 417 Center St., Lewiston, NY 14092 (716-754-4883), or in Canada at 40 Regal St., Guelph, Ont., N1K 1B5 (519-836-0102).

Cameras and Film

At every turn in the Northwest, you'll want to photograph the breaktaking scenery. Make sure your camera is in good shape before you go—repair on the road is likely to be rare, inexpert, expensive, or some combination of these hassles. Buy film before you leave, or in the big cities as you go. Often large discount department stores have the best deals. Avoid buying film in small towns or at tourist attractions, where prices are exorbitant. The sensitivity of film to light is measured by the ASA/ISO number: 64 or 100 is good for normal outdoor or indoor flash photography, 400 or higher is necessary for night photography. Consult a photo store for advice about the right film for special types of photography.

Even the greatest photographs cannot do the scenery perfect justice, so don't let the need to snap the perfect photo fill your every waking hour. Back home, sad to say, stacks of mountain or forest pictures without people in them will all start to look the same—keep this in mind and don't shoot too much scenery. To preserve some of the grandeur (and to save on processing costs), consider shooting slides instead of prints, or at least opt for larger prints (4 by 6 in.) when you get home.

Process your film after you return home; you will save money, and it's much simpler to carry rolls of film as you travel, rather than easily damaged boxes of slides or packages of prints and negatives. Protect exposed film from extreme heat and the sun.

Despite disclaimers, airport X-ray equipment can sometimes fog film, and the more sensitive the film, the more susceptible to damage. Ask security personnel to inspect your camera and film by hand. Serious photographers should purchase a lead-lined pouch for storing film.

Packing

Pack light—all the rest is commentary.

Traveling light will make your life easier in a number of ways. Obviously, the less you have to carry the less unpleasant it will be to go from place to place, and the less you will have to worry about belongings left somewhere while you step out. Furthermore, the fewer bags you have to lug around, the less you will look like (and thus be treated like) a tourist, and the more space you will have for gifts.

Your first decision is what kind of luggage you need: frame backpack, light suitcase, shoulder or duffle bag. If you'll be biking or hiking a great deal, a backpack may be in order. If you plan to stay in one city or town for awhile, you might prefer a suitcase. Large shoulder bags are good for stuffing into lockers, crowded baggage compartments, and all-purpose lugging. Whatever your main piece of baggage, be sure to have a small daypack. Daypacks are great for carrying a day's worth of food, camera, first-aid essentials, and valuables and documents. Anyone planning to cover a lot of ground on foot should have a sturdy backpack—see Tent Camping, Hiking, and Climbing below for advice on types of packs and good mail-order firms to buy from.

In the Northwest, be prepared for a wide range of weather conditions no matter what time of year you travel (see Climate for more details). To cover the most bases, stick with the "layer concept." Start with several T-shirts, over which you can wear a sweatshirt or sweater in cold or wet weather. Then pack a few pairs of shorts and a couple pairs of jeans. Add underwear and socks, and you've got your basic wardrobe. Stick with darker colors to avoid showing wear, tear, and dirt. Natural fibers and lightweight cottons are the best materials. Make sure your clothing can be washed in a sink and will survive a spin in the dryer. And don't forget a towel, swimwear, and a raincoat.

Shoes are very important whether you'll be doing serious hiking or not. Break your shoes in before you leave. Use talcum powder to prevent sores and to keep your feet fresh, and have some moleskin on hand for blister padding. Don't be caught without some type of rainproof footwear, from slipover rubbers to hiking boots, depending on your needs. Other odds and ends to consider bringing (in no particular order): first-aid kit (see Health), flashlight, pens and paper, travel alarm, canteen or water bottle, Ziplock bags, sewing kit, safety pins, pocketknife, sunglasses, assorted toiletries.

Pack light! (It's worth repeating.) Wrap sharper items in clothing so they won't stab you or puncture your luggage, and pack heavy items along the inside wall if you're carrying a backpack. Carry your luggage around the block a few times to simulate real travel—if beads of sweat start trickling down your brow, go home and take some things out. The neighbors may guffaw, but it'll give you a sense of how heavy your luggage really is.

Alternatives to Tourism

Work

Your best leads in the job hunt often are from local residents. You should also try employment offices, Chambers of Commerce, and temporary agencies. Consult the local newspapers once you've arrived, or check out the want-ads before you leave (many university and public libraries subscribe to the Northwest's major dailies). Keep your eyes peeled for notices put up on streetlights and telephone poles. Local college bulletin boards can also be very helpful, particularly for finding short-term jobs.

Paid employment can occasionally be found through the **U.S. Forest Service.** For information, contact the Alaska Regional Office, Federal Office Building, P.O. Box 21628-PAO, Juneau 99802 (907-568-8806), or the Pacific Northwest Regional Office, P.O. Box 3623, Portland, OR 97208 (503-326-2877). Agriculture in the Northwest generates a huge variety of temporary unskilled jobs, but expect low wages and poor conditions. Fruit pickers are always needed in Oregon, Washington, and BC's Okanagan Valley, since tons of fruit are lost each year due to never-ending shortages of workers. Those jobs that do pay well have their own draw-backs—seasonal fish cannery jobs on the coast of Alaska demand strenuous 16- to 18-hour days, non-stop for up to 45 days. As a crew member on an Alaskan fishing boat, you can make over $2000 per week baiting halibut hooks. However, the work is dangerous, and you can expect to sleep less than four hours per night. You may also be able to find seasonal work at resorts in the region or with companies that organize hiking, climbing, and boat trips.

Volunteer jobs are readily available almost everywhere. Some jobs provide room and board in exchange for labor. Send $5 plus $1 postage to CIEE for *Volunteer! The Comprehensive Guide to Voluntary Service in the U.S. and Abroad* (see Student Travel above for address). If you would like to volunteer in the national forests of Washington or Oregon, contact the US Forest Service, Pacific Northwest Region, Attn: Personnel Management, P.O. Box 3623, Portland, OR 97208 (503-326-3651). Ask for their publication *Pacific Northwest Volunteer.*

Many student travel organizations organize work-exchange programs. Both CIEE and the YMCA place students as summer camp counselors in the U.S. The **Association for International Practical Training (AIPT)** offers on-the-job training programs in agriculture, engineering, computer science, math, natural sciences, and architecture. The program is open to college students who have completed their sophomore year in a technical major. You must apply by December 10 for summer placement, six months in advance for other placements. There is a $75 non-refundable fee. Write to IAESTE Trainee Program (International Association for the Exchange of Students for Technology Experience), c/o AIPT, 320 Park View Bldg., 10480 Little Pautuxent Parkway, Columbia, MD 21044 (301-997-2200). If you are interested in working on an archaeological dig, contact the **Archaeological Institute of America,** 675 Commonwealth Ave., Boston, MA 02215 (617-353-9361) for a copy of their "Fieldwork Opportunities Bulletin" ($8).

Writer's Digest Books publishes the *1990 Summer Employment Directory of the United States* ($13). Contact Writer's Digest Books, Attn: Book Order Dept., 1507 Dana Ave., Cincinnati, OH 45207 (800-543-4644; in OH, 800-551-0884).

International visitors should see Visas below for regulations concerning work in the United States.

Study

Many colleges in the Pacific Northwest welcome visiting students. The colleges and universities listed below all offer summer terms (3-11 weeks). Direct all corre-spondence to the Director of Admissions.

University of Alaska, Fairbanks, Fairbanks, AK 99775-0060 (907-474-7821).

University of Alaska, Anchorage, 3211 Providence Dr., Anchorage, AK 99508 (907-786-1525).

Lewis and Clark College, Portland, OR 97219 (503-293-2679).

University of Oregon, 240 Oregon Hall, Eugene, OR 97403 (503-686-3201).

Oregon State University, Corvalis, OR 97331 (503-754-4411).

Reed College, 3203 SE Woodstock Blvd., Portland, OR 97202 (800-547-4750 or 503-777-7511).

University of Washington, 1400 NE Campus Pkwy., Seattle, WA 98195 (206-543-9686).

Washington State University, 342 French Administration Bldg., Pullman, WA 99164-1036 (509-335-5586).

University of Alberta, 1200 Administration Bldg., Edmonton, AB T6G 2M7 (403-492-3283).

University of Calgary, 2500 University Dr. NW, Calgary, AB T2N 1N4 (403-220-6640).

Simon Fraser University, Burnaby, BC V5A 1S6 (604-291-3224).

University of British Columbia, Vancouver, BC V6T 1Z2 (604-228-3014).

University of Victoria, Box 1700, Victoria, BC V8W 2Y2 (604-721-8111).

Many reference books revised each year provide summaries and evaluations of various colleges, describing their general atmosphere, fields of study, tuition, and enrollment data. Among the most useful are *The Insider's Guide to the Colleges* (St. Martin's Press, $12), the *Fiske Guide to Colleges,* by Edward Fiske (N.Y. Times Books, $11), and *Barron's Profiles of American Colleges* ($15).

International visitors interested in studying in the U.S. should also see For International Visitors below.

Keeping in Touch

In this age of postmodern mass communications, your friends and families will be able to keep in touch with you easily by phone or mail. To speak with the folks back home, it may be easiest for you to call them collect or with a credit card. To save everyone some money, you can try calling from a pay phone somewhere and having your interlocutors call you back. Many pay phones do not receive incoming calls, however, and they are usually so marked where the phone number is printed.

If you want to receive mail while you're on the road, it can be sent to you c/o General Delivery. Letters to you should be addressed with your name (last name capitalized and underlined, to ensure proper filing), the words "c/o General Delivery," the city/town and state/province, and the General Delivery ZIP or postal code for the town. *Let's Go* lists local ZIP and postal codes; for ZIPs in the U.S. you can also call 800-228-8777. Make sure the code is correct, or else the letter will end up in oblivion at some other post office in town. The envelope should also say "Please hold until . . . ," the blank filled in with a date a couple weeks after your correspondent expects you to pick up the letter. When you claim your mail, you'll have to present ID, and if you do not claim a letter within two to four weeks, it will be returned to its sender.

American Express cardholders and checkholders can receive letters at those AmEx Travel Service offices that provide "Client Letter Service." When you come to pick up your mail, you'll need to show your American Express card or traveler's checks plus one more form of ID. Contact the AmEx Travel Service office or affiliate in your area for more details and for the addresses of offices in the towns you plan to visit where you can collect your mail.

For information on how to use the U.S. and Canadian postal and phone systems, see Communication under For International Visitors (even if you are not from overseas).

Additional Concerns

Traveling Alone

The freedom to come and go at will, to backtrack or deviate from a schedule or route, is the solitary traveler's special prerogative. Traveling with even one other person can become stifling or even annoying at times, especially when separate desires and plans conflict. Pairs of travelers should consider splitting up for a few days, to satisfy personal desires and to meet other people. Often you'll come to appreciate each other more when you've been apart and have stories to tell. Hitchhiking is much easier for the lone traveler, although less safe, particularly for women. Traveling alone has its downside, though. Single accommodations are much more costly than doubles. In addition, if you do travel alone, you should be extremely careful about where you sleep. Outdoor locations make the lone traveler an easy target.

Even if you're alone, chances are you won't be hurting for company along the way. If you carry your copy of *Let's Go,* you might be noticed by others doing the same (sympathetically, we hope). Another trick for finding people with whom you may have some connection is to wear a baseball cap or T-shirt from your home state or college. Striking up acquaintances in this fashion might allow you to visit somewhere you hadn't considered, or to pool your resources and rent a car to reach out-of-the-way sights.

Women Travelers

Women traveling alone must take extra precautions. Forego cheap accommodations in city outskirts—the risks outweigh any savings—and stick to youth hostels, university accommodations, bed-and-breakfasts, and YWCAs. Religious organizations offering rooms for women only are another safe option. Hitching alone is dangerous; it's slightly better (though by no means safe) for two women to hitch together.

If you find yourself the object of catcalls or propositions, your best answer is no answer. Always look as if you know where you're going, and maintain an assertive, confident posture wherever you go. If you feel uncomfortable asking strangers for information or directions, it may be easier to approach other women or couples. Always carry enough change for a bus, taxi, or phone call. And in emergencies, don't hesitate to yell for help. Know the emergency numbers for the area you're visiting; *Let's Go* lists them in the Practical Information section of each area.

Gay and Lesbian Travelers

Generally, in the larger cities of the Pacific Northwest, you need not sacrifice much freedom or openness to enjoy your trip. However, more discretion is suggested in rural areas, where smaller communities may not be so receptive to gay and lesbian travelers. Wherever possible, *Let's Go* lists gay and lesbian information lines, community centers, bookshops, and special services. More extensive coverage of gay and lesbian bars, restaurants, accommodations, businesses, and medical services is available in the *Gayellow Pages* ($10), which covers both the United States and Canada. Order a copy from Renaissance House, P.O. Box 292, Village Station, New York, NY 10014 (212-674-0120). You can also contact Renaissance House for a copy of the *Spartacus Guide for Gay Men,* a worldwide touring guide.

Lesbians should consider buying a copy of *Gaia's Guide,* which lists local lesbian, gay, and feminist information numbers, as well as gay and lesbian hotels, restaurants, book stores, and publications, and women's cultural centers. If this guide isn't in your local bookstore, order by sending $12.50 (includes shipping) to **Giovanni's Room,** 345 S. 12th St. NE, Philadelphia, PA 19107 (800-222-6996 or 215-943-2960 in PA). Giovanni's Room also stocks all of the other books mentioned in this section, with the exception of the Gayellow Pages. Add $2.50 for shipping within the U.S., $3.50 to ship to Canada or Mexico.

Other general guides for lesbian and gay travelers include: *Odysseus: Accommodations and Travel Guide for the Gay Community* ($15); *Inn Places: USA and Worldwide Gay Accommodations* ($15); *Bob Damron's Address Book,* a guide for gay men ($14); and *Places of Interest,* which covers major cities in the U.S. and Canada ($8 for women's guide, $10 for men's guide, $11 for generic guide with maps), available as well from Ferrari Publications, P.O. Box 35575, Phoenix, AZ 85069 (602-863-2408).

Travelers without published material on gay and lesbian services can contact the **Gay/Lesbian Crisisline** (800-SOS-GAYS, i.e. 800-767-4297) which provides information about clubs, local gay/lesbian hotline numbers, counseling and support services in the U.S. and Canada, legal and medical advice, resources concerning AIDS, and information on dealing with homophobia.

Senior Citizens

Senior citizens enjoy a tremendous assortment of discounts on public transportation, museum, movie, theater, and concert admissions, accommodations, and even dining. To take advantage of these savings, you usually need an acceptable piece of identification proving your age, such as a driver's license, a Medicare card, or a membership card from a recognized society of retired people.

There is a whole slew of organizations that cater to senior citizens in general and senior travelers in particular. Membership in the **American Association of Retired**

Persons (AARP) is open to U.S. residents ages 50 and over. For the $5 annual membership fee (which includes spouse as well), AARP provides a ton of services and can help members save a lot of money. AARP's Purchase Privilege Program arranges discounts at major hotel/motel chains throughout the nation. In addition, older travelers receive discounts from car-rental and sight-seeing companies. For more information on these benefits, write AARP National Headquarters, Special Services Dept., 1909 K St. NW, Washington, DC 20049 (800-227-7737).

Membership in the **September Days Club (SDC)** (800-241-5050 or 800-344-3636) costs $12 per year and is also open to people over 50. Members enjoy a 15-50% discount at all Days Inns, discounts in restaurants and gift shops run by the chain, and a quarterly magazine. Senior citizens should also contact the **National Council of Senior Citizens,** 925 15th St. NW, Washington, DC 20005 (202-347-8800).

If you are academically inclined, look into **Elderhostel,** which offers residential academic programs for senior citizens at many colleges and universities in the Pacific Northwest, Western Canada, and Alaska. Participants pay a weekly sum to live in the dorms, take courses, and use the institution's various facilities. Programs are offered year-round, and you can register at any time. To participate you must be 60 or older; your companion may join you if he or she is over 50. For a free catalog, contact Elderhostel, 80 Boylston St., #480, Boston, MA 02116 (617-426-7788).

People over age 62 can acquire a free **Golden Age Passport,** which entitles them to free entry into U.S. National Parks, Monuments, and Recreation Areas, as well as 50% off Federal use fees for facilities and services at these parks. Golden Age Passports can be acquired on the spot wherever they can be used, or at Federal offices whose function concerns land, forests, or wildlife.

Helpful publications regarding travel for senior citizens abound. Many discounts and services are listed in the *Discount Guide for Travelers Over 55,* by Caroline and Walter Weintz, published by E.P. Dutton and available through Penguin USA, 120 Woodbine St., Bergenfield, NJ 07621 (800-331-4624). Pilot Books puts out two travel books for senior citizens: *Senior Citizen's Guide to Budget Travel in the United States and Canada* ($4), and *The International Health Guide for Senior Citizen Travelers* ($5). Order from Pilot Books, 103 Cooper St., Babylon, NY 11702 (516-422-2225) and add $1 for postage.

Disabled Travelers

Although easy-access facilities are often difficult to find, disabled travelers can still take advantage of *Let's Go* listings. Hotels and motels have become increasingly accessible to the disabled—consult the motel chains listed in Budget Chain Motels below. Most **Red Roof Inns** are wheelchair-accessible; call 800-843-7663 for information. If you are planning to visit a national park you should obtain a free **Golden Access Passport,** available at all park entrances and from Federal offices whose functions relate to land, forests, or wildlife. The Golden Access Passport entitles disabled travelers and their families to enter the park for free and provides a 50% reduction on all campsite fees.

Research the area you will be visiting before you leave. Call restaurants, hotels, parks, and other facilities to find out about the existence of ramps, the presence of easy trails, the width of doors, the dimensions of elevators, etc. Also inquire about restrictions on motorized wheelchairs.

Arrange transportation well in advance to ensure a smooth trip. If you give sufficient notice, some major car rental agencies have hand-controlled vehicles at certain locations. Call **Avis** (800-331-1212, at least 24 hours notice), **Hertz** (800-654-3131, 2-3 days notice), or **National** (800-328-4567, at least 24 hours notice). Both **Amtrak** and the airlines are now required to serve disabled passengers if notified in advance—simply tell the ticket agent when making reservations which services you'll need. **Greyhound** and **Trailways** will take on a disabled person and a companion for the price of a single fare. Special tickets require only a doctor's statement confirming that you need a companion to help you get on and off the bus. Both companies will count a non-motorized wheelchair as part of the 100-pound allotment for luggage. Hearing-impaired travelers may contact Greyhound (800-523-6590, in PA 800-843-7663) or Amtrak (800-345-3109, in PA 800-322-9537) using teletype printers. Many ferries that run up and down the Pacific coast can also accommodate disabled travelers; consult the companies listed below under By Ferry. For information on transportation availability for disabled people in any United States city, contact the **American Public Transit Association** (202-898-4000) in Washington, DC.

There are many special information services for disabled travelers. The **Travel Information Center** at the **Moss Rehabilitation Hospital**, 12th St. and Tabor Rd., Philadelphia, PA 19141 (215-329-5715, ext. 2233) is an excellent source of information (for a nominal postage fee if you request any mailings) on tourist sights, accommodations, and transportation for the disabled. The **Society for the Advancement of Travel for the Handicapped**, 26 Court St., Penthouse Suite, Brooklyn, NY 11242 (718-858-5483), provides several useful booklets as well as advice and assistance on trip planning. Membership is $40 per year, $25 for senior citizens and students. The **American Foundation for the Blind** recommends travel books and issues ID discount cards ($6) for the legally blind. For an ID application or for other information, contact the American Foundation for the Blind, 15 W. 16th St., New York, NY 10011 (800-232-5463). Other organizations specialize in arranging tours. **Directions Unlimited**, 720 N. Bedford Rd., Bedford Hills, NY 10507 (800-533-5343; in NY, 914-241-1700), also conducts tours for the physically disabled. To inquire about other organizations that plan tours for disabled travelers, write to the Handicapped Travel Division, National Tour Association, P.O. Box 3071, Lexington, KY 40596 (606-253-1036).

Several books are particularly helpful for disabled travelers. One good resource is *Access to the World,* by Louise Weiss ($13). For a copy, contact Facts on File, Inc., 460 Park Ave. S., New York, NY 10016 (212-683-2244). **Twin Peaks Press** publishes three books: *Directory for Travel Agencies for the Disabled* ($13), *Travel for the Disabled* ($10), and *Wheelchair Vagabond* ($10), which discusses camping and travel in cars, vans, and RVs. Order from Twin Peaks Press, P.O. Box 129, Vancouver, WA 98666 (800-637-2256). Add $2 shipping for a single book, $1 for each additional. Twin Peaks also operates a worldwide traveling nurse network.

Traveling with Children

There are plenty of opportunities in the Pacific Northwest to keep both you and your kids entertained, even all of you at the same time. Consult local newspapers or travel bureaus to find out about events that might be of special interest for young children, such as the Cannon Beach Sandcastle Festival in Oregon or the annual Magicazam magic show that visits Portland in the summer.

Parents generally find it easier to travel with children by car than by bus, train, or any other form of public transportation. With a car, you will have the freedom to make frequent stops, and children will have more room to spread out their toys, books, and selves in the back seat. Try to avoid areas with extreme climatic conditions, since children's bodies can be very sensitive, and they are more prone than you to frostbite, hypothermia, and heatstroke. (See Health for more information.) Before traveling, you might want to consult *Baby Travel* ($12), published by Hippocrene Books Inc., 171 Madison Ave., New York, NY 10016 (212-685-4371). **Wilderness Press** (see Camping and the Outdoors for address and phone) publishes *Backpacking with Babies and Small Children* ($9), *Sharing Nature With Children* ($7), and the companion *Sharing the Joy of Nature: Nature Activities for All Ages* ($10).

Vegetarian and Kosher Travelers

Vegetarians and observers of the laws of *kashrut* alike will find the Northwest highly felicitious. Fresh fish, fruits, and vegetables manifest themselves in both the larger cities and smaller towns of the region. Delicious apples and Chinook salmon are just a couple of the area's indigenous treats. Vegetarian travelers can obtain *The International Vegetarian Travel Guide* and *Vegetarian Times Guide to Natural Foods Restaurants in the U.S. and Canada* (each costs $9 plus $2 postage) from the **North American Vegetarian Society,** P.O. Box 72, Dolgeville, NY 13329 (518-568-7970).

Kosher travelers should contact synagogues in Seattle, Portland, Vancouver, Edmonton, and Calgary for information about kosher restaurants in those cities; your own synagogue or college Hillel should have access to lists of Jewish institutions across the continent. If you eat at nonkosher restaurants, you will have the most options available. According to some rabbis, you may eat anything at a restaurant as long as it does not contain any meat, and you may use the restaurant's utensils. Others restrict eating out to cold items such as cheeses and salads. Often you can ask to have ingredients that you would not eat left out of prepared dishes. Check to see whether foods are fried in vegetable oil and whether soups and sauces are meat-based. If you are more strict, consider preparing your own food. Bring along some sturdy plasticware, a pan, a small grill, and lots of aluminum foil; buy fresh fish, fruits, and vegetables along the way. You may need to bring your own bread—if so, bags of pita last longer than loaves of bread.

Getting There and Getting Around

By Air

The simplest and surest way to find a low airfare is to have a knowledgeable travel agent guide you through the inferno with his or her computer flight listings. In addition, check the weekend travel sections of major newspapers for bargain fares.

Many airlines offer special rates (often as high as 50-75% off regular fares) to children accompanied by an adult. Very few airlines offer discounts for senior citizens. Chances of receiving discount fares increase on competitive routes. Flying smaller airlines instead of the national giants can also save money. Check for specials on the following airlines:

Southwest, 800-531-5601.

Northwest, 800-225-2525.

Alaska, 800-426-0333.

Super Saver fares can save you hundreds of dollars over the regular coach fare. On the average, you can save up to 70% on the 30-day advance-purchase fare, 45% on the 14-day advance-purchase fare, and 30% on the 7-day advance-purchase fare. To obtain the cheapest Super Saver fare, buy a round-trip ticket (not necessarily returning to the same city) 30 days in advance and stay over at least one Saturday. Other restrictions to be aware of are pre-payment (the day your reservation is made, or 14 days after making your reservation) and up-to-50% penalties for either reservation changes or cancellation. Also check with your travel agent for system-wide air passes and excursion fares.

There are a few principles to keep in mind when booking a flight. Traveling at night and during the wee hours of the morning is generally cheaper than during the day, and traveling on a weekday (especially Tuesday or Wednesday) is usually cheaper than traveling on the weekend. Super Saver fares are an exception. Since airline travel peaks between June and August and around holidays, reserve a seat several months in advance for these times. Given the occasional appearance of sudden bargains and the availability of standby fares, advance purchase may not guarantee the lowest fare, but you will save some money and be assured a seat. The best deals usually appear between January and mid-May.

If all you need is a short flight, scout local airfields for prospective rides on private, non-commercial planes. Some airfields have ride boards. If not, a good place to begin is the operations counter, where pilots file their flight plans. Ask where they are headed and if they'd like a passenger. Remember that propeller planes have a much higher accident rate than their larger commercial counterparts; if the pilots seem even slightly reluctant because of the weather, think about heading back out to the highway.

For information on reaching the Northwest from a country other than the United States, see Transportation under For International Visitors.

By Bus

Buses generally offer the most frequent service between the cities and towns of the Pacific Northwest. Often the only way to reach smaller locales without a car is by bus. (Bus travel is almost nonexistent in Alaska and the Yukon, however.) Your biggest challenges when you travel by bus will involve scheduling. *Russell's Official National Motor Coach Guide* is an indispensible tool for constructing an itinerary. Updated each month, *Russell's Guide* contains schedules of literally every bus route between any two towns in the United States and Canada. Copies of the guide can be obtained for $8.35 plus 50¢ postage from Russell's Guides, Inc., P.O. Box 278, Cedar Rapids, IA 52406 (319-364-6138). Since schedules change frequently and the guide is updated monthly, a far better idea than purchasing the guide is to look at a copy in a library reference room.

In both the U.S. and Canada, **Greyhound** operates the largest number of lines. Recently Greyhound acquired its main rival, **Trailways,** but retains the Trailways name on many routes. Greyhound can get you both to and around the Northwest. Senior citizens receive a 10% discount, children ages 5-11 travel for half-fare, and younger children pay no fare at all. With a statement from a doctor, a disabled traveler and a companion may travel for the price of one. If you plan to travel a great deal by bus within the U.S., you may save money with the **Ameripass.** Passes can be purchased for seven days ($189), 15 days ($249), or 30 days ($349), and each can be extended for $10 per day. Before you purchase an Ameripass, you should have a pretty good idea of your itinerary; total up the separate bus fares between towns to make sure that you will in fact save with the pass. To contact Greyhound, call the local schedule and fare information number where you live.

By all means avoid spending the night in a bus station. Bus stations are often hangouts for dangerous or at least frightening characters. Try to arrange your arrivals for reasonable day or evening times. This will also make it easier for you to find transportation out of the station and a place to stay.

Greyhound allows passengers to carry two pieces of luggage weighing up to 100 pounds in total at no charge. Whatever you stow in the compartments underneath the bus should be clearly marked; try to get a claim check as well. As always, keep your essential documents and valuables on you, and carry a small bag onto the bus with you. Once on board, try to get a seat near the front. You'll see the scenery better and feel the motion of the bus less, and you may feel a bit safer near the driver. Nonsmokers will be farther away from the smoking area, which is confined to the last three rows of the bus (and forbidden altogether in Oregon, Washington, and Canada). If you intend to get off where there is no station—between towns, on a freeway—let the driver know when you get on.

For a more people-oriented, adventurous trip, consider **Green Tortoise.** Green Tortoise buses are remodeled diesel coaches done up with foam mattresses, sofa seats, and stereos. Bus drivers operate in teams so that one can drive and the other can point out sites and chat with passengers. In addition to the fare, each passenger contributes about $3 per day ($6 on longer trips) to a group kitty that goes for food, park entrance and use fees, and supplies. Meals are prepared communally. Green Tortoise can get you to San Francisco from Boston, Hartford, and New York City for $279. Buses run between San Francisco and Seattle, northbound on Monday and Friday, southbound on Thursday and Sunday. Between Seattle and San Francisco the fare is $59, less for shorter trips. For an extra $10 you can stay for a time between legs of a round trip. Deposits are generally required since space is tight and economy is an important goal for the group. For more information, write Green Tortoise, P.O. Box 24459, San Francisco, CA 94124 (800-227-4766, in CA 415-821-

Unique Journeys to Remote Places with Unforgettable People

Cost includes transportation and gourmet meals.

BLUE MOON ADVENTURES
P.O. Box 844, Forestville, CA 95436 • 707-887-7914

0803; in Boston, New York, Los Angeles, Vancouver, Seattle, Portland, and Eugene there are local agents).

By Train

A century ago, the train opened up the Pacific Northwest, Western Canada, and Alaska to a voracious young nation. Today the train is one of the cheapest and most comfortable ways to tour the area. Settle for one of the reclining seats rather than paying unnecessarily for a roomette or bedroom. Trains go one better than buses—you can walk from car to car to stretch your legs. Avoid the temptation to stop at the snack bar, though—prices are sometimes double those at a station (not to mention a grocery counter). Bring your own snacks on board instead.

Within the lower 48 states, **Amtrak** calculates fares based on a simple formula. Amtrak divides the U.S. into three regions and charges the same rate for both one way and round-trip travel: $189 within one region, $269 between two regions, $309 between three. Amtrak discounts allow children ages 2-11 to travel for half-fare when accompanied by an adult. Senior citizens and disabled travelers may save up to 25%. Watch for special holiday packages as well. For information and reservations, call 800-872-7245 or look up Amtrak's local number in your area.

VIA Rail, Amtrak's counterpart in Canada, makes British Columbia, Alberta, and the Yukon accessible to the northwestern traveler. Routes are as scenic as Amtrak's and the fares are often more affordable. If you'll be traveling by train a great deal or across the rest of Canada as well, you may save money with the **Canrailpass,** which allows unlimited travel and unlimited stops. Passes cost CDN$299 for 15 days, $434 for 30 days ($239 and $314 for students). For more information, call 800-561-7860. Travel by train in Alaska with the **Alaska Railroad Company (ARC).** ARC runs between Anchorage and Fairbanks for $176 round-trip (with a stop in Denali National Park) and between Anchorage and Seward for $35 one way, $60 round-trip. ARC also arranges transportation from Portage to Whittier, depending on demand. For more information, contact ARC, P.O. Box 107500, Anchorage, AK 99510 (800-544-0552).

In addition to the major lines, local and regional lines still thrive in some areas—check the yellow pages or else inquire at the local train station. Trains reach many fewer towns in the Northwest than buses do; keep this in mind as you plan. Regardless of which railway line you ride, always call to compare prices before purchasing a ticket.

By Car

If you plan to do a lot of driving within the U.S. during your trip, you might do well to join an automobile club. King of the hill, top of the heap is the **American Automobile Association (AAA)**, 811 Gatehouse Rd., Falls Church, VA 22047 (800-556-1166). Annual dues vary with the size and location of the local AAA club—call the toll-free number or contact your local club for details. Membership includes free maps and guidebooks, trip-planning services, emergency road service anywhere in the country, discounts on car rentals, the International Driver's License, and commission-free traveler's checks from American Express. Your membership card doubles as a $5000 bail bond (if you find yourself in jail) or a $200 arrest bond certificate (which you can use in lieu of being arrested for any motor vehicle offense except drunk driving, driving without a valid license, or failure to appear in court on a prior motor-vehicle arrest). Many clubs also have an "AAA Plus" membership program which provides more extensive emergency road service, insurance protection, and 100 miles of free towing (which may not be enough in rural areas, where AAA-affiliated garages are few and far between). *Let's Go* lists local AAA Emergency Road Service telephone numbers in the Practical Information sections.

Other automobile travel service organization are affiliated with oil companies or other large corporations. These include:

AMOCO Motor Club, P.O. Box 9014, Des Moines, IA 50306 (800-334-3300). $40 annual membership enrolls you, your spouse, and your car. Services include 24-hour towing and emergency road service.

Mobil Auto Club, P.O. Box 5039, North Suburban, IL 60194 (800-621-5581, in IL 800-572-5572). $39 membership includes you and one other person. Benefits include locksmith and other services on the road, as well as car-rental discounts with Hertz, Avis, and National.

Montgomery Ward Auto Club (800-621-5151). $45 membership includes entire family, covering children ages 16-23.

In Canada, automobile insurance is mandatory. If you are involved in a car accident and you don't have insurance, look out—the stiff fine won't make the experience any less harrowing. In Washington, British Columbia, and Alberta, you must wear seatbelts; in Oregon, children under 16 must wear wear them at all times.

See Documents and Formalities below under For International Visitors for information on the International Driver's License.

Learn a bit about minor automobile maintenance and repair before you leave. Easy-to-read manuals may at the very least help you survive long enough to reach a reputable garage. Practice changing your tire once or twice without help—you'll really have earned your driver's license once you've mastered this.

On the Road

Gas is generally cheaper in towns than at interstate service stops. Oil company credit cards are handy, but many stations charge for this service. MasterCard and Visa are not always accepted, and those stations that do accept them are often more expensive. Moral: always carry enough cash for gasoline emergencies.

When planning your budget, remember that the enormous travel distances of the Pacific Northwest will require you to spend more on gas than you might expect. Burn less money by burning less fuel. (To estimate roughly how much you'll spend on gas, figure 5¢ per mile or 3¢ per kilometre.) Tune up the car, make sure the tires are in good repair and properly inflated, check the oil frequently, avoid running the air conditioner unnecessarily, don't use roof luggage racks (they cause air drag), and don't drive over 55 miles/90 kilometres per hour (believe it or not, it *does* save gas).

Unlike the more densely populated regions of the continent, the Northwest does not have an extensive system of quality secondary roads. Older highways predominate; they merge with the main street of each town in their path, and are slower to drive—but far more rewarding—than most interstate freeways. Venture down unpaved roads for some unforgettable vistas, but be sure to have plenty of gas and a well-tuned driving machine. And before you hit the road, particularly during the winter, check out the road conditions.

Alaska Northwest Books puts out three valuable guides which include maps, detailed car routes, and general travel information. Send for *The Milepost*, a guide to Alaska and Western Canada, *Northwest Mileposts,* a guide to the U.S. Pacific Northwest and southwestern Canada, or *Alaska Wilderness Milepost* (each US$15, CDN$19). Order from Alaska Northwest Books, GTE Discovery Publications, Inc., 22026 20th Ave. SE, Bothell, WA 98021 (800-331-3510).

The greatest difficulty posed by interstates is not the state troopers, the other drivers, or even bad road conditions (although these are nothing to sneeze at)—it's the sheer boredom. Reading bumper stickers and playing auto license poker quickly become the nonpharmaceutical equivalent of NyQuil. To prevent "frozen vision," don't keep your eyes glued to the road. If you feel drowsy, pull off the road to take a break, even if there are no official rest areas in the vicinity. To avoid overexhaustion, start driving in the wee hours of the morning and stop early in the afternoon (this way, you'll also have more time to find accommodations). When you're driving with companions, insist that one of them is awake at all times, and keep talking. If you're driving by yourself, be extra careful. If you can't pull over, try listening to a radio talk show (music can be just as lulling as silence). Coffee in a thermos is also helpful. And remember that turning the heat up too high in the car can also make you sleepy.

Never drive if you've had anything alcoholic to drink or if you've used drugs. Avoid the open road on weekend nights and holidays, when more drivers are likely to be drunk.

Renting

Although the cost of renting a car for days at a time is often prohibitively expensive, renting for local trips is often reasonable, especially if several people share the cost. In general, automobile rental agencies fall into two categories: national companies with thousands of affiliated offices across the country, and local companies that serve only one city or area.

Major rental companies usually allow cars to be picked up in one city and dropped off in another without any hitch. Their toll-free numbers enable renters to reserve a reliable car anywhere in the country. Drawbacks include steep prices and high minimum ages for rentals (21 or even 25). If you have a major credit card in your name, you can avoid having to leave a large cash deposit at a rental agency, and you may be able to rent where the minimum age would otherwise rule you out. Student discounts are sometimes available. Some major companies: **Alamo** (800-327-9633), **Avis** (800-331-1212), **Budget** (800-527-0700), **Dollar** (800-421-6868), **Hertz** (800-654-3131), **National** (800-328-4567), and **Thrifty** (800-331-4200).

While many local companies observe similar age requirements, they often have more flexible policies. Some require smaller cash deposits, on the order of $50-100. Others will simply accept proof of employment (check stubs, etc.). Local companies often charge less than major companies, although you'll generally have to return to your point of origin to return the car. Companies with names like Rent-A-Wreck supply cars long past their prime. Sporting dents and inoperative radios, the cars sometimes get very poor mileage, but generally run. *Let's Go* gives the addresses and phone numbers of local rental agencies in most towns.

When dealing with any car rental company, make certain the price includes insurance against theft and collision. Although basic rental charges run from $15-30 per day for a compact car, plus 7-20¢ per mile, most companies offer special money-saving deals. Standard shift cars are usually a few dollars cheaper then automatics. All companies have special weekend rates, and renting by the week can save you even more. Most packages include a certain amount of free mileage that varies with the length of time you're renting for. If you'll be driving a long distance, ask for an unlimited-mileage deal. If you want to rent for longer than a week, look into automobile leasing. Leasing is cheaper than renting, but make sure the car is covered by a service plan, or you may end up stuck with outrageous repair bills.

Auto Transport Companies

If you don't have a car and can't afford to rent one for a long trip, you might consider registering with an automobile transport company. These outfits hire drivers on behalf of car owners who need their automobile moved from one city to another. You can let the companies know where you want to drive, and if one of them is asked to have a car driven there, you'll get a call. You are provided with the first tank of gas; all other expenses are yours (gas, food, lodging, tolls). Before you leave you have to pay a deposit, which is refunded to you when you deliver the car. If the car breaks down or is damaged, the insurance of the car transport company covers it. You must be at least 21 years old and have a valid driver's license. The following companies each have over 50 offices across the country:

Auto Caravan Corp. (800-221-0566). To be hired you must provide references and a record of employment. Deposit $100.

Auto Driveaway Co. (800-621-4155). Serves U.S. and Canada. Deposit $200. Arrival deadline can be negotiated, so you may be able to detour along the way.

Transporters, Inc. (212-594-2690). Call within a week of when you're available to depart—drivers hired on first-come, first-served basis. Deposit $200 (varies with distance). 9 days to travel coast-to-coast.

If offered a car, look it over first. Think twice about accepting a gas guzzler, since you're the one paying for gasoline. Driving for an auto transport company is most likely to bear fruit if your schedule is flexible; you may find a car within a week, or it may take several.

By Ferry

Along the Pacific coast, ferries are an exhilirating and occasionally indispensible way to travel. Some Alaskan towns can only be reached by water or air—Kodiak, for example, and many spots along the Panhandle. In addition to filling a need, the ferry system also allows travelers to view some of the area's most stunning sights. Travelers from land-locked parts will enjoy the wind in their faces and the beauty of the water and the coast. You can cruise past the remarkable Columbia Glacier on Alaska's *MV Bartlett* or *Tustumena,* or visit the San Juan Islands on the Washington State ferry to Victoria. Or gape at Sitka's volcano, "The Mount Fuji of Alaska," on the *LeConte* ferry. Ferry travel, however, is quite expensive, particularly when you bring a car along with you.

Alaska ferry travel is run by the **Alaska State Ferry System,** better known as the **Alaska Marine Highway.** There are three routes in the system. The southeastern route cruises from Seattle, WA, to Skagway, AK, via Prince Rupert, BC; this ferry stops in Juneau and a number of other small towns along the Alaskan panhandle. (In October 1989, a new terminus will open in Bellingham, WA.) The southcentral route runs between Cordova and Port Lions in Alaska. Much less frequent (only six scheduled voyages between May and October) is the southwestern route, which serves the Aleutian Islands. Alaska's ferry schedule is quite complicated, and changes every May and October. Fares are also subject to change. Fares are charged according to three categories: passengers (who ride on deck), cabins, and vehicles. Reservations are almost always required. Standby is available on a first-come, first-served basis, although once you and/or your vehicle is on board, the ferry still has the right to unload either of you before you reach your intended destination. Senior citizens ages 65 and over can obtain passes that entitle them to free ferry travel (subject to certain restrictions); passes are issued at any port of embarkation. Some ships are equipped for disabled travelers, who can also obtain a pass for free ferry travel by writing the central office in Juneau. Ferries do not stop at each port every day; doublecheck your itinerary with care, or you may find yourself unexpectedly grounded for days. For information and reservations, contact the Alaska Marine Highway, P.O. Box R, Juneau, AK 99811, 800-642-0066. See also the sections on the Alaska Marine Highway later in this book under Seattle and Alaska.

Ferries traveling along the coast also serve the area between Seattle, Vancouver Island, and the northern coast of British Columbia. Contact these companies for further information:

BC Ferries, 1112 Fort St., Victoria, BC V8V 4V2 (206-441-6865 in Seattle, 604-669-1211 in Vancouver, 604-386-3431 in Victoria). Operates *Queen of the North* between Port Hardy and Port Rupert year-round; during the summer, northbound and southbound routes on alternate days. Special facilities for disabled passengers.

BC Stena Line Ltd., 254 Belleville St., Victoria, BC V8V 1W9 (800-962-5984 in Seattle, 604-388-7397 in Victoria). Runs the *Vancouver Island Princess* and the *Princess Marguerite* between Seattle and Victoria. Two ferries per day in each direction; 1 per day fall to spring.

Black Ball Transport, 430 Belleville St., Victoria, BC V8V 1W9 (206-622-2222 in Seattle, 206-457-4491 in Port Angeles, 604-386-2202 in Victoria). Ferries every day between Port Angeles and Victoria.

Washington State Ferries, 206-464-6400; for information with touch tone phone outside WA 800-252-4550, then push 2840. Ferries between Anacortes, WA, and Sidney, BC, and between Seattle and points on the Kitsap Peninsula and San Juan Islands.

The **Alaska Northwest Travel Service, Inc.,** 130 2nd Ave. S., Edmonds, WA 98020 (206-775-4504), is an agent for Alaska and British Columbia ferries; they can book ferries and offer advice on itineraries. Ferry scheduling information can also be found in *The Milepost,* published by Alaska Northwest Publishing Co.; see By Car for information on how to obtain a copy.

Information about fares, reservations, vehicles, and schedules varies greatly during the various times of the year. *Let's Go* helps steer you through the morass in the sections of the book on Seattle and the areas of BC and Alaska served by ferries. Be sure to consult each ferry company to clear up any questions and help you piece together your own itinerary.

By Motorcycle

Well, it's cheaper than driving a car—but the physical and emotional wear and tear of motorcycling may cancel any financial gain. Fatigue and the small gas tank conspire to force the motorcyclist to stop more often on long trips; experienced riders are seldom on the road more than six hours per day. Lack of luggage space can also be a serious limitation. If you must carry a load, keep it low and forward where it won't distort the cycle's center of gravity. Fasten it either to the seat or over the rear axle in saddle or tank bags.

Annoyances are only a small part of the story. Despite their superior maneuverability, motorcycles are incredibly vulnerable. Major enemies are crosswinds, drunk drivers, and the blind spots of cars and trucks. *Always ride defensively.* The dangers skyrocket at night; travel only in the daytime. Half of all cyclists have an accident within their first month of riding. Even if you've never met a person who's had an accident on a motorcycle, realize that serious mishaps are remarkably common and often fatal. Always wear the best helmet you can get your hands on. For information on motorcycle emergencies, ask your State Department of Motor Vehicles for a motorcycle operator's manual.

Hitchhiking

Don't let the *Let's Go* logo fool you—hitchhiking is not the recommended way to travel on the North American continent. It's easily the least predictable and most risky way to get from place to place. Women should be especially cautious, and should never hitch alone.

While your thumb's extended, be prepared for the police as well as for free rides. In some places, hitchhiking is legal in the city but not in the suburbs. All states prohibit hitching while standing on the roadway itself or behind a posted freeway entrance sign. The law limits hitchers on interstates to thumbing from the access ramps only, and sometimes it's prohibited even there. An officer may ask you to move farther off the road, or to show picture identification. Hitching is illegal in some areas; in the wilds of Canada or Alaska it is especially risky and difficult because of the combination of fewer major highways and vast stretches of uninhabited land. If you hitch across the U.S.-Canada border, you will draw questions and suspicion.

If you decide hitchhiking is worth the risk, you should pay attention to a few strategic details when trying to get rides. Every city and road has a best and worst place for hitchhikers. Try stretches near a major intersection where many cars pass by. Since police regularly enforce laws against walking along limited access highways, a busy entrance ramp is the next best alternative. Hold a destination sign. Roads traveled almost exclusively by out-of-state tourists make for fruitless hitching; the drivers are out of their element and fear picking up hitchhikers.

Men and women alike should never accept a ride without sizing up the driver. Before you get in, ask the driver where he or she is going. Be wary if the driver opens the door quickly and enthusiastically offers to drive anywhere. Watch for drunk drivers, especially at night. These drivers may be more relaxed, and more likely to pick you up, but you will be placing yourself in real danger. Do not accept a ride if you feel uneasy for any reason. Make up an excuse and wait for another car to come along. If you do decide to get in, first make sure the passenger door opens from inside in case of an emergency. If there are several people in the car, do not sit in the middle. Always be in a position from which you can exit quickly. Do not let the driver place your belongings in the trunk. Once in the car, talk with the driver. Even idle chatter will make both driver and passenger more comfortable. Control the conversation by asking most of the questions, instead of answering them. Should a threatening or intimidating atmosphere develop during the ride, ask to be let out, even if the spot doesn't look like a promising place to get another ride. Don't worry about offending the driver or becoming embarrassed—*safety* before image.

Another strategy for getting a ride is to strike up a conversation with drivers parked at restaurants, gas stations, or scenic turnouts and simply ask for a ride. Your chances may be slightly higher this way, and you will have a chance to look each other over. On luckless days or in a dangerous situation, know when to call it quits and head for the bus or train station—always have these options available to you.

Accommodations

The Northwest has a pleasant variety of inexpensive alternatives to hotels and motels. Before you set out, try to locate places to stay along your route and make reservations, especially if you plan to travel during peak tourist seasons. If you are addicted to Hiltons and Marriotts beyond your means, consider joining **Discount Travel International**, 114 Forrest Ave., Ives Bldg., #205, Narberth, PA 19072 (215-668-2182). For an annual membership fee of $45, you and your household will have access to a clearing house of unsold hotel rooms (as well as airline tickets, cruises and the like), which can save you as much as 50%.

Youth Hostels

Youth hostels offer unbeatable deals on indoor lodging, and they are great places to meet other budget travelers from all over the world. Hostels generally are dorm-

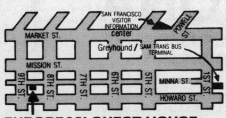

style accommodations where men and women sleep separately, often in large rooms with bunk beds. (Some hostels allow families and couples to have private rooms.) Prices are kept low since there are few frills. You have to bring your own sleep sack (two sheets sewn together); sleeping bags are often not allowed. Hostels often have kitchens and utensils for your use, and some have storage areas and laundry facilities.

In the United States, **American Youth Hostels (AYH)** maintains 31 hostels in Washington, Oregon, and Alaska. Most of them are near the coast, and they cluster around the major cities. Basic AYH rules: check-in between 5 and 8pm, check-out by 9:30am, maximum stay 3 days, no pets or alcohol allowed on the premises. All ages are welcome. Hostels differ in size, and fees range from $5-13 per night. Hostels are graded according to the number of facilities they offer and the overall level of quality—consult *Let's Go* evaluations for each town. Reservations may be necessary or advisable at some hostels, so check ahead of time. AYH membership is annual: $25, $15 for ages over 54, $10 for ages under 18, $35 for a family. Nonmembers who wish to stay at an AYH hostel pay $3 extra, which can be applied toward membership. IYHF memberships are recognized at all AYH hostels. For more information, contact AYH, P.O. Box 37613, Washington, DC 20013-7613 (202-783-6161). In Canada, the **Canadian Hostelling Association** is the counterpart to AYH. Most of the regulations are the same; fees range from CDN$4-13 per night. Membership costs CDN$21, CDN$12 for ages under 19, and CDN$42 for families. IYHF memberships are honored in Canada. For more information, contact Canadian Hostelling Association, National Office, 1600 James Naismith Dr., Gloucester, Ont. K1B 5N4 (613-748-5638).

Budget Chain Motels

Although many budget motels sport single digits in their names (e.g. Motel 6), the starting price of a single has escalated to about $20. Nevertheless, budget chain motels still cost significantly less than the larger chains such as Holiday Inn. Budget chains offer more consistency in cleanliness and comfort than their locally operated generic budget competitors; some budget motels even feature heated pools and pay-TVs. In bigger cities, budget motels are just off the highway, inconveniently far from the downtown area. If you don't have a car, you may well spend the difference between a budget motel and one downtown on transportation. Contact these chains for free directories:

Motel 6, 3391 S. Blvd, Rio Rancho, NM 87124 (505-891-6161).

Super 8 Motels, Inc., P.O. Box 4090, Aberdeen, SD 57402-4090 (800-843-1991).

Friendship Inns International, 2627 Paterson Plank Rd., North Bergen, NJ 07047 (800-453-4511).

Imperial 400 Motor Inns, 1000 Wilson Blvd., #820, Arlington, VA 22209 (800-368-4400; in VA, 800-572-2200).

College Dormitories

Many colleges and universities fling open their residence halls to travelers when term is not in session (some do so even while school is still in). No general policy covers all of these institutions, but rates tend to be low. *Let's Go* directs you to major educational institutions that offer accommodations. Since college dorms are popular with many travelers, you should write ahead for reservations if possible.

Students traveling through a college or university town while school is in session might try introducing themselves to friendly looking local students. At worst you'll receive a cold reception; at best, a good conversation might lead to an offer of a place to spend the night. Foreign visitors may have especially good luck here. In general, college campuses are some of the best sources for information on things

to do, places to stay, and possible rides out of town. In addition, dining halls often serve reasonably priced, reasonably edible all-you-can-eat meals.

Bed and Breakfasts

Bed and breakfasts (private homes with spare rooms available to travelers) are refreshing alternatives to impersonal hotel rooms, and some B&Bs provide an excellent way to explore with the help of a host who knows the region well. Some B&Bs go out of their way to be accommodating by accepting travelers with pets, arranging to meet the guest's plane, bus, or train (often for an added fee), giving personalized tours, and (best of all) preparing home-cooked breakfasts (and sometimes dinners). While many B&Bs do not provide phones, TVs, or showers with your room, they are usually delightful places that will remind you of home.

Prices vary widely. B&Bs in major cities are usually more expensive than those in out-of-the-way places. Doubles, with complete or continental breakfast, can cost anywhere from $20 to $300 per night. Most are in the $30-50 range. Some homes give special discounts to families or senior citizens. Reservations are almost always necessary, although in the off-season you can frequently find a room on short notice. Many bed-and-breakfasts close down during the winter, though.

For information on Pacific Northwest B&Bs, contact **Bed and Breakfast International,** 1181-B Solano Ave., Albany, CA 94706 (415-525-4569). Many B&B guidebooks are available in bookstore travel sections. Since many B&Bs are not listed in any guidebook, check local phonebooks and visitors bureaus.

Camping and the Outdoors

To many, the Northwest *is* the outdoors. Mountains, forests, rivers, and glaciers are accessible not only to the expert adventurer and naturalist but to the average

traveler. Indeed, if you haven't taken advantage of the great outdoors, you haven't really experienced the Northwest. Books and other writings about the region and its natural attractions are easy to find. Three publishers in particular put out a myriad of books that describe the parks and trails of the Northwest, as well as high quality books about camping, hiking, and biking in the area. Write or call to order or to receive a free catalog:

Sierra Club Books, Editorial Offices, 730 Polk St., San Francisco, CA 94109 (415-776-2211). Books about the national parks in the region, as well as *The Best About Backpacking* ($9), *Cooking for Camp and Trail* ($6), *Learning to Rock Climb* ($11), and *Wildwater* ($9).

The Mountaineers Books, 306 2nd Ave. W., Seattle, WA 98119 (800-553-4453 or 206-285-2665). Books too numerous to list individually include the *100 Hikes* series about trails in the region, as well as guides to bicycling in the Northwest and mountaineering medicine.

Wilderness Press, 2440 Bancroft Way, Berkeley, CA 94704-1676 (415-843-8080). Specializes in hiking guides and maps for the Western U.S. Also publishes the excellent *Backpacking Basics* and *Backpackers' Sourcebook* ($8 each).

Campers should run out and look at a copy of *Woodall's Campground Directory* (Western edition $9) and *Woodall's Tent Camping Guide* (Western edition $8). If you can't find a copy locally, contact **Woodall Publishing Company,** 100 Corporate N., #100, Bannockburn, IL 60015-1253 (800-323-9076 or 312-395-7799). For **topographical maps,** write the **U.S. Geological Survery,** Map Distribution, Box 25286, Federal Center, Denver, CO 80225 (call 703-648-6892 or 202-343-8073 with questions) or the **Canada Map Office,** 615 Booth St., Ottawa, Ont. K1A 0E9 (613-952-7000), which distributes geographical and aeronautical maps as well.

Parks and Forests

At the turn of the century, it may have seemed unnecessary to set aside parts of the vast American and Canadian wilderness as reserves, but today that action

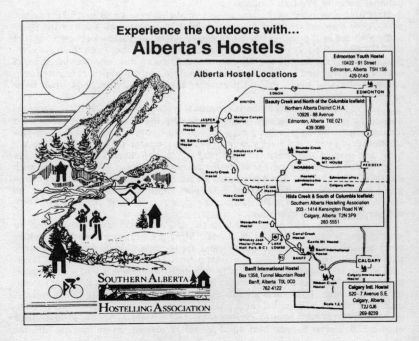

is recognized as a stroke of genius. The extensive system of government-protected parks in the Northwest provides a much-needed antidote to the silicon and concrete of the postmodern technopolis.

National parks protect some of America and Canada's most spectacular scenery. Breathtaking Mt. McKinley, glass-still Crater Lake, and the wilds of Jasper are treasures that will remain intact for generations. Though their official purpose is preservation, the parks make room for recreation as well. Many national parks have backcountry and developed tent camping; others welcome RVs, and a few allow opulent living in grand lodges. Internal road systems allow you to reach the interior and the major sights even if you are not a long-distance hiker. Ranger talks and guided hikes teach visitors about the parks. The larger and more popular national parks charge a $3-5 entry fee for vehicles, and sometimes a nominal one for pedestrians and cyclists as well. All U.S. parks accept the $25 **Golden Eagle Passport** (which most sell as well) in lieu of the fee. Visitors over 62 can obtain the free **Golden Age Passport,** which entitles them to free entry at national parks, monuments, and historical sites, as well as discounts on other park fees. Disabled travelers enjoy the same privileges with the **Golden Access Passport,** also free. For information about camping, accommodations, and regulations at national parks, contact any of the following agencies. For Washington and Oregon: **Pacific Northwest Regional Office, National Park Service,** 1018 1st Ave., Seattle, WA 98104 (206-442-0181). For Alberta and British Columbia: **Canadian Parks Service,** 220 4th Ave. SE, #552, Calgary, AB T2P 3H8 (403-292-4440). For the Yukon Territory: **Canadian Parks Service,** 457 Main St., 4th Floor, Winnipeg, Manitoba R3B 3E8 (204-983-2290). For Alaska: **Alaska Public Land Information Center,** 605 W. 4th Ave., #105, Anchorage, AK 99501 (907-271-2737). Visitor centers at parks offer excellent free literature and information, and the U.S. Government Printing Office publishes two useful pamphlets: *National Parks: Camping Guide* (S/N 024-005-01028-9; $3.50) and *National Parks: Lesser-Known Areas* (S/N 024-005-00911-6; $1.50). The Winnipeg office of the Canadian Parks Service distributes *Parks West,* a book about all the national parks of Western Canada.

State and provincial parks are, as one might expect, something like national parks, only they are operated by a lower level of government. Each of the states and provinces in the region has an extensive system of parks of its own, smaller than the national parks but much more numerous. While they cannot always compete with the grandeur of Mt. Rainier or Banff, many state and provincial parks offer some of the best camping around—handsome surroundings, elaborate facilities, and plenty of space. Prices for camping are almost always better than those at private campgrounds.

If you're really bothered by large crowds, stay away from the well-known parks during the peak tourist season, which is generally the summer. Many parks close for the winter, however, so you may not have this option. Don't let the presence of swarms of people dissuade you from visiting the large parks—these places are huge, and even at their most crowded they offer many chances for quiet and solitude. Reservations may be necessary for accommodations, especially those with solid walls (i.e., lodges). Even campsites are hard to come by at times; most campgrounds are first-come, first-pitched. Some parks limit the number of days you can stay in a campsite as well as the number of people you can have in your group (usually no more than 25 campers).

If you are a complete purist and even the national parks are too developed for your tastes, head for the **national forests.** Most are equipped only for primitive camping—pit toilets and no running water are the rule. Forests are less accessible than the parks, but less crowded as a consequence. They're also generally free. Backpackers can take advantage of specially designated **wilderness areas,** where regulations prohibit vehicles and there are no roads, making these areas even less accessible to the throngs. **Wilderness permits** are required for backcountry hiking and can usually be purchased at parks; check ahead to be on the safe side. One word of warning: Adventurers who plan to explore some real wilderness should always check in at a U.S. Forest Service field office for safety reasons before heading into the

woods. Many of these wilderness areas are difficult to find and therefore under-utilized—so write ahead for accurate, detailed maps. For general information, contact the **Pacific Northwest Regional Office, U.S. Forest Service,** P.O. Box 3623, Portland, OR 97208 (503-326-2877), or the **Alaska Regional Office, U.S. Forest Service,** Federal Office Bldg., P.O. Box 2168-PAO, Juneau, AK 99802 (907-568-8806).

The **Pacific Crest Trail,** which stretches from the Mexico-California border into Canada, is particularly attractive for one- or two-week hiking trips along its shorter segments. Heated cabins and some running tap water along the trails add convenience. Consult an area tourism bureau for maps of the trail. Another valuable source is *The Pacific Crest Trail,* Vol. 2 (Wilderness Press; $20), which covers Oregon and Washington.

Tent Camping, Hiking, and Climbing

To appreciate the beauty of the Northwest, to get a glimpse of the life that has been led in this region for centuries, to feel the grandeur of the landscape deep inside—you must go camping.

It's cheap, too.

Equipment

In the Northwest you and your equipment will be subject to weather conditions that may vary considerably even within a short time. The Climate section below has more detail about the weather, but always keep in mind the twin factors of cold and rain, and remember that areas west of the mountains are rained upon much more than parts just east. Here is a primer on the basic equipment you'll need to be a safe and happy camper.

At the core of your equipment is the **sleeping bag.** Which one you buy will depend on the climate in which you will be camping. Sleeping bags are rated according to the lowest outdoor temperature at which they will still protect you. If a bag's rating is not a temperature but a seasonal description, keep in mind that "summer" translates to a rating of 30-40°F, "three-season" can be anywhere from 5-30°F, and "four-season" means below 0°F. When you check specific sleeping bags, get the most specific temperature rating you can. To determine which bag to buy, figure out the lowest temperature you'll be sleeping in and subtract another few degrees. Sleeping bags are made either of down or of synthetic material. Down bags are warmer and lighter in weight, but they dry out less quickly when they get wet. Synthetic bags require more material to achieve the same level of warmth as down, and consequently weigh more, but they dry out well. Lowest prices for acceptable sleeping bags: $40 for a summer synthetic, $110 for a three-season synthetic, $135 for a three-season down bag, and upwards of $200 for a down sleeping bag you can use in the winter. If you're using a sleeping bag for serious camping, you should also have either a foam pad or an air mattress to cushion your back and neck. Inch-thick foam pads start at $10, while air mattresses cost around $50. Another good alternative is the **Therm-A-Rest,** which is part foam and part air-mattress and inflates to full padding when you unroll it (from $50).

When you select a **tent,** your major considerations should be shape and size. A-frame tents are the best all-around. When they are pitched, their internal space is almost entirely usable; this means little unnecessary bulk. Only one drawback: if you're caught in the rain and have to spend a day or two holed up inside your tent, A-frames can be cramped and claustrophobic. Dome and umbrella shapes offer more spacious living, but tend to be bulkier to carry around. As for size, two people can fit in a two-person tent but will find life more pleasant in a four-person tent. If you're traveling by car, go for the bigger tent. If you're hiking, stick with a smaller tent that weighs no more than 1.5 lbs./3.5kg. Good two-person tents cost about $85, $115 for a four-person. However, you can often find last year's version for half the price. Even expensive stores will slash the price of an "old" tent they find themselves stuck with, leaving it well within budget range. These deals pop up most often in the fall. **Eureka** is the classic manufacturer of tents.

If you intend to do a lot of hiking or biking, you should have a **frame backpack.** Buy a backpack with an internal frame if you'll be hiking on difficult trails that require a lot of bending and maneuvering—internal-frame packs mould better to your back, keep a lower center of gravity, and have enough give to follow you through your contortions. An internal-frame backpack is also good as an all-around travel pack, something you can carry by hand or on your back no matter how you travel. External-frame packs are more comfortable for long hikes over even terrain; since they keep the weight higher, walking upright will not cost you additional exertion. The size of a backpack is measured in cubic inches. Any serious backpacking requires at least 3300 of them, while longer trips require around 4000. Add an additional 500 cubic inches for internal-frame packs, since you'll have to pack your sleeping bag inside, rather than strap it on the outside as you do with an external-frame pack. Backpacks with many compartments generally turn a large space into many unusable small spaces. Packs that load from the front rather than the top allow you access to your stuff more easily. Some front-loading packs include a section that is attachable and detachable by zipper for use as a daypack. Sturdy backpacks start anywhere from $75-125. Anything cheaper may be less comfortable, and the straps are more likely to fray or rip quickly. Test-drive a backpack for comfort before you buy it.

Other necessities include: **battery-operated lantern** (never gas), **plastic groundcloth** for the floor of your tent, **nylon tarp** for general purposes, and a **"stuff bag"** to keep your sleeping bag dry. Don't go anywhere without a **canteen** or water bottle. Plastic models keep water cooler in the hot sun than metal ones do, although metal canteens are a bit sturdier and leak less. If you'll be away from parks with showers, bring **water sacks** and/or a **solar shower**, a small sack with an attachable shower head. Although most campgrounds provide campfire sites, you may want to bring a small **metal grate** of your own, and even a grill. For those places that forbid fires or the gathering of firewood, you'll need a **camp stove** (**Coleman** is the classic, and they start at $40). Make sure you have **waterproof matches.**

Shop around your area for the best deals on camping equipment. If you can, buy from a local retailer who can give you advice about using your equipment. Several mail-order firms offer lower prices, and they can also help you determine which item is the one you need. Call or write for a free catalog:

Campmor, 810 Rte. 17N, P.O. Box 997-P, Paramus, NJ 07653-0997 (800-526-4784).

L.L. Bean, 1 Casco St., Freeport, ME 04033 (800-341-4341).

Recreational Equipment, Inc. (REI), Commercial Sales, P.O. Box C-88126, Seattle, WA 98188 (800-426-4840).

The mail-order firms are guides to the lowest prices; if the prices at your local dealer are reasonable in comparison, buy from there (you could try bargaining if you're so inclined).

A good initial source of information on **recreational vehicles (RVs)** is the **Recreational Vehicle Industry Association,** 1986 Preston White Dr., P.O. Box 2999, Reston, VA 22090 (703-620-6003). For a free catalog that lists RV camping publications and state campground associations, send a self-addressed, stamped envelop to **Go Camping America Committee, P.O. Box 2669, Reston, VA 22090 (703-620-6003).**

Wilderness Concerns

Health, safety, and food should be your primary concerns as you camp. See Health above for information about basic medical concerns and first-aid. A comprehensive guide to outdoor survival is *How to Stay Alive in the Woods,* by Bradford Angier (Macmillan, $6). Many rivers, streams, and lakes are contaminated with bacteria such as *giardia,* which causes gas, diarrhea, cramps, and loss of appetite. To protect yourself from the effects of this invisible trip-wrecker, always boil water before drinking or cooking with it, and bring water purification pills along. *Never go camping or hiking any significant time or distance alone.* If you're going into an area that is not well-traveled or well-marked, let someone know where you're hiking and how long you intend to be out. If something unexpected occurs while you're unreachable, searchers will at least know where to look for you.

As you enjoy the wilderness, remember that with thousands of outdoor enthusiasts traipsing through the parks every year, the forests face being trampled to death. Be considerate, and take some steps to avoid marring the beauty of the wilderness. Because firewood is scarce in popular parks, campers are asked to make small fires (a campstove is preferable), and use only dead branches or brush. Check ahead to see if the park prohibits campfires altogether. To prevent repeated scarring of an area, make camp at least 100 feet from regularly used sites. Also, if there are no toilet facilities around, bury human waste 100 feet or more from any water supply to prevent contaminating lakes and streams. Keep soap or detergent away from bodies of water. Always burn your trash— *never* bury it. Bring whatever you cannot burn with you when you leave the campground. And remember that hunting is strictly prohibited in all national, state, and provincial parks.

Bear Necessities

No matter how tame a bear appears, don't be fooled—they're wild and dangerous animals, and they're just not impressed or intimidated by humans. To avoid an unbearable experience, never feed a bear, or tempt it with such delectables as open trash cans. They will come back for more and grow more aggressive every time. Keep your camp clean. Do not leave trash or food lying around camp. Burn waste to destroy its odors—never bury it. Store food in air-tight containers, then hang them in a tree 8 feet from the ground and 4 feet from the trunk. Avoid indulging in greasy foods, especially bacon and ham. Grease gets on everything, including your clothes and sleeping bag, and bears find it an alluring dressing for your equipment (even if you're in it). Burn all feminine hygiene materials as well—never throw these, or food, down a toilet. If you're lucky enough to be able to recognize a bear trail when you see one, don't camp on it. Park rangers can tell you more about how to identify bear trails. Bears are attracted to perfume smells; do without cologne, scented soap, and hairspray while camping. Stay away from dead animals and berry bushes—these are bear dinners. Always shine a flashlight when walking at night. When the bears see the light, they will take off before you arrive.

If you see a bear at a distance, calmly walk the other direction. If it seems interested, some suggest finding a long stick and waving it above your head; the general flailing creates the impression in the bear's eyes that you're much taller than a person, and it may decide that *you* are the menacing High Lord of the Forest. If you stumble upon a sweet-looking bear cub, leave immediately, no matter how cute it looks. Its mother will be right behind you, and she's *very* protective. If you find yourself face-to-face with a bear, don't run. Lie down and wait until the bear leaves. If the bear thinks you're dead, it may not feel the need to do the job itself.

Organized Adventure

If you're a novice outdoorsman, don't lose heart—many organized adventure tours are designed especially for amateurs. Be prepared to shell out some dough for the guidance, however. Before you sign up for any organized trip, make sure you have done a substantial amount of bargain shopping. Begin by consulting tourism bureaus, which can suggest parks and trails as well as outfitters and answer general questions. *Outside Magazine,* 1165 N. Clark St., Chicago, IL 60610, publishes an Expedition Services Directory in each issue.

The **Sierra Club,** 730 Polk St., San Francisco, CA 94109 (415-776-2211), plans many outings. So does **TrekAmerica,** P.O. Box 1338, Gardena, CA 90249 (800-221-0596 or 213-321-0734); call or write for information on their Canada and Alaska hikes. The **Pacific Crest Outward Bound School** (800-547-3312 or 503-243-1993) conducts courses in Oregon and Washington for adults and teenagers. These courses emphasize confidence building and communal cooperation. **Green Tortoise** organizes a two-month expedition to Alaska and the Canadian Rockies (see By Bus above for address and phone).

If the sight of Mt. Rainier brings you to the summit of excitement, take advantage of one of the many climbing schools in the Pacific Northwest. The **Lac Des Arcs Climbing School,** 1116 19 Ave. NW, Calgary, Alberta T2M 0Z9 (403-289-6795 or 403-240-6502), gives two- and four-day courses in rock climbing and mountaineering, which range in price from $100-250. Other trips and courses are offered by **Genet Expeditions, Inc.** (P.O. Box 230861, Anchorage, AK 99523; 800-334-3638 or 907-561-2123), and the Pacific Crest Outward Bound School. When you plan your climbing trips, remember that fatigue arrives faster at high altitudes. Let's be careful up there, and never go alone!

Bicycling

Assembling all the necessary equipment is, not surprisingly, the largest task you'll face as you prepare to tour by bike. Get in touch with a local biking club if you don't know a great deal about bicycle equipment and repair. When you shop around, compare knowledgeable local retailers to mail-order firms. If the disparity in price is modest, buy locally. Otherwise, order by phone or mail and make sure you have someone in town to consult with. Before you spend a cent, scan the pages of *Bicycling* magazine for low sale prices. **Bike Nashbar** almost always has the lowest prices—if you can find a nationally advertised price that's lower, they will beat it by 5¢. Contact them at P.O. Box 3449, Youngstown, OH 44513-3449 (800-627-4227). Their own line of products, including complete bicycles, is an excellent value. Another exceptional mail-order firm is **Bikecology,** P.O. Box 3900, Santa Monica, CA 90403 (800-326-2453).

Safe and secure riding requires a quality helmet and a quality lock. A **Bell** or **Tourlite** helmet costs about $40—much cheaper than critical head surgery (a la Mr. Gumby) or a well-appointed funeral. **Kryptonite** locks begin at $20, with insurance against theft either for one or two years or up to a certain amount of money, depending on where you buy it.

Long distance cyclists should get in touch with **Bikecentennial,** P.O. Box 8308, Missoula, MT 59807 (406-721-1776). This national, nonprofit organization researches and maps long-distance bicycle routes and organizes bike tours for members. Annual membership costs $22, $19 for students, and $25 for families. Members receive maps and guidebooks (write or call for a free catalog), route information, and nine issues of *BikeReport,* the organization's bicycle touring magazine. *Bicycling* magazine, noted above, is another good resource for bike travelers.

There are also a number of good books about bicycle touring and repair in general. *Bicycling* magazine publishes the compact but exhaustive *Bicycle Repair* ($5), available from Rodale Press, 33 E. Minor St., Emmaus, PA 18908 (215-967-5171). *Bicycle Touring* (Rodale Press, $5) and *Bike Touring* (Sierra Club, $11) both discuss how to equip oneself and plan for a bicycle trip. Both books begin with selecting the appropriate bike and other equipment, then move on to discuss how and what to pack, and how to plan the trip. *Bicycle Gearing: A Practical Guide* (The Mountaineers Books, $7) discusses in lay terms how bicycle gears work, covering everything you need to know in order to shift properly and get the maximum propulsion from the minimum exertion. Finally, 10-Speed Press publishes *The Bike Bag Book* ($4, or $3 plus 50¢ direct from publisher), a small and very cute book about the basics of bicycle repair; the authors suggest that the information found therein can be stretched a long way if you just add some common sense and creativity. Write 10-Speed Press, Box 7123, Berkeley, CA 94707.

Information about cycling in the region is available from tourist bureaus, which often distribute free maps. You can obtain the *Oregon Bicycling Guide* and *Oregon Coast Bike Route Map* from the Bikeway Program Manager, Oregon Department of Transportation, State Highway Division, Salem, OR 97310 (503-378-3432). The Mountaineers Books publishes a series about bicycling through Washington an Oregon. Another good guide is *Bicycle Touring in the Western United States,* by Karen and Gary Hawkins (Pantheon, $9). This book discusses planning and equipment as well as many things that seem obvious but never come to mind, such as road conditions and quality.

Bikers should remember that the Northwest possesses a less extensive network of well-paved backroads than other regions of the U.S. Between the coast and the mountains, bikers should also be wary of strong, prevailing winds from the northwest. You can transport your bike with you as you travel by bus, train, or air—check with each carrier about weight limits, packing requirements, insurance, and fees.

Organized bicycle trips take the burden of planning off your shoulders but leave you with substantial expenses. In the Yukon, Alberta, and British Columbia, contact **Rocky Mountain Cycle Tours,** Box 1978-H, Canmore, AB T0l 0M0 (403-678-6770). **Bicycle Adventures,** P.O. Box 7875, Olympia, WA 98507 (206-786-0989) organizes trips in Oregon, Washington, and British Columbia.

Outdoor Sports

Water Sports

The scores of fast-flowing rivers in the Pacific Northwest make the area ideal for canoeing, kayaking, and whitewater rafting. Throughout the book, boating opportunities are suggested in the Activities sections. Travel agents and tourism bureaus can recommend others.

The **River Travel Center,** Box 6, Pt. Arena, CA 95468 (800-882-7238), can place you in one of over 100 whitewater rafting trips, ranging in length from one to 18 days. They also organize kayaking trips. British Columbia rafting trips (1-6 days, $25-155) are planned by **Clearwater Expeditions Ltd.,** R.R. 2, Box 2506, Clearwater, BC V0E 1N0. **Hells Canyon Adventures, Inc.,** Box 159, Oxbow, OR 97840 (800-422-3568; in OR, 503-785-3352), is the place to call for Snake River whitewater rafting, whitewater jet boat tours, and fishing charters. One-day rafting trips cost $90 per person; three-day trips cost $330.

Sierra Club Books publishes a kayaking and whitewater rafting guide entitled *Wildwater* ($9). *Washington Whitewater* ($11 for each of two volumes) and *Canoe Routes: Northwest Oregon* ($9), published by The Mountaineers Books, might also interest you.

Snow Sports

In a region of the world that sprouts mountains at every turn, it is not surprising that so many people elect to spend so much time looking at the world from so many non-vertical perspectives. Winter sports enjoy enormous popularity in the Northwest. In an area where city dwellers can stare up at the mountain peaks from the streets, many people opt for skis or snow boots rather than sneakers. You'll find every imaginable way to enjoy the winter wonderland: the fast-paced can rent snowmobiles, the laid-back can shuffle along on snowshoes, and the courageous can even steer their own pack of sled dogs in Alaska or the Yukon.

Tourism bureaus can help you locate the best sports outfitters and ski areas. *Let's Go* suggests options in the Activities sections throughout the book. For Oregon and Washington skiing information, write the **Pacific Northwest Ski Association,** 640 NW Gilman Blvd., #104, Issaquah, WA 98027 (206-392-4220). The Sierra Club publishes *The Best Ski Touring in America* ($11), which includes Canada as well. The Mountaineers Books publishes good skiing guides for Oregon and Washington.

Always be aware of the health dangers of cold weather. Know the symptoms of hypothermia and frostbite (see Health), and bring along warm clothes and quick energy snacks such as candy bars and trail mix. Drinking alcohol in the cold can be particularly dangerous, even though it may help you feel warm—alcohol slows your body's ability to adjust to the temperature and therefore makes you more vulnerable to hypothermia. Send for the U.S. Government Printing Office's *Winter Recreation Safety Guide* (S/N 001-000-03856-7, $2; see Planning Your Trip for address and phone).

Fishing and Hunting

Fish seem quite willing to come on board your boat throughout the Pacific Northwest, Western Canada, and Alaska. Contact the appropriate department of fisheries for brochures that summarize regulations and make sport fishing predictions. Some fishing seasons are extremely short, so be sure to ask when the expected prime angling dates fall. Licenses are available from many tackle shops, or you can purchase them directly from the state or provincial department of fisheries. You need not reside in a state or province in order to hunt there, but steep license and tag fees will probably discourage you. If you must shoot, consult the appropriate departments of game to purchase licenses and receive regulations pamphlets.

Alaska: Fish and Game Licensing, 1111 W. 8th St., #108, Juneau, AK 99801 (907-465-2376). Nonresident fishing license $10 for 3 days, $20 for 14 days, $36 for a year. Nonresident hunting licenses $60, $96 for hunting and fishing. Big game tags, purchased before you hunt, range from $135 (deer) to $500 (musk ox).

Alberta: Fish and Wildlife Division, 9920 108th St., Edmonton T5K 2C9 (403-427-8580). Nonresident fishing license $7 for Canadians, $12 for non-Canadians. Nonresident hunting licenses: $15 wildlife certificate and resource development stamp, plus tags from $20 (wolf) to $275 (sheep).

British Columbia: Fish and Wildlife Division, Ministry of Environments, 810 Blanshard St., Victoria V8V 1X5 (604-387-4573). Nonresident fishing license US$15 for 6 days, US$27 for a year. Steelhead license US$42. Kootenay Rainbow Trout permit US$9 for 6 days, US$17 for a year.

Oregon: Department of Fish and Wildlife, 506 SW Mill St., P.O. Box 59, Portland 97207 (503-229-5403). Fishing licenses $12.50 for residents, $30.60 for nonresidents. Hunting licenses $9.50 for residents, $100.50 for nonresidents. Combination licenses $19.50 (residents only). Salmon and sturgeon tags $5.50.

Washington: Department of Fisheries, 11th and Columbia, 115 General Administration Bldg., Olympia 98504-0611 (206-753-6600). Licenses for food fish. Nonresident salmon and sturgeon licenses $3.50; personal use license required (residents $3.50, nonresidents $9.50). **Department of Game,** 600 N. Capitol Way, Olympia 98501-1091 (206-753-5700). Game fishing licenses $14 for residents, $40 for nonresidents. Hunting licenses $12 for residents, $125 for nonresidents. Combination licenses $24 (residents only).

Yukon: Department of Renewable Resources, Fish and Wildlife Branch, 10 Burns Rd., Whitehorse Y1A 4Y9 (403-667-5221). Nonresident fishing licenses $30 for Canadians, $35 for non-Canadians ($20 and $25 respectively for 3-day permits). Nonresident hunting licenses $75 for Canadians, $150 for non-Canadians.

Many outfitters plan fly-in fishing trips or boating trips designed for fishers. These expeditions are usually expensive. If you are interested, consult a travel agent or tourism bureau for possibilities.

Life in the Northwest

History

About 20,000 years ago, as the last Ice Age receded, the first people arrived in North America over a land bridge connecting eastern Asia with Alaska. They fanned out along the Pacific Coast and inland, blanketing the area from southeast Alaska to northern California. The groups they formed became the Native American tribes of the Northwest. Each group called itself *dene,* which means "people."

Two distinct types of society had emerged among the Native peoples by about 10,000 years ago. Between the mountain range and the coast, tribes made up of large extended families led a sedentary existence in settlements on the ocean. They sustained and supported themselves primarily from the sea, which provided their food and transportation. Coastal societies were complex and stratified. Men and women worked at distinct tasks, and authority was linked to property ownership. Professional artisans were supported by wealthy patrons. The central religious ceremony was the *potlatch*, regular festivals in which rights, privileges, and names were handed down. Although the various tribes along the coast became quite distinct, they developed a *lingua franca* for commerce, based on the language of the Chinook tribe. Farther inland, tribes were smaller and more nomadic. For three seasons a year, they would roam the plateaus for food. These tribes were much more egalitarian in nature; although men had a slight ascendancy over women, groups were governed consensually and food was shared. During the winter, groups of tribes would join together in permanent villages to conserve supplies and protect themselves from the cold.

Although the Spanish may have happened along the coast of Oregon in the 16th century, the first European explorers of the Northwest arrived from the same direction as the first immigrants. In 1741, Vitus Bering, a Dane employed by Peter the Great of Russia, discovered the coast of Alaska and explored the Aleutian Islands and the straits that bear his name. Bering's expedition brought the fur of sea otters back to Russia and inaugurated an intense competition for control of this lucrative trade. During the 1770s, Spain and Great Britain cluttered the Pacific coast with explorers in an attempt to secure a foothold in the region and stake a claim to its trade. Bruno Hezeta, a Spaniard, pushed up the coast to Alaska in 1775; a year later, James Cook of Great Britain arrived in Nootka Sound, in the no-man's land between Spanish and Russian holdings. Cook's expedition led to an explosion of British fur trading in the region, since his men had discovered the value of the sea otters' pelt in China on their way home.

Cook was also among the first explorers to search for a waterway (or "Northwest Passage") linking the Atlantic and the Pacific. British settlers in the eastern half of the continent suspected the existence of such a canal because Hudson Bay stretched so far to the west. By 1791, George Vancouver of Britain had abandoned that quest and turned to exploring the rivers that flowed into the Pacific. He hoped to discover a passage to the Great Plains. Others looked for the fabled connection between east and west in other ways. Alexander Mackenzie's quest led him to cross North America over land, in 1793—the first explorer to accomplish this feat.

For the three decades following 1780, the economic and political fortunes of the Northwest were in the hands of the large fur trading enterprises, which functioned not only as vast commercial empires but as quasi-governments as well. Great Britain's representative was the Hudson Bay Company, chartered by the crown long before Europe knew of the Pacific coast. The Company held a monopoly on British trading in "British North America"; it became the dominant force throughout what would become Canada with Britain's victory in 1763 in the French and Indian War. In 1779, a rival firm emerged, the North West Company. The "Nor'westers" quickly became legendary for their Mafia-like tactics. Rounding out the fur trade was John Jacob Astor, who founded the post of Fort Astoria (now Astoria) for the United States at the mouth of the Columbia River in 1811. Astoria surrendered to the Nor'westers without a fight at the end of the War of 1812, but the American presence remained and grew.

No one is quite certain of the origin of the name "Oregon," which gradually became attached to the area encompassing what is today Oregon, Washington, and much of British Columbia. Oregon emerged as the nub of the competition between the powers because of its many inland waterways: Puget Sound, and the Columbia, Willamette, Fraser, and Thompson Rivers. U.S. President Thomas Jefferson demonstrated that his country was serious about staking a claim in the region when he commissioned Meriwether Lewis and William Clark in 1803 to head overland toward the rivers near the coast. In 1818, the U.S. and Great Britain signed a treaty that ratified joint occupation of Oregon for 10 years. By the terms of the treaty, free competition was guaranteed to the settlers. During the following 15 years, the population of the area increased markedly. Vancouver Island and the Columbia and Willamette Valleys were thickly settled, and Protestant missionaries arrived to bring Western civilization to the Natives. In 1821, the Hudson Bay Company absorbed the North West Company in a merger, and in 1825, Russia agreed to limit its claim to the region north of 54°40' latitude. With the field of players steadily narrowing, Britain and the U.S. renewed their joint occupation treaty in 1827.

Five years later, the famous Oregon Trail opened. American pioneers gamboled in from the Midwest, braving the difficult winter, rivers to be forded, and Rocky Mountain passes. Missionaries such as Marcus and Narcissa Whitman (née Prentiss) and the Rev. and Mrs. Henry Spalding arrived over the Oregon Trail to teach the Natives, who initially welcomed and even asked for the missions. Between 1841 and 1843, U.S. settlement in the Willamette Valley exploded with new arrivals over the trail, and the British began to understand that their days south of the 49th parallel were numbered. In 1843, Britain judiciously moved its district capital from Fort Vancouver, on the Columbia, to newly constructed Victoria, on Vancouver Island. Around the same time, the American settlers began to clamor for self-rule and membership in the Union as a state. Initial attempts to form a government and write a constitution stalled, but an authority to rival that of the Hudson Bay Company took root in 1845. East of the Mississippi, Americans had begun to demand that the U.S. flag be hoisted from sea to shining sea. Democrat James K. Polk was elected president in 1844 with the slogan, "54°40' or Fight!"— indicating an intention to annex all the territory in Oregon under joint occupation. Once elected, Polk gobbled up territory in the Southwest from the ever-weakening Spanish, but began advocating compromise in Oregon. In 1846, the U.S. and Great Britain agreed to split Oregon by extending the 49th parallel boundary that divided the U.S. from Canada through the Rockies.

By 1853, the Oregon Territory, as the land assigned to the U.S. by the 1846 treaty was designated, had grown so large in population that the government determined to split it. Oregon became a state in 1866, while the Washington Territory, organized out of the remaining Oregon lands, gained statehood in 1889.

Far north, fur trading became less and less profitable to the Russians, and pressure increased on the U.S. to purchase Alaska. With a nod from President Andrew Johnson (perhaps dozing), Secretary of State William Seward led the charge. In 1867, Russia agreed to sell Alaska to the U.S. for $7.2 million, or less than 2¢ per acre. Many Americans derided the purchase as "Seward's Folly" or "Johnson's Polar Bear Garden," but the discovery of gold in the 1880s and 90s vindicated Secretary Seward's big splurge.

Gold was about to become what fur had previously been to the Northwest. In 1858, gold was discovered in British territory. When the Hudson Bay Company attempted to enforce the Company's monopoly rights with respect to the precious metal, Britain responded by creating the territories of New Caledonia and Vancouver Island. The next year a second gold rush, farther inland, brought new settlers and new pressures. In 1866 Britain wrested control of the area from the Company by merging the two colonies into the province of British Columbia. Now it was Britain that wanted to connect its possessions on the Atlantic and the Pacific, a desire that meshed with the settlers' demands for a transcontinental railroad. In 1885 the Canadian Pacific Railway was completed; its construction allowed the BC authorities to consolidate law and order in the West, and brought with it the fabled North West (now Royal Canadian) Mounted Police. The city of Vancouver was incorporated in 1887 as the terminus of the railroad and as a port on the Pacific. British Columbia boomed in the following years as other valuable natural resources were unearthed. The great Klondike gold rush of 1895-6 opened up much of the Yukon and Alaska; previously, gold had triggered a boom of sorts in eastern Washington as well.

Railroads led to the grabbing of the West in the U.S. as well as Canada. Back in 1853, Congress had authorized surveys to determine the most practical route for a railroad to Oregon. Residents of the Willamette Valley took matters into their own hands during the 1860s and attempted to raise money for track between Oregon and California. By 1883 the Northern Pacific Railroad had been completed, propelled in part by competition between the Portland and Seattle areas to be the terminus of the railroad. Washington's population grew with the completion of the new railroad, and Oregon's economy prospered. More lines linked the Northwest with parts east; the Canadian Northern reached Edmonton in 1905 and Vancouver in 1918.

As the 20th century began, the frontier began to close, and the Northwest was integrated more steadily into the rest of the United States and Canada. In 1898, the Yukon Territory was established. Alberta became a province in 1905, separated from British Columbia partly because of nativist sentiment against Albertan immigrants. (Alaska became a state only in 1959.) Uniformly across the region, the population increased steadily after 1900, and towns sprouted up along railway and highway routes. Natural resource industries predominated until World War II.

The Northwest was hospitable to populist and progressive politics in the first decades of the century. In 1911, Washington became the first U.S. state to organize a workers' compensation insurance fund, and through World War I Washington's legislature passed many other progressive acts as well. Oregon granted the vote to women in 1912. In the previous decade, William S. U'Ren created the "Oregon System." Legislation instituted initiative and referendum, direct primary elections, and popular recall of public officials. By 1917, women's suffrage had been adopted in Canada's western provinces as well, and Alberta selected the first woman magistrate in the history of the British empire. On a more populist note, the National Progressive Party catapulted to provincial parliamentary power in 1921 in Alberta, representing the protests of farmers. It governed the province until 1935 and left in place structures of cooperative agricultural marketing even after the party collapsed. Early in the 1930s, the Social Credit party was founded in Alberta by William Aberhart. Aberhart was a radio Bible preacher who proposed a simple (and ludicrous) way to increase everyone's buying power: the government should issue every citizen a "social dividend." Socreds ruled Alberta from 1935 to 1971, and governed in British Columbia from 1952 to 1972. After achieving power in each province, the Socreds realized that there was no money for their program, and took instead to budget cutting and cozying up to big business.

Since World War II, the Northwest has moved toward the frontiers of energy and technology. Alberta became the "Texas of Canada" after the discovery of oil in 1947, and the coastal states and provinces all look westward toward the Pacific Rim for future directions. In recent years, Oregon's state government has worked to develop trade links with the Pacific, hoping to link the fortunes of the agricultural interior with the growing commerce between the U.S. and Japan. Seattle has emerged as a technological center, and since World War II Washington has been home to the aircraft industry. Northwesterners have made their mark over the past decade in national politics as well: Joe Clark of Alberta succeeded Pierre Trudeau briefly as Prime Minister of Canada, and serves now in the government of Brian Mulroney; William O. Douglas of Washington was appointed to the Supreme Court from Franklin D. Roosevelt's inner circle and remained an unswerving liberal force on the Court into the 1970s; fellow Washingtonian Henry "Scoop" Jackson made a national name for himself in the U.S. Senate as a liberal on social issues who was also a fierce hawk on foreign policy; Tom Foley of Spokane, Washington, was elected Speaker of the U.S. House of Representatives in June 1989, after serving for many years as House majority leader.

Literature and the Arts

The Northwest has produced no literary school of its own, but many writers who have lived there or passed through testify to the liberating effect of the frontier and the mountains. Travelers such as John Muir and John McPhee have celebrated the natural wonders of the region and written detailed descriptions of travelers' struggles to stay alive. Stories and novels by Raymond Carver and Alice Munro provide a glimpse of the people and society of the region. Other authors, such as Ursula K. Leguin and Jean M. Auel, have simply drawn from the surroundings as they write about other matters completely. Poet Theodore Roethke taught at the University of Washington in Seattle, bequeathing his lyric sensibility to a generation of

Northwestern poets. Bernard Malamud taught for many years at Oregon State University as he wrote several of his best-known works.

What follows is a brief list of books by regional authors and about the region. In addition, look for *Finding the Boundaries: Poems and Short Stories by Alaskan Writers,* published by the Alaska State Council on the Arts. Check your local library for these books as well as other suggestions.

The Clan of the Cave Bear by Jean M. Auel

Ball Four by Jim Bouton

Cathedral by Raymond Carver

Go East, Young Man by William O. Douglas

Instructions to the Double by Tess Gallager

Adventures in the Alaska Skin Trade by John Hawkes

Notes from the Century Before: A Journal from British Columbia by Edward Hoagland

Selected Poems by Richard Hugo

Sometimes a Great Notion by Ken Kesey

The Moccasin Telegraph by W.P. Kinsella

The Left Hand of Darkness by Ursula K. Le Guin

Journals of Lewis and Clark by Merriwether Lewis and William Clark

The Call of the Wild by Jack London

Why Are We in Vietnam? by Norman Mailer

The Assistant by Bernard Malamud

Going to Extremes by Joe McGinness

Coming into the Country by John McPhee

Alaska and *Journey* by James Michener

Never Cry Wolf by Farley Mowat

Travels in Alaska by John Muir

Stories of Flo and Rose by Alice Munro

Zen and the Art of Motorcycle Maintenance by Robert Pirsig

Ten Days That Shook the World by John Reed

Another Roadside Attraction by Tom Robbins

The Lost Sun by Theodore Roethke

The Spell of the Yukon and Other Poems by Robert Service

Traveling Through the Dark by William Stafford

Staying Alive by David Wagoner

Theater and musical groups, museums and arts festivals make their home as well in the Northwest. During June and July, world-renowned Baroque authority Helmuth Rilling conducts some of the finest musicians in the United States in performances of Bach's cantatas and concerti at the Bach Festival in Eugene, OR. In August, the Mt. Hood Jazz Festival comes to Gresham, OR, near Portland, and brings to the stage some of America's favorite jazz musicians, including Wynton Marsalis and Stan Getz. Sitka, Alaska, draws renowned musicians each year for its Summer Music Festival, a series of chamber music concerts. In Alberta, two Jubilee Auditoriums attract visiting performers and groups year-round. The Seattle Opera deftly presents both classical and modern operas, gaining fame for an innovative and expert cycle of Wagner's *Ring*.

Afficianados of the theater should not miss the Oregon Shakespeare Festival in Ashland, OR. All summer long, the excellent company attracts troops of theater buffs to its outdoor performances. Drama is also highly acclaimed at the Contemporary Theater of Lewis and Clark College, in Portland, and at the School of Drama of the University of Washington, in Seattle. The Vancouver Art Gallery has a fine collection of classical and contemporary art and photography; British Columbia was the home of Emily Carr, a painter who blended British-influenced landscape painting with the patterns of Native American art. In Washington, the Seattle Art Museum presents an excellent collection of Asian art. The Portland Art Museum houses an especially fine exhibit of Pacific Northwest Native American art. Also in Portland, the Abanté Fine Arts Gallery houses original paintings by Picasso, Matisse, and Chagall.

Let's Go makes more detailed suggestions about art, music, and theater in the Sights and Entertainment sections throughout the book.

Climate

In the popular imagination, the Northwest is a frozen wasteland covered with snow for most of the year. In fact, you'll be able to enjoy warm temperatures in the summer just like at home, even if home is considerably farther south; rain may be more of a problem than snow.

In Alaska the weather varies from the coast inland. In general, though, summer and early fall (i.e. June-Sept.) are the warmest and sunniest times to visit. However, be prepared for wet, windy, and cold days even during the summer. In Anchorage, the average temperature is around 20°F in January and 60°F in July. In Alaska's interior, the temperatures can range from the 90s in the summers to the -70s in the winter. Remember also that as you progress farther north, summer days and winter nights become longer. In Barrow, at the top of Alaska, the sun does not set all summer, nor does it rise during the winter. Elsewhere in Alaska and the Yukon, summer days may last from 6am to 2am.

In Alberta, the north and south of the province differ in temperature, although the entire area tends to be dry and cool. In January, the average temperature is around 15°F in the south, closer to −20°F in the north; in the summer, both regions warm to around 70°F.

In British Columbia, Washington, and Oregon, the key weather-making factor is the mountains. The first rule of thumb is that west of the mountains it rains quite a bit, while to the east it rains relatively little. On the BC coast, the average temperature is about 35°F in January and a cool 65°F in the summer. Inland, winter temperatures hover around 0°F, while summer temperatures rise near 70°F. Temperatures in Washington range from an average of 35°F in January to 70°F in July—the west slightly colder, the east slightly warmer. In Oregon, temperatures are a little warmer than in Washington on average.

For International Visitors

Information Organizations

United States Tourist Offices, found in many foreign countries, offer a superpower-sized arsenal of free literature. If you can't find a U.S. Tourist Office in your area, write the **U.S. Travel and Tourism Administration,** Department of Commerce, 14th St. and Constitution Ave. NW, Washington, DC 20230 (202-377-4003 or 202-377-3811). USTTA has branches in Australia, Belgium, Canada, France, West Germany, Japan, Mexico, and the United Kingdom; contact the Washington office for information about the branch in your country. For general tourist information, you may also want to direct inquiries to the state, provincial and city tourist offices listed throughout the book and under Tourism Bureaus above. In Canada, contact **Travel CUTS,** 44 George St., Toronto, Ont. M5S 2E4 (416-979-2406).

The **Council on International Educational Exchange (CIEE)** has branches in Canada and overseas that sell charter airline tickets, International Student Identification Cards (ISICs), travel literature, and hostel cards. CIEE can arrange stays at private homes for up to four weeks. Branches can also help students secure work visas and find employment through their work-exchange programs. If you can't locate an affiliated office in your country, contact their main office: 205 E. 42nd St., New York, NY 10017 (212-661-1414; 800-223-7402 for charter flight tickets only). For details about other CIEE programs, see Student Travel, Safety and Insurance, and Work above.

Another excellent information source is the **Institute of International Education (IIE),** 809 United Nations Plaza, New York, NY 10017 (212-883-8200). The IIE administers fellowships and educational exchange programs worldwide and distributes several excellent publications. Summer visitors should study *Summer Learning Options USA: A Guide to Foreign Nationals.* The "Homestay Information Sheet" is also a good source. If you're interested in language and cultural programs, consult IIE's *English Language and Orientation Programs in the United States.*

The **Experiment in International Living** arranges homestays throughout the year for international visitors of all ages. Guests live with an American family for an extended time period. The Experiment also runs the International Student of English (ISE) Study Program, which offers language classes on select college campuses. Costs are fairly steep (about $1100 for a 4-week stay) but the experience is invaluable. For information on additional language training sessions, write to "Experiment" at Kipling Road, Brattleboro, VT 05301 (800-451-4465).

The **International Student Travel Conference (ISTC)** is extremely helpful for European students. ISTC arranges charter flights and discount air fares, provides travel insurance, publishes currency exchange rates weekly, issues the ISIC card, and sponsors the Student Air Travel Association for European students. Write for their *Student Travel Guide* at ISTC, Weinbergstrasse 31, CH-8006 Zurich, Switzerland (1-692769).

Founded to promote international peace and understanding, **Servas** matches hosts and travelers in about 90 countries. Stays are limited to two nights, unless your host invites you to stay longer; guests must complete their own arrangements with hosts. Travelers pay a $45 fee per year to Servas. No money is exchanged between travelers and hosts—rather, they share conversation and ideas. Travelers must provide two letters of reference and arrange for an interview at least one month before the trip. Contact the U.S. Servas Committee, 11 John St., #706, New York, NY 10038 (212-267-0252).

See also Student Travel, Youth Hostels, Work, and Study above for other organizations that may help foreign travelers.

Documents and Formalities

If you are coming to the U.S. from overseas, obtaining the proper documents before you leave home will take time. At a minimum, you will need some sort of visa to enter the U.S. In addition, legal documents and certain identification cards will save you time and money. To find out about the International Student Identity Card (ISIC), see Student Travel.

At the U.S.-Canadian border, people who are not citizens of either country will need a visa to cross in either direction, with the exception of citizens of Greenland, who can cross in either direction without a visa. Naturalized citizens should have their naturalization papers with them; occasionally officials will ask to see them. International visitors should have their papers handy and in good order, since customs officials on both sides of the border may be tough on anyone with a foreign accent.

Foreign visitors to the United States are required to have a **passport, visitor's visa,** and proof of plans to leave. Canadian citizens who are adults may enter the U.S. freely, while those under 18 need the written consent of a parent or guardian. Mexican citizens may cross into the U.S. with an I-186 form. Mexican border crossing cards (non-immigrant visas) prohibit you from staying more than 72 hours in the U.S. or straying more than 25 miles from the border.

Visas

To obtain a U.S. visa, contact the nearest **U.S. Embassy** or **Consulate.** Europeans can also write to the **Visa and Immigration Department,** 5 Upper Grosvenor St., London W1 (01-499-3443). **Visa Center, Inc.** secures visas to the United States and Canada for travelers from all countries. Cost varies with passport requirements. Contact Visa Center, Inc., 507 Fifth Ave., #904, New York, NY 10017 (212-986-0924) for information.

Most international visitors to the U.S. obtain a **B-2** or "pleasure tourist" visa, valid for six months. If you lose your visa once you reach the U.S., you must replace it through your country's embassy. If you lose your **I-94 form** (the arrival/departure certificate attached to your visa upon arrival), replace it at the nearest **U.S. Immigration and Naturalization Service** office; to do so, you will need forms I-34 and I-102. This office can also grant visa extensions up to six months for a fee of $35 when you file form I-539. For a list of offices, write the U.S. Immigration and Naturalization Service, Central Office Information Operations Unit, 425 I St. NW, #5044, Washington, DC 20536 (202-633-1900). Foreign visitors should be aware that working in the United States with only a B-2 visa is grounds for deportation. Before a **work visa** (the coveted "Green Card") can be issued to you, you must present the U.S. consulate in your country with a letter from an American employer stating that you have been offered a job and detailing your job's responsibilities, salary, and duration. Alternatively, an American employer can obtain an H visa (usually an H-2) for you.

To **study** in the United States, exchange students and full-time students enrolled in degree-granting programs must apply for an **F-1** or a **J-1** visa, respectively. F-1 and J-1 students may also apply for full-time **practical training** in employment closely related to the student's field of study, if such training is both beneficial to the student's professional development and unavailable in the home country. Requirements vary with each student visa.

Many colleges and universities in the U.S. and abroad have offices that give out specific advice and information on study and employment in the United States. Almost all American academic institutions accept applications from international students directly through their office of admission (for addresses and phones, see Study above). If English is not your first language, you will generally be required to take the **Test of English as a Foreign Language and Test of English as a Spoken Language (TOEFL/TSE),** which is administered in many countries. Each university determines its own requirements for how high you must score in order to be considered for admission. For more information, contact the TOEFL/TSE Application Office, P.O. Box 6151, Princeton, NJ 08541 (609-921-9000). See Study for additional information.

Before leaving the United States, foreigners holding J-1 Exchange Visitor visas, F-1 student visas, H-1 Temporary Worker visas, or immigrant visas must obtain a **"Sailing Permit."** This Certificate of Compliance will prove that you do not owe any income taxes to the U.S. government. The "Sailing Permit" must be obtained from the **Internal Revenue Service** within 30 days prior to departure. If you have any questions, write to Director of International Operations, Internal Revenue Service, Washington, DC 20225. Students with F-1 visas who have not received funding from any source in the U.S. during their stay, and others holding F-2, B-2, and H-4 visas, are not required to fill out a Sailing Permit.

International Driver's License

If you are considering renting or buying a car during your visit, you should obtain an **International Driver's License** from your national automobile association before leaving. To obtain a domestic U.S. driver's license, you must go through a testing process; some states require you to enroll in a certified drivers' education course before you can be tested. Some foreign driver's licenses will be valid here for up to one year—check before you leave. Even so, be careful; some local authorities may not realize that your foreign license is legal.

Customs

All travelers may bring the following into the U.S. without paying duty: 200 cigarettes, $100 worth of gifts, and personal belongings such as clothes and jewelry. Travelers aged 21 and over may also bring in up to one liter of alcohol if they have been outside the U.S. for at least 48 hours; otherwise the limit is 4 oz. (150ml). You can also bring any amount of currency into the U.S., but if you are carrying over $10,000 you must fill out a reporting form. If you have prescription drugs, make sure they are in clearly labeled containers, and have either a prescription or a written statement from your doctor ready to present to customs authorities.

Citizens of the U.S. returning from Canada may bring in up to $400 worth of items for personal or household use or as gifts. However, if you have been outside the U.S. for less than 48 hours, this exemption slips to $25, including 50 cigarettes and 4 oz. of alcohol. U.S. citizens may mail gifts to people in the U.S., provided no person receives more than $50 in value in a single day; gift packages should be marked "Unsolicited gift," and the nature and value of the gift should be marked as well. Duty for goods beyond the exempt amount is about 10%. For comprehensive information about U.S. customs, obtain a copy of *Know Before You Go,* from the U.S. Customs Service, 1301 Constitution Ave., Washington, DC 20229 (202-566-8195).

Canadian citizens may bring back goods worth up to CDN$20 after a 24-hr. absence, $100 after a 48-hr. absence, or $300 after a 7-day absence. Travelers who leave for only a day cannot bring back any liquor or tobacco, while all others can bring 200 cigarettes and either one 40-oz. bottle or 24 12-oz. bottles or cans of liquor. Duty beyond these amounts hovers around 20%. Canadians can use form Y-38 to mark valuables brought with them out of the country so that they can be brought back duty free. For more information, write for "I Declare/Je Declare" from Revenue Canada Customs and Excise Department, Communications Branch, Mackenzie Ave., Ottawa, Ont. K1A 0L5 (613-957-0275).

British citizens are allowed an exemption of £32, which includes 100 cigarettes, 2 litres of table wine, and 1 litre of alcohol over 22% by volume. Contact Her Majesty's Customs and Excise Office, New King's Beam House, 22 Upper Ground, London SE1 9PJ (01-382-54-68).

Exemptions for Australian citizens are AUS$400 for those 18 and over, and AUS$200 for those under 18. Travelers ages 18 and over may bring back 1 litre of alcohol and 250g of tobacco. All goods must be carried back into the country with you and not mailed. Australians should note that they may not export more than AUS$5000 from the country without permission from the Reserve Bank of Australia. "Customs Information for All Travellers" is available from local offices of the Collector of Customs (Sydney, Melbourne, Brisbane, Port Adelaide, Fremantle, Hobart, Darwin) or from Australian consulates abroad.

New Zealand citizens above age 16 are exempt from duty on the first NZ$500 worth of goods they bring back—up to 250g tobacco, 4.5 litre of beer or wine, and 1125ml of liquor. New or expensive items should be registered with a Customs Office to avoid their being taxed upon your return. "Customs Guides for Travellers" is available from local Customs Offices or New Zealand consulates abroad.

Currency and Exchange

In both the United States and Canada, the main unit of currency is the **dollar** ($). Both dollars are divided into 100 **cents** (¢). The two currencies use a decimal system based on the dollar ($). Paper money ("bills") comes primarily in six denominations, all of which are the same size and shape: $1, $5, $10, $20, $50, and $100. Occasionally you will encounter a $2 bill, more frequently in Canada than in the U.S. Coins vary in size and color, and each coin is worth a dollar or less. Pennies are worth 1¢ ($.01) and are made of copper. All other coins are silver: nickles, worth 5¢; dimes (smaller than pennies, strangely enough), worth 10¢; and quarters, worth 25¢. Half-dollar and dollar coins (known as silver dollars) exist but are rare.

In the United States, it is virtually impossible to pay for anything in foreign currency, and in some parts of the country you may even have trouble exchanging your currency for U.S. dollars. To avoid hassles, buy traveler's checks, and if you buy them in another currency, choose a widely known check. Some banks abroad offer their own traveler's checks, which may not be easily cashed here—see Money above for widely recognized traveler's checks. In addition, consider bringing along a credit card affiliated with an American company, such as Interbank (affiliated with MasterCard), Barclay Card (affiliated with Visa), and that old standby, American Express. These come in handy when paying for flights and car rentals, and sometimes can be used to pay for accommodations and food (although not at many places listed in *Let's Go*).

U.S. dollars can be used more easily in Canada, and since it is generally stronger than its Canadian counterpart, Canadian merchants will often be happy to accept your U.S. dollars and give you a good rate of exchange when you purchase with them. Still, this willingness is extremely idiosyncratic; you should not count on it without first familiarizing yourself with the attitudes of the area you're in.

In both the U.S. and Canada, coins and not tokens are used for public telephones and most laundromats, and drivers of local buses generally do not give change for dollar bills. Keep this in mind and make sure to carry coins with you.

See Money above for more information.

Sending Money

Sending money is a complicated and expensive process— avoid it if at all possible. Advance planning can reduce both the cost and problems inherent in transferring money overseas. If you think you'll need money sent to you while you are in the U.S., visit your bank before you leave for a list of its corresponding banks here. Before you leave, you can also arrange for your bank to send money from your account to specific correspondent banks on specific dates.

If you're pressed for money and need it quickly, **cable transfer** is the fastest way to send money. Usually it takes 48 hours for your money to reach you in a major city and slightly longer if you are in an out-of-the-way location. You pay cabling costs plus the commission charged by your home bank. If you do not have an account at the receiving bank, you may be delayed in receiving your money. Less expensive than cabling, but slower, is the **bank draft,** or international money order. You pay a commission (around US$20) on the draft, plus the cost of sending it airmail (preferably registered mail). Through **American Express** (800-543-4080), you can be cabled up to $10,000 from France or Great Britain and receive the money within one to three days. Neither you nor the person who sends you the money needs to be an AmEx cardholder. The fee for this service is US$35 for a $500 money gram, and increases gradually for larger amounts.

Finally, if you are stranded in the U.S. with no money and no other recourse, your consulate can wire home for you and deduct the cost from the money you receive. Consulates are often less than gracious about performing this service, however, so turn to them only in desperation.

Communication

Mail

The **United States Post Office** is a government-run organization. Individual offices are usually open Monday to Friday from 8am to 5pm and sometimes Saturday until noon or 12:30pm. All post offices are closed on national holidays (see When to Go above for a list). Postcards mailed within the U.S. or to Mexico cost 15¢, letters 25¢. Postcards to Canada cost 22¢, letters 30¢. Postcards mailed overseas cost 36¢, letters 45¢. Aerograms are available at the post office for 36¢—these can be sent all over the world. Mail within the U.S. takes between a day and a week (less time to closer destinations and only a day or two within the same city); to northern Europe, a week to 10 days; to southern Europe, North Africa, and the Middle East, two to three weeks; to South America, a week to 10 days. Service to other destinations may take even longer. Large city post offices offer **International Express Mail** service, in case you need to mail something to a major city overseas in less than 72 hours.

Canada Post requires a 37¢ Canadian postage stamp for all domestic first-class mail within the country. Letters or postcards sent to the U.S. cost 43¢. Mail headed elsewhere is, of course, considerably more costly—items mailed to Europe weighing less than 20g cost 74¢.

Both the U.S. and Canada are divided into postal zones. Each American postal zone has a five-digit ZIP code, while Canadian postal codes are composed of six letters and numbers (e.g. A1B 2C3). Some American businesses and governmental offices have nine-digit codes, the last four numerals set off by a dash (e.g. 02138-0987).

The normal form of address in both the United States and Canada is as follows:

J. Fred Muggs	(name)
Spira Consulting, Inc.	(name of organization, optional)
3080 Sesame St.	(address)
St. Paul, MN 55116	(city, state or province abbreviation, ZIP or postal code)
USA	(country, if mailed from different country)

When ordering books and materials from the U.S. and Canada, always include an **International Reply Coupon (IRC)** with your request. IRCs should be available from your home post office. Your coupon must have adequate postage to cover the cost of delivery.

See Keeping in Touch above for information about how others can write to you while you travel.

Telephone

Telephone numbers in the U.S. and Canada consist of a three-digit area code and a seven-digit number (divided into a group of 3 and a group of 4), written as 617-495-9659 or (617) 495-9659. Only the last seven digits are used in local calls. Within an area code, **non-local calls** require you to dial "1" before the seven-digit number. To make a **long-distance call**, dial "1", then the area code, then the number. For example, to call Let's Go in Cambridge, MA from another state or from another area code within the state, you would dial 1-617-495-9659.

Pay phones abound on street corners and in public areas such as restaurants, train stations, airports, and movie theaters. Most of them explain how to make both local and long-distance calls. To make a local call, deposit coins in the slot before dialing. Local calls cost 10-30¢, depending on the town, and in some places you will have to deposit additional coins if you speak longer than 3 minutes. If there is no answer or if you get a busy signal (a series of short beeps), your money will be returned when you hang up the receiver. Unlike pop machines, pay phones do not return excess change, so don't deposit more than you have to.

You can make a long-distance call to anywhere on the continent in any number of ways. The basic call is **station-to-station.** From a private phone, dial "1" plus the area code plus the number. From a pay phone, you usually do the same, and an operator will let you know how many coins to deposit and when. Otherwise, you can call **collect,** which means that the recipient of your call will be charged. Dial "0" plus the area code and number (you needn't deposit any coins), and tell the operator that you wish to make a collect call. The operator will ask for your name, and will ask whoever answers the phone if they will accept the call and the charges. Through the operator you can also make a **person-to-person** call—just specify to the operator the name of the person or people you wish to speak with, and if they are not home your call will be cancelled. Person-to-person calls can either be charged to you or made collect, and they cost more than station-to-station calls. Within North America, long-distance calls are discounted 35% between 5 and 11pm Sunday through Friday. This discount increases to 50% between 11pm and 8am during the week and from 11pm on Friday through 5pm Sunday.

International calls can be made from any phone. To call directly either from a private phone or with coins from a pay phone, dial 011, the country code, then the city code. From some phones you will need to dial "0" and give the number to the operator. To find out the cheapest time to call overseas, call the operator ("0").

To find out the number of a person or a business, call **directory assistance.** Directory assistance is a free call from any pay phone, although sometimes you will have to deposit a coin, which will be returned to you at the end of your call. To reach local directory assistance anywhere, dial 411; within your area code but farther away, 1-555-1212; outside your area code, 1-area code-555-1212. To find out a toll-free number, call 1-800-555-1212.

Most of the information you will need in order to use the telephones, along with the numbers of just about every home and business in town, can be found in any local phone book. The **White Pages** gives to private listings, while the **Yellow Pages** lists businesses by category. In larger cities, the White Pages and the Yellow Pages will be separate books, while in smaller towns, the two will be bound together in one book. Some pay phones have phone books nearby; otherwise, don't be afraid to call directory assistance or the operator, or to ask a local merchant if you can look at his phone book.

Telegrams

If a telephone call is impossible, cabling may be the only way to contact someone overseas quickly. A short message will usually reach its destination by the next day. **Western Union** charges about 25¢ per word, including name and address, for overseas telegrams. Call Western Union (800-325-6000) for general information and to check rates to specific countries.

Measurements and Time

In the United States, the antiquated British system of weights and measures is still in use, while Canada measures by the metric system. Here is a list of American units, their abbreviations, and their metric equivalents:

1 inch (in.) = 2.5 centimetres
1 foot (ft.; pl. "feet") = 0.3 metre
1 yard (yd.) = 0.9 metre
1 mile (mi.) = 1.6 kilometres
1 ounce (oz.) = 28 grams
1 pound (lb.) = 0.45 kilogram
1 quart (qt.), liquid = 0.9 litre

There are 12 inches in 1 foot, 3 feet in 1 yard, and 5280 feet in 1 mile. There are 16 ounces in 1 pound, 8 oz. (liquid) in 1 cup, 2 cups in 1 pint, 2 pints in 1 quart, and 4 quarts in 1 gallon.

The U.S. uses the **Fahrenheit** (FARE-en-hite) temperature scale, while Canada uses the **Celsius** scale. Those who are mathematically inclined can convert between them according to the following formulae: °C— 5(°F — 32)/9, °F—32 + 9°C/5. Others should just remember that 32°F is the freezing point of water, 212°F its boiling point, and 98.6°F the normal human body temperature. Room temperature typically hovers around 68°F.

The U.S. system of telling time is also slightly different from the European. America lives according to two 12-hour clocks, instead of one 24-hour clock. Hours between noon and midnight are *post meridiem* or **pm** (for example, 2pm); hours between midnight and noon are *ante meridiem* or **am.** Noon is 12pm and midnight is 12am; to avoid confusion, *Let's Go* says simply "noon" or "midnight."

The North American continent is divided into six **time zones.** Most of Oregon, Washington, British Columbia, and the Yukon are in the **Pacific** time zone (1 hr. behind Mountain, 2 behind Central, and 3 behind Eastern). Alberta is in the **Mountain time zone, and Alaska lives by Alaska** time (1 hr. behind Pacific), except for some of the Aleutian Island towns, which go by **Aleutian-Hawaii** time, one hour behind Alaska time. Shortly after midnight the first Sunday in April (April 1 in 1990), clocks are switched one hour forward to **daylight savings time**; on the last Sunday in October (Oct. 28 in 1990), again shortly after midnight, clocks are moved back one hour to **standard time.** When times are given with time-zone abbreviations, take this into account (e.g. PDT—Pacific Daylight Time, MST—Mountain Standard Time).

Electrical outlets throughout North American provide current at 117 volts, 60 cycles (Hertz). Appliances designed for a foreign electrical system will not operate without a converter or other adapter. If you intend to use an electric razor, contact lens disinfectant system, hair dryer, or other small appliance, consider purchasing a converter (US$15-20) and a plug adapter, available at many department, hardware, and electrical equipment stores.

Getting There

Transportation to the Pacific Northwest from other parts of the world will be the major expense of your trip. Only detailed calculations and advance planning can uncover the best way to go. When flying, always look for **Advance Purchase Excursion Fares (APEX)** and night fares, which will be easier on your wallet. The simplest and surest way to choose from among the options is to find a travel agent who keeps abreast of the chaos in airfares and whom you can trust to save you money. In addition, check the travel section of any major newspaper for bargain fares, and consult CIEE or your national student travel organization—they sometimes have special deals that regular travel agents can't offer. For information on flying within the United States, see By Air above.

From Canada and Mexico

For both Mexicans and Canadians, finding bargains on travel in the States may not be easy. Residents of North America are rarely eligible for the discounts that U.S. airlines, bus, and train companies offer visitors from overseas (see Getting Around: Discounts below).

From eastern Canada, the cheapest way to reach the Pacific Northwest is to drive or take the bus. Check major Canadian airlines for Super Saver discounts and standby fares accessible to student travelers. Students should contact **Travel CUTS (Canadian Universities Travel Service)**, 44 George St., Toronto, Ont. M5S 2E4 (416-979-2406) for information on special deals (see Student Travel above). **VIA Rail** and **Amtrak** offer scenic but expensive travel across Canada and the U.S., respectively. Canadians can reach the western United States on Amtrak from Montréal and Toronto via Chicago. VIA Rail also sells the **Canrailpass** for unlimited travel within Canada—see By Train above for further details.

Mexicans in particular may find travel within the United States a costly blow to their budget. Most buses and trains from Mexico travel no farther than the U.S. border, but it is possible to arrange connections at San Diego, CA, Nogales, AZ, and El Paso, Eagle Pass, Laredo, or Brownsville, TX. **Amtrak, Greyhound** and their subsidiaries serve the towns along the U.S.-Mexico border. From Mexico there are numerous flights on American and Mexican carriers to New York, Houston, Dallas, and Los Angeles. Because flying in the U.S. is expensive, it may be cheaper to fly on a Mexican airline to one of the border towns, and then to travel by train or bus from there. If you will be driving while in the United States or Canada, be aware that both countries require an international driver's license and proper insurance coverage (see Documents and Formalities above).

From Europe

Travelers from Europe will experience the least competition for inexpensive seats during the off-season. You don't have to travel in the dead of winter to save, either. Peak season rates are generally set on either May 15 or June 1 and run until about September 15. You can take advantage of cheap off-season flights within Europe to reach an advantageous port of departure for North America. London is an important connecting point for budget flights to the U.S. Once in the States, you can use the extensive system of coast-to-coast flights to make your way out west (see By Air above for details).

Charter flights can save you a lot of money. You can book charters up to the last minute, but many flights fill up well before their departure date. One major advantage is that they allow you to stay abroad for up to a year and to mix and match flights in and out of different cities. Charters do not, however, allow for changes of plan. You must choose your departure and return dates when you book, and you will lose all or most of your money if you cancel your ticket. (Travel agents will cover your losses only in case of sudden illness, death, or natural disaster.) Charter companies also reserve the right to change the dates of your flight or even cancel the flight a mere 48 hours in advance. Also be aware of delays, a common problem. To be safe, get your ticket as early as possible, and arrive at the airport well before departure time. When you're inquiring about charter options, try to investigate each charter company's reputation.

If you decide to fly with a scheduled airline, you'll be purchasing greater reliability, security, and flexibility. Major airlines offer two reduced-fare options, in addition to abundant **youth fares: standby** and **APEX (Advanced Purchase Excursion Fare).** Standby fares offer you maximum flexibility—you can come and go as you please. But the commercial air travel industry is becoming less flexible every year. Very few cities offer standby fares—you must check each city ahead of time. London offers the most standby opportunities; Pan Am, Northwestern, British Caledonian, and World Airways have about the same standby fares. Although you can purchase standby tickets in advance, you are not guaranteed a seat on any particular flight because seat availability is determined by cancellations and under-booking of flights. Some airlines, however, issue "predictions." The worst crunch for European flights comes during the summer, especially in August. At no time should you count on getting a seat immediately.

APEX is one of the more sensible reduced fare options. It provides you with confirmed reservations, and penalties for changing or cancelling your reservation are not as stiff as with charters. You can make connections through different cities and travel on different airlines. Drawbacks include restrictions on the length of your stay (from 7-14 days minimum to 60-90 days maximum) and the requirement that you make reservations three weeks in advance (hence the name). You might also investigate unusual airlines that undercut the major carriers on regularly scheduled flights to certain cities. **Virgin Atlantic** and **Icelandair** have particularly low fares. Competition for seats on these small carriers is usually fierce, so book early.

From Asia, Australia, and New Zealand

Whereas European travelers may choose from a variety of regular reduced fares, their counterparts in Asia and Australia must rely on APEX. While fares may seem astronomical ($1500 one way from Australia to California is not unusual), the West Coast remains one of the world's more accessible areas for Asian and Australian travelers.

From Japan, U.S. carriers such as **Northwest** and **United Airlines** generally offer cheaper flights than Japan Airlines. **Qantas, Air New Zealand, United, Continental, and UTA French Airlines** fly between Australia or New Zealand and the United States. Prices are roughly equivalent among the six, but the cities they serve differ. Super Saver fares from Australia have extremely tough restrictions. Many do not refund your money if you cancel. If you are uncertain about your plans, pay $100 extra for a Super Saver that has only a 50% penalty for cancellation.

Getting Around: Discounts

Airlines and bus and train companies offer special discounts to foreign visitors traveling within the U.S. Other discounts (for children, families, senior citizens, and disabled travelers) are noted in Getting There and Getting Around above. International travelers should realize that given the long distances between points within the United States and Canada, North Americans rely on buses and trains for travel much less than everyone else in the world. Bus and train stations may seem a little unusual at first, and bus and train riders not nearly as open to conversation as travelers in your home country. Expect, then, to rely on others less than you would at home.

Greyhound offers an **International Ameripass** to foreign students and faculty members and their families for unlimited bus travel. Passes can be used in the U.S. only, not in Canada, and they are sold primarily overseas, although they can be purchased in New York, Los Angeles, San Francisco, or Miami for a slightly higher price. Prices are $125 for 7 days ($135 if purchased in U.S.), $199 ($214 in the U.S.) for 15 days, and $279 ($299 in the U.S.) for 30 days. Unlike its domestic counterpart, this Ameripass cannot be extended past the duration originally purchased. To obtain a pass, you need a valid passport and proof of your student or faculty status. Call Greyhound (800-237-8211) or stop in at one of Greyhound's overseas offices to inquire about special deals and tour programs for international travelers or to request the *Visit USA Vacation Guide,* which details services for foreign travelers in the U.S.

Amtrak's **USA Rail Pass,** similar to the Eurailpass, entitles foreign visitors to unlimited travel anywhere in the U.S. A 45-day pass costs $299. If you plan to travel by train only in the Northwest, purchase a Regional Rail Pass for the Far West ($159). All USA Rail Passes are 50% off for children ages 2-11. With a valid passport, you can purchase the pass at home or in New York, Boston, Miami, Los Angeles, or San Francisco. Check with a travel agent or Amtrak representative in Europe, or write to Amtrak International Sales, 400 N. Capital St. NW, Washington, DC 20001. If you're already in the U.S., call Amtrak for information (800-872-7245). Be smart about buying passes—they are not a bargain unless you plan to travel almost every day, and remember that not all towns in the Pacific Northwest are accessible by train.

Many major airlines offer special "Visit USA" passes and fares to foreign travelers. Purchase these tickets in your own country; one price pays for a certain number of "flight coupons," each good for one flight segment on a particular airline's domestic system within a certain time period. Many different airlines offer these passes, but they come with innumerable restrictions and guidelines. Prices therefore vary a great deal. Consult a travel agent before you purchase any of these coupons to see whether you're really getting a good deal. Depending on the airline, the passes may be valid from 30 to 90 days. Some airlines allow those living 100 miles outside the U.S. to purchase the passes, so Canadians and Mexicans may be eligible. United Airlines offers special fares for travelers departing from many different regions of the world, including Asia, Europe, and Australia. When you purchase a pass, keep in mind the size of the airline. Eastern, United, and American have extensive systems covering the entire continent, while other airlines offer more limited or regional service. As always, a travel agent can help you work out the details.

OREGON

For decades, Oregon zealously protected its rocky shores and inland forests from interloping tourists and developers. The state today has adopted a more welcoming attitude toward the visitor. "Interpretive Centers" carry out their exegetical tasks almost everywhere, and excellent youth hostels operate in Ashland, Bandon, and Eugene. Scrambling for international renown, Oregon's Chambers of Commerce claim to guard the world's smallest park, tiniest navigable bay, and shortest river.

In recent years, Oregon's dusky forests have sparked considerable controversy. Environmentalists successfully halted logging in one-third of the state's timberland, arguing it would endanger the rare spotted owl. At the same time, rising exports of unmilled logs deprived local mills of business. To protest their predicament, angry timber workers drove enormous trucks through the downtown streets of Portland. The "logging crisis" seems to be abating now that the voters have banned the export of unmilled logs; the legislature is considering a compromise that would allow only the logging of the younger trees in Oregon's old-growth forests.

Lewis and Clark, Oregon's first tourists, slipped quietly down the Columbia River when their transcontinental trek brought them to Oregon; later, waves of settlers thronged the Oregon Trail. Today, most travelers devolve to the Pacific, gaping at waves and cliffs worthy of Big Sur. Handsome as the coastal route is, you must venture inland to see some of Oregon's greatest attractions—the prehistoric fossils at John Day National Monument, the volcanic cinder-cones near Crater Lake, and the yearly Shakespeare festival in Ashland. To escape the anomie of the countryside, head for Portland, an easy-going metropolis known for its public art, fertile elephants, and bemused tolerance of off-beat lifestyles.

Practical Information

Emergency: 911.

Postal Abbreviation: OR.

Capital: Salem.

Time Zone: Mostly Pacific (1 hr. behind Mountain, 2 behind Central, 3 behind Eastern). A small southeastern section is Mountain (1 hr. behind Central, 2 behind Eastern).

Drinking Age: 21.

Traffic Laws: Children under 16 must wear seatbelts at all times.

Visitor Information: State Tourist Office, 595 Cottage St. NE, Salem 97310 (800-547-7842). **Oregon State Parks,** 525 Trade St. SE, Salem 97310 (378-6305). **Department of Fish and Wildlife,** 506 SW Mill St., Portland 97208 (229-5403). **Oregon State Marine Board,** 3000 Market St. NE, #505, Salem 97310 (378-8587). **Statewide Road Conditions,** 976-7277.

Oregon Council American Youth Hostels: 99 W. 10th, #205, Eugene 97402 (683-3685).

Area Code: 503.

Impractical Information

Nickname: Beaver State.

Motto: The Union.

State Song: Oregon, My Oregon.

State Flower: Oregon Grape.

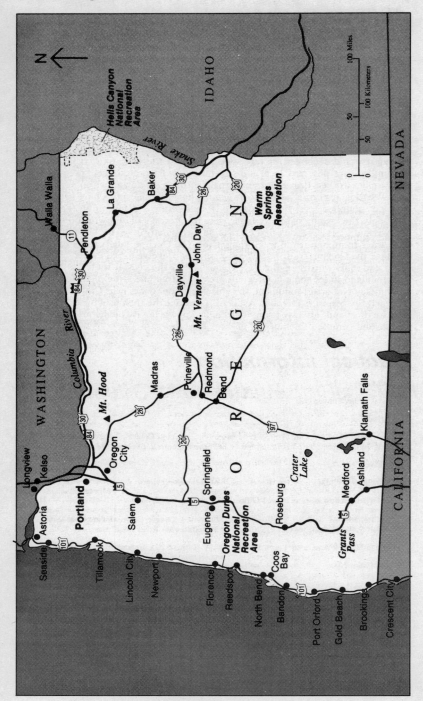

State Animal: Beaver.

State Fish: Chinook Salmon.

Portland

Nature keeps a watchful eye over Portland, as if the city's presence were only uneasily tolerated in Oregon's glorious wilderness. Mammoth Mt. Hood observes the eastern regions of the million-person metropolis while stubby Mt. St. Helens stares down from the north; the Willamette and Columbia Rivers encircle the city guardedly; and every so often an army of thunder clouds rumbles into town, just to keep everyone honest. The people of Portland are not intimidated by Nature's militant presence. Fanatic runners, hikers, and wind-surfers of Portland are as obsessed with the environment as with their own bodies. Development is carefully controlled and the entire city recently banned styrofoam. Portlanders are renowned for their somewhat unusual sense of humor. A local tavern owner posed for the notorious "Expose Yourself to Art" poster, depicting a man in a trenchcoat flashing a public sculpture. Shortly thereafter, he was elected mayor.

Portland is a city of roses and elephants. Every June, white-suited Royal Rosarians march in the streets during the Rose Festival. Meanwhile, the Washington Park Zoo breeds baby elephants with extraordinary success. But wait—there's more. In Old Town, the salty atmosphere of a 19th-century seaport survives. Secluded Reed College offers a first-rate liberal arts education. Portland also leads the nation in bank robberies per capita. A local official attributes this feat to the city's "open, airy, and inviting" banks. Oregon's leading city was originally a loggers' pit stop. In 1845, a toss of a coin at a dinner party gave Portland its name. If the coin had landed the other way, this casual and idiosyncratic city would have been named Boston.

Practical Information and Orientation

Visitor Information: Portland/Oregon Visitors Association, 26 SW Salmon St. (275-9750), at Front St. Brochures, pamphlets, maps, and advice. The free *Portland Book* contains maps, general information, and historical trivia. Open Mon.-Fri. 8:30am-5pm, Sat. 10am-3pm. Detailed city road maps are free at **Hertz,** 1009 SW 6th (249-5727), at Salmon.

Amtrak: 800 NW 6th Ave. (241-4290), at Hoyt St. Open daily 7:30am-5:30pm.

Greyhound-Trailways: 550 NW 6th Ave. (243-2323). Buses almost hourly to Seattle ($24 one way, 243-2313 for taped schedule) and to Eugene ($14 one way, 222-3361 for taped schedule). Ticket window open 5:30am-12:30am.

Green Tortoise: 225-0310. To Seattle (Tues. and Sat. at 4pm, $15) and San Francisco (Sun. and Thurs. at 12:30pm, $49).

City Buses: Tri-Met, Customer Service Center, #1 Pioneer Courthouse Sq., 701 SW 6th Ave. (233-3511). Open Mon.-Fri. 9am-5pm. Service generally 7am-midnight, reduced Sat.-Sun. 24-hour recorded information numbers ("Call-a-bus") for each bus: how to use the Call-a-bus system (231-3199); fare information (231-3198); updates, changes, and weather-related problems (231-3197); all-night information (231-3196); special needs transportation (238-4952, Mon.-Fri. 8:30am-4:30pm); lost and found (238-4855, Mon.-Fri. 10am-5pm); bicycle commuter service (233-0564). Fare 85¢-$1.15. **MAX** is Tri-Met's "light rail," the equivalent of an above-ground subway. It only serves one line (from downtown east to the city of Gresham, near Mt. Hood) but uses the same fare system as the buses. Buses and MAX are free within *Fareless Square,* a 300-square-block region downtown bounded by the Willamette River, NW Hoyt, and the I-405 freeway.

Taxi: Broadway Cab (227-1234), **New Rose City Cab Co.** (282-7707). Both charge $1.30 for the first mile plus $1.40 per additional mile.

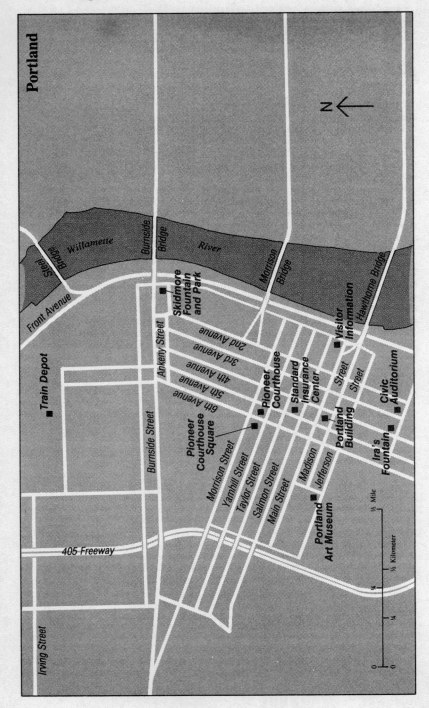

Portland

N

Willamette River

Steel Bridge

Burnside Bridge

Morrison Bridge

Hawthorne Bridge

Front Avenue

Skidmore Fountain and Park

Train Depot

Ankeny Street

2nd Avenue

3rd Avenue

4th Avenue

5th Avenue

6th Avenue

Burnside Street

Visitor Information

Pioneer Courthouse

Standard Insurance Center

Street

Street

Civic Auditorium

Pioneer Courthouse Square

Portland Building

Morrison Street

Yamhill Street

Taylor Street

Salmon Street

Main Street

Madison

Jefferson

Ira's Fountain

Portland Art Museum

405 Freeway

Irving Street

½ Mile

½ Kilometer

¼

¼

0
0

Car Rental: Rent-A-Wreck, 2838 NE Sandy (231-1640). $14 per day with 50 free miles, 15¢ per additional mile. Must be 25 or older. **Budget,** 2033 SW 4th (222-9123) and at the airport (249-4550). $46 per day, unlimited mileage. Must be 21. **Hertz,** 1009 SW 6th (249-5727), at Salmon. $48 per weekday with 100 free miles, 30¢ per additional mile; $23 daily on weekends with 150 free miles, 30¢ per additional mile. Must be 25.

Metropolitan Arts Commission: 1120 SW 5th St., #518 (796-5111).

Local Events Hotline: 233-3333.

Park Bureau/Public Recreation: 1120 SW 5th St. (796-5193 or 796-5100).

Laundromat: Suds 'n' Duds, 4820 NE 42nd (288-2489). Open Sun.-Thurs. 8am-9pm, Fri.-Sat. 8am-6pm.

Ski Conditions: Timberline: 222-2211. **Ski Bowl:** 222-2659. **Mt. Hood Meadows:** 227-7669.

Time/Weather: 778-6000.

Crisis Line: 223-6161.

Women's Crisis Lines: General/Rape Hotline (235-5333). Office at 3020 E. Burnside St. (232-9751). Open Mon.-Fri. 9am-4pm.

Women's Services: Women's Counseling of Portland, 19 SW Gibbs St. (242-0230). General counseling Mon.-Fri. 9am-5pm. **Women's Health Center,** 6510 SE Foster Rd. (777-7044). **West Women's Hotel Shelter,** 2010 NW Kearney St. (224-7718). **Women's Place Bookstore,** 1431 NE Broadway (284-1110). Local clearing house for area feminist events and services.

Men's Resource Center: 235-3433. Counseling. 24-hour recording for appointments.

Gay and Lesbian Information: Phoenix Rising, 333 SW 5th (223-8299). Counseling and referral for gay men and women. Open Mon.-Fri. 1-4pm.

Drug Counseling and Intervention: 230-9654. Mon.-Fri. 9am-5pm.

Senior Citizens' Services: County Committee on Aging (796-5269). **Senior Citizens' Crisis Line** (223-6161). **Oregon Retired Persons' Pharmacy,** 9800 Nimbus Ave., Beaverton (646-0591 for orders, 646-3500 for information). Open Mon.-Sat. 8:30am-5pm.

Child Care: Child Care Finders (244-1515). **Wee-Ba-Be Attendants** (661-5966).

24 Hour Nurse: 246-8773.

Police: 1111 SW 2nd (796-3097).

Post Office: 715 NW Hoyt St. (294-2424). General Delivery ZIP Code: 97208. Closer to the mall is the branch across the street from Pioneer Courthouse Square, 520 SW Morrison St. (221-0282). Both open Mon.-Fri. 7:30am-6:30pm, Sat. 8:30am-5pm.

Area Code: 503.

Portland sits just south of the Columbia River, about 75 miles inland from the Oregon coast. The city is 637 miles north of San Francisco; car travelers from the Bay Area should take Interstates 80, 505, and 5 north, or take the more scenic U.S. 101 north and cut inland via U.S. 26 from Cannon Beach. Portland lies 172 miles south of Seattle, and is reached directly from I-5 south. East of the city, I-84 (U.S. 30) follows the route of the Oregon Trail through the Columbia River Gorge. West of Portland, U.S. 30 follows the Columbia downstream to Astoria. I-405 curves around the west side of the business district to link I-5 with U.S. 30.

Portland is on the major north-south routes of both Amtrak and Greyhound. Both stations are located within Tri-Met's Fareless Square (see City Buses). Greyhound also runs out to the coast and to Spokane, WA, for connections east.

The cheapest way to reach downtown from **Portland International Airport** is to take Tri-Met bus #12, which will arrive going south on SW 5th Ave. (Fare 85¢.) **Raz Tranz** (246-4676 for taped info) provides an airport shuttle ($5, ages under 12 $1) that leaves every 20 minutes and takes 35 minutes to reach major downtown hotels and the Greyhound station. The shuttle runs from 5am to midnight.

Portland can be divided into five districts. **Burnside Street** divides the city into north and south, while east and west are separated by the Willamette River. **Wil-**

liams Avenue cuts off a corner of the northeast sector, which is called simply "North." The Southwest district is the city's hub, encompassing the downtown area, the southern end of historic Old Town, and a slice of the wealthier West Hills. The very center of the hub is the downtown mall area between SW 5th and 6th Ave. Car traffic is prohibited here; this is the transit system's turf. Streets in the Northwest district are named alphabetically beginning with Burnside and continuing with Couch (COOCH) through Wilson. The order is disrupted only where "X" and "Z" should be—you'll find Roosevelt and Reed St. instead. The Northwest district contains the northern end of Old Town. In the north this district is occupied by warehouses bordering the river; to the west it is residential, culminating in the upper class Northwestern Hills area. Most students enrolled in Portland's several colleges and universities live in the Northwest. The Southeast district is a poorer neighborhood. Factories and used-car dealers line the main streets and older houses occupy the residential areas. Anomalous amidst its poorer surroundings, Laurelhurst Park is a collection of posh houses around E. Burnside St. and SE 39th St. The North and Northeast districts are chiefly residential, punctuated by a few quiet, small parks, but are becoming increasingly commercial.

The Tri-Met bus system, one of the nation's better systems of mass transit, weaves together Portland's districts. In the downtown mall, 31 covered passenger shelters serve as both stops and information centers. Southbound buses pick up passengers along SW 5th Ave.; northbound passengers board on SW 6th Ave. Bus routes are grouped into seven regional service areas, each with its own individual totem: orange deer, yellow rose, green leaf, brown beaver, blue snow, red salmon, and purple rain. Shelters and buses are color-coded for their region. A few buses with black numbers on white backgrounds cross town north-south or east-west across color-coded boundaries.

Most of downtown, from NW Irving St. in the north to I-405 in the west and south and the Willamette River in the east, constitutes "Fareless Square." As the name suggests, the buses are free in this zone. The fare system divides the city into three zones defined by concentric circles around downtown. The center of the city on both sides of the river is Zone 1, a larger circle still within city limits is Zone 2, and outlying areas are Zone 3. Fare is 85¢ for one or two zones, $1.15 for three zones. Senior citizens and disabled riders pay 35¢ "Honored Citizen" fares. Pick up bus maps and schedules at the visitors center (see Practical Information), at Willamette Savings branches, or at the Tri-Met Customer Assistance Office along with monthly passes. Schedules can also be found at libraries, universities, and a few participating businesses. Buses generally run 7am to midnight, though Saturday and Sunday service is greatly reduced. Tri-Met also has special services for the disabled. Each of the 90 or so bus routes has its own 24-hour recorded information line, which will tell you where each bus goes and how frequently it operates. (See City Buses in Practical Information.)

Accommodations and Camping

As Portland gentrifies itself, cheap lodgings become increasingly uncommon. Northwest Bed and Breakfast, 610 SW Broadway, Portland 97205 (243-7616), has an extensive listing of member homes in the Portland area and throughout the Northwest. You must become a member for $25 per year to use their lists and reservation services. They promise singles from $25 to $40 and doubles from $30 to $60. All houses are clean, and breakfast is included.

The few remaining cheap hotels downtown are a little dingy and primitive but are generally good deals nonetheless. Parts of Old Town can be dangerous at night. Southwest of the city, several motels offer a few more conveniences for a few more dollars; you can also opt for the selection on N. Interstate Ave., where respectable motels happily cohabitate with pay-by-the-hour establishments. Campers can call the Oregon State Parks campsite info line at 238-7488, Mon.-Fri. 8am-4:30pm.

Portland International AYH Hostel, 3031 SE Hawthorne Blvd. (236-3380), at 31st Ave. Take bus #5 (brown beaver). Cheerful, clean, and crowded. Sleep inside or on the porch when it's warm. Kitchen facilities; laundromat across the street. Open 8-9:30am and 5-11pm. Members $8.75, nonmembers $11.75. Reservations necessary in summer.

Youth Hostel Portland International, 1024 SW 3rd St. (241-2513). Not as inviting, but more accessible. Washer and dryer in the lobby, laundromat a block away. Open 24 hours. Members $8.75, nonmembers $13-18; with private bath $18.

YWCA, 1111 SW 10th St. (223-6281). Women only. Situated on the park blocks, close to major sights. Clean and safe. Small rooms. Shared doubles $8.72. Singles $17.44, with bath $20.71.

Bel D'air Motel, 8355 N. Interstate Ave. (289-4800), just off I-5. Take bus #5 (red salmon) from 6th Ave. Its name is a bit pretentious; its decor is decidedly not. But hey, it has TVs. Very small, so call a week in advance. Singles $25. Doubles $30.52.

Aladdin Motor Inn, 8905 SW 30th St. (246-8241), at Barbur Blvd., about 10 min. from downtown. Take bus #12 (yellow rose) from 5th Ave. Clean and comfortable. A/C and kitchens available. Singles $32.70. Doubles $34.88.

Motel 6, 3104 SE Powell Blvd. (233-8811). Take bus #9 (brown beaver) from 5th Ave. Another cardboard box motel. Small, clean rooms, pool. Always full; call in advance. Singles $29.38. Doubles $35.92.

Portland Rose Motel, 8920 SW Barbur Blvd. (244-0107). Take bus #12 (yellow rose) from 5th Ave. Playground, laundromat, and wheelchair access. Singles $27.25. Doubles $38.15.

Mel's Motor Inn, 5205 N. Interstate Ave. (285-2556). Take bus #5 (red salmon) from 6th Ave. No aspirations to elegance, but clean and comfortable with A/C and HBO. Singles $26.16. Doubles $30.47.

The Unicorn Inn Motel, 3040 SE 82nd (774-1176), off I-205 at exit 19. A clean and comely (albeit obscure) hotel with TV, A/C, and wheelchair access. Singles $33.80. Doubles $39.25.

Jack London Hotel, 415 SW Alder St. (228-4303), downtown. Ask the management to discuss *White Fang* or *Call of the Wild,* and they'll stare at you as if you were insane. Not particularly clean, and female tenants are practically unknown, but it *is* downtown. Recommended only for the truly courageous. Singles $14.17, with bath $19.62. Doubles $17, with bath $21.80. $5 key deposit.

Ainsworth State Park, 37 miles east of Portland on I-84, up the Columbia River Gorge. Hot showers, flush toilets, and hiking trails along the gorge. Sites $8, with electrical $9, with full hookup $10.

Milo Molver State Park, 25 miles southeast of Portland, off Hwy. 211, 5 miles west of the town of Estacada. Fish, boat, and bicycle along the nearby Clackamas River. Hot showers and flush toilets, too. Sites $8, with electrical $9, with full hookup $10.

Food

Portland's restaurants reflect the health-conscious attitude of the people; it is sometimes easier to find a tofu burger on a whole wheat bun than a simple steak-and-potatoes dinner. Bear in mind that a restaurant's neighborhood is no indication of either its price or its quality. Some of the city's finest affordable restaurants adjoin pornographic bookstores or sleazy used-car dealerships, while truly down-and-out cafés somehow continue to survive next to upscale luxury hotels.

Some of the best produce in town is available at **Corno Foods,** 711 SE Union (232-3157), under the Morrison Bridge, a labyrinthine market skewed towards fruits and vegetables.

Southwest

Escape from New York Pizza, 913 SW Alder St. (226-4129). Best pizza in town. Good sized cheese slice $1, with pepperoni $1.35. Large cheese pie $7.75. Counter people have entertaining stories to tell renegade easterners. Open Mon.-Thurs. 11:30am-9pm, Fri.-Sat. 11:30am-11pm. Second location at 622 NW 23rd St. (227-5423).

Macheesmo Mouse, 715 SW Salmon St. (228-3491). Fast and healthy Mexican food in a setting somewhere between a Hard Rock Cafe and the Pompidou Center. The $2.65 veggie burrito stands out. Open Mon.-Sat. 11am-10pm, Sun. noon-9pm. Locations also at 811 NW 23rd St. (274-0500), 3553 SE Hawthorne Blvd. (232-6588, 5 blocks from the AYH hostel), and 1200 NE Broadway (249-0002).

Foothill Broiler, 33 NW 23rd Pl. (223-0287), in the Uptown Shopping Center. Take bus #20 (deer) up Burnside. Fantastic homemade food served by enterprising survivors of the 60s. Tasteful art on the walls, creative holiday decorations, and plants dangling from the ceiling. Some of the best burgers in the Northwest run from $2. Come off hours or be prepared to wait in line. Open Mon.-Fri. 7:30am-7pm, Sat. 7:30am-4pm.

Hamburger Mary's, 840 SW Park St. (223-0900), at Taylor. Good food near the museums and theaters, with a relaxed atmosphere and eclectic decor: floor lamps dangle upside-down from the ceiling. As popular with straights as it is with gay people (its original and most faithful clientele). Healthy burgers with everything and fries $4.80, some excellent vegetarian fare. Open daily 7am-midnight.

Jake's Famous Crawfish, 401 SW 12th St. (226-1419). Widely acclaimed as Portland's best restaurant; certainly the oldest. Jake's began in 1892 as a saloon, later metamorphosed into a soft-drink parlor during Prohibition, and then turned seaward for inspiration. The front dining room is plebeian, the rear two more formal. Fresh salmon, shrimp Creole, and fantastic steamed butter clams. Lunches around $6, dinners $10-15. Lunch Mon.-Fri. 11am-3pm. Dinner Mon.-Thurs. 5-11pm, Fri.-Sat. 5pm-midnight, Sun. 5-10pm. Call a week ahead for reservations.

Dan and Louie's Oyster Bar, 208 SW Ankeny St. (227-5906). Legendary since 1907, Dan and Louie's has its own Oyster Bay in Newport, OR. Lunch specials are especially cheap, and the older waitresses keep you giggling. Shrimp and Oyster Fry $8.50, crab cocktail $5.25, 4 "shuck 'em yourself oysters" $2.25. Open Sun.-Thurs. 11am-11pm, Fri.-Sat. 11am-midnight.

Yamhill Marketplace, 110 SW Yamhill (224-6705), at 1st St. A grocery and produce store operates on the first floor along with other food shops. International food stands amicably rub shoulders upstairs. Try the $3.50 shredded beef taco at **Carlos** or the colossal baked potato with broccoli ($2.75) at **Shelley's Chicago Deli.** Marketplace open Mon.-Sat. 7am-6pm, Sun. 10am-6pm.

Metro on Broadway, 911 SW Broadway (227-2746). A chic place in which to gaze and be gazed upon; also a good place to come alone and read. The piano player and espresso seduce an artsy crowd. A circle of stands serves a wide variety of above-average foods. Try Mexican chocolate at **Ears to You** ($1.50), chicken fried rice at **Orient Select** ($4), or yogurt milkshakes at **Split Decisions** ($2.25). Open Mon.-Thurs. 7am-11pm, Fri. 7am-midnight, Sat. 9am-midnight, Sun. 11am-7pm.

The Original Pancake House, 8600 SW Barbur Blvd. (246-9007). Take bus #12, 41, or 43 (all are yellow rose) to Barbur Transit Center. Great place for breakfast ($3.50-5). Hour-long lines on Sat. and Sun. morning. Open Wed.-Sun. 7am-3pm.

Maya's Tacqueria, 1000 SW Morrison St. (226-1946), at 10th. Genuinely Mexican, complete with wall-sized murals of Mayans doing Mayan things. Hearty chicken burrito $4.35. Open Mon.-Sat. 10:30am-10pm, Sun. 11am-7pm.

Northwest

Chang's Mongolian Grill, 1 SW 3rd St. (243-1991) at Burnside. Also at 2700 NW 185th (645-7718) and 1600 NE 122nd (253-3535). Ulan Bator's best cuisine in generous portions. All-you-can-eat lunches ($5.50) and dinners ($7.50). You select your meal from a buffet (fresh vegetables, meats, and fish), mix your own sauce to taste, and then watch your chef make a wild show of cooking it on a grill the size of a Volkswagen. Rice and hot-and-sour soup are included. Open daily 11:30am-2:30pm and 5-10pm.

Alexis, 215 W. Burnside St. (224-8577). Sincere Hellenic food served by a friendly Greek family in an east Mediterranean atmosphere. Lamb souvlaki $10. Open Mon.-Thurs. 11:30am-2pm and 5-10pm, Fri. 11:30am-2pm and 5-11pm, Sat. 5-11pm, Sun. 4:30-9pm.

Rose's Deli, 315 NW 23rd Ave. (227-5181), at Everett St. Take bus #15 (red salmon). Rose has her own cookbook now, but fame hasn't corrupted her cooking. She still serves up the city's best bagels in a noisy and crowded atmosphere. Great matzoh-ball soup ($2), cheese blintzes, and a pastry case that could fatten by osmosis. Luckily, the concave-mirrored interior makes you look skinny. Elephantine chocolate mousse cake $3, lunches $5-6.50. Open Mon.-Thurs. 7am-11pm, Fri. 7am-midnight, Sat. 8am-midnight, Sun. 8am-11pm.

Fuller's, 136 NW 9th (222-5608). The local regulars will stare at you; they're just surprised an outsider was smart enough to find this place. Breakfast ($3-4.50) and lunch at a counter. Not gourmet fare, but plenty of honest, down-to-earth Americana. Open Mon.-Fri. 6am-5pm, Sat.-Sun. 6am-2pm.

Fong Chong, 301 NW 4th (220-0235), in the heart of Chinatown. Portland's best *dim sum*. Unfortunately, selection is small and service varies. Still, it's worth a trip for the *fun gor* (crepes with pork) alone. Most dishes around $6. Open Mon.-Thurs. 10:30am-9pm, Fri.-Sun. 10:30am-10pm; *dim sum* daily 10:30am-3pm.

Southeast and Northeast

Jarra's Ethiopian Restaurant, 617 SE Morrison St. (230-8990). Take bus #15 (brown beaver). Authentic and hot cuisine served by a friendly staff. Eat with your fingers here, using spongy pancakes served on side plates to scoop up spicy mouthfuls. Main dishes, heaped on large *enjera* (which soak up the sauce and are consumed last), come with combinations of any 3 condiments: cottage cheese, mixed vegetables, or tomato salad with lettuce and collard greens. *Doro wat* (chicken in a spicy sauce) $6.50. Open Mon.-Tues. 5-10pm, Wed. 11:30am-2pm and 5-10pm, Thurs.-Fri. 5-10pm, Sat. 4-10pm.

Saigon Kitchen, 835 NE Broadway (281-3669), across from Lloyd Center. Fine Vietnamese and Thai food in a drab atmosphere. Daily lunch specials ($3.50) come with rice and soup. Open Mon.-Sat. 11am-10pm, Sun. noon-10pm.

Ice Cream and Pastries

Three Lions, 1138 SW Morrison St. (224-9039). The hip place to cheat on a diet, but those with willpower can always try the veggie sandwich ($3.50). Specialties include coffee cake and filled croissants (75¢-$1.20). Open Mon.-Fri. 7am-6pm, Sat. 7am-5pm.

Roberto's, 405 NW 23rd St. (248-9040). Deliciously dark chocolate ($20 per pound, $1 for a bite-sized morsel). Equally rich ice cream cones ($1.25) and truffle sundae ($2.90). Also at 921 SW Morrison (224-4234), in the Galleria. Open Mon.-Thurs. 11am-10pm, Fri. 11am-11pm, Sat. noon-11pm, Sun. noon-10pm.

Papa Haydn's, 2 locations. 701 NW 23rd (228-7317). The composer of *Die Schöpfung* would have smiled. Slightly overpriced lunch ($7) and desserts, but the palate is stronger than the wallet. 5829 SE Milwaukee (232-9440). Take bus #19 (brown beaver). Reed College hangout. Great soups and desserts. Open Tues.-Thurs. 11:30am-11pm, Fri.-Sat. 11:30am-midnight, Sun. 10am-3pm.

Rose's Bakery, 35 NW 20th Place (227-4875). A Viennese bakery of note, with wonderful aromas. Monstrous pastries $1, ft.-wide raised donuts $1.50. Branches in other parts of the city. **Rose's East,** 12329 NE Glissan (254-6545, take-out 254-6546). Open Mon.-Sat. 6:30am-6pm, Sun. 9am-5pm.

Sights and Activities

Portland can be exciting any time of year, but try to avoid the rains of fall, winter, and spring. Visit instead during the summer, when you can take advantage of the temperate weather and many free cultural events. This is also the best season in which to appreciate Portland's fountains, all of which seem to have long, intricate histories. The 20 bronze drinking fountains located on strategic street corners throughout Portland were dedicated to the city by Simon Benson, a wealthy Prohibition-era Portlander, ostensibly to ease the thirst of native loggers. **Benson Memorial Fountains'** four-spigoted heads pump cold "Bull Run" water, one of Portland's greatest natural assets. Other *objets d'art* dot the downtown area following the passage of a city law requiring that one percent of the costs of all construction and renovation work be devoted to public art projects.

Downtown

Portland's downtown area is centered on the **mall,** running north-south between 5th and 6th Ave., bounded on the north by W. Burnside St. and on the south by SW Madison St., and closed to all traffic except city buses. At 5th Ave. and Morrison St. sits the **Pioneer Courthouse,** the tribal elder of downtown landmarks. The monument now houses the U.S. Ninth Circuit Court of Appeals and is the centerpiece for **Pioneer Courthouse Square,** 701 SW 6th Ave. (223-1613), opened in 1983. Forty-eight thousand citizens supported its construction by sponsoring personalized bricks, and it seems as though all 48,000 make a daily pilgrimage to visit their gift to the city. Live jazz, folk, and ethnic music draws the rest of Portland to the square for the **Peanut Butter and Jam Sessions,** held in summer every Tuesday and Thursday from noon to 1pm.

At **Powell's Travel Bookstore** in Pioneer Courthouse Square (228-1108), you can rent the "Portland Downtown Discovery Walk," an 80-minute narrated tour on audio tape that highlights 90 historical downtown sites within 20 square blocks (tape plus solo player $7, with group player $10).

Certainly the most controversial building in the downtown area is Michael Graves's postmodern **Portland Building,** located on the mall. This amazing confection of pastel tile and concrete has been praised to the stars and condemned as an overgrown jukebox. Opened with great fanfare in 1984, the city celebrated by perching a full-sized inflatable King Kong on the building's roof. Since the building is surrounded by narrow streets and tall buildings, it can be difficult to obtain a good view of the exterior. Make sure to visit the interior, which looks like something out of *Blade Runner.* On a niche outside the building's second floor, *Portlandia,* an immense bronze statue of the trident-bearing woman on the state seal (which to many looks more like a man with breasts brandishing a large salad fork), reaches down to crowds below. The **Standard Insurance Center,** 900 SW 5th Ave., nearby, has also engendered controversy for the white marble sculpture out front, "The Quest." The sculpture is more commonly known to locals as "three groins in the fountain."

West of the mall are the **South Park Blocks,** a series of cool, shady parks down the middle of Park Ave. Facing the parks, the **Portland Art Museum,** 1219 SW Park Ave. (226-2811), at Jefferson St., has an especially fine exhibit of Pacific Northwest Native American art, including masks, textiles, and sacred objects. The Asian galleries also deserve notice, particularly the Chinese furniture. International exhibits and local artists' works are interspersed. (Open Tues.-Fri. 11am-7pm, Sat.-Sun. noon-5pm. Admission $3, senior citizens and students $1.50, under 12 50¢. Thurs. 5-9:30pm free.) The **Northwest Film and Video Center** (221-1156), in the same building, screens classics and off-beat flicks.

Across the street, the **Oregon Historical Society Museum and Library,** 1230 SW Park Ave. (222-1741), stores photographs, artifacts, and records of Oregon's past 200 years. The maritime exhibit is especially good. The library is open to the public for research. (Open Mon.-Sat. 10am-4:45pm. Free.)

On the eastern side of the Park Blocks is the **Portland Center for the Performing Arts,** at 1111 SW Broadway (248-4496). The Center consists of four theaters. The **Arlene Schnitzer Concert Hall,** a recently refurbished marble and granite wonder, shares the corner of Broadway and Main with the brick and glass **Dolores Winningstad Theatre** and the **Intermediate Theater.** The **Civic Auditorium** is the Center's fourth component. At 222 SW Clay St., the modern, glass-fronted, 3000-seat auditorium plays host to opera, ballet, and the occasional jazz or folk concert.

The view from the Civic Auditorium includes Lawrence Halprin's **Forecourt Fountain** (better known as Ira's Fountain), one of Portland's most popular footsoaking oases. This terraced waterfall, at SW 3rd Ave. and Clay St., circulates 13,000 gallons of water per minute. Retreat to a secluded niche behind the waterfall and discover for yourself what the back side of water looks like.

Old Town, to the north of the mall, was filled a century ago with drinking, shanghaiing sailors who docked in the ports from which the city takes its name. Redubbed Old Town by publicity-minded restorers, the district has been revived with large-scale refurbishment of store fronts, new "old brick," polished iron and brass, and a bevy of recently opened shops and restaurants. A popular people-watching vantage point, the **Skidmore Fountain** at SW 1st Ave. and SW Ankeny St., marks the entrance to the quarter. Had the city accepted resident draftsman Henry Weinhard's offer to run draft beer through the fountain, it would have been a truly cordial watering hole indeed. Old Town also marks the start of **Waterfront Park.** This enormous expanse of grass and flowers offers little shade, but provides great views of the Willamette River.

From March until Christmas, the area under the Burnside Bridge is given over to the **Saturday Market** (222-6072), 108 W. Burnside St. Saturdays from 10am to 5pm and Sundays from 11am to 4:30pm, the area is clogged with street musicians, artists, craftspeople, chefs, and produce sellers. Many of these artists and craftspeople sell their work in the city's studios and galleries during the week.

Portland's finest galleries are centered downtown. The **Image Gallery,** 1026 SW Morrison St. (224-9629), shows an international potpourri of Canadian Eskimo sculpture and Mexican and Japanese folk art. (Open Mon.-Fri. 10:30am-6pm, Sat. 11am-5pm.)

The Portland Children's Museum, 3037 SW 2nd Ave. (248-4587), at Wood St. (take bus #41 or 43, both yellow rose), schedules organized games, races, arts activities, and hands-on exhibits. (Open Tues.-Sat. 9am-5pm, Sun. 11am-5pm. Admission $2, children $1.50.) Sample some local lager at the **Blitz Weinhard Brewing Co.,** 1133 W. Burnside St. (222-4351), or take a stroll through all two feet of **Mill Ends Park,** at SW Front and Taylor St. The tiniest park in the world is the product of some journalist's desire to put some token greenery outside his window. It is now protected from iconoclasts by a chain hanging lazily between two iron columns.

Those in need of additional stimulation can stop by the **Electronic Poet** outside the Gap store on the corner of SW Morrison and SW 9th, or share brain waves with the **24-hour Computer Psychic** across from Dan and Louie's on SW Ankeny St. (see Food).

West Hills

Fewer than 2 miles west of downtown, these posh suburbs serve as a buffer zone between the soul-easing loveliness of the parks and the turmoil of the anomic city below. Take bus #63 (orange deer) or drive up SW Broadway to Clay St. and turn right onto Sunset Hwy. 26 (get off at zoo exit).

Washington Park and its nearby attractions are perhaps the handsomest sites in Portland. The park is open daily 7am-9pm and is crisscrossed with looping trails. "Bristlecone Pine" Trail is wheelchair accessible. Obtain trail maps at the information stand near the parking lot of the arboretum, or refer to the maps posted on the windows. **Hoyt Arboretum,** 4000 SW Fairview Blvd. (228-8732), at the crest of the hill above the other gardens, features many a conifer and "200 acres of trees and trails." (Free nature walks April-Oct. Sat.-Sun. at 2pm, and June-Aug. Tues 9:30am.) The walks last 60-90 minutes and cover 1-2 miles. The 3-mile "Wild Wood" Trail connects the arboretum to the zoo in the south. The **Japanese Gardens** (223-1321) arrange idyllic ponds and bridges into five contrasting formal patterns. Cherry blossoms ornament the park in summer, thanks to sibling city Sapporo, Japan. (Open daily 10am-6pm; Sept. 16-April 14 daily 10am-4pm. Admission $3.50, ages over 60 and under 12 $2.) Rows of roses await a few steps away at the **International Rose Test Garden,** 400 SW Kingston (248-4302). Stumble on prize-winning hybrids, marvel at the "miniature roses" gathered around the information kiosk, eat a hot dog, and survey the city from heights that would make an air force reconnaissance pilot giddy. Blooming season generally runs from June to November.

Below the Hoyt Arboretum lie many of Portland's most popular attractions. Although they can be crowded on hot summer days, they are certainly worth seeing. The **Washington Park Zoo** (226-1561 for a person, 226-7627 for a tape) is renowned for its successful elephant-breeding and its scrupulous re-creations of natural habitats. Whimsical murals decorate the #63 "zoo" bus connecting the park with Morrison St. in the downtown mall. A miniature railway also connects the Washington Park gardens with the zoo (fare $1.75). The zoo features a number of interesting "animal talks" at various times on weekends and has a pet-the-animals children's zoo. The zoo's countless elephants are world famous—several are represented by Mike Ovitz—so act deferentially towards them. (Open daily in summer 9:30am-7pm, call for winter hours. Admission $3, ages over 60 and under 12 $1.50. Tues. 3-7pm free.) Beginning in late June, the zoo sponsors **Your Zoo and All That Jazz,** a nine-week series of open-air jazz concerts (Wed. 6:30-8:30pm), free with zoo admission. Bring a picnic dinner. **Zoograss Concerts** features a 10-week series of bluegrass concerts (Thurs. 6:30-8:30pm), also free with admission.

Next to the zoo, the **Oregon Museum of Science and Industry (OMSI)**, 4015 SW Canyon Rd. (228-6674), will keep children and adults amused and bored with do-it-yourself science, computer, and medical exhibits. Don't miss the walk-through heart or the transparent woman. The **Kendall Planetarium** within the museum gives daily shows for 50¢ extra (228-7827 for taped planetarium info). The planetarium also puts on laser shows most evenings with painfully loud rock music and incredible laser special effects (admission $4.50, children $3.50); call 242-0723 for show times. Once overwhelmed by science, you can step outside into the small, immaculate garden of the Oregon Herb Society. Even in these oil-glutted days, the spirit of energy conservation lives on at **Terra One,** 3821 SW Canyon Rd. (222-2828, ext. 89), an avant-garde solar-heated residence operated by OMSI. (Open Mon.-Fri. 9am-5pm, Sat.-Sun. noon-5pm. Free.) The **World Forestry Center,** 4033 SW Canyon Rd. (228-1367), specializes in exhibits on Northwestern forestry and logging, although it is now taking on the entire world. Acquaintances of the Electronic Poet should hear the 70-foot "talking tree" continuously sprout information. (Open daily 10am-5pm. Admission $3, ages over 65 and under 12 $2.) Finally, the new and tastefully designed **Vietnam Memorial** is only a few steps up the hill.

Northwest, North, and Northeast

From Washington Park, you have easy access to sprawling **Forest Park,** the largest park completely within the confines of an American city. The park is laced by hiking trails and garnished with scenic picnic areas. The **Pittock Mansion,** 3229 NW Pittock Dr. (248-4469), within Forest Park, was built by Henry L. Pittock, the founder of Oregon's largest (and now only) daily newspaper, the *Oregonian.* From downtown take crosstown bus #20 (orange deer) to NW Barnes and W. Burnside St., and walk ½ mile up Pittock Ave. The 80-year-old structure, now owned by the city of Portland, will whisk you back to the French Renaissance. (Open daily 1-5pm. Admission $3, senior citizens $2.50, ages under 18 $1. Closed Jan. 1-21 for maintenance.)

Downtown on the edge of the Northwest district is **Powell's Book Store,** 1005 W. Burnside St. (228-4651), a cavernous establishment with an overwhelming collection of new and used books. Any book that's not here probably hasn't been written. (Open Mon.-Sat. 9am-11pm, Sun. 9am-9pm.) Enter Portland's small **Chinatown** at W. Burnside St. and NW 4th Ave., through the gate adorned with guardian lions and ornate arches. Take bus #4 (red salmon) to the **John Palmer House,** 4314 N. Mississippi Ave. (284-5893), another Victorian mansion restored to its 1890 splendor. Debts are apparently being settled by the exorbitant prices exacted by the bed-and-breakfast establishment inside. (Open for tours Thurs.-Sun. noon-5pm. Admission $3, senior citizens and students $2.)

Farther out, geographically and spiritually, is the **Grotto,** at the Sanctuary of Our Sorrowful Mother, NE 85th Ave. and NE Sandy Blvd. (254-7371). Take bus #12 (purple rain). The splendid grounds are decorated with the Stations of the Cross and Mary's Seven Sorrows. You can behold the Columbia River gorge from the cliff. (Open daily 8am-sunset. Admission by donation.)

Some find shopping a religious experience in the **Nob Hill** district. Fashionable boutiques run from Burnside to Thurman St., between NW 21st and NW 24th Ave. Shopping fanatics should also make sure to visit **Lloyd Center,** a shopping mall showcasing an open-air ice-skating rink. (Admission $3, skate rental $1.) Also noteworthy here is the award-winning **Lloyd Cinema,** an ultramodern multiplex equipped with comfortable contour chairs and plenty of neon. Next door, sample the delectable offerings at **Holladay Market,** a collection of fresh fruit, dessert, spice, and vegetable stands.

Southeast

Southeast Portland is largely a residential district. **Reed College,** a small liberal arts school founded in 1909, sponsors numerous cultural events. In 1968 this radiant enclave of progressive politics became the first undergraduate college to open a nuclear reactor. The ivy-covered campus encompasses a lake and a state wildlife refuge. Tours leave Eliot Hall, 3203 Woodstock Blvd. at SE 28th, twice per day during the school year. (Mon.-Fri. at 10am and 2pm or 10:30am and 2:30pm. Individual tours by appointment in summer. Call 771-7511.) The **Chamber Music Northwest** festival (294-6400), here every summer from late June to late July, holds concerts Mon., Thurs., Sat. at 8pm. Concerts sell out quickly; call ahead for tickets ($13, senior citizens and ages 7-14 $9). Across the street, in the lovely **Rhododendron Test Gardens,** SE 28th Ave. (796-5193), at Woodstock, 2500 rhododendrons surround a lake. The rhododendrons and azaleas are in full bloom April and May. (Open daily "in season" during daylight hours. Free, but $1 on Mother's Day. Sorry, Mom.)

Farther east in the southeast is **Mt. Tabor Park,** one of two city parks in the world on the site of an extinct volcano. More of a molehill than a mountain, the volcano is easily eclipsed by Mt. Tabor itself. Take bus #15 (brown beaver) from downtown, or drive down Hawthorne to SE 60th Ave. **Hawthorne Boulevard** has more antique shops, used book stores, and second-hand clothing stores than the other sectors of the city. A ritzier collection is found along **Old Sellwood Antique Row,** at the east end of Sellwood Bridge, on SE 13th Ave. between Bybee and Clatsop St. Over 30 curiosity shops showcase stained glass, rare books, and assorted "used" memorabilia at prices that may inspire you to hawk your own used items (face it, your *Batman* rhinestone jacket is becoming passé). (Hours vary, but all stores open Tues.-Sat.)

Sports

Contact the **Portland Park Bureau,** 1120 SW 5th Ave., #502 (796-5193), for a complete guide to Portland's many parks, which contain the usual hiking and cycling trails and lakes for swimming and sailing. Outdoor **tennis courts,** many of which are lighted for night play, are free and open to the public. The following parks have free **swimming pools:** Columbia, Creston, Dishman, Grant, Mt. Scott, Montavilla, Peninsula, Pier, and Sellwood. Special facilities and programs are provided for senior citizens and the disabled (call 248-4328).

The Oregon Road Runners Club (626-2348) sponsors several races each year. Most of the roads on the periphery of the city have ample bike lanes. The **Portland Beavers** (223-2837) play Class AAA baseball and aspire to become Minnesota Twins at Civic Stadium, 1844 SW Morrison St. (248-4345; tickets $3-5). The Coliseum, 1401 N. Wheeler (238-4636) is home to the **Trail Blazers** (234-9291) of the NBA and the **Winter Hawks** (238-6366) of the Western Hockey League. Take bus #9 (brown beaver) or take MAX.

Entertainment

Portland is no longer the hard-drinking, carousing port town of yore. The sea salt is out of the town's blood, and a newer, more sophisticated fluid now circulates. The best listings are in the Friday edition of the *Daily Oregonian* and in a number of free handouts: *Willamette Week, Multnomah Monthly,* the *Main Event, Clinton St. Quarterly,* and the *Downtowner.* The first of these caters to students, the last to the upwardly mobile. Each is available in restaurants downtown and in boxes on street corners.

Music

Oregon Symphony Orchestra plays in Arlene Schnitzer Concert Hall (228-1353) Sept.-April. Tickets $10-28. "Symphony Sunday" afternoon concerts $5-8.

Portland Civic Auditorium, 222 SW Clay St. (248-4496). Attracts the usual arena rock acts, as well as a few jazz and opera stars. Ticket prices vary.

Sack Lunch Concerts, 1422 SW 11th Ave. and Clay St. (222-2031), at the Old Church. Free concert every Wed. at noon (except in the event of rain).

Chamber Music Northwest performs summer concerts at Reed College Commons, 3203 SE Woodstock Ave. (223-3202). Classical music Mon., Thurs., Sat. 8pm. Admission $13, ages 7-14 $9.

Brown Bag Concerts, free public concerts given around the city in a summer 6-week series (at noon during the week and Tues. evenings). Check the *Oregonian* or call the Park Bureau at 796-5193.

Noon Lawn Concerts, at the Odell Manor Lawn, Lewis and Clark College (244-6161). Free classical concerts throughout June and July. Thurs. noon-1pm.

Peanut Butter and Jam Sessions at Pioneer Courthouse Square from noon to 1pm every Tues. and Thurs. during the summer months. A potpourri of rock, jazz, folk, and ethnic music.

Theater

Portland has many fine theaters, producing everything from off-Broadway to experimental plays.

Portland Civic Theater, 1530 SW Yamhill (226-3048). The mainstage often presents musical comedy, the smaller theater-in-the-round less traditional shows. Tickets $6.50 or $9.50.

Portland Civic Auditorium, 222 SW Clay St. (248-4496). Occasional big splashy touring shows, now part of the Portland Center for the Performing Arts (PCPA).

Oregon Shakespeare Festival/Portland (248-6309), at the Intermediate Theater of PCPA, corner of SW Broadway and SW Main. Five-play series, focusing on those of the Bard, runs Nov.-Feb. World-class productions.

New Rose Theater, 904 SW Main St. (222-2487), in the Park Blocks. Even mix of classic and contemporary productions. Tickets range from $9-14.

Artists Repertory Theater, SW 10th, on the 3rd floor of the YMCA. This small theater puts on excellent low-budget productions, many of them experimental. Tickets $10-15.

Portland State University Summer Festival Theater, at the Lincoln Hall Auditorium (229-4440). Schedules at the box office or the Portland Public Library. Performances mid-June to mid-July.

Oregon Contemporary Theater, 511 SW 10th St., Lewis and Clark College, Fir Acres Theater (241-3770). Considered one of Portland's most innovative companies.

Cinema

Most of Portland's countless movie theaters have half-price days or matinee shows. Consult the *Oregonian* and you will never have to pay the standard $5 ticket price for the average "major motion picture."

Movie House, 1220 SW Taylor (222-4595). Wine, cheese, and chess before art flicks. Tickets $5, ages over 62 and under 12 $3.

Cinema 21, 616 NW 21st (223-4515). Clean, attractive movie house showing mostly documentary, independent, and foreign films. Tickets $4, students and senior citizens $2; matinee seats $2.

Clinton Street Theater, 2522 SE Clinton St. (238-8899). Classic and foreign films $3, free popcorn Wed. nights. The execrable *Rocky Horror Picture Show* every Fri., Sat. at midnight.

Northwest Film and Video Center, 1219 SW Park Ave. (221-1156). Mostly documentary films on little-known places and peoples. Tickets $3.50, ages under 12 $2. Open Wed.-Sun.

Clubs and Bars

The best clubs in Portland are not the easiest ones to find. Neighborhood taverns and pubs may be tucked away on back roads, but they are also those with the most character and best music.

Flyers advertising upcoming shows are always plastered on telephone poles around town. Those with happy feet should foxtrot the length of 6th Ave. to find most of the dancing clubs. The under-21 crowd ought to head for the Confetti Club, 126 SW 2nd (274-0627; $6 cover, some $2 nights), for new-wave music, or try the Warehouse, 320 SE 2nd, for top-40 tunes (232-9645).

Produce Row Cafe, 204 SE Oak St. (232-8355). Bus #6 (red salmon) to SE Oak and SE Grand, then walk west along Oak towards the river. 21 beers on tap ($1), 72 bottled domestic and imported beers (ranging in origin from China to Belgium), and a lovely outdoor beer garden. Ask one of the friendly bartenders to mix you the house special, a Black Velvet (Guinness Stout and champagne, $1.85). Open Mon.-Fri. 11am-1am, Sat. noon-1am, Sun. 2pm-midnight.

Mission Theater and Pub, 1624 NW Glisan (223-4031). Serves excellent home-brewed ales as well as delicious and unusual sandwiches ($4.50). Also offers free showings of double features twice nightly. Relax in the balcony of this old moviehouse with a pitcher of Ruby, a fragrant raspberry ale named after one of Mick Jagger's creations ($1.25 glass, $6.50 pitcher). Open daily 5pm-1am.

Goose Hollow Inn, 1927 SW Jefferson (228-7010). Bus #57 or 59 (orange deer). Mayor Bud Clark's place, always a popular neighborhood tavern, is now wall-to-wall with aspiring progressives. No music, however. Sandwiches $3-6.50. Open daily 11:30am-1am.

Brasserie Montmarte, 626 SW Park (224-5552). A high-class, expensive joint with live jazz every night. Open Mon.-Fri. 11:30am-2:30pm for lunch (around $6); Mon.-Sat. 5:30-10pm, Sun. 5:30-9:30pm for dinner (around $10).

East Avenue Tavern, 727 E. Burnside St. (236-6900). Bus #12, 19, or 20 (all brown beaver). Folk music with open-mike nights that make for unexpected variety: Irish, French, flamenco, bluegrass. Cover $1-5, depending on the name and fame of the performer. Open Mon.-Sat. noon-midnight, Sun. 8pm-midnight.

Hobo's Inn Old Town, 120 NW 3rd Ave. (224-3285). Gay men's club playing a variety of music. A polished interior amid the squalor of 3rd Ave. Prime rib and seafood dinners $9-11. No cover. Open Mon.-Thurs. 4pm-1am, Fri.-Sat. 4pm-2:30am, Sun. 10am-2:30am.

Harrington's, 1001 SW 6th Ave. (243-2933), at Main St. A sight unto itself. Front door is a little gazebo and underground stairway in the middle of a downtown sidewalk. It's been listed as one of the nation's "top-10" bars by *Esquire*, which gives you an idea of the clientele. Look for Vladimir. Cover $1-5 Thurs.-Sat.; live music all week. Open Mon.-Fri. 11:30am-9pm. Take-out breakfast window opens at 7:30am.

Key Largo, 31 NW 1st Ave. (223-9919). Airy, tropical atmosphere. You can dance out on the patio when it's not raining. A variety of local and national bands. Rock, rhythm & blues, zydeco, and jazz. Cover $2-8. Open Mon.-Fri. 11am-2:30am, Sat.-Sun. noon-2:30am.

Seasonal Events

Rose Festival, first 3 weeks of June. The city bedecks itself in all its finery for Portland's premier summer event. Waterfront concerts, art festivals, parades, an air show, Navy ships, and Native American powwows. Unfortunately, with the influx of people comes an increase in crime—women walking alone at night should be careful. Call 248-7923 for taped info, 227-2681 for the offices.

Mt. Hood Festival of Jazz, Aug. 3-5, at Mt. Hood Community College in Gresham (666-3810). The premier jazz festival of the summer, with 20 hours of music over the course of a weekend; Stan Getz and Wynton Marsalis have been regulars in the past. Admission around $20 per day. Reserve well in advance. Write Mt. Hood Festival of Jazz, P.O. Box 696,

Gresham 97030. To reach the festival, take I-84 to Wood Village-Gresham exit and follow the signs, or follow the locals on MAX to the end of the line.

Artquake, Labor Day weekend. Music, mime, food, and neo-situationist hoopla in and around Pioneer Courthouse Square (227-2787).

Multnomah County Fair, late July-early Aug. Annual bash includes livestock fair, crafts, and country music at the Multnomah County Exposition Center in Portland. Call 285-7756.

Washington Park Festival, late July-early Aug. Pack a picnic supper and enjoy theater, music, and dance in the park's amphitheater. Check the *Oregonian* or call 796-5193 for information.

Magicazam, in early July. The largest traveling magic show in the U.S. stops at the Multnomah County Exposition Center (285-7756). Admission $4-5.

Near Portland

Many possible daytrips from Portland beckon you west to the coast and north into Washington. Cannon Beach, Tillamook, and Astoria are all within a day's drive through the serene Tillamook State Forest. In Washington, Mt. St. Helens is easily accessible from its southern side or, on a longer daytrip, from its northern side. (See Oregon Coast and Southwest Washington chapters.)

Sauvie Island and U.S. 30 West

Twenty minutes from downtown Portland nests Sauvie Island, a peaceful rural hideaway at the confluence of the Columbia and Willamette Rivers. On winter mornings, eagles and geese congregate along the roads, and in spring and summer, berries are everywhere. For many Portlanders, a trip to the island's **U-pick farms** (family operations announced by hand-lettered signs along the roads) is a berry season tradition. Visit the **James Bybee House and Agricultural Museum,** on Howell Park Rd., built in 1859 on the eve of Oregon's statehood. (Open June 1-Labor Day Wed.-Sun. noon-4:45pm.) In the island's northwestern corner, beaches and a wildlife management area open nature to fishermen, hikers, and solitude seekers. (Open daily 4am-10pm.) To reach Sauvie Island, take U.S. 30 west out of downtown.

Farther north on U.S. 30, some 42 miles from Portland, **Trojan Nuclear Power Plant** aims to convince tourists that nuclear power is "safe" and "efficient" The Trojan Visitors Center, 71760 Columbia River Hwy., Rainier (226-8510), has an exhibit on the mechanics of magnetism, electricity, and nuclear fission. Trojan is the only nuclear plant in the country that gives its visitors a look into the "Jane Fonda" room, so-named after the movie *The China Syndrome,* in which "Jane Fonda" witnessed the panic in the control room of a plant on the verge of a meltdown. (Visitors center open Mon.-Sat. 9am-5pm, Sun. noon-5pm; Labor Day-Memorial Day Wed.-Sat. 9am-5pm. Free.) Public tours of the plant itself are conducted several times per week; contact the visitors center for hours and reservations (which are usually necessary). If the visitors center or tour are not on your schedule, bring a picnic and dine with a view of the cooling tower; Trojan encourages recreational use of its 75-acre wooded area. U.S. 30 continues to follow the Columbia for about 35 miles to the river's mouth at Astoria.

Columbia River Gorge

Fifteen million years ago, massive flows of lava poured out of rifts in the earth, covering northern Oregon with 25,000 cubic miles of basalt. Then the Columbia River carved a narrow channel 3000 feet deep and 55 miles long. Walls of volcanic stone rise on either side of the Columbia as the grand river surges on its last lap to the sea. To follow the spectacular Columbia River Gorge, take I-84 east (old U.S. 30) to the Troutdale exit onto the **Columbia River Scenic Highway.** This highway, built in 1915, follows the crest of the gorge walls and affords legendary views. The famous **Vista House,** in Crown Point State Park, hangs on the edge of an outcropping cliff high above the river. A few meters past this house, a trail leaves the road to end on a rock spine, where you can view both gorge and Vista House in splendid solitude. Reach Crown Point from the Scenic Hwy. or from the Corbett exit off I-84.

About 2 miles farther east is **Latourell Falls,** where you can clamber over jagged black rock to stand behind a plume of falling spray. Six miles farther, **Multnomah Falls** crashes 620 feet into an astoundingly quiet pool at the bottom. The paved trail to the top of the falls is steep but rewarding. Hikers who would like to escape main-trail traffic can follow other paths into Mt. Hood National Forest. Get an inexpensive trail map from the Multnomah Falls gift shop. **Camping** is allowed at sites along the trails in **Ainsworth National Park** but accessibility varies seasonally. Check with posted regulations or with a Multnomah Falls park ranger for more information. For better prospects, try the Washington side of the river.

Exactly 44 miles east of Portland is the oldest of the Columbia River hydroelectric projects, the **Bonneville Dam.** Across the river on the Washington side, a **visitors center** presents tourists with a view of a fish ladder and of the dam's powerhouse and generator room. Follow the yellow arrows painted on the pavement to see the fish hatchery, where a little garden displays fishpools instead of flower beds. (Visitors center and hatchery both open daily 8am-8pm. Free.) Also on this side of the river, don't miss dramatic **Beacon Rock,** the 848-foot-high neck of an old volcano.

At the Cascade Locks, 4 miles past Bonneville, take a **paddleboat ride** aboard the *Columbia Gorge* (374-8474 or 374-8619, in Portland 223-3928), a replica of the sternwheelers that used to ply the Columbia and Willamette Rivers. (Rides 1 hr. and longer. Lowest fare $9, children $5.)

Thirty-four miles east of Multnomah Falls is **Hood River,** a town known for world-class windsurfing and sailing. **The Dalles,** just east of **Fort Dalles,** cradles a historical museum housed in the original 1856 surgeon's quarters; other 19th-century structures may be seen outside. For a free map including a walking tour, go to the **visitors center,** in an 1859 county courthouse. In late April, when the region's cherry trees are at the height of blossoming glory, The Dalles has a Cherry Festival. The third week in July brings **Fort Dalles Days and Rodeo,** a wild-west extravaganza.

Mount Hood

At the junction of U.S. 26 and Hwy. 35, 90 minutes from Portland and less than an hour from Hood River, is the glacier-topped volcano Mt. Hood. In early years Native Americans of the Willamette Valley—the Clackamas and Wasco—feared Mt. Hood's vile temper. Legend describes a brave warrior who tried to stop the devastating lava flows by hurling boulders into Mt. Hood's crater. The enraged mountain reportedly spit them back out, initiating a rock-throwing contest that lasted for four days. When the warrior realized that Hood's boulders were destroying his village below, he dropped to his knees in despair and was quickly swallowed up by lava. A huge rock outcropping called **Chief's Face** on Hood's northern side precisely marks this spot today.

The mountain has been behaving itself for quite some time. Skiers can take advantage of the winter trails at three ski areas: **Timberline, Ski Bowl Multorpor,** and **Mt. Hood Meadows.** All three offer night skiing, and Timberline allows summer skiing (you'll have to share the slopes with the U.S. national team, however). Rental of skis, poles, and boots runs under $20 (under $10 for children) and lift tickets generally cost under $20. All three areas offer ski lessons (averaging a hefty $10 per hr.). Timberline's Magic Mile lift carries nonskiers up above the clouds for spectacular views of the mountain and surrounding environs ($3, children $1.50). Experienced hikers can tackle the 11,000-foot mountain on foot (complete climbing equipment rental at Timberline $16.50).

Even if you decide to ski at Ski Bowl or Mt. Hood Meadows, turn up the 6-mile road just off **Government Camp** to the W.P.A.-style **Timberline Lodge** (800-452-1335, 231-5400 from Portland), site of the outdoor filming of Stanley Kubrick's flawless, metaphysically horrifying *The Shining*. The drive to the lodge allows spectacular views of the valley below. Next door is the **Day Lodge,** where skiers can store equipment without staying overnight, and the **Wy'east Kitchen,** a cafeteria alternative to the expensive dining at Timberline. Nonskiers can find non-stop fun on the mountain. Ski Bowl runs an alpine slide, a gheau-kart course, and groomed mountain-bicycle trails. In addition, hiking trails circle the mountain. The most popular is **Mirror Lake,** a 4-mile loop open June through October. Start at a parking lot off U.S. 26, 1 mile west of Government Camp. Ask at Timberline for a complete list of hiking trails.

From the Columbia River Gorge, you can also take Hwy. 35, south from Hood River, which wends through apple, pear, and cherry orchards. In April, when the trees are in bloom, the drive is particularly memorable. **Gray Line Tours,** 400 SW Broadway (226-6755), offers an eight-and-a-half-hour ride around Mt. Hood and through the Columbia River Gorge ($24, ages under 12 $12). Tours leave from the Imperial Hotel from mid-May to early October at 9am on Tuesdays, Thursdays, and Saturdays.

Oregon City

Originally the capital of the Oregon Territory, this once-burgeoning community was settled around the tremendous 42-foot-high Willamette Falls. Oregon City built a thriving transportation industry carrying cargo and people around the falls to new northern settlements such as Portland. As these settlements grew, Oregon City declined. Take bus #32, 33, or 35 (all green leaf) to Oregon City from 5th Ave. in downtown Portland, or drive down Hwy. 43 (20 min.). The **"End of the Trail" Interpretive Center,** 500 Washington St. (657-8287), celebrates the end of the 2170-mile Oregon Trail, which begins in Independence, MO. Pictures of covered wagons and tired, dusty-looking people inhabit this miniature museum. (Open Tues.-Sat. 10am-4pm, Sun. noon-4pm. Admission $2, senior citizens $1.50, children $1.) The **McLoughlin House,** 713 Center St. (656-5146), former home of beloved early Oregonian and fur trade baron Dr. John McLoughlin, has been restored with original furnishings. (Open Tues.-Sat. 10am-4pm. Admission $2.50, senior citizens $2, ages under 17 $1.)

The most distinctive structure in Oregon City is surely its **Municipal Elevator,** on Railroad St. at the end of 7th Ave. This dusty pink antique is built into a large hill and looks like something the Jetsons would design, only tackier. Nevertheless, rides are free and allow interesting views of the Smurfit paper mill. (Open Mon.-Sat. 7am-7pm.)

Come down from the dizzying heights to visit the less spectacular **Clackamas County Historical Society Museum,** 603 6th St. (655-2866). The generic exhibits feature pioneer and Native American relics. (Open Tues.-Sat. 10am-4pm. Admission $1.50.) If you sensibly decide to skip the museum, take the money you've saved and head for the **Sportcraft Marina,** 1701 Clackamette Dr. (656-6484), which rents boats and related equipment for reasonable prices; boats start at $20 per day. (Open daily 9am-6pm.) Oregon City's annual highlight is the **Riverfest** in mid-July, with a dunk tank, bingo games, and live bluegrass music.

What the city lacks in sights, it compensates for with a handful of down-to-earth restaurants that serve heavenly food. **Chris's Coffee Shop,** 210 7th St. (657-5111), serves imaginative burger specials ($2-4) and marvelous milkshakes ($1.50). City photos from the 40s adorn the walls. (Open Mon.-Fri. 6am-4pm, Sat. 7am-3pm.) **Main Street Eatery,** 716B Main St. (657-2865), serves soup and a sandwich for a reasonable $3.50. (Open Mon.-Fri. 6am-4pm, Sat. 8am-3pm.) Because of the easy access to Portland, there is absolutely no reason to spend the night in Oregon City. If trapped, stay at the **International Dunes Motor Inn,** 1900 Clackamette Dr. (655-7141); its luxurious rooms with VCR, cable, heated pool, and hot tub start at around $50 for a single.

The **Chamber of Commerce,** 500 Abernathy Rd. (656-1619), on the corner of Washington and 17th, has Oregon City road maps ($1.50), helpful staff, and many a pamphlet. (Open Mon.-Fri. 9am-noon and 1-5pm, Sat.-Sun. 11am-4pm.)

Oregon Coast

Oregon's western boundary deserves superlatives. The so-called "Pacific" hurls itself at the rocky shore with abandon, making a misty din. Only the most daring swim in its ice-cold surf; others are more than satisfied by the matchless views and huge stretches of unspoiled beach.

Possessively hugging the shore, **U.S. 101,** the renowned coastal highway, passes by a series of lofty viewpoints. From northernmost Astoria to Brookings in the south, the highway laces together the resorts and historic fishing villages that cluster around the mouths of rivers feeding into the Pacific. It is most breathtaking between the coastal towns, where hundreds of miles of state and national park allow direct access to the beach. Whenever the highway leaves the coast, look for a beach loop road. These are the "roads less traveled," which afford some of the finest scenery on the western seaboard.

Getting Around

Drive or bike for the best encounter with the coast. Remember that rain is frequent. The *Oregon Coast Bike Route Map* (available free from the Oregon Dept. of Transportation, Salem 97310, or at virtually any visitors center or Chamber of Commerce on the coast) provides invaluable information on campsites, hostels, bike repair facilities, temperatures, and wind speed.

For those without a car or bike, transportation becomes a bit tricky. **Greyhound's** coastal routes from Portland currently run only twice per day each way, with half of the routes running in the middle of the night. Along the southern coast, the 10-hour Portland-Brookings route stops at Lincoln City, Newport, Florence, Reedsport, Coos Bay, Bandon, Port Orford, Gold Beach, and every suburb between Portland and the coast. In the north, the Portland-Seaside-Astoria loop offers on-call service to Gearhart and Warrenton. Local public transportation goes from Tillamook to Astoria, but no public transportation links Tillamook and Lincoln City.

Gasoline and grocery prices on the coast are about 20% higher than in inland cities. Motorists may want to stock up and fill up before reaching the coast-bound highways.

Astoria

When the last of Astoria's many salmon canneries folded in the early 70s, the small city was left with no real industry; the dairy farms and lumber mills were long gone. Today, with the only new construction going on in Warrenton, a few miles south, Astoria's only shot at redemption lies in its formidable past. The first American city west of the Mississippi, Astoria looks over the infamous Columbia River sandbar, which Captain Gray's ship, the *Columbia,* successfully maneuvered around in 1792. Over 120 other ships have not been so lucky. In 1811, fur baron John Jacob Astor established Astoria for the purpose of shipping fur to China. Astor lost the post in the War of 1812 (during which he continued doing business with the British), but went on to extend his empire elsewhere. At his death, he was the richest man in America. Astoria is also near Lewis and Clark's western camp, Fort Clatsop.

Practical Information and Orientation

Visitor Information: Greater Astoria Chamber of Commerce, 111 W. Marine Dr. (325-6311), just east of the U.S. 101 toll bridge to Washington. P.O. Box 176, Astoria 97103. Thoroughly stocked with information on Astoria, the coast, and southwest Washington. Open Mon.-Sat. 8am-6pm, Sun. 9am-5pm; Oct.-April Mon.-Fri. 8am-5pm.

Greyhound (RAZ Transportation): 364 9th St. (325-5641), at Duane St. Leaves Astoria for Portland daily 9:30am and 6:30pm. Leaves Portland for Astoria daily 6am and 3:25pm (one way $13). Open Mon.-Sat. 8-11am and 4-7pm.

North Coast Transit: At the Greyhound station in Seaside (738-7083). Runs from Astoria to Seaside and back, serving towns in between. Leaves Astoria at 8:45am, 12:10pm, 3:20pm, and 5:40pm. To Seaside one way $2.25, round-trip $3.25.

Pacific Transit System: At the Greyhound terminal (206-642-4475, ext. 450). To Ilwaco and Chinook, WA. Fare 50¢. Buses flee Astoria daily at 7:30am, 11:40am, and 3pm.

TBR Transit: Also at the Greyhound terminal (325-3521 or 325-5189). Local bus service. One full city loop every hr. Fare 45¢, students and ages under 12 35¢. Service Mon.-Sat. 6:30am-7:15pm.

Laundromat: 127 Bond St., behind the visitors center. Open daily 8am-10pm.

Clatsop County Women's Crisis Services: 1250 Duane St. (325-5735). 24 hours.

Senior Citizens Information Service: 818 Commercial St. (325-0123). Legal services. Open Mon.-Fri. 8:30am-12:30pm. Also community recreational center.

Children's Services: 255-4811. While primarily crisis-oriented, this county-run service also advises on child care and education in the Astoria area.

Coast Guard: Clatsop Airport (861-2242), Warrenton. 24-hour marine and air emergency service.

Clatsop County Sheriff: 325-2061.

Post Office: in the Federal Bldg. (325-2141), at 8th and Commercial. Open Mon.-Fri. 8:30am-5pm. General Delivery ZIP Code: 97103.

Area Code: 503.

Astoria can be reached from the south by U.S. 101. From Portland, take U.S. 30 along the Columbia River, or U.S. 26 ("Sunset Highway"), which links Portland to U.S. 101 at Seaside.

Accommodations and Camping

For reasons unknown, motels in Astoria keep prices relatively high, and bargains are difficult to find. The 10-mile trek to Fort Stevens Park will let you pitch a tent in clean, albeit crowded, spaces.

Fort Columbia State Park Hostel (AYH), Fort Columbia, Chinook, WA (206-777-8755), within the park boundaries. Across the 4-mile bridge into Washington, 2 miles west on U.S. 101. Pacific Transit System will get you there for 50¢ (see Practical Information); otherwise you'll have to pay the $1.50 toll to cross the bridge. A practically deserted hostel located in the old army hospital of a turn-of-the-century fort. Glorious grounds, friendly staff, and a kitchen fire always lit on chilly evenings. Lockout 9am-5pm, but hours not strictly enforced. Members $5, nonmembers $8. Open year-round, but reservations should be made in winter.

Rivershore Motel, 59 W. Marine Dr. (325-2921), 1 mile east of the bridge, on U.S. 30 along the Columbia. Pleasant motel with TV, phones, and kitchenettes. Singles $37.65. Doubles $45.

Astoria City Center Motel, 495 Marine Dr. (325-4211). Nothing fancy, but clean and comfortable. Singles $34. Doubles $44.50. In winter, prices drop $5.

Rosebrian Inn, 636 14th St. (325-7427), at Franklin. A cozy bed and breakfast in a restored Victorian home. Doubles $40, breakfast included.

Fort Stevens State Park (861-2000), over Youngs Bay Bridge on U.S. 101 S., 10 miles west of Astoria. A huge park with rugged, desolate beaches. 223 sites, facilities for the disabled, and hot showers. Sites $7; in winter $6. For reservations, write Fort Stevens, Hammond 97121.

Food

Meals in Astoria are generally wholesome, though not especially fancy. The **Safeway**, 11th St. and Duane, is open 24 hours. The **Community Store**, 14th and Duane (325-0027), sells natural and bulk foods. (Open Mon.-Fri. 9am-5:30pm.)

Pacific Rim, 229 W. Marine Dr. (325-4481), near Washington Bridge. Great food, no frills. Ignore the ugly, diner-like decor and try the Sicilian-style ravioli with basil and blue cheese for an unusual culinary experience. Italian dinner $5-7, burgers $2-3. Open Sun.-Thurs. 11am-11pm, Fri.-Sat. 11am-midnight.

Columbian Cafe, 1114 Marine Dr. (325-2233). A real find for the vegetarian connoisseur. Fresh pasta made daily, dishes around $6.50, salads $3. Special seafood dinners, depending on the catch of the day. Open Mon.-Fri. 7am-2pm. Dinners served Wed.-Thurs. 5-8pm, Fri. 5-9pm. At the adjacent **Bordertown Burrito Bar**, the Columbian Cafe's eccentric chefs cook up delicious vegetarian Mexican food. Open daily 11am-6pm.

Little Denmark, 125 9th St. (325-2409), downtown on the waterfront. Authentically bland Danish food and homemade pastries. Assortment of entrees and open-faced sandwiches $4.50. Open Mon.-Fri. 10am-4pm, Sat.-Sun. 9am-4pm.

Sights and Activities

Astoria is a city that should be viewed from above, so climb the 165 or 166 steps (no one really knows) of the **Astoria Column** on Coxcomb Hill Rd. Erected in 1922, the column's outside spirals with friezes depicting the history of the area—the discovery of the Columbia by intrepid Robert Grey, the arrival of Lewis and Clark, the founding of Astoria, and the settlement of the territory. Open from dawn to dusk, it is accessible by the TBR bus (see Practical Information). However, a hike up 8th St. followed by a left turn on Franklin Ave. will be much more rewarding.

Since the early 19th century, the elite of Astoria have chosen to live in the area surrounding **Franklin Avenue**, between 10th and 18th St. The houses, still in pristine condition, are a monument to the splendor of the city's past. It is easy to forget the somewhat seamier atmosphere of the dock while you enjoy the vast panorama of mountains and water. The indefatigable should proceed 1 block higher to **Grand Avenue**, parallel to Franklin, for more magnificent houses and an equally stunning view.

Fort Astoria, at 15th and Exchange St., is a replica of the straightforward square blockhouse built by John Jacob Astor in 1811. You can't go in, but you can gape at the doorstep all day for free. Talks by informative guides are offered summer weekends at 11am, 12:30pm, 2pm, and 5:30pm. The **Flavel House**, 441 8th St. (325-2563), is a restored Victorian mansion. Although the house's original furnishings are gone, the replacements are from the right place and time. Wealthy Astorians had their furniture made in the east and shipped to them all the way around Cape Horn. At 16th and Exchange St., the **Clatsop County Heritage Museum** houses photographic exhibitions, the usual assortment of old things, a fascinating exhibit on Oregon's first Chinese settlers, and, strangely enough, a collection of ancient Persian artwork. (House and museum admission $3, students $2, children $1. Open daily 10am-5pm; Nov.-April Tues.-Sun. noon-4pm.)

Across from the museum, the eccentric, talkative owner of the **Shallon Winery**, 1598 Duane St. (325-5978), will give you a tour of his small winemaking facilities along with his interpretation of the area's history. Then he'll treat you to a taste of wines made from local berries and the only commercially produced whey wines around. (Usually open daily noon-6pm.) Nearby, the **Columbia River Maritime Museum**, 1793 Marine Dr. (325-2323), at the foot of 17th St., has, among a wide variety of nautical paraphernalia, sailing-ship models, early sea charts, and whaling exhibits. All displays are accompanied by well-written, detailed explanatory texts.

Plan on spending over an hour here. Anchored outside is the *Columbia,* the last lightship to see active duty at the mouth of the Columbia River. (Museum open daily 9:30am-5pm. Admission $3, senior citizens $2, ages 6-18 $1.50.)

In the third week of June, Astoria holds its **Scandinavian Festival.** The celebration includes a parade, tug of war, a profusion of ethnic foods, and folk dancing.

Six miles southwest of Astoria, the **Fort Clatsop National Memorial** (861-2471) reconstructs the winter headquarters of the ragtag Lewis and Clark expedition, based on descriptions in their detailed journal. The small, crude fort housed Lewis and Clark, 24 enlisted men, three officers, a few interpreters and guides, Clark's slave York, and Lewis's dog Scannon. By the end, Scannon wasn't the only one with fleas. The **visitors center** shows a good slide presentation and a few exhibits. Park rangers (clad in buckskin) give scheduled talks and demonstrations. (Open daily 8am-6pm; Labor Day to mid-June 8am-5pm. Admission $1, ages over 63 and under 13 free, families $3.)

Fort Stevens State Park (861-2000 or 800-452-5687), off U.S. 101 on a tiny peninsula 10 miles west of Astoria, has swimming, fishing, boating, beaches, and hiking trails. Fort Stevens was constructed in 1864 to guard against Confederate gun boats entering the Columbia. Within the park lie the skeletal remains of the *Peter Iredale,* lost in 1906. The battered hulk of this 287-foot British schooner makes a lonely and eerie sight at low tide. **Battery Russell,** also in the park, bears the dubious distinction of being the last mainland American fort to see active defensive duty since the war of 1812. At 10:30pm on June 22, 1942, a Japanese submarine offshore shelled the fort with 17 rounds. Today, in good sword-to-ploughshare fashion, the concrete gun emplacement has been taken out of service and converted to a playground.

Seaside

Seaside marks the farthest west Lewis and Clark traveled. Having finally reached the Pacific, they could think of nothing better to do than collect seawater to make salt. Seventy years later, the site was built up by eccentric Portland railroad and shipbuilding magnate Ben Holladay. Today Seaside is pure beachfront culture: families flock here for candy floss, corn dogs, arcades, and a piece of the crowded beach to spread their blankets on.

Practical Information and Orientation

Visitor Information: Chamber of Commerce, 7 N. Roosevelt St. (738-6391, in OR 800-444-6740), on U.S. 101 and Broadway. Well-versed staff ready to answer every question about this town. The Chamber of Commerce doubles as a booking agency for most local motels. Open daily 8am-6pm; Oct.-May 8am-5pm.

Greyhound (RAZ Transportation): 325 S. Holladay Dr. (738-5121, in Portland 246-3301), at Ave. C. Office in bike shop. Leaves Portland at 6am for Seaside (2 hr. 40 min.) and Astoria (3 hr. 10 min.), completing the loop to Portland in a full 6 hr. 20 min. (one way $12-14).

Citizens Better Transit: 738-5121; in Portland 232-1741. In summer the **Beach Bus** runs to Tillamook and Portland, with 10 stops along the coast. To Portland $13, ages under 12 $10. Reservations required. Leaves Seaside at 12:45pm.

North Coast Transit: 738-7083. Service between Seaside and Astoria with stops in Gearhart and Warrenton. The bus for Astoria leaves Rexall Drugs at Holladay and Broadway at 7:15am, 10:30am, 2:10pm, and 4:45pm. (45 min., $2.50, bikes 50¢).

Bike Rental: Prom Bike Shop, 325 S. Holladay (738-8257), at the Greyhound terminal (or, more accurately, *containing* the Greyhound terminal). Bikes, bike carts, roller skates, and beach tricycles $3 per hr.; tandem bicycles $4 per hr. Deposit and ID required. Open Mon.-Fri. 10am-5pm, Sat.-Sun. 10am-dusk.

Laundromat: 57 N. Holladay St., at 1st Ave. Open daily 6am-11pm.

Senior Citizens Information Service: 1225 Ave. A (738-7393).

Police: 1090 S. Roosevelt Dr. (738-6311).

Post Office: 300 Ave. A (738-5462). Open Mon.-Fri. 8:30am-5pm, Sat. for pickup 8-10am. General Delivery ZIP Code: 97138.

Area Code: 503.

Seaside lies 17 miles south of Astoria and 8 miles north of Cannon Beach along U.S. 101. It is most directly accessible from Portland via the 73-mile "Sunset Highway" (U.S. 26).

Accommodations

There are cheap rooms by the dozen at Seaside, but in summers more than enough tourists arrive to make the "vacancy" signs disappear. During peak tourist season (late July-Aug.), prices increase $4-10 per night, and reservations are crucial. The Chamber of Commerce coordinates information about room availability (see Practical Information).

Holladay and Mariner Motels, 426 and 429 S. Holladay Dr. (738-6529). Holladay Dr. parallels U.S. 101, beside the Necanicum River, toward the ocean. The same people own both; the front office and pool are located at the Mariner. Small, quaint rooms with bathrooms on the hall. Singles $30. Doubles $35. Sept. 16-May 23 rooms $5 less.

Riverside Inn, 430 S. Holladay Dr. (738-8254), next to the Holladay. Real bedrooms, with bookshelves and raftered ceilings. The rooms aren't large, however, and there is some noise from the road. Singles $33. Doubles $39. Nov.-April singles $29, doubles $35.

Anchor Motel, 1020 N. Holladay Dr. (738-8049), at the other end of town, in a quieter residential neighborhood. Small rooms, small TV, small price. A few have kitchens. Singles $27. Doubles $32. Mid-Sept. to May a few dollars less.

Royale Motel, 521 Ave. A (738-9541), 1 block from the arcades of Broadway. Friendly management and clean rooms. Cable TV. Rooms $35-42; Sept. 16-May 15 $30-36.

Camping

Private campgrounds around town are for RVs only, and the closest state parks are Fort Stevens, 21 miles north (see Astoria), and Saddle Mountain, 14 miles southeast from the coast. Sleeping on the beach is illegal, and the police do patrol. Camping on the dunes around Gearhart, 2 miles north of Seaside, is possible, but petty crime has been reported, so keep an eye on your belongings.

Saddle Mountain State Park, at Necanicum Jct., 14 miles east of Seaside off U.S. 26 on a winding 7½-mile road. Nine primitive campsites. Flush toilets, no showers. Pretty forest setting near base of Saddle Mountain hiking trail. Sites $7.

Kloochy Creek, 7½ miles southeast of Seaside, about 300 yards off U.S. 26. Nine primitive sites clustered around the world's largest Sitka Spruce tree. Sites $6.

Food

Corn dogs and pups will run you a dollar. Those who disdain such low-brow cuisine should avoid the tourist craziness and head about 2 miles north to the quiet streets of Gearhart.

White Lion Pizza and Bakery, 1445 S. Holladay (738-0157), on U.S. 101 south, as you leave Seaside. Loaf of fresh bread about $1. *New York Times* food critic James Beard once judged their European bread ($1.50 per loaf) the best in the country. Deli sandwiches and individual pizzas $3.50-4. Open daily 11am-10pm.

Dooger's Seafood and Grill, 505 Broadway St. (738-3773). The best clam chowder in town, unadulterated by flour or cornstarch thickeners. Lunch special of fried oysters, shrimp salad, and garlic bread $6. Open daily 11am-10pm; Oct.-May daily 11am-9pm.

Chicago Pan Pizza Co., 111 Broadway St. (738-5217). All-you-can-eat pizza and salad deal: lunch $4, dinner $5. Pizza made to order, not removed from under a heat lamp. Open daily 11am-9pm.

Sights and Seasonal Events

Seaside revolves around **Broadway,** a garish strip of arcades, shops, and salt water taffy stores running the ½ mile or so from Roosevelt (U.S. 101) to the beach. The arcades offer some of the few remaining 10¢ games of skee ball in this country. The **Turnaround** at the end of Broadway arbitrarily signals the end of the Lewis and Clark Trail. Eight short blocks south along Lewis and Clark Way, just off Prom St., is the **Lewis and Clark Salt Cairn,** a replica of the plant used to boil salt water down to salt. It is estimated that more than 40 gallons of water are evaporated here daily.

Travelers looking for Lewis and Clark will enjoy the **Lewis and Clark Historical Drama**—a re-enactment of the last leg of their journey. The drama does not relate Lewis and Clark's return east. Lewis went on to a violent death three years later, and Clark to a series of undistinguished positions. Tickets are available at the Chamber of Commerce and at some stores. (Tickets $7.50, senior citizens $6.50, ages 6-15 $3. Performances mid-July to Aug. Thurs.-Sat. 8pm, Mon.-Tues. 2pm.) A few blocks north of the beaten trail, the **Seaside Historical Museum,** 570 Necanicum Dr. (738-7065), houses a remarkably good exhibit of Clatsop Native American artifacts excavated by the Smithsonian Institution during the 70s. (Open daily 1-4pm; Oct.-April Wed.-Sun. 1-4pm.)

Seaside's beach is crowded but expansive. Three lifeguards are on duty from Memorial Day to Labor Day (daily 10am-6pm). On "red flag" days the surf is considered too rough for swimming (the water, of course, is always cold). For a quieter beach, head to **Gearhart.** No lifeguard is on duty here, and since a drowning accident in 1983 town officials have advised against swimming. You can, however, explore the long stretch of sand and dunes safely.

Saddle Mountain State Park, 14 miles southeast of Seaside on U.S. 26, is named for the highest peak in the coastal range. From Saddle Mountain's 3283-foot summit, the views of the Cascades to the north are astounding. The 6-mile trail, open March through December, is a good four-hour hike. Farther east on U.S. 26 lies the **Jewell Meadows Wildlife Area,** a wintering habitat for Roosevelt elk. Parking spaces throughout the refuge allow you to get out and wander about with the elk, present mostly in fall and winter. Black-tailed deer often show up in the spring and summer, and an occasional coyote may make an appearance any time of year. Take U.S. 26 to Jewell Jct., then head north on the unmarked state road for 9 miles to Jewell. Turn west and travel 1½ miles on Hwy. 202 to the refuge area.

Seven miles south of Seaside on U.S. 101, **Ecola State Park** (436-2844) marks yet another end of the Lewis and Clark Trail. That elusive first glimpse of the Pacific could not have been more arresting. From the high ground, you can see **Haystack Rock** anchored just a little offshore. Beyond it, the tenacious old **Tillamook Lighthouse** clings like a barnacle to a wave-swept rock. Construction of the lighthouse, begun in 1879, continued for years while storms kept blowing the foundations away. Decommissioned in 1957 because of damage caused by storm-tossed rocks, the now privately owned lighthouse can be reached only by helicopter and only for the purpose of depositing ashes of the dead. So far, this has not been a lucrative commercial venture.

From Ecola State Park, you can take the 12-mile round-trip hike to **Tillamook Head,** from which you can sometimes glimpse migrating whales. In the fall, ask a knowledgeable local to point out chanterelle mushrooms along the path. The trail is open year-round.

In late February, the **Trail's End Marathon** is run from Seaside's Turnaround Hallway to Astoria and back to Seaside. The marathon is one of the flattest, coolest, and fastest in the nation. Call the Chamber of Commerce for information. In mid-August, the **Seaside Beach Run** leaves the same spot for an 8-mile race on the Oregon sand. Thousands of people from all over the country assemble for these races. Contact the Parks and Recreation Service for information.

Cannon Beach

A rusty cannon from the shipwrecked schooner *Shark,* which washed ashore at Ecola State Park, gave this town its name. Distinguished from Seaside by its romance and subtlety, and from Astoria by its lack of any real history, Cannon Beach is tasteful and expensive. The town tries to blend inconspicuously with the grandeur of the northern Oregon coast, camouflaging its houses in thickets of trees and maintaining an unobtrusive beach front. Aesthetic sensibility runs amok in Cannon Beach: art galleries, pseudo-bohemian shops, and theater groups outnumber fastfood joints and neon signs. Here wealthy Portlanders summer.

Practical Information and Orientation

Visitor Information: Cannon Beach Chamber of Commerce, 201 E. 2nd (436-2623), at Spruce St. P.O. Box 64, Cannon Beach 97110. Run by an extremely helpful manager. Maps of the area. Open Mon.-Sat. 11am-5pm, Sun. 11am-4pm; sometimes closed on winter weekends.

Citizens Better Transit: 738-5121, in Seaside. In summer, the **Beach Bus** runs from Portland to Seaside and back via Hwy. 6 and U.S. 101, serving towns in between. Bus leaves Cannon Beach for Portland at 2:12pm ($13, ages under 12 $10). Reservations required for some of the stops.

Bike Rental: Mike's Bike Shop, 248 N. Spruce St. (436-1266), around the corner from the Chamber of Commerce. Maps of routes along old, untraveled logging roads. Mountain bikes and cruisers $4 per hr., beach tricycles $5 per 90 min. Theoretically open in summer Mon., Wed.-Thurs., and Sat. 10am-6pm, Fri. 10am-7pm, Sun. noon-5pm, but Mike's hours change at the drop of an inner tube; call first.

Post Office: 155 N. Hemlock St. (436-2822). Open Mon.-Fri. 9am-5pm. General Delivery ZIP Code: 97110.

Area Code: 503.

Cannon Beach lies 8 miles south of Seaside and 42 miles north of Tillamook on U.S. 101; it is 80 miles from Portland via U.S. 26.

Accommodations and Food

Cannon Beach has a variety of pleasant motels, few of which are affordable. The budget-conscious might wish to camp out at **Oswald West** (see Cannon Beach to Tillamook), just south of town.

In keeping with Cannon Beach's character, the food here is served for the most part in trendy and pricy cafes. Be especially wary of the town's several overpriced bakeries. You will, however, find a few budget treasures.

McBee Court, S. Hemlock and Van Buren Rd. (436-2569), at old U.S. 101, ½ block from the ocean near Haystack Rock. A little south of the commercial center of town, but still on a noisy main street. Pleasant rooms 1 block from the beach. 1 bed $27, 1 bed with hide-a-bed $36, 2 double beds $38. Separate 2-story coach house with kitchen, fireplace, 1 double bed, 3 twins, and hide-a-bed $65. A few dollars less in winter.

Blue Gull Motel, 632 S. Hemlock St. (436-2714). Big clean rooms decorated with heavy-handed oil paintings of crashing surf. Set back from the street. TV with cable. Singles and doubles $36; in off-season $30.

Hidden Villa, 188 E. Van Buren Rd. (436-2237), 2 blocks from beach. Singles $30. Doubles $34. In winter, rooms $5 less. Discounts for stays of longer than one night.

Lazy Susan Cafe, 126 N. Hemlock St. (436-2816). A gorgeous health food restaurant that serves your foodin sturdy crockery. Sandwiches $4-5, variety of omelettes $5. Make sure to order the waffles and fruit special ($4.50) when it's available. Open Thurs.-Sat. 7:30am-2:30pm and 5:30-9:30pm, Sun. 8am-2pm for brunch only.

Osburn's Deli and Grocery, 240 N. Hemlock St. (436-2234). Great hearty sandwiches to take out ($3.75, available 11am-5pm). Open daily 8:30am-8:30pm; Labor Day-June 9am-7:30pm. **Osburn's Ice Creamery,** next door, dishes out cones for 95¢. The fresh strawberry shake ($3), available in season, is like the nectar of the gods. Open daily 11am-6pm.

Mariner Market, 139 N. Hemlock St. (436-2442). About the least expensive grocery store in town—which isn't saying much. Open daily 9am-9pm.

Brass Lantern, 1116 S. Hemlock St. (436-2412), at the other end of town. Recognized as the best restaurant in the area. Mouth-watering red snapper with mushrooms and artichoke hearts $10.50. Tender scallops $13. Generous desserts. Open Mon.-Sat. 5-9pm.

Cannon Beach Seafood Co., 123 S. Hemlock St. (436-2272). Great prices for fresh seafood. Large shrimp cocktail $3. Fish and chips $3.37. Open daily 11am-6pm.

Sights and Activities

Rather than browse in the art galleries, you should spend a morning walking on the 7-mile beach and admiring the hulking **Haystack Rock.** The bay's 235-foot centerpiece is spotted with gulls, puffins, barnacles, anemones, and an occasional sea lion. The tide pools below are usually teeming with colorful sea life. Tidal charts, available at the Chamber of Commerce, indicate good times and best methods for digging clams.

The **Coaster Theater** (436-1242), on Hemlock, stages three semi-professional productions from late June through August. (Box office hours July-Aug. Thurs.-Sat. noon-8pm. Or write Coaster Theater, P.O. Box 643, Cannon Beach 97110. Performances Thurs.-Sat. at 8pm. Admission $10.)

Try to schedule your itinerary around the **Sand Castle Competition.** Contestants pour in from hundreds of miles away and begin building early in the morning, creating ornate sculptures from wet sand. In the evening, the high tide washes everything away, leaving photographs the sole testimony to the staggering amount of creative energy expended during the day. The photos are prominently displayed in the Chamber of Commerce. Past creations have included Humpty Dumpty, King Tut, and Ozymandias, as well as numerous enchanted castles and dreadful monsters. Contact the Chamber of Commerce for the date of the 1990 competition.

In December, locals celebrate Christmas with a three-week festival, opening officially with a lamplighting ceremony on the first Friday of the month. A proclamation is read and the public ushers in the holiday season with songs and cider guzzling.

Cannon Beach to Tillamook

Tillamook County has been in various stages of convalescence since the summer of 1933, when a hellish fire raged for over a week, reducing 500 square miles of the world's finest timber to a charred pile of sticks. Fifty-six years later, Tillamook State Forest has finally been nursed back to health. The sedate beaches and trees of Tillamook County accommodate spillover from the more popular resorts to the north and south. Small towns strung out along the coastline—Manzanita, Nehalem, Rockaway, and Garibaldi—are generally uncrowded and peaceful. Tourist information for these towns is available at the visitors information bureau in Tillamook or the **Rockaway Beach Chamber of Commerce,** 216 N. U.S. 101 (355-8108). The **Beach Bus,** run by **Citizens Better Transit** in Tillamook, serves Manzanita, Wheeler, Rockaway Beach, and Garibaldi. Call 503-842-5848 for information.

Oswald West State Park, 10 miles south of Cannon Beach, is a headland rain forest with huge spruce and cedar trees. The park is accessible only by foot on a ¼-mile trail off U.S. 101. This doesn't quite qualify as "roughing it," for the State Parks Division is at hand to provide wheelbarrows for pushing gear from the U.S. 101 parking area to the 36 uncrowded, primitive campsites near the beach. The overnight camping season lasts from mid-May to October, and sites cost $7. From the park, take the 4-mile **Cape Falcon** hiking trail farther out toward the water, or just follow the path from the campground down to one of Oregon's only surfing beaches.

Five miles south of Oswald, self-consciously quaint **Manzanita** sleeps on a long expanse of uncrowded beach. The **San Dune Motel,** 428 Dorcas Lane (368-5163), just off Laneda St., the main drag through town, has inexpensive, pleasant rooms 5 blocks from the shore. Suites cost $25-60, and most rooms have fully equipped kitchens. It's best to cook in your room, since the few restaurants in town are expensive.

Nehalem, a few miles south, is little more than a handful of "made in Oregon" shops lining U.S. 101. Stop in at the **Bayway Eatery** (368-6495) for excellent $3.25 fish and chips. The slightly grubby diner is a favorite Nehalem hangout. (Open Mon.-Sat. 6am-9pm, Sun. 7am-4pm.) The **Nehalem Food Mart** stocks an impressive selection of imported beers. (Open Mon.-Tues. 9am-7pm, Wed.-Sat. 9am-9pm, Sun. 10am-6pm.) Three miles away, the **Nehalem Bay Winery,** 34965 Hwy. 53 (368-5300), hands out samples of local specialties. (Open daily 10am-5pm.)

A few miles south of Nehalem, just north of Wheeler, **Nehalem Bay State Park** offers 292 sites ($8), including some hiker/biker sites ($1), and hot showers. If you prefer indoor accommodations, stop at the small **Webfoot Motel,** 580 Marine Dr. (368-5858), on U.S. 101 at the bayfront in **Wheeler.** On busy summer weekends, clean, baby-blue rooms with kitchens go for $35; on weekdays and in off-season $25. The town joke is on display across the street at the **Wheeler Inn,** 675 Nehalem Blvd. (368-9108). Above the doorway, a life-sized figure of a man pushes a woman in a wheelbarrow ("Wheel her in"—get it?). If you can stomach that, you'll also enjoy the local lounge and the seafood/steak restaurant fare offered inside. The food is much better than the joke. Next door, the **Bayfront Bakery and Deli,** 468 Nehalem Blvd. (368-6599), serves baked goods hot out of the oven, as well as $3.25 lunch sandwiches. (Open Tues.-Sat. 8:30am-5:30pm.) A 2-hour train ride might be the most relaxed way to get from Wheeler to Tillamook. Call **Coast Line Express** (842-2768) for times. ($15, senior citizens $12, children $8.)

Rockaway, about 8 miles south of Wheeler, is a quiet retirement town with a long stretch of lonely beach, and, mysteriously, about five penny arcades. The friendly, knowledgeable manager at the **Sand Dollar Motel,** on U.S. 101 (355-2301), offers clean rooms with showers from $24 (discount for senior citizens). This is one of the few affordable seaside motels in the state.

The larger town of **Garibaldi,** roughly 6 miles south of Rockaway, is named after the glamorous unifier of Italy who, it seems, was a fisherman in his early years. A highly developed marina juts into the bay at Garibaldi, wooing boaters but minimizing ocean and beach access for landlubbers. There are a few good places to eat in town. The **Bayfront Bakery and Deli,** 302 Garibaldi (322-3787), on U.S. 101, has a more extensive menu than its Wheeler branch, including BBQ ribs, pizza, and salads. The pies and baked goods still win out. (Open Tues.-Sat. 5:30am-5:30pm, Sun. 7am-4pm.) The **Old Mill Restaurant,** 3rd and Americana St. (322-0222), overlooks the boats and water from the old mill marina. Turn west off U.S. 101 over the railroad tracks and follow the signs to the left. This faded wooden building contains an ordinary family-style restaurant. The daily lunch special costs $4, and they leave the skins on their french fries. A razor clam dinner is $8.50. (Open daily 4:30am-10pm.)

Tillamook

Oregon's finest cheeses are cultured at the eastern shore of Tillamook Bay, well out of sight of the hungry ocean. The residential nook called Tillamook is bordered on three sides by cow pastures. Some visitors enjoy a brief jaunt through the surrounding bucolic countryside, but most are content with a hunk of cheese.

Practical Information and Orientation

Visitor Information: Tillamook County Chamber of Commerce, 3705 U.S. 101 N. (842-7525), next to the Tillamook Cheese Factory. Open Mon.-Fri. 9am-5pm, Sat. 1-5pm; mid-June to Sept. also open Sun. 9:30am-2:30pm.

Parks and Recreation: 322-3477.

Citizens Better Transit: 604 Main St. (842-5848), in the Jiffy Market. In summer, the **Beach Bus** runs from Portland to Seaside and back via Hwy. 6 and U.S. 101, serving towns in between. To Portland $10, ages under 12 $7.50. Reservations required for some of the stops. Call for exact departure times.

Tillamook Crisis and Resource Center: 842-9486.

Ambulance: 842-4444.

County Sheriff: 842-2561.

Post Office: 2200 1st St. Open Mon.-Fri. 8:30am-5pm. General Delivery ZIP Code: 97191.

Area Code: 503.

Tillamook lies 49 miles south of Seaside and 44 miles north of Lincoln City on U.S. 101. The most direct route from Portland is to take U.S. 26 to Hwy. 6 (74 miles).

Accommodations, Camping, and Food

Tillamook's main occupation is to sate cheese-crazed tourists, so expect inflated seasonal lodging prices. A large-scale reforestation project has opened camping and hiking trails in the coastal range. For the most part, those who frown on fast food will be happiest buying cheese and sausage and making a picnic in the nearby valley.

El Ranch Motel, 1810 U.S. 101 N. (842-4413), between the center of town and the Tillamook Cheese Factory. Generic motel rooms, sometimes disturbed by noise from the highway. Free coffee. Guests pay $1.50 to use tanning salon. Singles $30. Doubles $32. Rates may be lower off-season. Senior citizen discount.

Greenacres Motel, 3615 U.S. 101 N. (842-2731), next to the Cheese Factory. Reserve these small, dingy rooms well in advance in summer. Singles $22. Doubles $26.

Kilchis County Park, 8 miles northeast of Tillamook, along Kilchis River Rd. 40 primitive sites near the river and the county ball field. Pets allowed. Tentsites $6.

Cape Lookout State Park. Hot showers, flush toilets. Hiker/biker sites $6. (See Tillamook to Lincoln City.)

La Casa Medello (842-5768), north of town on U.S. 101, down the street from El Ranch Motel. Pleasant, but hardly authentic. Mild Mexican food prepared to order. Tacos $2, burritos $3.50. Dinners (about $7) come with rice, beans, and chips. Open Mon.-Fri. 11am-9pm, Sat.-Sun. 11am-10pm; in winter Mon.-Fri. 11am-8pm, Sat.-Sun. 11am-10pm.

Hadley House, 2203 3rd St. (842-2101), across from the courthouse. More-than-generous helpings of sea and cheese products, as well as American standbys. Kitchen clatter competes with conversation, but the bread is always fresh from the oven. Sandwich and soup $4, full dinner $5.50-11.

Tillamook Cheese Factory, 4175 U.S. 101 N. (842-4481). Cheap breakfasts served 8-11am. Lunch specials $3.50. Homemade ice cream 75¢. Open daily 8am-8pm; Sept. to mid-June 8am-5pm.

Sights and Activities

In Native American parlance, Tillamook means "land of many waters." Whether these original inhabitants were referring to the frequent downpours or not remains a mystery. But in any case, the place can be very wet. That perhaps explains why so many of Tillamook's tourist attractions are indoors. The most visited of these is undoubtedly the **Tillamook Cheese Factory,** at 4175 U.S. 101 N. (842-4481). The primary reason for the building's popularity seems not to lie in the self-guided tour, but rather in the adjacent ice cream parlor, where a cone of the local specialty goes for 75¢. The place is usually packed in summer. (Open daily 8am-8pm; Sept. to mid-June 9am-5pm.) Somewhat less crowded is the **Blue Heron French Cheese Factory,** 2001 Blue Heron Dr. (842-8281), 1 mile south of the Tillamook factory on the east side of U.S. 101. The "factory" is little more than a room full of dairy tubs, but the sales room is more open to tasting than at Tillamook and features basket after basket of cheesy goodies to sample. Four bucks will buy you a wheel of their excellent brie. Next door, visit **Debbie D's Sausage Factory** (842-2622) to pick up some delicious meat for picnicking. (Both factories open daily 9am-6pm.)

West of the highway, in downtown Tillamook, the **Tillamook County Pioneer Museum,** 2106 2nd St. (842-4553), features all manner of household and industrial goods from the pioneer era, labeled with yellowed donation cards. (Open Mon.-Sat. 8:30am-5pm, Sun. noon-5pm; Oct.-April Tues.-Sat. 8:30am-5pm, Sun. noon-5pm. Admission $1, ages 12-17 50¢, families $5.)

The first weekend in March, Tillamook pays tribute to some of its earliest settlers in the **Swiss Festival** celebration. In addition to the "oompah" band, arts, crafts, and European foods are displayed and consumed.

Tillamook to Lincoln City

Between Tillamook and Lincoln City, U.S. 101 wanders eastward into forest land out of sight of the ocean. Consider taking instead the **Three Capes Loop,** a 35-mile circle to the west that connects a trio of spectacular promontories—Cape Meares, Cape Lookout, and Cape Kiwanda State Parks. The beaches are secluded, and the scenery is worth the uncrowded drive. Cyclists especially will appreciate the reduction in car traffic, but should also note that the roads are narrow, winding, and poorly maintained.

Cape Meares, at the tip of the promontory jutting out from Tillamook, is home to the **Octopus Tree,** a twisted Sitka spruce with several trunks. Also at the park is the **Cape Meares Lighthouse,** built in 1890, which now operates as a historically invaded interpretive center. Climb to the top for sweeping views and a peek at the original lens of the big light. (Open May-Sept. Thurs.-Mon. 11am-6pm. Free.)

From here, continue 12 miles southwest to **Cape Lookout** (842-4981), a reservation park with 193 tentsites and 53 full hookups for $7-9 ($5-7 in winter). The park is also equipped with showers, trails, and facilities for the disabled. For reservations, write Cape Lookout, 13000 Whiskey Creek Rd., Tillamook 97141.

Cape Kiwanda, the third promontory on the loop, is for day-use only. (Open 8am-dusk.) On sunny, windy days, hang gliders gather to test their skill at negotiating the wave-carved sandstone cliffs. The sheltered cape draws skin divers, and beach hikers come to sink their toes into the dunes. Whether hang glider, skin diver, or beach hiker, you'll find your thing in Cape Kiwanda. A state park trail overlooks the top of the cape before reaching the ocean. On the cape, just barely north of Pacific City, massive rock outcroppings in a small bay mark the launching pad of the flat-bottomed **dory fleet,** one of a few fleets in the world that launches beachside directly onto the surf. If you bring your own fishing gear down to the cape most mornings around 5am, you can probably convince someone to take you out; the fee will nearly always be lower than those of commercial outfitters. If you want to guarantee a catch, or don't have your own gear, let **Pacific City Sporting Goods** (965-6466) take you salmon- or bottom-fishing ($40 per day). Make reservations, and be prepared to leave by 6am. The required one-day license can be purchased at the store for $4. There is a two-fish limit on salmon.

Pacific City is a delightful town unknown to most U.S. 101 travelers. The **Turn-around Motel,** 5985 Pacific Ave. (965-6496), has a few handsome suites with kitchens, living rooms, and excellent views (doubles $30). The undisputed summit of gustation in the area is the **Riverhouse Restaurant,** 34450 Brooten Rd. (965-6722), overlooking the Nestucca River. Chowder and piled-high sandwiches cost $5.50. At dinner try the oysters Kirkpatrick, oven-broiled with swiss cheese, bacon, and tomato, for $11. (Open Tues.-Thurs. 11am-9pm, Fri.-Sat. 11am-10pm, Sun. 10am-9pm.) The **Chamber of Commerce** (965-6161) does not operate a regular office but does have a complete information sign and map posted at 34960 Brooten Rd., in the middle of nowhere.

Back on U.S. 101 about 8 miles south, **Neskowin** appears little more than a motel by the side of the road. Squeezed into this parking lot complex, however, is the **Deli** at **Neskowin,** 4505 Salem Ave. (392-3838), a refuge for homesick New Yorkers (and Minnesotans). Pastrami sandwiches go for $4, and the pickled Oregon salmon combines the best of both worlds. (Open Sun.-Fri. 8am-9pm, Sat. 7am-9pm.) Driving south of Neskowin on U.S. 101, you should watch for signs of the **Siuslaw National Forest.** An 11-mile road leaves U.S. 101 and passes by huge old trees dripping with moss (this is a northern rain forest). Five and a half miles down the road from Neskowin is **Neskowin Creek Campground** (392-3131), where 12 primitive tentsites (outhouse only) are maintained for free camping.

U.S. 101 crosses Hwy. 18 at **Otis.** Stop here at the **Otis Cafe** (994-2813) for some of the best home-style rhubarb pie around. The place is often crowded; don't expect to get in and out quickly during peak hours. Your patience will be rewarded by $2 sandwiches on freshly baked bread and breakfast specials for $1.65. (Open Mon.-Wed. 7am-3pm, Thurs.-Sat. 7am-9pm, Sun. 8am-9pm.)

A dozen wineries line Hwy. 18 on the way to Portland. A 9-mile detour via Hwy. 99 W. and Hwy. 47 will take you to **Carlton,** home of the **Chateau Benoit Winery,** Mineral Springs Rd. (864-2991 or 864-3666). From Hwy. 47 in Carlton, take Rd. 204 1.3 miles east, then go 2½ miles south on Mineral Springs. The winery specializes in Pinot Noir, Chardonnay, and Riesling. (Tasting hours Mon.-Fri. 11am-5pm, Sat.-Sun. noon-5pm.)

Lincoln City

Lincoln City is actually five towns incorporated into one, all conspiring to make you drive at 30 miles per hour past 7 miles of motels, gas stations, and tourist traps. Bicyclists will find it hellish, and hikers might do better to cut 3 blocks west to the shore. There is little reason for drivers to stop in what is perhaps the crassest city on the Oregon coast except to fill their gas tanks and stomachs, or maybe spend the night in a cheap motel.

Practical Information

Visitor Information: Lincoln City Chamber of Commerce, 3939 NW U.S. 101 (994-3070 or 800-452-2151). Brochures covering everything in Lincoln City. Open Mon.-Fri. 9am-5pm, Sat. 9am-4pm, Sun. 10am-5pm.

Greyhound: 316 SE U.S. 101 (994-8418), behind the bowling alley. To Portland $12. Open daily 9am-7pm.

Taxi: 996-2772 or 994-8070.

Car Rental: Robben-Rent-A-Car, 3232 NE U.S. 101 (867-3615). Additional location at airport (994-5530). $27 per day plus 25¢ per mile. Must be 21 with major credit card.

Community Swimming Pool: 994-5208 or 994-2131. Nonresidents $1.50, showers 75¢.

Coast Guard: In Depoe Bay (765-2123).

Post Office: E. Devil's Lake Rd. (994-2148), 2 blocks east of U.S. 101. Open Mon.-Fri. 8:30am-5pm. General Delivery ZIP Code: 97367.

Area Code: 503.

Accommodations and Camping

The cheaper motels are located along noisy U.S. 101. Camping is available within walking distance of Lincoln City, but arrive as early as possible—the sites fill by mid-afternoon almost every day during the summer.

City Center Motel, 1014 NE U.S. 101 (994-2612). Straightforward, immaculate rooms, on the highway. Cable TV. Some rooms with kitchens. Singles $23. Doubles $25. Late Oct.-Memorial Day prices $3 lower.

Budget Inn, 1713 NW 21st St. (994-5281). Still on the highway. First-floor rooms are protected from the noise by a bank of earth; 3rd-floor rooms have balconies with sea views. Singles $25. Doubles $29.

Captain Cook's Motel, 2626 NE U.S. 101 (994-2522), 3 blocks from the ocean. Big rooms with big TVs. Bring your earplugs: the highway practically runs through the lobby. One bed $22-26. Two beds $30-32.

Bel-Aire Motel, 2945 NW U.S. 101 (994-2984), at the north end of town. Singles $23. Doubles $25. Rates in winter $2 less.

Southshore Motel, 1070 SE 1st (994-7559), on the D River, a little off the highway. Pleasant rooms. Cable TV, spa, sauna. Singles $29. Doubles $32.

Devil's Lake State Park, 1452 NE 6th St., Lincoln City 97367. Clearly marked turn east off U.S. 101. 100 closely spaced sites. Showers, flush toilets, facilities for the disabled. Sites $8, RVs $10, hiker/biker camp $1. Write for reservations. Open April-Oct.

Food

Head down to Depoe Bay or Newport for better seafood. The **Safeway** market on U.S. 101 is the only establishment that stays open 24 hours.

Foon Hing Yuen, Inc., 3819 SE U.S. 101 (996-3831). Generous portions of good Chinese food. Try the *pork chow yuk* ($5.25), a delicious vegetable dish. The only restaurant in town that doesn't close before 10pm. Take-out available. Open Mon.-Fri. noon-midnight, Sat.-Sun. noon-2am.

René's Place, 660 SE U.S. 101 (996-4161). René cooks, while his wife serves the varied continental menu, with complete dinners ($9-12) and full lunches ($5). A local favorite. Daily specials. Open Wed.-Sun. noon-8pm.

Colonial Bakery, 1734 NE U.S. 101 (994-5919). This could be any bakery anywhere in the United States. Still, it's hard to go wrong with the three S's: sugar, starch, and satisfaction. Coffee 35¢, apple fritters 45¢, glazed doughnuts 35¢. Open daily 6:30am-6pm.

A lil' Cheesecake Restaurant and Bakery, 2156 NE U.S. 101 (994-7323). Dumb name but good food. Sauteed shrimp in eggs with croissant and home fries $5.25. Spaghetti or tortellini with homemade bread $5. Open daily 7am-2:30pm.

Lighthouse Brew Pub, 9157 U.S. 101 (994-7238), in Lighthouse Sq. at the north end of town. Six in-house beers $2.10 a pint. Sandwiches and burgers $3-5. Ask about tours of the brewery. Open Sun.-Thurs. 11am-11pm, Fri.-Sat. 11am-1am.

Sights and Activities

Lincoln City's focal point and rather dubious claim to fame is the **D.** All public routes to the beach cross the D, and streets in Lincoln City are numbered from it. Marketed as "the world's shortest river," the D is a 100- to 300-yard overflow from Devil's Lake. Thousands of tourists each year pull over, snap a picture, and zoom off faster than you can say "Trilling."

A pleasant detour on **East Devil's Lake Road** leads around the lake to quiet, clearly marked fishing and picnic sites. You can windsurf at Devil's Lake. If, and only if, you have passed a certification course, you can rent equipment from **Windsurfing Oregon,** 4933 SW U.S. 101 (996-3957). The certification course lasts four hours and costs $55 (for 4 or more people $40 each). Because of legal ins-and-outs, you must buy the equipment (sailboards, boogie boards, wetsuits, etc.) rather than rent it. Then, according to a buy-back guarantee, the store buys it back for nearly what you paid for it.

Film buffs should know that *Sometimes a Great Notion* (based on the Ken Kesey novel) was shot in Lincoln City. The fake old house that was used as the set can be seen by turning east off U.S. 101 onto the Siletz River Hwy. A jumbled assortment of more than 4000 dolls stares from behind dusty glass at **Lacey's Doll and Antique Museum,** 3400 NE U.S. 101 (994-2392). (Open daily 8am-5pm; during the school year 9am-4pm. Admission $1.50, ages under 10 25¢.)

Two Oregon wineries maintain tasting rooms in Lincoln City. **Honeywood Winery,** 30 SE U.S. 101 (994-2755), across from the D, is open daily from 10am to 6pm. The **Oak Knoll Winery,** 3521 SW U.S. 101 (996-3221), is open Monday through Saturday from 11am-5pm, Sunday from noon-5pm.

Lincoln City is the self-inflicted "Kite Capital of the World." The last week of September sees the D River beach overrun with kite flyers. Everyone is welcome to participate. Call the Chamber of Commerce for information.

Lincoln City to Newport

Between Lincoln City and Newport the state park system gets down to business. There are rest stops every few miles and one overnight state park. Off County Rte. 229 to Forest Service Rte. 19 is the free **North Creek Campground,** a small area within the Siuslaw National Forest (drinking water not available). Just south on U.S. 101 and around the corner from the Salishan Lodge, the **Alder House Glassblowing Factory** is open for public viewing. The artisans explain the process as they blow and shape vases, bowls, and paperweights. Of course, they also encourage you to buy their priceless artwork, in the "low-low price range" of $10-50. (Open Tues.-Sun. 10am-5pm.) A few hundred yards up the road, **Mossy Creek Pottery** hawks imaginative clay creations (mugs $5) with similar deftness. (Open daily 10am-5:30pm.)

Boiler Bay Wayside, 5 miles south of Salishan, takes its name from the remnant of a locally famous disaster. In 1910, the wooden schooner *J.J. Marhoffer* burst into flames and burned at sea. The captain, his wife, and 21 crew members watched from safety as the hulk washed up on shore. Only the charred remains of the *Marhoffer's* boiler—still visible at low tide—survived.

A few miles south, diminutive **Depoe Bay,** seeking to surpass Portland's "smallest park" and Lincoln City's "smallest river," claims to have the smallest navigable harbor in the world. The motels charge hefty rates (in the $35-50 range for singles). Stop for lunch at the **Chowder Bowl,** on U.S. 101 (765-2300), an off-shoot of the famous Newport restaurant (see Newport Food). The excellent chowder ($2.50) is a meal in itself. (Open daily 11:30am-7:30pm.)

Watching the life of the sea, rather than just eating it, is also popular in Depoe Bay. The best gray whale viewing points in this important "whale watching capital of the Oregon coast" are along the seawall in town, at the Depoe Bay State Park Wayside, and at the **Observatory Lookout,** 4½ miles south of town. Go out early in the morning on a cloudy, calm day between December and May for the best chance of spotting the huge grays. Gray whales have the longest known migration of any mammal: 12,000 miles round-trip each year from the Arctic waters of the north to the coastal waters of Baja California in Mexico, where the females let the little ones loose.

Several outfitters charter fishing trips from Depoe Bay. **Deep Sea Trollers,** in the Spouting Horn Restaurant (765-2248), provides five-hour trips for $35 per person. Trips leave at 5 and 10:30am. Reservations can be made by writing to P.O. Box 513, Depoe Bay 97341. **Depoe Bay Sportfishing and Charters,** on U.S. 101 (765-2222), at the north end of the Depoe Bay Bridge, also heads out for five-hour trips for the same price. Reservations are always necessary for charter trips. Both companies also run hour-long **whale-watching excursions** for as little as $5. Depoe Bay holds a popular **Salmon Bake** at Fogarty Creek State Park on the third Saturday of September. (Admission $9.) Call the Chamber of Commerce at 765-2361 for more information.

Just south of Depoe Bay, take the famous **Otter Crest Loop,** a twisting 4-mile drive high above the shore, which (as you'd expect) allows spectacular vistas at every bend. At **Cape Foulweather,** Captain James Cook first struck the North American mainland in 1778. A high storm greeted his expedition and won the cape its name. Cook wasn't kidding; winds at this 500-foot elevation sometimes reach 100 miles per hour. A lookout at the wayside has telescopes for spotting sea lions on the rocks below—weather permitting, of course. Also on the loop, **Devil's Punchbowl** demonstrates the brutal force of the waves. The roof of a cave here has collapsed, leaving arched walls standing to create a voluminous cauldron. The waters churn in and out of this huge double boiler at your feet.

Just south of Devil's Punchbowl, the road returns to U.S. 101 and brings the eager camper to **Beverly Beach State Park,** a year-round reservation campground in gorgeous, rugged terrain. Swimming in the crashing surf here is forbidden even to the lunatics who might try it; the views from the hiking trails will satisfy most visitors anyway. Hot showers and facilities for the disabled are available, as well as a few hiker/biker spots. (Sites $8, hookups $10.) For reservations during the summer, write the park at Star Rte. N., Box 684, Newport 97365. Farther down the road, just past Salishan, **Gleneden Beach State Park** has showerless sites for $7.

New Age sportsmen shouldn't miss **Agate Beach Wayside,** an excellent place, as is the entire Newport Area, to hunt for semi-precious stones. The Newport Chamber of Commerce (see Newport Practical Information) puts out a free pamphlet entitled *Agates: Their Formation and How to Hunt for Them.* The brochure recommends October through May as prime hunting months, although the stones can be found here year-round.

Just north of Agate Beach is the **Yaquina Head Lighthouse,** a photogenic coastal landmark. Said to be the brightest on the coast of Oregon, this lighthouse is haunted by the ghosts of used flashbulbs. (Open daily noon-5pm; Labor Day-Memorial Day Mon.-Fri. noon-5pm. Admission 50¢.) A seabird-, seal-, and whale-watching nature station has recently been unleashed onto the area.

Newport

Part tourist mill, part fishing village, part logging town, Newport offers an escape from U.S. 101's malls and gas stations. Recently refurbished, the town's waterfront is a-flutter with quaint tourist traps. Originally a turn-of-the-century sea town where wealthy Portlanders could go to escape the mosquitoes, Newport has matured into a late 20th-century sea town where wealthy Portlanders can go to escape the mosquitoes.

Practical Information

Visitor Information: **Chamber of Commerce,** 555 SW Coast Hwy. (265-8801). Friendly office with a free, thorough guide and map to Newport. On the weekends, the volunteers may know less about Newport than you do. Open daily 8:30am-5pm; Nov.-Jan. Mon.-Fri. 8:30am-5pm.

Newport Parks and Recreation Office: 169 SW Coast Hwy. (265-7783).

Greyhound: 956 SW 10th St. (265-2253). To Portland ($8) and San Francisco ($86).

Newport Area Transit (NAT): 265-8088. Runs a 1-hr. route around Newport daily 7am-7pm. Fare 50¢; 3 rides for $1.25. Map available at the Chamber of Commerce.

Taxi: Yaquina Cab Company, 265-9552. 24 hours.

Newport Public Library: 35 NW Nye St. (265-2153). Open Mon. and Wed. 1-8pm, Tues. and Thurs. 10am-8pm, Fri.-Sat. 1-6pm.

Post Office: 310 SW 2nd St. (265-5542). Open Mon.-Fri. 8:30am-5pm. General Delivery ZIP Code: 97365.

Area Code: 503.

Accommodations and Camping

God is in His heaven, but the motel situation in Newport is dismal. The cheapest ones are on U.S. 101, with predictable consequences. **Bed and breakfasts** are a tempting alternative, but the prices may be prohibitive (about $50).

Penny Saver Motel, 710 N. Coast Hwy. (265-6631). The name speaks volumes. Kitchens, telephones, and queen-sized beds. No view, of course. Color TV. Free coffee and fruit. Singles $26. Doubles $30.

Sands Motor Lodge, 206 N. Coast Hwy. (265-5321). Less noise than at Penny Saver, and lower prices in winter. Doubles and singles $28 in summer. Room-sharing (4-6 people) allowed for cheaper rates.

Willers Motel, 754 SW Coast Hwy. (265-2241 or 800-433-2639). Free HBO. Singles and doubles $28-36; Nov. to mid-June $22. Rooms for groups available at lower rates per person.

Money Saver Motel, 861 SW U.S. 101 (265-2277). Pleasant rooms, cable TV, some kitchens. Singles $26. Doubles $30.

Finding a place to pitch your tent near Newport can prove tricky. The few private campgrounds are overrun by RVs, and campground owners have established facilities geared exclusively toward these monstrosities. Campers should escape to the many state campgrounds along U.S. 101, where sites average $7 and hookups go for $9. **South Beach State Park,** P.O. Box 1350, Newport 97366 (867-4715), 2 miles south of town, has 254 full-hookup sites and showers ($9). Just north of town, **Beverly Beach State Park,** HC 63, Box 684, Newport (265-9278), has 279 sites, 152 specifically for tents ($8). Both campgrounds are usually full by noon.

Food

The eating is excellent and expensive in Newport, both at Nye Beach and on the bay.

The Chowder Bowl, 728 NW Beach Dr. (265-7477), at Nye Beach. Renowned bowls of chowder $2.75. Huge shrimp basket with fries and garlic bread $7.50. Pies are also famous ($1.50 per slice). Open Mon.-Thurs. 11am-8pm, Fri.-Sat. 11am-9pm, Sun. noon-8pm. Also at 434 S.W. Bay Blvd. (265-5575), on the same block as the Whale's Tale. *Gelato* is the specialty here (95¢ per cone).

Don Petrie's Italian Food Company, 613 NW 3rd (265-3663), across the street from the Chowder Bowl. Incredible vegetarian manicotti ($6) includes cheesy garlic bread. Spinach fettuccine ($5.50) is equally good. For dessert, try the chocolate torte ($2.50). In summer, there's often free live entertainment on weekends. Open Mon.-Thurs. and Sun. 4:30-9pm, Fri.-Sat. 4:30-9:30pm; in winter daily 4:30-8pm.

The Whale's Tale, 452 SW Bay Blvd. (265-8660), on the bayfront at the corner of Fall St. This famous place is great fun—decorated with local art and mismatched old wooden chairs and tables. For breakfast, try the internationally celebrated $6.50 Eggs Newport: Oregon shrimp and 2 poached eggs on an English muffin, topped with Bearnaise sauce, plus home fries. Or how about the oft-praised poppy seed pancakes for $2.75? Dinners can be expensive (*cioppino* $10.25), but good sandwiches start at $4.25. Live local music Sat. night and during Sun. brunch. Open Mon.-Fri. 7am-9pm, Sat.-Sun. 9am-9pm; Nov.-May Thurs.-Tues. only.

Canyon Way Bookstore and Restaurant, 1216 SW Canyon Way (265-8319), up the hill from the bayfront. 45¢ espresso whimsically cheaper than 50¢ regular coffee. Extensive wine and beer list. Imported beer $1.50-2. Lunch $3-8. Open daily 11am-3pm and 5-9pm; Sun. brunch 10am-3pm. Deli open all day. Reservations suggested.

Oceana Food Coop, 415 NW Coast St., Nye Beach (265-8285). Health food store with a gourmet backspin. The fresh cream cheese puts brand names to shame. You pay for the quality, however, and nonmembers must add 10% to the listed prices.

Sights and Activities

Among the many cookie-cutter West Coast pioneer museums (my goodness, there seems to be one in *every* seaside town), Newport's **Lincoln County Historical Museum and Burrows House,** 545 SW 9th (265-7509), stands apart. For once, the exhibits *are* unusual, especially the room devoted to Newport Bay's shipwrecks. (Open Tues.-Sun. 10am-5pm; Sept.-May Tues.-Sun. 11am-4pm. Free.)

From the museum, take Abbey St. 2 blocks down to the waterfront and Mariner Sq. The **Wax Works, Ripley's Believe It or Not,** and the **Undersea Gardens** are all within 100m of each other at 250 SW Bay Blvd. Although the three museums apparently attract a majority of Newport's tourists, none is really worth the price of admission ($4.50, discounts for senior citizens, youth, and children). (All open daily 9am-8pm; in winter 10am-5pm.)

The **Mark O. Hatfield Marine Science Center** (867-3011), across the bridge to the south on Marine Science Dr., is the hub of Oregon State University's coastal research. The Center's aquarium and museum explain current research and display Pacific Northwest marine animals in their natural environment. Beginning the third week of June, the center (named after Oregon's eminent U.S. senator) offers a free educational program called Seataugua, in which marine biologists give talks, show films, and lead nature walks. Call the center (ext. 226) for a complete schedule. (Open daily 10am-6pm; Nov.-April 10am-4pm. Free.)

If you want to take part in local activity, try **salmon-** or **bottom-fishing** with one of Newport's charter companies. **Newport Tradewinds,** 653 SW Bay Blvd. (265-2101, 24 hours), offers a variety of trips year-round. (A 5-hr. crabbing run costs $40, a 12-hr. run $96.) Fishing runs last five or eight hours. Whale-watching trips last only two and a half hours, and cost $15. These leave daily at 6am, 11:30am, 2:30pm, and 3:30pm. **Cape Perpetua Charters,** 839 SW Bay Blvd. (265-7777, 24 hours), is another good company, and clearly the better catch. (5-hr. trip $35; 8-hr. trip $55. 10% discount for senior citizens and ages 11-17.) The local bird watchers club, **Yaquina Birders and Naturalists,** leads free field trips, and welcomes guests. (Usually 1 trip per month.) Call 265-2965 for more information. For those who'd like to put a little zest into their day, **Alpine Vineyards** has constructed a tasting room at 818 SW Bay Blvd. in Newport. (Open daily noon-5:30pm; Sept. 16-June 14 call 265-6843 to check hours.)

Some of the sheltered coves in the area, especially those to the north around Depoe Bay, are excellent for scuba diving. Rent equipment and get tips from **Deep Sea John's,** S. Jetty Rd., South Beach (867-3742), at the south end of the bridge. (Open daily 6am-6pm. Full top-of-the-line gear rental about $55 per day, depending on amount of equipment.)

Popular festivals in Newport include the **Newport Seafood and Wine Festival** in mid-February, featuring Oregon wines, food, music, and crafts (with a focus on the wine and food) and **Newport Loyalty Days and Sea Fair Festival,** in early May, with rides, parades, fried chicken, and sailboat races. Contact the Newport Chamber of Commerce (see Practical Information) for more information on both events. The **Yaquina Bay Open** is a 5- or 10-kilometer road race held on the beach in mid-June, usually on Fathers' Day, to benefit the American Cancer Society. At least 300 runners compete each year. To run or to find out about other local races, contact the Newport Bay Club, 1111 SW 10th St. (265-9225).

Newport to Florence

In the 50 miles between Newport and Florence, the vistas remain vast and voluptuous as the towns dwindle in size. The **Siuslaw National Forest,** on the coast nearby, provides even more camping than usual, some of it free. Take the time to drive inland on the forest service roads for gorgeous, wooded scenery. As you leave the stoplights of Newport behind, you will come upon **South Beach State Park,** 2 miles south, off U.S. 101. South Beach has 254 crowded sites (including a few for the hiker/biker set), hot showers, hiking trails, and facilities for the disabled. Reservations can be made by writing P.O. Box 1350, Newport 97365. (Sites $8.)

Farther south is the town of **Waldport** on Alsea Bay. In Waldport, the tiny **Pine Beach Motel,** 8090 U.S. 101 (563-2155), has a cozy atmosphere and color TV. Although not right on the water, the motel has access to a nice beach, good for agate and driftwood collecting. (Singles $20. Doubles $25.) In the **Waldport Motel** (536-3035) on U.S. 101 (across another great WPA bridge), seashell collages decorate the walls. Everything here is a tiny bit imperfect, but nothing is seriously damaged; ignore it while you enjoy the A/C and HBO. (Singles and doubles $28.50; in off-season $22.) The baked goods at **The City Bakery,** U.S. 101 (563-3621), are unbelievably cheap (doughnuts 40¢, fresh loaves of bread 85¢), and there's plenty of eye-opening coffee. (Open Mon.-Sat. 4am-6pm.) **Leroy's Blue Whale Too,** across the street (563-2050), has excellent fish and chips for $4.25. (Open Mon.-Sat. 6am-9pm, Sun. 6am-8pm.) The **Continental Deli** (563-2050) serves great clam chowder and excellent sandwiches—vegetarian $2.25, giant reuben $4.35. (Open daily 11am-8pm.) In mid-June, Waldport hosts the **Beachcomber Days and Speed Boat Races** (563-2198), featuring parades and children's events, all highlighted by a 5-mile beach run from Patterson State Park. The **Chamber of Commerce** (563-2133) operates a visitors information booth here (open Memorial Day-Sept. daily 10am-4pm). Pick up general information on camping in the Siuslaw National Forest, or stop by the **Waldport Ranger Station** (563-3211).

Four miles south of Waldport, camp at **Beachside State Park,** which has 60 sites and hot showers (no hiker/biker spots). Beachside is a reservation park; write P.O. Box 1350, Newport 97365. Less than 1 mile south, the forest service operates **Tillicum Beach,** with 58 sites and drinking water. (Sites $7.)

The name of **Yachats** (YAH-hots) is derived from a Chinook word meaning "dark waters at the foot of the mountain." This tiny town gains a measure of renown from its position at the mouth of the Yachats River. The original **Leroy's Blue Whale** (547-3399), right on the highway in the center of town, is a cafeteria-style restaurant with tasty fish and chips ($4.25). For something new, try squid and chips for the same price. (Open daily 7am-10pm.) Head west 2 blocks to reach **Rock Park Cottages** (547-3214 or 343-4782). The five delightful cabins are well-equipped with kitchens and dishes, bookshelves, board games, and lovely wood paneling. Right on the beach, the cabins are quiet and available at weekly rates. (Doubles $28-38; in winter $22-32. Extra double bed $4 per night.) Three miles south of Yachats, on U.S. 101, there are several hiker/biker campsites in **Neptune State Park.** The second weekend of July, the town indulges in the **Yachats Smelt Fry,** during which 700 pounds of delicate smelt are served on the grounds of the Yachats School. For information, contact the Chamber of Commerce. In early November, the skies fill with kites at the **Yachats Kite Festival.** Competitions are held on the beach. Contact Robert Oxley, P.O. Box 346, Yachats 97498. The **Chamber of Commerce,** P.O. Box 174, Yachats 97498 (547-3530), in the center of town, has information on the village, the national forest, and local beaches. In an **emergency,** call 547-3119.

The **Cape Perpetua Visitors Center,** P.O. Box 274, Yachats 97498 (547-3289), is located midway down the Siuslaw National Forest's shoreline. High on a basalt cliff, the center grants mesmeric views of the capes and surf below. A number of hiking trails lead to other viewing points, or down to coves and tidal pools. The forest service offers free lectures and hikes throughout the summer, and the center itself features dioramas and displays explaining the geology and biology of the area. Unless the weather is really lousy, don't bother with the free 15-minute film, *Forces of Nature.* The visuals are all right, but on clear days you can walk down to the water to see the crashing waves for yourself. (Center open daily 9am-5pm; Labor Day-Memorial Day Fri.-Sun. 10am-4pm. Sites $6.) Especially impressive is **Devil's Churn,** where lava flows have formed a basin for the waves to crash in at high tide. From the center, take the **Cape Perpetua Auto Tour,** a 22-mile loop through the forest on forest service roads; signs along the way describe the local flora. The equally enchanting **Cummins Ridge Trail** leaves just south of the visitors center and winds 2½ miles down to the beach.

Two miles south of Cape Perpetua, the **Gull Haven Lodge,** 94770 U.S. 101 (547-3583), clings to the cliff high above the gorgeous sea. When reserving a room, ask for "the nest," a tastefully decorated cabin perched alone right over the beach. The bathroom is in the main house, but otherwise the cabin is idyllic—kitchenette, Native American woven bedspreads, butcher block tables, hanging plants, and large plate-glass windows, all for only $35. Equally nice units in the main building start at $26. Reservations are essential in the summer. Nearby **Ocean Beach State Park** forbids camping, but its silky sands make for an excellent daytrip. Campers can instead try **Rock Creek campground,** run by the forest service (16 sites, $6). But the real winner is **Carl G. Washburne State Park,** 12 miles south of Yachats. The park has excellent hiking, fishing, and swimming, as well as campsites with hot showers. (Tents $7, RVs $11. Open Memorial Day-Labor Day.) To tour the **Haceta Head Lighthouse** in the park, you must first call the Coast Guard (997-3631). Between here and Florence, the forest service operates three more campgrounds: Alder Lake Dune, Sutton Lake, and Sutton Creek. Nearly all state parks provide drinking water for parched throats, but no showers for parched souls.

C & M Stables, 90241 U.S. 101 N. (997-7540), 8 miles north of Florence, keeps horses for beach or trail rides. The rate is $18 for 90 minutes or $23 for two hours. Call ahead for reservations. (Stables open daily 9am-sunset. Hours vary; call ahead.)

From Newport to Florence, U.S. 101 is studded with signs pointing the way to the **Sea Lion Caves** (547-3415 or 547-3111), 12 miles north of Florence. Elevators ride down to one of the largest caves on the coast, a sea lion riviera. The ride costs $5, but the caves are spectacular. You can stop at the overlook a few hundred yards north on U.S. 101, just before the tunnel, for a free view of the slippery seals below.

Florence

When a nameplate from an old shipwreck washed ashore in 1870 with the word Florence inscribed on it, the 300 newly arrived villagers decided the name was as good as any other. The Tuscan title has stuck to this day.

If all you did was pass through Florence on U.S. 101 to the dunes, you'd think it was just like any other strip clinging to the highway. But if you go 2 blocks off the highway to Bay St., you'll discover the tiny, reconstructed Old Town, lair of health stores, charming craft shops, and superb seafood.

Practical Information

Visitor Information: Chamber of Commerce, 270 U.S. 101 (997-3128), 3 blocks north of the Siuslaw River Bridge. Open daily 9am-5pm.

Greyhound: 478 U.S. 101 (997-8782), just north of the Florence city center. Open Mon.-Fri. 9am-5pm, Sat. 9am-1pm. To Portland ($15) and San Francisco ($80).

Hospital: Western Lane, 1525 12th St. (997-3411).

Post Office: 770 Maple St. (997-2533). Open Mon.-Fri. 8am-5pm. General Delivery ZIP Code: 97439.

Area Code: 503.

Accommodations

Motels here are generally a few dollars more than in the neighboring towns.

Ocean Breeze Motel, 85165 U.S. 101 (997-2642), 1 mile south of the bridge. Small but immaculate rooms. Singles and doubles $26.

Silver Sands Motel, 1499 U.S. 101 (977-3459). Color TV and a tiny kidney-shaped outdoor pool. Doubles $32; Oct.-April $28.

Florence Coast Motel, 155 U.S. 101 (997-3221), across from the Chamber of Commerce. Congenial owner and homey lobby with fireplace. Free coffee and cable TV. Singles and doubles $32; Sept.-May $24.

Villa West Motel, 901 U.S. 101 (977-3457), at 9th St. Clean rooms and pleasant bathrooms. Friendly management. Other features include queen-sized beds, TV, and noise from the highway. Singles and doubles $44; Oct.-May $38.

Money Saver Motel, 170 U.S. 101 (997-7131), adjacent to Old Town. Does not live up to its name. Cable TV and coffee. Singles $40. Doubles $42. In winter singles $36, doubles $38.

Food

Almost all of the restaurants in Florence line **Bay Street** along the waterfront.

Mo's, 1436 Bay St. (997-2185), in the heart of Old Town. Good food and low prices have turned this upscale restaurant into a chain with links all along the coast. Tables overlook a dreamy river. Fish and chips $5. All dinners include fries, homemade bread, and chowder or salad. The $8 halibut dinner is the most expensive item on the menu. Open daily 11am-9pm.

Bridgewater Seafood Restaurant and Oyster Bay, 1297 Bay St. (997-9405), at Laurel St. This gorgeous restaurant is in the 1901 Kyle Bldg., which was used until 1961 as the general store. It has been restored in a style reminiscent of a 1930s seaside resort: ceiling fans, straw basket chairs, overstuffed art-deco couches in the bar. In the dining room full dinners cost $9-14, but in the oyster bar a shrimp and avocado sandwich goes for $5.75, steamed clams $4. The whole shebang is open daily 9am-10pm; Sept.-March 9am-9pm.

Weber's Fish Market and Restaurant, 802 U.S. 101 (997-8886), at the junction with Hwy. 126. Straightforward, inexpensive seafood. The rich oyster stew is worth the $3.25. Blueberry pancakes $2.75. Open Sun.-Fri. 7:30am-8pm, Sat. 7:30am-9pm.

Seafood Market and Cafe, 1368 Bay St. Small and plain. Good for a quick fix of cheap seafood: cup of chowder $1, oyster stew $2.50, fish and chips $3.25. Open Wed.-Mon. 11am-6pm.

Pizza Express, 1285 Bay St. (997-8073). Follow your nose to the only homemade pizza in Florence—and deep dish at that. Interesting toppings include smoked oyster. Medium pizzas $7, large garden salad $2.25. Free delivery within a 4-mile radius, 25¢ per mile thereafter. Open daily 11am-midnight.

Sights and Activities

Florence's major attraction is its **Old Town;** wander about its one street, or climb the stairs from Bay St. for a closer look at Florence's **bridge.** Built in 1936 by a WPA crew, the bridge is one of the many along the coast with intriguing art-deco detail work. The bridge spans the harbor and lifeline of the city, Siuslaw River, named for the Siuslaw natives who once populated this area. In 1855, the Siuslaw signed a treaty to sell much of their land to the U.S. government; when the money never came, the Siuslaw took the government to court—and lost. They never received remuneration for a million acres of land. In 1860, they were granted homesteading tracts of 160 acres each. Only three tracts amd seven Siuslaws survive today. Some artifacts from this vanished people, as well as from the white settlers who usurped their place, are on display at the **Siuslaw Pioneer Museum,** 85290 U.S. 101, 1 mile south of the bridge.

Cross the bridge and head west on South Jetty Rd. for easy access to the beach and dunes; waterfowl and deer frequent the marshlands along this road. At the last parking lot on the road is the **Beached Whale Memorial,** a tribute to the 41 tragic whales who beached themselves and died here in 1979.

Crabbing, clamming, and fishing equipment can be rented at **Port of Siuslaw Marina** harbor at 1st St. (997-3040), where salmon charters leave daily. During the third week in May, Florence holds its annual **Rhododendron Festival.** Begun in 1908 to celebrate the blooming of the flowers, the festival includes a parade, a carnival, boat races, a rhododendron show, and a popular road race.

Reedsport and the Dunes

For 42 miles between Florence and Coos Bay, the beach widens considerably to form the **Oregon Dunes National Recreation Area.** Shifting hills of sand rise to 500 feet and extend inland up to 3 miles (often to the brink of U.S. 101), clogging mountain streams and forming numerous small lakes. The dunes were created by glaciation 15,000 years ago and reached their maximum development 9000 years later. A constant, unidirectional wind maintains their shape. Hiking trails wind around the lakes, through the coastal forests, and up to the dunes themselves. In many places, no grasses or shrubs grow, and you can see only bare sand and sky. Other places, however, feel more like the Gator Bowl parking lot than the Gobi Desert. Campgrounds fill up early with dune buggy and motorcycle morons, especially on summer weekends. The blaring radios, thrumming engines, and swarms of drunk people might drive you into the sands seeking eternal truth—or at least a quiet place to crash.

Practical Information

Visitor Information: Oregon Dunes National Recreation Area Information Center, 855 U.S. 101, Reedsport (271-3611), just south of the Umpqua River Bridge. The U.S. Forest Service runs this center with typical aplomb. During the summer, staff is somewhat brusque, but their free guide answers most of your questions anyway by detailing camping, hiking, fishing, boating, wildlife observation, environmental exploration, and dune buggy access for each site the NRA maintains. Ask to see the wonderful movie on Mt. St. Helens. Open Mon.-Fri. 8am-4:30pm, Sat.-Sun. 9am-5pm; Labor Day-Memorial Day Mon.-Fri. 8am-4:30pm. Reedsport Chamber of Commerce, U.S. 101 and Hwy. 38 (271-3495), across the street from the NRA office. Open Mon.-Fri. 9am-5pm.

Greyhound: 1625 U.S. 101 (271-8423), at the 1-stop convenience store.

Coast Guard: near the end of the harbor, at the foot of the mountain in Winchester Bay (271-2138).

Taxi: Reedsport Taxi (271-5112). The only way to get to the Dunes without a car.

Post Office: 301 Fir St. (271-2521). Open Mon.-Fri. 9am-5pm. General Delivery ZIP Code: 97467.

Area Code: 503.

Accommodations

Whether you prefer motels or campsites, for a peaceful night's rest you should head to Winchester Bay, 3 miles south of Reedsport. During fishing season, try to reserve a spot; arrive in the morning if you can't.

Harbor View Motel, Beach Blvd. (271-3352), across from the Winchester Bay waterfront. A little shabby, but fairly clean. Color TV and some kitchenettes. Singles $21. Doubles $26. Mid-Sept. to April singles $18.50, doubles $23.

Winchester Bay Motel, at the end of Broadway (271-4871), on 4th St. past dock A in Winchester Bay. This clean, quiet 50-room motel is a good place to blow dough after weeks of camping out and feeling grungy. Color TV and free coffee. Singles $28. Doubles $35. Prices go up on weekends. Labor Day-Memorial Day singles $25, doubles $30.

Fir Grove Motel, 2178 Winchester Ave., Reedsport (271-4848). Winchester Ave. runs to the east diagonal to U.S. 101, intersecting the highway just before the Scholfield Creek Bridge; the motel is at the intersection. The rooms are rather small. Color TV, free coffee, outdoor pool. Singles $34. Doubles $38. In winter singles $25, doubles $28.

Western Hills Motel, 1821 Winchester Ave. (271-2149), just south of Greyhound. Standard rooms. TV, small pool. Singles $30. Doubles $34. Prices may be negotiable.

Camping

This national recreation area is subsumed under the Siuslaw National Forest, so the forest service's pamphlet *Campgrounds in the Siuslaw National Forest* covers those in the dunes. The sites closest to Reedsport are in Winchester Bay. The campgrounds that allow dune buggy access—South Jetty, Lagoon, Waxmyrtle, Driftwood II, Horsfall, and Bluebill—are generally loud and rowdy.

Surfwood Campground, ½ mile north of Winchester Bay on U.S. 101 (271-4020). Great campground with all the luxuries of (some people's) home: laundromat, heated pool, grocery store, sauna, tennis court, and hot showers. Sites $6, full hookups $9.50. Call at least a week in advance during the summer.

Windy Cove Campground (271-5634), adjacent to Salmon Harbor in Winchester Bay. A fog-horn will keep you company all night long. A county park with rather steep rates for tent camping. 75 sites with drinking water, hot showers, flush toilets, and beach access. Sites $7.35.

Umpqua Lighthouse (271-3546) and **William H. Tugman,** 5 and 8 miles south of Reedsport, respectively. Hot showers, boat launches, hiker/biker sites. The Umpqua site is on **Lake Marie,** a cold but swimmable lake with a beach. Tugman has facilities for the disabled. Sites $9.

Tahkenitch Landing, 7 miles north of Reedsport, has 27 sites with pit toilets and drinking water. Swimming, boating, and fishing on nearby Tahkenitch Lake. Sites $7.

Food

Winchester Bay again wins the contest with Reedsport for charm and originality. Restauranteurs pride themselves on their seafood, especially salmon.

Seven Seas Cafe, Dock A, Winchester Bay (271-4381), at the end of Broadway at 4th St. A small diner crowded with marine memorabilia and navigational charts. The local fishing crowd gathers here to trade big fish stories. The cafe is, in fact, the self-proclaimed "haunt of the liars." The seafood comes in huge helpings—don't order the $6 Captain's seafood platter unless you plan not to move for quite some time. Fish and chips $4, deep-fried prawns $5.75, coffee 35¢. Open Fri.-Tues. 8am-2pm.

Seafood Grotto and Restaurant, 8th St. and Broadway, Winchester Bay (271-4250). A peaceful restaurant with excellent seafood and a large Victorian doll house. *Cioppino* with rich tomato sauce $11. Large salmon steak $10. Dinners include clam chowder or salad, and a baked potato or rice. Open Sun.-Thurs. 8am-9pm.

Pepper Pot Deli, 1061 U.S. 101, Reedsport (271-5114), a few blocks south of the information centers. Too antiseptic to qualify as a *true* deli but the sandwiches are fine nonetheless. Reuben or pastrami $3.25. Open Mon.-Sat. 10:30am-6pm. Winter hours may be shorter.

Sugar Shack Bakery and Restaurant, 145 N. 3rd, Reedsport (271-3514). Won't win any medals for cleanliness, but has delicious sweets and fast meals. Try the buttermilk donuts (45¢). Sandwiches $3. Open daily 7am-6pm.

Activities

Romp in the dunes—why else are you here? Many visitors to this miniature Sahara-by-the-sea take to driving *over* the dunes. **Sand Dunes Frontier,** 83960 U.S. 101 S. (997-3544), 4 miles south of Florence, gives 25-minute **dune buggy rides** ($5, under 11 $2.50, under 5 free). The Frontier also has mini-golf for $3 and men's bathroom stalls decorated with endearing slogans. A more personable place, 1 mile south of Sand Dunes Frontier, is **Lawrence of Florence,** cleverly named after both the British bedouin *and* the 20s film star Florence Lawrence. Camel rides in a pen cost $3 for adults, $2 for children. (Open daily in summer from 10am.) If you really want to experience the dunes, shell out $25 for the first hour and $15 per additional hour on your own dune buggy; **Dunes Odyssey,** on U.S. 101 in Winchester Bay (271-4011), and **Spinreel Park,** Wildwood Dr., 8 miles south on U.S. 101 (759-3313; open daily 8am-6pm), both offer rentals at the same prices. The best access to the dunes for actual contact is at **Eel Creek Campground,** 11 miles south of Reedsport. Leave your car in the parking lot of the day-use area and hike a short and easy distance through scrubby pines and grasses; suddenly, the dune piles will tower above you. It's easy to get lost wandering from one identical, stark rise to the next. The ocean is another 2 miles to the west.

Inside **Umpqua Lighthouse State Park,** 6 miles south of Reedsport, the Douglas County Park Department operates the **coastal visitor center** (440-4500), in the old Coast Guard administration building. The center has small exhibits on the shipping and timber industries of the turn-of-the-century era. (Open May-Sept. Wed.-Sat. 10am-5pm, Sun. 1-5pm. Free.)

When you tire of dune doodling and museum dawdling, go deep-sea fishing from Winchester Bay. **Main Charters,** 4th and Beach St. (271-3800), is the cheapest company on the coast. Four-hour salmon trips cost $30 per person, five-hour bottom-fishing expeditions $32 per person. The required one-day license for salmon fishing ($4) may also be purchased there. Trips leave at 6am, 10am, and 2pm. Call the day before for reservations.

The Roosevelt Elk, Oregon's largest land mammal, can be seen from the safety of your automobile at the **Dean Creek Elk Viewing Area,** 2 miles east of Reedsport on Hwy. 38.

Coos Bay/North Bend

Largest city on the Oregon Coast, the industrial lumber town of Coos Bay has suffered greatly from recent closings of local plants. Staggering under an unemployment rate near 20%, the town has faced an exodus of local workers. Its downtown shopping mall seems almost deserted. Nevertheless, Coos Bay has managed to retain the character of its seafront, what with its rattling traps, rolling logs, and smelly fish. The town also offers the best places to stay while you inch farther down the coast toward Bandon.

Practical Information

Visitor Information: Chamber of Commerce, 50 E. Central (269-0215 or 800-824-8486; in OR 800-762-6278), 5 blocks west from U.S. 101, off Commercial Ave. in Coos Bay. Not as well-stocked as the Chamber of Commerce in Bandon. Good county map $1. Open Mon.-Fri. 9am-7pm, Sat.-Sun. 10am-4pm; Sept.-May Mon.-Fri. 9am-5pm, Sat. 10am-4pm. **North Bend Information Center,** 138 Sherman Ave. (756-4613), on U.S. 101, just south of the harbor bridge in North Bend. Open Mon.-Fri. 8:30am-5:30pm, Sat. 10am-3pm; Labor Day-Memorial Day Mon.-Fri. 8:30am-5pm.

Oregon State Parks Information: 1155 S. 5th St. (269-9410).

Coos County Parks Department: 267-7009, toll-free from Coos Bay.

Greyhound: 275 N. Broadway (267-6517), at the Tioga Hotel, in a seedy neighborhood. To Portland ($21) and San Francisco ($76). Open Mon.-Fri. 7am-4:30pm, Sat. 7am-3pm, Sun. 7-8am. In North Bend, flag down buses at the corner of Virginia and Sherman.

The Shuttle: 267-4521. Low-cost transportation within Coos Bay/North Bend and environs. Scenic and historical tours. No set schedule. On call 24 hours. Any round-trip within city limits (i.e. Coos Bay or North Bend) $5. To Shore Acres State Park one way $7.

Taxi: Yellow Cab, 267-3111. 24 hours. Senior citizen and student discount.

Coos Bay Public Library: 525 W. Anderson (267-1101). Open Mon.-Thurs. 10am-9pm, Fri. 10am-5pm, Sat. noon-5pm.

Help Line: 269-5910. 24 hours.

Coast Guard: 888-3266 (in Charleston).

Medical Emergency: Tel-Med, 1775 Thompson Rd. (269-2313). **Ambulance** (269-1151).

Police: 269-1151.

Post Office: 4th and Golden (267-4514). Open Mon.-Fri. 8:30am-5pm. General Delivery ZIP Code: 97420.

Area Code: 503.

Accommodations

City Center Motel, 750 Connecticut St., North Bend (756-5118), off U.S. 101. Pleasant rooms for low rates. Telephones and HBO in every room. Singles from $25.

Tradewinds Motel, 1504 Sherman Ave., North Bend (756-6398), on U.S. 101. Small, faded rooms with color TV. Singles $24. Doubles $28. In winter, about $4 less. Reservations recommended.

Captain John's Motel, 8061 Kingfisher Dr., Charleston (888-4041). Next to the small boat basin in Charleston, 9 miles from Coos Bay, closer to state parks and beaches. Within walking distance of the docks. The management is protective toward young travelers. Singles and doubles $30.

Camping

The state-run and private campgrounds make full use of the breathtaking coast. Always obtain reservations for summer.

Bluebill Forest Service Campground, off U.S. 101, 4 miles northwest of North Bend, in the Horsfall Beach area. 19 sites. Trails lead to the ocean and dunes. Sites $7.

Sunset Bay State Park (888-4902), 12 miles south of Coos Bay and 3½ miles west of Charleston on the Coos Bay/Bandon loop. Akin to camping in a parking lot, but the cove looks like Club Med. 108 sites with hot showers and facilities for the disabled. Sites $8, with hookups $10, RVs $10. Reservations accepted by mail. Write 13030 Cape Arago Hwy., Coos Bay 97420. Open mid-April to Oct.

Cape Arago, 2 miles farther south. A few hiker/biker sites. Excellent views. Hike down to the ocean to commune with the sea lions on Simpson Reef, visible from the sheltered north cove. Phone Sunset Bay (888-4902) for information.

Bastendorff Beach Park (888-5353). A county park 10 miles southwest of Coos Bay. Highly developed sites including hot showers (25¢), flush toilets, and hiking trails. Sites $7. No reservations. Open year-round.

Food

Coos Bay is definitely not a gourmet paradise, but the budget restaurants downtown can satisfy you. The reliable racks of **Safeway Supermarket** can be found at 4th and Commercial St. (267-3512), opposite the post office.

El Sol, 525 Newport St. (U.S. 101), Coos Bay. Excellent authentic Mexican cuisine. Different $4 lunch special every weekday. Wide selection of Mexican beers. Try the *chimichangas* (fried burritos, $6.75) if you are ready for spice, or the tacos, burritos, or enchiladas ($2.50) for milder tastes. Open Tues.-Thurs. 11:30am-9:30pm, Fri.-Sat. 11:30am-10pm, Sun. 11:30am-8:30pm.

Seventh Wave Cafe, 1740 NW Ocean Blvd. (888-9531). A 10-min. ride from the center of town. Follow signs to Ocean Beaches. Excellent decor—an ambitious attempt to bring art deco to Coos Bay. Oriental stir-fry $4.50. Catch of the day $6.75. Games, too—chess, backgammon, and big-time poker.

Sea Basket, in Charleston Boat Basin (888-5711), 9 miles west of Coos Bay. Head south on Cape Arago Hwy. Baskets of local oysters, prawns, or scallops ($4.50)—not to mention steaks and an amazing salad bar—have won this new restaurant an enthusiastic clientele. Open daily 6am-8pm.

Carolyn's Breakfast Barn, in Charlestown Boat Basin (888-4512). Local fishermen's hangout. Inexpensive egg dishes in a diner setting. Special senior citizen breakfasts $1. Open daily 4am-5pm; mid-Sept. to mid-May Thurs.-Tues. 6am-2pm.

The Blue Heron, 100 Commercial St., Coos Bay (267-3933), at the corner of U.S. 101, Charleston turn-off. Friendly atmosphere and a good magazine rack. Famous for its wholesome homemade foods—pastas, seafood, fresh fruits, vegetables, and a great chocolate cheesecake ($2). Not cheap; seafood dinners $9-11, eggs florentine $5. Open Mon.-Sat. 7am-10pm, Sun. 9am-3pm; open until midnight for coffee and snacks after Oregon Coast Music Festival concerts in July.

Woodie's Quik Wok, 3385 Broadway, North Bend (756-7275). Chinese food with a minimum of grease and no MSG. Lunch combos from $3. Open Mon.-Thurs. 11am-9pm, Fri.-Sat. noon-9:30pm.

Sights and Activities

In Coos Bay, you may wish to visit the **Coos Art Museum,** 235 Anderson Ave. (267-3901), which displays changing exhibits of the work of local and state artists, ranging from classical painting to weaving and jewelry. Or you may not. Classes and lectures are often held at the museum. (Open Tues.-Fri. 11am-5pm, Sat.-Sun. noon-4pm.) South of here is the **Marshfield Sun Printing Museum,** 1049 N. Front St. (269-1363), at the corner of Front and U.S. 101. The first floor has been preserved in its early 20th-century configuration. Some of the equipment dates to the paper's beginning in 1891. Upstairs are exhibits on the history of printing, American newspapers, and early Coos Bay, formerly Marshfield. Don't walk here alone, even in daytime; it's in a bad neighborhood. (Open June-Aug. Mon., Wed., and Fri. 1-4pm. Free.)

In North Bend, the **Little Theatre on the Bay,** corner of Sherman and Washington St., presents musical cabaret with a regional flavor on Saturday nights. Phone 756-4336 for reservations. Also in North Bend is the **Coos County Historical Museum,** in Simpson Park (756-6320), just off U.S. 101 south of McCullough Bridge. The museum houses exhibits on local Native and pioneer history, with a special emphasis on the logging and fishing industries and on pioneer children. A 1922 logging train engine stands at the entrance, and inside is an especially fine collection of spinning wheels. (Open Tues.-Sat. 10am-4pm, Sun. 1-4pm; Oct.-Memorial Day Tues.-Sat. 10am-4pm. Admission 50¢, ages under 13 25¢.) Between North Bend and Coos Bay, the Coast Guard cutter *Citrus* (269-5859) is moored along U.S. 101. (Free tours daily 1-7pm. Call for reservations.)

So much for rainy-day activities. When the weather is fine, drive northeast from Eastside on the Coos River Rd. past the town of Allegany to **Golden and Silver Falls State Park.** There, ¾ mile in from the road, twin falls (about 1 mile apart) crash 200 feet in a grove of red alder and Douglas fir. South from Coos Bay on the Cape Arago Hwy., follow the signs out of town to **Charleston,** a pleasant (albeit slightly seedy) town that caters to its residents rather than highway tourists. A few taverns feature rowdy local rock 'n' roll. While in town, you can tour the **Coast Guard Lifeboat Station** (888-3266), in the Charleston Marina. (Tours Mon.-Fri. 1-3pm, Sat.-Sun. 1-4pm. Reservations required.) West of Charleston 4½ miles, the lumber tycoon Louis J. Simpson built a country home in 1906. Although the mansion was razed by fire, the botanical gardens have survived through restoration as **Shore Acres State Park.** The wheelchair-accessible gardens contain an interpretive shelter detailing their history, and a greenhouse for rare plants accustomed to warmer climates. The egret sculptures are the artistry of inmates in the Oregon State Correctional Institution. (Admission to the gardens $1 per car.)

Fishing charters pullulate in Charleston. **B&B Charters,** 7788 Albacore Lane (888-4139), at the small marina, has five-hour fishing trips for $35, leaving daily at 5:30 and 10:30am. **Charleston Charters,** P.O. Box 5457 (888-4846; 24 hours), organizes different types of cruises, including whale watches, ocean cruises for tracking sea lions and lighthouses, and shorter cruises along the Coos Bay waterfront. (Boats leave the dock at 6 and 11:30am for 5-hr. fishing trips. Bay cruises $15, fishing cruises $35.) All river charters require reservations, especially on weekends and holidays; some require a $5 deposit to confirm the reservation.

When the tide recedes at **Cape Arago,** 1 mile south of Shore Acres, large pools of water are trapped by dikes of sand. Probe the tidal pools for starfish, urchins, crabs, and other ocean life. The cape is believed to be the "bad bay" where Sir Francis Drake temporarily anchored in 1579. Nearby, the **South Slough Sanctuary** (888-5558) makes an interesting side trip from the coastal drive. The sanctuary protects 4400 acres of estuaries and tideflats. Turn south off Cape Arago Hwy. onto Seven Devils Rd. and travel 4 miles to the new visitors center and headquarters. The Slough area teems with wildlife, from sand shrimp to deer. Numerous hiking trails weave through the sanctuary. A visitors center explains the ecology of the estuarine environment. (Open daily 8:30am-4:30pm; Sept.-May Mon.-Fri. 8:30am-4:30pm. Free.) The trails are always open.

On Cape Arago Hwy. at Whiskey Run stands the **Pacific Power and Light Company Wind Turbine,** the world's largest and most expensive "wind farm." Although, the operation is closed to the public, the interpretive center explains the proceedings. Part of an experiment in alternative energy sources, the turbines are still not sufficient for large-scale operation, but they have supplied a few hundred homes with subsidized electricity for several years.

Seasonal Events

The annual **North Bend Air Show** is held the first week of August. The event takes off each day at 8am with a pancake feed and continues until 5pm. The air shows occur between noon and 3pm. For further information, write to the North Bend Air Show, Inc., 1321-D Airport Way, North Bend 97459, or call 756-1723 (days) or 267-7330 (evenings). At the **Coos Bay Speedway,** south of Coos Bay (near Coquille), each Sunday afternoon (1-5:30pm), sports enthusiasts cheer local heroes in open competition, street-stock, and jalopy-style racing. (Admission $8, senior citizens and ages 7-12 $6, under 7 free. Call 267-7045 for more information.)

The **Oregon Coast Music Festival** (269-4150), in mid-July, includes a series of classical, jazz, and folk performances at sites around town and in Bandon and Reedsport. (Tickets $8-10, senior citizens and ages 6-18 $6-7.) For ticket information, write the Music Enrichment Association, P.O. Box 663, Coos Bay 97420. In late August, Coos Bay celebrates a native fruit with the **Blackberry Arts Festival.** Downtown is crowded with square dancing, wine tasting, concerts, and crafts. In early September, Oregon memorializes its favorite son in the **Steve Prefontaine 10K Road Race,** named after the great Olympic athlete who died in an automobile accident at the height of his career. The race attracts dozens of world-class runners to the area. For information on both these events, contact the Chamber of Commerce.

Bandon

As U.S. 101 reaches Bandon, the traffic thins and slows to look at the spectacular coastal scenery. Bandon welcomes visitors without the obnoxious trinket trade shared by so many of its neighbors. Concentrate on the fresh-fish stores and boutiques of Old Town, a reconstruction of the original Bandon settlement. Bandon is also an excellent place to do your own clamming.

Practical Information

Visitor Information: Chamber of Commerce, 2nd and Chicago (347-9616). Well-equipped with useful maps of the town and surrounding area. Ask about touring the Myrtlewood shops and about wood-carving classes. Arranges tours to Glen Flora Cranberry Bogs, Magness Woods, and Seagull Myrtlewood. The guide to the town is mysteriously 63 pages long. Open Mon.-Sat. 10am-5pm, Sun. noon-5pm.

Greyhound: 610 2nd St. (347-3324). Bus stop is 1½ blocks from the hostel. To Portland ($24) and San Francisco ($70). Open Mon.-Sat. 9am-5:30pm.

Bicycle Rental: Bandon Ticket Booth, 1st St. (347-9093). Bikes $2.50 per hr., $7 per 4 hr.

Coast Guard Summer Patrol: 347-3122 or 888-3266.

Post Office: 105 12th St. (347-3406), 1 block east of U.S. 101. Open Mon.-Fri. 9am-5pm. General Delivery ZIP Code: 97411.

Area Code: 503.

Accommodations and Camping

Staying at the hostel is the best (and cheapest) way to remain in the middle of things. If you need privacy and an ocean view, try the guesthouse or a motel on Beach Loop Drive.

Sea Star Hostel (AYH), 375 2nd St. (347-9533). A fine wooden building with a quiet courtyard, a clean, well-equipped kitchen, and a common area flooded with sunshine from the skylight. Three "couple rooms" (private lodgings with loft-beds for 2) available at no extra charge. People come for a night and end up staying the week. No lockout and no curfew. Members $7, nonmembers $10. Reservations recommended.

Sea Star Guest House, 370 1st St. (347-9632). The folks who brought you the hostel present lovely rooms facing the water. TV, A/C, some kitchens. Rooms from $29, in winter $4 less.

Table Rock Motel, 840 Beach Loop Dr. (347-2700). Follow 1st St. west as it curves south, becoming Beach Loop Dr. Overlooks the water, but the small rooms have no views. Beach access. Singles and doubles $26-30.

Sunset Motel, 1755 Beach Loop Dr. (347-2453), just down the road from the Table Rock. Lovely wood-paneled rooms with color TV, free coffee, and spanking clean bathrooms. The more expensive rooms have sliding floor-to-ceiling glass doors that frame tremendous ocean scenes. Singles and doubles $27-35. Family suites from $35.

Bandon Wayside Motel, Hwy. 42 S. (347-3421), 3 blocks east of U.S. 101. Comfortable and clean, with hard-to-beat prices. Far on the other side of town. Singles $22. Doubles $28-30.

Bullards Beach (347-2209), 1 block and a bridge north of town on U.S. 101. Approximately 100 sites, a few of which are hiker/biker. Wheelchair-accessible, with hot showers. Reserve well in advance. Sites $9, hookups $10.

Blue Jay Campground (347-3258), 3 miles south of town on Beach Loop Dr. Quiet sites for both tenters and RVs. Hot showers. Sites $8. Open summers only.

Driftwood Shores RV Park, U.S. 101 and Hwy. 42 (347-4122). RVs only. Clean showers and a laundromat. Sites with full hookups $11.

Food

If you have money, Bandon's excellent restaurants are good places to spend it. If you have no money, the Cheese and Cranberry factories give out free samples.

Sea Star International Coffeehouse, 375 2nd St. (347-9632), in the front of the hostel building. A great place to mix with the locals. All sorts of coffees (from 50¢ for the house brand to $1.70 for a double Mexican espresso). Sandwiches $1.90-2.90. Delicious desert crepes $1.25-1.60. Open Mon.-Fri. 8am-11pm, Sat.-Sun. 8am-midnight.

Chicago St. Eatery, 130 Chicago St. (347-4215), in Old Town. Mostly Italian (entrees $4.50-10). Relax while the superlative staff guides you through (for example) a spicy vegetarian minestrone soup (garnished with popcorn), a hearty Parmesan salad, the main course, and coffee. Open daily 11am-9pm.

Andrea's Old Town Cafe, 160 Baltimore Ave. (347-3022), between 1st and 2nd St., 1½ blocks west of the hostel. Gourmet food in a far-out atmosphere—a huge mural à la Maurice Sendak covers half a wall. Favorites are raspberry blintzes ($5 in season) and curried lamb crepes ($6). Lunch salads $5. Fruit, cheese, and meat plate $6. Dinner menus always include at least 1 vegetarian dish, and average $12. Sat. night and Sun. brunch occasionally accompanied by classical guitar, folk music, or jazz. Open Mon.-Sat. 9am-9pm, Sun. 10am-2:30pm. Reservations recommended.

Minute Cafe, 145 N. 2nd St. (347-2707). Diner-style food at the local hangout. Fresh salmon $6. Excellent $2 breakfasts. Try the $1.25 cream pies. Open Mon.-Sat. 6am-10pm, Sun. 7am-10pm; Nov.-May Mon.-Sat. 7am-9pm.

Bandon Fish Market, 1st St. (347-4282). From the sea to the frying pan to your mouth—fresh, delicious seafood cooked at a snail's pace. Clam chowder $1.50, fish and chips $3.35. Picnic tables outside. Open daily 11am-8pm.

Riverside National Grocery, 125 Baltimore St. (347-2293). Bulk goods, flour, various grains, and olive oil available here in any volume. 12% discount for ages over 60 on Sat. and Mon. Open Mon.-Sat. 10am-6pm.

Bandon Boatworks, South Jetty Rd. (347-2111). Seafood overlooking the Coquille River. Dinner is expensive but at lunch, sauteed fish with slaw and garlic bread is $4.25. Open Tues.-Sat. 11:30am-2:30pm, Sun. 11:30am-9pm.

Ragtime Pizza, 490 Hwy. 101 (347-3911), 2 blocks north of Old Town. Nothing special, but the all-you-can-eat pizza and salad bar is a great deal (Mon.-Fri. 11:30am-1:30pm $3.75, ages under 12 $2.75). Open Mon.-Sat. 11am-10pm, Sun. 1-10pm.

Sights and Activities

Bandon's **Old Town** is home to two highly touted food factories: the **Cheddar Cheese Factory** (recently reopened after a 2-year hiatus) and **Cranberry Sweets.** The Cheese Factory on 2nd St. distributes an enormous range of free samples. Picnickers should pick up a pound of flavored cheddar for $3.35. Come in the morning if you want to see the cheese made. (Open Mon.-Sat. 8:30am-6pm, Sun. 9am-5pm.) Don't leave town without also trying the samples at Cranberry Sweets, at the corner of 1st and Chicago; especially delicious are the mocha fudge and lemon-meringue-pie candies. (Open daily 9am-5:30pm.)

Only 1 mile downstream from the Old Town, the surf leaps up against islands scattered in typical Oregon-coast fashion. At low tide, neon-orange starfish and bright green anemones are revealed clinging to the lower surfaces of gigantic rocks. Mussels grow in grotesquely large colonies and can be harvested at low tide (6 dozen max. per person per day).

Pick up clamming brochures and information at the youth hostel. To catch crabs, buy bait and purchase or rent a crab net for $3.50 at the **Bandon Bait Shop,** 1st and Alabama St. (347-3905), on the waterfront. (Open April-Nov. daily, depending on weather, 8am-7pm. $25 deposit required.) Observe the laws regulating the crabs and fish you can keep; carry a ruler, and keep only male crabs over 4 inches. If you're unsure, ask anyone at the bait shop or on the docks.

The **Dixie Lee Riverboat** will take you from the docks on a tour of the Coquille (co-KEEL) River and estuary, past a series of historic sites—Native American burial grounds, an old barge ruin, and fish weirs among them. The daily two-hour cruises leave at 12:30 and 3pm. (Fare $8, ages 4-12 $5, under 4 $1.) Dinner cruises leave on weekends (3 hr., $16 per person). The boat can accommodate 90 passengers; call ahead on warm, sunny days. The ticket office (347-3942) is on the waterfront in Old Town, 1 block north of U.S. 101. (Open daily 11am-3pm.) Two blocks west of Old Town on 1st St., the Bandon Historical Society operates the **Coquille River Museum** (347-2164), in the old Coast Guard building. Photographs of the 1936 fire that leveled Bandon stand out among the usual relics from previous settlements. (Open Tues.-Sun. 1-4pm; in winter Fri.-Sun. 1-4pm. Free.) **Harbor Hall,** 210 E. 2nd St. (347-9712), in Old Town, is a recent addition to Bandon's nightlife. On occasional Thursday, Friday, and Saturday nights, the Hall hosts concerts at 8pm. (Tickets $3-15, depending on the performer.) During the day, the hall is used for workshops, meetings, ceremonies, and community events.

Bandon's most striking geographical feature is **Bullard's Beach State Park,** 1 mile north of town on U.S. 101. Bullard's plunges the visitor into miles of gorgeous walking and beachcombing territory. Fishing and boating are also good here, and there is a fully developed campground. The 1896 **Coquille Lighthouse,** inside the park on a spit, is 10 miles away from Old Town by land, but only 2 to 3 miles by water. (Open in summer only.) Four miles north of town on U.S. 101 are the **cranberry bogs,** on Randolph Rd.

Beach Loop Drive leaves the town heading south, clings to the coast, and traverses a series of state parks (day use only) and beaches. **Bandon Beach Loop Stables** (347-9242), 4 miles from Old Town just past Crooked Creek, rents horses by the hour, day, or week for beach trail rides. They give lessons as well. Horses gallop across the beach for $10 per hour, and children can sit atop a pony for 15 minutes ($2). **Crooked Creek** is one of several state parks along the coast. Just north are **Bandon** and **Bandon Ocean State Parks,** both staging dramatic views of off-shore rocks.

Beach access roads lead from Beach Loop Dr. to several rocky promontories just north of the state parks, including **Face Rock.** North of Coquille Point are more rock stacks with names such as Table Rock, Garden of Gods Rocks, Cat and Hatton's Rocks, Monk's Rock, and the Sisters' Rock. **Free Flight,** the Betty Ford Center of our fine feathered friends, is southwest Oregon's bird rehabilitation home (347-3886). Bird sanctuaries exist at Elephant and Table Rock and the Coquille River Estuary. North of the Sisters, where the river mouth opens to the sea, is the site of the 1915 wreck of the *S.S. Fifield*. North of the mouth, near the lighthouse, the *Oliver Olsen* sank decades later. Part of the wreck is still visible on clear days at low tide, although, given the history, you might prefer to roam elsewhere.

Bandon's hoopla happens at the end of September each year at the **Cranberry Festival** (347-2257). The very red berry is celebrated with a food fair, spellbinding exhibits on "cranberries through history," parades, square dances, jam sessions, and a 7-mile run from Bullard's Beach. The food alone should make it worthwhile.

Seven miles south of Gold Beach on U.S. 101, **Cape Sebastian State Park** has a good trail down to a remarkable overlook on the ocean. There are no rest rooms or drinking water at the park.

Port Orford

The good people of Port Orford, the westernmost city in the Lower 48, boast that their town is the earliest pioneer settlement on Oregon's southern coast. In 1851, nine early settlers lost a skirmish at the aptly named Battle Rock to 400 Native Americans. After a short heyday, from which time many of the historic buildings date, the city lost its allure as a seaport. Today it is too tiny to deserve even the appellation "small town." There is no reason to eat or sleep here, but why not stop to marvel at the surrounding cliff-cropped beaches?

Practical Information

Visitor Information: Information Center (332-8055), at Battle Rock, the southernmost point of town on the west side of U.S. 101. More brochures than one would expect a town this size could produce.

Greyhound: (332-1685), at the K store, across from the Port Orford Motel. Open only when buses pass through (but someone is usually there, since it's at a variety store). To Portland ($24) and San Francisco ($70).

Post Office: Jackson and 7th St. (332-4251). General Delivery ZIP Code: 97465.

Area Code: 503.

Accommodations and Camping

Summer motel prices in Port Orford generally exceed budget range, though some bargains do exist.

Shoreline Motel, P.O. Box 426 (332-2901), across the street from the information center. Outstanding view. Clean rooms. A/C, TV with cable. Singles $32. Doubles $34. Prices lower in winter. Senior discount $2.

Port Orford Motel, 1034 Oregon St. (332-1685). Cheaper than the Shoreline, and for a reason: it's beginning to fall apart. The landscaping, however, is lovely (all roses and calla lilies). About 10 min. from the beach. Laundry machines (50¢). Singles $27. Doubles $29. In winter singles $20, doubles $25.

Humbug Mountain State Park (332-6774), 7 miles south of Port Orford. 80 tentsites. Stunning scenery, excellent showers, flush toilets. Mosquitoes will keep you company at the hiker/biker sites ($2 per person); grassy $8 sites are a 10-min. walk down the road. No reservations accepted. Hookups $10.

Cape Blanco State Park (332-6774), 9 miles north of Port Orford, off U.S. 101. Showers, flush toilets. Sites $9, hiker/biker sites $1.

Elk River Campground (332-2255), on Elk River Rd. off U.S. 101. Excellent, clean sites with hot showers. Sites $6, full hookups $9.

Food

It seems as though every other building in Port Orford houses a restaurant; unfortunately, most of these specialize in greasy burgers.

The Truculent Oyster, 236 6th St. (332-9461). Excellent, if assertive, seafood. The prices may be a little hard to swallow. Sauteed oysters with vegetables $8.50. Open Mon.-Sat. 11am-10pm, Sun. 2-10pm.

Golden Owl Deli, 775 U.S. 101 (332-6595). Superb sandwiches in a tiny building plastered with misspelled slogans and posters. Vegetarian $2.50, ½-sandwich $1.50. Try the BBQ beef hoagie $3. Open Mon.-Sat. 10am-8pm, Sun. 11am-5pm.

The Wheelhouse Restaurant, 521 Jefferson St. (332-1605). Locals flock here. Burgers, home-made soups, and pies. Continental breakfast $1.75. Open daily 7am-8pm.

Sights

The view of the ocean from **Battle Rock** ranks among the most melodramatic on the entire Oregon coast. Be prepared to turn at the visitors center or else you will speed by and have to make a dangerous U-turn. Head down to the beach and take the short, well-worn path to the top of the mammoth rock outcropping. Port Orford's beach is quite windy, so bring a jacket. Turn your back to the wind and watch the sand blow in huge, feathery plumes straight into the crashing waves. For other magnificent views, take a walk through **Humbug Mountain State Park,** 7 miles south of town. Survivors of the 3-mile hike up the mountain are rewarded with a tremendous panorama of the entire area. **Fishing** in the two nearby rivers (the Sixes and the Elk) is fantastic. Ask at the information center for details. **Scuba divers** come for Port Orford's protected coves, where the water temperature rises to a mild 50°F and water clarity ranges from 10 to 50 feet in summer.

The town itself is small and pleasant. The brochure *Port Orford's History in its Architecture* is an enlightening companion to a relaxed 10-minute stroll through the town. Several houses date back to the end of the 19th century. The most impressive building in the area, 9 miles outside of town, is the restored **Hughes House** built by Per Johan Lindberg, locally famed Swedish carpenter. (Open in summer daily 9am-5:30pm.)

Halfway down the road to Gold Beach, 13 miles south on U.S. 101, the frontispiece of the **Prehistoric Gardens,** 36848 U.S. 101 (332-4463), arrests visitors unprepared for a full-sized Tyrannosaurus Rex with a yellow underbelly. The Rex is one of over 20 life-sized prehistoric animals carved by sculptor E.V. Nelson. Despite earnest attempts to recall the golden days of dinosaurs, he garnished his creations with splendorless 1970s facades. Your six-year old will never forgive you if you don't spend the $2 to visit.

Gold Beach

Gold Beach is Kodak Instamatic country. From Port Orford south to the California border, the green hills shade to a golden brown, interspersed with the yellow and lavender of wildflowers. The jagged coastline in this area is some of the most sublime on the coast. Through the middle of this splendor cuts the wild Rogue River, slow and peaceful by the time it reaches Gold Beach. Just inland, the Siskiyou National Forest smiles upon hikers and photographers with scenery lifted from a coffee-table book.

Practical Information

Visitor Information: Chamber of Commerce, 510 S. Ellensburg (247-7526; 800-452-2334 outside OR). Friendly, but do not expect a volcano of information. Open Mon.-Fri. 9am-5pm, Sat. 10am-4pm.

Gold Beach Ranger District Office: 1225 S. Ellensburg (247-6651), on U.S. 101. Free packet details camping and recreation in the district. Open Mon.-Fri. 7:30am-5pm.

Greyhound: 310 Colvin St. (247-7710). Tiny smoke-filled box. Better to wait across the street in the public library. Two per day to Portland ($29) and San Francisco ($65). Open Mon.-Sat. 11am-5pm.

Taxi: Gold Beach Cab (247-2205).

Gold Beach Public Library: Colvin St. (247-7246). Well-stocked with recent magazines, but no rest rooms. Fresh air despite proximity to Greyhound. Open Mon.-Thurs. 10am-8pm, Fri.-Sat. 10am-6pm.

Laundromat: Stonsell's Coin-op Laundry, U.S. 101 S., near 8th St.

Post Office: Moore St. (247-7610). Open Mon.-Fri. 8:30am-5pm. General Delivery ZIP Code: 97444.

Area Code: 503.

Accommodations and Camping

Unfortunately, cheap motels seem to go out of business in this town, and most of the campgrounds are overpriced.

Oregon Trail Lodge, 550 N. Ellensburg, Box 721 (247-6030). Rooms are clean and average-sized. Probably the cheapest in the area. Singles $27. Doubles $30. Senior citizens $20.

City Center Motel, 150 Harlow St. (247-6675). Queen-sized beds in smallish rooms. Singles $26. Doubles $32-34. In off-season singles $21, doubles $23.

Western Village Motel, 9755 S. Ellensburg (247-6611). Large, clean rooms. HBO, A/C. Singles $30. Doubles $32. Prices may be negotiable.

Friendship Inn, U.S. 101 and Jerry's Flat Rd. (247-4533 or 800-453-4511). Handsome rooms with river views (and some with kitchenettes). Extremely friendly management makes it worth the extra dough. Singles $44. Doubles $48.

Indian Creek Campground, 94680 Jerry's Flat Rd. (247-7704). All the friendly amenities of a KOA, and the high prices, too. Showers could easily pass inspection in a ritzy hotel. A recreation room and laundromat, emblazoned with "spiritually uplifting" poetry. Tent sites (isolated from the roar of RV engines) $8. Full hookups $10.

Arizona Beach Campground (332-6491), 2 miles north of Gold Beach on U.S. 101. A nice place, but not cheap. Tent sites $10.

Food

Restaurants here are expensive. Head away from the port for more reasonable prices.

Grant's Pancake and Omelette House, Jerry's Flat Rd. (247-7208), next to Indian Creek Camp. A good 20-min. walk from the port. A favorite among locals. Undoubtedly the best breakfasts in town. The "ranch cakes"—2 buttermilk pancakes, 2 strips of bacon, and 1 egg—go for just $2.50. Open daily 6am-2pm.

Spada's, 1020 S. Ellensburg (247-7732). A huge menu in a family-style restaurant. Try to drop in for the Sun. champagne brunch, an all-you-can-eat arrangement ranging from standard breakfast fare to beef teriyaki ($6, children $4). Open daily 6am-10pm.

The Golden Egg, 710 S. Ellensburg (247-7528). A Nietzchean superhen could lay an omelette selection this varied. Try the avocado and cheese ($4.50). Typical burger lunches $4-5, steak-and-seafood dinners under $10. Open daily 6am-9pm.

Ethel's Fine Foods, 347 N. Ellensburg (247-7713), next to the movie theater. The usual burgers and sandwiches, but also fish, with and without shells. Grilled fresh oysters $7, 16-oz. steak $8.25. Open Mon.-Fri. 5:30am-10pm, Sat. 7am-8pm; in winter Mon.-Fri. 6am-9pm.

Activities

Gold Beach's main appeal lies in the Rogue River and its spectacular approach through rugged canyonlands to the sea. A free pamphlet at the ranger station outlines a self-guided **auto tour** through the Siskiyou. The tour begins on Hunter Creek Rd. just south of Gold Beach and loops north through the forest, eventually following the course of the Rogue back into town. The drive takes approximately three hours.

You can leave your car behind to hike the famed **Rogue River Trail,** which follows the 65-mile river through the canyon past threatening rapids, massive rock outcroppings, and dense forests. Reach the trail by crossing the Lobster Creek Bridge, across from the Quosatana campground (4¼ miles northeast on U.S. 595, then 10 miles northeast on U.S. 33), and starting east on Silver Creek Rd. The trail terminates at Grave Creek, 27 miles northwest of Grants Pass.

The best way to see all this rugged glory without much exertion is to take a jet boat up the river. **Jerry's Rogue River Jet Boats,** just across the bridge to the west of U.S. 101 (247-4571 or 800-458-3511), runs trips from May through October in large motorboats. A 64-mile round-trip run goes all the way as far as the town of Agness and takes in much of the wildlife and scenery. (Fare $25, ages 4-11 $10.) The 104-mile round-trip run goes up the river to the base of the infamous "Blossom Bar" rapid, crashing through many more rapids on the way up. (Fare $50, ages 4-11 $20.) Both trips have a stop for lunch (not included in the fare). Jerry's staff is friendly and informative. Reservations are recommended. Send a 25% deposit to P.O. Box 1011, Gold Beach 97444. (Office open May-Oct. daily 7am-9pm.)

Daily from April through October, **Courts River Running White Water Trips** (247-6676 or 800-367-5687) runs the same routes, leaving from Jots' Resort at the north end of the Rogue River Bridge, west of U.S. 101. The 64-mile, six-hour trip includes lunch or dinner in Agness. (Fare $22.50, ages 5-12 $10, under 5 free.) The 104-mile, eight-hour trip stops briefly in Agness and longer at the Paradise Bar Lodge. (Fare $45, ages 6-12 $20, under 5 free.) You may stay the night and resume the trip the next day. (Singles at the lodge are $65 May-June and Oct., $75 July-Sept. 4 meals included.)

If you are not up to the rigors of "runnin' the Rogue," **Indian Creek Trail Rides,** Jerry's Flat Rd. (247-7704), guides sturdy horses over the river and through the woods. (Rides cost $12 per hr., $20 per 2 hr.) Before you leave Gold Beach, stop at the **Curry County Museum,** 920 S. Ellensburg (247-6113), which illustrates the history of the area. Excellent old photographs and Native American petroglyphs give a brief but fascinating picture of days gone by. (Open June-Sept. Wed.-Sun. 1-5pm; Oct.-May Fri.-Sat. noon-4pm. Free.) Seven miles south of Gold Beach on U.S. 101, **Cape Sebastian State Park** has a good trail down to a remarkable ocean overlook. There are no rest rooms or water facilities at the park.

From late June to late August, visitors can enjoy **Gold Beach Summer Theatre** at the Curry County Campgrounds. The theater presents serious drama and light comedy, usually modern. (Admission $6.50, senior citizens $5, students and ages 4-12 $2.50.) Contact Gold Beach Summer Theatre Inc., P.O. Box 1324, Gold Beach 97444 (800-542-2334; in OR, 800-452-2334).

Brookings

Few reasons to spend time in Brookings come to mind. Surrounded by comely parks and beaches, the tiny town itself has little to offer. It does, however, serve as a convenient first port of call for those heading north up the coast from California.

In **Azalea State Park,** downtown, lawns are encircled by large native azaleas, some of which are over 300 years old. Two rare weeping spruce trees also grace the park's grounds. Picnic areas and facilities for the disabled are provided. The pride of Brookings is its annual **Azalea Festival,** held in the park during Memorial Day weekend. The **Chetco Valley Historical Society Museum,** 15461 Museum Rd. (469-6651), 2½ miles south of the Chetco River, occupies the oldest building in Brookings. Some of the better exhibits include the patchwork quilts and wedding dresses of white settlers and Native American basketwork. (Open Tues.-Sat. 2-6pm, Sun. noon-6pm; Nov. to mid-May Fri.-Sun. 9am-5pm. Free.)

Stay at the **Chetco Inn Hotel,** 417 Fern Ave. (469-9984), behind the Shell station on a hill overlooking the town. A clean and gracious interior is hidden by the dilapidated facade. **Harris Beach State Park,** 2 miles north of Brookings, has 66 tentsites in the midst of a grand natural setting. The park is equipped with showers, hiker/biker sites, and facilities for the disabled. (Open year-round. Sites $8.) **Samuel Broadman State Park,** 2 miles farther north, has a few hiker/biker sites, and **Loeb State Park,** 8 miles east of Brookings, has good swimming, fishing, tent, and hiker/biker sites. (Sites at both campgrounds $9.) For more unspoiled campsites off the beaten path, continue past 7 more miles past Loeb to the charming **Little Redwood** campground (sites $4).

Choosing a place to eat should not perplex you. **Mama's Authentic Italian Food,** 703 Chetco Ave. (469-7611), in the Central Mall, is nirvana for the hungry traveler. "Mama" delights in stuffing her clientele with homemade bread and pasta. Entrees include a choice of soup or salad, and garlic bread. Try the delicious *fettuccine alfredo* ($5.25). Those without feminist sensibilities should look into special "Heman" portions for an extra buck. (Open Mon.-Sat. 11am-9pm, Sun. 3-8:30pm.) **Lyn's Country Tea Room,** 1240 Chetco Ave. (469-7020), is noteworthy for its homebaked pastries and bread. (Open Mon.-Sat. 7am-3pm.)

The **Oregon State Department of Economic Development Information Center,** 1650 U.S. 101 (469-4117), a well-stocked office just north of Brookings, answers questions regarding the Oregon coast. (Open May-Nov. Mon.-Sat. 9am-6pm, Sun. 9am-5pm.) The town's **Chamber of Commerce,** 97949 Shopping Center Rd. (469-3818), is across the bridge to the south, just off the highway. (Open Mon.-Fri. 9am-5pm; call for weekend hours.) The **Chetco Ranger Station,** 555 5th St. (469-2196), distributes information on this area of the Siskiyou National Forest. (Open Mon.-Fri. 7:30am-4:30pm.) The **Greyhound** station is at Tanburk and Railroad (469-3326). The **Laundramat** [sic], open daily 7am-11pm, is known to locals by its sobriquet "The Old Wash House"; you'll find it near the Chamber of Commerce, at the Brookings Harbor Shopping Center. The **post office,** 711 Spruce St. (469-2318), is open Mon.-Fri. 9am-5pm (General Delivery ZIP Code: 97415).

Inland Valleys

While the jagged cliffs and coastal surf seduce tourists and nature lovers to the Oregon coast, the lush inland valleys are the state's breadbaskets. The bulk of Oregonians live in the Willamette, Rogue, and Umpqua river valleys, where vast tracts of fertile land and huge forests support a large agricultural industry and immense lumber mills.

Interstate 5, which runs north and south through the three West Coast states, traverses rolling agricultural land that is punctuated by comparatively barren urban centers. Farthest south, the **Rogue River Valley,** from Ashland to Grants Pass, is generally hot and dry in the summer—the temperature climbs to well over 100°F on many days. Whitewater rafting, fishing, and spelunking offer refuge from the heat. Eugene, Oregon's second largest city and bawdiest college town, rests at the southern extreme of the temperate **Willamette Valley.** This carpet of agricultural land extends about 20 miles on either side of the highway and runs 80 miles or so north until it bumps into the suburban hills that house Portland's bedroom communities.

It is possible to travel the 250-mile stretch of I-5 from tip to toe in less than six hours, but lead-foot out-of-staters should be wary—Oregonians obey speed limits, and the highways are of poor quality. To make matters worse, the snowy winters make road construction possible only in summer; you may well find yourself steaming behind the wheel in traffic jams in 100° weather. But don't despair; the Oregon Parks and Recreation Department maintains rest areas every 30 to 40 miles along the interstate. Public rest rooms, phones, picnic tables, and "animal exercise areas" are available. Rest areas are shaded, grassy, and generally well-kept, but travelers may want to bring their own toilet paper. Tents may not be pitched in public rest areas, but those motorists who have developed the talent for slumbering on a back seat may park for up to 18 hours.

Salem

Salem is a small town trying to dress up for its job as the state capital. While the downtown area is brand new, much of Salem retains the look and flavor of the missionary settlement it was in 1851, when it beat Oregon City in the competition to be capital.

Practical Information and Orientation

Visitor Information: Visitors Center, 1313 Mill St. SE (581-4325), part of the Mission Mill Village complex (see Sights). Brochures on Salem and other parts of the state. Open Mon.-Fri. 8:30am-5pm, Sat. 10am-4pm, Sun. 1-4pm; in fall and winter Mon.-Fri. 8:30am-5pm. **Chamber of Commerce,** 220 Cottage St. NE (581-1466).

Amtrak: 13th St. and Oak St. SE (588-1551), across from Willamette University. One train per day to Portland ($11).

Greyhound: 450 Church St. NE (362-2428), at Center St. To Portland $6. Open daily 6:45am-8:45pm.

Local Transportation: Cherriots (Salem Area Transit) (588-2877). 18 buses originate from High St.; terminals are in front of the courthouse. Fares 25-50¢, depending on distance. Service Mon.-Fri. 6am-6:15pm (buses every ½-hr. during rush hours), Sat. 7:45am-6:15pm (every hr.).

Taxi: Salem Yellow Cab Co., 362-2411.

Car Rental: National, 695 Liberty St. NE (585-4226 or 800-227-7368). Open Mon.-Fri. 8am-6pm.

Women's Crisis Center: 399-7722.

Emergency: 911.

Police: 555 Liberty St. SE (588-6123), in City Hall.

Post Office: 1050 25th St. (370-4700). Open Mon.-Fri. 9am-5:30pm. General Delivery ZIP Code: 97301-9999.

Area Code: 503.

Halfway between the equator and the North Pole, bordered on the west by the Willamette River and on the east by I-5, Salem is 47 miles south of Portland.

Accommodations and Camping

Since the closest camping is 26 miles north of town, the only good deal downtown is the women-only Y. The cheaper motels are a long hike from the center of town.

YWCA, 768 State St. (581-9922), next to Willamette U. and Capital Park. Women only. A scenic and safe location. Bunks $12.72. Key deposit $3. If you have your own sleeping bag, the price drops to $8.48.

Friendship City Center Motel, 510 Liberty St. SE (364-0121), about ½ mile from the Capitol. Singles $35. Doubles $37.

Motel 6, 2250 Mission St. SE (588-7191), 1 mile east of town. Singles $27.20. Doubles $33.74.

Super 8 Motel, 1288 Hawthorne NE (370-8888), 1 mile northeast of city center, exit 256 off I-5. More luxurious than most. Singles $36. Doubles $40.

All-Star Inn, 1401 Hawthorne NE (371-8024), a standard motel chain. Singles $24. Doubles $31.

Silver Falls State Park, 20024 Silver Falls SE (Hwy. 214), Sublimity (873-8681), 26 miles from Salem. Oregon's largest state park offers swimming, hiking trails, and views of multitudinous waterfalls, the tallest (spectacular Double Falls) crashing 178 ft. Campsites $7, with electricity and water use $8.

Food

Restaurants in Salem are generally overpriced and not particularly good. Better options send up smoke signals near **Willamette University. Commercial Street SE** is neon America's version of Main St., lined on both sides with chain supermarkets, franchise restaurants, and "Drive-up Divorce" booths.

Ram Border Cafe and Sports Bar, 515 SE 12th St. (363-1904). Sports freaks can watch football on TV as they eat inside, but most will prefer the shady outdoor patio overlooking the river. Tex-Mex lunches average $6, dinners $10. Mexican brunch on weekends 11:30am-2pm ($5). Open Mon.-Sat. 11:30am-10pm, Sun. 11:30am-midnight.

La Casa Réal, 698 12th St. SE (588-0700). An inexpensive, family-style restaurant. Average Mexican dinners $6. Open Mon.-Thurs. 11am-10pm, Fri.-Sat. 11am-11pm.

Chelsea Restaurant and Pie Shop, 4053 Commercial SE (585-1175), on the outskirts of town, about 1 mile from the I-5 southbound on-ramp. Big, clean, and modern. Worth the trek off the interstate for the glorious dessert menu. Pies $1.75 per slice. New York Chocolate Cheesecake $2.25. Standard American lunches and dinners $5-10. Open Sun.-Thurs. 6:30am-10pm, Fri.-Sat. 6:30am-11pm.

Sights

The **State Capitol** (378-4423), on Court St. between W. Summer and E. Summer St., is capped by a 24-foot gold-leaf statue of the quintessential "Oregon Pioneer." The combination of this statue with big blocks of white Vermont marble and large murals gives the Capitol an imposing, temple-like appearance; the whole structure is vaguely reminiscent of government buildings found in foreign dictatorships. Fortunately, the Capitol's interior is much more personable. Despite persistent conflicts between loggers and environmentalists, the legislative chambers are designed for laid-back lawmaking. The carpet on the Senate floor is checkered with salmon and sheaves of wheat, while the House's carpet depicts a forest of Christmas trees. There are temporary art exhibits on the main floor. Although the tower has recently been closed due to the not-at-all-exaggerated perils of asbestos, the gold-plated pioneer atop the tower remains steadfast. The Capitol is open for roaming Sat. 9am-4pm, Sun. noon-4pm.

Across the street is **Willamette University,** 900 State St. (370-6300). Founded by Methodist missionaries in 1842, it is billed as "the oldest university of the West."

The **Reed Opera House Shopping Mall,** on Liberty St. between Court and State, symbolizes the fate of the Old West. The building's brick facade and long windows remain intact, but its insides have been gutted and remodeled with clothing stores and specialty shops that wear the structure's history like a period costume. Those who can't bear to see this elegant old building tarted up in neon should head for **Mission Mill Village,** 1313 Mill St. SE (585-7012), a group of historic houses where employees in pioneer garb demonstrate forest cooking, carving, and hunting. The village includes a reasonably interesting woolen mill/museum and several stores more closely tied to the contemporary consumer economy. Tours of the houses and mill leave hourly ($3, senior citizens and children $2.50). The **Marion Museum of History** (364-2128) is part of the village but charges a separate admission fee. Inside survive rare relics of the Kalpuyans, a Native American tribe destroyed by 19th-century settlers. (Open daily 1:30-4:30pm. Admission $1, senior citizens and children 50¢.)

The **Enchanted Forest** (363-3060), a smaller and tamer Disneyland, is 7 miles south of Salem on I-5. The park's displays bring nursery rhymes to life, where they no doubt belong. (Open March 15-Sept. 30 daily 9:30am-5:30pm. Admission $3.50, children $3, plus 50¢ for the haunted house and 75¢ for the bobsled.)

Bush's Pasture Park, 600 Mission St. SE, is an 80-acre park with rose gardens, tennis courts, and lots of shade. The park—perhaps emblematic of America in 1990—is an ideal picnic spot. The **Bush House** (363-4714) is a well-restored Victorian mansion built in 1877 by a banker and newspaper publisher. Hourly tours Tues.-Sun. noon-5pm ($1.50, senior citizens $1, students 75¢). Taste Oregon's fruit and wines at the **Honeywood Winery** (362-4111), the oldest winery in the state (1934). Tasting room open Mon.-Fri. 9am-5pm, Sat. 10am-5pm, Sun. 1-5pm. Call in advance for tours. The winery will be changing location in spring of 1990.

Eugene and Springfield

Nestled between the Siuslaw (see-YOU-slaw) and the Willamette National Forests, Oregon's second largest city sits astride the Willamette River, touching tiny Springfield to the east. Not small or quaint enough to be a town, not big or (despite its efforts) sophisticated enough to be a metropolis, Eugene is a city open to interpretation. City slickers can shop and dine in downtown's Pedestrian Mall and 5th Street Market. Outdoor types can raft the river, bike and run on its banks, or hike in one of the large parks near the city. And as home to the University of Oregon, Eugene crawls with art museums, ice cream parlors, and all the other trappings of a college town in the age of mass academia.

The footloose and fancy free have dubbed Eugene "the running capital of the universe." Only in this city could the annual Bach Festival (in late June) be accompanied by the "Bach Run," a 1- to 5-kilometer dash through the city's downtown area. Nike, Johann Sebastian's favorite brand of footwear, sponsors the event, which culminates in a performance of the so-called "Sports Cantata" (BWV 12 "Weinen, Klagen, Laufen," or "Weeping, Lamenting, Running").

Practical Information and Orientation

Visitor Information: Eugene-Springfield Convention and Visitors Bureau, 305 W. 7th (484-5307 or 800-452-3670; outside OR 800-547-5445), between Lincoln and Lawrence St. downtown. Maps, brochures, listings, and guides to everything you might want to do in the 2 cities. Open Mon.-Fri. 8:30am-5pm.

Park Information: Willamette National Forest Service, 211 E. 7th Ave. (687-6521). **Eugene Parks and Recreation Dept.,** 858 Pearl St. (687-5333 for general information, 687-5360 for athletics, 341-5850 for arts, 687-5311 for specialized recreation for the disabled), in City Hall. Open Mon.-Fri. 7:45am-5pm. Also at 777 High St. (687-5333).

University of Oregon Switchboard: 795 Willamette St. (686-3111). Referral for just about everything—rides, housing, emergency services. Open Mon.-Fri. 8am-5pm.

Amtrak: 4th and Willamette St. (485-1092).

Greyhound: 9th and Pearl St. (344-6265). Nine buses north, 6 south per day. Open daily 6am-10:30pm. Storage lockers $1 per day.

Green Tortoise: 937-3603. Three buses per week head south from Seattle to San Francisco, and 3 head north on the same route. Half the price of Greyhound. Call for details.

Lane Transit District (LTD): 10th and Willamette St. (687-5555). Provides public transportation throughout the towns of Eugene and Springfield. Pick up a map and timetables at the Convention and Visitors Bureau, the LTD Service Center, or 7-Eleven stores. Many routes are wheelchair-accessible—look for the international accessibility symbol. Fares Mon.-Fri. 60¢, Sat.-Sun. 30¢; senior citizens and children ½-price.

Ride Board: Erb Memorial Union (EMU) basement (345-4600), University of Oregon. Open during the school year daily 7am-11:30pm; mid-June to mid-Sept. 7am-7pm.

Bike Rental: Pedal Power, 6th and High St. (687-1775), downtown. 6-speeds $2 per hr., $10 per day, $30 per week. 10-speeds $10 per day, $40 per week. Tandems $5 per hr., $20 per day. Children's bikes available. Baby seats provided for 3-speeds at no extra cost. $100 deposit necessary for 10-speeds rented for more than 24 hours. Open Mon.-Sat. 9am-6pm, Sun. 10am-5pm.

Bike Tools: The River House, 301 N. Adams (687-5329). Handled by the Park Service. A bicycle tool "library" that lends tools to the public free of charge for 2-day periods. A cash deposit of the tool's worth is required, and refunded upon return of the tools. Open Mon.-Fri. 10am-4:30pm.

University Events and Activities Line: 686-4636. 24 hours.

Laundromat: 365 13th St. (344-0550). Open daily 8am-11:30pm.

Rape Crisis Network: 650 W. 12th St. (485-6700). Crisis intervention for rape, abuse, and sexual harassment. Open Mon.-Thurs. 9am-5pm. Answering service 24 hours.

Women's Referral and Resource Service: EMU, #336 (686-3327), University of Oregon. Open during the school year Mon.-Fri. 9am-5pm; erratic hours in summer.

Gay Hotline: 485-1075. Confidential crisis intervention and referral. Open Thurs.-Sun. 8pm-midnight.

Post Office: In Eugene, 5th and Willamette St. (341-3611), or in the EMU Bldg. at the university. Open Mon.-Fri. 8am-5:30pm, Sat. 9am-noon. General Delivery ZIP Code: 97401. In **Springfield,** 760 N. Ave. (747-3383). General Delivery ZIP Code: 97477.

Area Code: 503.

Eugene sleeps 100 miles south of Portland on the I-5 corridor. The University of Oregon campus lies in the southeastern corner of town, bordered on the north by Franklin Boulevard, which runs from the city center to I-5 and Springfield. First Avenue mostly parallels the winding Willamette River, and Willamette Avenue intersects the river, dividing the city into east and west.

Accommodations

Eugene has the usual assortment of motels; the cheapest are on E. Broadway and W. 7th St. The hostel, though far from downtown, is the least expensive and most interesting place to stay. The closest legal camping is 12 miles away, although it is said that people camp by the river (especially in the wild and woolly northeastern side, near Springfield). Most park hours are officially 6am to midnight. Lone women should avoid the university campus vicinity at night—sexual assaults have grown more frequent in the area.

The Green House Home Hostel, 1117 W. 11th St. (344-5296). This newly opened 5-bed hostel serves also as a private residence, a community meeting place, and headquarters for the Green Party. It is on its way to becoming a self-sufficient, alternative-energy, global-village eco-home. Always a hive of activity, so much so that hostelers might feel lost in the shuffle. Never boring, however. Check-in before 11pm. Kitchen open 4:30-6:30pm. Curfew and kitchen hours flexible. Members and nonmembers $7. Reservations essential.

Broadway Motel, 659 E. Broadway (344-3761). Paper-thin walls help you share your neighbors' experiences, but the rooms are mercifully clean. TV, A/C. Singles $18. Doubles $20.

Eugene Motor Lodge Motel, 476 E. Broadway (344-5233). Comfortable rooms with firm beds. A/C, some rooms with kitchenettes. Pool and adjacent cafe open 24 hours. Singles $24. Doubles $28.

Timbers Motel, 1015 Pearl St. (343-3345), ½-block from Greyhound. 24-hour desk, so these clean and small rooms are perfect for late-night bus arrivals. Cable TV, A/C. Singles $25. Doubles $29.

Downtown Motel, 361 W. 7th Ave. (345-8739). Coffee shop next door. Cable TV, A/C. Singles $23. Doubles $27.

Fantasyland, 568 W. 7th Ave. (687-0531). Most rooms here are generic and comfortable, but a few more dollars will buy a trip to fantasyland—suites with leather waterbeds, heart-shaped tubs, and velvet wallpaper. VCR rentals for $9 include unlimited free films (adult or otherwise). Singles $22. Doubles $24.

Camping

Campers with cars should drive the 20 miles down Hwy. 58 into the Willamette National Forest, where lovely marshland sites with water are available along the river for $3. The swamp fungus turns the tree bark and ferns an eerie phosphorescent color in some seasons, especially in the **Black Canyon** campground.

Fern Ridge Lake, 12 miles west of Eugene on Hwy. 126. Campgrounds on the southwest spit of land that projects into the lake at Fern Ridge Shores. Sites $7.

Fall Creek Lake, Lookout Point Lake, and **Hills Creek Lake,** 20 miles southeast of Eugene on Hwy. 58. Overnight camping allowed on all 3 lakes. Sites $7.

Dorena Lake and **Cottage Grove,** 20 miles south of Eugene on I-5. Park manager's office 942-5631. Equipped for camping. **Schwarz Park,** at the west end of Dorena Lake, is one of the few free campgrounds. Generally no piped-in water.

Food

Around the university, Eugene's food is college-town all the way. On this island of all-nighters and financial aid recipients, the natives want their food fast and soaked in saturated fats—and when all else fails, there's pizza. Some of the best food in the city's real world (a/k/a downtown) awaits snarfing in the enormous open-air **City Center Mall,** anchored on E. 11th and Willamette St. For a more penurious repast, poke past the street vendors who peddle more frugal vittles in the area.

Downtown

Keystone Cafe, 395 W. 5th St. (342-2075). Don't let the shabby building fool you—this co-op serves some incredible food made from homegrown ingredients. Two deluxe burritos $2.50. Tofu burrito $2.50. Huge slices of fresh pie $1.50. Open daily 7am-9pm.

De Frisco's, 99 W. 10th St. (484-2263). Pleasantly terraced. Pitchers about $3, large sandwiches $2.50. Open daily 11am-1am.

Kestrel Cafe, 454 Willamette St. (344-4794). Lots of excellent vegetarian and Creole food. Lunch special $3. Open Tues.-Sat. 7am-3pm and 5-9pm.

Allann Bros. Bakery, 152 W. 5th Ave. (342-3378). Delicious baked goods and salads in a bright, airy atmosphere. Lunch specials $3-4. Open daily 6am-midnight.

Tom's Teahouse, 788 W. 7th Ave. (343-7658). All-you-can-eat Chinese buffet every weekday at lunch. Moreover, the food's not bad at all. Open Mon.-Fri. 11:30am-2pm and 5-9:30pm, Sat.-Sun. 5-9:30pm.

Prince Pücker's Ice Cream Parlor, 861 Willamette St. (343-2621). Homemade ice cream from all-natural ingredients. Best ice cream in Eugene—try the raspberry truffle. "Baby" size (really 1 scoop) 50¢. Open Mon.-Thurs. 11:30am-11pm, Fri. 11:30am-midnight, Sat. noon-midnight, Sun. noon-11pm.

University Area

Taylor's Bayou Kitchen (Louisiana Cookin'), 894 E. 13th St. (344-1212), right across from the university. Low-key, low-priced; friendly waiters, plenty of beer. Spare ribs smothered in spicy Louisiana sauce at 85¢ per bone are probably the best deal. On Mon., try the *Jambalaya* with slaw and French bread ($4.25). At 8pm nightly, this mild-mannered restaurant rocks with live music that echoes throughout the campus. Restaurant open Mon.-Sat. 11am-8pm. Nightclub open 8pm-3am.

Guido's, 801 E. 13th St. (343-0681). Good Italian dinners that average $6. Open daily 8:30am-noon and 5-10pm. Move around vacantly to top-40 tunes Wed. and Fri.-Sat. 10pm-2:30am.

Stuff-It, 1219 Alder St. (343-3062). Filling pita-bread sandwiches with groan-inducing names. Pita the Great, a gyro, is $2.75; Pita Sellers, a falafel, is $2.50. Open Mon.-Sat. 11am-11pm, Sun. 3-11pm.

Sights and Activities

Mad dogs and Eugeneans go out in the midday sun. Despite the roasting temperatures of a Willamette Valley summer, noon is when recreational centers and museums open. Even the Saturday market drags its feet until the sun reaches the magical meridian.

If the day is painfully young, you can set off south on Willamette St. to see **Spencer Butte,** the base of which is approximately 44 blocks south of downtown. The

3½-mile **South Hills Ridgeline Hiking Trail** starts at the intersection of 52nd Ave. and Willamette St., and extends east to Dillard Rd. As it winds upward, the trail gives breathtaking views of the Cascade Peaks (maps at the Parks Office).

Closer to and north of downtown is **Skinner's Butte Park,** on the southwest side of the river. Named for the city's founder, it gazes on his lifework: Eugene and the river valley. Just to the east is **Alton Baker Park,** the main drag for runners. Ride or jog east along the bank of the Willamette River to the point where N. Adams St. intersects the bike path. Here the **River House** contains the offices for the city's outdoor program and is a meeting place for outdoor activities. The nearby **Owen Memorial Rose Garden,** just under the I-5 overpass, is perfect for a picnic (particularly in June), despite the rattle of mid-afternoon traffic.

The **Lane County Historical Museum,** 740 W. 13th Ave. (687-4239), arranges a more formal, historical, exalting look at the city than old Skinner's. (Open Tues.-Sat. 10am-5pm. Admission $1, senior citizens 75¢, children 50¢.)

Reception centers for the University of Oregon are deployed to handle tours and distribute campus maps at **Oregon Hall,** E. 13th Ave. and Agate St., and at the visitors parking and information booth, just left of the main entrance on Franklin Blvd. The spacious lawns of the campus befit picnics. The **University Museum of Art** (686-3027), on 13th St. between Kincaid and University St., houses contemporary Northwest and American art, as well as an extensive collection from the Pacific Basin. (Open Sept.-June Wed.-Sun. noon-5pm. Free. Call the museum office for tours.) A few blocks away, the **Museum of Natural History,** 1680 E. 15th Ave. (686-3024), at Agate, shows a collection of relics from the peoples of the Pacific Rim and the Pacific Northwest that includes a 7000-year-old pair of running shoes. (Open Wed.-Sun. noon-5pm. Free.)

Museum Park, a large tract of land across the river, was originally intended to house all of the city's museums. Plans for this mammoth complex, however, have apparently been shelved. The **Willamette Science and Technology Center,** 2300 Centennial Blvd. (687-3619), is the lone survivor of this bureaucratic tangle. Planetarium shows are given Tues.-Fri. at 3pm and Sat.-Sun. at 1pm and 3pm. (Open Tues.-Sun. noon-5pm. Admission $2, senior citizens and students $1, children 75¢. Planetarium shows $1.50, senior citizens and students $1.)

Downtown, store browsers mill around the mall between 8th and 10th St., at the north end of Willamette; punks gather at the central fountain. Nearby, the $26 million **Hult Performing Arts Center,** the city's crown jewel, resides at One Eugene Center (687-5000), 6th and Willamette St., and features a spectrum of music from the blues to Bartók. (Free tours in summer Fri.-Sat. at noon; in winter Sat. at noon. Call 687-5087 for information and reservations.) The Community Center for the Performing Arts, better known as **WOW Hall,** 291 W. 8th St. (687-2746), is an old Wobblie (International Workers of the World) meeting hall that for years has sponsored concerts by lesser-known artists. When Emma Goldman asserted, "If I can't dance, I don't want your revolution," little did she know that one day her era's most radical organization would leave behind only a dance hall.

In the heart of tourist country lurks the highly acclaimed **Fifth Street Market** (484-0383), at 5th and High St. This collection of overpriced boutiques and eateries attracts both those who consider "foreign" food to be superior, no matter how hastily prepared, and those who actually believe that British cuisine is "gourmet." The leafy central courtyard is a pleasant place to linger over a cup of coffee. Instead of falling victim to this labyrinth of pseudo-sophistication, head to the **Saturday Market** at 8th and Oak, held weekly between March 30 and Christmas (call 686-8885 for more information). The food here (ranging from blintzes to berries to burritos) is tastier, healthier and cheaper than that at Fifth. Far from the chains of wage-slavery, this crafts market has survived since 1969.

In and around the two cities are a bevy of tours for the industrial-minded. One of the more popular is the **Weyerhaeuser Pulp and Paper Mill,** 785 N. 42nd St., Springfield (746-2511). Tours start at the plant entrance in summer Mon.-Fri. at 9am; winter hours vary and require advance notice. The **Hinman Vineyards,** 27012 Briggs Hill Rd., Eugene (345-1945), organizes tours by appointment only; speak to Doyle Hinman. (Tastings and tours Feb.-Dec. noon-5pm. The tasting area is occasionally closed on weekends in the summer when concerts are held.) **Forgeron Vineyards,** 89697 Sheffler Rd., Elmira (935-1117), has daily visiting hours (June-Sept. noon-5pm; Oct.-Dec. and Feb.-May Sat.-Sun. noon-5pm). A **bluegrass festival** takes place here the third weekend in July. The **Williams Bakery,** 1760 E. 13th St., Eugene (485-8211), offers tours during the school year (Sun., Mon., and Wed.-Fri. 9am-3pm). Call in advance for reservations. **Oregon Aqua Foods,** 88700 Marcola Rd., Springfield (746-4484), a salmon hatchery, gives tours from late May to mid-September. Call ahead for dates, times, and reservations.

Ouzel Outfitters, P.O. Box 11217, Eugene 97440 (947-2236), leads reputable and enjoyable trips on the Willamette. They also rent rafts and inflatable kayaks. In Springfield, **McKenzie River Rafts** (726-6078) gives tours starting at 9:30am near the lower river and ending at around 5pm ($30 per person and up). The visitor information center can supply a list of several other companies. Reservations are recommended on weekends. Check local river conditions and maps, since there are some dangerous areas on the Willamette near Eugene.

If you just have an afternoon hour to spare, canoe or kayak the **Millrace Canal,** which parallels the Willamette for 3 or 4 miles. This shallow waterway passes under many small foot bridges and through several pipes. While not clean enough to swim in, the river is perfect for lazing in the sun. Rent canoes or kayaks (life vests and paddles but no spray skirts) from **EMU Waterworks Company,** 1395 Franklin Blvd. (686-4386, 686-3705, or 686-3711), run by University of Oregon students. (Open in summer daily noon-dusk.)

University sports facilities are open to the public from mid-June to mid-August ($1 per day). The pool, indoor tennis courts, and outdoor racquetball courts are open daily. Gyms, weight rooms, and indoor racquetball courts are open Monday through Friday only. Pick up a list of exact times from the information desk or from the recreation office at 103 Gerlinger Hall (686-4113). You can rent miscellaneous sports equipment (bats, balls) from various community centers. (Duffle bags of equipment, called "picnic kits," available for $5 per day with deposit. Contact the Department of Parks. See Practical Information.)

Seasonal Events

There are several annual festivals worthy of note: the **Irish Festival** around St. Patrick's Day in March, the **Springfield Springfest** during the second week of May, and the two-week **Bach Festival** beginning the last week of June. Helmuth Rilling, world-renowned authority on baroque music, travels here each year from his native West Germany to lead some of the country's finest musicians in performances of Bach's cantatas and concerti. (Write to the Hult Center Ticket Office, One Eugene Center 97401; or call 687-5000 for reservations or further information. Tickets run from $5-25.) The enormous **Oregon Country Fair** takes place in the middle of June and lasts three days. (Admission $6 per day; $5 for the 1st day only.) To discourage driving and the inevitable traffic jams, Lane County Transit provides bus service (25¢) to and from the fairgrounds in Veneta. Buses leave every ½ hour in the morning from the LTD Customer Service Center, and take off again before the fairgrounds close at 7pm. The fair is a huge crafts-and-music happening, characterized by some as the entire 1960s squashed into one weekend. For information, exact dates, and other festivals, especially in the summer and fall, call the Eugene Visitors Center or the Springfield Chamber of Commerce (746-1651).

Near Eugene and Springfield

Eugene and Springfield lie at the southern end of the Willamette Valley, whose fertile floor and richly forested hills attracted Oregon's waves of pioneer settlers. Relics of pioneer days and dollops of the wilderness await those who venture off I-5. One of the favored drives in the area runs from Hwy. 126 to U.S. 20 and then back to 126. The 50-mile loop surveys the McKenzie Valley and the McKenzie Pass, where lava outcroppings served as a training site for astronauts preparing to walk on the moon.

Fifty miles from Eugene is the **Willamette National Forest** and the start of the 13-mile McKenzie River Trail. The trailhead is 55 miles northeast of Eugene on Hwy. 126, 1.2 miles past McKenzie Bridge. Five **campgrounds** are in the area. Contact the Parks Department or the Willamette National Forest Service (see Eugene and Springfield Practical Information).

The small-town scenes in National Lampoon's *Animal House* were filmed in **Cottage Grove,** 20 miles south of Eugene off I-5, and the town couldn't have needed more than a spit-polish for its big-screen debut. Maps for self-guided car tours of a nearby **ghost town** and its **Bohemian Mines** are available at the **Chamber of Commerce,** 710 Row River Rd. (942-2411). The trip is best made between May and October, as snow clogs the rough road to Bohemia during other months. **The Goose,** a 1914 steam engine, departs for a two-hour sweep through the Cascade Mountains on summer weekends, leaving Cottage Grove at 10am and 2pm. (Rides $7.50, ages 2-11 $3.75.) The Oregon Pacific and Eastern Railroad depot (942-3368), which runs The Goose, is impossible to miss—it's the noisiest spot in town.

Twenty miles north of Eugene by exit 216, a whitewashed sign boldly marks the "Brownsville Historic Museum" (officially the **Linn County Historic Museum;** 466-3390), a meager display hall surrounded by three boxcars in the old depot. (Open Mon.-Sat. 11am-4pm, Sun. 1-5pm, or upon request at city hall.) The small town of **Brownsville's** fate was sealed when I-5 made obsolete the iron horse that had once been the town's lifeblood. Today it keeps its false storefronts polished in hopes of wooing wayward motorists.

Overnight camping along the shady creek banks is allowed at Brownsville's **Pioneer Park,** 1 block west of Main on Park. Sites are $3, trailer and RV sites $6. Clean public toilets are maintained by the city, and campfires are permitted in designated areas. Serving the tiny community with a common kitchen, a performance stage, a Little League baseball diamond, and a dirt-bike track, the main park closes its gates at dusk. Call for reservations at 466-5666. From Brownsville, Main Street meanders idyllically northward into a backroad that eventually reaches I-5. When the road forks, keep to the left, and when in doubt, follow the signs directing you to Albany or Lebanon. A left onto Hwy. 34 leads straight to I-5. Go at sunset—hum a tune, pick a wildflower, watch a tractor plow, or say "moo" to a cow.

Grants Pass

Workers building a road through the Oregon mountains in 1863 were so excited by the news of General Ulysses Grant's victory at Vicksburg that they decided to name the town after the burly alcoholic and president-to-be. Today both tourists and locals find the town an excellent base camp from which to attack the mountains. Grants Pass has a bazaar of outfitters, river runners, and adventure travel companies—as well as its share of cheap motels and fast food joints.

Practical Information and Orientation

Visitor Information: Visitor and Convention Bureau (476-7717 in OR, or 800-547-5927). Brochures about all of Josephine County. Eager and pleasant volunteer staff. Open Mon.-Fri. 9am-5pm, Sat.-Sun. 11am-6pm.

Greyhound: 460 Agness Ave. (476-4513), at the east end of town. To Portland ($55) and San Francisco ($39). A limited number of storage lockers (75¢ per 24 hours) can be found next to the station. Open Mon.-Fri. 7:30am-6:45pm, Sat. 7:30am-2pm.

Taxi: Grants Pass Taxi (476-6444).

Women's Crisis Support Team: 479-9349.

Hospital: 476-6831.

Police: 479-3311.

Post Office: 132 NW 6th St. Open Mon.-Fri. 9am-5pm. General Delivery ZIP Code: 97526.

Area Code: 503.

Whether an address is marked east or west depends on whether it's on the east or west side of the street. The railroad tracks (around 6th St.) divide the town into north and south.

Accommodations and Camping

Grants Pass has a stupefying number of standard and ugly motels, although the rates are among the lowest in Oregon.

As with the rest of the Inland Valleys, Grants Pass suffers from a shortage of campgrounds. There are free campsites at **Rogue State Park,** 16 miles east on I-5, and grassy, quiet sites at **Les Clare RV Park,** 2956 U.S. 99 (479-0046; sites $8, hookups $12). Another option is **Schroeder Campgrounds,** 4 miles south of town; take Hwy. 199 to Willow Lane; then follow the signs 1 mile to the campground. Call 474-5285 for information on this and other Josephine County parks. Sites are fine and the showers excellent, but the campground is often full by the mid-afternoon. (Sites $8, hookups $10.)

Fordson Home Hostel (AYH), 250 Robinson Rd., Cave Junction 97523 (592-3203). 37 miles southwest on U.S. 199. Only 3 beds. Reservations necessary. Bunks $4, in winter $5.

The Flamingo Motel, 728 NW 6th St. (476-6601). Wonderfully tacky landscaping. Clean rooms. Small pool. HBO. Singles $25, with 2 beds $29.

Motel 6, 1800 NE 7th St. (474-1331). Low prices without having to worry whether you have been properly vaccinated. Cable TV, swimming pool, and A/C. Singles $26. Doubles $32.

Hawks Inn, 1464 NW 6th St. (479-4057). A real bargain. Swimming pool, A/C, and HBO. Singles and doubles $21.20.

City Center Motel, 741 NE 6th St. (476-6134). Large modern rooms. A/C, cable TV. Singles $22. Doubles $29.

Food

In Grants Pass, the hegemony of the fast-food industry is not absolute. A number of tasty surprises have fallen through the cracks.

Pongsri's, 1571 NE 6th St. (479-1345). Authentic Thai-Chinese cuisine. Excellent food, reasonable prices. Pleasant atmosphere. The dishes marked "spicy" and "very spicy" aren't really, so go for it. Lunch special $3 (served Tues.-Fri.). Open Tues.-Sun. 11am-9pm.

J.J. North's Chuck Wagon, 1150 NE E St. (479-5331), in Grants Pass Shopping Center. Huge buffet lunch $3.85, dinner $6. The locals come here to "pork out." Senior citizens get discounts. The corn bread is worth the price. Open Mon.-Sat. 11am-3:30pm and 4-8pm, Sun. 8:30-11:30am and 2-8pm.

Joy's Kitchen, 428 SW 6th St. (479-1814). Not at all Lithuanian, but tasty. Good breakfast special ($2). Fresh strawberry crepes ($2.49) until 11am. Homemade soups, baked goods, veggie burgers. Lunch special $4. In summer box lunches are available for $3. Open Mon.-Fri. 6:30am-2:30pm, Sat. 8am-2:30pm.

Matsukaze, 1675 NE 7th St. (479-2961). Standard Japanese food in nice setting. Lunch specials Mon.-Fri., chicken teriyaki, *mahi mahi* ($3-3.65). Open Mon.-Thurs. 11am-2pm and 5-8:30pm, Fri. 11am-2pm and 5-9pm, Sat. 5-9pm.

Black Forest, 820 NE E St. (474-2353). A family favorite. Burgers and stuff $3-4. Belgian waffles ($2.45) will sustain you for decades. Open daily 6am-10pm.

Near Grants Pass

A few miles east of Grants Pass in the town of **Rogue River** is the **Valley of the Rogue State Park** (see Accommodations and Camping). You can savor the Rogue (one of the few rivers in the United States to be protected by the government as a "Wild and Scenic River") by raft, jetboat, mail boat, fishing poles, or a walk along the banks. Possible excursions range from two-hour scenic tours (**Hellgate Excursions, Inc.,** 479-7204; $12, ages 4-11 $6) to four-day fishing outings (**Rogue Excursions Unlimited,** 773-5983).

When you're so sated with rafting that a Class IV rapid draws no more than a yawn, you can hike in the Rogue State Park or visit one of the following attractions if you have a car. The **Oregon Vortex/House of Mystery** (855-1543) is 20 miles east on I-5 in Gold Hill. Here, balls roll uphill, pendulums hang at an angle, and people seem to vary in height depending on where they stand. The bizarre phenomena are supposedly due to a local perturbation of the earth's magnetic field. (Open June-Aug. daily 9am-4:45pm; March 4-Oct. 15 Thurs.-Tues. 9am-4:45pm. Admission $3.)

For another geocuriosity, see the **Oregon Caves National Monument** by taking U.S. 199 south 30 miles to Cave Junction, then following Hwy. 46 east for 20 miles. Here in the belly of the ancient Siskiyous, limestone compressed to marble was carved out by acidic waters. Dissolved and redeposited, the limestone filled huge open chambers with exotic formations, whose slow growth is nurtured by the constant climate of 39-43°F. This place is *cold.* (75-minute tours are conducted as groups of 16 form. Tours mid-June to Aug. daily 8am-7pm; May to mid-June and Sept. daily 9am-5pm; Oct.-April daily at 10:30am, 12:30pm, 2pm, and 3:30pm. Admission $4.75, ages under 12 $2.50, ages under 6 not admitted. Call 592-3400 for more information.) Also in Gold Hill, near the Oregon Vortex, is the **Old Oregon Historical Museum,** 2345 Sardine Creek Rd. (855-1043), displaying a vast collection of Native American pottery and basketry from early in this century. (Open March 15-Sept. 15 daily 10am-6pm. Donation $2.50, ages 12-18 75¢, under 12 free.)

Jacksonville

The biggest of Oregon's gold boomtowns, Jacksonville played the role of rich and lawless frontier outpost with appropriate debauchery and zest. But the town's salad days were doomed to brevity. Gold dwindled, the railroad and stagecoach lines took Jacksonville off their routes, and the city lost the county seat to Medford. On the brink of oblivion, Jacksonville was rescued by nostalgia. During the 50s, the town was rehabilitated; today, it is a national historic landmark. A stroll down Main Street will unveil views of several balustraded, century-old buildings: the U.S. National Bank, the Methodist-Episcopal Church, and the Wolf Creek Tavern.

The town's greatest attractions are the costumed guided tour that occurs daily from 1 to 5pm at the **Beekman House** and the informative lecture on 19th-century banking at the **Beekman Bank** on California St., four blocks south. Visit the **Jacksonville Museum** in the County Courthouse on 5th St. (899-1847; open daily 9am-5pm; Labor Day-May Tues.-Sun. 9am-5pm; free), and the **Children's Museum,** in the old jail next door. Climb into a covered wagon, lock yourself in the county jail, or strike up a tune on the old-fashioned organ—all amid the din of children doing likewise (same hours as the museum next door). Checking out free museums is thirsty work, and sampling free wine is the perfect remedy. The **Tasting Room,** at 690 N. 5th St., offers vintages from the nearby Valley View Vineyard. (Open daily 11am-5pm.)

For an excellent overview of the town's sights, catch the 30-minute trolley tour at the Beekman Bank, 3rd and California St. (Runs daily 10am-5:30pm on the hr. Fare $2.50, ages under 12 $1.) Those who don't want to hike into the hills can make a trip to **Siskiyou Llama Expeditions,** P.O. Box 1330 (899-1696), which rents and sells llamas as beasts of burden for wilderness treks.

The **Peter Britt Music Festival** (really three festivals in one), takes Jacksonville by storm every summer. Throughout July and August, the town is flooded with tourists and artists from all over the world. The music runs the gamut from classical to jazz to bluegrass. Tickets are $10-18, with discounts at some concerts for those over 65 or under 25. Passes for the entire festival are also available. For information write Peter Britt Festival, P.O. Box 1124, Medford 97501 (773-6077 in OR, or 800-882-7488).

Try to avoid spending the night in town. There are no campgrounds, and the **Jacksonville Inn,** 175 E. California St. (899-1900), for all its charm and free Belgian-waffle breakfasts, costs $45 for a single (doubles $68). You can savor pasta or salads ($5-6) in the inn's elegant dining room, or grab some chow at the **Mustard Seed,** 5th and C St., which broils thick burgers for $2. For a more varied menu at some of the cheapest prices in town, grab a cup of chili ($1.35) or a burrito ($2) at **The Claim Jumper's,** an outdoor cafe at 115 W. California St. (Open daily 10:30am-5pm.)

Drop by the **visitors center** in the old railway station on Oregon St., where the eager staff will supply you with directions and pamphlets. The **post office** is right next door at 175 Oregon St. (Open Mon.-Fri. 8:30am-5pm; ZIP code: 97530.)

To reach Jacksonville (or "J-ville" as residents affectionately call it), take Hwy. 238 southwest from Medford. Or catch the #30 bus at 6th and Bartlett in Medford (buses Mon.-Sat.—see Medford Practical Information). Jacksonville can be reached by bus from Ashland only via Medford.

Medford

In former days, Jacksonville was the center of the Rogue River Valley and nearby Medford was just a bend in the river. Then came the railroads, offering jobs, trade, and growth. Jacksonville refused to pay the $25,000 "bonus" demanded by the self-confident leaders of the new industry and so, to spite the county seat, the lines were laid in Medford instead. Within 20 years, the community of log cabins and trappers had seized power from Jacksonville. Today, Medford, a heavily industrialized city of 40,000, makes the money while Jacksonville, still small and rustic, draws in the tourists.

Practical Information

Visitor Information: Medford Visitors and Convention Bureau, 304 S. Central Ave. (772-6293), at 10th St. Enthusiastically helpful, with piles of maps and directories. Open Mon.-Fri. 9am-5pm. After hours, a small packet of information, including a city map and sealed with teddy bear and heart stickers, is left by the door.

Medford-Jackson County Airport: 770-5314. Off Biddle Rd., north of town. Served by United Airlines and a variety of regional carriers.

Greyhound: 212 Bartlett St. (779-2103), at 5th St. Five per day to Portland ($58) and San Francisco ($86). Open daily 6am-midnight.

Rogue Valley Transportation: 3200 Crater Lake Ave. (799-2988). Connects Medford with Jacksonville, Phoenix, White City, Talent, and Ashland. Buses leave 6th and Bartlett Mon.-Fri. 8am-5pm. Limited service Sat. 9am-5pm. Fare 55¢, senior citizens and grades 1-12 pay ½-price.

Cascade Bus Lines: 664-4801. Service to Eagle Point and White City.

Taxi: 773-6665.

Car Rental: Budget, 773-7023. **National,** 779-4863. Both are at the airport.

Public Library: 413 W. Main St. (776-7281), at Holly St. Open Mon.-Thurs. 9:30am-8pm, Fri.-Sat. 9:30am-5pm.

Hospital: Providence, 773-6611. Emergency care 24 hours.

Fire: 770-4460.

Police: 770-4783.

Post Office: 333 W. 8th (776-3604), at Holly St. Open Mon.-Fri. 8:30am-5:30pm. General Delivery ZIP Code: 97501.

Area Code: 503.

Accommodations

Medford is filled with small, clean motels, most along Central Ave.; many are cheaper than the benchmark Motel 6. These are good places to take a break from camping, but terrible places to spend a week. There are no campgrounds within 15 miles of town, just several grassy areas styled "day-use parks" with wooden picnic tables.

Valli Hai Motel, 1034 Court St. (772-6183). A nice place run by a friendly couple. Pleasant, well-scrubbed rooms with dark wood ceilings. Singles $21. Doubles $26.

Sierra Inn Motel, 345 S. Central Ave. (773-7727). Better-than-average rooms. Laundry and kitchen facilities available. Singles $26.50. Doubles $30.

City Center Motel, 324 S. Central Ave. (773-6248). Next door to the information center. Dukes it out with Motel 6 in Medford's lodgings cellar—slightly larger and more interesting rooms, with free HBO a retort to the Motel 6 swimming pool. Singles $21. Doubles $24.

Motel 6, 950 Alba Dr. (773-4290), on the northwest edge of town. Inconvenient for those without cars. Singles $23. Doubles $29.

Food

Medford's unofficial specialties are burgers and beer. Most restaurants are in the downtown area, where businesses go under early and often.

Yellow Submarine Sandwich Shop, 137 S. Central Ave. (779-7589), at 9th St. A great place to pick up a picnic for Crater Lake. Subs up to 2' long cost $9; an 8" is only $3.25. Open Mon.-Sat. 10am-5pm.

Kim's, 2321 Hwy. 99 (773-3653), 1 mile south of Medford. Chinese dishes $4.50-6.75. American cuisine as well. Open Sun.-Thurs. 11am-1am, Fri.-Sat. 11am-2am.

Bobbio's, 317 E. Main St. (773-7173). Neo-50s decor, and '57 pink Chevy on your right as you walk in. Square pan pizza. Calzone $4. Sandwiches $2.30-3.65. "Old-fashion" shakes and sodas $1.35. Open Mon.-Thurs. 11am-11pm, Fri.-Sat. 11am-1am, Sun. 11am-10pm.

Sights

Slightly north of the city limits, the **Medford Corporation,** on North Pacific Hwy. (773-7491), allows free self-guided tours of its sawmill operations. The tours reveal the strange secrets of plywood production. (Tours Mon.-Fri. 7am-3pm.) On Hwy. 62 in the nearby town of **Trail,** the **Cole Rivers Fish Hatchery** (878-2335) has self-guided tours Mon.-Fri. 8:30am-4pm. The hatchery is an important part of the ongoing effort to repopulate the Rogue. The **Valley View Vineyard,** 1000 Applegate Rd. (899-8468), just south of the town of **Ruch,** gives wine tasting and vineyard tours by appointment. (Open daily 11am-5pm; Jan.-April 14 Sat.-Sun. 1-5pm.)

Crater Lake is as accessible from Medford as it is from Klamath Falls. Follow Hwy. 62 east. On the way, you should stop at **Beckie's Café** (560-3563), at the Union Creek Resort. This friendly, wood-paneled restaurant has lunches ($3-5) and delicious homemade pies ($1.50). Any of the berry pies will be a delight to the palate.

For a sensationalist alternative to the nearby Shakespeare Festival, check out the old-fashioned **melodrama** in **Talent,** between Medford and Ashland. Hiss at the villain ("You *must* pay the rent!"), and sigh in sympathy with the damsel in distress ("I *can't* pay the rent!"). The festivities take place from June through Labor Day on Fridays and Saturdays at 8pm in the **Minshall Theatre,** 101 Talent Ave., P.O. Box 353, Talent 97540 (535-5250). (Admission $6, ages under 12 $3.50.)

Ashland

Ashland's main draw is its annual Shakespeare festival. Before their expropriation by the guardians of gentility, Shakespeare's plays were common knowledge to 19th-century Americans. Ashland's informal, rural setting returns the plays to this forgotten context. Over a 55-year history, the fesitval has sired delightful shops, lodgings, and restaurants. Although more expensive than its neighbors, Ashland is very reasonable when compared with other towns in the U.S. of similar charm and elegance. From February to October, the festival puts on an astonishing number of plays with a roster of excellent performers. While the repertory is by no means limited to the 16th century, Shakespeare's works dominate the three stages. Ashland's wonderful climate allows for nightly performances in the outdoor Elizabethan theater, with a money-back guarantee in case of rain.

The influx of tourists for the festival is only a season in Ashland's yearly cycle. October's rains see the last of the Shakespeare buffs, and bring in the Southern Oregon State College students. Come Thanksgiving, the nearby Siskiyou Mountains are blanketed with snow and sprinkled with cross-country skiers. Spring thaw brings in the hikers, bikers, and rafters, even as the skiers leave. And yea, the cycle beginneth anew when Shakespeare, Elvis-like, wakes to walk again.

Practical Information

Visitor Information: Chamber of Commerce, 110 E. Main St. (482-3486). Play schedules and brochures, several of which contain small but adequate maps. Does not sell tickets to performances. Open Mon.-Fri. 9am-5pm. **Information Kiosk,** center of Lithia Park Plaza, open June to mid-Sept. 9am-8pm.

Oregon Shakespearean Festival Box Office: P.O. Box 158, Ashland 97520 (482-4331). Next to the Elizabethan Theater. Rush tickets (½-price) occasionally available ½-hr. before performances that aren't sold out.

Greyhound: 91 Oak St. (482-2516), between Lithia Way and E. Main St. 3 departures north and 4 south per day. To Portland ($49) and San Francisco ($51). Open Mon.-Sat. 8am-5pm.

Rogue Valley Transportation: 779-2877, in Medford. Schedules available at the Chamber of Commerce. Fare 55¢, plus 10¢ for each zone change. The #10 bus serving Ashland runs every ½ hr. 5:03am-8:03pm. Service Mon.-Sat. to Medford, and from there to Jacksonville (on bus #30).

Taxi: 482-3065. 24 hours.

Car Rental: Executive Rent-A-Car, Butler Ford, 1977 Hwy. 99 N. (482-2521). Ashland's only rental agency picks up and delivers anywhere in Medford or Ashland. A used car goes for $9 per day plus 8¢ per mile. Reservations advised in summer.

Police: 482-5211.

Post Office: Lithia Way and 1st St. (482-3986). General Delivery ZIP Code: 97520.

Area Code: 503.

Accommodations and Camping

Definitely shoot for the hostel, although in winter, at least, you don't have to worry: Ashland is stocked with inexpensive hotels. In summer, rates double in practically every hotel. Ashland is not rich in campgrounds.

Ashland Hostel (AYH), 150 N. Main St. (482-9217), a few blocks west of Greyhound. In May and June this well-kept hostel swarms with school groups in town for a little culture. The wonderful owner-managers will help you any way they can, from tracking down theater tix to suggesting activities on days when the play's not the thing. Laundry facilities. Members $7.50, nonmembers $10.50. Reservations advised.

Vista 6 Motel, 535 Clover Lane (482-4423), on I-5 at exit 14. Small rooms. One of the few motels in town where prices don't skyrocket each summer. Friendly management. A/C, small pool. Singles $24.35. Doubles $27.50. Winter and spring discounts.

Columbia Hotel, 262½ E. Main St. (482-3726). A cozy little inn 1½ blocks from the theaters. Splendid decor is straight from the 1940s. Rates are the same for 1 or 2 people. Bathroom down the hall. Doubles from $36; Nov. to mid-June $28. Children under 12 free.

Manor Motel, 476 N. Main St. (482-2246), at Hwy. 99, 6 blocks northwest of the theaters. Quiet with A/C and TV. Family suites available. Singles $30. Doubles $32. Nov. to mid-June singles $24, doubles $26.

Jackson Hot Springs, 2253 Hwy. 99N (482-3776), off exit 19 from I-5, down Valley View Rd. to Hwy. 99 N. The closest campground to downtown, with a separate tent area. Tent rentals available. Hot showers. Sites $8, hookups $9.

Glenyan KOA, 5310 Hwy. 66 (482-4138), 5 miles out of town southeast on Hwy. 66, exit 14 from I-5. Typical high quality (and high price) of a KOA. Showers, laundromat, and a petite grocery store. Sites $12.75, hookups $14.75.

Emigrant Lake (776-7001), 6 miles southeast on Hwy. 66, exit 14 off I-5. Hot showers and laundromat. Sites $8. Open April 15-Oct. 15.

Food

Thanks to the festival, Ashland offers more interesting menus than other towns in the region. Unfortunately, the steep prices reflect the wealth of the typical Ashland theatergoer. The hostel has kitchen facilities; **Sentry Market,** 310 Oak St. (482-3521), stays open until 9pm.

China Station, 75 N. Main (488-0101). Faithful Chinese and Thai food. Dinners are expensive but the $3.50 lunch special is a good deal. Open Mon.-Thurs. noon-10pm, Fri.-Sat. noon-11pm, Sun. 4:30-10pm.

Thai Pepper, 84 N. Main (482-8058). Curries and seafood prepared exquisitely in an elegant environment. An antidote to weeks of bland and greasy grub. Dinners $8-12. Open Mon.-Thurs. 11:30am-2pm and 5:30-9pm, Fri. 11:30am-2pm and 5-9:30pm, Sat. 5-9:30pm, Sun. 5-8pm.

Teresa's Cantina, 76 N. Pioneer St. (482-1107), at Main. Delicious Mexican food in a congenial atmosphere. Try the 1-lb. *cantina burrito* ($6) smothered in salsa with some of the best home-made guacamole this side of the border. Excellent place to bring children: the management *looooves* them. 10% discount for senior citizens. Open Tues.-Sat. 11am-9pm.

The Bakery Cafe, 38 E. Main St. (482-2117). *The* breakfast place. Four buckwheat pancakes served with genuine maple syrup cost $3.50, and should only be attempted by the famished. Normal appetites will be satisfied with a short stack ($2.50). The "peasant scramble" leaves peasants scrambling for cash at $4, but is a tasty mélange of scrambled eggs and veggies. Open daily 7am-9pm.

Geppetto's, 345 E. Main St. (482-1138). A local favorite, but the food is unexceptional. Dinner entrees average $8. Try the baked snapper with tomatoes and wine sauce ($10.25) or the eggplant burger ($3). Open daily 8am-midnight.

Key of C Coffee House, 116 Lithia Way (488-5012). Sit with an espresso (75¢) and read one of the magazines. Authentic homemade bagels to go at 75¢. Open daily 7am-4pm.

Sights and Entertainment

The **Shakespeare Festival** was the brainchild of local teacher Angus Bowmer and began with two plays performed by schoolchildren. Today, four Shakespeare plays and a host of other classics are performed by professional actors February through October on indoor and outdoor stages. Backstage tours ($6, call 482-4331), lectures, and workshops enhance appreciation of the elaborate productions. *The Many Wives of Windsor, Henry V, The Comedy of Errors, The Winter's Tale,* Ibsen's *Peer Gynt,* and several modern pieces make up the 1990 lineup.

Due to the tremendous popularity of the productions, reservations are recommended one to two months in advance. (Admission $10, $14, and $18. For complete ticket information, write Oregon Shakespeare Festival, Ashland 97520, or call 482-2111.) From March to May, half-price rush tickets may often be bought an hour before every performance that is not sold out. In the summer, obtaining tickets can be a real bitch; be at the box office by 9:30am on the day of any show. Locals occasionally leave their shoes to hold their place in line, and you should respect this tradition. At 9:30am, the box office releases any unsold tickets for the day's performances. If no tickets are available, you will be given a priority number, entitling you to a place in line when the very few tickets that members have returned are released (1pm for matinees, 6pm for evening performances). The box-office will sell a limited number of standing-room seats for the outdoor Elizabethan theater ($6).

In addition to the major productions on the three large stages, Ashland hosts several smaller, less conventional theaters. The **Cabaret Theater** (488-2902), at 1st and Hagarcline, stages several light musicals in a sophisticated setting with drinks and hors d'oeuvres. (Weekday tickets $8.50, $10.50. Weekends $10.50, $12.50.) The **Ashland Resident Theater** (482-4117) stages dramas sporadically throughout the summer. The **Schneider Museum of Art,** on the Southern Oregon State campus (482-6245), displays college-sponsored contemporary art exhibits that change every two weeks. (Open Tues.-Fri. 11am-5pm, Sat.-Sun. 1-5pm. Free.) For less-renowned art at reasonable prices, try the **Saturday Marketplace** on Guanajuato Way behind the plaza. (Open May-Sept. Sat. 10am-6pm.)

Before it had Shakespeare, Ashland had **lithia water,** which was reputed to have miraculous healing powers. The noisome mineral springs have given their name to the well-tended **Lithia Park,** west of the plaza off Main St. To sample the vaunted water itself, head for the circle of fountains in the center of the plaza, under the statue of horse and rider—the water is as delicious as sulphur.

The daily events taking place in Lithia Park are tabulated in brochures and described at the Plaza Kiosk. The park itself has hiking trails, picnic grounds, a Japanese garden, duck and swan ponds, and a creek that trips over itself in ecstatic little waterfalls. If the park and its infamous waters fail to refresh you, find your way to the **Valley View Tasting Room,** 52 E. Main St. (482-8964), where 14 different wines are laid out for your sampling pleasure. As a mere sip is never enough, the wines are also sold by the glass ($1). (Open daily 10am-6pm.)

If your muscles are calling for a little abuse after all this R&R, you can join the **Pacific Crest Trail** from here. Or take advantage of the variety of **raft** companies that offer daytrips on local rivers. **Noah's** offers full- and half-day trips for both beginners and experts (write P.O. Box 11, 97520, or call 488-2811). For a tamer experience, try the double-flumed, 280-foot waterslide at **Emigrant Lake Park** (10 slides for $3.50), or just practice your freestyle in the lake. The park also offers sailing lessons through the **Hobie House Marina** (488-0595). (Open in summer 10am-6pm; sailboard $10, Hobie Cat $25, lessons $15 per hr., full-day rental $50-80 with a $25-50 deposit.) There is also swimming in the town pool (50¢); ask about it at a hotel or kiosk.

Equipment for most outdoor activities can be bought or rented from **Ashland Mountain Supply,** 31 N. Main St. (488-2749), at The Plaza. You will pay top dollar here, but the help is friendly, the equipment new, and the location central. Tents $10 for 2 days; Farmer John wetsuits $7 per day; mountain bikes $9 for 2 hr., $20 per day. Varying deposit required. Ice axes and crampons also for rent. (Open daily 10am-5:30pm.) **Headwaters River Adventures** (488-0583) operates out of the store and runs daily river trips for $55 and up.

Mount Ashland has 22 ski trails of varying intensity (from moguls to bunny slopes), with two chair lifts and three surface lifts. (Open Thanksgiving-April. Day skiing daily 9am-4pm, night skiing Thurs.-Sat. 4-10pm. Full-day ticket $9 weekdays, $18 weekends. Full rental $12.) Daily buses run to Ashland and Medford. Contact **Ski Ashland,** P.O. Box 220, Ashland 97520 (482-2897; snow conditions 482-2754). **Jackson Hot Springs,** 2 miles north of Ashland on Hwy. 99 (482-3776), gives year-round private mineral baths.

Fourth of July celebrations in Ashland include a parade, food and game booths in Lithia Park, music, and, oddly enough, fireworks. **Halloween** is a trick-or-treating excuse for mass drunkenness; the town sponsors a free shuttle that transfers ghosts and goblins from one bar to another. In summer, the **Ashland City Band** sets up every Thursday at 7:30pm in Lithia Park (information 482-9215).

Bars and Dancing

Jazmin's, 180 C St. (488-0883). Locals set the tone. Sidewalk café, dance floor, and live music Thurs.-Sat. 9:30pm. Cover from $1. Dinners $6-13. Restaurant open daily 4-10pm. Bar open Thurs.-Sat. 4pm-2:30am.

Backporch BBQ, 92 N. Main St. (482-4131), north of The Plaza, above the creek. Smashing in the summer. Texas-style BBQ ($7-9) and margaritas ($2.50) consumed outside to the tune of a bubbling creek. Live music until 2am on summer weekends. Restaurant open June-Aug. daily 11am-10pm. Bar open until 2am. In winter, open 5-10pm.

Cook's, 66 E. Main St. (482-5145). Pool table, small dance floor. Sandwiches $2.50. The bar in the front is a gay scene on weekends after 9pm. Open daily noon-2:30am.

Log Cabin Tavern, 41 N. Main St. (482-9701). The cheapest brew around: $1.50 per pitcher, 35¢ per glass. An older crowd. Open daily 10am-2:30am.

Eastern Oregon

The triangle of land between Portland, Bend, and John Day was once one of the great centers of volcanic activity on the North American continent. The nearby snow-capped Cascades, which run just west of center through Oregon, were spat forth hundreds of millions of years ago by volcanic eruptions, then honed to their present figure by glaciation. In more recent history, the jagged mountain range was the last obstacle between pioneers on the Oregon Trail and the coast. Since then, the Cascades have become a vast wilderness recreation area, with forests, mountain streams, steep slopes, and caves that attract hikers, fishermen, and spelunkers year-round.

East of the Cascades, most of Oregon's principal sights are in the upper half of the state. The desert area is sliced by several rivers, including the John Day, much of which rakes alongside U.S. 26 through Malheur National Forest. In the state's northeast corner, beyond the Blue Mountains, the area's population is concentrated in the city of Pendleton. Hells Canyon National Recreation Area hems the Idaho border. In this region a car is a boon—distances are great, buses take roundabout routes, and hitching is slow.

Klamath Falls and Crater Lake

The Klamath Falls and Crater Lake area was one of the most popular luxury resort regions between Seattle and San Francisco in the first decades of this century of excess. The wealthy crowds are gone, but the region retains a silent scenic glory. Mirror-blue Crater Lake, Oregon's only National Park, is a true natural wonder. Iceless in winter and flawlessly circular, from an elevation of over 6000 feet it plunges to a depth of 2000 feet, making it the nation's deepest lake.

Practical Information and Orientation

The **Greyhound Station** in Klamath Falls is at 1200 Klamath Ave. (882-4616). (Open Mon.-Fri. 6am-6pm and 11:30pm-12:30am, Sat. 6am-3:15pm.) The **Klamath County Chamber of Commerce,** 125 N. 8th (884-5193) is not much help. The **Klamath Cab Company** can be reached at 882-7875, and the Police emergency number is 883-5333.

Klamath Falls is accessible from the north or the east on Greyhound via **U.S. 97.** Crater Lake can be reached only by car. A charter limousine service from Klamath Falls run by **W.W. Enterprises** (884-7433) charges $45 for two people and a more reasonable $55-60 for larger groups (up to 9 people).

Highway 62 through Crater Lake National Park is open year-round, but its services and accommodations are available only during the summer. After its jaunt around the lake, Hwy. 62 heads west to Medford and east to Klamath Falls. To reach the park from Portland, take I-5 to Eugene, then Hwy. 58 east to U.S. 97 south. Many roads leading to the park are closed or dangerous during the winter; call ahead for road conditions (1-238-8400).

Admission to the park (charged only in summer) is $5 for cars, $3 for hikers and bikers. The tiny **visitors center** (594-2211) on the lake shore at **Rim Village,** distributes books and maps on hiking and camping. (Open daily 8am-7pm.) Rangers conduct nightly talks in the **Rim Center** across the street starting at 8pm; check a schedule for the night's topic. In winter, advice and amusement are scarce.

Accommodations and Camping

The only hotel in the park is **Crater Lake Lodge,** Rim Village (594-2511), open from June to September. Call far in advance for reservations: renovations due to safety hazards have closed parts of the lodge for extended periods of time. Staying here will put a crater in your wallet; cottages start at $36, and $47 is the minimum for a room with a view of the lakes.

Inexpensive campsites may be found along U.S. 97 to the north. Klamath Falls has several affordable hotels; you may be wise to sack out in the town and base your visits to Crater Lake from there.

Pony Pass Motel, 75 Main St. (884-7735), in Klamath Falls. Clean, comfortable rooms at the edge of town with A/C and HBO. Free coffee. Singles $32. Doubles $34.

Maverick Motel, 1220 Main St. (882-6688), down the street from Greyhound in Klamath Falls. Right in the center of town. A helpful 24-hour staff. TV, A/C, and a handkerchief-sized pool. Singles $24.60. Doubles $27.50.

Molatore's Motel, 100 Main St. (882-4666), across the street from the Pony Pass. This well-maintained, 104-unit motel caters mostly to business travelers. Large pool, immense rooms with A/C. TV and coffee. Singles from $30.75. Doubles $33.90.

Mazama Campground (594-2211), in Crater Lake National Park. The 200 sites in this monster facility are usually usurped in summer by equally mammoth RVs, with the ambience more of a parking lot than the wilderness. Sites $7.

Lost Creek Campground (594-2211), in Crater Lake National Park. Hidden at the southwest corner of the park, this campground has only 12 sites. Best to secure a spot in the morning hours.

Food

Eating inexpensively in Crater Lake is difficult. Crater Lake Lodge has a small dining room, and Rim Village has several groceries that charge high prices for a skimpy array of foodstuffs. As in most national parks, the best plan is to buy supplies in nearby towns and cook your own meals once inside. If you're coming from the south, **Fort Klamath** is the final food frontier before the park. Stock up here at the **Old Fort Store** (381-2345; open daily 8am-8pm). There are several affordable restaurants in Klamath Falls listed below.

McPherson's Old Town Pizza Co., 722 Main St. (884-8858), between 7th and 8th. Housed in a building combining Roman architecture and reliefs of cows' skulls, this local favorite has some of the cheapest and tastiest food in the area. Try the small taco pizza ($3). Personal pizzas from $2.55. Lunch buffet $5. Open daily 11am-11pm.

Hobo Junction, 636 Main St. (882-8013) at 7th St. The perfect place to stock up for a picnic or simply to relax with *Critical Inquiry* among the potted plants. Good deli fare, with hearty $1 bowls of chili and 22 varieties of hot dogs including the specialty of the house, the box-car dog (a ¼-lb. cheese dog with chili and onions, $3). Open Mon.-Thurs. 11am-4pm, Fri. 11am-7pm, Sat. 11am-3pm.

The Blue Ox, 835 Main St. (884-5308). A must for famished travelers. A buffet with desserts and drinks included that changes daily. Lunch (until 4pm) $3.75. Dinner $5. Open daily 11am-8pm.

Sights

Down by its surface, Crater Lake resembles any other lake, and the sky and mountains are the show. Higher up, however, the lake's reflected blue seems almost unreal in its placidity. This grand, serene mountain was the source of a prehistoric cataclysm—one of the most destructive of Earth's volcanic eruptions. Thousands of square miles in the western U.S. were obliterated by a deep layer of ash. **Rim Drive,** open only in summer, is a 33-mile route high above the lake. Points along the drive offer views and trailheads for hiking. Among the most spectacular are **Discovery Point Trail** (from which the first pioneer saw the lake in 1853), **Garfield Peak Trail,** and **Watchman Lookout.**

The hike up **Scott Peak,** the park's highest (just a tad under 9000 ft.), begins from the drive near the lake's eastern edge. Although steep, the 7½-mile trail to the top gives the persevering hiker a unique view of the lake that repays the sweat spent getting there. Steep **Cleetwood Trail,** a 1-mile switchback, is the only trail that leads down to the water's edge. From here a boat tours the lake (fare $8.50, ages 12 and under $5; check with the lodge for times). Both **Wizard Island,** a cinder cone 760 feet above lake level, and **Phantom Ship Rock** are fragile and tiny specks when viewed from above, yet they prove surprisingly large from the surface of the water. Picnics and fishing are allowed, as is swimming, although you must withstand the frigid 50°F temperature. Park rangers lead free walking tours daily in the summer and periodically during the winter (on snowshoes). Call the visitors center at Rim Village for exact times.

If pressed for time, walk the easy 100 yards from the visitors center down to the **Sinnott Memorial Overlook.** The view is the area's best and most accessible. For a short lecture on the area's history, attend a ranger talk or catch a 15-minute film at Rim Village.

Make the effort to spend some time in charming Klamath Falls. For adults and children alike, the free 45-minute historical and architectural tour of the city in a restored 1906 trolley is a definite must. Bounce along happily as the driver tips his period bowler hat to passing locals and points out such sights as the first replica of an Egyptian temple built on the West Coast (which is now—prosaically enough—a former Ford dealership showroom). Catch the trolley at either the **Baldwin Hotel Museum,** 31 Main St. (883-4207; open Tues.-Sat. 10am-5pm) or at the larger, more exciting **Klamath County Museum,** 1451 Main St. (883-4208; open Tues.-Sat. 10am-6pm). Both museums are free and mix local history with archaeology in a fascinating mishmash. Also worth a drive is the **Weyerhauser Sawmill** (884-2241), which offers a chance to follow the transformation of trees from their natural state into plywood. Take a free tour of the world's largest producer of pine lumber. Although interesting, the tour takes a whopping 2½ hours. (Tours June-Sept. Mon.-Fri. 10am.)

Bend

Bend has always been in the middle of things. Originally the site of Native American trail junctures, Bend is now a hub of central Oregon's highway system, with U.S. 97 and U.S. 20 intersecting here. In Bend you will find what's missing from the rest of eastern Oregon: fast-food restaurants, traffic jams, and *people.* With 19,000 inhabitants, the city has the state's largest population east of the Cascades, and more cultural, athletic, and culinary options than many of its neighbors. Bordered by Mt. Bachelor, the Deschutes River, and a national forest, Bend makes an ideal way station for hikers and bicyclists. The lofty peaks of the Cascades, snow-capped even in August, will lure you out of town to the west. The town itself, however, is a budgetarian's dream, with many affordable hotels and cheap meals.

Practical Information

Visitor Information: Chamber of Commerce, 164 NW Hawthorne (382-3221), on a quiet street near downtown. Maps and brochures can be picked up at the door on weekends and after hours. Open Mon.-Fri. 9am-5pm.

Greyhound: 2045 E. Highway 20 (382-2151), a few miles east of town. Changing location in late 1989. Open Mon.-Sat. 7:30am-9pm.

Taxi: Owl Taxi, 1283 NW Wall St. (382-3311). 24 hours.

AAA: 20360 Anderson Rd. (382-1303).

Camping Equipment: Bend Rental Helps, 353 SE 3rd St. (382-2792). Tents $14 per day, lanterns $5 per day. Open Mon.-Sat. 7:30am-6pm, Sun. hours vary.

Laundromat: Nelson's, 407 SE 3rd St. One block from Royal Gateway. Open daily 7am-10:30pm.

Ambulance: 388-5522.

Police: 388-5555.

Post Office: 2300 NE 4th St. (388-1971), at Webster. Open Mon.-Fri. 9am-5pm. General Delivery ZIP Code: 97709.

Area Code: 503.

Accommodations and Camping

Bend's flock of cheap motels proceed down 3rd St. (U.S. 97). A price war has driven most singles to around $20. Campgrounds proliferate in the **Deschutes National Forest,** where you can stay for free if you tote your own water. Contact the **National Forest Office,** 1645 E. Hwy. 20 (388-2715), for details.

Royal Gateway Motel, 475 SE 3rd St. (382-5631). The rooms are clean but small, with Movie Channel and A/C. Singles $20. Doubles $24.

Edelweiss Motel, 2346 NE Division (382-6222), near the northern intersection with 3rd St. The owners couldn't be more pleasant, the rooms nicer, or the bathrooms cleaner. Singles $20. Doubles $23.

Chalet Motel, 510 SE 3rd (382-6124), at the southern end of town. A/C and TV cramped into small rooms. Singles $18. Doubles $21.

Holiday Motel, 880 SE 3rd St. (382-4620). Clean and comfortable. Discounts for senior citizens and commerical travelers. Cable TV, A/C, outdoor hot tub. Singles $20. Doubles $24.

Tumalo State Park, 5 miles northwest of town on U.S. 20 (382-3586). 88 sites along the Deschutes River, 20 with water and electricity. Facilities include hot showers and flush toilets. Open April 15-Oct.; reservations recommended. Sites $6.

Elk Lake Recreation Area, on Forest Service Road 46, 30 miles from Bend in the national forest. 53 sites with pit toilets; no drinking water. Open June-Sept.

Bend KOA Kampground, 63615 N. U.S. 97 (382-7728), 2 miles north of Bend. Typical KOA. Sites $10, with full hookup $13.

Food

The Hong Kong, 480 SE 3rd St., across from the Royal Gateway. Above-average Chinese and American food. A few Szechuan dishes. Average portions. Combination plate $5. Open Mon.-Thurs. 11am-10pm, Fri. 11am-11pm, Sat. noon-11pm, Sun. noon-10pm.

Sargent's Cafe, 719 SE 3rd St. (382-3916). Standard diner fare. All-you-can-eat spaghetti $4.50. 20%-off coupons available at nearby motels. Open daily 6am-9pm.

Rolaine's Cantina, 785 SE 3rd St. (382-4944), across from Albertson's. Mexican specials of almost frightening proportions. Try the vegetarian *burrito rolaine* ($5.20), and garnish it with gobs of "killer" salsa (available upon request). Open Mon.-Fri. 11:30am-10pm, Sat.-Sun. noon-10pm.

D&D Bar and Grill, 927 NW Bond (382-4592), downtown. For the *really* hungry. Home of some of the best specials in central Oregon. $8 buys a 16-oz. steak, baked potato, a mountain of vegetables, and a glass of wine. Grab a friend and share the "2 fer" special (2 8-oz. steaks, 2 salads, 2 baked potatoes, and 2 cheese breads, all for only $10). The debonair clink of pool balls, the pulsating rock anthems, and the chatter of sated locals add the finishing touches to this find. Open daily 6am-9pm.

De Nicola's Pizza, 811 NW Wall (389-7364). The pies are not quite Italian, but they satisfy the younger crowd that eats here. Slices available until 4pm. 10-inch pizza $5.25. Open Mon.-Fri. 11am-9pm, Sat. 11:30am-9pm.

Arvard's Lounge and Cafe, 928 NW Bond (389-0990), across the street from D&D. A clean, standard coffee shop. A sandwich and a stomach-full of fries is $4. Open Mon.-Sat. 7am-9pm, Sun. 7am-7pm.

Deschutes Brewery and Public House, 1044 NW Bond St. (382-4242). Delicious food and beer. Daily special $4.75, daily homemade sausage special $14.50. Pint of ale, bitters, or stout brewed on the premises $2. Open Mon.-Sat. 11am-11:30pm, Sun. 1-10pm.

Sights and Events

Just east of the intersection of U.S. 97 and 20, **Pilot Butte State Park** spreads 101 acres around Pilot Butte, a 511-foot cinder cone. Climb to the top for an excellent view of the Cascade Range. Six miles south of Bend on U.S. 97, the **High Desert Museum** (382-4754) shines as one of central Oregon's feature attractions, maintaining live exhibits on the fragile ecosystem of the Oregon plateau. The museum humorously presents facts (a horned owl's eyeball is bigger than its brain) and explanations of the geological history of the area. The main building is solar-heated and contains a lecture hall in which park rangers hold forth upon Oregon's ecology. Especially interesting are the otter feedings (10:30am, 1pm, 3:30pm), although small children may be distressed to see the otters hunt down and then shred live fish. The museum also features a 15-min. desert slide show, offered every hour on the half-hour. (Open daily 9am-5pm. Admission $3, ages 12 and under $1.50.)

The rest of Bend's sights are dots on the map of Deschutes National Forest. West of Bend, **Century Drive** (Cascade Lakes Hwy.) makes its dramatic 100-mile loop over Mt. Bachelor, through the forest, and past the Crane Prairie Reservoir before rejoining U.S. 97. Thirty campgrounds, fishing areas, and hiking trails pockmark the countryside. Leave a full day for the spectacular drive, and pack a picnic lunch. (Bend has several supermarkets.)

Ten miles south of the city on U.S. 97 is **Lava Butte,** which resembles Pilot Butte in height and geology. The **Lava Lands Visitor Center** (593-2421), at the base of the butte, offers interpretive dioramas and information. The **Lava River Caves,** 2 miles farther on U.S. 97, were formed by age-old lava flow from the nearby volcanoes. In the midst of endless juniper bushes, the caves are a welcome change of scenery. A self-guided 1.2-mile tour allows you to explore on your own. Ask about shorter trails at the visitor center. (Open May 15-late Sept. daily 8:30am-5pm. Admission $1, ages 12 and under free.)

Class A baseball hits Bend from June to September as the **Bend Bucks** try to fight their way to the majors in Vince Genna Stadium, 401 SE Roosevelt, just off 3rd St. (Admission $2.50.) Would-be super-men and wonder-women compete in the **Pole, Pedal, Paddle Race** every May (389-0399). Contestants ski, bike, canoe, and run to finish this grueling answer to the triathlon. June brings the **Cascade Festival of Music** with a wide variety of concerts. Write 842 NW Wall St., #6, for tickets and info. On the third weekend of July, local visual and performing artists aestheticize at the **Festival of the Arts** in Drake Park.

U.S. 20 and 26

To get from the Willamette Valley through the Cascades, take U.S. 20 to Bend, avoiding U.S. 26's soporific traversal of the Warm Springs Indian Reservation. East of the Bend area, U.S. 26 is the prettier of your two options. While U.S. 20 crosses eastern Oregon's vast expanse of high desert, U.S. 26 winds through the foothills of the scenic **Blue Mountains** en route to the two roads' final junction in Vale, some 250 miles east of Bend.

U.S. 20

Starting inland from Newport on the Oregon Coast, U.S. 20 crosses I-5 at Corvallis, entering the Cascade Range along the South Santiam River. Just past Cascadia, U.S. 20 cuts through the towering Douglas firs of **Willamette National Forest,** whose well-marked fishing and hiking areas extend roughly south to Hwy. 126 and north to Hwy. 22 and Detroit Lake. **Detroit Lake State Park** (854-3346), 3½ miles west of Detroit on Hwy. 22, has 300 sites with flush toilets and hot showers for $7 (with electrical hookup $8, with full hookup $9). East and south of Detroit Lake is the **Mount Jefferson Wilderness,** in the southernmost corner of Mount Hood National Forest. The 10,000-foot peak of Mount Jefferson actually lies within the Warm Springs Indian Reservation. Trailheads for hikes through the wilderness area are reached easily from Hwy. 22.

East of U.S. 20's junction with Hwy. 22, in the area between the North, Middle, and South Santiam Rivers, the heavily forested **Santiam Pass** rises 4817 feet, opening the way to the **Mount Washington Wilderness.** The McKenzie Pass Highway (Hwy. 126) meets U.S. 20 on its way to Bend at **Sisters,** a charming (if rather self-consciously quaint) village that is an important supply station for backpackers on the Pacific Crest Trail. Sisters hosts one of the better rodeos in the area during the second weekend of June. Reserve tickets ($7-9) with the **Sisters Rodeo Association,** P.O. Box 1018, Sisters 97759 (549-0121). For wilderness information, stop at the **ranger station,** on the highway at the west end of town, and pick up directions to **Lava Lake Camp,** a magnicently isolated, free campsite located among lava fields about 20 miles out of Sisters.

For 40 miles, Hwy. 126 follows the McKenzie River. Chinook salmon attract anglers here from all over. For more information visit the **Sisters Chamber of Commerce** (549-0251; open Mon.-Fri. 9am-5pm).

Below Sisters, U.S. 20 continues along the edge of the **Deschutes National Forest** (duh-SHOOTS), which extends south almost to Crater Lake. The forest features five wilderness areas, fishing lakes, canoeing rivers, and skiing on Mt. Bachelor, one of the Northwest's top ski resorts. (Prices vary; call 382-8334.) Camp at whim in the forest. The Deschutes National Forest Office, 1645 E. U.S. 20, Bend (388-2715), administers the area. (Open Mon.-Fri. 7:45am-4:30pm.)

U.S. 26

From Portland, U.S. 26 runs through the forested Cascades and, north of U.S. 20, the scorching deserts of central and eastern Oregon. After threading through the Mount Hood Wilderness Area, the highway enters **Warm Springs Indian Reservation,** a transition region from national forest to eastern desert about 100 miles east of Portland. Beware of the overpriced curio shops. The nearest legitimate vacation draw is the **Kan-Nee-Ta Resort,** about 15 miles north. Originally intended to offer the "life of another culture," the resort has deteriorated into an ultra-American lodge with a golf course and the works. Luxurious rooms start at $32 per person (call 553-1112 or 800-831-0100 if you are so moved).

Every Sunday at 1pm, a Don Ho-like emcee leads a group of Native American dancers through a performance in the main plaza of **Warm Springs.** It smacks of Englebert Humperdinck hosting an Indian cabaret—you won't kick yourself for missing it. Instead, head for the weekly **salmon bake,** held every Saturday night from 5 to 7pm. The price is a bit steep ($16.50, children $10.50), but you can gorge yourself while you watch Native Americans in full regalia. In general, the Warm Springs Reservation is not the best spot to appreciate native culture.

Another expensive way to amuse yourself in Warm Springs is to raft down the Deschutes River. Call **Rainbow Rafting** (553-1663) to reserve a six-person raft ($33 per day) or to find a spot for yourself with another group.

Madras lies on U.S. 26 about 10 miles past Warm Springs and 40 miles short of Bend. "Rockhounds," who excavate for rocks and fossils, dominate the area. You can dig alongside them at the **Richardson Recreational Ranch,** Gateway Rd. (475-2680), 11 miles north of town on U.S. 97. Ten miles south of town, the **Cove Palisades State Park** claims a man-made lake alongside slabs of frozen lava 80 feet thick. The **Madras Chamber of Commerce,** 4th and D St. (475-2350), seems about as big as the town itself. (Open Mon.-Fri. 9am-5pm, Sat. 10am-2pm; off-season Mon.-Fri. 9am-5pm.)

John Day Fossil Beds National Monument

U.S. 26 passes by two of the three units that comprise the vast and barren **John Day Fossil Beds National Monument. Sheep Rocks,** 5 miles northwest of Dayville on Hwy. 19 near its junction with U.S. 26, offers a peek at 25-million-year-old remains. The bones of sabertooth tigers and other more docile creatures are buried under volcanic ash. The monument's main **Visitors Center,** 2 miles north at the junction of Hwy. 19 and U.S. 26, exhibits dozens of fossils. (Open March 15-Oct. 15 daily 9am-5pm.) The **Painted Hills** unit, 6 miles northwest of Mitchell off U.S. 26, retains the red, green, and black stains of lava flows from the good old days. **Clarno,** the last unit, 23 miles west of Fossil on Hwy. 218 (best approached from U.S. 26 via U.S. 97 in Madras to Hwy. 218), reveals the fossils of nuts, seeds, and rhinoceri buried by mud slides 40 million years ago (Tuesday). The best way to see and make sense of all this is to follow one of the many trails blazed by the Parks Department. Large groups might ask the visitors center for a ranger as a guide. You can lead yourself around with the free trail guide that also describes the fossilization process during the Cenozoic Era. Most trails are short but rugged, ranging from ¼ to 2 miles. Further information is available at the entrance to each unit of the monument.

The monument headquarters is in the **Parks Department,** a large pink building at 420 W. Main St., John Day (575-0721; open Mon.-Fri. 8am-4:30pm). The staff will tell you all you ever wanted to know about fossils but were afraid to ask. The **Grant County Visitors Information Center,** at 710 S. Canyon Blvd., overflows with information on Oregon in general (575-0547; open Mon.-Fri. 9am-5pm.). For more area-specific facts, try the **Malheur National Forest** ranger station on the eastern edge of town at 139 NE Dayton (575-1731; open Mon.-Fri. 7:15am-5pm), or the Parks Department. If you stay overnight in John Day, try **Little Mac's Motel,** 250 E. Main (575-1751), for clean (if worn-out) rooms. Beware of the extremely hot showers. TV and A/C. (Singles $24. Doubles $28.) Eat at the **Mother Lode Restaurant,** 241 W. Main (575-2714) for hearty but unexceptional food. Good breakfasts $2-4. Senior citizens receive a substantial discount. Open Mon.-Fri. 5am-9pm, Sat.-Sun. 6am-9pm.

"Nobody here likes it indoors," quips one resident of the sleepy timber, ranching, and mining town of John Day (pop. 1200). During hunting season (Sept.-Nov.), the town heads for the mountains in the **Malheur National Forest** (mal-HERE). Ask at the ranger station about licenses to kill black bears, bighorn sheep, mule deer, salmon, steelhead, and trout. Camp wherever you please in the forest—except, of course, where forbidden by No Trespassing signs. Established sites do not exist. Some areas in the forest boast vault toilets and drinkable water. The more adventurous might penetrate the two government-regulated wilderness areas, **Strawberry Mountain** and **Monument Rock.** You must get maps and guidance from the ranger station before venturing out.

In John Day itself, the **Kam Wah Chung and Co. Museum,** on Canton St. near City Park, showcases personal possessions Chinese immigrants brought to Grant County during the 1862 gold rush. The highlight is a large collection of herbal medicines. (Open May 1-Oct. 31 Mon.-Thurs. 9am-noon and 1-5pm, Sat.-Sun. 1-5pm. Admission $1.50, children 50¢.)

Prineville

Prineville, the oldest city in Central Oregon, may well qualify as the quintessential Oregon town. Clean and friendly streets, burger and steak restaurants, a historical museum, a yearly rodeo, and proximity to outdoor activities all contribute to its anytown atmosphere. Perhaps the most distinguishing feature is the profusion of churches—23 for a population of 5000.

Practical Information and Orientation

Visitor Information: Prineville Crook County Chamber of Commerce, 390 N. Fairview (447-6304), off 3rd. The usual pamphlets and a very friendly staff. Open Mon.-Fri. 9am-5pm.

Greyhound: 1825 E. 3rd (447-5516), about a mile east of town.

Taxi: County Cab. Co. (447-4884), 24 hours.

Dial-a-Ride: 447-6429.

Rape Crisis Line: 389-7021.

Hospital: Pioneer Memorial, 1201 N. Elm (447-6254).

Police Emergency: 447-4168.

Post Office: Federal Building (447-5652). General Delivery ZIP Code: 97754.

Prineville is at the junction of U.S. 26 and Hwy. 126, just west of the **Ochoco National Forest** (OH-chuh-coe), 36 miles northeast of Bend and 148 miles southeast of Portland.

Accommodations and Camping

Almost all motels are along 3rd St. and are slightly above budget range. You can camp anywhere in the forest for free as long as you leave no trace of your stay. Many campgrounds dot the area, with fees from $3-5. Contact the Forest Supervisor at Ochoco National Forest, P.O. Box 490, Prineville 97754-0490, for details.

Ochoco Inn, 123 E. 3rd (447-6231). Better-than-average rooms, TV, A/C. They also run the **Ochoco Motel,** 3 blocks down, at the same prices. Singles $31.50. Doubles $35.50.

City Center Motel, 509 E. 3rd (447-5522). Standard clean rooms. Coffee, A/C, TV. Single $25.20. Double $31.50.

Caroliner Motel, 1050 E. 3rd (447-4152). Small rooms, a little out of the way, friendly, and cheap. Singles $25.30. Doubles $29.40. Special family rates: 6 beds for $52.

Food

Makin' Bacon, 323 N. Main (447-7679). Design your own sandwiches ($3) in the cutesy atmosphere. Large homemade soup $2. Open Mon.-Fri. 9:30am-5:30pm, Sat. 9am-5pm.

The Coffee Pot, 386 W. Main (447-1043). Burgers "from A to Z": 26 varieties served with fries or tater tots ($2-4). Tasty and filling. Try the jalapeño burger. Open daily 6am-10pm.

Arnold's Drive-In, 36 E. 3rd (447-9920). Beef ribs with all the trimmings ($4) will bring you happy days. Also large subs ($5). Open Mon.-Sat. 11am-6pm.

Sights and Events

Prineville's star attraction is the **Bowman Museum,** 246 N. Main (447-3715), at the corner of 3rd St. Its collection of tobacco cans, bank books, and Bibles once belonged to 19th-century Prineville folk. Artfully arranged to affect your sense of nostalgia, the Bowman includes a 1908 Sears Roebuck catalog and a portion of the first Japanese plane shot down in World War II (over Hawaii, not Prineville). (Open April-Dec. Mon.-Fri. 10am-5pm, Sat. noon-5pm. Donations only.)

The second weekend in July brings the **Crooked River Roundup** into Prineville. Write for tickets ($5-8) at P.O. Box 536, Prineville 97754, or call 447-6335 for info. In the Ochocos one can hunt, fish, and ski. Contact the ranger for details.

Baker

When gold was discovered in the hills south of the Powder River Valley in 1861, a settlement sprang up where the river intersected the Oregon Trail. Today, Baker is a rest stop for truckers, a base for hikers and wilderness lovers, and a fine spot for an afternoon stroll.

Practical Information and Orientation

Visitor Information: Baker County Chamber of Commerce, 490 Campbell St. (523-5855, 800-523-1235 from outside OR). Pamphlets cover not only Baker County, but the rest of Oregon and the surrounding states as well. Small museum upstairs. Open Mon.-Sat. 8am-6pm.

Greyhound: 512 Campbell St. (523-5011), in the Truck Corral Café. Buses east (2 per day) and west (2 per day). Open Mon.-Sat. 6:30-10:30am and 4-7pm, Sun. 6:30-9am and 4-6:30pm.

Taxi: Baker Cab Co., 515 Campbell St. (523-6070). Up to $3.25 within Baker, $1 per mile outside city limits. The best way to get from a motel to the bus station, but you might have to call twice, since the dispatchers are not always reliable.

Laundromat: Coin-Op Laundry, 2690 Broadway.

Help Inc. Senior Services: 523-6591.

Hospital: St. Elizabeth, 3325 Pocahontas Rd. (523-6461). 24 hours.

Police Emergency: 523-3644.

Post Office: 1550 Dewey Ave. (523-4237). Open Mon.-Fri. 8:30am-5pm, Sat. 10am-noon. General Delivery ZIP Code: 97814.

Baker is at the intersection of I-84 and Hwy. 30 in northeast Oregon. Main Street, Campbell Street, Broadway Avenue, and 10th Street are the principal thoroughfares.

Accommodations and Camping

Baker has several motels, most of which are a little above budget range. Most places will knock off a few dollars for commercial travelers. Camping is easy and free—just find a comfortable spot by the Powder River. For more information about where you can and can't camp, call the U.S. Forest Service at 523-6391.

Hereford Motor Inn, 134 Bridge St. (523-6571), just off Main St. The rooms are bigger and plusher than in the costlier motels. Limited room service, outdoor jacuzzi, continental breakfast, cable TV, A/C, phone. Singles $24.50. Doubles $26.

Oregon Trail Motel, 211 Bridge St. (523-5844), right across from Hereford. Call a few days ahead for these spotless rooms. Sauna, heated pool, cable TV, and A/C. Senior citizen rates available. Singles $26. Doubles $29.

El Dorado Motel, 695 Campbell St. (523-6494), right next to Greyhound. Clean, with neo-Conquistador architecture. Big rooms with matador paintings on the walls. Indoor pool and jacuzzi, TV, A/C. Singles $29. Doubles $32. Family (2 adjoining rooms) $40.

Mt. View Campground, 9th and Hughes Lane (523-4824), exit 302 off I-84. A clean, spacious campground and trailer park in the hub of things. Showers, heated pool, water, and electric hookups available. Prices hover around $10.25.

Union Creek Campground, Box 54, Baker (894-2210), at Phillips Lake. Follow signs to Sumpter, and go 20 miles down Hwy. 7. Beach, but no shower. Sites $6, with full hookup $10. Heater or A/C $1 per day.

Food

The Brass Parrot, 2190 Main St. (523-4266). Try the Mexican food for a refreshing change from eastern Oregon's slimy hamburgers. Relax in a cool dining room with a delicious frozen strawberry-wine margarita ($1.50) and an immense burrito ($3.25). Open Mon.-Sat. 11am-9pm.

The Gold Skillet, 781 Campbell St. (523-4657) and 2300 Broadway, at 4th (523-2716). "Just Good Food," they claim—a fair enough self-assessment. Truckers and families drop in for $4-5 lunches and $5-6 dinners. Open daily 6am-2am.

Oregon Trail Restaurant, 211 Bridge St. (523-5844, ext. 179). The usual sandwiches, burgers, and steaks. Dinners from $5. Five clocks on the wall mark the time in Baker, Boise, Anchorage, Omaha, and New York. Milk shakes $1.25. Open daily 7am-9pm.

Truck Corral Café, 515 Campbell St. (523-4657), at the Greyhound. Uplifting atmosphere, at least for a truck stop. Big breakfasts $3-5, sandwiches $3-5, full dinners $5-9. Open 24 hours.

Sights and Seasonal Events

Baker's greatest attraction is the surrounding hills, which turn almost supernaturally green in the summer months. Pack a picnic lunch and hike in almost any direction. Twenty minutes east or west should take you far enough. Within Baker itself, the five-year-old **Oregon Trail Regional Museum,** 2490 Grove St. (523-9308), off Campbell St., is the center of attention. Century-old artifacts from the area are displayed alongside items from one of the largest private semi-precious stone collections in the world, a collection to rival the Smithsonian's. "Isophere Cochrane's hand-made wedding dress" hangs next to the world's largest cluster of fluorite and quartz. Tucked away at the back of the museum is a black-lit room with a shelf of phosphorescent rocks. (Open May-Sept. daily 10am-4pm. Suggested donation $1, children 50¢.) The **U.S. Bank,** 2000 Main St. (523-7791), at Washington St., has a glass case in the corner filled with Baker County gold. An 80-ounce nugget is the centerpiece. (Open Mon.-Thurs. 10am-5pm, Fri. 10am-6pm.) The Chamber of Commerce sells a guide to several walking tours of the city ($3), which indicates all the "century" houses. If the kids get bored, take them to **Geiser Pollman Park,** a big field with a playground, two blocks from Main St. along the river. Next to the park, the **Public Library** (523-6870), on Resort St., has a huge selection of children's books. (Open Mon.-Thurs. 10am-9pm, Fri. 10am-5pm, Sat. 10am-4pm, Sun. 1-4pm.)

The **Miners' Jubilee,** the third weekend of July, stages a hot air balloon race, a triathlon, and the world championship porcupine sprints. Porcupines train all year for this big event and wish to introduce it into the 1992 Olympics. The largest flea market in eastern Oregon buzzes in nearby **Sumpter** three times per year: Memorial Day weekend, Independence Day weekend, and Labor Day weekend. Sumpter also preserves a 100-year-old train that still gives rides.

Hells Canyon National Recreation Area

Spectacular, wild, and well-nigh inaccessible, Hells Canyon is truly rewarding for those brave enough to enter its gaping maw. Bighorn sheep, the tempestuous **Snake River,** spectacular "Grand Canyonic" vistas, and unspoiled archaeological sites all harmonically converge in an area thankfully untouched by the tourist steamroller. From the summit of Idaho's **Seven Devils** mountains to the frothing river below, is a dizzying 8000-foot drop—Hells Canyon is the deepest gorge on the continent. The Snake River Canyon's gorge gained dubious renown when Evel Knievel attempted to jump it on a motorcycle in the late 70s. (Don't try this at home.)

Settlers—including Lewis and Clark—have historically chosen to steer clear of the region, which straddles the borders of Idaho, Washington, and Oregon and encompasses the Snake, Imnaha, and Rapid Rivers. Consequently, getting to Hells Canyon remains, well, hell. From the Oregon side, take either Hwy. 82 to **Enterprise** or Hwy. 86 through Halfway to Hells Canyon Dam. Several U.S. Forest Service roads descend from U.S. 95 on the Idaho side, near Riggins. Public transportation to the area is practically nonexistent. If there is absolutely no way for you to obtain a car, contact the **Wallowa Valley Stage** (503-569-2284). Wallowa runs one van per day from La Grande to Enterprise, and conducts occasional group tours to the lookouts on the Oregon side.

If you come to Enterprise or to U.S. 95 with a car, make sure your vehicle is solid and safe, since the roads to the viewpoints are awful at best. For a view of the Canyon (and the Imnaha River), take the gravel-paved Zumwalt Road (County Rd. 697) out of Enterprise some 40 miles to the **Buckhorn Lookout.** Views of the legendary Snake River are harder to find. From Enterprise, drive through **Joseph** to **Imnaha.** From Imnaha, it's an extremely rough, 24-mile, two-hour drive to the 90-foot observation tower at **Hat Point Lookout,** but the view of the canyon, the river, and the Seven Devils beyond makes it worth shattering your nerves. From Idaho, Forest Service Rd. 517 departs U.S. 95 just south of Riggins and leads to **Heavens Gate Lookout,** in the heart of the Seven Devils. Heavens Gate provides a rare angle: the Snake *without* the Seven Devils in the background. Before setting out on any of the roads listed above, visit or contact the **U.S. Forest Service** stations in Enterprise, right on Hwy. 82 (503-426-3151), or in Riggins, on Hwy. 95 (208-628-3916). The helpful rangers will tell you which roads are passable and which are vacationing as waterslides. Primitive, cheap ($3 or free) **campsites** abound along all of the area's roads. Pick up a full listing of campsites at either of the Forest Service stations, or call the ranger station to reserve roomy cabins ($20 per couple, $5 per additional person). **Wallowa Llamas** offers several different trips through the Wallowa mountains and into Hells Canyon. They range from easy to strenuous, and from three to seven days. Tents, meals, and llamas are supplied; you provide sleeping bags, stamina, and between $225 and $600. Write Rt. 1, Box 84, Halfway 97834 or call 742-2961 or 742-4930.

A view is nice, but true recreation can only be had by plunging into the canyon or slithering down the Snake. The Forest Service maintains only some of the 900 miles of trail running through the canyon; the unmaintained miles are hard to use (let alone find). As with the local roads, inquire about trail conditions at the Forest Service offices. It's easier, and perhaps more exciting, to view the canyon from the water itself. A wide range of both **jet boat** and **raft trips** are available for the adventurer willing to shell out $45-90 per day. **Hells Canyon Adventures** offers the most varied options and a toll-free number (800-422-3568). For a complete list of boat runners and rafting groups, contact the **Hells Canyon Chamber of Commerce,** P.O. Box 841, Halfway 97834 (503-785-3393).

La Grande

Historical and cultural sensitivity aside, if you try to pronounce "La Grande" with even the slightest hint of a French accent when talking to locals, you might as well be speaking Urdu. In the mid-1800s, La Grande served as a pit stop for pioneers on the Oregon Trail; today it serves a similar function for West Coast truckers. The location is *de rigueur;* La Grande claims the Blue Mountains and the Grande Ronde River as its backyard.

As one strolls down Adams Avenue, a picture-postcard rendition of an American small town, one cannot but agree with the assertion made by most of La Grande's tourist brochures: "La Grande: An All-American City."

Practical Information and Orientation

Visitor Information: La Grande-Union County Chamber of Commerce, 1502 N. Pine Ave. (963-8588), off Spruce. The pamphlet selection will assuage your fears—there is much more to do in the surrounding area than in La Grande itself. Open Mon.-Fri. 8:30am-5pm.

Ranger Station: U.S. 30 (963-7186).

Greyhound: 2108 Cove Ave. (963-5165), off U.S. 82 in the northeast corner of town. Buses east (2 per day) and west (2 per day). Open Mon.-Fri. 8am-noon and 2-6pm, Sat. 8am-noon and 4-5pm.

Taxi: Rainbow Cab Co., 1609 Albany (936-6960). Anywhere within the city $3.

Laundromat: Stein's Wash Haus, Island City Strip (963-9629). Open Mon.-Fri. 7am-5:30pm.

Senior Citizen Services: Union County Senior Center, 1504 Albany Ave. (963-7532).

Crisis Action Team: 1906 3rd St. (963-6850).

Hospital: Grande Ronde Hospital, 900 Sunset Dr. (963-8421).

Police: 963-9110.

Post Office: 1202 Washington (963-2041). General Delivery ZIP code: 97850.

Area Code: 503.

La Grande is on I-84, halfway between Pendleton and Baker. The two main roads are Adams Avenue, which runs into U.S. 30, and Highway 82, which contains the Island City Strip.

Accommodations and Camping

Almost every motel is along Adams Ave. In summer, square dancers and other conventioneers book the motels quite solidly; call a day in advance to ensure a room. Camping is free and generally unrestricted—pitch a tent anywhere in the mountains. Closer to town, try **Morgan Lake,** 2 miles outside La Grande on B Ave., or **Hillgard Park,** at the edge of the Umatilla Forest, 8 miles west on U.S. 30. Camping along the Grande Ronde River is permitted.

Broken Arrow Lodge, 2215 Adams Ave. (963-7116). A clean room, free continental breakfast, cable TV, free coffee, and A/C. A courtesy car will pick you up at the bus station. Singles $24.50. Doubles $28.

Orchard Motel, 2206 Adams Ave. (963-6160). Small but comfortable wood-paneled rooms, some with kitchenettes. HBO, A/C, free continental breakfast. Singles $21. Doubles $26.25.

Stardust Lodge, 402 Adams Ave. (963-4166). The owner is a leading and enthusiastic expert on the Oregon Trail. Huge rooms, HBO, A/C, heated pool, and courtesy car from station. Singles $23.10. Doubles $27.30. Senior citizens and military personnel $22, students $20, under 16 free.

Moon Motel, 2116 Adams Ave. (963-2724). Cheaper, but not quite as clean or accommodating as the more expensive motels. Tiny rooms. Cable TV, A/C, and free coffee. Singles $19. Doubles $21.

Food

Fast-food joints, family restaurants, and greasy drive-ins are the extent of La Grande's cuisine.

Mamacita's, 110 Depot St. (936-6223). Incongruously funky and Mexican. Dinners $4-7. Open Tues.-Thurs. 11am-2pm and 5:30-9pm, Fri. 11am-2pm and 5:30-10pm, Sat. 5:30-10pm, Sun. 5:30-9pm.

Farm House Restaurant, 401 Adams Ave. (963-9318). Popular with the over-60 crowd. The terrific spicy apple pie ($1) makes La Grande worthwhile. Sandwiches $3, dinners $6. Open daily 6am-9pm.

DeBorde's Cafe, 1414 Adams Ave. (963-6439), in Pat's Alley, a mini-mall. This tiny restaurant with brown-toned decor could be any coffeeshop anywhere in the country, both in appearance and in food. Singular in its unsingularity. Breakfast and lunch $2-3, dinner $7. Open Mon.-Fri. 6am-10pm, Sat. 6am-8pm.

Sights and Activities

Let your imagination run free, and the **Oregon Trail** will be loads of fun. If you squint, the Toyotas of I-84 might become hyperkinetic horse-drawn wagons, hell-bent from Missouri to the Pacific. To hike along a substantial portion of the trail, you must contact the Chamber of Commerce (963-8588) for a special tour, because much of the trail crosses private property.

The **Hot Lake,** (963-5587), about 10 miles southeast of town on Hwy. 203, is a 185° steambath that occasions an annual pilgrimage of panacea hunters. Associated with turn-of-the-century quackery, mineral bathing now allegedly soothes the pains of cancer, arthritis, and other diseases. (Write Hot Lake Co., Box 1601, La Grande 97850 for details on Hot Lake's miracle cure. Open Wed.-Sun. 1-9pm. Admission $6.)

Hunters roam the area from October through February, destroying mule deer and Rocky Mountain elk. Skiers drive the 41 miles to **Anthony Lakes** on I-84, where they can ski all day for $14. (Write P.O. Box 3040, La Grande 97850 or call 963-8282.) Those who seek ultimate thrills can traverse the Wallowa-Whitman National Forest atop a llama. The 4-hour ride is $15 complete with riding lesson. (Contact **Hurricane Creek Llamas,** Rte. 1, Box 123, Enterprise 97828, 432-4455.)

The **Timber Festival,** held in the third week of June, stars the town's three world-champion lumberjacks in tree topping, axe throwing, speed climbing, and straight chopping competitions. For three weeks beginning in mid-August, the **Oregon Trail Pageant** summons forth the past with dramatic reenactments and dancing performances.

Pendleton

Pendleton is as close to a true Western town as one can find these days. Men who wear cowboy hats and talk about horses here wouldn't be caught dead in a Marlboro ad. When the **Pendleton Round-Up** rolls around in mid-September, the town falls into the ecstasy of rodeo. 45,000 rodeo fans ride up, causing room rates to double and bars to serve anything that walks. The rest of the year Pendleton is less zany, with a few interesting places to eat and visit.

Practical Information and Orientation

Visitor Information: Pendleton Chamber of Commerce, 25 SE Dorion Ave. (276-7411). A brusque staff flings out pamphlets galore. Open Mon.-Fri. 9am-5pm.

Greyhound: 320 SW Court Ave. (276-1551), a few blocks west of the city center. To Boise (3 per day, $46), Salt Lake City (3 per day, $92), and Portland (3 per day, $25). Open Mon.-Sat. 6am-8pm, buses only on Sun.

Taxi: JB's Taxi Service, 30 W. Beebe (567-8811).

Car Rental: Ugly Duckling Rent-a-Car, 309 SW Emigrant Ave. (276-1498). The only way to enjoy the Blue or Wallowa Mts. without your own car. $20 per day plus 20¢ per mile. $50 deposit or credit card required to rent for more than 1 day. Must be over 21. Open Mon.-Fri. 8am-5pm, Sat. 8am-noon.

Rape Crisis Line: 278-0241.

Hospital: St. Anthony's, 1601 SE Court Ave. (276-5121).

Police: 276-4411.

Post Office: Federal Building, 104 SW Dorion Ave. (278-0203), at SW 1st. Open Mon.-Fri. 8:30am-5pm. General Delivery ZIP Code: 97801.

Area Code: 503.

Pendleton is on **I-84,** just under the Washington border, about the same distance (220-260 miles) from Portland, Seattle, Spokane, and Boise. **Raley Park,** home of the Round-Up Grounds, is the spiritual center of town, while Main Street is the physical one. Hitchhikers should know that towns are few and far between in this area.

Be aware of the peculiarities of Pendleton's street design. The city has many streets (running east to west) which are named with startling originality—1st St., 2nd St., and so on. Take the directional notations seriously; unfortunately, there are *two* 1st Streets, one SE and one SW, *two* 2nd Streets, etc., which are parallel to each other.

Accommodations and Camping

During most of the year, lodging in Pendleton is inexpensive. To stay here during the Round-Up, however, you must reserve rooms six months in advance. Rates double, and prices on everything from hamburgers to commemorative cowboy hats become celestial. Pendleton has no camping areas nearby. For more information on camping around here, contact the **State Highway Division,** 104 SE 12th St. (276-1241).

Longhorn Motel, 411 SW Dorion Ave. (276-7531), around the corner from the bus station. The management will tell you what you've been dying to know: how to get the most out of Pendleton. You get the biggest rooms in town, with bathroom, cable TV, and A/C. Singles $20. Doubles $26.

The Ranch Motel (276-4711), 5 miles west of town at exit 202 off I-84. Horribly inconvenient for travelers without a car, but the swimming pool is a blessing in Pendleton's summer heat and the rates are low. Singles $18. Doubles $22.

Motel 6, 325 SE Nye Ave. (276-3160), on the south side of town. Not in the middle of things, but easy access to I-84. Cable TV, A/C, and heated pool. Singles $24.60. Doubles $30.50.

Tapadera Inn, 105 SE Court Ave. (276-3231). A little above budget range, but with gorgeous rooms, A/C, HBO, a nice restaurant, and access to a health club for $4, it may be worth it. Singles $34.25. Doubles $39.60.

Emigrant Springs State Park, 26 miles southeast of Pendleton on I-84. The best campground within 50 miles. Once a favorite stopping place on the Oregon Trail, the park now offers numerous sites (and hot showers) in a shady grove of ponderosa pines.

Food

Pendleton proffers classic American dining in all its gaudy splendor. Sit at a long counter and enjoy a patty melt or Saturday stew served by a waitress named Roz or Bea.

Bread Board, 141 S. Main St. (276-4520). Great $2 sandwiches and 75¢ cinnamon rolls in a friendly atmosphere, with national newspapers strewn about. Try the $2.25 French Fantasy for breakfast—croissant, eggs, ham, and cheese. Open Mon.-Fri. 8am-3:30pm.

The Circle S, 210 SE 5th St. (276-9637). Don't let the 3-ft. axe door handle scare you away from a great Western BBQ restaurant. Drink beverages from Mason jars while you enjoy a BBQ sandwich and fries ($3.50) and a creme de menthe shake ($1.75). 72-oz. sirloin $35. If you can eat it all in an hour, like John Candy in *The Great Outdoors,* it's free. Smaller portions available. Open Tues.-Fri. 6am-10pm, Sat. 7am-10pm, Sun. 7am-3pm.

Rainbow Café, 209 S. Main St. (276-4120). Where the cowboys chow down. Classic American diner setting with rodeo decor. Good, hearty food. Burger and beer $3-4. Open daily 6am-2:30am.

The Club Café, 138 Main St. (276-9825), across from the Bread Board. The food isn't great, but the regulars don't seem to mind. Sit at the counter and watch TV. Filling breakfasts $2-3. Open Mon.-Fri. 5am-6pm, Sat. 6am-6pm.

Sights and Activities

The **Pendleton Round-Up** (276-2553), a premier event on the nation's rodeo circuit, draws ranchers from all over the U.S. For "four glorious days and nights," yahoo at steer roping, saddle-bronc riding, bulldogging, and bareback riding, not to mention non-equine attractions such as lying contests, buffalo-chip tosses, quick draws, and greased pig chases. For more information or tickets ($5-10), write to the Pendleton Round-Up Association, P.O. Box 609, Pendleton 97801. The **Round-Up Hall of Fame,** SW Court Ave. (276-2553), at SW 13th St., gives tours by appointment during the week. The hall has captured some of the rodeo's action for all eternity, including Pendleton's best preserved Round-Up hero, a stuffed horse named "War Paint."

Two other "attractions" will leave you desperately searching for excuses to leave in the middle of a guided tour, unless you have a special interest in wool or wood. Just outside the city center, **Pendleton Woolen Mills,** 1307 SE Court Ave. (276-6911), exposes its world-famous, top-secret blanket-making process to the public. Tours conclude, naturally, with a visit to the gift shop, where you can purchase a genuine Pendleton wool cap. (Tours Mon.-Fri. at 9am, 11am, 1:30pm, and 3pm. Free.) **Harris Pine Mills,** 2203 SW Court Ave. (276-1421), offers free tours of its facilities. You can witness the transubstantiation of wood from plain pine into chairs and tables! (Tours Mon.-Thurs. at 9:30am and 2:30pm, Fri. at 9:30am. Free.)

The second floor of **Hamley's Western Store,** 30 SE Court Ave. (276-2321), is an art gallery. On display are bronze sculptures of men, bronze sculptures of horses, and bronze sculptures of men on horses, not to mention a small collection of contemporary Native Art. Ask in front for someone to show you part (surely not all) of the 80-hour saddlemaking process that goes on at the back of the store. (Open Mon.-Sat. 9am-5:30pm. Free.) **The Corio Shop,** 142 S. Main (276-4434), is an eclectic store that sells everything from Native jewelry and sports pennants to hunting knives and sex aids.

Pendleton was once an important stop on the ol' **Oregon Trail.** Thousands of weary westward-bound pioneers stopped their caravans at what is now **Emigrant Springs State Park,** 25 miles southeast of town on I-84. Exhausted from thousands of miles of prairie and desert, wagon trains could rest here before the final push to general apotheosis in Portland. The wagon trains are gone now, but big game hunting remains popular in the Blue Mountains; mule deer and Rocky Mountain elk are favorite victims.

WASHINGTON

Washington has two personalities, clearly split by the Cascade Range. The western ridge of the range blocks Pacific moisture heading east and hurls it back toward the ocean, bathing the Olympic Peninsula with an average annual rainfall of 135 inches (compared to 15 inches inland). The Peninsula is carpeted with rain forests, while wheat fields drape the eastern region near Spokane.

Most of Washington's population is clustered around Puget Sound, an area that prides itself on its opera and its aerospace industry. The east is far less congested; residents and tourists can enjoy its rolling countryside without jostling for space. Native American reservations and rodeos are among the distinguishing features of the sunnier side of the state.

Though raindrops keep falling on its head, the wet portion of Washington not only sings in the rain, but takes fitting pride in its seafood. Seattle is perhaps best known for salmon and crabs, available at the Pike Place Market on the waterfront. Crabs are also sold directly from the ocean for gastronomes willing to journey as far as Dungeness on the Olympic Peninsula. Fans of the great Chinook salmon can make a killing in winter or spring when the 20-pounders gather to spawn near the Columbia River. But pity not the residents of eastern Washington, blessed with seafood thanks only to the miracle of modern refrigeration. Time that might otherwise be devoted to cracking crab shells can be spent savoring fresh fruit in Yakima.

Washington runs the gamut of terrain; deserts, volcanoes, untouched Pacific Ocean beaches, and the world's only non-tropical rain forest await exploration. There's rafting on the Skagit, Suiattle, Sauk, Yakima, and Wenatchee Rivers; sea kayaking in the San Juan Islands; and sand castle building on the Strait of Juan de Fuca (beware of razor clams). Beach bums can sleep on the banks of the Columbia or the shores of the Pacific. Mount Rainier has fantastic hiking, while the Cascades boast perfect conditions for nearly any winter activity. Seattle and Spokane drape themselves over equally handsome green landscapes, showing that botany and bottom line can still intersect. Best of all, Washington is a compact state by Western standards—everything is less than a daytrip away.

Practical Information

Emergency: 911.

Capital: Olympia.

Visitor Information: State Tourist Office, Tourism Development Division, 101 General Administration Bldg., Olympia 98504 (206-753-5600). **Washington State Parks and Recreation Commission,** 7150 Cleanwater Lane, Olympia 98504 (206-753-2027, during summer in WA 800-562-0990). **Forest Service/National Park Service Outdoor Recreation Information Office,** 1018 1st. Ave., Seattle 98104 (206-442-0170).

Time Zone: Pacific (3 hr. behind Eastern).

Postal Abbreviation: WA.

Drinking Age: 21.

Traffic Laws: Mandatory seatbelt law.

Area: 68,192 square miles.

Area Codes: 206 in western Washington, 509 in eastern Washington.

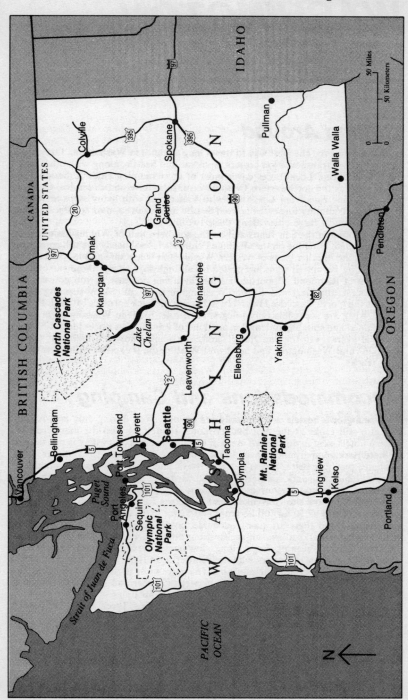

Impractical Information

Nickname: Evergreen State.

Motto: Alki (which means "by and by" in a Native American language).

State Song: Washington, My Home.

State Flower: Coast Rhododendron.

Getting Around

Bus remains the cheapest way to travel long distance in Washington. Greyhound serves the two transportation centers, Spokane and Seattle, along with other major cities in between. Local buses cover most of the remaining cities, although a few areas (such as the northwestern Olympic Peninsula) have no bus service. One Amtrak **train** line runs from Los Angeles to Vancouver with many stops in western Washington; another line extends from Seattle to Spokane and on to Chicago. Amtrak serves most large cities along these two lines.

Hitchhiking in the San Juans and on the southern half of Whidbey Island is locally accepted. Hitching on the Olympic Peninsula is less speedy but still considered safe; hitching in other parts of western Washington is less safe and less speedy. No Hitchhiking Permitted signs are posted on all highways except those surrounding the town of Raymond. Opportunities for thumbing decrease as you go east.

Of course, the ideal way to tour Washington is by **car.** Many startling drives, such as the North Cascades Hwy. (Hwy. 20) and the back entrance into Mt. Rainier (Hwy. 410), are accessible only to cars. As a rule, roads in Washington are well-maintained and suitable for travel in any kind of vehicle. Gas prices jump 10% over national averages in the San Juan Islands. Two-lane undivided highways are the norm in rural Washington, and northwest Washington is overrun with massive logging trucks.

Accommodations and Camping

Washington's **hostels** are generally uncrowded, even during July and August. Motel 6 still ranks as the best budget motel, though it's also the most crowded. Cheap hotels exist in downtown areas of most large cities, but safety is not assured.

State park campgrounds have cheaper, more secluded sites than private campgrounds; they give better access to trails, rivers, and lakes. Drivers and hitchhikers alike will find state park campgrounds (standard sites $6) more accessible than Department of Natural Resources (DNR) and national forest campgrounds. Most campgrounds have sites for hikers and bicyclists for $3. The state park system charges an extra $2.50 for full hookups and $2 for extra vehicles. Six-minute showers cost 25¢, but there are many adequate, colder spigots throughout the campgrounds. Some parks allow self-registration; others have rangers register campers at their sites in the evening. Expect long, slow lines if the campground requires registration at the office. Campers who arrive after 9 or 10pm needn't register until a ranger checks the sites in the morning. The gates close at 10pm. Most parks stay open year-round, although some close between October and March. Pets must be on an 8-foot leash and accompanied by owners at all times.

Be aware that several state parks—including Belfair, Birch Bay, Fort Flagler, Steamboat Rock, Fort Canby, Twin Harbors/Grayland Beach, Lake Chelan, Pearrygin Lake, and Moran—accept reservations for Memorial Day through Labor Day and may be filled up weeks in advance, especially during July and August. Reservations can be made beginning in January, and must be made two weeks in advance. Fort Worden, near Port Townsend, also accepts reservations, but only for full-hookup sites.

National forest and DNR sites abound but are impractical for hitchhikers. Drivers can enjoy the solitude and price—while some national forest campgrounds cost $5, most cost $2-4, and many others are free. National park campgrounds accessible by road cost $4-6 and are generally in the best settings. Olympic National Park has some free campgrounds accessible by car. Campgrounds that can be reached only by trail are usually free.

Seattle

A city in the shadow of a mountain, Seattle is both physically and spiritually an odd fusion of alpine candor and urban illusion. Here octogenarian architects tote backpacks, thirtysomething accountants wear clogs, and everyone else paws through the fresh greens and sea creatures at the Pike Place Market. No one culture dominates the city. Like other major cities in the West, Seattle has long welcomed immigrants from Asia. In the International District, Chinese, Japanese, and Vietnamese communities preserve their traditional ways of life without exploitation in the name of tourism.

Seattle the unnoticed beauty spends nearly three quarters of the year blanketed by clouds. Prompted by a hometown organization called Lesser Seattle, many inhabitants ballyhoo their city's reputation as the rain capital of the U.S. in an effort to keep the city to themselves. (In reality, Seattle catches less precipitation each year than quite a few other major cities.) Undaunted by precipitation, residents spend as much time as possible in the great outdoors. Diversions include ferry rides across the Sound to Bainbridge Island and bike rides in Seattle's parks, which are closed to motorized vehicles on Sundays. Visitors will find Seattle a convenient base for longer excursions into the wilderness. The Cascades just east of the city offer fine climbing and spectacular landscapes. And every day 747s (a product of the city's largest employer, Boeing) and ferries leave for the United States' last wilds in Alaska.

A movement is afoot to build—or rebuild—a city that can compete with San Francisco in arts and culture. Local bands like Mud Honey, recorded on the city's Sub Pop label, spew out some of the rawest guitar rock in the country. Residents who support an already lively and responsive cultural life lament efforts to put a polish on what has served the city so well with a minimum of marketing savvy. You can wander among large-scale museums and parks, small galleries, and bistros. There is more to Seattle than is visible from the top of the Space Needle.

Practical Information

Visitor Information: Seattle-King County Visitors Bureau, 666 Stewart St. (461-5890), in the Vance Hotel near Greyhound. Well-stocked with maps, brochures, newspapers, and transit schedules. Information on the rest of WA. Staff is helpful, though somewhat harried during the summer. Open Mon.-Fri. 8:30am-5pm, Sat. 10am-4pm. From 5-7:30pm, call the airport branch at 433-5218. **Tourism BC,** 720 Olive Way, Seattle 98101 (623-5937, 9am-4pm). Information on travel to British Columbia. Open Mon.-Fri. 8:30am-1pm and 2-4:30pm.

Seattle Parks and Recreation Department: 5201 Green Lake Way N., Seattle 98103 (684-4075). Open Mon.-Fri. 8am-6pm. **National Park Service, Pacific Northwest Region,** 83 S. King St., 3rd floor (442-4830).

Currency Exchange: Seattle Airport Hilton, 17260 Pacific Hwy. S. (244-4800). Open 24 hours. Try major downtown banks as well.

Airport: Seattle-Tacoma International (Sea-Tac), on Federal Way, south of Seattle proper. General information 433-5217. **Sea-Tac Visitors Information Center** (433-5218), in the central baggage claim area across from carousel 10. Helps with initial transportation questions. Open daily 9:30am-7:30pm. Foreign visitors should contact **Operation Welcome** (433-5367),

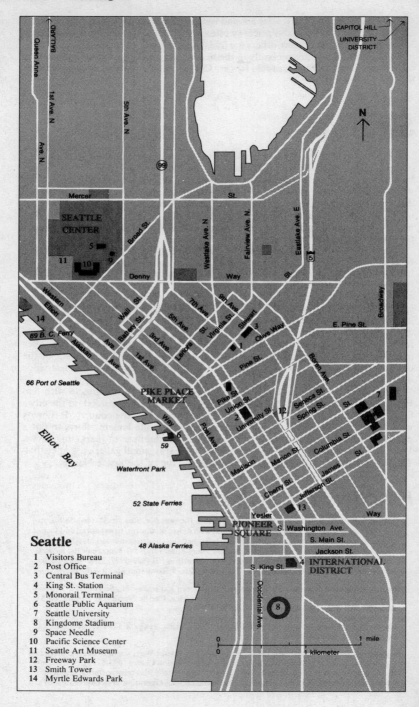

Seattle

1   Visitors Bureau
2   Post Office
3   Central Bus Terminal
4   King St. Station
5   Monorail Terminal
6   Seattle Public Aquarium
7   Seattle University
8   Kingdome Stadium
9   Space Needle
10 Pacific Science Center
11 Seattle Art Museum
12 Freeway Park
13 Smith Tower
14 Myrtle Edwards Park

at the Information Center, where multilingual staff members answer questions on customs, immigration, and foreign language services.

Amtrak: King Street Station, 3rd and Jackson St. (464-1930 or 800-872-7245). Trains to Portland (3 per day, $27), Everett ($6), Tacoma ($9), Centralia ($15), Kelso-Longview ($20), Vancouver, WA ($27), San Francisco ($139), and Chicago ($250). Station open daily 6am-10pm; ticket office 6am-5:30pm.

Greyhound: 8th Ave. and Stewart St. (624-3456). To Sea-Tac Airport (5 per day, $2.50), Vancouver (2 per day, $23), and Portland (2 per day, $23). Open daily 5:45am-7:45pm, 10-10:30pm, and 11:45pm-1:20am.

Green Tortoise Alternative Travel: 324-7433 or 800-227-4766. Buses leave from NE Campus Parkway and 15th Ave. NE in the U District and then swing by the downtown Greyhound station. Trips leave Thurs. and Sun. at 8am for Portland (5 hr., $15), Eugene, OR (7½ hr., $25), Berkeley, CA (26 hr., $49), San Francisco (27 hr., $59), and Los Angeles ($75). Reservations required. See Getting Around By Bus in the General Introduction for more information.

Metro Transit: Customer Assistance Office, 821 2nd Ave., in the Exchange Building downtown. Open Mon. 8am-5:30pm, Tues.-Fri. 8am-5pm. 24-hour information 447-4800. TTY service 447-4826. Complaints and suggestions 447-4824. Fare 55¢; during weekday peak hours 75¢. Buy an All-Day Pass ($2.50, includes 2 monorail tickets) and *really* explore the city. Ride free in the area bordered by Jackson St. on the south, 6th Ave. and I-5 on the east, Battery St. on the north, and the waterfront on the west. Transfers valid for 1 hr. and for Waterfront Streetcars as well.

Ferries: Washington State Ferries, Colman Dock, Pier 52 (464-6400; in WA 800-542-0810 or 800-542-7052). Service to Bremerton on Kitsap Peninsula and Winslow on Bainbridge Island. Ferries leave frequently daily 6am-midnight. Fares from $1.65, car and driver $6.65. **BC Stena Line,** Pier 69, 2700 Alaskan Way (624-6663). Daily cruises on the *Princess Marguerite* and the *Vancouver Island Princess* to Victoria, BC, early May-late Sept. One way $22, round-trip $32; ages over 65 one way $19, round-trip $28; ages 5-11 one way $11, round-trip $16. Bikes $3, motorcycles $11. Car and driver $40.

Car Rental: Five & Ten, 14120 Pacific Hwy. S. (246-4434). $18 per day with 100 free miles plus 5¢ per additional mile. Must be 21 with credit card or $120 deposit. Airport pickup. Open Mon.-Sat. 8am-6pm, Sun. 12:30-6pm. **A-19.95-Rent-A-Car,** 365-1995. $20 per day with 100 free miles plus 15¢ per additional mile. Free delivery. Qualified drivers under 21 welcome; call ahead for appointment.

Automobile Club of Washington (AAA): 330 6th Ave. N. (448-5353). Provides maps, tourbooks, and Triptycks to AAA members. Open Mon.-Fri. 8am-6pm.

Bike Rentals: Gregg's, 7007 Woodlawn Ave. NE (523-1822). 10-speeds and mountain bikes $25 per day; other bikes $3.50 per hr. $20 deposit or credit card. Open Mon.-Fri. 9:30am-9pm, Sat.-Sun. 9:30am-6pm. **The Bicycle Center,** 4529 Sand Point Way (523-8300). 10-speeds only. $4 per hr., $13 per 24 hours. Credit card or license required as deposit. Open Mon.-Thurs. 10am-8pm, Fri.-Sat. 10am-6pm, Sun. noon-5pm. **Alki Bikes,** 2722 Alki Ave. SW (938-3322). Mountain bikes $7 per hr., $17 per day; 10-speeds $4 per hr., $13 per day. Credit card or license required as deposit. Open Mon.-Thurs. 10am-7pm, Fri. 10am-8pm, Sat. 10am-6pm, Sun. 10am-5pm; Oct.-April daily 10am-6pm.

Bookstores: University Book Store, 4326 University Way NE (634-3400). Stocks the entire white male canon and more. Open Mon.-Wed. and Fri.-Sat. 9am-6pm, Thurs. 9am-9pm. **Left Bank Books,** 92 Pike St. (622-0195), in the Pike Place Market. A large leftist bookstore lazily awaiting the revolution in its pleasant and relaxed quarters. Good prices on new and used books. Open Mon.-Sat. 10am-9pm, Sun. noon-5pm. **Shorey's Book Store,** 110 Union St. (624-0221), downtown. One of the oldest and largest bookstores in the Northwest, Shorey's sells new, used, and rare books. Open Mon.-Sat. 9am-6pm, Sun. noon-6pm. **Beatty Book Store,** 1925 3rd Ave. (728-2665). An eye-catching selection of used books, with an especially robust poetry section. Great for browsing. Open Mon.-Sat. 11am-5pm.

Seattle Public Library: 1000 4th Ave. (386-4636). Quiet and relaxed modern facility. Pick up a copy of the SPL *Events* newsletter for listings of free lectures, films, and programs. Tours leave the information desk Wed. and Sat. at 2pm. Open Mon.-Thurs. 9am-9pm, Fri.-Sat. 9am-6pm, Sun. 1-5pm; June-Aug. Mon.-Sat. only.

Ticket Agency: Ticket Master, 201 S. King St. #38, Seattle 98104 (628-0888). Open Mon.-Sat. 10am-10pm, Sun. 10am-6pm.

Jazz Hotline: 102 S. Jackson (624-5277). Recorded information on area happenings.

Arts Hotline: 447-2787.

Laundromat: Downtown-St. Regis, 116 Stewart St., attached to the St. Regis Hotel (see Accommodations). A shady, sometimes dangerous area, so bring a friend and watch your laundry. Open 24 hours.

Crisis Clinics: 461-3222.

Suicide Prevention: 447-3222. 24 hours.

Seattle Rape Relief: 1825 S. Jackson St., #102 (632-RAPE; 632-7273). 24 hours. Crisis counseling, advocacy and prevention training.

University of Washington Women's Information Center: 545-1090. Monthly calendar, networking, and referral for women's groups throughout the Seattle area. Open Mon.-Wed. and Fri. 9am-5pm, Thurs. 9am-8pm.

Senior Citizen Information and Referral: 100 W. Roy (285-3110). Open Mon.-Fri. 9am-5pm.

Travelers Aid: 909 4th Ave., #630 (461-3888), at Marion, in the YMCA. Free services for stranded travelers with lost wallets, lost relatives, or lost heads. Open Mon.-Fri. 8:30am-9pm, Sat.-Sun. and holidays 1-5pm.

Operation Nightwatch: 1315½ 1st Ave. (448-8804). Emergency aid in the downtown area. Street ministry operates nightly 9:30pm-2am. Answering machine 24 hours.

International District Emergency Center: 623-3321. Multilingual counselors available. 24 hours.

Fremont Public Association: 3410 Fremont N. (632-1285). Food bank and free legal clinic. Open Mon.-Fri. 8:30am-5pm.

Poison Information: 526-2121.

AIDS Hotline: 587-4999.

Gay Counseling: Dorian Group, 340 15th Ave. E. (322-1501). Support and referral for gay men and women. Open Mon.-Fri. 9am-midnight.

Lesbian Resource Center: 1208 E. Pine (322-3953). Peer counseling, drop-in center, workshops, and referrals. Open Mon. and Thurs. 2-7pm, Tues. 2-5pm, Wed. 10am-7pm, Fri.-Sat. 1-5pm.

Health Care: Aradia Women's Health Center, 112 Boylston St. E. (323-9388). Appointments necessary. Staff will refer you elsewhere when booked. Open Mon.-Fri. 10am-6pm. **Country Doctor Community Clinic,** 500 19th Ave. E. (461-4503). Family care. Open Mon.-Tues. and Thurs.-Fri. 9am-1pm and 2-5pm, Wed. 1-5pm and 6:30-9pm. **Harborview V.D. Clinic,** Clinic #11, 325 9th Ave. (223-3590), in the Harborview Medical Complex. Walk-in only. Open Mon.-Fri. 7:30am-1pm.

Post Office: Union St. and 3rd Ave. (442-6255), downtown. Open Mon.-Fri. 8am-5:30pm. General Delivery ZIP Code: 98101.

Area Code: 206.

Getting There and Getting Around

Midway between Washington's northern and southern borders, Seattle lies intertwined with the inlets of Puget Sound. The city is easily accessible by **car** via I-5, which runs north-south through the downtown area, and by I-90 from the east, which ends its path from Boston just south of the city center. From I-5, take the Stewart St. or Union St. exit to downtown (including Pioneer Square, Pike Place Market, and the waterfront). Take the Mercer St./Fairview Ave. exit to the Seattle Center. The Denny Way exit leads to Capitol Hill, and farther north, the 45th St. exit will take you to the University District. Getting back on the freeway from the downtown area is a challenge, even for long-time residents. The freeway is always visible; just drive around until you spot a blue I-5 sign.

Transportation options from the mammoth **Seattle-Tacoma International Airport (Sea-Tac)** are numerous. Gray Line **coaches** and **limousines** both will whisk you to and from downtown ($5 each way, $9 round-trip). Metro buses #174 and 194 are cheaper and run daily every half-hour from 6am-1am. (Fare $1.25 during peak hours, 85¢ off-peak; ages under 18 75¢ during peak hours, 55¢ off-peak.)

Seattle is a long, skinny city stretched out north to south between long, skinny **Puget Sound** on the west and long, skinny **Lake Washington** on the east. The head of the city is cut from its torso by Lake Union and a string of locks, canals, and bays. This waterway links the saltwater of Puget Sound with the freshwater of Lake Washington. In the downtown area, avenues run northwest to southeast and streets southwest to northeast. Outside the downtown area everything is vastly simplified: avenues run north to south and streets east to west, with only a few exceptions. The city is split into quadrants: 1000 1st Ave. NW is a far cry from 1000 1st Ave. S. All maps of the city and all telephone books include grids that impart spatial significance to these alphanumeric designations.

Seattle's **Metro Transit** system provides extensive, reliable, and inexpensive service by bus and electric trolley throughout the city and major suburbs. The monorail operates in Seattle Center only. The hassles of downtown traffic jams and expensive parking are avoided by taking the bus, but making connections all across the city often entails long waits, especially in the evening.

Buses operate daily from 6am to 1 or 2am. A few buses offer "night owl service" from 1:30-4:30am. Express buses do not run on weekends. Fares are based on a two-zone system. Zone 1 includes everything within the city limits (65¢ during peak hours, 55¢ off-peak); Zone 2 comprises anything outside the city limits ($1.25 peak, 85¢ off-peak). Ages 5-17 pay 75¢ peak and 55¢ off-peak in either zone. Ages over 64 and disabled people with reduced fare permits pay 25¢ anywhere at all times. Peak hours in both zones are generally weekdays 6-9am and 3-6pm. Everyone rides free in the **Magic Carpet Zone** downtown, from Jackson St. to Battery St. and between 6th Ave. and the waterfront. Drivers usually announce when the bus passes out of the free zone. Transfers are free and valid for one hour anywhere in Zone 1 if you board in that zone, or in either Zone 1 or 2 if you board in Zone 2. By 1990, a transit tunnel should make downtown buses a whole lot faster and more convenient.

A number of pass options are also available. The **All-Day Pass** provides unlimited travel in both zones on Saturday, Sunday, and holidays only. (Available from the driver, $2.50.) Families should note that on Sundays and holidays two children ages 5-15 ride free with an adult. For long-term visitors, the **Monthly Pass Plus** is an inspiration. Two-zone unlimited travel for one month costs $29.25, one-zone just $19.50. The pass is valid at all times and comes with a wealth of discounts on theater tickets, restaurants, museums, health clubs, shops, and travel agencies. Senior citizens and disabled riders can obtain a $2 monthly sticker to go on their reduced fare permit, allowing them to travel anywhere in the system for free. Monthly passes are good on the waterfront streetcar but not on the monorail. All passes, as well as timetables and a free, comprehensive map, are available from the Metro Customer Assistance Office (see Practical Information). **Timetables** and **maps** are also available at public libraries, 7-11 stores, Wendy's, Albertson's, the visitors bureau, and on buses.

Routes and buses equipped with lifts are marked by blue **wheelchair accessibility** signs. **Bike racks** for two bicycles are also placed on the front of a few buses that run from downtown Seattle to Bellevue and Kirkland. During the week, buses #226, 253, and 255 have bike racks; on weekends, buses #210, 266, and 227 are so equipped. Bikes can be loaded only at designated stops, so check with the Metro ahead of time.

Metro slides easily into Seattle's outskirts, covering the whole of King County as far east as North Bend and Carnation, south to Enumclaw, and north to Snohomish County, where Metro bus #6 hooks up with Community Transit. This line runs to Everett, Stanwood, and well into the Cascades. Another link occurs in Federal Way, where Metro bus #174 connects to Tacoma's Pierce County System. (See Tacoma and Near Seattle for more information on those buses.)

Accommodations

Staying in downtown Seattle, as in so many other American metropolises, reduces to a choice between spending in the vicinity of $100 per night or bedding down in an unsafe and unpleasant dive. The Seattle International Hostel is undoubtedly the best option for the budget traveler. For those tired of the urban scene, the Vashon Island Hostel is ideal. (Take bus #54, 118, or 119 from downtown. See Tacoma Accommodations.) **Pacific Bed and Breakfast,** 701 NW 60th St., Seattle 98107 (784-0539), can set you up with an interesting B&B in the $30-85 range. (Open Mon.-Fri. 9am-5pm.)

Downtown

Seattle International Hostel (AYH), 84 Union St. (622-5443), at Western Ave. 125 beds in sterile rooms, immaculate facilities, plenty of modern amenities, and a friendly, knowledge-able staff. Check-in may be tedious and security tight, but the location is convenient and the crowd alluring. Loads of information about Seattle in the library and on the brochure racks. The view of the bay will mollify your temper when the traffic gets too loud. Sleep sacks required. Open daily 7-10am and 5pm-midnight. Extended curfew on weekend nights (until 2am; $1 fee). Members $11, nonmembers $14.

YMCA, 909 4th Ave. (382-5000), near the Madison St. intersection. Men and women welcome; must be over 17. Luxury lodgings for the budget traveler. Good location. Free local calls from phone in room, TV lounge on each floor, laundry facilities, and use of swimming pool and fitness facilities. Well-run, clean, and friendly. No curfew. Singles from $22. Doubles from $26. Weekly: singles from $78, doubles from $96. AYH members pay $12 for a dorm bunk, or 10% off the regular price.

YWCA, 1118 5th Ave. (461-4888), near the YMCA. Take any 4th Ave. bus to Seneca St. Women only, ages under 18 require advance arrangement. Great security and location, but an older facility than the YMCA with smaller rooms. Housing desk open 24 hours. No curfew. Singles $22, with bath $27. Doubles $33, with bath $38. Weekly: singles $124, with bath $150. Additional charge for health center use. Key deposit $2.

Commodore Hotel, 2013 2nd Ave. (448-8868), at Virginia. Where the hostel sends its overflow. Those with AYH card and sleep sack can get a dorm bed for $9. Tight security and fairly clean. Private room for 2 $31.50.

Pacific Hotel, 317 Marion St. (622-3985), between 3rd and 4th Ave., across from the YMCA. Quiet and safe location—not the usual downtown sleaze. The small rooms are very small but the large singles can hold 2 people. No visitors after 10pm. Small singles $24. Large singles $25, with bath $30. Doubles $27, with bath $32. Key deposit $2.

St. Regis Hotel, 116 Stewart St. (448-6366), conveniently located 2 blocks from the Pike Place Market. The rooms are dark and your lamp may not work, but the place is clean and the management pleasant. The neighborhood, however, is not the safest after dark. Laundromat on the first floor. Singles $22, with bath $28. Doubles $27, with bath $34.

Other Neighborhoods

Hillside Motel, 2451 Aurora Ave. N. (285-7860). Take bus #6 or 16. One of a number of relatively inexpensive motels along noisy Aurora. 11 units with hot plates. Singles $23. Doubles $27.

Park Plaza Hotel, 4401 Aurora Ave. N. (632-2101). Another option along this endless strip of car dealerships and fast-food joints. Clean rooms, in-room coffee, cable TV. Singles $25. Doubles $27.

Nites Inn, 11746 Aurora Ave. N. (365-3216). Yet another Aurora abode. Large rooms. Movie channel. Singles $30. Doubles $32.

Bush Hotel, 621 S. Jackson (623-8079). Take bus #1, 7, or 14. In the heart of the International District. 24-hour desk staff. Newly remodeled, but still not particularly presidential or safe. Singles from $17. Doubles from $20. Key deposit $5.

Motel 6, 18900 47th Ave. S. (241-1648), exit 152 off I-5. Take bus #170 during peak hours; otherwise take #174 to Sea-Tac. Noisy but clean. Pool and TV. Singles $25. Doubles $32.

The College Inn, 4000 University Way NE (633-4441). European-style B&B in the University District. Breakfast served in a lovely refinished attic. Antiques and individual wash basins in every room. Service not always reliable. Singles from $44. Doubles from $52.

Food

By a Sound full of fish and in a state tacked in place by orchards, Seattle rivals San Francisco in culinary excitement and eclecticism. City center eateries range from ritzy shops along 5th Ave. to skid-row coffee houses along 1st. Avoid the many boring diners and pseudo-health-food rip-offs. Seafood and produce here are always fresh in season. If you want to eat in, buy fish right off the boats at **Fisherman's Wharf,** at NW 54th St. and 30th Ave. NW in Ballard, along bus route #43. The wharf is usually open from 8am to 3 or 4pm. Or visit one of Seattle's active **food coops,** such as those located at 6518 Fremont N. in Greenlake and at 6504 20th NE in the Ravenna District north of the university. Also in Ravenna is a fine produce stand, **Rising Sun Farms and Produce,** 6505 15th Ave. NE (524-9741).

Pike Place Market

Farmers have been selling their own produce here since 1907, when angry Seattle citizens demanded an alternative to the middle merchant. A nasty fire in 1941, the draft, and the internment of Japanese-Americans during World War II almost did away with the market, but in the last 15 years, a rehabilitation drive has restored it. Crazy fishmongers and produce sellers yell at customers and at each other while street performers do their thing and unsuspecting tourists wonder what they've walked into. Seattlites accept the whole affair with equanimity and sail through at day's end in search of something special for dinner. The market's interesting conglomeration of self- and full-service restaurants allows you to avoid the crowds. Chic shops and restaurants develop in increasing numbers, but the farmers and fishmongers are the mainstays of the market. Hunt around for end-of-the-day specials on produce, and call the **Produce Hotline** (344-7988) for tips on best buys. The monthly *Pike Place Market News,* available free throughout the market, has a map of the market, and the low-down on the latest events, new merchants, and old-timers. An information table in front of the bakery in the main market can answer your questions. (Table and market open Mon.-Sat. 9am-6pm; many stands also open Sun.)

El Puerco Lloron, 1501 Western Ave. (624-0541), at the 2nd level of the Hillclimb overlooking the waterfront. Some of the best Mexican food in Seattle—no nachos here. The entire place has been transported from Tijuana, down to the wooden masks, bird cages, Mexican beer bottle *piñatas,* card tables, and folding chairs. *Tacos de carne asada* (charcoal-broiled flank steak in soft tortillas) $4. Small helpings. Open Mon.-Sat. 11:30am-9pm, Sun. noon-8pm.

Soundview Cafe (623-5700), on the mezzanine level in the Main Arcade. This wholesome self-serve sandwich-and-salad bar offers fresh food, a spectacular view of the Sound, and occasional poetry readings. Buy a large green salad ($3), try the West African nut stew ($2), or bring a brown-bag lunch—the cafe provides public seating as a public service. Open Mon.-Sat. 7am-5pm, Sun. 9am-2pm.

The Market Cafe, 1523 1st Ave. (624-2598). A good diner with big portions. Breakfasts are especially overwhelming—the $5 *huevos rancheros* keep you going until the next morning. Lunches $3.50-4.50. They make their own salsa here, and the coffee is always fresh. Open Mon.-Fri. 7am-5pm, Sat. 8am-5pm.

Blue Goose Cafe, 94 Stewart St. (441-4121). Black-and-white checkerboard tiles accented with occasional brushstrokes of color distinguish this bright and trendy cafe from the rest. The pricy breakfast special ($3.75) isn't so special, but the hot 8-grain cereal ($2) and fresh muffins and scones (95¢) make a perfect and affordable morning meal. Open Mon.-Fri. 7am-4pm, Sat. 7:40am-4pm, Sun. 7:30am-2pm.

Copacabana, 1520½ Pike Pl. (622-6359), in the Triangle Market. Watch the harried crowds below from your table on the veranda. Bolivian *salteñas,* the house specialty, are meat and vegetable pies ($3). Sample *paella* madness for $7.50. Open daily 11:30am-4pm.

World Class Chili, 1411 1st Ave. (623-3678), in the South Arcade. Order up a Texas-sized portion of Seattle's best chili here ($3.19) and quickly grab a stool at the crowded bar. Four different kinds to choose from; California-style contains chicken instead of beef. Wash it all down with a cold Michelob on tap ($1.25). Open Mon.-Sat. 11am-6pm.

Athenian Inn, 1517 Pike Pl. (624-7166), in the main market. Dinners cost up to $12, although a hefty plate of fish and chips is only $4.25. You may just want to skip the food and go for the caffeine and alcohol. Coffee 60¢ (refills 15¢). The 16 varieties of beer on tap (and pages of bottled beer) are half-price at the bar 7am-noon. Highballs from the well 99¢ noon-7pm. Open daily 7am-7pm.

The Pink Door, 1919 Post Alley (682-3241), in the alley. Unmarked; look for the pink door. A tastefully decorated Italian restaurant, worth the price. Dinners cost up to $12, but you can eat lunch for $6. Outdoor dining. Open Tues.-Sat. 11:30am-10pm.

Roos' Market, 1543 Pike Pl. (624-2945), in the Triangle Market on the corner of Pine St. 50¢ for day-old bread, rye or pita 55¢. Open Mon.-Sat. 9am-6pm.

El Mercado Latino, 1514 Pike Pl. (622-1033), just behind the Triangle Market. This Caribbean, South American, and Creole grocery carries at least 5 different kinds of homemade hot sauce, each for about $2.50. The corn chips are a starchy mainstay at $1.40 per bag. Open Mon.-Sat. 9am-6pm.

International District

Between the Kingdome and I-5, Seattle's International District crowds together immigrants—and chefs—from China, Japan, the Philippines, and Southeast Asia. Fierce competition keeps prices low and quality high. Don't shy away from a shabby exterior—inside you may find the tastiest meals. **Uwajimaya,** the largest Asian retail store in the Pacific Northwest, is at 519 6th Ave. S. (624-6248). A huge selection of Japanese staples such as rice, fish, and soup base, a wide variety of dried and/or instant foods (great for camping), a sushi bar, and a bakery make this Seattle institution a must. Don't forget the gift shop and bookstore upstairs. (Open daily 9am-6pm). Take bus #1, 7, or 14.

Ying Hei Restaurant, 664 S. King St. (622-4229). A spacious place decorated with paper lanterns and a fish tank. Excellent barbecue and soy sauce chicken. Try the individual portion soups or shrimp with black bean sauce ($5.75). Good seafood selection. Few choices for the vegetarian. Open Mon.-Wed. and Fri.-Sun. 11:30am-8:30pm, Thurs. 11:30am-4pm.

Viet My Restaurant, 129 Prefontaine Pl. S. (464-8681). Not the place for a first date, but consistently delicious Vietnamese food at great prices. Try *la lot* (beef in rice pancakes, $3.50), or shrimp curry ($4.25). Open Mon.-Sat. 11am-8pm.

Lao Chorearn Restaurant, 121 Prefontaine Pl. S. (223-9456). Exquisite Laotian cuisine. Slightly pricier (albeit slightly snazzier) than the Viet My next door. Experience *soom tun* (green papaya salad with peanuts, shrimp, chili, and lime) for $3. Open Mon.-Fri. 11am-3pm and 5-9pm, Sat. 1-9pm.

Phnom Penh Noodle Soup House, 414 Maynard Ave. S. (682-5690). Excellent Cambodian cuisine. Head to the upstairs dining room for a good view of the park and a spicy, steaming bowl of *battambany* noodles ($3.75). What appears to be an extensive menu simmers down to 7 wild varieties of soup. Open Mon.-Fri. 8:30am-7pm, Sat.-Sun. 9am-7pm.

Ho Ho Seafood Restaurant, 653 S. Weller St. (382-9671). Elegant yet laid-back. Generous portions. Hungry diners should try the whole steamed rock cod ($10). Open Sun.-Thurs. 11am-1am, Fri.-Sat. 11am-2am.

House of Hong Restaurant, 409 8th Ave. S. (622-7997), at Jackson. May not look like much from the outside, but nonetheless serves up the best Chinese food in the city. Dinners around $10. *Dim sum* 11am-3pm. Open Sun.-Thurs. 11am-10pm, Fri.-Sat. 11am-midnight. Reservations recommended.

Pioneer Square

Historic Pioneer Square is an area of *haute couture* and high prices. The best strategy is to pack a lunch and picnic in Occidental Park or Waterfall Park, along with the myriad street people.

Ivar's Fish Bar, Pier 54 (624-6852), on the waterfront. One of a string of seafood restaurants owned by and named for Seattle celebrity Ivar Haglund. This locals' favorite charges $2.89 for fish and chips, 5¢ extra for packets of ketchup and tartar sauce. Dine with the gulls and pigeons in outdoor (covered) booths. Open daily 11am-2am.

Elliott Bay Book Company and Cafe, 101 S. Main St. (682-6664). Free coffee refills to get you through the duller patches of *Middlemarch*. Sandwiches $3.50-4.50. Bookstore open Mon.-Sat. 9am-11pm, Sun. noon-6pm. Café open Mon.-Fri. 7am-10:30pm, Sat. 10am-10:30pm, Sun. noon-5pm.

The Bakery, 214 1st Ave. S. (622-3644). Soups ($1.25 per cup, $2.30 per bowl), sandwiches ($3.35-3.80), and heated cinnamon rolls ($1.16). Come early—these famous pastries sell out fast. Eat at outdoor tables in the Grand Arcade or Occidental Park. Open Mon.-Fri. 7am-6pm, Sat.-Sun. 9am-5pm. Espresso ($1.50) bar open daily 11am-5pm.

Trattoria Mitchelli, 84 Yesler Way (623-3883), toward the waterfront. Good breakfasts. Lunch on a large antipasto ($5) or the pasta of the week ($4-5). Dinners from $9. Open Mon. 7am-11pm, Tues.-Fri. 7am-4am, Sat. 8am-4am, Sun. 8am-11pm.

Umberto Ristorante Italiano, 100 S. King (621-0575). Another chi-chi Italian place with live entertainment. Go for happy hour (5-7pm) when the drinks are $1 and the hors d'oeuvres free. Express lunches from $4, full dinners from $6. Pizza and pasta at the bar when the kitchen is closed. Open Mon.-Thurs. 11:30am-2:30pm and 5-10pm, Fri. 11:30am-2:30pm and 5-11pm, Sat. 5-11pm, Sun. 4:30-9pm.

Fran-Glor's Creole Cafe, 547 1st Ave. (682-1578). Genuine gumbo with crabmeat, sausage, and who knows what else. The bric-a-brac and the jazz are classic New Orleans. Lunches from $4.50. Open Mon.-Sat. noon-9:30pm.

Alvin's Restaurant, 1600 1st Ave. (441-6184). Not exactly in Pioneer Sq. proper, but close enough (and good enough) to merit a stroll. How you dare miss the Filipino breakfast ($3). Open Mon.-Fri. 7am-7pm.

Capitol Hill

Climb the low hill northeast of downtown and scout the blocks along Broadway between Seattle University and Volunteer Park for Fellini-esque frolics. The imaginative shops, elegant clubs, and espresso houses which drape Capitol Hill are particularly popular among Seattle's gay community. Follow the dance steps on the sidewalk to hoity-toity night spots, or skirt the edges of the area for more reasonably priced entertainment. Bus #7 goes along Broadway, #10 along 15th St.

Deluxe Bar and Grill, 625 Broadway E. (324-9697). A jazzy indoor/outdoor joint where you can enjoy great breakfasts for under $4. Pound a pint of Bud Lite or Rainier for $1 during HaHa hours—Mon.-Tues. and Thurs.-Fri. 3-7pm. Open Mon.-Thurs. 10am-11pm, Fri. 10am-1am, Sat. 9am-1am, Sun. 9am-11pm. Bar open Mon.-Wed. 10am-1am, Thurs.-Sat. 9am-2am, Sun. 9am-1am.

Andy's Cafe, 214 Broadway E. (323-2554). The gaudy lamps, soiled menus, and low prices here seem out of place among the glitzy neon cafes along Broadway. Nonetheless, this wood-paneled diner is packed around the clock. Try the roast tom turkey dinner ($4) or the #4 breakfast special (3 pancakes, 2 eggs, hash browns, and toast, $2.65). Open daily 6am-9pm.

Piecora's Pizzeria, 1401 E. Madison St. (322-9411), a few blocks southeast of most of the action. Your basic New York-style pizza parlor, replete with olive oil and Brooklyn accents. Big 17-in. pizzas $8, toppings 75¢-$1 each. Open daily 5-11pm.

Kokeb Restaurant, 926 12th Ave. (322-0485). Behind Seattle University at the far south end of Capitol Hill, near the First Hill neighborhood. An intriguing Ethiopian restaurant that serves hot and spicy meat stews on *enjera*, a soft bread. Colorful decor. Lunch $3.50-5, dinner $5-6.50. Open Mon.-Thurs. 11:30am-9pm, Fri.-Sat. 4-10pm, Sun. 11:30am-3pm and 6-9pm.

The Cause Celebre, 524 E. 15th Ave. (323-1888), at Mercer St., at the other end of Capitol Hill. The special province of Seattle's well-fed left. Stay away if you don't like feminist music or neighboring discussions on Bob Avakian and the struggle for Chinese succession. The homemade ice cream and baked goods are sublime. Free evening entertainment. Great Sun. brunch. Lunch sandwiches $3-6. Open Mon.-Thurs. 7:30am-9:30pm, Fri. 7:30am-midnight, Sat. 8am-midnight, Sun. 8am-9:30pm.

University District

The titanic **University of Washington,** between Union and Portage Bays (north of downtown), supports a colorful neighborhood of funky shops, ethnic restaurants, and above all, coffeehouses. Most of the good restaurants, jazz clubs, cinemas, and cafes are within a few blocks of **University Way.** To reach the university, take buses #70-74 from downtown. Buses #7 and 43 get there via Capitol Hill.

Last Exit on Brooklyn, 3930 Brooklyn Ave. NE (545-9873), 1 block west of University Way at NE 40th St. Sandwiches $2-3. Hang out forever and play backgammon with the local musicians. Open mike Mon. at 9pm. Open Mon.-Thurs. 7am-midnight, Fri. 7am-2am, Sat. 11am-2am, Sun. 11am-midnight.

Lox, Stock and Bagel, 4552 University Way NE (634-3144). In spite of a somewhat pricy menu—bagels go for 75¢ each—Huskies flock to the Stock nightly. $1 well drinks and $2.75 pitchers between 4-7pm may contribute to their zeal. Your best option is the $4 lunch special. High ceilings and low hanging lamps add to the cool, relaxed atmosphere. Open Mon.-Sat. 9am-2am.

Espresso Roma Cafe, 4201 University Way NE (633-2534). Rather like an undecorated basement. Students and professors study, chat, and watch the crowds walk by from outdoor streetside tables. Croissants 95¢. Interesting nonalcoholic drinks. Open Mon.-Fri. 7am-midnight, Sat.-Sun. 8am-midnight.

Asia Deli, 4235 University Way NE (632-2364). No corned beef here—this atypical deli offers quick service and generous portions of delicious Vietnamese and Thai food (mostly of the noodle variety). Try the vegetable *pad thai* ($3), and don't forget the banana with tapioca in coconut milk (90¢) for a superb palate cleanser. Open Mon.-Sat. 11am-9pm, Sun. noon-8pm.

Arnold's Fun Food and Games, 3947 University Way NE (633-2181). An updated version of its *Happy Days* namesake, this cheap hamburger joint has become a hangout for local Joanies and Potsies. Two eggs, hash browns, and toast for $2, a doughnut and coffee for 25¢, and the all-American cheeseburger and fries for $1.50. You can waste all the money you save on the virtual jungle of video games. Open Sun.-Thurs. 7am-midnight, Fri.-Sat. 7am-2am.

Grand Illusion Cinema and Espresso, 1405 50th St. NE (525-9573), at University Way. Relaxing coffeehouse with an overstuffed green couch in front of the working fireplace. Small wooden terrace and in-house theater (see Entertainment). Hot and cold coffees and other drinks 60¢-$1.75. Open Mon.-Sat. 8:30am-11:30pm, Sun. 8:30am-10:30pm.

The Unicorn Restaurant, 4550 University Ave. (634-1115). Renowned for its large collection of obscure English ales ($2.50-3), the Unicorn also cooks up a mean steak-and-kidney pie ($7). Open Mon.-Sat. 11:30am-10pm, Sun. 4-9pm.

Other Neighborhoods

Hattie's Hat Restaurant, 5231 Ballard Ave. NW (784-0175), in the southern part of Ballard, just a few blocks from the canal. A funky hangout with a bright dining room, a dark quiet bar, and a weird Swedish mural looming over the counter. Popular with Ballard's locals. Sandwiches $2-5, Swedish pancakes $3.10, dinners $4-11. Open Mon.-Thurs. 6am-8pm, Fri.-Sat. 24 hours, Sun. 8am-2pm. Bar open daily 6am-2am.

Zesto's Burger and Fish House, 6416 15th NW (783-3350). This Ballard High hangout has been serving students and frying fish since 1952, and even local fishermen rave about Zesto's "oriental-style" batter. Filling fish and chips dinners run $5.25, and unique "snowshoe" fries make the deal a good one. Good burgers ($1.70-4.85), too. Open Mon.-Fri. 9am-11pm, Sat.-Sun. 11am-11pm.

Burk's Cafe-Creole and Cajun, 5411 Ballard Ave. (782-0091). A relaxed Creole cafe. Lunch sandwiches reasonably priced at $5, dinners $7-11. If your palate can endure the infamous southern vegetable, try the chicken, sausage, and okra gumbo ($8). Open Mon.-Sat. 11am-10pm.

Greenlake Jake's, 7918 E. Greenlake Dr. N. (523-4747), on the north shore of Green Lake. A favorite drive-in (or roll-in) for the lake's runners, skateboarders, and roller skaters. Tasty burgers. Gourmands can try the mushroom burger ($2.75). Blueberry muffins (2 for $1.15) at breakfast. Open Mon.-Sat. 7am-9pm, Sun. 8am-9pm.

Spud, 6860 E. Greenlake Way N., across the lake from Greenlake Jake's. Serving the Seattle staple of fish and chips ($2) for 52 years. Clams and chips $2.10. Open Sun.-Thurs. 11am-10pm, Fri.-Sat. 11am-11pm.

The Dog House, 2230 7th Ave. (624-2741), 3 blocks north of Greyhound between Bell and Blanchard St. This 24-hour Seattle institution (featuring a classic sexist 1934 mural) is perfect for the night you arrive at Greyhound with no place to go. The waitresses will call you "honey" and Dick Dickerson will serenade you on the electric organ Wed.-Sun. 9pm-1:30am. Although the diner caters almost exclusively to locals, the prices run high. Try the Mutt Burger ($3.50). Full bar open daily 6am-2am.

Julia's 14 Carrot Cafe, 2305 Eastlake E. (324-1442), between Lake Union and I-5 at Lynn St. Julia's has the only edible nut burgers ($3.50) in the world—they don't crumble, dry up, or stick in the back of your throat. Great baked goods, too. Open Mon. 7am-2pm, Tues.-Sat. 7am-10pm, Sun. 8am-3pm.

Sights and Activities

If you are a latter-day Phineas Fogg with only a day to spare in Seattle, despair not. In one day of dedicated sightseeing you can cover a good deal of the city. Many sights are within walking distance of each other, or are within Metro's free zone. You can easily explore the market, waterfront, Pioneer Square, and International District in one excursion, or do the city's museums in a day. But how you dare ignore Seattle's soothing natural scenery! Head out to Seward Park for a late afternoon dip in Lake Washington, or cycle along the lake's western bank.

The Waterfront, Downtown, and Seattle Center

The **Pike Place Market,** at the bottom of Pike St. between 1st and Western Ave., somehow crowds produce stands, fish vendors, bakeries, craft sellers, restaurants, and boutiques into a 3-block indoor/outdoor area. An information table at the corner of Pike St. and Pike Place (in front of the bakery) provides information about market history as well as shop (and rest room) locations. (Market open Mon.-Sat. 9am-6pm. Information booth open Mon.-Sat. 10am-5pm.) **Freeway Park,** a delightful oasis of greenery on Seneca St. at 7th Ave., is a smashing place for picnicking. Its waterfall and playground are built right on top of I-5, in the midst of Seattle's high-rises. At the south end of the market begins the **Pike Place Hillclimb,** a set of staircases leading down past more chic shops and ethnic restaurants to Alaskan Way and the **waterfront.** (An elevator is also available.)

The waterfront docks once played Ellis Island to shiploads of gold coming in from the 1897 Klondike gold rush. Today, on a pier full of shops and restaurants, the credit card is firmly established as standard currency. On Pier 59 at the base of the hillclimb, the **Seattle Aquarium** (625-4357) rationcinates the history of marine life in Puget Sound and the effects of tidal action. Outdoor tanks re-create the ecosystems of salt marshes and tidal pools, employing marine birds and mammals as well as members of the finny tribe. Don't miss the daily 11:30am feeding. (Open daily 10am-7pm; Labor Day-Memorial Day 10am-5pm. Admission $3.25, senior citizens and ages 13-18 $1.50, ages 6-12 75¢.)

Abreast the Aquarium is Seattle's big-screen movie theater, the **Omnidome** (622-1868). The films shown here on the half-hour are short (30 min.), science-oriented dramas designed especially for the giant, wrap-around screen. *The Eruption of Mt. St. Helens* provides a haunting look at the events of May 18, 1980. It alternates with *Nomads of the Deep,* a film about frolicking humpback whales. (Films shown daily 10am-8pm. Tickets to 2 movies $5, senior citizens and students $4, ages 6-12 $3; with admission to aquarium $7.50, students $5.)

Pier 59 and the aquarium are geographically in the middle of the waterfront district. Explore north or south by foot or by **streetcar**. The circa 1927 cars were imported from Melbourne, Australia in 1982; Seattle sold its original streetcars to San Francisco, where they now enjoy international fame. (Streetcars run every 20 min. Mon.-Sat. 7am-11pm, Sun. 10:15am-9:45pm; in winter every ½-hr. until 6pm. 60¢ for 1½ hour of unlimited travel. One-day, three-day, and monthly Metro passes are good on the streetcar. On Sun. ages under 16 ride free with 1 paying passenger.)

North of Pier 70's expensive shopping arcade, **Myrtle Edwards Park** stretches along the water to the granaries on Piers 90 and 91. Despite lovely grassy areas and equally good views, Myrtle Edwards is frequented less than other downtown parks (perhaps it's the name).

Four blocks inland from Pier 70 you'll find **Seattle Center.** The 74-acre, pedestrians-only park was originally constructed for the 1962 World's Fair and still attracts thousands of sightseers daily. Located between Denny Way and W. Mercer St., and 1st and 5th Ave., the Center has eight gates, each equipped with a model of the Center and a key to its facilities. Take the monorail from Pine St. and 5th Ave. downtown. (Fare 60¢, senior citizens and children 25¢.) The **Pacific Science Center** (443-2001), within the park, houses a **laserium** (443-2850) and IMAX theater (443-4629) in addition to exhibits on modern technology. (Science Center open daily 10am-6pm; Labor Day-June Mon.-Fri. 10am-5pm, Sat.-Sun. 10am-6pm. Admission $4.50, senior citizens and students $3.50, ages 2-5 $1.50. Laser shows $5, $2.50 on Tues. evenings.) The **Space Needle** (443-2100), sometimes known as "the world's tackiest monument," has an observation tower and restaurant. On clear days, the view from atop is without peer; on cloudy days, forget it. (Admission $4.25, ages 5-12 $2.) After working up an appetite in the Center's amusement park, head next door to the **Center House,** home to dozens of shops and restaurants. Exciting food offerings range from Mongolian to Mexican. (Open in summer daily 11am-9pm; in spring 11am-7pm; in fall and winter Sun.-Thurs. 11am-6pm, Fri.-Sat. 11am-9pm.)

Although Seattlites generally disdain the Center (leaving it to tourists and suburbanites), they do turn out for the frequently held performances, special exhibits, and festivals. For recorded information regarding special events and permanent attractions at the Center, call 684-7165. The Center has an **information desk** (625-4234) on the court level in the Center House. (Open daily 11am-7pm.) The visitors bureau (447-4244) also runs an **information booth** next to the monorail terminal. (Open Memorial Day-Labor Day daily 10am-6pm.) See Seasonal Events for information on the ever-popular Folklife Festival and Bumbershoot, both held annually at the Center.

Pier 57 is also home to Seattle's new maritime museum, **The Water Link** (624-4975). Wallow in Seattle's waterfront history or probe the geological mysteries of the ocean floor. (Open May 17-Sept. 30 Tues.-Sun. noon-6pm. Admission $1.) From Pier 56, **Harbor Tours** (623-1445) leaves for a one-hour cruise south to look at the docks and Coast Guard outposts around Harbor Island (June-Sept. 5 per day; May and Oct. 3 per day. Fare $6.50, senior citizens $6, children $3). A recent entrant into the historic harbor tour niche, **Major Marine Tours** (783-8873) departs on the hour from Pier 54. (June-Sept. fare $6.50, senior citizens $5.50, children $4.)

Colman Dock, Pier 52, is now the departure point for the Washington State Ferries to Bremerton and Bainbridge Island (see Getting There). Taking a ferry to Bremerton or Winslow (on Bainbridge Island) is a glorious way to see Seattle, even if you just turn around and come back. Round-trip fare is $3.30 for a pedestrian, $6.15 for a car and driver. The dock has gone through a number of incarnations and was at one time the home base of the Mosquito Fleet. Pick up a free copy of the *Historic Old Colman Dock* pamphlet inside the terminal for stories of the dock's—and Seattle's—past. Today, Colman Dock pales in comparison to its picaresque past; in fact, it's pretty boring.

Pioneer Square and International District

From the waterfront, it's just 2 blocks to historic Pioneer Square, where 19th-century warehouses and office buildings were restored in a tantrum of prosperity during the 70s. The *Compleat Browser's Guide to Pioneer Square,* available in area bookstores, provides a short history and walking tour, not to mention listings of all the shops, galleries, restaurants, and museums in the square. After an aborted attempt by pioneers to claim the land on Alki Beach (now West Seattle) in 1851, the settlers settled instead on the site which is today Pioneer Square; this area quickly became Seattle's first city center. "Doc" Maynard, a notorious early resident, gave a plot of land here to one Henry Yesler, on the condition that he build a steam-powered lumber mill. No sooner said than done, the mill was fed with logs dragged down the steep grade of Yesler Way, earning that street the epithet "Skid Row." Years later, the center of activity moved north, sending Pioneer Square into decline and popularizing "skid row" as a nationwide term for a neighborhood of utter poverty and despair.

When Seattle nearly burned to the ground in 1889, an ordinance was passed to raise the city 35 feet. At first, shops below the elevated streets remained open for business and were moored to the upper city by an elaborate network of stairs. In 1907 the city moved upstairs permanently, and the underground city was sealed off. Tours of the vast underworld are now given by **Bill Speidel's Underground Tours** (682-4646). Speidel spearheaded the movement to save Pioneer Square from the apocalypse of renewal. The tours are informative and irreverent glimpses at Seattle's beginnings; just ignore the rats that infest the tunnels. Tours (1½ hr.) leave from Doc Maynard's Pub at 610 1st Ave. (March-Sept. 6 per day 10am-6pm. Reservations strongly recommended. Admission $4, senior citizens $2.75, students $3.25. ages 6-12 $2.)

Once back above ground, learn about the next major event in the city's history at the **Klondike Gold Rush National Historic Park,** 117 S. Main St. (442-7220). Not really a park, this "interpretive center" (as the Park Service would have it) depicts the lives and fortunes of the miners. A slide show weaves together seven photographers' recordings of the mostly unsuccessful ventures of the miners. Saturday and Sunday at 3pm, the park screens Charlie Chaplin's 1925 classic, *The Gold Rush.* (Open daily 9am-5pm. Free.)

While in Pioneer Square, browse through the 31 local art galleries, distributors for many of the Northwest's prominent artists. A few of the square's notable galleries are the **Flury and Co. Gallery,** 322 1st Ave. S. (587-0260), which features vintage photographic portraits of Native American life (open Tues.-Sat. 11am-6pm); **Linda Farris Gallery,** 320 2nd Ave. S. (623-1110), which promotes innovative Seattle artists (open Tues.-Sat. 11:30am-5pm, Sun. 1-5pm); **Native Design Gallery,** 108 Jackson St. (624-9985), housing imported art from Africa, South America, and India (open Tues.-Sat. 11am-5pm); and **Sacred Circle Gallery,** 607 1st Ave. (285-4425), guardian of a loudly applauded collection of contemporary Native American art (open Tues.-Sat. 9am-5pm). Stop in also at the **Seattle Indian Arts and Crafts Shop,** 113 Cherry St. (621-0655), run by the American Indian Women's Service League. A nonprofit business, the shop features Native American art of the Pacific Northwest. Proceeds go toward scholarships for Native American students and food and shelter for needy Native Americans. (Open Mon.-Fri. 10am-5pm, Sat. 11am-4pm.) Another important landmark of the Pioneer Square area is the **Smith Tower,** for years the tallest building in the city. The 21-story tower was commissioned in 1911 by L. C. Smith at a total cost of $1,500,000. The building was later owned by local celebrity Ivar Haglund, who launched a popular fish-and-chips empire.

Many Seattlites consider the **Kingdome,** down 1st Ave. (340-2100 or 340-2128), the only serious challenger to the Boeing field as the city's ugliest building. Tours of the stadium include a stop at the **Royal Brougham Sports Museum.** (Tours leave daily from Gate D on the north side of the dome at 11am, 1pm, and 3pm; Nov.-

April at 1 and 3pm. Otherwise, stadium only open during sporting events. Admission $2.50, senior citizens and children $1.25.)

Three blocks east of Pioneer Square, up Jackson on King St., is Seattle's **International District**. Though sometimes still called Chinatown by Seattlites, this area is home to peoples from all over Asia. The 45-minute slideshow *Seattle's Other History*, presented at the **Nippon Kan Theater**, 628 Washington St. (624-8801), explores the years of discrimination endured by Seattle's Asian community. (Presentation given whenever large enough groups accumulate; call ahead. Admission $2.) Whether or not you see the show, pick up the brochure *Chinatown Tour: Seattle's Other History*, which is available for free at the Nippon Kan Theater, itself a good place to start your tour of the district. The theater was built in 1909 to house weddings and cultural events. An advertising screen dating from the same period is painted with the symbols and names of various Japanese merchants, some of whom are still doing business in the district today. The Nippon Kan fell into disrepair during World War II and was only restored and reopened in 1981.

Behold also the **Tsutakawa Sculpture** at the corner of S. Jackson and Maynard St., the gigantic dragon mural in **Hing Hay Park** at S. King and Maynard St., and especially the **Wing Luke Memorial Museum**, 414 8th St. (623-5124). The tiny museum houses constantly changing exhibits of Asian folk art, which are well displayed and explained. Occasional free demonstrations of traditional crafts are also scheduled. (Open Tues.-Fri. 11am-4:30pm, Sat.-Sun. noon-4pm. Admission $1.50, students and children 50¢.)

Capitol Hill

Capitol Hill inspires extreme reactions from both its residents and its neighbors. The former wouldn't live anywhere else, while the latter never go near the place. The district's leftist and gay communities set the tone for its nightspots (see Entertainment), while the retail outlets include a large number of collectives and radical bookstores. Saunter down Broadway or its cross streets to window-shop, or walk a few blocks east and north for a stroll down the hill's lovely residential streets, lined with well-maintained Victorian homes. Bus #10 runs along 15th St. and #7 cruises along Broadway.

Volunteer Park, between 11th and 17th Ave. at E. Ward St., north of the main Broadway activity, beckons tourists to travel east of the city center. Named for the "brave volunteers who gave their lives to liberate the oppressed people of Cuba and the Philippines," the park boasts lovely lawns and an outdoor running track. Climb the water tower at the 14th Ave. entrance for stunning 360° views of the city and the Olympic Range. The views rival those from the Space Needle, and what's more, they are free. On rainy days, languish amid the orchids inside the free glass conservatory. The **Seattle Art Museum**, 14th St. E. and Prospect (625-8901), houses an excellent permanent collection of Asian art. Pick up a program listing or call 443-4670 for information about special exhibits, lectures, demonstrations, and films at the museum. (Open Tues.-Wed. and Fri.-Sat. 10am-5pm, Thurs. 10am-9pm, Sun. noon-5pm. Admission $2, students, ages over 64 and under 12 $1; free Thurs.)

The **University of Washington Arboretum** (325-4510), 10 blocks east of Volunteer Park, has superb cycling and running trails. Lake Washington Blvd., a popular paved road among bicyclists, runs the arboretum's length north to south and then continues along the western shore of Lake Washington as far south as Seward Park. The tranquil **Japanese Garden** (684-4725) is in the southern end of the arboretum at E. Helen St. Take bus #43 from downtown. The nine acres of sculpted gardens include fruit trees, a reflecting pool, and a traditional tea house. (Open March-Nov. daily 10am-5pm. Admission $1.50, senior citizens, disabled people, and ages under 19 75¢. Arboretum open daily dawn to dusk; greenhouse open Mon.-Fri. 10am-4pm.)

North of the arboretum near Union Bay sits the **Seattle Historical Society Museum of Science and History**, 2161 E. Hamlin St. (324-1125). The museum includes exhibits on Seattle's and King County's earliest pioneer settlers and relates amusing anecdotes of the city's slow beginnings. (Open Mon.-Sat. 10am-5pm, Sun. noon-5pm.)

University District

With 35,000 students, the **University of Washington** is the state's cultural and educational center of gravity. The "U District" swarms with students year-round, and other Seattlites also take advantage of the many bookstores, shops, taverns, and restaurants. Stop by the friendly and helpful **visitors information center,** 4014 University Way NE (543-9198), to pick up a map of the campus and to obtain information on the university. (Open Mon.-Fri. 8am-5pm.)

On the campus, visit the **Thomas Burke Memorial Washington State Museum,** NE 45th St. and 17th Ave. NE (543-5590), in the northwest corner of the campus. The museum houses artifacts of the Pacific Northwest's Native American tribes. Especially good are the scrimshaw displays. (Open Mon.-Fri. 11am-5:30pm, Sat. 9am-4:30pm.) The **Henry Art Gallery,** 15th Ave. NE and NE 41st St. (543-2256), houses a collection of 18th- to 20th-century European and American art. The foyer is a dramatic dome inscribed with quotations on the function of art. (Open Tues.-Wed. and Fri. 10am-5pm, Thurs. 10am-7pm, Sat.-Sun. 11-5pm. Admission $2, senior citizens and students $1.) The Astronomy Department's **observatory** is open to the public for viewings on clear nights (543-0126). The **UW Arts Ticket Office,** 4001 University Way NE, has information and tickets for all events. (Open Mon.-Fri. 10:30am-4:30pm.) To reach the U-District, take buses #71-74 from downtown, #7 or 43 from Capitol Hill.

Waterways and Parks

A string of attractions festoon the waterways linking Lake Washington and Puget Sound. Houseboats and sailboats fill **Lake Union.** Here, the **Center for Wooden Boats,** 1010 Valley St. (382-2628), maintains a moored flotilla of new and restored small craft for rental. (Sailboats $7.50-8.50 per hr., 15-min. check of your sailing skills $2.50. Must be 16; no deposit required. Open Mon.-Fri. noon-8pm, Sat.-Sun. 10am-8pm.) **Kelly's Landing,** 1401 NE Boat St. (547-9909), below the UW campus, rents canoes for outings on Lake Union. ($4.50 per hr., $15 per 5 hr.; $100, a credit card, or car keys required for deposit.) Tour the houseboat moorings along Lake Union's shores or go through the Montlake Cut to Lake Washington. **Gasworks Park,** a much-bruited kite-flying spot at the north end of the lake, was reopened a few years ago by the EPA after being shut down due to an excess of toxins. **Gasworks Kite Shop,** 1915 N. 34th St. (633-4780), is 1 block north of the park. To reach the park, take bus #26 from downtown to N. 35th St. and Wallingford Ave. N.

But wait—there's a **public boat ramp** at N. 36th St. and Northlake Way, northeast of Gasworks Park. The popular **Burke-Gilman Trail** runs from Latona St. at NE Northlake, just next to the Washington Ship Canal Bridge and I-5, through the university, past Sand Point and Magnuson Park, north to NE 145th. Since the trail prohibits motorized traffic, it is adored by cyclists, runners, and walkers.

Farther west, the **Hiram M. Chittenden Locks** are movers and shakers of ships. On fine summer days, good-sized crowds surge forth to watch their boat-loving neighbors jockeying for position in the locks. A circus atmosphere develops at peak hours, as *all* boats traveling between Puget Sound and Lake Washington try to cross over. (Viewing hours 7am-9pm.) If listening to the cries of frustrated skippers doesn't amuse you, proceed at once to the **Fish Ladder** on the south side of the locks to watch trout and salmon as they struggle on their journey from the sea. Take bus #43 from the U District or #17 from downtown. The busiest salmon runs occur from June to November; steelhead trout run in the winter, cutthroat trout run in the fall. After watching the fish hurl themselves over 21 concrete steps, go to the lectures held in the visitors center (783-7059) during the summer Tuesdays at 7:30pm. The frivolous U.S. Army Corps of Engineers gives talks with names like

"The Corps Cares About Fish" and "A Beaver in Your Backyard?" (Visitors center open daily 11am-8pm; Sept. 16-June 14 Thurs.-Mon. 11am-5pm.)

Farther north, on the northwestern shore of the city, lies the **Golden Gardens Park,** in the Loyal Heights neighborhood, between NW 80th and NW 95th. The beach is for the brave. A small boat ramp is at the southern end of the park. All will enjoy a picnic supper eaten as the sun sets over Shilshole Bay. Several expensive restaurants are located on the piers to the south, and the unobstructed views of the Olympics almost make their uniformly excellent seafood worth the price (see Food).

Ethnic historians passing through the Scandinavian neighborhood of **Ballard** may want to stop at the **Nordic Heritage Museum,** 3014 NW 67th St. (789-5707). Take bus #17. (Open Tues.-Sat. 10am-4pm, Sun. noon-4pm. Admission $2.50, senior citizens $1.50, children $1.)

Directly north of Lake Union, the beautiful people run, roller skate, and skateboard around **Green Lake.** Take bus #16 from downtown Seattle to Green Lake. The lake is also given high marks by windsurfers, but woe to those who lose their balance. Whoever named Green Lake wasn't kidding; even a quick dunk results in gobs of green algae clinging to your body and hair. Next door is Woodland Park and the **Woodland Park Zoo,** 5500 Phinney Ave. N. (789-7919), best reached from Hwy. 99 or N. 50th St. Take bus #5 from downtown. The park itself is shaggy, but this makes the animals' habitats seem all the more realistic. The African Savannah and Gorilla Houses reproduce the wilds, while the Nocturnal House reveals what really goes on when the lights go out. (Open daily 8:30am-6pm; in winter 8:30am-4pm. Admission $2.50, ages 13-17 $1, senior citizens, disabled people, and ages 6-12 50¢.)

A number of other worthwhile parks and attractions are spattered across the city. **Discovery Park** (625-4636), on a lonely point west of the Magnolia district and south of Golden Gardens Park, at 36th Ave. W. and Government Way W., is comprised of acres of minimally tended grassy fields and steep bluffs atop Puget Sound. At its northern end is the **Indian Cultural Center** (285-4425), operated by the United Indians of All Tribes Foundation. (Open Mon.-Fri. 8:30am-5pm, Sat.-Sun. 10am-5pm. Free.)

Seward Park is the southern endpoint of a string of beaches and park land along the western shore of Lake Washington. Take bus #39 during peak hours; bus #31 Mon.-Fri. 9am-3pm and Sat. 6am-7pm. The park has a number of beaches, wooded areas, and walking and biking trails. It also brandishes a fishing pier, picnic shelters, tennis courts, and an arts center (723-5780). After exercising in the park, refresh yourself with a tour of the **Rainier Brewery Co.,** 3100 Airport Way S. (622-2600), off I-5 at the West Seattle Bridge. Take bus #123. Attentiveness is rewarded with free beer (root beer for those under 21) and cheese and crackers. (Tours Mon.-Fri. 1-6pm. Free.)

Directly to the west is **Alki Beach Park,** a thin strip of beach wrapped around residential West Seattle. The water is cold, but the views of downtown Seattle in one direction and of the Olympics in the other are scrumptious. The Coast Guard's **Alki Point Lighthouse,** 3201 Alki Ave. SW (932-5800), is open for tours Monday through Friday by appointment only (call one day in advance). The first white settlers of Seattle set up camp here in 1851, naming their new home New York Alki (Alki is a Native American word meaning "by and by"). By the time the settlement moved to Pioneer Square, new arrival Doc Maynard suggested that perhaps "New York by and by" was too deferential a name and that the city should be named for his friend Chief Sealth, whose name was eventually mangled into Seattle. A monument to the city's birthplace is located along Alki Beach at 63rd Ave. SW. South of Alki, **Lincoln Park,** along Fauntleroy Way, is the departure point for ferries to Vashon Island (see Near Tacoma). Take bus #18 to Lincoln Park. The park has a number of playing fields, tennis courts, picnic tables, swimming beaches, bicycling trails, and the Colman Pool, open only during the summer.

Sports and Recreation

Seattle parks are a relentless carnival of running and cycling trails, tennis courts, and playing fields. Pick up a copy of the pamphlet *Your Seattle Parks and Recreation Guide,* available at the visitors bureau or the Parks Department. Ned David types will also want to get their hands on a free copy of the monthly *Sports Northwest,* available from area sports outfitters. The paper includes calendars of competitive events in the Northwest, as well as book reviews and recreation suggestions.

More than 200 road races each summer in the Northwest will excite runners. Distance bicyclists should note the 192-mile **Seattle to Portland Race,** in which 1600 people compete annually. Call the **bike hotline** (522-2453) for more information. The Seattle Parks Department also holds a monthly **Bicycle Sunday** from May to September, when Lake Washington Blvd. is open only to cyclists from 10am-5pm. Contact the Parks Department's Citywide Sports Office (684-7092) for more information. Dear to the heart of many Seattle cyclists is **Marymoor Velodrome** (282-8356), in Redmond off Hwy. 520 at the Hwy. 901 exit. Take bus #268 during peak hours only. The velodrome is open to the public when not in use for competition, and offers classes on the ways of the track. Watch the sweaty races sponsored by the Washington State Bicycling Association from May through August on Friday nights at 7:30pm. Pack a picnic supper and sit on the lawn.

The **Northwest Outdoor Center,** 1009 NE Boat St. (632-1984), on Lake Union, holds a number of instructional programs in whitewater and sea kayaking during the spring, summer, and fall. (3-day introduction to sea touring $25 if you have your own boat. Equipment rentals available.) The center also leads a number of excursions—sea kayaking through the San Juan Islands or backpacking and paddling through the North Cascades. (Open Mon.-Fri. 10am-8pm, Sat.-Sun. 10am-6pm.)

Whitewater rafting has become extremely popular in Washington in the last decade. While the navigable rivers all lie at least two hours from Seattle by car, many outfitters are based in the Seattle area. River running is currently unregulated, and over 50 companies compete for a growing market. The best way to secure an inexpensive trip is to call some outfitters and compare competitors' prices; they are often willing to undercut one another. Look under "Guides" in the Yellow Pages. In recent years rafting companies have attempted to subject themselves to a regulatory bureaucracy of their own making, **River Outfitters of Washington (ROW)** (485-1427), which sets safety guidelines for its members. Even if your outfitter does not belong to ROW, be sure it lives up to ROW's basic safety standards. Under no circumstances should a single raft navigate a river unaccompanied; guides should possess basic water and safety skills and should have been trained at least twice on each river that they run commercially; all guides should have Standard First Aid and CPR certification; and all rafts should be rigged with bail buckets, throw lines, and extra paddles. Some of the larger companies have on-shore support staff at all times. Spend the extra dollars to ensure the highest level of safety. Private boaters should remember that whitewater is unpredictable and potentially dangerous. Even if you are schooled in the ways of wild water, scout out new rivers before running them. ROW has a list of tips for private boaters, and outfitters can give you an idea of the navigable Washington rivers.

Catch the NBA basketball team, the **Supersonics,** at the coliseum in Seattle Center (281-5800). Successors to the ill-supported Pilots (who moved to Milwaukee in 1970 after just one year in Seattle), the **Mariners** play the Minnesota Twins and other lesser American League baseball clubs at the Kingdome from April to early October (628-0888; tickets $2-8.50). The **Seahawks** play football in the Kingdome (827-9766; tickets $7-24). (Never confuse Jim Zorn, former southpaw quarterback of the Seahawks, with the avant-garde saxophonist.) Intercollegiate sports at the University of Washington are open to the public; call the Athletic Ticket Office (543-2200) for schedules and price information.

South of Seattle, the 30-year-old **Longacres** track (226-3131) still has classic thoroughbred racing (April-Oct. Wed.-Sun.). From Seattle, take I-5 south to exit 157 Empire Way. Or take Metro's Longacres Special direct service from 2nd and Pine downtown. (One way $3, round-trip $3.50; no passes or transfers accepted. Departure times vary, so pick up a schedule.) Once per month, Saturday morning workouts are free to the public. Talk to jockeys, watch a film, and receive free souvenirs of your visit. Meet at 8am at the north end of the grandstand. Every Saturday and Sunday, free tours of Longacres are conducted by an ex-jockey. Reservations are required. (Grandstand admission $3, clubhouse $5, ages under 10 free.)

Since the days of the Klondike rush, Seattle has been one of the foremost cities in the world for supplying expeditions into the wilds. Besides a host of ordinary army-navy surplus stores and campers' supply shops, Seattle is home to many world-class outfitters. **Recreational Equipment Inc. Coop (REI Coop)**, 1525 11th Ave. (323-8333), is the favored place to buy high-quality mountaineering and water recreation gear. Take bus #10. Their semiannual sales are gala events in themselves—shoppers line up all morning on opening day. For a few dollars you can join the coop and receive a year-end rebate on your purchases. REI also offers its own backpacking and climbing trips and clinics, and presents free slide shows and lectures on trekking in Nepal, bicycling in Ireland, improving your fly-fishing techniques, &c. Call or stop by the store for a full schedule. (Open Mon.-Tues. and Sat. 9:30am-6pm, Wed.-Fri. 9:30am-9pm, Sun. noon-5pm.) **Second Wind**, 300 Queen Anne N. (329-5921), sells much cheaper second-hand equipment, and **North Face**, 4560 University Way NE (574-6276), also has its headquarters in Seattle (open Mon.-Fri. 10am-8pm, Sat.-Sun. 10am-6pm).

Entertainment

Obtain a copy of *The Weekly*, 75¢ at newsstands and in boxes on the street, for a complete calendar of music, theater, exhibits, and special events. The free *Rocket*, available in music stores throughout the city, is a monthly off-beat guide to the popular music scene around the Puget Sound area. *Seattle Gay News*, 25¢ in boxes on the street, lists events and musical happenings relevant to the gay community. The *Area 206* Friday insert of the *Seattle Post-Intelligencer* has a "Hot Tix" column on free performances and discount tickets.

During summertime lunch hours downtown, city-sponsored free entertainment incarnates itself as the **"Out to Lunch"** series (623-0340), bringing everything from reggae to folk dancing to the parks and squares of Seattle. The **Seattle Public Library** (625-2665) shows free films as part of this program, and also has a daily schedule of other free events, such as poetry readings and children's book-reading competitions. *Events*, published every two months, has a calendar of the library's offerings; it is available at libraries throughout the city.

Music and Dance

The **Seattle Opera** (443-4700) performs in the Opera House in the Seattle Center throughout the winter. In 1990, this imaginative and expert company will put on *Daughter of the Regiment* and *Tales of Hoffman*, among other works. The popularity of the program requires that you order tickets well in advance, although rush tickets are sometimes available 15 minutes before curtain ($8 and up). Write to the Seattle Opera, P.O. Box 9248, Seattle 98109. The **Seattle Symphony Orchestra** (447-4747), also in Seattle Center's Opera House, performs a regular subscription series September through June (rush tickets $4 and up) under the often uninspired baton of Gerard Schwarz, as well as special pops and children's series. More recently, the symphony has been playing summer series in the gorgeous, renovated Fifth Avenue Theater. The **Pacific Northwest Ballet** (547-5900) starts its season at the Seattle Center in December with a production of the "Nutcracker." The season continues through May with a slate of four or five productions. The University

of Washington offers its own program of student recitals and concerts by visiting
artists. Call the Meany Hall box office at 543-4880.

Theater

Seattle specializes in excellent small theaters, though it has recently worked to
attract large-scale touring shows fresh from Broadway.

A Contemporary Theater (ACT), 100 W. Roy (285-5110), at the base of Queen Anne Hill.
One of Seattle's more established and traditional theaters. Performances May-Oct.

Seattle Repertory Theater, 225 Mercer (443-2222), in the Bagley Wright Theater in Seattle
Center. Classic and contemporary theater with at least one premier Oct.-May.

Fifth Avenue Theater, 1308 5th Ave. (625-1418). This well-restored theater attracts many
of the big name touring shows.

Seattle Group Theatre, 3940 Brooklyn NE (543-4327), in the U District, next to the Last
Exit on Brooklyn. Home to **The Group,** one of Seattle's most innovative small theater ensembles, performing original and avant-garde works.

Paul Robeson Community Theater, 500 30th S. (322-7080). Performs works by Black artists,
often at the Langston Hughes Cultural Center.

New City Theater, 1634 11th Ave. (323-6800), on Capitol Hill. Home of the incisive **Off the
Wall Players,** Seattle's well-established improvisational group. The Players' quick wit produces immediate gratification. You can also watch them for free on KING-TV's *Rev* show,
Sat. at 4pm and Sun. at 1am.

University of Washington School of Drama Theaters (543-4880). The 3 UW theaters—the
Penthouse, Meany Hall, and Glenn Hughes Playhouse—offer a wide variety of works, from
children's shows to classical and contemporary theater. Call for information on the wide variety of UW cultural activities.

The Empty Space Theatre, 95 S. Jackson St. (467-6000), in Pioneer Sq. An exciting selection
of modern comic dramas fills the void.

Pioneer Square Theatre, 512 2nd Ave. (622-2016). This popular theater's mainstage has been
home for the last 6 years to *Angry Housewives,* a modern suburban-punk musical comedy.
The theater's **Firststage,** at 107 Occidental Ave., produces an eclectic series of mostly witty
new works.

Taverns and Clubs

One of the joys of living in Seattle is the abundance of community taverns dedicated not to inebriating or scoping, but rather to providing a relaxed environment
for dancing and spending time with friends. In Washington a tavern serves only
beer and wine; a fully licensed bar or cocktail lounge must adjoin a restaurant. You
must be 21 to enter bars and taverns. The Northwest produces a variety of local
beers, none bottled, including **Grant's, Imperial Russian Stout, India Pale Ale, Red
Hook, Ballard Bitter,** and **Black Hook.**

For $4 or so, catch an evening of live stand-up comedy in one of Seattle's comedy
clubs, such as Pioneer Square's **Swannie's Comedy Underground,** 222 S. Main St.
(628-0303; acts Wed.-Sun. 9:30 and 11pm).

The University Bistro, 4315 University Way NE (547-8010). Live music (everything from
blues to reggae) nightly. Happy hour (4-7pm) finds schooners of Bud for 75¢, well drinks
$1.25. Cover Tues. $2, Wed.-Sat. $3-5, no cover Sun.-Mon. Open daily 10am-2am; in summer
Tues.-Sat. 10am-2am.

Murphy's Pub, 2110 N. 45th St. (634-2110), in Wallingford, west of the U District. Take
bus #43. A classic Irish pub with a mile-long beer list. Popular with the folkie crowd, Murphy's has live Irish and folk music nightly with no cover charge. Open daily 2pm-2am.

Central Tavern, 207 1st Ave. S. (622-0209). One of several good live rock 'n' roll taverns
in Pioneer Sq. On weekends, walk around the square to find a tavern to your liking; many
charge no cover. Open Mon.-Thurs. 11:30am-midnight, Fri.-Sat. 2pm-2am, Sun. 2-10pm.

Virginia Inn, 1937 1st Ave. (624-3173), right downtown at 1st and Virginia. The VI is a famous, almost new-wave tavern frequented by all types of drinkers. Guinness and Grant's on tap. Open Mon.-Tues. 11am-1am, Wed.-Sat. 11am-2am, Sun. noon-midnight.

Squid Row Tavern, 518 E. Pine (322-2031). Bizarre paintings, black booths, a bar, and earfuls of delightful punk rock. Cover $4. Open Mon.-Fri. noon-2am, Sat. 4pm-2am.

The Borderline, 608 1st Ave. (624-3316), in the heart of Pioneer Sq. Under-25 crowd dances to a mix of music from Motown to new-wave. Occasional live bands. Happy hour (8-10pm) features 50¢ pints of Bud and Bud Lite and free snacks. Fri.-Sat. cover $2 for men, $1 for women. Open Thurs.-Sat. 8pm-2am.

The Double Header, 407 2nd Ave. in Pioneer Sq. (464-9918). Claims to be the oldest gay bar in the country. An oom-pah band plays nightly to a mostly middle-aged crowd of gay men and women. A Seattle institution. Open daily 10am-2am. No cover.

The Frontier, 2203 1st Ave. (441-3377), just north of the VI in Belltown. Free dancing nightly to a live DJ. The new sound system in this go-go attracts both gay and straight crowds. Bar open daily 10am-2am. Dancing Wed.-Sat. 10pm-2am. Restaurant open Mon.-Fri. 6am-10pm, Sat. 10am-10pm, Sun. 10am-6pm.

New Melody Tavern and Dance Hall, 5213 Ballard Ave. NW (782-3480), in Ballard. Along with beer and well drinks, this out-of-the-way dance bar delivers some of Seattle's best jazz and bluegrass. Open Mon.-Fri. 5pm-2am, Sat. 6pm-2am. Cover $3-9.

Cinema

Most of the theaters that screen non-Hollywood films are on Capitol Hill and in the University District. Expect to pay $5. Seven Gables has recently bought up the Metro, the Neptune, and others. They sell admission to any five films at any of their theaters for $17.50.

The Egyptian, 801 E. Pine St. (323-4978), at Harvard, on Capitol Hill. This handsome art-deco theater shows arty films and is best known for putting on the Seattle Film Festival throughout May. The festival includes a retrospective of one director's work and a personal appearance by the featured director. Festival series tickets are available at a discount.

The Harvard Exit, 807 E. Roy (323-8986), on Capitol Hill. Quality classic and foreign films. Half the fun of seeing a movie here is the theater itself, a converted old house—the lobby was once the living room. Arrive early for complimentary cheese and crackers over a game of chess, checkers, or backgammon. Admission $5, senior citizens and children $3.

The Broadway Theatre, 201 E. Broadway (323-1085), on Capitol Hill. Take bus #7. Plays long-run art films. Sometimes dispenses umbrellas and coffee to customers waiting in line in the rain. Admission $3.50, senior citizens and children $2.50.

Grand Illusion Cinema, 1403 NE 50th St. (523-3935), in the U District at University Way. A tiny theater attached to an espresso bar, showing low budget films. Admission $5, senior citizens and students $4, matinees $4.

Neptune, 1303 NE 45th St. (633-5545), just off University Way. A repertory theater, with double features that change daily. Admission $4.50, senior citizens and children $3.50.

Seven Gables Theater, 911 NE 50th St. (632-8820), in the U District, just off Roosevelt, a short walk west from University Way. Another cinema in an old house. Shows independent and classic films. Admission $5, senior citizens and children $3.

Market Theater, 1428 Post Alley (382-1171), downstairs from the Pike Place Market. Shows foreign flicks like *Airfeet of Desire* and *Attack of the Killer Ice Cream Sandwiches*. Admission $5.50, senior citizens $4.50, children $2.75.

Metro Cinemas, 45th St. and Roosevelt Way NE (663-0055), in the U District. A large, generic 10-theater complex. Half the screens show mainstream teen movies, the other half are reserved for contemporary art films. Admission $5, senior citizens and children $3.

Seasonal Events

Seattlites never let the rain dampen their spirits. To the contrary! Pick up a copy of the Seattle-King County visitors center brochure *Coming Events,* published every season, for an exact listing of innumerable area happenings. One of the most notable events is the **Northwest Folklife Festival** (689-7300), held on Memorial Day weekend at the Seattle Center. Artists, musicians, and dancers congregate to celebrate the heritage of the area. The Japanese celebrate their cultural tradition in the **Bon Odori** festival (623-7100) in the International District the third week of July. Temples are opened to the public and there are traditional dances in the street. **Street fairs** throughout the city are popular conglomerations of crafts and food stands, street music, and theater. Especially of note are those in the University District during mid- to late May, the Pike Place Market (625-4762) over Memorial Day weekend, and the Fremont District (633-4409) in mid-June. The **Bite of Seattle** (232-2982) is an extremely popular smattering of food (*sans* Jamie), held in mid-July at Greenlake. The summer is capped off with the massive **Bumbershoot** (683-7337), held in the Seattle Center over Labor Day weekend. This fantastic arts festival attracts big-name bands, street musicians, and an exuberant crowd. (Fri. free, Sat.-Sun. $4 at the door, $3 in advance.)

Seattle is most joyous, however, when it dances the dance of the sea. At the beginning of May, the **opening day** of yachting season sees Puget Sound and the lakes swarming with sails of all descriptions. The third week of May is **Maritime Week** (467-6340 or 329-5700), and in mid-August the **Seattle Boats Afloat Show** (634-0911) gives area boaters a chance to show off their craft. At the beginning of July, the Center for Wooden Boats sponsors the free **Wooden Boat Show** (382-2628) on Lake Union. The show includes a floating display of over 100 traditional wooden boats and a demonstration of boat-building skills. The crowning event is the **Quick and Daring Boatbuilding Contest,** in which teams race to build and sail a wooden boat of their own design using a limited kit of tools and materials. Plenty of music and food accompanies the naval exercises.

The biggest and zaniest festival of them all is the **Seattle Seafair** (623-7100, hotline 421-5012), spread out over three weeks from mid-July to early August. The whole city contributes with street fairs, big parades, little parades, ethnic parades, balloon races, musical entertainment, and a seafood fest. The festival ends with the totally insane Emerald City Unlimited Hydroplane Races, in which everybody grabs anything that will float and heads to Lake Washington for front row seats. As the sun shines more often than not during these weeks, half the city seems to turn out in inner tubes. Zowie!

The year ends with the annual **Christmas Cruise** of brightly lit boats in early December.

Near Seattle

Simply by crossing one of the two floating bridges over Lake Washington, tourists fatigued by the hectic city pace may easily reach a biker's and picnicker's Eden. In general, these towns are of no interest to the sightseer, but the spacious parklands and miles of country roads delight those especially dedicated to the outdoors. Seattle's outskirts are astonishingly rural; only **Bellevue** across Lake Washington has developed anything akin to urban flair. Although bowling and movie-going draw the big evening crowds in this affluent suburb, Bellevue is beginning to show sparks of a nightlife in its downtown restaurants and clubs. The July **Bellevue Jazz Festival** (455-6885) has grown to significant proportions as well.

If nothing else, a jaunt to suburbia grants a fine view of Seattle against a mountainous backdrop. The hills due east of the city, known affectionately as the **"Issaquah Alps,"** are crocheted with good hiking trails and superb views of Seattle and Puget Sound.

Head farther out for lovely country excursions. Take I-90 to **Lake Sammamish State Park,** off exit 15, for excellent swimming and waterskiing. The park also has volleyball courts and playing fields. You might want to continue onward to the towns of **Snoqualmie** and **North Bend,** 29 miles east of Seattle. In Snoqualmie, the **Puget Sound Railroad Museum,** 109 King St. (746-4025), on Hwy. 202, features a collection of still-working early steam and electric trains. The impressive equipment is housed in the classic old Snoqualmie Depot. Train rides on these old beasts run to North Bend, offering views of Snoqualmie Falls. (Open April-Sept. Sat.-Sun. 11am-5pm. Round-trip rides $7, senior citizens $5, children $3.) In North Bend, the **Snoqualmie Valley Museum,** 320 North Bend Blvd. S. (888-3200 or 888-0062), resurrects a *fin-de-siècle* parlor and kitchen, and displays locally retrieved Native American artifacts. (Open Sat.-Sun. 1-5pm.) North Bend operates a **visitors information booth** in summer at the corner of North Bend Blvd. and Park Ave. (888-1678).

Twenty-four miles east, I-90 climbs to Snoqualmie Pass and some of the most popular **skiing** in the state. Four resorts share the slopes, often offering interchangeable lift tickets and free shuttles, during the November to April season. Restaurants, ski schools, night skiing, and a ski shop complete the facilities. Each resort takes a different day of rest; skiing is thus available seven days per week. Contact each resort separately: **Alpental** (236-1600), **Snoqualmie** (232-8182), **Ski Acres** (434-6671 or 232-8182), and **Pacific West** (462-7669).

Back in North Bend, take bus #210 or Hwy. 202 north to view the astounding **Snoqualmie Falls.** Washington State residents are quick to mention that they are 100 feet higher than Niagara. The falls were formerly a sacred place for coastal Native Americans, who called them *Sdokwalbu.* Now Puget Power has the capacity to turn the falls on and off depending on the secular needs of the hydroelectric plant (née 1898). Puget Power maintains public picnic facilities at the falls.

In the spring and summer, a number of **U-Pick berry farms** lining Hwy. 202 north along the Snoqualmie River open for the season. In Woodinville is the **Ste. Michelle Vintners,** 14111 NE 145th St. (488-7733), the leaders in the recent move to popularize Washington wines. From downtown Seattle take bus #310 during peak hours only. The 45-minute tours of the facility, which resembles a French château, finish with wine tasting for those 21 and over. (Tours Mon.-Thurs. 10am-4:30pm, Fri.-Sun. 10am-6pm.)

The Seattle area is heavily garnished by the many facilities of the **Boeing Aircraft Industry,** Seattle's most prominent employer. When last seen in the 1950s, Thomas Pynchon was working for this glittering jewel of the military-industrial complex, writing technical manuals. Free tours of one Boeing plant are given 25 miles north of Seattle in **Everett.** Take I-5 to exit 189, then Hwy. 526 west. (Tours 9am-2pm. Reservations required. Call the Everett Tour Center at 342-4801 for more information.) At Boeing Field to the south of Seattle is the **Museum of Flight,** 9404 E. Marginal Way S. (767-7373). Take I-5 south to exit 158 and turn north onto E. Marginal Way S., or take bus #123. The museum is in the restored Red Barn where William E. Boeing founded the company in 1916. Inside, photographs and artifacts trace the history of flight from its beginnings through the 30s. Included is an operating replica of the Wright Brothers' wind tunnel. Rare aircraft sometimes participate in special events on the grounds nearby. (Open Sat.-Wed. 10am-5pm, Thurs.-Fri. 10am-9pm. Admission $4, senior citizens and ages 13-19 $3, ages 6-12 $2.)

Just south of Des Moines on Hwy. 509 off Hwy. 99 is **Saltwater State Park.** Take bus #130. The park has extensive foot trails through the Kent Smith Canyon, a beach for swimming and clamming, and 53 campsites with pay showers and flush toilets. (Sites $7.)

From Pier 56, ferries leave for **Blake Island Marine State Park** twice per day during the summer. After a narrated tour of the harbor, the ferry docks at **Tillicum Village,** where you'll eat "Indian-style" salmon in a long house, visit a wood carver, and watch a "rare presentation" of Native dance and other Native activities. The package (with dinner) lasts 4 hours and costs $32 (senior citizens $29, youths $21, children $12). Call 443-1244 for more details. From Colman Dock (Pier 52) on Seattle's waterfront, ferries run to the town of **Bremerton,** on the Kitsap Peninsula, which serves as the Puget Sound Naval Shipyard (see Kitsap Peninsula).

Ferries also depart from Colman Dock for the town of **Winslow** on Bainbridge Island, a charmingly rural area. In Winslow visit the **Bainbridge Island Historical Museum** on Highschool Rd. (open Sat. 10am-4pm; free), or head for one of the island's state parks. **Fort Ward,** southwest of Winslow on Hwy. 305, is a day-use only park, with boat launches, picnic facilities, and an underwater park for scuba divers. **Fay-Bainbridge,** on the northern end of the island, has good fishing and 36 **campsites** with pay showers and flush toilets. (Sites $6. Ferries daily about every 45 min.)

The Alaska Marine Highway

Since the days of the Alaska Gold Rush, Seattle has served as the most important link for trade and transportation to Alaska. The M.V. *Columbia* (623-1149) sails out of Pier 48 on Seattle's waterfront and stops at **Prince Rupert, BC, Ketchikan, Wrangell, Petersburg, Juneau,** and **Haines** before arriving in **Skagway** on Monday afternoon; you can make stopovers at any port along the way. This well-equipped vessel offers a spectacular trip to the north for travelers with some time and money to spare. Reservations for all passengers out of Seattle are required, as well as reservations for berths. Summer passages are booked six months in advance, but you may be able to find space on a standby basis. (Standby fare identical to regular fare.) The wait list for standby passengers opens at 8:30am on the Monday before Friday's departure. Walk-ons are virtually guaranteed a ride if they sign up before Thursday, though space for vehicles is less certain. Reserved vehicles must check in at the Seattle terminal three hours prior to departure or at the Prince Rupert terminal two hours prior to departure. Cabins are never available standby; sleeping bags in the lounges are a happy, and free, alternative. (Departures May-Sept. Fri. at 9pm. To Skagway $198 and Haines $192. Dorm-room berth an extra $87 or $93, respectively. To Skagway cars up to 10 ft. $210, 10-15 ft. $478. Senior citizens travel free standby Oct.-April with a pass, available with proof of age at port of embarkation. Pets $10 extra, health certificate required.) For reservations, write to the Alaska Marine Highway, P.O. Box R, Juneau, AK 99811 (800-642-0066 or 907-465-3941). Stop by the Pier 48 terminal for current schedules and general information on all the Marine Highway's services (open Mon.-Fri. 8:30am-5pm), or write the **Alaska State Division of Tourism,** P.O. Box E, Juneau, AK 99811 (907-465-2010).

The weekend-long ride is a Fantastic Voyage past glaciers, wooded islands, and snow-capped peaks. Whales, seals, and eagles are commonplace. The **Tongass National Forest** even trots out an interpretive program when ferries sail by its holdings.

If Seattle's Friday departures are inconvenient, you can catch one of the highway's many ships leaving Prince Rupert in British Columbia Wednesday through Monday. Alaska Motorcoaches makes regular connections between Seattle and Prince Rupert, and those who can reach Prince Rupert by land will save $106 on the Seattle-Skagway passage.

Puget Sound

According to Native American legend, Puget Sound was created when Ocean, wishing to keep his children Cloud and Rain close to home, gouged out a trough in western Washington and molded the dirt into a wall of mountains. Ever since then, Cloud and Rain have kept near the sea, rarely venturing across the Cascade Range to the interior tablelands. Most of Washington's residents also stick close by the water, making their homes in the Sound's labyrinth of inlets, bays, and harbors.

From Bellingham in the north through Seattle to industrial Tacoma, cities and towns form an almost continuous megalopolis along I-5. The bay's southern shore curves around past Lacey to Olympia, the state capital, and beyond that to the Olympic Peninsula. A few dozen islands speckle the Sound, providing tranquil retreats to harried city dwellers. The San Juan Islands, off Anacortes, catch the brunt of the tourist traffic. Vashon Island, between Seattle and Tacoma, remains quiet.

Puget Sound attracts as many water breathers as city dwellers. **Greenpeace Northwest,** 4649 Sunnyside Ave. N., Seattle 98103 (633-6020), runs a dozen weekend daytrips throughout the summer to view killer whales, porpoises, puffins, seals, sea lions, and eagles ($40-45). Although pods of orcas can be sighted anywhere in the Sound, the southwest coast of San Juan Island is the favorite haunt of the highly intelligent, black-and-white cetaceans.

An extensive web of roads and ferries ensnares the cities and islands of Puget Sound. Information on ferries to specific destinations is given in the Getting There and Practical Information sections of each city or area. If you're driving, you should arrive at the ferry terminal early and get in the line that matches your destination (cars are boarded according to their exit points). Cyclists and pedestrians travel cheaply and never have to wait in line. Try to avoid ferries across the Sound during commuter rush hours and the San Juan ferry on Friday afternoons. Larger cars and RVs may have to wait for a place; RVs pay an extra fee.

Olympia

Olympia was once a peaceful, easy-going fishing and oystering port at the southernmost end of Puget Sound. Today, as the home of K records and the shy trio Beat Happening, Olympia is the world capital of the primitive pop music underground. Since 1856, it has also served as the capital of Washington. The imposing architecture of the Capitol Group commands attention from its hilltop location, just south of the port. Evergreen State College, an experiment in "ecotopian" idealism, is just west of the city center. The combination of impressive Capitol buildings, Evergreen "events," and tattered folk-rock make Olympia worth a detour.

Practical Information and Orientation

Visitor Information: Olympia-Thurston Co. Chamber of Commerce, 1000 Plum St. (357-3362). Plenty of brochures, information, and good advice about seeing Olympia on a budget. Open Mon.-Fri. 9am-5pm. **Department of Trade and Economic Development, Tourism Division,** General Administration Bldg., #G-3 (800-541-9274, in WA 800-562-4570). Choose your brochure with care. **City of Olympia Parks and Recreation Department,** 222 N. Columbia Ave. (753-8380). Open Mon.-Fri. 8am-9pm.

Washington State Parks and Recreation Commission: 7150 Clearwater Lane (753-5755; in summer 800-562-0990 Mon.-Fri. 8am-5pm). All the latest on the state parks. Immensely helpful staff.

Department of Natural Resources (DNR): John Cherbert Bldg. (753-5327 or 800-527-3305), in the Capitol Group on Water St. between 15th and 16th St. The *Guide to Camp and Picnic Sites* describes all the free DNR sites throughout the state. Ask for *Your Public Beaches,* about waterfront areas in the Puget Sound area. Open Mon.-Fri. 8am-5pm.

Department of Fisheries: 115 General Administration Bldg. (753-6600), just outside the Capitol Group at Columbia and 11th St. Information on saltwater fishing and shellfish, including season and limit designations. Open Mon.-Fri. 8am-5pm.

Department of Wildlife: 600 N. Capitol Way (753-5700). Information and licensing for freshwater fishing and game hunting. Open Mon.-Fri. 8am-5pm.

Greyhound: 107 E. 7th St. (357-5541). To Seattle (9 per day, $8.70), Portland (7 per day, $5), and Spokane (4 per day, $31). Open daily 7am-8:45pm.

Buses: Intercity Transit, 526 S. Pattison (786-1881). Office open Mon.-Fri. 9am-5pm; phone staffed Mon.-Fri. 7am-6pm, Sat. 9am-5pm. Buses run Mon.-Sat. 5:50am-8pm. Fare 35¢, ages 6-17 25¢; senior citizens and disabled people 10¢ with IT reduced-fare cards ($2) available from the IT office. Day passes are 75¢, youths 50¢, senior citizens and the disabled 20¢. Everyone rides free 11am-2pm in the downtown zone (bounded by the Capitol Group and the port). All buses begin and end their routes at 4th and Columbia.

Taxi: Red Top Taxi, 357-3700. **South Sound Taxi,** 357-5757.

Car Rental: Rent-A-Dent, Olympia Airport (786-8333). $21 per day with 100 free miles plus 15¢ per additional mile. Must be 21 with credit card or $100 deposit. Open daily 8am-6pm.

Bike Rental: Olympic Outfitters, 407 E. 4th Ave. (943-1997). Mountain bikes $15 per day, 10-speeds $12.50 per day. Deposit $25. This enormous sports shop also rents tents, skis, mountain climbing gear, and sailboards. Open Mon.-Fri. 10am-8pm, Sat. 10am-6pm, Sun. noon-4pm.

Public Library: E. 8th and S. Franklin St. (352-0595). Open Mon.-Thurs. 10am-9pm, Fri.-Sat. 10am-5pm.

Lesbian Resource Center: Evergreen State College, CAB 305 (866-6000, ext. 6544). For the gay and lesbian community. Open during the school year Tues.-Thurs. 10am-4pm.

Women's Shelter: Safeplace, 754-6300. 24-hour counseling and housing referral.

Women's Health Clinic: Evergreen State College CAB 305 (866-6000, ext. 6200). 24 hours.

Post Office: 900 S. Jefferson St. (753-9474). Open Mon.-Fri. 7:30am-6pm. General Delivery ZIP Code: 98501.

Area Code: 206.

Greyhound stops in downtown Olympia on its way up and down I-5. The Amtrak depot is almost 8 miles southeast of the city, and there is no bus service to downtown. Intercity Transit provides limited service to the three "capital cities": Olympia, Tumwater, and Lacey (see listing above). Supplementary transport is provided for senior citizens and the disabled by **Special Mobility Services** at 825 Legion Way SE (754-9393).

Accommodations and Camping

The hotels and motels in Olympia generally cater to lobbyists and lawyers, not to tourists. Since the nearest hostel is all the way out in Tacoma, and the two local universities need all their rooms for their own students, your options here are limited.

Holly Motel, 2816 Martin Way (943-3000), on a main east-west drag, east of town. Take exit 109 off I-5, or bus #61 or 62. The beds are a little narrow, but the TVs add a little color. Small pool. Singles $22, with TV $29. Doubles with TV $31.

Bailey Motor Inn, 3333 Martin Way (491-7515), just off exit 107. Clean, comfortable rooms, and an indoor heated pool to boot. Singles from $25. Doubles from $29.

Super 8 Motel, 4615 Martin Way (459-8888), just outside Olympia in Lacey, but still accessible by exit 109 off I-5. More upscale than Motel 6 (by at least 2 points), but essentially a bland representative of the national chain. Singles $34. Doubles $37.

Motel 6, 400 W. Lee St. (754-7320), in Tumwater. Take exit 102 off I-5 and head east on Trosper Rd., then south on Capitol Blvd. Head west again, after 1 block, on W. Lee St. Or take bus #13 from downtown. Comfortable rooms right next to the freeway. Color TV and swimming pool. Singles $22. Doubles $28. Each additional person $6.

Millersylvania State Park, 12245 Tilly Rd. S. (753-1519), 10 miles south of Olympia, off I-5. The park's old-growth forest will outlive the swimmers and campers who use it. 216 crowded sites for camping, with pay showers and flush toilets. Facilities for the disabled. Primitive hiker/biker sites available. Standard sites $7, RV hookups $9.

Capital Forest Multiple Use Area, 15 miles west of Olympia. Administered by the DNR. 50 campsites scattered among 6 campgrounds. Camping is free and requires no notification or permit. Pick up a forest map at the visitors bureau or at the state Department of Natural Resources office (see Practical Information).

Food

There are a few good eating possibilities along bohemian 4th Ave., east of Columbia. The pace picks up during the school year. The **farmer's market** (866-6835), at Capital Way and Thurston Ave., allows the farmer and the consumer to be friends. (Open May-Oct. Thurs.-Sun. 10am-3pm.)

Barb's BBQ Soul Cuisine, 203 W. 4th Ave. (786-8758). Check out the pictures of Black political and musical figures on the wall while Barb cooks up her fabulous soul food. The dinners ($6.50) overflow with beans, rice, veggies, and incredible cornbread. Try the ribs or the catfish. Occasional live jazz Thurs.-Sat. at 8pm. Open Mon.-Thurs. 6-8:30pm, Fri. 6-11pm, Sat. 6pm-midnight.

Sonny's Capital City Cafe, 1023 S. Capitol Way (754-5152). Drop a dime in the Wurlitzer jukebox and bop back to the 50s and its sensational salads, burgers, and sandwiches. Meatloaf with potato salad $5. Dinners $7. Open Mon.-Thurs. 9:30am-9pm, Fri. 9:30am-10pm, Sat. 11:30am-10pm.

Smithfield Cafe, 212 W. 4th Ave. (786-1725). This cozy café serves coffee (65¢), cappuccino ($1.20), and espresso (90¢). The relaxed and eclectic crowd also digs the fresh pastries, especially the blueberry bran muffins (90¢) and cherry turnovers ($1). Open Mon.-Fri. 7am-10pm, Sat. 8am-10pm, Sun. 8am-8pm.

Jo Mama's Restaurant, 120 N. Pear St. (943-9849), in an old house on the corner of State and Pear. Homemade pizza served in an all-wood, "old-tavern" atmosphere. The food is somewhat overpriced (8-in. vegetarian pizza $11.25—feeds 2 hungry people), but the ambience compensates. Pitchers of Olympia beer cost only $1.25 on Mon. and Sat. Open Mon.-Thurs. 11am-11pm, Fri. 11am-midnight, Sat. 4pm-midnight.

The Falls Terrace Restaurant, 106 S. Deschutes Way (943-7830). Take exit 103 off I-5. Very elegant. Dinner prices are out of sight, but you can enjoy the great view of Tumwater Falls over a $6 lunch. Open Mon.-Fri. 11am-10pm, Sat. 4:30-10:30pm, Sun. noon-9pm. Make reservations.

Sights

Begin your exploration of the capitol area at the **State Capitol Information Center,** on Capitol Way between 12th and 14th Ave. (586-3460). The staff here can provide you with information on the Capitol Group and save you a trip to the Chamber of Commerce. (Open Mon.-Fri. 8am-5pm.) Take a free tour of the **Legislative Building** (586-8687) to get a peek at the public realm. You may even venture into the governor's office, but you must use your imagination when picturing the layout of the Senate's and House of Representatives' respective "locker rooms." The building's spectacular dome (the fifth tallest of its type in the world) is even more spectacular now that the $40 million renovations for Washington's 1989 centennial are complete. An enormous wool, velvet, and velour carpet covers over 1200 square feet of the State Reception Room's teakwood floor; when the handpainted rug was completed, the original pattern was destroyed so it could never be used elsewhere. Even those who don't find large carpets particularly exciting will enjoy the informative tours given by a knowledgeable corps of tour guides (45-min., Mon.-Fri. 10am-4pm, Sat.-Sun. 10am-3pm). Committed sightseers should arrive on Wednesday afternoon to complete the double feature with a short tour of the nearby **Governor's mansion** (586-8687; 15-min. tours Wed. 1-2:30pm, otherwise by appointment only).

Capitol Lake Park, next to the Legislative Building, is a favorite spot for runners, sailors, and swimmers. Spawning salmon head for Tumwater Falls late August through October; you can spot the lox-to-be leaping through the air as they cross the lake. The **State Capitol Museum,** 211 W. 21st Ave. (753-2580), exhibits local artwork and historical fragments. (Open Tues.-Fri. 10am-4pm, Sat.-Sun. noon-4pm. Free.)

The city offers a number of budget deals after dark. The **State Theater,** 204 E. 4th Ave. (357-4010), shows movies for $1. During the summer, the city schedules free jazz, ensemble, and symphony concerts (Wed. at 7:30pm and Fri. at noon; call 753-8183). Evergreen State College earns honors for the best low-cost entertainment in town; call 866-6000 for information on musical and theatrical performances. The **Evergreen Summer Repertory Theater** (866-6833) produces four high-quality shows over the summer.

Near Olympia

The **Mima Mounds** (753-2400), an unusual geologic formation, have been preserved in a Department of Natural Resources prairie park 10 miles south of Olympia. The self-guided interpretive trails are wheelchair-accessible. (Open daily 8am-dusk.) Take I-5 south to exit 95; 1 mile west of Littlerock, follow Wadell Creek Rd. west.

The **Nisqually National Wildlife Refuge** (753-9467), located off I-5 between Olympia and Tacoma (exit 114), has recently set neighbor against neighbor in the quiet Nisqually delta. While environmentalists treasure the delta as the home of diverse marsh and marine life, developers hope to cast some of their bread upon the water and its environs. For the time being you can watch the protected wildlife from blinds or walk the trails through the preserve. (Open Mon.-Fri. 7:30am-4pm. Free.)

Olympia Beer (754-5177), actually brewed south of the capital city in **Tumwater,** has recently been taken over by the Pabst Company, which now produces a number of different beers on the premises. Tour the facility and have a brewski on the house. (Open daily 8am-4:30pm. Free.) The brewery, visible from I-5, can be reached from exit 103 in Tumwater. Nearby, **Tumwater Falls Park** practically begs for picnickers.

Elma, a small town 26 miles west of Olympia on Hwy. 12, proudly sponsors a **Slug Festival,** held the first weekend in August. The festival features a parade, a street fair, and, for the *grande finale,* slug races. Rarely does the winner of the race slime the full 1/3 furlong before the five-minute time limit is called.

Tacoma

Boston has its Worcester, New England has its Midwest, St. Paul has its Minneapolis, Manhattan has New Jersey, LA has itself, and Seattle has its Tacoma. Seattlites will advise the traveler to avoid this industrial port city. Yet though it may be only a Triple-A town compared to its glamorous major league sibling on the Sound, Tacoma is hardly shabby. Brightest of its gems is Point Defiance Park at the northern tip of the city.

Practical Information and Orientation

Visitor Information: Tacoma/Pierce County Visitor Information Center, 950 Pacific Ave., #450 (627-2836), on the 4th floor of the Seafirst Center. Volunteers can interpret local bus schedules, calendars of events, and city maps. Open daily 9am-4:30pm. For more detailed information, take the elevator down to the 3rd floor, where the staff of the **Tacoma/Pierce County Chamber of Commerce** (627-2715) will be glad to assist. Open Mon.-Fri. 8:30am-5pm.

Amtrak: 1001 Puyallup (627-8141 or 800-872-7245). Take bus #400 or 401. To Seattle (3 per day) and Portland (3 per day). Two trains per day persevere south to San Francisco and Los Angeles. Open daily 6:30am-8:30pm.

Greyhound: 1319 Pacific Ave. (383-4621), in Tacoma's least gem-like area. Buses virtually every hour to Seattle (one way $6) and Portland (one way $16.75). Open daily 7am-8:30pm.

Pierce County Transit: 3701 96th St. SW (581-8000). Economical transportation throughout the city and county. Buses run daily 5am-1am, depending on route number. Fare 65¢; weekdays after 6pm and weekends 50¢. Pick up a map and schedule at the Chamber of Commerce or at the bus stop at 904 Broadway, downtown. Bus service for the disabled also available (call 593-4563). The #601X Olympia Express will take you to Olympia for $1.25. Office open Mon.-Fri. 8am-5pm.

Taxi: Yellow Cab, 472-3303. **United Taxi Co.,** 531-7489.

Car Rental: Rent-A-Dent, 10619 Pacific Ave. (531-3058). $20 per day with 100 free miles plus 15¢ per additional mile. Must be 21 with credit card or $100 deposit. **U-Save Auto Rental,** 7201 S. Tacoma Way (475-1050 or 475-3165). $25 per day with 100 free miles plus 16¢ per additional mile. Must be 21 with credit card. Open Mon.-Sat. 8:30am-6:30pm, Sun. 11am-4pm.

Laundromat: Daisy Laundry and Dry Cleaning, 5909 6th Ave. (564-4949).

Time and Weather: 922-3333.

Pierce County Park and Recreation: 9112 Lakewood Dr. SW (593-4176).

Help Lines: Coast Guard, 800-592-9911. 24 hours. **Rape Relief,** 474-7273. 24 hours. **Tacoma Area Coalition for Individuals with Disabilities (TACID),** 565-9000. Open Mon.-Fri. 8:30am-5pm. **Crisis Line,** 759-6700. **Poison Center,** 594-1414.

YWCA Support Shelter for Battered Women: 383-2593.

Post Office: 11th and A St. Open Mon.-Fri. 8am-5:30pm. General Delivery ZIP Code: 98402.

Area Code: 206.

Tacoma lies on everyone's north-south route through Washington. Both Amtrak and Greyhound pass through, and I-5 skirts the downtown area. From Seattle, take **local transit** and save some money. Hop on Metro bus #174 during off-peak hours (#171 or 175-7 during peak hours) from 2nd and Pike St. to the Federal Way Park and Ride. Transfer here to Pierce Transit bus #500, which will take you downtown. Federal Way is within Metro's two-zone area. The fare is 90¢ during peak hours, 75¢ off-peak.

The city center is accessible from exit 133 off I-5. **Pacific Avenue** is the main drag, passing by the Greyhound and Trailways depots, the post office, and the landmark Old City Hall. Downtown streets run east-west, avenues north-south up to **Division Avenue.** The deep water harbor is at the southeast end of **Commencement Bay,** Tacoma's *raison d'être.* The port waterfront extends along **Ruston Way** to **Point Defiance,** then turns sharply south along **The Narrows,** which is less built up. To navigate these twisted streets, pick up a map from the Chamber of Commerce. Avoid the unsavory area near the Greyhound station, especially after business hours.

Accommodations and Camping

Camping on Mt. Rainier, reveling in Seattle, or relaxing in a small town somewhere on Puget Sound are all more appealing options than spending your money on the expensive hotels and sleazy motels of Tacoma. The two hostels near Tacoma are undoubtedly your best option; hop the ferry to Vashon Island to escape the brouhaha of the metropolises on the Sound.

Vashon Island Hostel (AYH), Cove Rd. (463-2592), at 121st Ave. SW, in nearby Vashon Island. Take the ferry from Point Defiance and then bus #118 (which leaves only at 4:15 and 6:30pm, so timing is important). After waking up in a comfortable log cabin or teepee, fix breakfast with the complimentary pancake mix and have a chat with the friendly owner. Don't forget to explore Vashon (see Near Tacoma). Bikes can be rented from the hostel. Seldom crowded. Check-in 5-10pm. Members $7, nonmembers $10. Open May-Sept.

Clara's Home Hostel (AYH), 5535 Frances (952-4640), 7 miles north of the city. Clara will take great care of you; just be sure to write or call ahead for reservations. Kitchen facilities, washer and dryer, a gorgeous view of Puget Sound. Families with children welcome. Members $5.

Portage Inn, 3021 Pacific Hwy. E. (922-3500), exit 136B off I-5. Clean, convenient, and—best of all—cheap. A/C, color TV. Transportation to Sea-Tac. Singles $24. Doubles $28.

Motel 6, 1811 76th (473-7100). Your basic comfortable sterility. A/C and TV, but at prices somewhat higher than most of its nationwide namesakes. Singles $29.. Doubles $32.

Olympus Hotel, 815 Pacific Ave. (272-7895), in the city center. An impressive lobby serves as a false front for an otherwise dirty hotel. Dining room attached. See a room before putting your money down. Singles $23. Doubles $28. Key deposit $5.

Dash Point State Park (593-2206), on Hwy. 509 across Commencement Bay, in the northeast corner of the city. Take bus #63. A thick forest, a wide beach, and a terrific view are this park's attractions. Sites $7.

Kopachuck State Park (265-3606), on Henderson Bay across the Narrows, about 12 miles northwest of the city center, west of Hwy. 16 on local roads. Take bus #100. Specializes in water recreation, including clamming. Sites $7.

Food

Antique Sandwich Company, 5102 N. Pearl St. (752-4069), near Point Defiance. A gathering place for local folk musicians and aimless recent college graduates. Homemade soups as well as whole-wheat honey desserts. Waffles $1.50. For a richer meal, try the "poor boy sandwich" ($5). Open mike Tues. at 7pm. The restaurant's bulletin board chronicles local happenings. Open Mon., Wed.-Thurs., and Sat. 7am-8pm, Tues. 7am-10pm, Fri. 7am-9pm, Sun. 8:30am-7pm.

Bob's Java Jive, 2102 S. Tacoma Way (475-9843), south of downtown and directly below the I-5 skyway. Take bus #300 from Jefferson and Broadway downtown. A cabaret-cafe shaped like a teapot. Two monkeys (Java and Jive) live in a cage in the back room. A family café until 8pm, when the cabaret starts. Hamburgers and sandwiches around $2. Open Mon. 11:30am-midnight, Tues.-Thurs. 3pm-midnight, Fri. 11:30am-2am, Sat. 6pm-2am.

O'Shea's, 786 Commerce St. (383-8855), downtown. *The* place for lunching shipping executives. Interesting lunches alter daily ($5). Breakfasts of waffles or pancakes with fresh fruit $3. Delicious baked goods—try the white chocolate brownie ($1). Open Mon.-Fri. 7am-3pm.

Tacoma Salmon House, 2611 Pacific (627-0141), near I-5. Good seafood in a woodsy atmosphere. Lunch specials from $4 Mon.-Fri. 11am-3pm. Open daily 11am-8pm.

Moctezuma's Restaurant, corner of 56th and Tyler (474-5593), 1063 miles north of the border. Above-par burritos, tostadas, and enchiladas ($3.50-4). Open Mon.-Thurs. 11am-10pm, Fri.-Sat. 11am-11pm.

Mrs. Frisbee's Bakery Deli and Coffee Shop, 710 S. 38th St. (475-8450 or 472-7591). Sure, you can get a ham-and-cheese sandwich for $2, but leave money for dessert—sublime neopolitans cost 99¢, enormous day-old apple cinnamon muffins only 30¢. Open Mon.-Sat. 6am-6pm, Sun. 10am-4pm.

Sights and Activities

Predictably, the most attractive sights in Tacoma line up along the waterfront. Huge freighters steam out of the sprawling port to bring the lumber and paper products of the central Cascades to the world. Survey the activity from a vantage point in **Commencement Park** or **Marine Park,** both on **Ruston Way** just north of downtown. The city has developed much of Ruston Way's 2-mile waterfront along Commencement Bay as a recreational area for biking, hiking, scuba diving, and boating. On a clear day, this road offers a great view of Mt. Rainier as it looms over Tacoma's skyline.

For the traveler, Tacoma's most valuable waterfront real estate is the 700-acre **Point Defiance Park.** Miles of woodland trails and roads promise tranquility and wistful vistas of Puget Sound's islands and waterways. The **Point Defiance Zoo and Aquarium** (591-5335) features a polar bear complex, an aquarium, and a reproduction of Southeast Asia. (Open daily 10am-7pm; in winter 10am-4pm. Admission $2.50, ages over 62 and under 18 $1.50.) **Camp Six Logging Museum** (752-0047) retrieves an entire 19th-century logging camp from the dustbin of history. The camp includes buildings and equipment, and offers a 1-mile ride on an original steam logging engine. (Open Memorial Day-Labor Day Sat.-Sun. 11am-6pm. Admission $1.50, senior citizens and children 75¢.)

Also in the park is the meticulously restored **Fort Nisqually** (591-5339). The British Hudson's Bay Company built the fort in 1832 to offset growing commercial competition from Americans. The project backfired when the company began to sell supplies to the American settlers. The indoor **museum** dips the fort into the Sound's history. (Fort open daily 11am-7pm; Labor Day-Memorial Day Wed.-Sun. 9am-5pm. Museum open daily noon-6pm; Labor Day-Memorial Day Wed.-Sun. 1-4pm. Both free.)

Tacoma's excellent **Washington State Historical Museum,** 315 N. Stadium (593-2830), has comprehensive exhibits on Washington's natural and human history.

(Open Tues.-Sat. 9:30am-5pm, Sun. 2-5pm. Free.) The **Pantages Center** (591-5890), on the Broadway Mall downtown, is a recently rejuvenated cultural center in an old-fashioned building. It embraces both local rep companies and national touring shows. (Tours offered on the hour Tues. 10am-1pm and Thurs. 1-4pm. Ticket office open Mon.-Fri. 11:30am-4pm.) The basement of the Pantages is the current home of the **Bing Crosby Historical Society** (627-2947). Bing spent his first three years in Tacoma, and this display casts a retrospective glance on those auspicious times. Devotees should shuffle east to the Crosby Library in Spokane to see a piece of Bing's right index finger bone. (Open Mon.-Fri. 11am-3pm.) The city sponsors free outdoor concerts in summer, including a regular schedule of noon and evening performances by the **Tacoma Symphony,** and jazz and classical artists. Contact the Chamber of Commerce for more information. Aesthetes should make a quick stop at the convenient **Tacoma Art Museum** (272-4258), at 12th and Pacific Ave. downtown. This eclectic collection brings a needed dose of local artwork to Tacoma's depressed downtown area. (Open Mon.-Sat. 10am-5pm, Sun. noon-5pm. Admission $2, senior citizens and students $1. Tues. free.)

Near Tacoma: Vashon Island

Only a short ferry ride from Seattle or Tacoma, vision-quenching Vashon Island is, for the moment anyway, spared the scourge of tourism. Of the many ways a day might be spent on Vashon, most are free. **Biking** is rapturous throughout the island—the Westside Highway is particularly flat and sunny. The **Wax Orchards,** 204th and 131st St. (463-9735), processes all-natural preserves and other fruity items. Take a self-guided tour of the orchards and processing facilities. (Open daily 8:30am-4:30pm.) Skiing buffs should examine the famed **K2 Ski Factory,** located in the town of Vashon (463-3631; tours given Mon.-Fri. 7am-5pm). With one out of every 10 residents of the island a professional artist, aesthetic praxis is common. **Blue Heron Arts** coordinates most of these activities. Call 463-5131 for a tour or details on upcoming classes and events. The "really big show" on Vashon is the **Strawberry Festival,** the second or third weekend of July. Enjoy miles of food and craft booths, a parade, and, of course, all known strawberry products.

The best budget accommodation on Vashon Island is unquestionably the hostel (see Tacoma Accommodations). There are no campgrounds on the island, but you can put up a tent on the hostel's lawn and use its facilities for $10 per night.

In an **emergency,** call the Coast Guard at 463-2951. In a **medical emergency,** call 463-3696 Tues.-Sat. 9am-5pm; otherwise phone Seattle. The **post office** is in downtown Vashon (463-9390) and is open Mon.-Fri. 9am-5pm. The General Delivery ZIP Code is 98070.

Bellingham

Local poet Ella Higginson once bragged that she had lived in three different cities without ever having moved a block. Founded by loggers and coal miners in the 1850s, Bellingham was originally called Whatcom, and the town's name changed to Sehome before the powers that be settled on the current name (which presumably will hold out at least until the turn of the century). Together with Fairhaven, its southern neighbor, Bellingham set its sights on becoming the terminus of the transcontinental railroad. So hell-bent were the residents on capturing that ultimate spike that when the famed feminist-anarchist Emma Goldman blew into town, they trooped en masse to jeer her, fearful that her intent was to smear Bellingham's all-American image as the promised land of free enterprise. The townspeople's enthusiasm and spleen went for naught, however—the sea was to lap at the railroad's heels 90 miles to the south.

Yet Bellingham survived this setback and is now in the process of gentrification. Western Washington University is the town's largest single employer, but aluminum and paper mills are close seconds. The city itself is aesthetically uninspiring, but Whatcom County's gorgeous scenery and older logging communities provide a pleasing backdrop.

Practical Information and Orientation

Visitor Information: 904 Potter St. (671-3990). Take the Lakeway exit from I-5. Prepare yourself for a flood of Whatcom County paraphernalia. Extremely helpful staff. Open daily 9am-6pm; in winter 8:30am-5:30pm. **Bellingham Parks and Recreation Department,** 3424 Meridian St. (676-6985).

Greyhound: 1329 N. State St. (733-5251). To Seattle (7 per day, $10), Vancouver (5 per day, $8), and Mt. Vernon (7 per day, $4). Open Mon.-Fri. 6am-6pm, Sat.-Sun. 8am-5pm.

Whatcom County Transit: 676-7433. All buses originate at the terminal in the Railroad Ave. mall on Magnolia St., where maps and schedules are available. Fare 25¢, senior citizens 10¢; no free transfers. Buses run every 15-30 min. Mon.-Fri. 7am-6pm, reduced service Sat. 9am-5pm.

Lummi Island Ferry: 676-6730. 26 trips back and forth each day. The first leaves the island at 6:50am; the last departs the mainland at 12:10am. Fare $1, driver and car $2.

Taxi: Superior Cabs, 734-3478. **Bellingham Taxi,** 676-0445. Both 24 hours.

Car Rental: U-Save Auto Rental, 1100 Iowa (671-3687). Cars from $18 per day with 100 free miles, 20¢ per additional mile. Must be 21 with credit card or $250 deposit. Open Mon.-Fri. 9am-6pm, Sat. 9am-5pm.

Ski Report: 671-0211 or 733-8180 (second number also gives windsurfing conditions in summer).

Mountain Pass Conditions: 1-976-7623. Nov.-March 24 hours. Toll call.

Ride Board: Viking Union at Western Washington University. Rides most often to Seattle and eastern Washington, but also to diverse regions of the continent.

Senior Services: Information and assistance 733-4033 (city), 398-1995 (county).

Crisis Centers: Bellingham, 734-7271. Whatcom County, 384-1485. Both open 24 hours.

Pharmacy: Fountain Super Drug Store, 2416 Meridian (733-6200). Open Mon.-Sat. 9am-10pm, Sun. 10am-7pm.

Hospital: St. Luke's General, 734-8300. Open 24 hours.

Post Office: 315 Prospect (676-8303). Open Mon.-Fri. 8am-5pm. General Delivery ZIP Code: 98225.

Area Code: 206.

Bellingham lies along I-5, 90 miles north of Seattle and 57 miles south of Vancouver. Bellingham's downtown is a small shopping and business area centered on Holly St. and Cornwall Ave., perfumed by the aromatic Georgia Pacific paper plant. Western Washington University climbs a hill to the south along Indian St., and Old Fairhaven Village (the "South Side" to the locals) fronts the south end of the bay along South State St. Suburbs and 130 acres of city parks circle the city. **Whatcom County Transit** provides service throughout the area.

Reach **Fairhaven** either by heading south along State St. from downtown or by taking the Fairhaven exit (#250) off I-5. From the south, consider taking the bayside **Chuckanut Drive** (Hwy. 11) instead of I-5. Chuckanut leaves I-5 at exit 231 in Skagit County and follows the water and mountains into Fairhaven Village. Larrabee State Park is along this drive. Startling views of the San Juan Islands and sparkling Puget Sound appear through the trees. This route is not recommended for cyclists, since the road is extremely narrow and seems to be a favorite show-off spot for hotrodders. Instead, cyclists should stick to Hwy. 9, a more manageable stretch that pops up on the east side of I-5. Fairhaven is also on Bellingham bus lines 1A, 1B, 2B, 5A, and 7B.

Accommodations and Camping

Most of Bellingham's motels serve traveling salespeople and other itinerants, and the rooms lack both tranquility and a bay view. One alternative is the local bed-and-breakfast association **Babs**, P.O. Box 5025, Bellingham 98227 (733-8642), which offers doubles averaging $50.

YWCA, 1026 N. Forest St. (734-4820), up the hill, 1 block east of State St., about 4 blocks from Greyhound. Only women over 18 allowed. A pleasant, older building. Some rooms have views. Large rooms with sink; bathroom down the hall. Check-in Mon.-Fri. 8am-9pm, Sat. 9am-5pm. No curfew. Singles $10-15.

Mac's Motel, 1215 E. Maple St. (734-7570), at Samish Way. Large clean rooms. Pleasant management lets cats loaf all over the office. Singles $25. Doubles $30.

Motel 6, 3701 Byron Ave. (671-4494), Samish Way exit off I-5, between Denny's and the Calico Inn Pancake House. Noisy location on freeway. Singles $25. Doubles $31. Reservations sometimes necessary in summer.

Bell Motel, 208 N. Samish Way (733-2520), on the strip. Hard beds and plain decor. Free local calls. Refrigerator in most rooms. Singles $30. Doubles $35. Kitchens $5. Winter rates $5 less.

Larrabee State Park, Chuckanut Dr. (676-2093), 7 miles south of Bellingham. 100 sites on Samish Bay. Near tidal pools and short hikes to alpine lakes. For your listening pleasure, trains thunder by nightly; tracks separate the campground from the bay. The 3 walk-in tentsites are the most appealing option. Sites $7. Hookups $9.50.

Food

Stock up naturally at the **Community Food Co-op**, 1059 N. State St. (734-8158), at Maple. (Open Mon.-Sat. 9am-8pm, Sun. 11am-6pm.) Pineapples and coconuts are unaccountably common throughout the city.

The Bagelry, 1319 Railroad Ave. (676-5288), 1 block south of the City Transit terminal. Order a veggie-laden bagel sandwich for $3, or just have a bagel (8 kinds) with cream cheese (9 flavors) for $1.60. The pumpernickel-pineapple combination is not recommended. Open Mon.-Fri. 7am-5pm, Sat. 8am-5pm, Sun. 9am-4pm.

Bullie's Restaurant, 1200 Harris (734-2855), in the Fairhaven Marketplace. An old gas pump converted into a cylindrical fish bowl. Burgers $5, Tex-Mex, and Potato Skin Dinners ($6). Don't pass up a chance to experience the Aloha pineapple burger. Massive beer selection. Open Mon.-Sat. 6am-10pm, Sun. 6am-9pm.

Tony's Coffees and Tea Shop, 1101 Harris Ave., Fairhaven Village (733-6319), just down the hill from S. State St. This Fairhaven institution is at once café and coffee market. Some tables are inlaid with hand-painted tiles, and local artists display their work on the walls. Coffee, bagels, and pastries surrounded by sitar music, a sea of paisley, and a pierced nose or two. Serves something called a "toxic milkshake" ($1.65). Free live music Fri. and Sat. nights. Open daily 7:30am-11pm. Same cinnamon rolls for ½-price at the **Great Harvest Bakery** in the Bellingham Mall (671-0873), on Samish Way. Bakery open Tues.-Sat. 9:30am-6pm.

GJK Greek Cafe, 1219 Cornwall Ave. (676-5554). White plaster and Greek accents. Gyros $4, *souvlaki*, baklava, and more esoteric dishes. Open Mon.-Sat. 10am-10pm.

Mexican Village Cafe, 2010 N. State St. (676-8033), 5 blocks northeast of downtown. Full meals $5-7, tacos $1.50. Open Tues.-Sun. 4:30-8:30pm.

The High Country, 119 N. Commercial St. (733-3443), at the top of the Bellingham Towers downtown. Elevated dining at elevated prices; go up merely for a drink and the views. Faborama panorama. Open Mon.-Fri. 11:30am-2pm and 5:30-9:30pm, Sat.-Sun. 5:30-10:30pm.

Sights and Activities

When Bellingham and nearby Fairhaven lost their bid to become the terminus of the transcontinental railroad, construction stopped short and many buildings, especially in Fairhaven, were left uncompleted. Fairhaven was later incorporated into Bellingham and left to rot. After a developer caught sight of Fairhaven's decaying buildings about 10 years ago, the South Side began to revitalize.

Old railway cars frequently serve as restaurants and shops, especially in the fully restored **Marketplace,** at Harris Ave. and 12th St. This is also the setting for the annual **Christmas Arts and Crafts Fair** (Sat.-Sun. for 3 weeks before Christmas). The fair imports live music and other forms of entertainment. *Fairhaven,* a free brochure available from the visitors center, describes a short walking tour through the area.

The **Whatcom Museum of History and Art,** 121 Prospect St. (676-6981), between Holly, Prospect, and Central St. downtown, dates from the same boom era as the South Side buildings. The towering red Victorian, once the city hall, is visible from most of downtown. It now displays first-rate exhibitions of modern art and local history. The exhibits are impeccably presented, a rare achievement for a county museum. There is absolutely no reason to miss a free museum of this caliber. How you dare. (Open Tues.-Sun. noon-5pm.)

Many choose to live in Bellingham for its distance from the anomie of late-capitalist brouhaha. Hike up **Chuckanut Mountain** through a quiet forest for great views of the islands that fill the bay. You can occasionally spot Mt. Rainier to the south. A 2½-mile hike uphill leaves from Old Samish Hwy. about 1 mile south of the city limits. The beach at **Lake Padden Park,** 4882 Samish Way (676-6989), delights those who find Puget Sound a little chilly. Take bus #5B or 10A 1 mile south of downtown. A lifeguard stands guard Memorial Day through Labor Day. The park also has miles of hiking trails, a boat launch (no motors allowed), tennis courts, and playing fields. The park is wheelchair-accessible. (Open daily 6am-10pm.)

Whatcom Falls Park, 1401 Electric Ave., due east of town, also has fantastic hiking trails, picnic facilities, and tennis courts. Upper Whatcom Falls trail (1.6 miles) leads to the falls themselves, converted into an unofficial waterslide by the young people. Take bus #4A or 11A. (Open daily 6am-10pm.) Fishing is good in both these lakes and also in **Lake Samish** and **Silver Lake,** north of the town of Maple Falls off the Mt. Baker Hwy. (See Near Bellingham for information on Silver Lake County Park.) The lake trout season opens the third Sunday in April. **Fishing licenses** ($3) are available from the Department of Fisheries (586-1425), at any sporting goods store, and at some hardware stores.

Popular with South Side residents, **Interurban trail** runs 6.6 miles from Fairhaven Park to Larrabee State Park along the route of the old Interurban Electric Railway. The trail is less developed than those at Padden and Whatcom Lakes and follows a creek through the forest. Occasional breaks in the trees permit views of the San Juan Islands. More information on these and other city parks is available from the Parks and Recreation Department (see Practical Information).

Western Washington University (676-3000) is the nexus of much of the activity in and around the Bellingham area. A sylvan setting and extensive outdoor sculpture collection ease one's soul. Take bus #3B, 7B, or 8A to reach the campus. Friday nights, a program of concerts aptly titled **Mama Sundays** takes place in the Viking Union on campus. Top-notch folk and bluegrass are the norm ($1-5). The campus displays 16 pieces of outdoor sculpture, commissioned from local and nationally known artists. The free brochure, *Western's Outdoor Museum,* locates sculpture on a map, with descriptions. The brochure is available at the **Western Visitors Center,** at the entrance to the college on South College Dr., and at the Whatcom County Visitors Center in Blaine.

Near Bellingham

The *pièce de résistance* of Whatcom County is certainly **Mount Baker,** which dominates the landscape and the recreational economy of the area. Exit 255 off I-5, just north of Bellingham, leads to Hwy. 542, the Mt. Baker Highway. Fifty-six miles of roadway jog through the foothills, bestowing spectacular views of Baker and the other peaks in the range. Crowning the Mt. Baker-Snoqualmie National Forest, Mt. Baker coos over its excellent downhill and cross-country facilities, usually open from late October through mid-May. The peak reaches 10,778 feet and the longest downhill run plummets 6500 feet. Call 734-6771 in Bellingham for more information on the operation and resort. On your way to the mountain, stop at the **Mount Bakery,** 3706 Mt. Baker Hwy. (592-5703), for gigantic apple fritters and other muffins, donuts, and pastries (under 50¢). (Open Mon.-Sat. 6am-6pm.)

Mount Baker Vineyards, 4298 Mt. Baker Hwy. (592-2300), fewer than 10 miles outside the city limits, is one of a number of successful vineyards in Washington. The processing and storage areas are open to the public and guided tours are conducted daily. (Open Wed.-Sun. 11am-5pm; Jan.-March Sat.-Sun. 11am-5pm.)

Silver Lake Park, 9006 Silver Lake Rd. (599-2776), 28 miles east of Bellingham on the Mt. Baker Hwy. and 3 miles north of Maple Falls, is operated by the Whatcom County Parks and Recreation Department. The park tends 113 campsites near the lake along with facilities for swimming, hiking, and fishing. (Tentsites $6. Hookups $7.50.)

The *cogniscenti* flee the town of **Lynden,** which gained local notoriety when it outlawed public dancing wherever liquor is served. Blue suede shoes may have gone by the wayside, but clogging is still esteemed by the town's Dutch community, which also keeps a steady supply of tulips and miniature windmills on display. **Holland Days,** in early May, features a wooden shoe race. The **Lynden Pioneer Museum,** 217 Front St. (354-3675), owns a fine collection of over 100 buggies, tractors, and old cars. (Open Mon.-Sat. 10am-5pm; Nov.-March Thurs.-Sat. noon-4pm. Free.) Just down the street, **Dutch Mother's Restaurant and Bakery,** 405 Front St. (354-2174), celebrates Lynden's gastronomic heritage with Dutch baked goods and servers in full Netherlandish costume. (Breakfast under $5, lunch and dinner also served.) Reach Lynden via I-5: going south, turn east off exit 270; going north, head north off exit 256.

Lummi Island, off the coast of Bellingham, was for centuries the fishing and hunting ground of the Lummi nation of Native Americans. Now the Lummis are confined to a reservation on the northwestern side of Bellingham Bay, and the island has been overrun by palefaces in search of neo-Thoreaudian solitude. The island is distinctly rural, with paved roads only on the northern half. Old logging roads chessboarding the rest of the island are perfect for hiking up to Lummi Mountain or down to the island's various bays and tidal pools. Bicyclists will find the island roads peaceful; traffic is unbearably light and fairly slow. The Department of Natural Resources (DNR) operates a 5-site campground on the southeast tip of the island, accessible only by boat.

Lummi Island can be reached by **ferry** from Gooseberry Point on the Lummi Indian Reservation, 15 miles from Bellingham. Take I-5 north to exit 260; left on Hwy. 540 will lead you west about 3½ miles to Haxton Way. Turn south and follow signs to the ferry terminal. For 10 days in June each year, the ferry is sent to Seattle for maintenance. During this interlude a walk-on ferry is substituted, so don't plan on taking your car. Call ferry information (676-6730) for exact dates.

The border town of **Blaine,** 20 miles north of Bellingham, is a famous overnight spot for those who get turned away at the Canadian border. Heavily geared toward tourism, Blaine's pier is a popular fishing spot for locals and out-of-towners.

Although much-touted, **Peace Arch State Park Heritage Site** (332-8221; open for day-use only) does not warrant a special trip. Embracing the Canada-U.S. border from both sides, the park commemorates a century of peaceful relations between the two nations. The lawns and picnic areas are lovely when the flowers are in bloom, but such inscriptions as "Children of a Common Mother" and "Brethren Dwelling Together in Unity" seem less than earth-shattering in these days of Free Trade and acid rain. Park officers have not yet reacted to a recent poll finding that while Americans most commonly describe Canadians as "friendly," Canadians most commonly describe Americans as "snobs." (Open daily 6:30am-10pm; Oct. 16-March 8am-5pm.)

Supervised by the Whatcom County Parks and Recreation Department, **Semiahmoo Park** on the neck of Semiahmoo Spit (371-5513), 1 mile south of Blaine, is somewhat more interesting. Take Drayton Harbor Rd. around to the southwestern side of Drayton Harbor. The spit was first inhabited by the coastal Salish people, who harvested shellfish when the tide was low. Clam digging is still a popular activity. Buckets and shovels may be rented from the park, and a $3 license is required. Three buildings from the former Alaska Packers Association cannery, which operated on the spit for 74 years, are now used by the park as an **interpretive center,** vacuum-packing the history of both the local canning industries and the natural environment. (Open mid-Feb. to Dec. Wed.-Sun. 1-5pm. Admission $3.) The park also hosts such events as wool-spinning and weaving shows and traditional salmon bakes. For information on all Whatcom County Parks, contact the Parks and Recreation Board Headquarters and Information Center, 3373 Mt. Baker Hwy. (733-2900).

If you end up staying in Blaine, stop in first at the **Blaine Visitors Center,** 900 Portal Dr. (332-4544), where the helpful staff can load you up with maps, brochures, and newspapers. Some remote but rewarding places lurk in their brochure racks. (Open daily 8am-7pm.) Then head to the **Harbor Cafe,** on Marine Dr. (332-5176), halfway down the pier, for some of the best seafood in the county. The $6 fish and chips, salad bar and roll included, is hard to resist. The **Westview Motel,** 1300 Peace Portal Dr. (332-5501), has TV, fridges, and peaceful management. (Singles $23. Doubles $27.)

For camping, **Birch Bay State Park,** 5105 Helwig Rd. (371-2800), 10 miles south of Blaine, operates 156 sites near the water. The Semiahmoo Native Americans used this area and the marshland at the southern end of the park to gather shellfish and hunt waterfowl. Three hundred species of birds live in the **Terrell Creek Estuary.** The park is also a good area for crabbing, scuba diving, waterskiing, and swimming. To reach the park, take the Birch Bay-Lynden exit off I-5 and turn south onto Blaine Rd. When you run out of road, turn east onto Bay Rd. Turn south on Jackson Rd. and take it to Helwig Rd. The way is well-marked from the freeway. (Sites $7. Open year-round.)

Nearby is the **Birch Bay Hostel (AYH),** stationed on the former Blaine Air Force Base (371-2180). Take either the Birch Bay-Lynden Rd. exit or the Grandview Rd. exit off I-5 and head west. Blaine Rd. will take you to the Alderson Rd. entrance to the Air Force base. The hostel is building #630. There are 24 beds in small, non-dorm rooms. (Members only, $6.50. Open June-Sept.)

While in Blaine or Birch Bay, dial 911 for **fire, ambulance, or police,** and 384-5390 for the **Whatcom County Sheriff.**

Seasonal Events

Whatcom County has a number of annual fairs and festivals that celebrate its modestly colorful past. Held on Gooseberry Point in the Lummi Island Reservation, the **Lummi Stommish Indian Water Carnival** (758-7221) is entering its 43rd year. The three-day carnival at the end of June stages traditional dances and war-canoe races, arts and crafts sales, and a salmon barbecue.

Loggers succeeded Natives in Whatcom County, but fête themselves earlier in June at the 27-year old **Deming Logging Show** (592-2423). Amateur logging stunt-people migrate here from throughout the region to compete in such elaborations of their trade as axe-throwing, log-rolling, and speed climbing. To reach the Show-grounds, take Mt. Baker Hwy. 12 miles east to Cedarville Rd. and head north. Signs beckon you to the grounds.

The crowning event of the two-week **Ski to Sea Festival** (734-1330) is an 85-mile relay race from Mt. Baker to Bellingham Bay over Memorial Day weekend. Team members ski, run, bicycle, canoe, and sail to the finish line. Joyful parades precede the event.

The **Northwest Washington Fairgrounds** (354-4111), in Lynden, hosts a number of wing-dings throughout the summer, including the **Lynden Spring Fair,** at the end of June (with its old-fashioned draft-horse-plowing competition) and the **Northwest Washington Fair,** in mid-August.

San Juan Islands

The San Juan Islands are an uncorrupted treasure. Bald eagles spiral above haggard hillsides and family farms, pods of killer whales spout offshore, and the sun shines perpetually. To travelers approaching from summer resorts infested with vacationers, the islands will seem blissfully quiet. Even in mid-summer, it is possible to drive the back roads and pass another car just once every hour. For this reason, islanders don't begrudge admission to their towns and campsites. Although tension is starting to build between the locals and the Seattle vacationers who are buying up huge chunks of the islands at exorbitant prices, quiet, well-behaved tourists and their dollars are still very welcome on the San Juans.

An excellent guide to the area is *The San Juan Islands Afoot and Afloat* by Marge Mueller ($10), available at bookstores and outfitting stores on the islands and in Seattle. *The San Juans Beckon* is published annually by the *Islands Sounder,* the local paper, to provide up-to-date information on island recreation. You can pick it up free on the ferries and in island stores. The *San Juanderer* is another freebie available on the ferries and at visitors centers.

Getting There

Washington State Ferries serve the islands daily from **Anacortes** on the mainland. To reach Anacortes, take I-5 north from Seattle to Mt. Vernon. From there, Hwy. 20 heads west; the way to the ferry is well-marked. **Evergreen Trailways** buses to Anacortes depart Seattle from the Greyhound depot at 8th Ave. and Stewart St. twice per day. Call 728-5955 for exact times.

Of the 172 islands in the San Juan archipelago, only four are accessible by ferry. Ferries leave about every other hour for Lopez, Shaw, Orcas, and San Juan Island. In summer, two additional ferries per day travel directly to San Juan Island. One ferry per day continues year-round from San Juan Island to the town of Sidney, BC, just north of Victoria on Vancouver Island. The ferry system publishes its schedule every season.

In Anacortes, you can purchase a ticket to Lopez, Shaw, Orcas, or San Juan Island. You pay only on westbound trips to or between the islands; no charge is levied on eastbound traffic. (In effect, any ticket to the islands is a round-trip ticket.) You can thus save money by traveling directly to the westernmost island on your itinerary and then making your way back island by island. The ferry unloads first at Lopez Island, then at Shaw, Orcas, and finally San Juan. It is possible to purchase one-way tickets to Sidney, or from Sidney to the islands. Foot passengers travel in either direction between the islands free of charge. Fares from Anacortes to San Juan Island are $4.65 for pedestrians ($2.35 for senior citizens and ages 5-11), $6.25 for bikes, and $9.50 for motorcycles; cars cost $19. Fares to the other islands en route are generally a few dollars cheaper. Inter-island fares average $2.25 for bikes and motorcycles, $7.75 for cars. The one-way fare to Sidney is $6.05 for pedestrians, $8.55 for bikes, $13.15 for motorcycles, and $31.25 for cars in summer ($26.05 in winter). Some car spaces are available from the islands to Sidney, but reservations are recommended. Call before noon the day before your trip to ensure a space. For specific departure times and rates, call Washington State Ferries (206-464-6400; in WA 800-542-0810). The ferry authorities only accept cash or in-state checks as payment. You may park your vehicle for free in Anacortes at the parking lot on the corner of 30th and T St. A free, reliable shuttle then whisks you 4 miles to the terminal.

San Juan Island

Although San Juan is the last stop on the ferry's route, it is the most frequently visited island and home to the largest town in the group, **Friday Harbor.** Since the ferry docks right in town, the island is the easiest to explore. San Juan was the site of the Pig War, which pitted the U.S. against England in a phony war for control of the islands. The 1846 Treaty of Oregon did not assign the San Juans to either Canada or the U.S., and when the Canadian Hudson's Bay Company established a salmon-curing station and a sheep farm on the island, the Company assumed its ownership would go undisputed. The Territorial Congress of Oregon, oblivious to British intentions, declared the islands its own in 1853. By 1859, 25 Americans lived on San Juan Island. When an American farmer shot a British pig rooting in his garden, the situation became intolerable and both countries had no choice but to send in troops, thus initiating perhaps the least-known international dispute in U.S. history. For 12 years, two thoroughly bored garrisons stared across the island at each other, occasionally convening for horse races and Christmas dances. Their descendants now sublimate their energies into more peaceful pursuits, primarily the bustling tourist industry on this island.

Practical Information

Visitor Information: National Park Service Information Center and **Chamber of Commerce Information Center,** 1st and Spring (378-2240). Answers to questions about the British and American camps (see below). Open Mon.-Fri. 8am-4:30pm, Sat.-Sun. 10:30am-3:30pm.

U.S. Customs: 271 Front St. (378-2080). Open 24 hours.

Ferry Terminal: 378-4777. Open 24 hours.

Taxi: Island Taxi, 378-5545. **Primo Taxi,** 378-3550.

Car Rental: Friday Harbor Rentals, 410 Spring St. (378-4351), in the Friday Harbor Motor Inn. $30 per day. 50 miles free, 25¢ per additional mile. Major credit card or $200 cash deposit required. Must be 21.

Bike Rental: Island Bicycles, 180 West St., Friday Harbor (378-4941), and Roche Harbor Resort (378-4222). 1-speeds $2 per hr., $8 per day; 5-speeds $3 per hr., $12 per day; 10-speeds $4 per hr., $16 per day; mountain bikes $5 per hr., $20 per day. Also rents child carriers, trailers, and panniers. Provides maps of the island and suggests bike routes. (Most roads are hilly and narrow, so exercise caution.) Open Mon.-Sat. 10am-5:30pm, Sun. noon-5:30pm; Labor Day-Memorial Day Thurs.-Sat. 10am-5:30pm.

Moped Rental: Susie's Mopeds, 410 Spring St. (378-5244), up a short hill from the ferry, at the Friday Harbor Motor Inn. Mopeds $9 per hr., $35 per day. Credit card or $100 deposit required. Open March-Oct. daily 10am-6pm.

Tours: San Juan Island Tour and Transit (378-5545) stops at the yellow bench next to the ferry in the summer. Hourly trips to Lakedale/Duck Soup ($3, $5 round-trip) and Roche Harbor ($4, $6 round-trip) daily 8:30am-9pm. **Friday Harbor Motor Inn,** 410 Spring St. (378-4351), sends a double-decker bus ($7) around the island via English Camp and Lime Kiln Park (for whalewatching).

Laundromat: Up a wooden alley on Spring St. between 1st and Front. Open daily 7:30am-9pm.

Pharmacy: Friday Harbor Drug, 210 Spring (378-4421).

Sheriff: 911 emergency, 378-4151 nonemergency. (You be the judge.)

Post Office: Blair and Reed St. (378-4511). Open Mon.-Fri. 8:30am-4:30pm. General Delivery ZIP Code: 98250.

Area Code: 206.

With a youth hostel and bicycle, car, and boat rentals all just one block from the ferry terminal, Friday Harbor makes an ideal starting point for exploration of all the islands. Miles of road traverse all corners of the island from Friday Harbor's eastern hub. Unfortunately, the roads aren't well-marked, so plot your course carefully on one of the maps available free at the information center in Friday Harbor (see Practical Information). **Hitching** is fairly common, and it's a relatively safe means of travel on the island.

Accommodations and Camping

San Juan's campgrounds have become wildly popular of late; show up early in the afternoon.

Friday Harbor Youth Hostel (AYH), 35 1st St. (378-5555), in the Elite Hotel. No kitchen facilities or common areas, but cafe downstairs. Earns low scores for cleanliness, elegance, and security, but its location can't be beat. Check in at the novelty store downstairs, or at the manager's residence (3rd floor). No curfew. Members $9, nonmembers $14.

San Juan County Park, 380 Westside Rd. (378-2992), 10 miles west of Friday Harbor on Smallpox and Andrews Bays. Public campgrounds. Sit on the bay where Native Americans with smallpox fever swam to cool themselves (thereby catching pneumonia). Cold water and flush toilets. Bikers and hikers $3; cars, campers, and trailers $10.

Lakedale Campgrounds, 2627 Roche Harbor Rd. (378-2350), 4 miles from Friday Harbor. San Juan Tours and Transit provides service. Pay showers, fishing, and swimming in freshwater lakes. Bikers and hikers $3.50, vehicles $8 plus $1.50 per person. Canoe rentals $16 per day, plus $10 refundable deposit. Swimming available to noncampers for $1.50 per day, ages under 6 75¢.

Food

The parks and shoreline drives beg you to pack a picnic lunch and leave Friday Harbor behind. Stock up on bread and cheese at **King's Market,** 160 Spring St. (378-4505; open daily 8am-10pm).

Friday Harbor Bistro, 35 1st St. (378-3076), in the same building as the hostel. A cheap pizza place gone upscale. 10-in. pizzas and Italian dinners $8.25. Open Sun.-Thurs. 11am-10pm, Fri.-Sat. 11am-10:30pm.

Driftwood Drive-In, corner of 2nd and Court. Put on your jeans, lumberjack shirt, caterpillar tractor hat, and *Batman* rhinestone jacket and join the locals for a burger ($2) and chocolate shake ($1.30). Hours vary, but open late.

The Hungry Clam, on 1st St. near Spring. The unmistakable spout of the fast-food leviathan. Clam basket $5, burger $3.25. Open Mon.-Fri. 11am-8pm, Sat. 11am-9pm, Sun. noon-6pm.

San Juan Donut Shop, 209 Spring St. (378-2271). Another local hangout. Breakfast under $5, with plenty of bagels and croissants. Cheeseburger $2. Open Mon.-Sat. 5am-5pm, Sun. 6am-noon.

Funk 'n' Junk Bakery, 65 Nickel St., behind the antique store. The truly bold opt for the jalapeño jack cheese croissant ($1.75); the rest settle for nutty chocolate chip cookies. Hours vary.

Sights and Activities

Friday Harbor is less than charming when the tourists are out in full force, but quite appealing in the winter. Take the time to poke around the galleries, craft shops, and bookstores. The **Whale Museum**, 62 1st St. (378-4710), will teach you more than you ever wanted to know about the giant cetaceans, starring skeletons, sculptures, and information on new research. The museum even has a **whale hotline** (800-562-8832) so you can report sightings and strandings. (Open daily in summer 10am-5pm, in winter 11am-4pm. Admission $2.50, senior citizens and students $2, ages under 12 $1.) The free **San Juan Historical Museum,** in the old King House at 405 Price St. (378-4587), across from the St. Francis Catholic church, explodes with exhibits, furnishings, and photographs from the late 1800s. (Open June-Labor Day Wed.-Sat. 1-4pm.)

A drive around the perimeter of the island takes about 90 minutes. The route is flat enough to keep cyclists happy. The **West Side Road** traverses gorgeous scenery and allows your best chance of sighting orcas (killer whales) offshore. For those without private transportation, **San Juan Tours and Transit Co.** (378-5545) runs two sight-seeing tours of the island every afternoon. The two-hour tours circle the island, stopping at Roche Harbor, English and American Camps, and Lime Kiln Lighthouse (see Practical Information).

To begin a loop of the island, head south out of Friday Harbor on Argyle Rd., which merges into Cattle Point Rd. on the way to **American Camp** (378-2240), 5 miles south of Friday Harbor. The camp dates to the aforementioned Pig War of 1859, when the U.S. and England were at loggerheads over possession of the islands. Two of the camp's buildings still stand. An interpretive shelter near the entrance to the park explains the history of the war; there is also a self-guided exegetical trail from the shelter through the buildings and past the site of the English sheep farm. Watch your footing; gigantic rabbits have rampaged across this terrain in recent years. (Free.) A ½-mile jaunt farther down the road to **Cattle Point** rewards you with blissful, quiet clear-weather views of the distant Olympic Mountains.

Returning north on Cattle Point Rd., consider taking the gravel False Bay Rd. to the west. The road will guide you to **False Bay,** a true bay that is home to a large number of nesting bald eagles. A University of Washington biology preserve, the bay is the site of many student projects, each indicated by markers. False Bay is almost a guaranteed spot for eagle watching. During the spring and summer at low tide, walk quietly along the northwestern shore (to your right as you face the water) to see the nesting national emblems.

Whale-watching at **Lime Kiln Point State Park,** a few miles north, is best during salmon runs in the summer. Check the whale museum for day-to-day information on your chances of sighting the orcas and minkes looming off-shore.

Farther north on False Bay Rd., you'll run into **Bailer Hill Road,** which turns into West Side Rd. when it reaches Haro Straight. (You can also reach Bailer Hill Rd. by taking Cattle Point Rd. to Little Rd.) Sloping hills blanketed with wild-flowers rise to one side, and rocky shores fall to the other. **San Juan County Park** on Smallpox Bay offers a convenient opportunity to stop and examine this Manichaean scenery more closely.

The Pig War casts a comic pallor over **English Camp,** the second half of San Juan National Historical Park. The camp lies on West Valley Rd. on the sheltered Garrison Bay. From West Side Rd., take Mitchell Bay Rd. east to West Valley Rd. Here, four original buildings have been preserved, including the barracks, now used as an **interpretive center.** The center explains the history of the "war" and sells guides to the island. It also shows a relatively interesting 10-minute slide show on the struggle. (Park open year-round; buildings open Memorial Day-Labor Day daily 9am-6pm. Free.)

Roche Harbor Resort, Roche Harbor Rd. (378-2155), on the northern side of the island, began as a lime mine and kiln, built by the British during their occupation. Bought up by industrialist John S. McMillan in 1886, Roche Harbor became a full-fledged company town. McMillan paid his workers in scrip, redeemable only at the company store (still standing today), and apparently had no qualms about firing his whole crew when a strike broke out. In 1956, the entire town was bought from the company and turned into a resort. The **Hotel de Haro,** built by McMillan in 1887 to accommodate clients, is the center of the resort. Stop by the information kiosk in front for a copy of the $1 brochure, *A Walking Tour of Historic Roche Harbor,* which tosses a little history of the "town" in with architectural and social commentary. Much of the grounds is open to the public. Don't miss the bizarre **mausoleum** that McMillan had built for himself and his family. The Masonic symbolism that garnishes the structure is explained in the *Walking Tour.* (Grounds open 24 hours. Tennis courts and swimming pool open only to those staying at the resort.)

Those eager to **fish** or **clam** ought to pick up a copy of the Department of Fisheries pamphlet, *Salmon, Shellfish, Marine Fish Sport Fishing Guide,* for details on regulations and limits. The guide is available free at Friday Harbor **Hardware and Marine,** 270 Spring St. (378-4622). Free hunting and fishing licenses are required on the islands, and can be obtained from the hardware store. (Open Mon.-Sat. 8am-6pm,

Sun. 10am-4pm.) Check with the **red tide hotline** (800-562-5632) if you'll be harvesting shellfish; the nasty bacteria can wreak satanic horrors on your intestines.

Several small-scale entrepreneurs rent out or charter boats to visitors for expeditions on the water or to neighboring small islands. **San Juan Kayak Expeditions** (378-4436) leads two- to four-day trips in stable two-person sea kayaks. These excursions (given June-Sept.) offer a peaceful and personal way to see the hidden niches of the archipelago. You give them money; they supply equipment and camping gear. ($125 for a 2-day trip, $175 for a 3-day trip, and $225 for a 4-day trip, including 2 hot meals per day.) Make reservations early by contacting the company at 3090-B Roche Harbor Rd., Friday Harbor 98250.

The annual **San Juan Island Traditional Jazz Festival** brings several swing bands to Friday and Roche Harbors on the last weekend in July. A $35 badge ($40 if purchased after July 1) will gain you admission to all performances, but you'll have just as much fun for free by joining the festive crowd of revelers in the alleys outside the clubs. Don't expect Cecil Taylor. For more information, contact San Juan Island Goodtime Classic Jazz Association, P.O. Box 1666, Friday Harbor 98250 (378-5509).

Orcas Island

Mount Constitution overlooks much of Puget Sound from its 2409-foot peak atop Orcas Island, the largest of the San Juan chain. In the mountain's shadow dwells a small population of retirees, artists, and farmers amidst understated homes and surprisingly few tourists. Surprising, because with its state park and youth hostel, Orcas has perhaps the best tourist facilities of all the islands. Stop in one of the shops at the landing to get a free map. (Most shops open daily 8:30am-6:30pm.)

Practical Information and Orientation

Visitor Information: Chamber of Commerce, North Beach Rd. (376-2273), just north of Eastsound Sq. and Doty's (see Food). An unimpressive shack, but it distributes an excellent map of Orcas (all you'll need to explore). Open Mon.-Sat. noon-4pm.

Ferry Terminal: 376-4389 or 376-2134. Open daily 6am-8pm.

Bike Rental: Island Chainsaw (376-2586), in the Sears Bldg. on Prune Alley in Eastsound. No, we're not steering you into *The Washington Chainsaw Massacre*—they rent bicycles too. 6-speed bikes $3 first hr., $1.50 per additional hr., $12 per day, $40 per week. Mountain bikes $4 per hr., $18 per day. $10 deposit required. **Wildlife Cycle,** in Eastsound, rents 18-speeds for $5 per hr., $20 per day. Open Mon.-Sat. 10:30am-5:30pm.

Moped Rental: Key Moped Rentals (376-2474), at the ferry landing, Eastsound, or Rosario Resort. Mopeds $9 per hr., $35 per 8-hr. day. Driver's license required. $10 deposit. Open in summer daily 10am-6pm.

Library: On Horseshoe Hwy., across from Emmanuel Church in Eastsound (376-4985). Open Tues.-Wed. 10am-7pm, Thurs. 10am-9pm, Sat. 10am-4pm.

Pharmacy: Ray's, next to Templin's in Eastsound (376-2230). Open Mon.-Sat. 9am-6pm, Sun. 11am-2pm.

Fire and Ambulance: 376-2341. Staffed with Emergency Medical Technicians and paramedics in case of medical emergency. Open 24 hours.

Sheriff: 376-2207. 24 hours.

Post Office: A St., in Eastsound Market Place (376-4121), ½ block north of the Chamber of Commerce. Open Mon.-Fri. 9am-4:30pm. General Delivery ZIP Code: 98245.

Area Code: 206.

Because Orcas is shaped like a horseshoe, getting around is a bit of a chore. The ferry lands on the southwest tip. Travel 9 miles northeast up the horseshoe to reach Eastsound, the island's main town. Olga and Doe Bay are yet another 8 and 11 miles from Eastsound, respectively, down the eastern side of the horseshoe. Gas prices on Orcas often run 40¢ more per gallon than on the mainland. Tank up in Anacortes, if not sooner. The only gas stations on the island are located in Deer Harbor, Eastsound, and the ferry landing.

Accommodations and Camping

Avoid the nine bed and breakfasts (upwards of $60 per day) of the "Healing Island" and stay at the hostel. If the hostel is full, the campgrounds are the next best way to get a feel for Orcas.

Doe Bay Village Resort (AYH), Star Rte. 86, Olga 98279 (376-2291 or 376-4755), off Horseshoe Hwy. On a secluded bay. The resort comes with kitchen facilities, a health food store, and plenty of grounds to wander. The crowning attraction, however, is the steam sauna and mineral bath, available to hostelers at $3 per day. (Nonlodgers $5. Bathing suits are optional.) Members $9.50, nonmembers $10.50. Camping $7.50. Cottages from $26.50. Guided kayak trips $25 per half-day. Reservations are recommended. Open year-round.

Outlook Inn (376-2200), on the north side of Horseshoe Hwy. in the center of Eastsound. Consider draining your wallet into this renovated Victorian inn; all rooms are decorated in period antiques. Singles from $55. Doubles $60. Reservations required in summer. Write P.O. Box 210, Eastsound 98245.

Moran State Park, Star Rte. Box 22, Eastsound 98245 (376-2326). Follow Horseshoe Hwy. straight into the park. Four different campgrounds with a total of 151 sites. About 12 sites remain open year-round, as do the restrooms. Backcountry camping not permitted. All the best of San Juan fun—swimming, fishing, and hiking. Arresting grounds, amiable staff. Rowboats $6 per hr., paddleboats $7 per hr. Standard sites, hot showers $7; hiker/biker sites $3. **Information booth** at park entrance open Memorial Day-Labor Day daily 8am-10pm. Park open daily 6:30am-dusk; Sept.-March 8am-dusk. Reservations strongly recommended May-Labor Day. Write to the park (do not call), and include $11 ($7 site + $4 reservation fee).

Obstruction Pass: DNR maintains 9 primitive sites, accessible only by boat or foot. Just past Olga, turn off Horseshoe Hwy. and hang a right to head south on Obstruction Pass Rd. Soon you'll come to a dirt road marked "Obstruction Pass Trailhead." Follow the road for about 1 mile. The sites are a ½-mile hike from the end of the road. No drinking water, so bring plenty. Sites free.

Food

All the essentials can be found at **Templin's General Store** in the middle of Eastsound (376-2101; open Mon.-Sat. 8am-8pm, Sun. 10am-6pm). Also try the **Farmers' Market** in front of the museum (see Sights), every Saturday at 10am.

Sunny Side Espresso (376-2828), in Eastsound Sq. Upbeat, offbeat staff serve up croissants ($1.15) and sandwiches ($4.25). Buy day-old pastry bags at half-price. Open Mon.-Sat. 8am-6pm, Sun. 10am-3pm.

La Famiglia, Prune Alley, Eastsound (376-2335). Relaxed Italian cooking and seafood in a tasty atmosphere. Sunny veranda with flower boxes everywhere. Great cheesecake. Seafood special changes daily. Lunches $5.50, dinners $7.50. Open Mon.-Sat. 11:30am-2:30pm and 5-9pm, Sun. 5-9pm. Reduced hours in winter.

Doty's A-1 Drive-In and Bakery (376-2593), across from the Chamber of Commerce. Pure diner atmosphere, pure diner food. Breakfast $4. Freshly baked breads and pastry. Open Mon.-Sat. 6:30am-8pm, Sun. 7am-4pm.

The Shoals, behind the Old Orcas Hotel at the ferry landing. Cheap yet mediocre. Burgers $3.15, deli sandwiches $4. Watch the ferries dock. Open daily 6:30am-7:30pm.

The Lower Tavern, Horseshoe Hwy., Eastsound (376-4848). Admire the trophies precariously mounted overhead as you try to eat the full "catastrophe" meal ($5.75). Don't choke. Open Mon.-Sat. 11am-midnight, Sun. noon-8pm.

Cafe Olga (376-4408), in the Orcas Island Artworks Bldg. at the Olga crossing, a few miles beyond Moran State Park. A cooperative gallery converted into an artsy and overpriced coffeehouse. Chicken cashew sandwich $5.65, blackberry pie $2.50. Open March-Dec. daily 10am-6pm.

Sights and Activities

Moran State Park is unquestionably Orcas's greatest attraction. Over 21 miles of hiking trails cover the park, ranging in difficulty from a one-hour jaunt around Mountain Lake to a day-long hike up the south face of Mt. Constitution. Pick up a copy of the trail guide from the rangers. Whatever else you do, be sure to reach the top of **Mount Constitution,** the highest peak in the islands. From here you can see other islands in the group, as well as the Olympic and Cascade Ranges, Vancouver Island, and Mt. Rainier. The stone tower at the top was built in 1936 by the Civilian Conservation Corps as a fire lookout and tourist observation tower. A road leads to the top for those who opt against the steep 3-mile hike. You can swim in either of two freshwater lakes easily accessible from the highway, or rent rowboats ($6 per hr.) and paddleboats ($7 per hr.) from the park. Watch the frolicking deer and somnolent otters.

Olga is a miniscule collection of buildings that strains the very definition of "town." At the Olga crossing stands an old strawberry-packing plant, now converted by an artists' cooperative into **Orcas Island Artworks** (376-4408), a shop carrying high-quality, high-priced local crafts and clothing. (Open March-Dec. daily 10am-6pm.) Continue along Horseshoe Hwy. to **Doe Bay Village Resorts** (376-2291), where you can soak in the natural mineral waters, sweat in the sauna, and see prophetic visions as you jump into the cold bath. (See Accommodations and Camping.) The resort grounds are secluded and make for good wandering. Check first with the manager to learn the perimeters and parameters of the resort.

Eastsound, smack at the top of the horseshoe, offers great views from the highway and from the adjacent beach. Stop into the picturesque and peaceful **Emmanuel Church** (1885) on Main St. (376-2352), just across from the library. Islanders ignore sectarian differences and worship in the same building. The Episcopalians, who own the church, hold their services at 8 and 10am on Sundays; Lutherans move in at 2pm and Roman Catholics at 4:30pm. Around the corner, two doors from the Chamber of Commerce on North Beach Rd., is the delightfully anarchical **Orcas Island Historical Society Museum** (376-4849). A number of log cabins have been moved from their original sites and fitted together to make this museum. Information on the history of the cabins is available and accurate; displays, however, are jumbled, and many items unmarked. What labels there are seem somewhat lacking in scholarly precision (for example, "very old fishing rod"). Don't miss the foot-powered dental drill—one of the finest of its kind in a Washington museum. The staff bequeaths a wealth of information on the island. (Open Memorial Day-Labor Day Mon.-Fri. 1-4pm, Sat. 10am-4pm. Admission $1, children 50¢, families $3.)

Lopez Island

Smaller than either Orcas or San Juan, Lopez is an island of 1200 fishermen and farmers. Lopez lacks some of the tourist facilities of the other islands and some of the tourists as well; you know, therefore, that the amiability of the locals is genuine. Hitching on the island is safe and rapid; it's also the only way to get from the ferry terminal (376-2326) into Lopez Village without your own car or bicycle.

Lopez Island is best for those who seek solitary beach walking or tranquil bicycling. Since Lopez Village (with all of 8 buildings, the largest town on the island) is 3½ miles from the ferry, it's best to BYOB (bring your own bicycle). If you need to rent a bike, head to **Lopez Bicycle Works** (468-2847), south of the village, next to the island's Marine Center. The cheerful staff will give you a detailed map of island roads, complete with distances, even if you don't rent. Ten-speeds cost $3.50 per hr. or $16 per day; mountain bikes cost $5 per hr. or $20 per day. (Open daily 10am-6pm; May and Sept. Thurs.-Mon. 10am-5pm; April Thurs.-Sun. 10am-5pm.)

Small, day-use parks on the south end of the island, **Agate Beach Park** and **Mud Bay Park** offer a change from mainland campgrounds. The only other "sight" is the **Lopez Island Historical Society Museum** in Lopez Village (468-2049), 1½ blocks from the New Bay, across from the San Juan County Bank. Besides exhibits on island history, this new facility boasts an open shed filled with old canoes and obsolete farm equipment. (Open Fri-Sun. noon-4pm and by appointment. Free.)

Accommodations, Camping, and Food

Lopez supports two bed and breakfasts: **MacKaye Harbor Inn** (468-2253), and **Inn at Swift's Bay** (468-3636). Reservations are generally required far in advance for the summer season, and $65-75 per night is the rule. Bring your tent instead. Canned asparagus and croissant pizza thrive at **Lopez Village Market** in the village (open Mon.-Sat. 9am-7pm, Sun. 10am-6pm).

Odlin Park (468-2496), just off the road, a little over a mile from the ferry terminal. 21 sites. Little privacy, but fine facilities: kitchen, boat launch, volleyball net, and softball diamond. Day-use daily 6am-9pm. Sites $6 per vehicle up to 4 people, each additional person $1.50. A grassy lawn provides some hiker/biker sites at $1.50.

Spencer Spit State Park (468-2251), on the northeast corner of the island, about 3½ miles from the ferry terminal. 24 sites, with a mile of beachfront that provides good clamming year-round. No hookups. Flush toilets, but no showers. Standard sites $7. 8-bunk covered shelters $9.50. Thirty hiker/biker sites (some on the beach) $3.

Hummel Haven Bicycle Camp, on Center Rd. just south of Hummel Lake (468-2217), 4¼ miles from the ferry landing. This quiet bike camp prohibits motorized vehicles, though you can park outside the grounds. Swim or fish in the lake. Boat rental $3.50 per hr.; bike rental $10 per day. Reservations recommended in summer. Contact the camp at Rte. 2, Box 3940, Lopez 98261. No deposit needed. Sites $2.50 per person.

Bay Cafe, Fisherman Bay Rd. (468-2204), across from the post office in Lopez Village. Enjoy the creative omelettes while you listen to soft music—with whale songs dubbed over it, for heaven's sake. Open Wed.-Sat. 11:30am-2pm and 6-8pm, Sun. 8am-noon and 6-8pm.

Holly B's, Lopez Plaza (468-2133). Nothin' says lovin' like pastries and bread from the oven, especially for only 55¢ and up. Starbuck's coffee 60¢, refills 25¢. Open Thurs.-Mon. 8am-6pm.

Gail's Restaurant and Delicatessen, across the road from Lopez Plaza (468-2150). Young urban professionals will find familiar food, atmosphere, and prices. Deli sandwiches $4.50, seafood dinners $12.50. Open in summer Sun.-Fri. 8am-3pm and 6-8pm, Sat. 8am-4pm and 6-9pm; reduced hours in winter.

The Fogged Inn (468-2281), at the ferry landing. A burger shack disguised as an RV. Standard burgers $3. Open Mon.-Sat. 6:30am-7pm, Sun. 7:30am-7:30pm.

Whidbey Island

Locals like to point out two things about telephone-receiver-shaped Whidbey Island: it is the second largest island in the contiguous U.S., and it sits in the rain shadow of the Olympic Mountains. The clouds are wrung dry by the time they finally pass over Whidbey; merely 25" of rain pitter patter on Whidbey per year, leaving the island with one of America's highest sunshine slugging averages. Rocky beaches are bounded by bluffs blooming with wild roses and crawling with blackberry brambles.

The island was originally inhabited by the Skagit nation of Native Americans, whose peaceful ways and gradual obliteration are not often recalled today on Whidbey. In stark contrast, the history of European settlement and development is prominently displayed. The island was named in 1792 for Captain Joseph Whidbey, who sailed through Deception Pass, north of the island, on the *H.M.S. Discovery.* Pioneer homesteaders followed in the mid-19th century. The town of Coupeville has been designated a national historic reserve, maintaining nearly 100 original homes and commercial buildings.

In 1941, the U.S. Navy placed a massive air station outside Oak Harbor, irrevocably changing that community of 600 on the island's northern tip. Of the 10,000 current residents, 7200 are Navy affiliates. Since the time of this abrupt shift, the inhabitants of the lower two-thirds of the island have become quick to assert that they live on *South* Whidbey Island.

Practical Information

Oak Harbor Public Library: 3075 300th W. (675-5115), in City Hall, lower level. Open Mon.-Thurs. noon-9pm, Fri.-Sat. 9am-5pm.

Laundromat: Coupeville, 11 Front St. Well-stocked with *Opera News* and *Runner's World* for literate laundering. Open daily 8am-8pm.

Crisis Center: 678-5555 or 321-4868. 24 hours.

Pharmacy: Penn Cove, 402 N. Main (678-2200), across from Whidbey Island Bank. Open Mon.-Sat. 9am-7pm, Sun. 10am-4pm.

Hospital: Whidbey General, 101 Main St. (678-5151), in Coupeville.

Police/Fire: 911.

Post Office: Langley, 115 2nd St. (321-4113). General Delivery ZIP Code: 98260. **Coupeville,** 201 NW Coveland (678-5353). General Delivery ZIP Code: 98239. **Oak Harbor,** 7035 70th NW (675-6621). General Delivery ZIP Code: 98277.

Area Code: 206.

Getting There and Getting Around

The southern tip of Whidbey Island lies 40 miles north of Seattle as the African swallow flies. The 20-minute **ferry** to Clinton, at the southern end of the island, leaves from Mukilteo (mu-kul-TEE-o), a small community just south of Everett. Take I-5 north from Seattle and follow the large signs to the ferry. Avoid commuter traffic eastbound in the morning and westbound at night. Ferries leave Mukilteo every half-hour from 6am to 11pm, and leave Clinton every half-hour from 5:30am to 11:30pm. The exact schedule changes with the seasons; call Washington State Ferries at 800-542-7052 for detailed information. (Car and passenger $3.75, each additional passenger $1; bicycle and rider $3. Walk-on $1.65; ages over 65, 5-12, and disabled travelers 50¢; under 5 free.) Small surcharges are added in summer.

Whidbey Island can also be reached from Port Townsend on the Olympic Peninsula. Ferries leave the terminal in downtown Port Townsend for Keystone, on the west side of the island, eight times per day between 7am and 5:45pm. Ferries return from Keystone to Port Townsend eight times per day between 7:45am and 6:30pm. Throughout the summer, ferries run later at night and more frequently on weekends, and extra daily ferries are added in August. (35 min. Car and passenger $5.55; bicycle riders $3.50. Walk-on $1.65; ages over 64, 5-12, and disabled travelers 80¢; under 5 free.) For more information, call Washington State Ferries.

To reach Whidbey from the north, take exit 189 off I-5 and head west toward Anacortes. Be sure to stay on Hwy. 20 when it heads south through stunning Deception Pass State Park (signs will direct you); otherwise you will continue on to Anacortes. **Evergreen Trailways** runs a bus to Whidbey from Seattle. The bus leaves Seattle at 4:30pm and arrives in Anacortes at 8pm (Mon, Wed., and Fri.). It returns to Seattle from the Anacortes ferry dock at 8:25am, leaving downtown Anacortes at 8:35am and arriving in Seattle at 11:55am (Mon., Wed., Fri.).

Unfortunately, **Island Transit** (678-7771 or 321-6688) runs only one intra-island bus line—thus the automobile still reigns. There is, however, only one main road: Hwy. 525 on the southern half of the island, which transmutes itself into Hwy. 20 around Coupeville. **Hitching** is therefore fairly good, but, as always, not recommended for women traveling alone, especially in the northern part of the island. **The Pedaler,** 1504 E. Hwy. 525, Freeland (321-5040), 7 miles from Clinton, rents bicycles by the hour ($3), by the day ($14.50), and by the week ($43.50). Bicycle helmets are provided at no extra cost. Transporting bikes on the ferry is also easy and inexpensive (see above). Bicyclists will have safer and more scenic rides away from Hwy. 525/20 (where motorists are often unmindful of speed limits and shoulders are narrow).

The 1990 Let's Go® Travel Catalogue

your one stop travel store

LET'S GO Travel

one source for all your needs

Feel Confident, You'll Have The Basics.

1990 American Youth Hostel Card (AYH): Often required and frequently discounted at youth hostels, we recommend it to every hosteler.
10022 AYH Card $25.00 ($.75)
10023 Plastic Case $.75
FREE directory of hostels in the USA.

1990 International Student Identification Cards (ISIC): Available to currently enrolled full-time students, provides accident/medical insurance, discount air fares, countless discounts on cultural events, accomodations, and more.
10020 ISIC $10.00 ($.75)
FREE "International Student Travel Guide"

1990 Youth International Educational Exchange Card (YIEE): All the same benefits of ISIC (above), for non students under 26 years of age.
10021 YIEE $10.00 ($.75)
FREE "Discounts for Youth Travel," a 200 page guide to discounts all around the world.

1990 International Teacher Identification Card (ITIC): Same benefits as the ISIC. Applicants must be full time teachers at a school or university.
10024 ITIC $10.00 ($.75)

Eurail Pass: (Please include an additional $4.00 for Certified Mail)

First Class

10025	15 Day	**$340**
10026	21 Day	**$440**
10027	1 Month	**$550**
10028	2 Months	**$750**
10029	3 Months	**$930**

Flexipass

10030	5 Days within 15	**$198**
10031	9 Days within 21	**$360**
10032	14 Days in 1 month	**$458**

Eurail Youth Pass (Under 26)

10033	1 Month	**$380**
10034	2 Months	**$500**

All Eurail Pass orders include FREE: Eurail Map, Pocket Timetable, and Traveler's Guide.

LET'S G✊ Travel

THE travel authority for 30 years

Postage prices are within parentheses.

Now You're Covered.

PLEASE follow these instructions carefully. Incomplete applications will be returned. Failure to follow directions causes needless processing delays.

Application for International Student Identity Card enclose: 1) Dated proof of current student status (copy of transcript or letter from registrar stating that you are currently a full-time student). The proof should be from a registered educational institution and CLEARLY indicate that you are a full-time student. 2) One small picture (1 1/2" x 2") signed on the reverse side. Applicants must be at least 12 years old.

Application for the Youth International Exchange Card enclose: 1) Proof of birthdate (copy of birth certificate or passport). Applicants must be under 26. 2) One small picture (1 1/2" x 2") signed on reverse side. 3) Passport number _____ 4) Sex: M F

Last Name _____

First Name _____ Middle Initial_____

US addresses only. We do not mail overseas.

Street _____

City _____ State_____ Zip Code_____

Home Phone (area code) _____

Date of Birth _____ Citizenship_____

School/College _____

Date of Departure _____

ITEM NUMBER	DESCRIPTION	QUANT.	POSTAGE TOTAL	UNIT OR SET PRICE dollars	cents	TOTAL PRICE dollars	cents
	TOTAL MERCHANDISE PRICE						
	TOTAL POSTAGE						
	EXPRESS MAIL HANDLING $13.95 in lieu of postage						
	MASS. RESIDENTS (5% on Gear, Books & Maps)						

Please photocopy this form so others may use it.

TOTAL

☐ **CHECK HERE** for more information on Travel Gear, charter flights, car rental, Britrail and France Vacances passes, travel guides and maps.

PLEASE ALLOW AT LEAST 2 WEEKS FOR DELIVERY (unless rush service) **PAYMENT**: Enclose check or money order payable to LET'S GO TRAVEL.

LET'S GO Travel

Harvard Student Agencies, Inc.   Thayer Hall-B   Cambridge, MA   02138

(617) 495-9649   1-800-5LETSGO

Stop at one of the real estate offices in Clinton, or in any one of the state parks, to pick up a free detailed **map** of the island. None of the roads is well-marked, and it's easy to become hopelessly lost.

Accommodations

Inexpensive motels are few and far between on Whidbey, and those that do exist are frequently a little run-down. Still, reservations are always sensible, especially rain-free July and August.

A number of bed and breakfasts offer elegant rooms for a few more dollars. Contact **Whidbey Island Bed and Breakfast Association**, P.O. Box 259, Langley 98260 (321-6272), for a full listing; reservations are necessary.

Tyee Motel and Cafe, 405 S. Main St., Coupeville (678-6616), across Hwy. 20 from the town proper, toward the Keystone ferry. Clean, straightforward rooms; showers, but no tubs. The setting is bleak—you'll forget you're on an island—but it's within walking distance of Coupeville center and the water. Cafe open daily 6:30am-9pm. Singles $24, each additional person $2.

Crossroads Motel, 5622 Hwy. 20 (675-3145), on northern edge of Oak Harbor. Cinderblock construction suggests a past as cheap military housing, but the rooms are immaculately kept and comfortable. Fully equipped kitchens available. Singles $28. Doubles $39. Rooms with kitchens $43.

Acorn Motor Inn, 8066 Hwy. 20 (675-6646), in Oak Harbor, across the street from Safeway. A well-maintained motel run by pleasant managment. A step up from most in elegance. Singles $36. Doubles $39. Continental breakfast included.

Camping

Considering the motel scenario, you may want to "do Whidbey" in a tent. Four state parks on a 50-mile-long island can hardly be passed up. They are listed here south to north.

South Whidbey State Park, 4128 S. Smuggler's Cove Rd. (321-4559), 7 miles northwest of Freeland via Bush Point Rd. and Smuggler's Cove Rd. On a cliff in a virgin stand of Douglas fir. Steep ¼-mile trail leads down to a broad but rocky beach. 46 sites, deer rub noses with RVs. Sites $7. Open year-round.

Fort Casey State Park, 1280 S. Fort Casey Rd. (678-4519), right next to the Keystone ferry terminal, 3 miles south of Coupeville on Fort Casey Rd. 35 sites interspersed with *fin-de-siècle* military memorabilia. Sites aren't too pretty, but it fills early in summer because the ferry is close. Sites $7. Open year-round.

Fort Ebey State Park, 395 N. Fort Ebey Rd. (678-4636). North of Fort Casey and just west of Coupeville. Take Libbey Rd. turn-off from Hwy. 20. Miles of hiking trails and easy access to a pebbly beach make this, the island's newest campground, also the island's best. 50 sites for cars and RVs ($7), 3 sites for hikers and bikers ($3). Open year-round.

Deception Pass State Park, 5175 N. Hwy. 525 (675-2417), 8 miles north of Oak Harbor. The highway passes right through the park on Deception Pass Bridge. The park has 8½ miles of hiking trails and freshwater fishing and swimming. Jets flying overhead from Oak Harbor Naval Air Station will lull you to sleep. 250 standard sites ($7), 4 rustic sites for hikers and bikers ($3). Open year-round.

Food

Smoked salmon is the dish of choice on Whidbey; every town (and every milepost along the highway) has its share of salmon shacks. The restaurants below are listed from south to north.

Hong Kong Gardens, 4643 S. Hwy. 525 (221-2828), in Clinton, across from Tara Properties, up a steep hill to the right as you leave town. Turn-off marked by a nearly gone-with-the-wind "restaurant" sign. The tables overlook the sound and the mainland to the east. Go up for a drink ($1.25-2), even if you skip the food. Try the *chow sai foon,* a Cantonese mix of shrimp, pork, mushrooms, and tiny noodles ($5.75). Open Sun.-Thurs. 11:30am-11:30pm, Fri.-Sat. 11:30am-2am.

Doghouse Tavern, 230 1st St. (321-9996), in Langley, on the main drag of a 1-block town. A local hangout that serves 10¢ 6-oz. beers with lunch (limit 2). Eat $4 sandwiches and $4.55 corn soup out of an edible bread bowl, either in the tavern or around the back in the "family restaurant" (singles presumably welcome). Open Mon.-Sat. 11am-1am, Sun. noon-1am.

Mike's Place, 215 1st St. (321-6575), in Langley, right across the street from the Doghouse. Although Mike's only opened in 1985, its $2.25 clam chowder is already considered the best on the island. The nightly all-you-can-eat specials are also highly recommended. Monstrous but mediocre cheese blintzes $4.55, lunches $4-6, dinners under $10. Open Mon.-Fri. 7am-10pm, Sat.-Sun. 8am-10pm.

Knead and Feed, 2 Front St. (678-5431), in Coupeville, at the east end of the main commercial street in town, within walking distance of everything. Open for lunch only. Great homemade food in tiny portions. Whole sandwich $4.15. All kinds of amazingly good baked goods. Open Mon. and Wed.-Fri. 10:30am-3pm, Sat.-Sun. 10am-4pm.

Toby's Tavern, 8 Front St. (678-4222), Coupeville, in the 1890 Whidbey Mercantile Company Bldg., less than 1 block west of the Knead. Like everything else in Coupeville, the building is a historical landmark. Inside, the tavern (a favorite with locals) serves $3.50 burgers, $4.50 sandwiches, and beer. Open Sun.-Thurs. 11:30am-10:30pm, Fri.-Sat. 11:30am-midnight.

Jason's (679-3535), Hwy. 20 at Goldie Rd. in Oak Harbor, across from the Crossroads Motel. Standard chain-restaurant fare: burgers, steaks, and spaghetti. Locals swear by the mushroom burger ($4.50). Breakfast under $5, lunch $3-4, dinner $5-8. Open 24 hours.

Sights and Activities

You could spend days exploring Whidbey Island, or only a few hours as you wait for transport connections. Whichever interval you choose, spend no more time in **Clinton** than it requires to get off the ferry and up the hill. In general, the island's interior regions are nothing special; the island's real beauty lies along its circle of beaches.

Less than 3 miles from the center of Clinton, Langley Rd. heads north to the little town of **Langley.** Located just to the west of a small shopping plaza, the road to the town is not well marked. If you make it to Langley, poke around the various arts and crafts shops on 1st St. Langley has capitalized on the Old West motif—wooden sidewalks connect false fronts of antique shops and taverns. The ensemble is not overdone, however, and the change from run-down small town to *Gunsmoke* set isn't too tacky.

Cast a cold eye on the bronze child guarding the stairs leading to the beach, then climb down to **Seawall Park** for a picnic on the grassy stretch along the water. Upstairs from the Doghouse Tavern, the **First Street Theater** hosts poetry readings, concerts, and theatrical productions. The **Clyde Theater** (321-5525), across the street, puts on the annual **Fool's Show**, an original musical produced by the townspeople that opens each April Fool's Day. The Clyde charges $3.50 for first-run movies that change every weekend (Sun., Wed.-Fri. 8pm; Sat. 7 and 9:15pm). For more information about Langley, contact the **Chamber of Commerce**, P.O. Box 403, Langley 98260 (321-6765).

Useless Bay remains useful to the soul in its very uselessness as a bay. On the west side of the bay, uninterrupted beach stretches from Bayview Beach along **Double Bluff Park** to the tip of the Double Bluff Peninsula. Comb the 1½-mile beach, explore the bluffs, or just soak up the sun. Perhaps the single most impressive vista on the island is the view of Seattle and Mt. Rainier from the parking lot at the end of Double Bluff Rd. The bay can be reached on Double Bluff Rd., about 5 miles west of Langley Rd. and 1 mile east of Freeland.

The town of **Freeland**, at the south end of Holmes Harbor, is not particularly interesting. Take E. Harbor Rd. off Main St. toward the water. Freeland's pleasant grassy beach along Bayview St. has a public boat launch and picnic tables. The views here are tame in comparison to those on the western shore. The beach is more accessible for the disabled.

Another ideal spot for the blithe spirit is **South Whidbey State Park,** 4128 S. Smuggler's Cove Rd. (321-4559), about 7 miles north of Freeland. The park wraps around the west coast of the island, covering 87 acres of virgin forest. Park by the tiny outdoor amphitheater and walk down the bluff to the beach (10 min.). Wander along the pebbly beach approximately 1½ miles in either direction—to Lagoon Point in the north or to a lighthouse on Bush Point in the south. (See Camping for the park's overnight facilities.)

Around the bend to the north, Fort Casey and Fort Ebey State Parks sustain the Park Service's domination of Whidbey's western shore. **Fort Casey State Park,** 1280 S. Fort Casey Rd. (678-4519), is right next to the Keystone ferry terminal, 3 miles south of Coupeville. The park is situated on the site of a late 1890s fort designed, along with Fort Worden and Fort Flagler on the mainland, to defend against a long-anticipated attack from the west. The fort was updated and reactivated with the onset of each major war until the military lost patience with its prospective enemies in 1956 and sold the property to the Park Service. The **Admiralty Head Lighthouse,** also dating from the turn of the century, now operates as an **interpretive center,** expounding on the history of the fort. (Open Wed.-Sun. 10am-6pm.) Tours of what remains of the fort are given Sundays at 2pm and start at the main gun sites. For the less militarily inclined, Fort Casey also operates recreational facilities: underwater reserve, boat launch, camping facilities, and shower rooms for scuba divers. (Interpretive center open in winter only for large groups by appointment. The rest of the park is open year-round.)

Public beach lands extend north of the ferry landing all the way to Partridge Point, north of Fort Ebey State Park. This is perfect territory for an all-day beach expedition. Access to the beach is also permitted at **Ebey's Landing,** halfway between the two state parks, at the site of the original 1852 pioneer settlement. Isaac Ebey, who was subsequently decapitated by members of the Haida nation (of coastal Vancouver Island) to avenge one of their leaders, led the small group of settlers to Whidbey Island.

Fort Ebey State Park, 395 N. Fort Ebey Rd. (678-4636), is accessible from Libbey Rd. off Hwy. 20 north of Coupeville, by Valley Drive's park entrance. The way from the highway to the park is well marked, but the way back to the highway from the park is not—remember your route. The park is also the driest spot on the island; prickly pear cacti grow on the parched bluffs. The park facilities (nine years old) are still new and clean. Signs explaining the causes of erosion (and probably contributing to the process) crop up on dunes which shrink daily.

Both parks and the town of Coupeville are contained within **Ebey's Landing National Historical Reserve,** established by the Federal Government for the "preservation and protection of a rural community." Many of Coupeville's homes and commercial establishments date from the 19th century. The town extends along East Front St. between two blockhouses. Constructed in 1855, the blockhouses were meant to withstand a predicted Skagit uprising that never occurred. Two of the zealously fortified buildings remain standing: the **John Alexander Blockhouse,** at the west end of town, and the **Davis Blockhouse,** at the edge of the town's cemetery.

The **Island County Historical Museum,** at Alexander and Coveland St., across from the Alexander Blockhouse, houses an interesting, if small, collection of Northwest Native American baskets and dolls. (Open May-Sept. daily noon-4pm; April Sat.-Sun. only. Free.) The 10¢ brochure *A Walk Through History* narrates a walking tour of Coupeville's Victorian buildings. A detailed island map is available for 10¢.

Two miles southeast of Coupeville, on Hwy. 20, DNR's Rhododendron Park has picnic areas and six free campsites, which almost always fill early during summer months. Coupeville's **City Park,** 1 block west of the wharf, also operates picnic areas and a reservable community kitchen. During the second weekend in August, Coupeville hosts a popular **Arts and Crafts Festival** (678-4126), drawing artists from all over the Northwest. For information on other Coupevilliana, contact the **Central Whidbey Chamber of Commerce,** P.O. Box 152, Coupeville 98239 (678-5434).

The Navy's EA-6B Prowler jets, designed for tactical electronic warfare, keep the peace near the town of **Oak Harbor,** on Oak Harbor Bay at the northern end of the island. The town was named for the Garry oaks that once dominated the landscape. The Chamber of Commerce insists that the influence of early Dutch settlers can still be felt, but fast-food restaurants generally make more of an impact. **City Beach Park,** downtown, maintains a free swimming pool, kitchens, and tennis courts. (Buildings and facilities open April-Nov.; park open year-round.) During the last weekend in April, Oak Harbor plants tulips and puts on wooden shoes for the annual **Holland Happenings.** In mid-July the city sponsors **Whidbey Island Race Week,** a colorful yacht regatta.

A few miles north on Hwy. 20, fruit fields and aviation aficionados peacefully coexist at the **U-Pick Strawberry Farms.** The roar from low-flying Navy jets virtually rattles the fruit from the plants.

When the Skagit tribe lived and fished around Deception Pass, it was often raided by the Haida tribe from the north. A bear totem of the Haidas now stands on the north end of West Beach in **Deception Pass State Park,** 5175 N. Hwy. 20 (675-2417). Make sure to visit the WPA bridge on Hwy. 20 E. for the view of the crashing waves. The pass itself was named by Captain George Vancouver, who found the tangled geography of Puget Sound as confusing as most visitors do today. The trails and shelters were developed during the Depression by the Civilian Conservation Corps. A brand-new interpretive center in the Bowman area, just north of the bridge, gives a good overview of the environmental army that built so many of the park facilities in the Pacific Northwest. This is the most heavily used of Whidbey's four state parks, and its views are breathtaking. There are camping facilities, a salt-water boat launch, and a freshwater lake for swimming, fishing, and boating. Eight and a half miles of trails allow a closer look at the tidal pools, beaches, and beasts of the area. (A fishing license, available at most hardware stores, is required for fishing in the lake; the season runs from mid-April to Oct. Park open year-round.)

Near Whidbey Island

Posh galleries, stylish boutiques, gelato emporiums—these are **La Conner,** an old fishing village on the Swinomish Channel. La Conner lies 4 miles south of Hwy. 20 on La Conner-Whitney Rd. Take Hwy. 20 east from Whidbey Island to the mainland. Since the rustic waterfront houses and picturesque harbor have lured tourists and developers to La Conner, prices have risen.

The **Skagit County Historical Museum,** 501 4th St. (466-3365), at the top of the hill in La Conner, shows exhibits on settler life in Skagit county. Behind the ugly concrete exterior stand full-scale replicas of an old-time general store, a blacksmith's shop, a bedroom, and a kitchen. (Open Wed.-Sun. 1-5pm. Admission $1; ages under 13 50¢.) **Gaches Mansion,** 2nd and Calhoun St. (466-4288), a restored Victorian mansion built in 1891, also houses the **Valley Museum of Northwest Art.** (Open April-Oct. Fri.-Sun. 1-5pm; Nov.-March 1-4pm. Free.) The **La Conner Volunteer Firefighter Museum,** 615 1st St., sets the sirens of small-town Americana a-wailing. The displays, visible through a street-level window (you can't enter the one-room building), include a horse-drawn pumper "used in the 1906 San Fransisco [sic] fire."

The few places to stay in La Conner are expensive, but if you can afford it, try **Katy's Inn Bed and Breakfast,** 3rd and Washington (466-3366). The elegantly furnished rooms ($55; up to 2 people) include a jar of candy at every bedside. Budgetarians should head for the campgrounds on Whidbey Island, less than 10 miles away.

The **Calico Cupboard,** 720 S. 1st St. (466-4451), emphasizes baked goods and vegetarian delights. The interior looks like an oversized dollhouse with its quaint country decor. (Breakfast and sandwiches around $5. Open Sun.-Thurs. 8am-11pm, Fri.-Sat. 8am-11:30pm. Tea served 2:30-5pm.) **At's A Pizza,** 201 E. Morris (466-4406), serves less elaborate fare, such as cold sandwiches (including vegetarian) and strictly mediocre pizza, in a tavern-like atmosphere. (Open Sun.-Thurs. 11am-10pm, Fri.-Sat. 11am-midnight.)

The **Rhododendron Cafe,** 553 Chuckanut Dr. in Bow (766-6667), at the crossroads of Hwy. 11 and 237, north of La Conner, serves unusual food in a subdued setting. A refurbished gas station, the restaurant provides a break from the old hamburger-and-fries routine. The food is superb and the prices generally under $10.

Vegetarian specials are served nightly, and the pan-fried oysters ($9) are recommended. (Open Wed.-Thurs. 4-9pm, Fri.-Sat. 11am-3pm and 4-9pm, Sun. 10am-3pm and 4-9pm.)

A few miles inland on I-5, the city of **Mt. Vernon** hosts the two-day Mt. Vernon/Skagit Valley Tulip Festival in early April. Fertile Skagit Valley is best known for its tulips, which bloom in April; daffodils bloom in March, irises in late May. Display gardens are operated by area bulb producers. **West Shore Acres,** 956 Downey Rd. (466-3158), 1 mile west of La Conner-Whitney Rd. on Downey Rd., tends display gardens and sells flowers and bulbs. (Open March 23-April daily 10am-6pm.) **Westwinds Motel,** 2020 Riverside Dr., Mt. Vernon (424-4224), peddles spacious rooms past their prime. (Singles $30.)

The La Conner **post office** (General Delivery ZIP code: 98257) is at 1st and Washington St. The **area code** is 206.

Other Islands

With one store and 100 residents, **Shaw Island** was not designed with tourists in mind. Only one building serves island visitors: a combination ferry terminal/general store/post office/dock/gas station, run by Franciscan nuns. The island's 11 miles of public roads, however, endear it to hikers and bikers. The library and museum, near the center of the island, at the intersection of Blind Bay and Hoffman Cove Rd., are open only on Mondays and Saturdays. A little red schoolhouse stands on the other side of the untraveled road. **Shaw Island County Park,** on the south side of the island, has eight campsites ($6), which fill quickly. There are no other accommodations on the island.

Washington State Parks operates over 15 **marine parks** on some of the smaller islands in the archipelago. These islands, accessible by private craft only, have anywhere from one to 51 mainly primitive campsites. The park system publishes a pamphlet on its marine facilities, available at other island parks or hardware and supply stores. One of the most popular is **Sucia Island,** site of gorgeous scenery and torturous geology. Canoes and kayaks can easily navigate the archipelago when the water is calm, but when the wind whips up the surf, only larger boats (at least 16 ft.) are safe. Navigational maps are essential to avoid the reefs and nasty hidden rocks that surround the islands.

The Department of Natural Resources operates three parks; each has three to six free campsites bestowed with toilets but no drinking water. Cypress Head on **Cypress Island** has wheelchair-accessible facilities.

Olympic Peninsula

In the fishing villages and logging towns of the Olympic Peninsula, locals jest about having webbed feet and using Rustoleum instead of suntan oil. The area's heavy rainfall (up to 200" per year on Mt. Olympus) is wrenched out of the moist Pacific air by the Olympic Mountains. While this torrent supports bona fide rain forests in the peninsula's western river valleys, towns such as Sequim in the range's rain shadow are the driest in all of Washington, with as little as 17 inches of rain in a typical year.

Extremes of climate are matched by extremes of geography. The beaches along the Pacific strip are a hiker's paradise—isolated, windy, and wildly sublime. The glaciated peaks of the Olympic range exhibit spectacular alpine scenery; the network of trails covers an area the size of Rhode Island. These wild, woody mountains resisted exploration well into the 20th century.

Because it compresses such variety into a relatively small area, the Olympic Peninsula is one of Washington's best destinations for those seeking accessible wilderness and outdoor recreation. U.S. 101 loops around the peninsula, stringing together scattered towns and attractions on the nape of the mountains. The numerous secondary roads departing from 101 were designed with exploration in mind, although many are gravel-covered, making biking into the heart of the park difficult. Heart o' the Hills Road to Hurricane Ridge makes a particularly good detour, providing an unbeatable panorama of the mountains. Highway 112 follows the Strait of Juan de Fuca out to Neah Bay, the driftwood-laden coastal town near Cape Flattery. Greyhound runs only as far as Port Angeles to the north and Aberdeen/Hoquiam to the south. Although local transit systems extend public transportation a little farther, the western portion of the peninsula and the southern portion of Hood Canal are not on any regular routes.

Hitchhiking is illegal on U.S. 101 southwest of Olympia. Elsewhere, thumbing can often be slow, and you may be stranded in the rain for hours. On one of summer's many sunny days, you can often catch a ride with a forester, fisherman, or tourist making a loop of the peninsula. Bicycling is dangerous in some spots, particularly along Crescent Lake just west of Port Angeles—the shoulders are narrow or nonexistent, the curves are sharp, and the roads serve as race tracks for any number of speeding logging trucks. Motoring suits the peninsula best, although some of the beaches and mountain wilds can be reached only on foot. Extended backpacking trips are particularly rewarding.

Camping

Although many towns on the peninsula cater to tourists with motels and resorts, the great outdoors make camping the more attractive option. The Olympic National Forest, the state of Washington, and Olympic National Park all maintain a number of free campgrounds. In addition, the national park has many standard campgrounds (sites $5). The numerous **state parks** along Hood Canal and the eastern rim charge $4 per night, with an occasional site for tenters at only $1-3 per night. The national forest and the park services welcome **backcountry camping** (free everywhere), but a permit, available at any ranger station, is required within the park. Camping on the beaches is especially easy, although you should be sure to pack a supply of water. The beaches in the westernmost corner of Neah Bay and from the town of Queets to Moclips farther south fall within Native American reserve land. Visitors should be aware that reservation land is private property—travelers are welcome, but local regulations prohibiting alcohol, fishing without a tribal permit, and beachcombing should be obeyed. The Quinault Indian Reservation gained fame 20 years ago by forcibly ousting vandals trespassing on their beaches.

Washington's **Department of Natural Resources (DNR)** manages the proverbial huge tracts of land on the Kitsap Peninsula and along the Hoh and Clearwater Rivers near the western shore, as well as smaller, individual campsites sprinkled around the peninsula. In DNR areas, camping is generally free and uncrowded; no reservations are required. Some of these sites allow RVs, some do not have drinking water, and most have good fishing. Unfortunately, many sites cannot be found without a map. The DNR publishes a guide to all its Washington sites, and additional maps of its Multiple Use Areas (MUAs). Maps of Hoh-Clearwater MUA and Tahuya MUA (on the Kitsap Peninsula) are available from DNR, Olympic Area, Rte. 1, P.O. Box 1375, Forks 98331 (206-374-6131), and at most DNR campgrounds.

Keep an eye out for other camping possibilities, such as county and city parks and ITT Rayonier's **Tumbling Rapids Park** off U.S. 101 in Sappho, 55 miles west of Port Angeles. This campground with rest rooms, picnic area, and community kitchen is maintained by the giant company for public use.

Be warned: in the summer, competition for campground space is fierce. From late June on, most sites are taken by 2 or 3pm, so start hunting early; in the more popular areas of the national parks (such as the Hoh River), find a site before noon, or plan on sleeping somewhere else.

Hood Canal

Originally named Lord Hood's Channel by early English explorers, the long ribbon of water that separates the Kitsap and Olympic Peninsulas was transformed into the Hood Canal by lazy or careless mapmakers. Today, U.S. 101 parallels the west bank of the canal, from **Potlatch State Park** in the south to **Quilcene** in the north. This flat, scenic road, highlighted by a challengingly steep pass just outside Quilcene, is every bicyclist's dream.

West of the canal, the **Olympic National Forest** rims the eastern edge of the national park. Much of the forest is more developed and more accessible than the park and gives those with little time or small appetites for the outdoors a "taste" of the peninsula's wildlife. Stop by one of the forest's **ranger stations** along the canal to pick up information on camping and trails in the forest. The two stations are in **Hoodsport**, P.O. Box 68 (877-5254; open Memorial Day to Labor Day daily 8am-4:30pm) and **Quilcene**, U.S. 101 S. (765-3368; open Mon.-Fri. 7:30am-5pm, Sat.-Sun. 8:30am-5pm). Both are clearly marked with signs on the highway. Many of the forest service **campgrounds** cost only $4, including **Hamma Hamma**, on Forest Service Rd. 25, 7 miles northwest of Eldon; **Lena Creek**, 2 miles beyond Hamma Hamma; **Elkhorn**, on Forest Service Rd. 2610, 11 miles northwest of Brinnon; and **Collins**, on Forest Service Rd. 2515, 8 miles west of Brinnon. All are marked on U.S. 101 and have drinking water, as well as good fishing, hiking, and gorgeous scenery. Unfortunately, many of these are accessible only by gravel roads, which are difficult, if not impossible, to navigate by bicycle. U.S. 101 in Hoodsport passes by **Linda Lee's**, creator of strictly average ice cream ($1.20 per scoop) and sandwiches. Adjacent to the Hoodsport Ranger Station is a **post office** (877-5552; open Mon.-Fri. 8am-12:30pm and 1:30-5pm, Sat. 8:30am-11:30pm; General Delivery ZIP Code: 98548).

Lake Cushman State Park (877-5491), 7 miles west of Hoodsport on Lake Cushman Rd., stretches by a comely lake with good swimming beaches. The park is also popular as a base camp for extended backpacking trips into the national forest and park. Lake Cushman has 80 sites ($6 per site, $8.50 with full hookup) with flush toilets and pay showers. Clinging to a quiet cove is **Mike's Beach Resort and Hostel**, N. 38470 U.S. 101 (877-5324), just north of Eldon. The hostel lacks a kitchen, and too many bunks crowd its tiny rooms, but it does have a small grocery store. (Members $5, nonmembers $7.50. Open May 15-Oct. 1.) The **Hungry Bear Cafe**, in Eldon (877-5527), serves the Hood Canal specialty—geoduck (GOO-ey-duck) steak ($8)—in a small cafe inhabited by scores of stuffed bears, doubtless courtesy of the local taxidermist. Adventurous eaters will find that the geoduck, a giant bivalve that lives 2½ to 7 feet below the surface of Hood Canal's beaches, has a taste somewhere between that of a razor clam and a scallop—and is especially delectable when (as here) served with mounds of great french fries and some of the best homemade tartar sauce anywhere. Those feeling less daring might want to stick with the tamer hamburger ($1.50-5). (Open Mon.-Thurs. 9am-7pm, Fri. 9am-8pm, Sat. 8am-8pm, Sun. 8am-7pm.)

Kitsap Peninsula

Topologically, the amorphous Kitsap Peninsula resembles a half-completed landfill project jutting into Puget Sound. Especially on the section encircled by the Hood Canal, a plethora of backroads and campgrounds lay out the blueprints for a cyclist's paradise.

The Hood Canal bridge crosses the northern end of Hood Canal and links the Kitsap Peninsula with the towns along the Strait of Juan de Fuca; no pedestrian traffic is allowed, but hitchhiking across is easy. Kitsap can also be reached by ferry: from Seattle to Bremerton or Winslow on connected Bainbridge Island, or from Edmonds, north of Seattle, to Kingston on the northern end of the peninsula.

Bremerton is an overgrown repair shop for United States Navy ships, and the site of numerous naval homecomings. You'll swear that you have stepped into the backdrop of a Tom Clancy novel; every third person has a Navy security pass swinging from his or her neck. After you take shore leave from the ferry, stop at the **Bremerton-Naval Museum,** 130 Washington St. (479-3588), next to the visitors bureau. The museum displays photos and large models of naval ships, of interest only to military fanatics. The museum also showcases the world's oldest surviving cannon: a wicker model from Korea, dated 1377. (Open Tues.-Sat. 10am-5pm, Sun. 1-5pm.) The Kitsap's most appealing attraction, however, is the **Suquamish Museum** (598-3311), 6 miles north of Winslow, just over the Agate Pass Bridge on Hwy. 305. Run by the Port Madison Indian Reservation, the very small museum is devoted entirely to the history and culture of the Puget Sound Salish Native Americans. Arrestingly displayed photographs, artifacts, and quotes from tribal elders piece together the lives of those who inhabited the peninsula before the arrival of the white invaders. (Open daily 10 am-5pm. Admission $2, senior citizens $1.50, ages under 12 $1.) Chief Sealth, for whom Seattle was named, belonged to the Salish nation; his nearby grave is marked by raised painted canoes. Next to the gravesite is a Suquamish city park that was once the site of **Old Man House,** a cedar loghouse burned by federal agents in 1870 as part of an attempt to eliminate communal living by Native Americans.

The **Kitsap County Historical Museum** (692-1949), on NW Byron and Washington in Silverdale, is your average small town museum. The displays dilate on boats, logging, and daily life on the peninsula. (Open Tues.-Sat. 10am-5pm. Admission $1, families $2.)

The major hotel chains are scattered along Kitsap Way. **Scenic Beach State Park,** near the village of Seabeck on the west coast of the peninsula, has 50 campsites with water and bathrooms (sites $7, walk-in sites $3). From Silverdale, take Anderson Hill Rd. or Newberry Hill Rd. west to Seabeck Hwy., then follow the highway 7 miles south to the Scenic Beach turnoff. Cyclists should beware of the staggering hills along this route.

Bremerton has its share of quotidian greasy spoon spots, but locals recommend the slightly upscale **Boat Shed,** 101 Shore Dr. (377-2600), on the water immediately below the northeast side of the Manette Bridge. Good seafood and sandwiches ($5) and super nachos ($5). Open Mon.-Thurs. 11am-midnight, Fri.-Sat. 11am-1am, Sun. 3-10pm.

The Bremerton Kitsap County Visitor and Convention Bureau, 120 Washington St. (479-3588), is just up the hill from the ferry terminal. The office supports a flotilla of pamphlets on Bremerton and nearby towns, and the lively staff tries hard to cover up the city's fundamental drabness. (Open Mon.-Fri. 9am-5pm.) The **post office** is stationed at 602 Pacific St. (373-1456; General Delivery ZIP Code: 98310).

Strait of Juan de Fuca

From Port Townsend to Cape Flattery, the northern rim of the Olympic Peninsula defines the U.S. side of the Strait of Juan de Fuca. This passage of sapphire, from the Pacific Ocean to Puget Sound, was named for a legendary explorer, supposedly the first European to enter the ocean inlet. The shores are dotted with small towns, many of them old salmon fishing ports still hankering after bounties of the past.

Port Townsend

Two things stand out in Port Townsend: its Victorian architecture and its sailors. The town's buildings have been fabulously restored to their original condition. The lace and upright charm are intact; not a cracked window or loose shingle is to be found. The entire business district of this "peninsula off a peninsula" has been declared a national landmark. Seen from a ferry boat in the strait, Port Townsend's

Victorian houses on the overhanging bluff obscure the highway behind, creating the illusion of a town that time forgot.

With their beards, fisherman's caps, and scruffed denim jackets, the town's sailors and amateur boat-builders seem like incarnations of the stereotypical old salt. But if you keep a close eye on these old pirates, you may see them stop in at bars only to forego the traditional beer and crackers in favor of cappuccino and Celtic folk music.

Practical Information and Orientation

Visitor Information: Chamber of Commerce, 2437 Sims Way, Port Townsend 98368 (385-2722), about 10 blocks from the center of town on Hwy. 20. The free map and visitors guide, enthusiastically distributed, fulfill your needs. Open Mon.-Fri. 9am-5pm, Sat. 10am-4pm, Sun. 11am-4pm.

Jefferson County Transit: 425 Washington St. (385-4777). Also the number to call for **Greyhound** information. Jefferson County Transit's Greyhound connection bus stops in Port Ludlow several times daily.

Ferries: Washington State Ferry (800-542-0810). Runs from the dock at Water St., west of downtown. **Northcat Transportation Inc.,** 1322 Washington St. (385-3590). 2-hr. trips to Edmonds via Kingston (5am, 10:15am, and 3:30pm). $6.65 one way. No cars. Runs year-round.

Taxi: Key City Transport, 385-5972. 24 hours.

Bike Rental: Coast to Coast, 1102 Water St. (385-5900). Mountain bikes and 10-speeds $3 per hr., $15 per day. Credit card or $30 deposit required.

Boat Rental: Field Dock, Port Ludlow Marina (437-2222), in Port Ludlow, south of Port Townsend. Sailboats $6 per hr., $18 per 4 hr.

Public Library: 1220 Lawrence (385-3181), uptown. Open Tues. 1-9pm, Wed.-Thurs. 10am-9pm, Fri. 1-5:30pm, Sat. 1-5pm.

Jefferson County Crisis Line: 385-0321. 24 hours.

Senior Services: Olympic Area Agency on Aging, 385-2564. **Senior Assistance,** 385-2552.

Pharmacy: Don's, 1151 Water St. (385-2622). Open Mon.-Fri. 9am-7pm, Sat. 9am-6pm, Sun. 11am-5pm.

Hospital: Jefferson General, 385-2200. **Emergency Medical Care,** 385-4622.

Police: 607 Water St. (385-2322).

Post Office: 1322 Washington St. (385-1600). Open Mon.-Fri. 9am-5pm. General Delivery ZIP Code: 98368.

Area Code: 206.

Port Townsend can be reached by ferry from the town of Keystone on Whidbey Island, or by car either from U.S. 101 along Hood Canal or from the Kitsap Peninsula across the Hood Canal Bridge. **Greyhound's** daily Seattle to Port Angeles run hooks up with **Jefferson County Transit** in the town of Port Ludlow for the last leg to Port Townsend. Jefferson County Transit serves the Port Townsend area Monday through Friday from 8am to 6pm, weekends for the link with Greyhound only. A Port Townsend shuttle bus loops around the town itself, and other service extends west along the strait to Sequim. (Fare 50¢, senior citizens and students 25¢, under 6 free. Daily passes $1.50.)

From Victoria, BC, two ferries per day run to Port Angeles (4 in summer), a mere $1 bus ride from Port Townsend. To reach Port Angeles from Port Townsend, hop on Jefferson County Transit bus #8 (at Water and Quincy St.) to Sequim (30 min.), where you can catch Clallam Transit System bus #30 to Port Angeles (30 min.).

Accommodations and Camping

Port Townsend's hostel and campground rest near the town. So many cheap beds in such a small town doesn't make sense, but who's arguing?

Fort Worden Youth Hostel (AYH), Fort Worden State Park (385-0655), 2 miles from downtown. The bulletin boards and trekkers' log are sterling sources of information on budget travel around the Olympics and elsewhere. Kitchen facilities. Check-in 4:30-9pm. Check-out 9:30am. Curfew 11pm. Members $6, nonmembers $9. Family rates available. Open Jan. 4-Dec. 14.

Fort Flagler Youth Hostel (AYH), Fort Flagler State Park (385-1288), on handsome Marrowstone Island, 20 miles from Port Townsend. Fantastic for cyclists—miles of pastoral bike routes weave through Marrowstone. Hostel virtually unoccupied, even in summer. Members $6, nonmembers $7.50. Reservations required in winter.

Point Hudson Resort, Point Hudson Harbor (385-2828), at the end of Jefferson St. Fading wooden structures tell of a past when Point Hudson was the major resort in the area. Today, boat-builders hammer away outside your window, and an obnoxious buoy clangs constantly. Rooms more elegant than most and very clean. Singles and doubles $42.

Camping: You can camp at **Fort Worden State Park** (385-4730) for $9.50 per night, or at **Old Fort Townsend State Park** (385-4730) for $7 per night. The latter is 5 miles south of Port Townsend just off Hwy. 20. Fort Worden is open year-round; Old Fort Townsend mid-May to mid-Sept. Or camp along the beach at **Fort Flagler State Park** (753-2027) for $7.

Food and Entertainment

Strap on your Birkenstocks and gather your organic essentials while you may at **The Food Co-op,** 1033 Lawrence (385-2883), at Polk. But watch out: only national co-op members pay the marked price; others pay 10% more. A **Safeway** serves those reluctant to co-op-erate.

Landfall, 412 Water St. (385-5814), on Point Hudson. Seafood, salads, and Mexican food. Expensive dinners, but reasonable for lunch and breakfast. A huge bowl of homemade fish and chips $4.75. Good sourdough french toast $2.50. The boat-making crowd hangs out here, seasoning their food with shoptalk about lamination and wind resistance. Open Mon.-Tues. 7am-3pm, Wed.-Sun. 7am-9pm.

Lighthouse Cafe, 955 Water St. (385-1165). Some of the cheapest seafood in town, but uninspiring breakfasts. Fried oysters and fries $5. Open daily 6am-9pm.

Bread and Roses Bakery and Deli, 230 Quincy St. (385-1044). Monstrous raspberry $1.50, turkey and swiss croissant $1.75. Open Mon.-Sat. 7:30am-5pm, Sun. 7:30am-4pm.

Salal Cafe, 634 Water St. (385-6532). The service is spotty and the food only a step above mediocre, but the numerous vegetarian dishes are very popular with the locals. Tofu reuben $4.75, veggie omelette $4.50. Open Sun.-Thurs. 7am-2pm, Fri.-Sat. 7am-2pm and 6-10pm.

Elevated Ice Cream Co., 627 Water St. (385-1156). Friendly owners receptive to the half-respectable traveler. Delicious homemade ice cream and decent espresso (75¢). One scoop of ice cream or 2 mini-scoops of Italian ice $1.05. Open daily 9:30am-10pm; in winter 11am-10pm.

Town Tavern, 939 Water St., down the block from the Salal Cafe at Quincy St. Mellow pool players and live entertainment on weekends: Irish, folk, and rock. $2-3 cover. Open daily 10am-2am.

The Back Alley Tavern, 923 Washington St. (385-6536). Reggae and rock. Cover $2.50-4. Jam sessions Sun. evenings.

Sights and Seasonal Events

Port Townsend's early pioneer settlers built sturdy maritime-style houses, but their wealthier successors preferred huge Queen Anne and Victorian mansions. Of the over 200 restored homes in the area, some have been converted into quaint and costly bed and breakfasts; others are open to tours. The 1868 **Rothschild House,** at Franklin and Taylor St., has period furnishings and herbal and flower gardens. (Open daily 10am-5pm; Sept. 16-May 14 Sat.-Sun. 11am-4pm. Admission $1.)

Take the steps on Taylor St. down to Water St., the town's quaint main artery. Here, the brick buildings of the 1890s are interspersed with newer shops and cafés in the old-style motif. The **Jefferson County Museum**, at Madison and Water St. (385-1003), holds vestiges of the town's wild past. Highlights include a kayak parka made of seal intestines and the ubiquitous pedal-powered dentist's drill. (Open Mon.-Sat. 11am-4pm, Sun. 1-4pm. Donations $1.)

The red **bell tower** on Jefferson St. alerted firefighters in Port Townsend for 80 years. No one goes up to ring the bell these days, but the base of the tower grandly overlooks the town, the caves and inlets of Port Townsend Bay, and the mountains beyond. An old Romanesque clock tower hovers over the **County Courthouse**, at Jefferson and Walker St. You can tour the tower only by making an appointment with the custodian in the basement. Farther southwest is the **Manresa Castle** on Sheridan St. (385-5750), built in 1892 and used as a Jesuit school for 42 years. Now a hotel, it is open for wandering and gawking.

Point Hudson, the hub of the small shipbuilding area, forms the corner of Port Townsend, where Admiralty Inlet and Port Townsend Bay meet. North of Point Hudson are several miles of beach, Chetzemolka Park, and the larger Fort Worden State Park. **Fort Worden** (385-4730), a strategic military post dating from the turn of the century, guards the mouth of Puget Sound, conjuring up fine views of the sound and the Cascades. The fort was pressed into service in 1981 as a set for the movie *An Officer and a Gentleman*. Miles of trails and tunnels string through **Chetzemolka Park.** The **Marine Science Center** on the Fort Worden Dock (385-5582) keeps live sea creatures to touch and observe; if you've never seen a live sand dollar, this is your chance. (Open Sun. and Wed.-Fri. noon-5pm, Sat. noon-9pm. Free.)

South of town on Marrowstone Island, **Fort Flagler State Park,** another retired military post, has slightly more run-down barracks than Fort Worden, but only a fraction of the tourists. Explore the gun emplacements, watch the sailboats on Puget Sound from the outpost high above the water, or stroll along the almost deserted beach down below. This is the life.

From mid-June to early September, the **Centrum Foundation** sponsors a series of festivals in Fort Worden Park. The foundation kindly supports bluegrass, jazz, folk, and classical music along with poetry readings, dance performances, and painting displays. Two of the most popular events are the **Fiddle Tunes Festival** in early July and **Jazz Port Townsend** in late July. Tickets are $6 for most single events; combination tickets can be purchased to cover the whole of each festival. For a schedule, write the Centrum Foundation, P.O. Box 1158, Port Townsend 98368 (385-3102). The **Rhododendron Festival,** held in mid-May, hosts arts and crafts displays, a clambake, bathtub race, parade, and fireworks. Contact the Chamber of Commerce for more information.

Port Angeles

Port Angeles, the last major town on the peninsula before Aberdeen, is a rather cheerless industrial complex dominated by paper and plywood mills. Perhaps its greatest asset is an unparalleled view of the gorgeous blue bay below. Stop here for information, transportation connections, or before driving up to the stupendous Hurricane Ridge, but don't stay around long—the rest of the peninsula awaits.

Practical Information and Orientation

Visitor Information: Chamber of Commerce, 121 E. Railroad (452-2363), next to the ferry terminal. Stands ready to arm tourists with literature and schedules. In addition to lists of lodgings, the center provides a free telephone for calling motels. Open daily 7am-10pm; in winter 10am-4pm. **Clallam County Parks and Recreation Department,** Courthouse Bldg. (452-7831, ext. 291), at Lincoln and 4th St. Open Mon.-Fri. 8:30am-4:30pm.

Buses: Greyhound, 215 N. Laurel (452-7611), near the ferry dock. To Seattle (2 per weekday, $15). **Clallam Transit System,** 694 Monroe Rd. (452-4511 or 800-858-3747). Open Mon.-Sat. 5am-9pm.

Ferries: Black Ball Transport (457-4491), foot of Laurel St.

Taxis: Blue Top Cab Company, 452-2223. 24 hours.

Car Rental: Birdwell Ford, 1527 E. Front St. (457-3333). $18 per day plus 15¢ per mile. Must be 21 with credit card. **All-Star,** 602 E. Front St. (452-8001 or 800-522-3009), in Aggie's Motel complex. $20 per day. Must be 21 and pay rental in advance. Credit card or $100 deposit required. Call for 24-hour service. **Budget,** 111 E. Front St. (452-4774), has rentals with unlimited mileage for $10 per hr. Open daily 7am-6pm.

Camping Supplies: Browns, 112 W. Front St. (457-4150), between Laurel and Oak. Well-stocked, with friendly service from knowledgeable salespeople. Open Mon.-Sat. 9am-5:30pm.

Public Library: 207 S. Lincoln St. (452-9253). Open Mon.-Wed. 10am-8pm, Thurs.-Sat. 10am-5pm.

Senior Citizen's Center: 452-3221.

Laundromat: Peabody Street Coin Laundry, 212 Peabody St. Open 24 hours.

Weather: 457-6533. 24 hours.

Pharmacy: Jim's, 221 Peabody St. (452-4200). Open Mon.-Fri. 8:30am-7pm, Sat. 8:30am-5pm.

Crisis Line: Rape Relief/Safehome, 452-4357. 24 hours. **County Crisis Line:** 683-0111.

Coast Guard: 457-4404 in emergencies. 24 hours.

Post Office: 424 E. 1st St. (452-9275), at Vine. General Delivery ZIP Code: 98362.

Area Code: 206.

Ferry service between Port Angeles and Victoria, BC, is provided by **Black Ball Transport** (457-4491). (June 16-Sept. 19 4 per day; May 19-Sept. 30 2 per day. Fare $5.75, ages under 12 $2.90, car and driver $23, motorcycle and driver $12.75, bicycle and rider $8.25.) **Clallam Transit System ("The Bus")** serves the Port Angeles area and connects with Jefferson Transit in Sequim. (Buses run Mon.-Fri. 6am-7:30pm, Sat. 9am-5pm. Fare 50¢.)

Accommodations and Camping

Port Angeles' dumpy hotels linger as a reminder of the town's long-standing tradition as a rough-and-tumble port town. Fortunately, cheap camping abounds in the scenic environs.

All-View Motel, 214 E. Lauridsen Blvd. (457-7779), on U.S. 101 at Lincoln St. Take bus #22 from Oak and Railroad to Lincoln and Lauridsen. Quiet, residential neighborhood. Well-equipped rooms: cable TV, laundry facilities, some kitchens. Discounts for senior citizens. Singles or doubles in summer from $31; in winter $23.

Dan Dee Motel, 132 E. Lauridsen Blvd. (457-5404), on U.S. 101. Take bus #22 from Oak and Railroad to Lincoln and Lauridsen. Relatively clean rooms with fuzzy color TV, some with kitchenettes. Singles $24. Doubles $30.

Heart o' the Hills Campground (452-2713), 5½ miles from Port Angeles inside Olympic National Park. Go up Race Rd. past the park's visitors center and toward Hurricane Ridge. 105 idyllic campsites. Drinking water and toilets, but no showers. Sites $5. Open year-round.

Elwha Campground (452-9191), 3 miles up Elwha River Rd., which leaves U.S. 101 9 miles west of Port Angeles. Not as lovely a setting as Heart o' the Hills, but not as crowded. Sites $5. Open year-round.

Altaire Campground, another 2 miles up Elwha River Rd. A near Xerox of Elwha Campground, only higher on the hill. Sites $5. Open year-round.

Boulder Creek Campground, at the end of Elwha River Rd., 8 miles past Altaire. The closest free campground to Port Angeles. Park at the end of the road, and hike 2 miles along an abandoned road. You'll need a free backcountry permit (available at the trailhead). 50 sites.

House of Health Hostel, 511 E. 1st St (452-7494). Opened in May 1989, this hostel has a large kitchen, lockers, comfortable beds, and friendly management. Located above a health food store and steambath emporium. Reception 7-10am and 5-10pm. $9.50 per night, $2 linen rental. Open April-Oct. 31.

Food

In a town that makes its living off the sea, the absence of cheap seafood is inexplicable. In fact, there is a severe shortage of any cheap food at all. If you're low on money but feel that you must eat, you can always fall back on the fast-food chains that line the eastern half of Front and 1st St.

First Street Haven, 107 E. 1st St. (457-0352). The best price-to-quality ratio. Jam-packed in the morning, but if you can elbow your way in, try the strawberry belgian waffle ($4) or any of the cheesy scrambles. Sandwiches run in the $5 range. Open Mon.-Fri. 7am-4pm, Sat. 8am-4pm, Sun. 8am-2pm.

It's All Greek to Me, 1506 E. 1st St. (452-5964). The gyros ($2.55) look suspiciously mass-produced, and the food is not strictly hellenic, but it's inexpensive and tasty nonetheless. Open Mon.-Wed. 6:30am-7pm, Thurs.-Sat. 6:30am-9pm.

Steve's Bakery, 110 E. 1st St. (457-4003). Foot-long maple bars (65¢), cake donuts (15¢), and healthy-looking loaves of bread ($1). Open Tues.-Fri. 7am-5pm, Sat. 7am-4pm.

Sights and Activities

The town's charms are few. To watch the sunset, go west on Front St. to **Ediz Hook,** a long sand spit jutting into the strait. The city pier (right next to the visitors center) houses Peninsula College's **Arthur D. Feiro Marine Laboratory** (452-9277, ext. 264). The lab offers touch tanks and excellent displays of local marine life. (Open daily 10am-8pm; in winter Sat.-Sun. noon-4pm. Admission $1, ages under 12 50¢.) Also on the pier is an observation tower with great views of a drab port. (Open daily 6am-10pm.) The **Clallam County Museum,** 223 E. 4th St. (452-7831, ext. 364), on the second floor of the old Clallam Courthouse, lets you get up close to a lighthouse light, a stereopticon with shelves full of picture-cards, and a fully preserved turn-of-the-century courtroom. (Open Mon.-Sat. 10am-4pm; in winter Mon.-Fri. 10am-4pm. Free.) As you walk the streets, keep your eyes peeled for the occasionally ambulatory ferret.

No visit to Port Angeles is complete without a drive up Hurricane Ridge Rd. to **Hurricane Ridge.** Thick populations of bear and deer roam the woods to the side of the thrilling thoroughfare, as alpine meadows leap straight out of *The Sound of Music.* The often-crowded ridge is the easiest point from which to grab a hiker's view of the range. However, on the many trails that begin here (including some for senior citizens or the disabled), the crowds quickly dissipate. Be alert while in the tourist-ridden parking area: deer, grown brazen, often graze in the parking lot. Hitching to the top is not an ordeal; you might stop in at the visitors center, at the base of the road, and ask around for a ride. Although the snow is too heavy and wet to be much good for winter sports, the park service nonetheless runs cross-country and downhill skiing on Hurricane Ridge during the winter (lift ticket $12). Sledding is discouraged because of injuries in the past.

The **visitors center,** 3200 Mt. Angeles Rd. (452-4501, ext. 230), at Race St., dispenses free wilderness permits for backcountry camping. (Open daily 8am-6pm, shorter hours in winter.) The **Pioneer Memorial Museum,** near the visitors center, strips bare the life of the early logger and displays pressed specimens of park flora. (Open same hours as visitors center. Free.)

Near Port Angeles

Jutting into the Strait of Juan de Fuca, some 15 miles east of Port Angeles and 6 miles from the tiny town of Sequim (pronounced SKWIM), the **Dungeness Spit National Wildlife Refuge** protects seals, waterfowl, shellfish, and the occasional human on its 7-mile stretch of beach. Unfortunately, the refuge is so isolated that it is virtually inaccessible to travelers without vehicles of their own. Although you can reach Sequim from Seattle via Greyhound ($11), from Port Townsend via Jefferson County Transit, or from Port Angeles via the Clallam Transit System, you still must walk the remaining 6 miles to the refuge; Sequim does not include a bicycle rental shop among its attractions. Cars are not allowed on the spit itself, and a $2 entrance fee is charged.

Sequim, an oasis of dry weather in a soggy region, has seen rapid growth in the last few years as a retirement center. The **Sequim-Dungeness Museum,** 175 W. Cedar (683-8100), in the old post office, exhibits local historical artifacts, including handiwork by the Klallam and Lummi nations. (Open Wed.-Sun. noon-4pm.) Drink your fill at the **Neuharth Winery,** 148 Still Rd. (683-9652 or 683-3706), which opens its cellars for tasting and tours. (Open daily 9:30am-5:30pm; in winter Wed.-Sun. noon-5pm.) If you hunger for English pastries, why aren't you going to **Scarborough Fayre,** 126 E. Washington St. (683-7861), in the Olde Sequim Marketplace? Sandwiches with soup or salad $5, sausage pastry $1.50. (Open Mon.-Sat. 10am-4pm.) Afterward, you may want to follow the signs to the **Olympic Game Farm,** 383 Ward Rd. (683-4295), where you can meet face-to-face with wild animals, some of whom are celebrities (Disney shoots many of its animal films here). A walking or driving tour costs $4, $3 for senior citizens and children. (Open daily 9am-7pm; in winter 9am-5pm.) Sequim's **Chamber of Commerce** (683-6197), ½-mile east of town on the corner of U.S. 101 and Rhodofer Rd., is awash with pamphlets. The Sequim **post office** is one block south of U.S. 101 on Sunnyside (General Delivery ZIP Code: 98382), and the local **area code** is 206.

Camping sites are plentiful. **Sequim Bay State Park** (683-4235), 4 miles east of Sequim on U.S. 101, has 86 sites and is wheelchair-accessible. (Sites $7, $9.50 with full hookup.) Eleven miles south of Sequim on Forest Service Rd. 2958 is **Dungeness Forks,** a free Forest Service campground. The site has pit toilets, running water, and hiking trails. The most popular spot in the area, however, is the **Dungeness Recreation Area** (683-5847), a Clallam County Park. Turn north on Kitchen-Dick Rd. off 101 to reach the home of the famous Dungeness crab. Clamming, crabbing, and beachcombing are major activities. Before collecting any shellfish, however, be sure to call the Washington State Red Tide Hotline at 800-562-5632. (Sites $5 resident, $7 nonresident. Open Jan. 15-Oct. 9.)

West of the city, accessible via U.S. 101 and Soleduck Rd., the **Sol Duc Hot Springs** (327-3583) smolder. You'll pay $3.50 per day for a soak in the warm mineral pools. (Springs open May-Aug. daily 8am-9pm; Sept. 9am-7pm.)

Five miles west of Port Angeles, the highway divides and U.S. 101 heads south, away from the coast. Hwy. 112 continues along the Strait of Juan de Fuca for 63 miles to Neah Bay. Clallam County Parks runs two well-developed campgrounds along Hwy. 112. **Salt Creek Recreation Area** (928-3441), 14 miles west of Port Angeles, has a marine life sanctuary, hiking trails, hot showers, and horseshoe pits. (Sites $6. Open year-round.) **Pillar Point Fishing Camp** (928-3201), another 26 miles west of Salt Creek, is much smaller, with running water and flush toilets, but no showers. (Sites $6. Open May 15-Sept. 15.) Clallam County Transit bus #10 travels Hwy. 112 as far as the town of Joyce, with a stop at Lake Crescent.

At the westernmost point on the strait within Washington State is **Neah Bay,** the only town in the Makah Indian Reservation. On the pier, six tables grace the **Windsong Café,** which offers burgers for $2.25-4.75 and clam chowder for $2. The Clallam Transit System reaches Neah Bay via Sappho. Take bus #14 from Oak St. in Port Angeles to Sappho (60 min.). Then take bus #16 to Neah Bay (60 min.). Check schedules to avoid excessive layovers. In Neah Bay, call 645-2701 in an **emergency,** 645-2236 in a **marine emergency.** Neah Bay's **ZIP code** is 98357.

Cape Flattery, the northwesternmost point in the contiguous United States, sits in the corner of Neah Bay's backyard, but the dirt road out is hard to follow. Watch for signs reading "cape trails" at the west end of town. Follow the signs (and the dirt road) about 8 miles to a dead end, where a well-marked trailhead sends you toward Cape Flattery. The half-hour hike rewards those willing to risk twisted ankles with fantastic views of Tatoosh Island just off the coast and Vancouver Island across the strait. A few miles south of Cape Flattery is **Hobuck Beach,** where camping and picnicking are accessible by car. South of here begin the most deserted beaches, which can be reached only on foot. The whole area is private property; visitors are welcome, but should stop at the cultural center in Neah Bay for reservation regulations.

Unlike the Native Americans of eastern Washington, the Makah nation (whose recorded history goes back 2000 years) still lives, fishes, and produces magnificent art work on its original land. The **Makah Cultural and Research Center** (645-2711) houses artifacts from the archaeological site at Cape Alava, where a huge mudslide 500 years ago buried and preserved an entire settlement. A 70-foot-long house, the famous slope-roofed shelter ideally suited to this rainy environment, has been replicated at the museum. (Open daily 10am-5pm; in winter Wed.-Sun. 10am-5pm. Admission $3, senior citizens and students $2.)

The **Makah Days** celebration in late August features a salmon bake, canoe races, traditional dances, and sports events, all in traditional Native American style. Tribes from throughout the Northwest gather to participate in these events and in the bone games, a form of gambling. Contact the cultural center for more information.

The town of **Forks** has a sporting goods store, several motels, and a shopping center. Stay at the **Rainforest Home Hostel (AYH)** between mileposts 169 and 170 on U.S. 101 (374-2270). Check-in starts at 5pm. Members $6, in winter $7.50; add $3 for nonmembers. Reservations are required; call or write Jim Conomos, HC 80, P.O. Box 870, Forks 98331. Use Forks as a base for exploring Olympic National Park's rain forests and the rugged coastline of the peninsula's western side. Before taking off into the wilderness, however, sample the scrumptious pies at **Pacific Pizza,** on U.S. 101 in Forks (374-2626). Seafood lovers should try the shrimp pizza ($4), fruit lovers the apple pizza ($4), and purists the all-American 8-inch cheese pizza ($3). A small pitcher of soda pop costs $1. (Open Sun.-Thurs. 11am-10pm, Fri.-Sat. 11am-11pm.)

Olympic National Park

Lodged among the august Olympic mountains, Olympic National Park unites 900,000 acres of velvet-green rainforest, jagged snow-covered peaks, and ominously dense evergreen forest. This enormous region at the center of the peninsula allows limited access to four-wheeled traffic. No scenic loops or roads cross the park, and only a handful of secondary roads attempt to penetrate the interior. The roads that do exist serve as trailheads for over 600 miles of hiking trails. The only people who seem not to enjoy this wildly diverse wilderness are those who come unprepared for rain; a parka, good boots, and a waterproof tent are essential in this area.

Practical Information and Orientation

Visitor Information: Park Service Visitors Center, 3002 Mt. Angeles Rd., Port Angeles (452-4501, ext. 230), off Race St. Main information center; fields questions about the whole park—camping, backcountry hiking, and fishing. Wilderness permits and map of the locations of other park ranger stations. Also houses the **Pioneer Memorial Museum** (see Port Angeles Sights). Open daily 8am-6pm, reduced hours in winter.

Park Superintendent: 600 E. Park Ave., Port Angeles (452-4501, ext. 217). Open daily 8am-5pm.

Park Weather: 452-9235. 24 hours.

Park Emergency: 452-4501. Operates 8am-2pm.

The perimeters of the park are well developed. The park service runs **interpretive programs** such as guided forest walks, tidal pool walks, and campfire programs out of its various ranger stations (all free). For a full schedule of events throughout the park, obtain a copy of the park newspaper, from ranger stations or the visitors center. A $3 entrance fee per car is charged at the more popular entrances, such as the Hoh, Heart O' the Hills, and Elwaha. The fee buys an entrance permit good for 7 days. A similar pass for hiker/bikers costs $1.

July, August, and September are the best months for visiting Olympic National Park, since much of the backcountry often remains snowed-in until late June, and only the summer has a good number of rainless days. **Backpackers** should come prepared for a potpourri of weather conditions at any time. Always wear a wool hat in winter; hypothermia is a leading cause of death in the backcountry (see Health in the General Introduction for more details). Backcountry camping requires a free wilderness permit, available at ranger stations and trailheads. The park service's backcountry shelters are for emergencies only; large concentrations of people attract bears.

Never, ever drink untreated water in the park. *Giardia*, a very nasty microscopic parasite, lives in all these waters and causes severe diarrhea, gas, and abdominal cramps. Symptoms often don't appear for weeks after ingestion and make life more miserable than you ever thought possible. Carry your own water supply, or boil local water for five minutes before drinking it. Dogs are not allowed in the backcountry and must be restrained at all times within the park.

Mountain climbing is tricky business in the Olympic Range. Although the peaks are not high in absolute terms (Mt. Olympus is only 7915 ft. above sea level), they are steep and their proximity to the sea makes them prone to nasty weather. The quality of rock is poor, and most ascents require sophisticated equipment. Climbers are required to check in at a ranger station before any summit attempt. The rangers urge novices to buddy up with experienced climbers who are "wise in the ways of Northwest mountaineering."

Berry picking ranks high on the list of summer activities, and is easy as pie on the peninsula. Newly cleared regions and roadside areas have the best pickings; raspberries, strawberries, blueberries, and huckleberries are all common. Bears are also fond of this fruit. If one stumbles onto your favorite berry patch, be polite.

Fishing within park boundaries requires no permit, but you must obtain a state game department punch card for salmon and steelhead trout at outfitting and hardware stores locally, or at the game department in Olympia. The **Elwha River** is best for trout.

Eastern Rim

The eastern section of the park is accessible through the Olympic National Forest from U.S. 101 along Hood Canal. (See Hood Canal for information on camping in the forest.) The auto campgrounds are popular with hikers, who use them as trailheads to the interior of the park. **Staircase Campground** (877-5569), 19 miles northwest of Hoodsport at the head of Lake Cushman, has a ranger station that offers interpretive programs on weekends. (63 sites open year-round, $5.) **Dosewallips,** on a road that leaves U.S. 101 3 miles north of Brinnon (27 miles north of Hoodsport), has 33 free but less well-developed sites. The ranger station, open from June through September only, has no electricity or telephone. A spectacular trail leads from here across the park to Hurricane Ridge.

Northern Rim

Heart o' the Hills (452-2713; 105 sites) and **Elwha Valley** (452-9191; 41 sites) campgrounds both have interpretive programs and ranger stations (see Port Angeles), as does **Fairholm Campground** (928-3380, 87 sites), 30 miles west of Port Angeles at the western tip of Lake Crescent. (Sites $5. Open year-round.) The **Lake Crescent** station (928-3380) has an extensive interpretive program but no camping. The **information booth** here is open Memorial Day to Labor Day daily from 11:30am-4:30pm. **Soleduck Hotsprings Campground** (327-3534), to the southeast of Lake Crescent, 13 miles off U.S. 101, is adjacent to the commercial hot springs resort (see Port Angeles Sights and Activities). A roving naturalist is on duty in the afternoon, and there are scheduled programs in the evening. (Sites $5.) The grounds are shut down when (not if) it snows.

The main attraction of the northern area, especially for those not planning back-country trips, is **Hurricane Ridge,** with its magnificent views of Mt. Olympus, the Bailey Range, and Canada on clear days. (See Port Angeles Sights and Activities.)

Rain Forests

Washington is home to the only temperate (as opposed to tropical) rain forests in the world. The rain forests along the Hoh and Queets rivers are canopied by par-ticularly lush growths of gigantic trees, ferns, and mosses. Although the forest floor is congested with unusual foliage and fallen trees, the Park Service keeps the many walking trails clear and well-marked. The first campgrounds along the Hoh River Rd., which leaves U.S. 101 13 miles south of the town of Forks, are administered by the Department of Natural Resources (DNR), and accept no reservations. Drinking water is available at the **Cottonwood** and **Minnie Patterson** sites only. They are usually much less crowded than the Hoh, and the sites are about twice as roomy. You can obtain a separate map of the Hoh-Clearwater Multiple Use Area (MUA) from the DNR main office in Forks or at Minnie Patterson (see Olympic Peninsula Camping.)

At the top of the Hoh River Rd. is the park service's **Hoh Rain Forest Camp-ground and Visitors Center** (374-6925). The center is wheelchair-accessible, as is a trail leading from the center into the rain forest. Camping is available year-round and costs $5. (Visitors center open in summer daily 9am-5pm.) Try to camp near the riverbed in loop A. Deer stroll casually through your campsite here, and herds of elk can often be spotted in the riverbed early in the morning.

Farther south, after U.S. 101 rejoins the coast (see Ocean Beaches below), the park's boundaries extend southwest to edge the banks of the **Queets River.** The road here is unpaved and the campground at the top is free. (26 sites; open June-Sept.) The park and forest services share the land surrounding **Quinault Lake** and **River.** The park service land is accessible only by foot. The forest service operates a day-use beach and an information center in the **Quinault Ranger Station,** South Shore Rd. (288-2444; open daily 7:30am-5pm; in winter Mon.-Fri. 7:30am-5pm).

Ocean Beaches

The rugged and deserted beaches along the peninsula's western edge are espe-cially magnificent during winter storms. Hike miles out of civilization's reach (with the exception of a few shelters around Mora), but beware of incoming tides that can trap you against steep cliffs (clip and carry a tide chart from a local newspaper). Bald eagles rise to greet windy days in this area; whales and seals tear through the gong-tormented sea.

Mora (374-5460), near the Quillayute Indian fishing village of **La Push,** and **Ka-laloch** (962-2283), have campgrounds (sites $5) and ranger stations. The Kalaloch (kuh-LAY-lok) Center, including lodge, general store, and gas station, is the more scenic, with 195 sites near the ocean.

Southwest Washington

At the climax of its Washington odyssey, the Columbia River makes a breathtak-ing descent into the Columbia River Gorge. As it moves seaward, the river becomes a border between Oregon and Washington for several hundred miles before ending in the Pacific. Resort towns conspire at the mouth of the river and around the bays and fishing ports to the north. The towns are small and rarely dovetail smooth-ly—wild marshlands and grasslands intercept, harboring coastal fauna in several good state parks and wildlife refuges. For information about the area, contact the

Tourist Regional Information Program, SW Washington, P.O. Box 128, Longview 98632. In an emergency, call the state police (206-577-2050). From Memorial Day to Labor Day, call 800-562-0990 for Washington Park information.

Longview/Kelso

The twin towns of Kelso and Longview hold hands over the Cowlitz River near its confluence with the Columbia, just across from Rainier, OR. Longview was the first planned city west of the Rockies, and Kelso was founded by Highland Scots. Today, neither urban planning nor bagpipes define the sister cities as definitively as do their convention centers. Although there are a few sights worth seeing, Kelso and Longview together warrant no more than a day's visit.

Practical Information

Visitor Information: Longview Chamber of Commerce, 1563 Olympia Way (423-8400). Open Mon.-Fri. 9am-5pm. Very helpful. **Kelso Chamber of Commerce,** 105 Miner Rd. (577-8058), exit 39 off I-5, near Kelso Rd. With its diagrams and dioramas, it's a good source of Mt. St. Helens information. Open daily 9am-5pm.

Greyhound: 1109 Broadway, in Broadway Hotel, Longview (423-7380). Buses to Portland (6 per day, $6.50), Olympia (7 per day, $9), Seattle (7 per day, $13), and Vancouver, BC (4 per day, $50).

Community Urban Bus: 577-3399. Runs Mon.-Fri. 7am-6pm, Sat. 9am-6pm. Buses leave "Triangle Center" on the west bank of the Cowlitz in Longview every hr. on the hr. Fare 50¢, day pass $1. Free transfers.

Pacific Ferry: 800-542-7042 or 800-542-0810. Puget Island to Oregon (8 min., $2 per car).

Police: In Longview, 577-3157. In Kelso, 423-1270.

General Delivery ZIP Code: Longview: 98632. Kelso: 98626.

Area Code: 206.

Accommodations, Camping, and Food

Motel 6, 1505 Allen St., Kelso (636-3660), across from the Chamber of Commerce. So immaculate it is often used as a convention center by soap salespeople. Cable, pool, and A/C. Singles $28. Doubles $34.

Electra Motel, 1744 10th Ave., Longview (423-5040). Color TV, kitchen, and living room in your single make up for peeling paint. No reservations. Singles $20. Doubles $25.

Oaks Trailer and RV Park, 636 California Way, Longview (425-2708), exit 36 off I-5. Deluxe accoutrements include, of all things, free cable TV. Sites $10.50.

Commerce Cafe, Commerce Plaza, 1338 Commerce Ave. (577-0115). Average prices (breakfast $2-3). Open Mon.-Thurs. 7am-9pm, Fri. 7am-10pm, Sat. 9am-10pm.

Hilander Restaurant, 1509 Allen St., Kelso (423-1500), near Motel 6 across from Volcano Center. Breakfast $2. Burgers $3-4. An adjacent bowling alley provides striking accompaniment to your meal. Open Sun.-Thurs. 7am-10pm, Fri.-Sat. 7am-11pm.

Sights

Famous for its January and February **smelt run,** when thousands of the tiny fish take the kamikaze trip from the ocean to the river, Kelso has earned the dubious title of "Smelt Capital of the World." Local civic groups sponsor a deranged annual "smelt eating contest" the first Sunday in March. For a few dollars, watch the local champions compete for prizes by stuffing themselves silly with phenomenal numbers of smelt. Contestants are said to fast for days in advance.

See a display of reconstructed pioneer-era buildings, Cowlitz and Chinook Indian artifacts, and a new exhibit on the role of transportation in the history of Washington at the **Cowlitz County Historical Museum,** 405 Allen St. (577-3119). (Open Tues.-Sat. 9am-5pm, Sun. 1-5pm.) At the museum, a pamphlet details a walking tour of Kelso's century houses. The **Volcano Information Center,** in the same building as the Chamber of Commerce, features detailed accounts of the eruption of nearby Mt. St. Helens and dramatic pictures of rescue attempts. (Open daily 9am-5pm; Nov.-April Wed.-Sun. 9am-5pm.)

The **Reynolds Metal Co. Plant,** 4029 Industrial Way (425-2800), near the Columbia River, reveals the inner workings of metallurgy in a 90-minute tour Thursdays at 1pm. To protect against industrial espionage, no cameras are allowed. Reynolds suggests that visitors wear long sleeves. Take another inside view of Washington's natural-industrial complex at the **Weyerhauser Company Mill Site,** Industrial Way (425-2150). Hour-long tours depart from the gatehouse just inside the main gate. (Tours given Mon.-Fri. 9:30am and 1:30pm; Labor Day to mid-June only on Fri. by appointment. Ages under 10 not allowed.)

The **Highlander Festival,** held during the third week of September, celebrates Kelso's Scottish heritage. Kelso residents cap off a day of bagpiping with an exciting round of canine weight-pulling. From featherweights to heavyweights, dogs see how much they can drag by their teeth. Oh wow.

Longview was named after its wealthy founder, R.A. Long, who fancied himself a visionary. Now a logging town and major deep-water port of declining population, Longview is not the stuff of visions. There is, however, a pleasant wooded park surrounding mile-long **Lake Sacajawea** in the center of town. Relax here or tour Longview port. (One-hr. tours daily 10am-1pm. Call 425-3305.) The innocuous **Monticello Convention Site,** at 18th, Maple, and Olympic Ave., commemorates the 1852 political gathering that made Washington a state.

Longview/Kelso to the Pacific

Access to the beaches on the coast from Longview and Kelso is smooth. From Naselle, **Highway 401** rambles south past the mouth of the Columbia, a more scenic road than either Hwy. 4 or U.S. 101. By car, take exit 39 off I-5 and follow Hwy. 4 (Ocean Beach Highway) west. The latter allows good bicycling along the scenic Columbia River. When hitching, avoid Hwy. 4 and cross the bridge to Rainier, OR, where extroverted U.S. 30 continues to Astoria.

Although much of the **Willapa Hills** area, along Hwy. 4, is owned by timber companies, it still explodes with bears, deer, geefels, gonks, and other wildlife. The **Columbian White-Tailed Deer National Wildlife Refuge** covers 9800 acres of island and mainland around **Cathlamet.** From headquarters (795-3915), 2 miles off Hwy. 4, a walk or drive on the local roads yields close-up sightings of park deer. Connected to Cathlamet (see below) by Hwy. 409, rural **Puget Island** is prime bicycling country in the middle of the Columbia. The **Wahkiakum County Historical Museum,** a folksy, crowded collection of local memorabilia, beckons just 1 block from Hwy. 4 on River St. The delightfully unpretentious museum shows old photos of the logging operations and of above average Scandinavian immigrants. (Open Tues.-Sun. 1-4pm; Dec.-March Thurs.-Sun. 1-4pm.) There are numerous little parks along the Columbia River. Watch for huge ocean-bound vessels navigating the currents.

Just west of Cathlamet on Hwy. 4, **Skamokawa** (ska-MOCK-away) is a riverside village that has changed little since the turn of the century. Across the creek from town, **Skamokawa Vista Park** (789-8605) permits picnics, camping with tents or RVs, and enjoyment of the playgrounds and tennis park next to the Columbia River. **Grays River,** part of which flows under Washington's only remaining covered bridge, is a convenient starting point for a bike trip to the old fishing village of **Altoona,** south of Hwy. 403 on the northern bank of the widened Columbia River.

Columbia River Mouth and Long Beach Peninsula

Over 230 vessels have been wrecked, stranded, or sunk where the Columbia meets the ocean—a region aptly dubbed the "graveyard of the Pacific." One British fur trader in the 18th century, chagrined after his repeated failure to cross the treacherous Columbia River Bar, named the large promontory guarding the river's mouth **Cape Disappointment.**

Fort Columbia State Park (777-8221 or 777-8358) is on U.S. 101 northwest of the Astoria Megler Bridge and 1 mile east of Chinook. An interesting complex of buildings and historical sites, the fort was built in 1895 and armed with huge guns to protect the mouth of the river from enemies who never arrived. The park's **interpretive center** entertainingly re-creates life at the fort. The art gallery next door features local artists' work as well as a permanent collection of intriguing old photographs and sketches. A mile-long woodland trail takes you past several historical sites, including an abandoned observation station. (Park open daily 6:30am-dusk; Oct. 16-March Wed.-Sun. 8am-dusk.) What was once the hospital is now the **Fort Columbia Youth Hostel,** P.O. Box 224, Chinook (777-8755). The hostel is run by a talkative ranger and is rarely full. There are some rooms available for couples and families. (Members $5, nonmembers $7. Open June 6-Sept. 15.) The only drawbacks are a military atmosphere and a 9am check-out time. The park locks up at dusk, even though the hostel is only open for registration from 5:30-10pm. You can get to Fort Columbia from Astoria on bus #14.

In nearby Ilwaco, **Fort Canby State Park** offers camping and more Lewis-and-Clarkana. Given the treacherous river entrance, it is not surprising that two lighthouses are found here; one is the Northwest's oldest. The U.S. Coast Guard maintains a **Lifeboat Station and Surf School** in the park, where arduous training in rough winter surf pays off in summer; this is one of the busiest search-and-rescue stations in the United States.

You can watch the Coast Guard's perilous training maneuvers or fetch views of the distant lighthouses from many angles. The Cape Disappointment Lighthouse, built in 1856, and the North Head Lighthouse, built in 1898, are both in the park and accessible by 4-mile forest trails. **Waikiki Beach** the lesser is in a sheltered area near the park's center, ideal for swimming in summer, beachcombing after storms in winter, and ship-watching day in and day out. It is near the park's main attraction, the **Lewis and Clark Interpretive Center** (642-3029 or 642-3078). Here the legendary expedition is depicted through journal entries, photos, and equipment. The center also delves into Native American lore and probes Cape Disappointment's recent role as a strategic military stronghold. (Open daily 9am-6pm; Oct.-May Wed.-Sun. 9am-5pm.) The park lets 194 tentsites ($6-11), which fill up on summer weekends. To reserve a site, write Fort Canby State Park, P.O. Box 488, Ilwaco 98624, or call the park office in Ilwaco (642-3078). To reach the park, exit U.S. 101 at Ilwaco and head 2 miles southwest. Ignore the many signs pointing right—that road is a mile longer. **Pacific Transit** buses (642-4475) connect Ilwaco with the north Washington coast and with Astoria, OR. (Fare 35-50¢.) From Ilwaco you can hitchhike or walk the 2 miles to the park.

In Ilwaco, the **Heritage Museum,** 115 SE Lake St., lines up the usual suspects: Native crafts, pioneer memorabilia, and a rotating display of local artwork. (Open Mon.-Sat. 9am-5pm, Sun. 1-4pm. Admission $1.25, senior citizens and children 50¢.) For something completely different, the restored railway depot behind the museum runs a model train through a scale model of the peninsula as it looked in the 20s. Charter fishing is really hot in Ilwaco. The best deal is **Reel 'Em In Charters and Cafe** at the Port of Ilwaco. Eight-hour salmon tours including coffee, lunch, and tackle start at $41 (Sun.-Thurs. at 5am). Write P.O. Box 489, Ilwaco 98624 for reservations, or call either 642-8511 or 642-3511. Stay at **Heidi's Inn,** 126 Spruce

(642-2837), for its cable TV and kitchen and laundry facilities. (Singles $26. Doubles $34.)

Long Beach Peninsula, with its 28 miles of unbroken beach, seems a private riviera. Fishing, swimming, boating, and kite-flying fill in the seasons between pounding winter storms on this uncrowded stretch. **Beachcombing** for peculiar pieces of driftwood and glass balls from Japanese fishing nets relaxes and rewards. Beachcombers need a permit for gathering driftwood in state parks. Driving on the beach is common and legal on the hard, wet sand above the lower clam beds. From October to mid-March, look for people trying to catch the limit of 15 meaty razor clams. Outwitting the tasty, fast-digging bivalves is an art, but it involves standard techniques. If you're willing to shell out $10 for an annual nonresident license and spend a few days learning the ropes, you may harvest a seafood feast. The *Chinook Observer's* Long Beach Peninsula Guide and the **state fisheries** (Ocean Park, 753-6600) advise clammers. Consult fisheries' regulations before digging in. Free tide tables are available at information centers and many places of business. These are useful both for clamming and to avoid being marooned.

Berry picking keeps many travelers well-fed in late summer; look for wild varieties in the weeds along the peninsula's roadsides. Be careful about picking on private property and watch for bears.

Limited transportation is provided by **Pacific Transit** (in Raymond 642-4475, in Naselle 484-7136, farther north 875-6541). For 85¢ and a transfer, you can take a bus as far north as Aberdeen. Flag down buses anywhere along their routes. Schedules are available in post offices and visitors centers. (Service Mon.-Fri. 2-3 times per day.)

In **Seaview,** about 10 miles north on the peninsula, the **visitors information center** (642-2400), at the intersection of U.S. 101 and Hwy. 103, welcomes tourists Mon.-Sat. 10am-5pm and Sun. 10am-4pm.

Farther north, the city of Long Beach draws the serious traveler to its strip of video arcades, bumper cars, kiddie rides, and junk food. Right in the middle of things lurks **Marsh's Free Museum,** 409 S. Pacific Ave. (642-2188), really a large store selling myriad geegaws and *tchatchkes.* The promised "exhibits" in the back are mostly old coin-operated peepshows or player pianos. Don't miss "Jake," however—this mummified half-man, half-crocodile is a local cult favorite. (Open daily 9am-10pm.) Two blocks west of Pacific Ave. you'll find the beach. Here you can ride bumper boats or rent a horse at **Double D Ranch**—it costs $10 per hour and a wrangler goes with you to make sure you don't gallop into the ocean. Late July brings the **Sand Castle Festival** to Long Beach. In 1989, a world record was challenged when participants built a three-mile-long fortress of sand. The cheapest place to sleep is the **Sand-Lo-Motel,** 1906 Pacific Hwy. (642-2600). The large, clean rooms can be yours for $22 (singles) or $28 (doubles).

Continuing up the peninsula, the quiet residential community of **Ocean Park** is home to **Jack's Country Store,** at Bay and Veron (665-4988), *the* place for groceries, hardware, and just about anything else. Prices are reasonable and the store is run by a gregarious former math professor. (Open daily 8am-8pm.) **Grub 'n' Stuff,** Bay St. (665-4224), a block from the beach, serves cheap and tasty grub such as burgers on homemade buns ($2.75-3.45). As for the stuff: $10 per hour, a $20 deposit, and a driver's licence can rent you a moped—a perfect way to see Oysterville and Nahcotta.

Oysterville is a preserved 1854 town. For a walking tour of this two-street hamlet, pick up a free guide at the church. Don't get too close to the houses, though—people still live in them. For once, the past has not been tainted by commercialism—there's no way to spend money in Oysterville.

Nearby **Nahcotta** relies on the oyster for both entertainment and financial solvency. Nahcotta's sole claim to fame is **The Ark,** easily the finest restaurant in the area. Dinner might cost over $15 but it will deluge you with fresh seafood, homemade baked goods and pastries, and Northwest specialties, all elegantly prepared and served. (Open Tues.-Sun. for dinner and Sun. for brunch.) Reservations are required—call 665-4133.

Leadbetter Point State Park, on the Long Beach peninsula's northernmost tip, is a favorite with photographers, nature lovers, and mosquitoes. Bring bug repellent and make sure that your kids and small pets aren't devoured by the insect multitudes. The park is a mosaic of marsh, grass, forest, pond, and dune; it is quite wet despite all the sand. Farther down the peninsula, **Pacific Pines** and **Loomis Lake State Parks** are good spots for hiking, picnicking, and surf fishing. Stay at one of the several cheap motels along the road; the state's seven Pacific beaches join the parks in forbidding campsites.

Willapa Bay and Grays Harbor

Willapa Bay, just north of Long Beach, is known for its wildlife but not its wild life. A drive up U.S. 101 and west on Hwy. 105 at Raymond offers stunning scenery, compensating for the protected bay's deficiencies as a swimming and sunning spot. The small towns along the peninsula gear themselves to tourists and bristle with the usual array of souvenir shops and overpriced seafood restaurants. The state parks that clutter the region are all for day use only. (All parks open daily 6:30am-dusk; Nov.-March 8am-dusk. Call 665-5557 for information.)

Your first stop heading north on U.S. 101 should be the **Willapa National Wildlife Refuge,** a sanctuary for seabirds and waterfowl. You'll need a car to get there, but once you've arrived, plan to spend two or three hours of wet hiking in the swamplands. **South Bend** (accessible by Pacific Transit) claims to be the oyster capital of the world. You can tour the fully automated **Coast Oyster Company** (875-5557); the oysters are great but they cost as much as pearls. **Bob's Pizza and Seafood** is a family-type place with average prices. The **South Bend Chamber of Commerce** (875-5231) has local and area-wide information, as well as advice on places to camp overnight. (Open Mon.-Sat. 11:30am-4pm.) While walking through the streets at night, try not to look too closely at the benches dedicated to the local dead; they are waiting to be included in a new Stephen King novel.

Raymond, 4 miles from South Bend, is another quiet roadside logging town. The town relives its heyday during its annual **Loggers Fest,** held the first weekend of August. **Pizza Loft,** 226 Duryea (942-5109), serves obligatto pizza and sandwiches. (Lunch special Mon.-Fri. $2.75. All-you-can-eat spaghetti Mon. nights $4.75. Open Mon.-Sat. 11am-10pm, Sun. noon-9pm.) **Maunu's Mountcastle Motel,** 524 3rd St., is just about the only place to stay in the area; its clean rooms include color TV and A/C. (Singles $28. Doubles $32.) The **Raymond Visitor Information Center** is not very helpful and is located in the Century 21 building at 625 Heath St., just off U.S. 101. (942-5419; open daily 9am-5pm.)

If you still have gas or gumption, drive west to **Tokeland** for good beaches and better beachcombing. **Frances,** a ghost town on Hwy. 6, 15 miles east of Raymond, suddenly comes alive with tourists twice per year for its Swiss-American celebrations. The first week in July is time for the **Schwingfest** ("schwinging" is Swiss wrestling), where you can watch the competitions, eat bratwurst, and polka down.

North of Willapa Bay at the far southwest corner of the Olympic Peninsula, the restless waters of Grays Harbor make a sizable dent in Washington's coastline. Long sandbars protect the harbor, itself undistinguished. The spits also extend north and south of the bay, forming wide, fine-grained beaches that stretch for miles in both directions. The inevitably resulting resort area extends north to Moclips near the **Quinault Indian Reservation.** Mobs of vacationers invaded the turf of the Quinault nation until August of 1969, when the Quinault people booted the littering and vandalizing visitors off their tribal beaches. The bold move brought a flood of letters supportive of the Quinault's action. A small museum (276-8211) up the coast in **Taholah,** in the office of the Quinault Historical Foundation, exhibits these political memoranda alongside more ethnological displays. (Open Mon.-Fri. 10am-4pm.) You'll see more if the staff is on hand, so call ahead to arrange a guided tour, as well as to get directions—it's a little tough to find. Grays Harbor Transit's Rte. 50 stops in Taholah.

On Grays Harbor's Southern Spit, **Westport** and **Grayland** are known for salmon and cranberries, respectively. Focus your attention on Westport. At least every other storefront by the waterside Westhaven Dr. is devoted to charter fishing. Besides salmon fishing, most companies offer bottom fishing, tuna fishing, and whale watching tours. **Deep Sea Charters,** across from float six (800-562-0151), is one of the cheapest, with full day trips at $50, plus $6 for tackle. But prices vary; get a list from the Chamber of Commerce and call around.

Generic clam strips and chowder joints are almost as common as charters. For a more serious dining experience, try **Arthur's,** 2681 Westhaven Dr. (268-9292). Lunches start at around $5. Dinners are costlier: a plate of salmon costs $13 and an oyster stew $6. The dining room is cozy and tastefully appointed. (Open Tues.-Sun. 11:30am-2pm and 5-9pm.)

The **Maritime Museum,** 2201 Westhaven Dr. (268-0078), is a fun mix of old seafaring equipment and other mundane objects. The museum is run by an ensemble of elderly women, one of whose 3rd grade report card is on display. (Open Wed.-Sun. noon-4pm; Sept.-May Sat.-Sun. noon-4pm.) Several notches up the tackiness scale, the **Westport Aquarium and Giftshop,** 321 Harbor St. (268-0471), emphasizes the gift shop. A wayward shark and a tired octopus more or less comprise the entire aquarium. (Admission $2, children $1.50.)

Dozens of cheap motels line Hwy. 105 in Westport. Slightly pricier are the motels on the waterfront. The **Chamber of Commerce,** 1200 N. Montesano St. (268-9422), is only too eager to help you out. (Open daily 9am-5pm.)

Buses for Taholah, Westport, even Raymond and Olympia, originate from the **Aberdeen Station,** Wishkah and G St. (800-562-9730). The fare is only 25¢ ($1 to Olympia). Surrounding the station is the heavily industrialized city of **Aberdeen,** which, along with its sister city **Hoquiam,** suffers from a bad reputation. The residents of the rest of Washington call these port towns the mud puddles of the Northwest—not only a reference to the torrents of rain. In the drier summer, however, their strategic location and low prices make them fine places to rest and refuel between the Olympic beaches and the more expensive inland mountains and cities.

The main point of interest in these villified villages is **Hoquiam's Castle,** 515 Chenault Ave. (533-2005), a large Victorian home that stores trinkets and antiques from the area. (Open daily 11am-5pm; in winter by appointment only. Admission $2, ages under 16 $1.) The **Aberdeen Museum of History,** 111 E. 3rd St. (533-1976), brandishes slide shows and antique firefighting equipment. (Open Wed.-Sun. 11am-4pm; Sept.-May Sat.-Sun. noon-4pm.) If you haven't been camping long enough to yearn for the comforts of a cheap motel, make a stop in **Montesano,** a small town about 20 minutes east of Aberdeen on Hwy. 12. From Montesano, you can waltz into the hills for an overnight stay and a swim at **Lake Sylvia.** (Sites $6. Park closes to noncampers at 8pm.)

A string of inexpensive motels bequeaths cheap rooms to those stopping overnight. In Aberdeen, your best bet is undoubtedly the **Towne Motel,** 712 E. Wishkah (533-2340), a few blocks east of the bus station. Ignore the slightly dilapidated exterior—these small, tidy rooms have it all: cable TV with HBO, A/C, in-room coffee, minifridges, and a potted plant. (Singles $23. Doubles $24.) The **TraveLure Motel,** 623 W. Wishkah, has larger rooms and movies available. (Singles $25. Doubles $30.) For more information on this area, say hello to the **Grays Harbor Chamber of Commerce,** 2704 Sumner Ave., Aberdeen 98520 (532-1924).

Cascade Range

Forged by centuries of volcanic activity, the relatively young Cascade Range is still evolving—as the 1980 eruption of Mt. St. Helens attests. While a handful of white-domed beauties attract the most interest, the bulk of the range consists of smaller systems that together form a natural barrier from the Columbia Gorge to

Canada. The mountain wall intercepts moist Pacific air, and is responsible both for Seattle's cloudy weather and the 300 rainless days per year in the plains of eastern Washington.

Although much of the heavily forested range is accessible only to hikers and horseback riders, four major roads cut through the mountains along river valleys, each offering good trailheads and impressive scenery. **Highway 12** through White Pass goes nearest Mt. Rainier National Park; **Interstate 90** sends four lanes past the major ski resorts of Snoqualmie Pass; scenic **Highway 2** leaves Everett for Stevens Pass and descends along the Wenatchee River, a favorite of whitewater rafters; **Highway 20**, the **North Cascades Highway**, provides access to North Cascades National Park from spring to fall. These last two roads are often traveled in sequence as the **Cascade Loop.**

Greyhound covers the routes over Stevens and Snoqualmie Passes to and from Seattle, while **Amtrak** cuts between Ellensburg and Puget Sound. Rainstorms and evening traffic can slow **hitchhiking** down; locals warn against thumbing across Hwy. 20, where a few hapless hitchers have apparently vanished over the last decade. The mountains are most accessible in the clear months of July, August, and September; many high mountain passes are snowed-in the rest of the year. The best source of general information on the Cascades is the joint **National Park/National Forest Information Service**, 915 2nd Ave., Seattle 98174 (442-0181 or 442-0170).

North Cascades

The North Cascades, an aggregation of dramatic peaks north of Stevens Pass on Hwy. 2, is administered by a number of different agencies. Pasayten and Glacier Peak are designated **wilderness areas,** each attracting hardy numbers of large backpackers and mountain climbers. Ross Lake Recreation Area surrounds the Hwy. 20 corridor, and North Cascades National Park extends north and south of Hwy. 20. The Mt. Baker/Snoqualmie National Forest borders the park on the west, the Okanogan National Forest to the east, and Wenatchee National Forest to the south. Highway 20, the North Cascades Highway (open April-Nov., weather permitting), provides the major access to the area, as well as astounding views past each new curve in the road. The North Cascades remain one of the last great expanses of relatively untouched land in the continental states—deer, mountain goats, and black bears (maybe even some grizzlies) continue to make their homes here.

A wide selection of books can help plan a hike in the North Cascades. Ira Springs's *101 Hikes in the North Cascades* (The Mountaineers Press) ranks among the most readable for recreational hikers, while Fred Beckley's *Cascade Alpine Guide* (The Mountaineers Press) interests the more serious high-country traveler and mountain climber.

Practical Information and Orientation

North Cascades National Park: 2105 Hwy. 20, Sedro Woolley 98284 (206-856-5700). Open Sun.-Thurs. 8am-4:30pm, Fri.-Sat. 8am-6pm.

Mt. Baker/Snoqualmie National Forest: 1018 First Ave., Seattle 98104 (206-442-0170).

Okanogan National Forest: 1240 2nd Ave. S., P.O. Box 950, Okanogan 98840 (509-422-2704).

Wenatchee National Forest: 301 Yakima St., P.O. Box 811, Wenatchee 98801 (509-662-4335).

Area Code: 206 west of the Cascades, 509 to the east.

Highway 20 (exit 230 on I-5) gives the best first impression of the North Cascades. A feat of modern engineering, Hwy. 20 follows the Skagit River to the Skagit Dams and lakes, whose hydroelectric energy powers Seattle; then it crosses the Cascade

Crest at Rainy Pass (4860 ft.) and Washington Pass (5477 ft.), finally descending to the Methow River and the dry Okanogan rangeland of eastern Washington.

Greyhound stops in Burlington once per day on the Seattle-Portland route, and **Empire Lines** (affiliated with Greyhound) serves Okanogan, Pateros, and Chelan on the eastern slope. Hitching can be quite frustrating, since nervous RV owners generally blow wind in your face. Local traffic, your only hope, completely vanishes at night.

Skagit Valley

Sedro Woolley, though situated in the rich farmland of the lower Skagit Valley, is primarily a logging town. Locals turn out in droves for the annual **Sedro Woolley Loggerodeo,** which occupies five rowdy days around the Fourth of July. Axe-throwing, pole-climbing, and sawing competitions vie with free-flowing beer for center stage. For information write the Sedro Woolley Chamber of Commerce, 714 Metcalf, Sedro Woolley 98284 (855-1841). North Cascades National Park Headquarters (856-5700) is on Hwy. 20 (open Sun.-Thurs. 8am-4:30pm, Fri.-Sat. 8am-6pm).

Highway 9 leads north of town through inspiring forested countryside, providing somewhat indirect access to **Mount Baker** via the forks at the Nooksack River and Hwy. 542. Mt. Baker (10,778 ft.) has been belching since 1975, and in winter, jets of steam often snort from its dome. The snow tarries long enough here to extend the ski season to the Fourth of July, when the zany **Slush Cup** challenges skiers of both alpine and water persuasions.

You would only have to sneeze four times in succession to miss the town of **Concrete** and its three neighbors—and perhaps you may want to do so. If you do feel compelled to stop by, you will certainly be welcome; the ratio of Welcome to Concrete signs to inhabitants is comically high. If you drive through at lunchtime, stop at the **Mount Baker Cafe,** 119 E. Main (853-8200; open Mon.-Sat. 6am-4pm). The road from Concrete to Mt. Baker runs past the lakes created by the Upper and Lower Baker Dams. Concrete information and solid help are available from the **Concrete Chamber of Commerce** (853-8400), tucked away in the old depot between Main St. and Hwy. 20 (follow the railroad tracks east upon entering town). (Open Sat.-Sun. 9am-4pm.) The information center can tell you if the **Puget Power Fish Facility's** salmon taxi service is in operation. After all, salmon don't have wheels of their own. Spawning salmon are taken from the water east of town and transported to the top of Lower Baker Dam. If you come to Concrete in late August, you'll be just in time for the **Good Olde Days Celebration,** whose high pitch of excitement is reached during a scarecrow-judging contest.

Neighboring **Rockport** borders **Rockport State Park,** a park blessed by magnificent Douglas firs, a trail that accommodates wheelchairs, and 50 campsites ($7, with full hookup $9.50). These last are fully developed, densely wooded, and among the nicest in the state. The surrounding **Mount Baker National Forest** permits free camping closer to the high peaks. From Rockport, Hwy. 530 stems south to **Darrington,** home to a large population of displaced North Carolinians and therefore host to a rapidly growing **Bluegrass Festival** on the third weekend of July. Darrington's **ranger station** (436-1155) is on Hwy. 530 at the north end of town. (Open Mon.-Fri. 6:45am-4:30pm; in winter also open Sat.-Sun. 8am-5pm.) If Rockport is full, continue 1 mile east to Skagit County's **Howard Miller Steelhead Park** and its 20 $7 sites on the fast-flowing Skagit River.

Stop in **Marblemont** to dine at the **Mountain Song Restaurant,** 5860 Hwy. 20 (873-2461). The Mountain Song serves hearty and healthy meals—try the trout dinner ($8.50) or the BLT ($4.25, emphasis on L and T). Open daily 8am-9pm.

Pitch your tent at the free sites in the **Cascade Islands Campground,** on the south side of the Cascade River. Bring heavy-duty repellant to ward off the swarms of mosquitoes. Ask for directions in town or you'll end up wandering around for hours with hordes of starving insects on your heels.

From Marblemount, drive up Cascade Rd. for a short hike over **Cascade Pass,** and catch the Park Service's **shuttle** from Cottonwood or High Bridge to Stehekin on the eastern slope. (Shuttle runs 3 times daily from mid-June to mid-Sept. 2 hrs., one way $4.) Always check at the **Marblemount Ranger Station** (873-4590), 1 mile north of Marblemount on a well-marked road from the west end of town, to see if the shuttle is running. (Open daily 8am-4:30pm.) See Lake Chelan for information on Stehekin and the southern section of the national park.

Skagit Dams to Washington Pass

Newhalem is the first town in the **Ross Lake National Recreation Area,** a buffer zone between Hwy. 20 and North Cascades National Park where videotapes of *Brazil* play endlessly and the music of Sir Arnold Bax resounds through the trees. A small grocery store and hiking trails to the dams and lakes nearby are the highlights of Newhalem, most of which is owned by Seattle City Light Power Company. Information is available at the **visitors center,** on Hwy. 20. (Open late June-early Sept. Thurs.-Mon. 8am-4pm. At other times, stop by the general store; open daily 8am-8pm.)

The artificial expanse of **Ross Lake** (plugged up by Ross Dam on the west) extends back into the mountains as far as the Canadian border and is ringed by 15 campgrounds—some accessible only by boat, others by trail. The trail along Big Beaver Creek, a few miles north of Hwy. 20, leads from Ross Lake into the Picket Range and eventually to Mt. Baker and the **Northern Unit** of North Cascades National Park. The **Sourdough Mountain** and **Desolation Peak** lookout towers near Ross Lake offer eagle's-eye views of the range.

The National Park's **Goodell Creek Campground,** just south of Newhalem, has 22 sites suitable for tents and trailers and a launch site for whitewater rafting on the Skagit River. (Drinking water and pit toilets. Sites $3. Open year-round.) **Colonial Creek Campground,** 10 miles to the east, is a fully developed, vehicle-accessible campground with flush toilets, a dump station, and campfire programs every evening. (Open mid-May to Nov.; 164 sites, $5.) **Newhalem Creek Campground,** another National Park facility, keeps 50 developed sites ($5).

Diablo Lake lies directly to the west of Ross Lake. The foot of Ross Dam acts as its eastern shore. The town of **Diablo Lake,** on the lake's northeast shore, is the main trailhead for hikes into the southern unit of North Cascades National Park. The Thunder Creek Trail traverses Park Creek Pass to Stehekin River Rd., in Lake Chelan National Recreation Area. Diablo Lake supports a boathouse and a lodge that sells groceries and gas.

The **Pacific Crest Trail** crosses **Rainy Pass,** 30 miles farther on the North Cascades Hwy., on one of the most scenic and challenging legs of its 2500-mile Canada-to-Mexico span. The trail leads up to **Pasayten Wilderness** in the north and down to **Glacier Peak** (10,541 ft.), which commands the central portion of the range. (Glacier Peak can also be approached from the secondary roads extending northward from the Lake Wenatchee area near Coles Corner on U.S. 2, or from Hwy. 530 to Darrington.) An overlook at Washington Pass rewards a very short hike with a flabbergasting view of the red rocks of upper Early Winters Creek's Copper Basin. The vista is perhaps the single most dramatic in the state, if not the entire Pacific Northwest. Look for rock climbers on Liberty Bell Mountain across the pass to the south. (For information on the eastern slopes of the North Cascades, see Okanogan County.)

The town of **Winthrop** was named in 1891 after John Winthrop, first governor of Massachusetts. Despite the Puritan moniker, the town now strikes up a Wild West theme. The one row of restaurants, stores, and hotels along the main street—all made of weather-beaten wood with corrugated tin roofs—features creaky wooden sidewalks and painted signs.

The great billows of hickory-scented smoke draw customers to the **Riverside Rib Co. Bar B-Q,** 207 Riverside (996-2001), which serves fantastic ribs in a convertible prairie schooner (i.e., covered wagon); it also presents a filling vegetarian dinner for $6.25. (Open daily 11am-9pm.) Across the street is the **Winthrop Information Station** (996-2125), on the corner of Hwy. 20 and Riverside. (Open Memorial Day-Labor Day 9am-5pm.)

While in Winthrop, mark time at the **Shafer Museum,** 285 Castle Ave. (996-2712), up the hill overlooking the town, 1 block west of Riverside Ave. The museum deploys all sorts of pioneer paraphernalia in a log cabin built in 1897. (Open daily 10am-5pm. Free.) You can rent horses at the **Rocking Horse Ranch** (996-2768), 9 miles north of Winthrop on the North Cascade Hwy. ($10 per hr.) Mountain bikes are available at the **Virginian Hotel,** just east of town on Hwy. 20 ($4.50 1st hour, $3 per additional hour, $20 full day). The **Winthrop Ranger Station,** P.O. Box 158 (996-2266), up a marked dirt road at the west end of town, dispenses information on camping in the National Forest. (Open Mon.-Fri. 7:45am-5pm, Sat. 8:30am-5pm.) North of Winthrop, the **Early Winters Visitor Center** (996-2534), outside Mazama, is a-flutter with information about the Pasayten Wilderness, an area whose relatively gentle terrain and mild climate endear it to hikers and equestrians. (Open in summer Sun.-Thurs. 9am-5pm, Fri.-Sat. 9am-6pm; in winter weekends only.)

Fourteen miles west of Winthrop on Hwy. 2, **Early Winters** has 15 campsites ($5). **Klipchuk,** 1 mile farther west, tends 39 better developed sites ($5). Cool off at **Pearrygin Lake State Park** beach. From Riverside west of town, take Pearrygin Lake Rd. for 4 miles. Sites ($6) by the lake have flush toilets and pay showers. Arrive early, since the campground fills up in the early afternoon.

Flee Winthrop's prohibitively expensive hotel world and sleep in **Twisp,** the town that should have been a breakfast cereal. Nine miles south of Winthrop on Hwy. 20, this peaceful town offers low prices and far fewer tourists. Stay at **The Sportsman Motel,** 1010 E. Hwy. 20 (997-2911), whose barracks-like exterior masks tastefully decorated rooms and kitchens. (Singles $26. Doubles $30. Oct. 31-June 15 singles $18, doubles $23.) The **Blue Spruce Motel** (997-8852) offers more spartan accommodations just a ½ block away. (Singles $21. Doubles $32.) The **Twisp Ranger Station,** 502 Glover St. (997-2131), employs an extremely helpful staff ready to strafe you with trail and campground guides. (Open Mon.-Fri. 7:45am-4:30pm, Sat. 10am-2pm.) The **Methow Valley Tourist Information Office,** in the community center-*cum*-karate school at the corner of Hwy. 20 and 3rd, dispenses area brochures. (Open Mon.-Fri. 8am-noon and 1-5pm.)

The **Methow Valley Farmer's Market** sells produce from 9am to noon on Saturdays (April-Oct.) in front of the community center. Join local workers and their families at **Rosey's Branding Iron,** 123 Glover St. (997-3576), in the center of town. The Iron offers special menus for dieters, senior citizens, and children, along with wonderfully droll service. All-you-can-eat soup and salad $6. (Open daily 5am-9pm.)

Five miles east of Twisp, the Forest Service operates an advanced training station for **Smoke Jumpers,** firefighters who parachute into the middle of blazing forest fires. Occasionally the service gives tours and runs training sessions that the public can watch. Call the station at 997-2031 for details.

Leavenworth

"Willkommen zu Leavenworth" proclaims the polite wooden sign at the entrance to this curious resort. Once a dying mill town, Leavenworth "went Bavarian" in the mid-60s at the suggestion of solicitous German emigrés. Despite the town's only meager resemblance to Oberammergau (the sibling city in the old country, location of the first *Let's Go* listing ever), merchants have been raking in the proceeds from beer steins and dinners served by a phalanx of waiters dressed in *lederhosen* or *dirndl*.

The town's establishments frequently sport names that are freakish fusions of German and English. Have your hair cut at Das Klip und Kurl, and shop at a crenelated Safeway market. The German gimmick lures skiers during the peak season from November to March; in the slow summer months, this *kleines Dorf* survives on profits from taste-tests between local Mt. Rainier beer and German brew. The locals take their Bavarianization seriously. Never mind that no one speaks German; this town is postmodern.

Practical Information and Orientation

Visitor Information: Chamber of Commerce, 703 U.S. 2 (548-5807), in the Innsbrucker Bldg. Very helpful and knowledgeable staff, many of whom see nothing amusing in their town's gimmick. Open Mon.-Sat. 9am-noon and 1-5pm, Sun. 11am-4pm; Labor Day-Feb. 15 and April 15-Memorial Day Mon.-Sat. 9am-5pm; Feb. 16-April 14 Mon.-Fri. 9am-5pm.

Ranger Station: 600 Sherbourne (782-1413), just off U.S. 2. Pick up a well-organized guide to trails in Wenatchee National Forest and a list of the 8 developed campgrounds within 20 miles of Leavenworth. Families should consult the 1-page "list of relatively easy, short hikes." The Enchantment Lakes trail is the most popular, but be sure to apply for a permit before tackling this treacherous route. Open daily 7:45am-4:30pm; in winter Mon.-Fri. 7:45am-4:30pm.

Greyhound: on U.S. 2 (548-7414), at the Kountry Kitchen Drive-In. Three buses per day to Spokane ($25.15) and Seattle ($18.80). Open daily 10am-9pm.

Bike Rental: Icicle Bicycle Rentals (548-7864), on U.S. 2 west of town. Tandems and mountain bikes at reasonable rates.

Laundromat: Die Wäscherei, intersection of Front St. and U.S. 2, at the east end of town. Open daily 7am-10pm.

Hospital: Cascade Medical Center, 817 Commercial Ave. (548-5815). Formerly named "General Hospital."

Emergency: 911.

Post Office: 960 U.S. 2 (548-7212). Open Mon.-Fri. 9:30am-5pm, Sat. 9:30-10:30am. General Delivery ZIP Code: 98826.

Area Code: 509.

The route from Ellensburg to Wenatchee leads across Swauk Pass on U.S. 97. At the junction with U.S. 2, take a 5-mile detour to Leavenworth. U.S. 2 is the city's main artery, and pseudo-Germanic activity is centered on Front Street, 1 block from and parallel to the highway.

Accommodations and Camping

If you can't get a room at the Hotel Edelweiss or the Bavarian Inn, consider leaving town; most hotels start at $40 for a single. Call ahead for reservations on weekends.

Camping is plentiful in Wenatchee National Forest. **Icicle Creek Road,** the last left in town on U.S. 2 heading toward to Seattle, climbs the mountainside, following the creek. Ten miles from town, a series of Forest Service campgrounds squeeze between the creek and the road. The first five all have drinking water and cost $5 per site, while the last two cost only $4. You will find more isolated spots by pulling off the road and hauling your gear down the banks of the Icicle. Even this area is popular, however; if you seek solitude, avoid weekends after Memorial Day. In any case, come early, or you may not find a spot.

Hotel Edelweiss, 843 Front St. (548-7015), downtown. Bless my hotel forever. Plain but clean rooms; bar and cocktail lounge downstairs. Room 14 has no TV, bath, or windows, but it's cheap ($15). Room 10, graced with a TV and a window, but no bath or sink, costs $16. Other singles with bath and TV from $24.

Bavarian Inn, 100 U.S. 2 (548-4760). All rooms in this immaculate, 5-room inn have TV, bath, A/C, and an elegant glass table. Four rooms have 2 large beds; one has 3. Rooms start at $35. Try bargaining with the outgoing manager, especially on weekdays. Reservations recommended.

Chalet Park, Duncan Rd. (548-4578), off U.S. 2, next to Duncan's Orchards fruit market. This small campground is close to the highway but otherwise quiet. Sites $9.15 for 1 or 2 people, full hookups $10.50. Baths and showers included. Open April 15-Oct. 15.

KOA Kampground, 11401 Riverbend Dr. (548-7709), ¼ mile east of town on U.S. 2. A vacationland in itself, with laundry, basketball, volleyball, playground, swimming pool, pool table, video games, and a well-stocked convenience store. Quiet hours 11pm-8am. Two people $14.45, each additional adult $4. Electrical hookup $3.50, sewer $2. Kamping Kabin (a wooden shack) $24. Klean bath, showers inkluded. Open March-Dec.

Food

Predictably, Leavenworth's food mimics German cuisine; unpredictably, it often succeeds. Those who wish to avoid burgers and hot dogs and swallow some *schnitzel,* however, should prepare to pay $8-12 for a full dinner. But don't fret—if you get bored of bratwurst and the entire German leitmotif, you can always opt for pizza, Mexican, or even Thai.

Winzig's Burger Haus, 701 U.S. 2 (548-5397). The younger set eats here, cramming down $1.89 burgers with a *wunderschön* spicy house sauce and 45¢ soft ice cream cones. Open Sun.-Thurs. 11am-7pm, Fri.-Sat. 11am-8pm.

Oberland Bakery and Cafe, 703 Front St. (548-7216). The pop music and modern decor are a refreshing change. $3.75 buys the rights to a generous sub. All-you-can-eat brunch on Sun. 10am-2pm ($7). Open in summer daily 9am-5:30pm.

Hansel und Gretel Delicatessen, 819 Front St. (548-7721). Tasty bratwurst and "knackwurst" ($2.75). The sandwiches are the wurst. Mingle with the Americans who stop by on their lunch break. Open daily 7am-9pm.

Wolfe's, 220 8th St. (548-7580). American fast-food synthesized with German efficiency. Try the beer-battered onion rings for $1, hot dog "a la American" (why not *auf Amerika?*) for $1.50, or super-deluxe cheeseburger for $2.70. Sit outside or carry your grub and grog to the gazebo downtown. Open Mon.-Fri. 11am-5pm, Sat.-Sun. 11am-6pm.

Sala Thai, 894 U.S. 2 (548-5935). Probably the least Bavarian food in town. Try #26 (tofu in spicy peanut sauce on a bed of spinach, $7). Other entrees $6-7. Open Tues.-Sun. 10am-2pm and 5-9pm.

Mini-Market, 285 U.S. 2 (548-5027). An otherwise run-of-the-mill convenience store specializes in 10¢ coffee and 50¢ hot cider or hot egg nog. Open daily 6am-midnight.

Sights and Entertainment

Whitewater **raft trips** on the Wenatchee River are expensive thrills—the cheapest one-day trips are $39. Individuals can sign up at short notice; groups must call in advance. (Try **Wenatchee Whitewater,** P.O. Box 12, Cashmere 98815; 800-423-8639 ext. 162 or 782-2254.) Downhill skiing during the winter can be found 58 miles away at **Stevens Pass** (206-973-2441).

For slower joy rides, try the **Eagle Creek Ranch** (north on Hwy. 209, right on Eagle Creek Rd. for 5½ miles; 548-7798) or the **Red Tail Canyon Farm** (11780 Freund Canyon Rd., 2½ miles up Hwy. 209; 548-4512). The former takes kids under 10 on sleigh rides ($4) and hay rides ($10). Parents come along for $10 each. The latter also offers hay rides ($6; ages under 12 $4).

On your way up Icicle Rd., stop at the **Leavenworth National Fish Hatchery** (548-7641) to see exhibits on local river life. In the summer, adult salmon (sometimes reaching 30 lbs.) fill the holding ponds. (Open daily 7:30am-4pm.)

On your way south to the U.S. 97 junction, stop in **Cashmere** at the **Aplets and Cotlets Factory,** 117 Mission St. (782-2191), for free tours of the plant and samples of the gooey candies. (Open Mon.-Fri. 8am-6pm, Sat.-Sun. 10am-4pm; Nov.-May Mon.-Sat. 8-11:45am and 1-4:45pm.) On U.S. 2 in Cashmere, the **Chelan County Museum** (782-3230) displays artifacts of the Native Americans whose land this used to be.

In Leavenworth, the **Historic Movie and Photo Gallery** at 801 Front St. continuously shows a 30-minute history of the Bavarian village. The **Washington State Leaf**

Festival, a celebration of autumn, runs for nine days beginning in late September. It includes a "Grand Parade," as well as art shows, flea markets, and street dances. "Smooshing," a four-person race run on wooden two-by-fours, is the highlight of the **Great Bavarian Ice Fest,** held on Martin Luther King Day weekend. (Yeah, right.) **Maifest,** held during the second weekend in May, celebrates the spring with appropriate German bombast. Featured events include a *Volksmarch,* street dances, a Maypole dance, and earfuls of polka music.

Wenatchee

In the self-proclaimed "Apple Capital of the World," the enormous fruit weighs down the branches in the orchards so much that the trees must be propped. In the signs of stores and businesses, the letter "O" is often replaced with a big, red Wenatchee apple. Aside from the Apple Blossom Festival in the spring, however, Wenatchee has little to offer—unless you consider countless used car dealerships and 300 days of sunshine per year enough incentive to visit. Although Wenatchee is the largest metropolitan area in northcentral Washington, it serves primarily as a gateway to the wilderness of the Cascades for hikers, fishermen, skiers, campers, and mountain climbers.

Practical Information and Orientation

Visitor Information: Visitor and Convention Center, 2 S. Chelan Ave. (662-4774), at Douglas St. Literally bushels of brochures. Staff members are very proud of their hometown. Open Mon.-Fri. 9am-5pm. Apple aficionados should stop at the **Washington Apple Commission Visitors Center,** 2900 Euclid Ave. (663-9600), on the northern outskirts of Wenatchee, for more juicy details on the state's largest agricultural industry. Open Mon.-Fri. 8am-5pm, Sat. 9am-5pm, Sun. 11am-5pm; Nov.-April Mon.-Fri. 8am-5pm.

Amtrak: 315 N. Mission (663-0781 or 663-1101). One train per day to Seattle ($28) and 1 to Spokane ($31.50).

Greyhound: 301 First St. (662-2183), corner of Chelan. Open Mon.-Fri. 6am-7pm, Sat.-Sun. 6am-noon and 4-7pm.

Taxi: Woody's Cab, 109 S. Kittitas St. (884-0358).

Car Rental: John Clark Motors/U-Save Auto Rental, 908 S. Wenatchee Ave. (663-1512). Rates start at $24 per day with 50 free miles plus 16¢ per additional mile. Must be 21. Open Mon.-Fri. 8:30am-5:30pm, Sat. 9am-noon.

AAA: 221 N. Mission St. (662-8550).

Job Service Center: at Bridge and Mission St. (662-8167). Call to get a job picking peaches, apricots, pears, or apples.

Laundromat: Wash Works, Inc. 907 S. Wenatchee Ave. (662-3582). Open daily 7am-10pm.

Crisis Line: 662-7105. 24 hours.

Senior Citizens Hospitality Center: 215 Orondo St. (662-7036). Open Mon.-Sat. 9:30am-4pm, Sun. 12:30-4pm.

Hospital: Central Washington, 1300 Fuller St. (662-1511). 24 hours.

Police: 662-6173. 24 hours.

Post Office: 301 Yakima St. (662-7663). General Delivery ZIP Code: 98801.

Area Code: 509.

Wenatchee is at the intersection of U.S. 2 and U.S. 97, 138 miles east of Seattle and 164 miles west of Spokane. The downtown area centers around Wenatchee Avenue, Mission Street, and Chelan Avenue, which all run parallel to the Columbia River. Hitchhikers in this area are not held in high regard, but their chosen profession is legal on the state highways.

Accommodations

Motels are strafed along the main streets of Wenatchee. The closest campgrounds lie to the west on U.S. 2 in Stevens Pass and Blewett Pass.

Travel Lodge, 232 N. Wenatchee Ave. (800-255-3050). Immaculate rooms with cable TV, A/C, private bath, and queen-sized beds. Singles $35. Doubles $40.

Burgerbeer's, 821 N. Wenatchee Ave. (662-8208). Trim your beard and press that shirt, lest the wary management turn you away. Color TV. Aquamaniacs should inquire about the room with the waterbed. All rooms $20. No charge for additional people.

EconoLodge, 700 N. Wenatchee Ave. (663-8133). Basic wood-paneled units with small bathrooms, cable TV, and large beds. Streetside pool for the immodest. Singles $23. Doubles $27.

Lyle's Motel, 924 N. Wenatchee Ave. (663-5155). Large, polished rooms with cable TV. Forget the occasionally aggravating street noise in a soak in the hot tub. Singles $23. Doubles $30.

Food

Surprisingly, Wenatchee restaurants have not capitalized on the city's fruity reputation. Instead of innovative apple dishes, restaurants serve the standard fare. Thorough searching, however, may uncover a few gourmet treats and maybe even an apple muffin or pie.

The Greenhouse, 10 N. Chelan (663-7932), across from the visitor center. All sandwiches served on thick slices of homebaked bread ($3.15). Also try the homemade cookies and desserts. Travelers from more exotic places will love the "rajun' cajun" submarine sandwich (beef or turkey, onion, mushroom, and bell peppers grilled with cheese and special "cajun heat" spices, $3.75).

Sodbuster Restaurant and Bakery, 731 N. Wenatchee Ave. (662-1118). A family-style restaurant with mediocre but plentiful servings. Line up at dinnertime for early-bird special suppers that include *everything.* Extraordinary cream pie $1.25. Open Sun.-Thurs. 6am-11pm, Fri.-Sat. 6am-midnight.

The Cellar, 202 N. Wenatchee Ave. (662-1722). Some of the most exotic food in town. Dine in the dark, subdued deli, or take your meal outside to a table in the sun. Quiche, guacamole, and $3.75 vegetarian sandwiches. Open Mon.-Fri. 11am-5:30pm, Sat. 11am-4pm.

Hoss's Little Brick Cafe, 234 S. Wenatchee Ave. (662-9622). Great for local flavor and "hoss"pitality. Down-home dinners such as boneless chicken or fish and chips ($4) include an enormous bowl of soup. For breakfast, try the biscuits with sausage gravy ($2). Open Tues.-Sat. 6am-3pm, Sun. 7am-1pm.

Bob's Classic Brass and Brew, 110 2nd St. (663-3954). Try the $2 budget lunch on weekdays, or a juicy 20-oz. porterhouse steak for $8. Every Wed. from 6-9pm you can buy either 4 tacos, a pitcher of beer, or a margarita for $2. Open Mon.-Sat. 11am-midnight, Sun. 1-10pm. Happy hour 4:30-6:30pm.

The Spaghetti Works, 29 N. Columbia (662-8975). The only choice here is among sauces for your pasta. Ten options from $5-6. Dinners include salad, bread, and spumoni. Open Wed.-Sat. from 4:30pm until around 10pm depending on business, Sun. from 12:30pm.

Sights and Entertainment

Be sure to grab a free copy of the weekly *Kiosk,* the arts and entertainment guide for northcentral Washington. Also pick up "What's Happening in Wenatchee" at the Chamber of Commerce.

Winters in Wenatchee are wonderful, especially for skiers. **Mission Ridge** (663-3200) offers 30 acres of lighted trails in a convenient location, just 20 minutes from downtown by car. Rent skis (both downhill and cross-country) at **Arlberg Sports,** on the mountain or downtown at 25 N. Wenatchee Ave. (663-7401).

The **North Central Washington Museum,** at 125-7 S. Mission (662-5989), features exhibits on the development of fruit packing, a topic as boring as it sounds, along with a film depicting the city's rise from pioneer town to apple kingdom. (Open Mon.-Fri. 10am-4pm, Sat.-Sun. 1-4pm.) The **Victorian Village** is a short walk away, at 611 S. Mission. A poorly disguised attempt to lure tourists, the "village" is simply a strip of about 10 overpriced boutiques in flimsy cottages that don't even look Victorian. (Open Mon.-Sat. 10am-5pm.) The gorgeous **Ohme Gardens** (OH-me), 3327 Ohme Rd. (662-5785), 3 miles north of the city, comprise 9 acres of alpine gardens, rock gardens, and pools. The gardens offer a view of Wenatchee in all its ripe majesty. (Open daily 9am-7pm; Oct. 16-April 14 9am-6pm. Admission $4, children $2.)

The **Apple Blossom Festival** is the undeniable apogee of Wenatchee's diurnal round. A potpourri of exhibits, contests, fairs, and shows are splattered across 11 days starting at the end of April. A more modest undertaking is the **Wenatchee Valley Arts Festival,** held in the third weekend of September, with a juried street fair and a fine arts show. (Call 662-1213 for information.)

Mount Rainier National Park

Pete Seeger, the stalwart folksinger, called it "that great strawberry ice cream cone in the sky." Mt. Rainier rises elegantly over the other Cascade mountains, 2 miles taller than many of the surrounding foothills. Residents of Washington refer to it simply as "The Mountain."

Be prepared for rain. Warm ocean air condenses when it reaches Rainier and falls on the mountain at least 200 days of the year. When the sun does shine, you will understand why Native Americans called Mt. Rainier "Tahoma" (Mountain of God).

Although an expedition to the summit is exhilarating, if you remain at slightly lower elevations you will lessen cost and personal risk without diminishing epiphany—midnight views of the mountain silhouetted against the moon, inner-tube rides down the slick sides in winter, romps in alpine meadows full of unparalleled wildflower displays. Despite the beauty below, 2500 determined climbers ascend to Rainier's peak each year.

Practical Information and Orientation

Visitor Information: Longmire Museum and Hikers' Center. Lodging, food, exhibits, and souvenirs. Open daily 8am-5:30pm; mid-Sept. to mid-June 9am-5pm. **Paradise Visitor Center.** Lodging, food, souvenirs. Open daily 9am-6pm; mid-Sept. to mid-June hours depend on funding. **Sunrise Visitors Center.** Snacks and gift shop. Open same hours as Paradise. **Ohanapecosh Visitors Center.** Information only. Open same hours as Paradise. All centers can be contacted ℅ Superintendent, Mt. Rainier National Park, Ashford 98304, or telephoned through the park's central operator (569-2211).

Park Headquarters: Tahoma Woods, Star Rte., Ashford 98304 (569-2211). Open Mon.-Fri. 8am-4:30pm.

Gray Line Bus Service: 2411 4th Ave., Seattle (343-2000). Excursions from Seattle to Rainier daily May 15-Oct. 15 ($20 single-day round-trip, ages under 13 $10; $3 surcharge to reserve a return on a later bus). Buses leave from the Space Needle in Seattle Center at 9:15am and return around 7pm, leaving you 2 hr. at the mountain.

Recorded Weather Information: 569-2343. Weather forecasts and mountain conditions are also posted once per day at all ranger stations.

Park Emergency: 569-2211 (Mon.-Fri. 8am-4:30pm), 569-2662 (Mon.-Fri. 4:30pm-8am, Sat.-Sun. 24 hours).

Post Office: In the National Park Inn, Longmire. Open Mon.-Sat. 9am-5pm. General Delivery ZIP Code: 98397.

Area Code: 206.

To reach Mt. Rainier from the west, drive south from Seattle on I-5 to Tacoma, then go east on Hwy. 512, south on Hwy. 7, and east on Hwy. 706. This scenic road meanders through the town of Ashford and into the park by the Nisqually entrance. Hwy. 706 is the only access road kept open throughout the year; snow usually closes all other park roads from November through May. The total distance

New York's Favorite Bedtime Story. $15.

No, it's not Sleeping Beauty, but it's close. It's YMCA's Sloane House in the heart of midtown Manhattan. Get a bed in a clean, comfortable, two-bed room for just $15 a night.

No reservations accepted at this price. Just bring in or mention this ad.

And after a good night's sleep, you'll wake up close to all the sights, including Madison Square Garden, Macy's, the Empire State Building, Times Square and Greenwich Village.

Now what could be a better bedtime story than that!

YMCA SLOANE HOUSE

THE AFFORDABLE WAY TO STAY IN NEW YORK CITY.

For regular reservations,
call or telex our Y's Way office:
Tel.: 212-760-5856. Telex: 237581 YVUT.

356 West 34th Steet, New York 10001

CALIFORNIA

**YOU'RE A LONG WAY
FROM HOME,**

**BUT YOUR DAUGHTER'S
STILL WITH YOU.
CALL HOME.**

Wherever you go, you can
stay as close to your daughter
as you'd like. With AT&T, you
can pick up the phone and be
together again.

AT&T

from Tacoma is 65 miles. You can also take I-90 from Seattle east to Bellevue, then Hwy. 405 south to Renton, and Hwy. 169 south through Maple Valley and the town of Black Diamond. At Enumclaw, head east on Hwy. 410 through the Wenatchee National Forest and into Mt. Rainier National Park by the White River entrance. The distance from Seattle is approximately 60 miles.

The city of Yakima is the eastern gateway to the park. Take I-82 from the center of town to U.S. 12 heading west. At the junction of the Naches and Tieton Rivers, go either left on U.S. 12 or continue straight up Hwy. 410. U.S. 12 runs past Rimrock Lake, over White Pass to Hwy. 123, where a right turn leads to the Stevens Canyon entrance to Rainier. Hwy. 410 ascends Chinook Pass and ultimately runs north-south inside Rainier Park. The change in vegetation and terrain on the eastern ascent to the park is remarkable: dry plains around Yakima are followed by canyons lined with ponderosa pine, then stands of Douglas fir take center stage. Hwy. 410 offers more scenic views, but Hwy. 123 is 10 miles closer to Yakima.

Hitchhiking along the mountain roads is exceptionally good. Park Service employees will often give lifts to stranded hikers. Don't hesitate to ask a person in uniform for assistance; personnel here are as helpful and friendly as they come, especially when the peak is visible and spirits are high.

Summer temperatures stay warm during the day, but become chilly at night. You should be prepared for rapid changes in weather. (See Camping in the General Introduction.) The park is staffed with emergency medical technicians and owns a number of emergency vans. Rangers can provide first-aid. The nearest medical facilities are in Morton (40 miles from Longmire) and Enumclaw (50 miles from Sunrise).

Admission to the park is $5 per car or $2 per hiker. Gates are open 24 hours, with free admission in the evenings. The park has four **visitors centers** (see Practical Information). If you're interested in working in the national park, contact **Mt. Rainier Guest Services, Inc.,** which runs the concessions at the visitors centers and has openings each summer. Write or call the Personnel Department, Mt. Rainier Guest Services, P.O. Box 108, Ashford 98304 (206-569-2275). Pay is minimum wage minus $1.35 per hour for room and board. Guest Services headquarters are 3 miles west of the Nisqually entrance toward Ashford, off Hwy. 7 on Kernahan Rd.

The **Gifford Pinchot National Forest** is headquartered at 500 W. 12th St., Vancouver 98660 (696-7500). The section of the Mt. Baker-Snoqualmie National Forest that adjoins Mt. Rainier is administered by the **Wenatchee National Forest,** P.O. Box 811, Wenatchee 98801 (509-662-4335). Closer ranger stations are at 16680 Hwy. 410, Naches 98937 (509-658-2435 or 658-2436) and at Star Rte., P.O. Box 189, Naches 98937 (509-672-4101 or 672-4111).

Accommodations, Camping, and Food

The towns of **Packwood** and **Ashford** have a few motels near the park. For general lodging information and reservations within the park, call 569-2275.

Paradise Inn, Paradise (569-2291). This rustic inn, built in 1917 from Alaskan cedar, offers heavenly views of the mountain. Wake up early to hike the Skyline Trail, which starts in the heavenly parking lot. Small singles and doubles with shared bath $43 plus 9% tax, each additional person $8. Open late May-early Oct. Reservations required.

National Park Inn, Longmire (569-2706). Less dramatic view than in Paradise, but convenient for cross-country skiing. Singles and doubles with shared bath $38, each additional person $8. Reservations required for weekends and recommended for weekdays. The inn should reopen after renovations in May 1990.

Camping at the auto campsites between mid-June and late Sept. requires a do-it-yourself permit ($6), available at the campsites. **Alpine** and **cross-country camping** requires free permits year-round and is subject to certain restrictions. Be sure to pick up a copy of the *Backcountry Trip Planner* at any ranger station or hikers' center before you set off. Alpine and cross-country permits are strictly controlled to prevent environmental damage, but auto camping permits are easy to come by.

The best developed auto campgrounds are at **Sunshine Point** near the Nisqually entrance, at **Cougar Rock** near Longmire, at **Ohanapecosh**, at **White River** in the northeast corner, and at **Carbon River.** Open on a first-come, first-camped basis, they fill up only on the busiest summer weekends. Sunshine Point is the only auto campground open throughout the year. With a permit, cross-country hikers can use any of the free, well-established **trailside camps** that are scattered throughout the park's backcountry. Most camps have toilet facilities and a nearby water source; some have shelters. Most of these sites are in the low forests, although some are found high up the mountain on the glaciers and snow fields. More adventurous cross-country hikers can test their survival skills in the vast cross-country zones in any of the low forests, and in the sub-alpine zone. In both areas, fires are prohibited and there are limits on the number of members in a party. Talk to a ranger for details. Mountain- and glacier-climbers must always register in person at ranger stations in order to be granted permits.

The **national forests** outside Rainier Park provide both developed sites (free to $5) and thousands of acres of campable countryside (free). Avoid eroded lakesides and riverbanks. Minimum-impact camping fire permits, which allow hikers to use small fires that don't sterilize the soil, are available at national forest ranger stations (see Practical Information). Don't count on receiving one, however, since the small number of backcountry sites limits the supply of permits.

There is no middle ground for food prices. Edible items within the park are either very expensive (at the Longmire, Paradise, and Sunrise concession stands) or free (no fishing permits are required for any of the park's lakes or streams, but contact a ranger about seasons and catch limits). The towns in the immediate vicinity of Rainier are equally overpriced; stock up on supplies in Seattle, Tacoma, or Yakima before entering the park.

Sights and Activities

Much of the activity in Rainier occurs at the park's four visitors centers (see Practical Information). Each has displays, a wealth of literature on everything from hiking to natural history, postings on trail and road conditions, and a ranger to fill in any gaps. Naturalist-guided trips and talks, campfire programs, and slide presentations are given at the visitors centers and vehicle campgrounds throughout the park. Check at a visitors center or pick up a copy of the free annual newsletter, *Tahoma,* for details.

A car tour provides a good introduction to the park. All major roads offer scenic views of the mountain and have numerous roadside sites for camera-clicking and general gawking. The roads to Paradise and Sunrise are especially picturesque. **Stevens Canyon Road** connects the southeast corner of the national park with Paradise, Longmire, and the Nisqually entrance, unfolding truly spectacular vistas of Rainier and the rugged Tatoosh Range. Mt. Adams and Mt. St. Helens, not visible from the road, can be seen clearly from the mountain trails.

Several less developed roads provide access to more isolated regions, often meeting trailheads that crisscross the park or lead to the summit. Cross-country hiking and camping outside designated campsites is permissible through most regions of the park, but a permit is always required for overnight backpacking trips. The **Hikers Center** at Longmire has information on day and backcountry hikes through the park and dispenses camping permits. (Open June 15-Sept. 30 daily 7am-7pm.)

A segment of the **Pacific Crest Trail (PCT),** running between the Columbia River and the Canadian border, crosses through the southeast corner of the park. Geared for both hikers and horse riders, the PCT is maintained by the U.S. Forest Service. Primitive campsites and shelters line the trail; no permit is required for camping, although you should contact the nearest ranger station for information on site and trail conditions. The trail, sometimes overlooking the snow-covered peaks of the Cascades, snakes through delightful wildlife areas.

A trip to the summit of Mt. Rainier requires a fair amount of special preparation and expense. The ascent involves a vertical rise of 9000 feet, usually taking two days, with an overnight stay at Camp Muir on the south side (10,000 ft.) or Camp Schurman on the north side (9500 ft.). Shelters are provided, but climbers should be prepared to camp if these are full.

Experienced climbers may form their own expeditions if they complete a fairly detailed application; consult a climbing ranger at Paradise, Carbon River, or White River stations. Solo climbing requires the consent of the superintendent. Novices can sign up for a **summit climb. Rainier Mountaineering, Inc. (RMI)** offers a one-day basic climbing course followed by a two-day guided climb; the package costs $225 and requires good physical fitness. Headquartered in their Guide House in Paradise (569-2227), RMI is also the only organization in the park that rents equipment: ice axes, crampons, boots, packs, and helmets, at about $6.50 per day per item. You must bring your own sleeping bag, headlamp, and rain jacket and pants, and carry four meals in addition to hiking gear. For more information, contact park headquarters or RMI at (Oct.-May) 535 Dock St, #209, Tacoma 98402 (206-627-6242 or 206-569-2227); (June-Sept.) RMI, Paradise 98398 (206-569-2227).

Less ambitious, ranger-led **interpretive hikes** interpret everything from local wildflowers to area history. Each visitors center (see Practical Information) conducts its own hikes and each has a different schedule. The hikes, lasting anywhere from 20 minutes to all day, are ideal outings for families with young children. These free hikes complement evening campfire programs, also conducted by each visitors center.

Longmire

Longmire's **museum** dwells modestly on Rainier's past. The rooms are filled with exhibits on local natural history and the history of human encounters with the mountain. One interesting display depressingly reveals the secret of the mountain's name: "Rainier" has nothing to do with either a weather report or Monaco's monarch, but rather derives from a forgotten Tory politician who never even saw the peak. See Practical Information for hours.

Longmire-area walks and programs run by the visitors center typically include night meadow walks and hikes into the surrounding dense forest. The **Hikers Center** is an excellent source of information and guidance for all backcountry trips except summit attempts. Free information sheets are available for specific day and overnight hikes throughout the park. Look closely at the relief model of the mountain before plunging into the woods. Remember that a permit is required for backcountry camping.

Longmire remains open during the winter, and serves as a base for snowshoeing, cross-country skiing, and other alpine activities. **Guest Services, Inc.,** runs a **cross-country ski center;** a typical package costs $8. The trails are difficult, but snowshoeing can be enjoyed eight months out of the year. Some diehards even enjoy winter hiking and climbing out of Longmire.

Paradise

Whatever Joni Mitchell might say, Paradise is not a parking lot but rather a town in southern Washington. The area was introduced to the world by the Longmire family, who thought the vast meadows of wildflowers and breathtaking scenery were the Northwest's answer to the Elysian Fields. Those who visit Paradise on a clear, sunny day will probably agree. It is situated well above the timberline, and even in mid-June the sparkling snowfields blind visitors staring down at the forest canyons thousands of feet below. The road from the Nisqually entrance to Paradise is open year-round, but the road east through Stevens Canyon is open only from mid-June through October, weather permitting. The **Paradise Visitors Center** offers radiant choirs, audiovisual programs, and an observation deck. From January to mid-April, park naturalists lead **snowshoe hikes** to explore winter ecology around Paradise. (Sat.-Sun. at 10:30am, 12:30pm, and 2:30pm. Snowshoe rental $1.) You'll need snowshoes: the world record for snowfall in one season (93 ft.!) was set here in the winter of 1971-72.

Paradise serves as the starting point for a number of trails heading through the meadows to the nearby Nisqually Glacier, or up the mountain to the summit. Many trails allow up-close views of Mt. Rainier's glaciers. The 4½-mile **Skyline Trail** is the longest of the loop trails out of Paradise (3-hr. walk). The marked trail starts at the Paradise Inn, climbing above the treeline. Skyline is probably the closest a casual hiker will come to climbing the mountain. The first leg of the trail is often hiked by climbing parties headed for Camp Muir (the base camp for most ascents to the summit). The trail turns off before reaching Camp Muir, rising to its highest elevation at **Panorama Point.** Although only halfway up the mountain, the point has views of the glaciers, with the summit appearing deceptively close. Turn around to witness rows and rows of blue-gray mountaintops, with Mt. St. Helens and Mt. Adams presiding over the horizon. Heading back down the trail, you will cross a few snow fields and do some boulder-hopping. Boots are highly recommended, although the hike can be accomplished in sneakers. Since route conditions vary a great deal, contact a ranger station at Paradise, White River, Sunrise, or Longmire for information on crevice and rockfall conditions.

The mildly strenuous, half-day hike up to **Pinnacle Peak,** which begins across the road from Reflection Lakes (just east of Paradise), presents a clear view of Rainier.

Ohanapecosh and Carbon River

The **Ohanapecosh Visitor Center** and campground are located in a lush forest along a river valley in the park's southeast corner. The **Grove of the Patriarchs** here is one of the oldest stands of original trees in Washington. These 500- to 1000-year-old Douglas firs, cedars, and hemlocks create a serene spot for easy hiking. The visitors center has displays on the forest and naturalist programs that include walks to the grove, Silver Falls, and Ohanapecosh Hot Springs.

Carbon River Valley, in the northwest corner of the park, is one of the only true rain forests in the continental U.S. The Carbon River Rd. entrance is accessible from Hwy. 165. Several good hiking trails beginning on Carbon River Rd. offer the solitude missing from the Longmire and Paradise areas in summer.

Sunrise

The winding road to Sunrise alternates vistas of the Pacific Ocean, Mt. Baker, and the heavily glaciated eastern side of Mt. Rainier. Nine out of ten experts agree that the mountain views from Sunrise are among the best in the park.

Wonderland Trail passes through Sunrise on its way around the mountain. A popular 95-mile trek circumscribing Rainier, the trail traverses ridges and valleys; the lakes and streams near the path are populated by trout. The entire circuit takes 10-14 days, involving several brutal ascents and descents. Be careful of early snow storms in September, snow-blocked passes in June, and muddy trails in July. Rangers can provide information on weather and trail conditions; they also can store food caches for you at ranger stations along the trail.

The hike from Fryingpan Creek Bridge (3 miles from the White River entrance) to Summerland is popular for its views of Mt. Rainier and the Little Tahoma Crag; behold elk and mountain goats grazing on the surrounding slopes. The circuit runs 4.2 miles from the road along Fryingpan Creek to the Sunrise campground, ranger station, and meadows.

Cowlitz Valley

The Cowlitz River winds through miles of unspoiled territory on its journey west and south to the Columbia River. Fed by streams tumbling out of the Cascade Crest, the river forms part of the waterbed for both the **Mount Adams** and **Goat Rocks Wilderness Areas** (to the west and northwest of Mt. St. Helens, respectively). Both areas are superlative hiking country (accessible only on foot or horseback) and count the **Pacific Crest Trail** among their excellent trail networks. The rugged Goat

Rocks area is famed for its herd of mountain goats, while Mt. Adams seduces hundreds of climbers each year to its snowcapped summit (12,307 ft.). Contact the U.S. Forest Service for trail guides and other information on these wilderness areas.

The Cowlitz passes closest to Mt. St. Helens near the town of **Morton.** This logging town is served by U.S. 12 from the east and west (I-15 exit 68), Hwy. 508 from the west (I-5 exit 71), and Hwy. 7 from the north. Hitching on U.S. 12 is generally good. Try asking a logging truck for a ride when it stops to get weighed.

Morton hosts an annual **Logger's Jubilee** in the second weekend of August. Admission ($4) entitles you to join the crowds cheering sawyers, climbers, and choppers on their way to glory; parades, a carnival, and a barbecue contribute to the festive atmosphere.

Morton and other towns near Mt. St. Helens have capitalized on the public interest in the somewhat *passé* 1980 eruption. All the stores sell containers of ash and other St. Helens *dreck.* The Morton airfield is one of several that offer $40 flights to view Mt. St. Helens. Good places to gawk at the mountain along the Cowlitz include the Hopkins Hill/Short Road viewpoint off U.S. 12, 2 miles west of Morton. Look for the turn-off on the northern side of the road. Revive yourself in Morton at the **Cody Cafe**, on Main St. (496-5787). This classic hometown diner serves a whopping stack of pancakes for $2. Lunches run $3-5. (Open daily 6am-8pm.) The **Morton Chamber of Commerce**, P.O. Box 10, can be reached at 496-3260. The **post office** is on Hwy. 7 (General Delivery ZIP Code: 98356).

The Cowlitz River, once wild and treacherous, has been tamed considerably by the Tacoma City Light hydroelectric project. The Mayfield and Mossyrock Dams back water up into the river gorge to create two lakes, Mayfield and Riffe, both major recreation areas. **Ike Kinswa State Park** and **Mayfield Lake County Park,** on Mayfield Lake off U.S. 12, each offer camping and excellent rainbow- and silver-trout fishing year-round. Public boat launches provide access to Mayfield, the lower of the two lakes.

Riffe Lake, much larger than Mayfield, was named in memory of Riffe, a town flooded by the creation of the enormous Mossyrock Dam. Scuba divers come here to explore the remains of this and another town, Kosmos, which was also washed out so the city of Tacoma could read at night. Hang gliders leap off the ridge behind the lake near the town of **Glenoma,** riding near-ideal wind currents for phenomenal distances. Mossyrock Park campers on the south shore can drop by the display at Hydro Vista next to the dam. Tacoma City Light offers free guided tours of the whole Cowlitz River Development complex by reservation (383-2471 in Tacoma).

One of the more interesting features of the complex is the **Cowlitz Salmon Hatchery,** south of the town of Salkum just off U.S. 12. The free self-guided tours of the facility include views of fish ladders, the spawning center, and the tanks where the salmon are kept. This facility releases 17.5 million chinooks (young salmon) each year. Displays show the tragic life cycle of the salmon—born in the rivers, fattened in the ocean, and finally propelled upstream to spawn and die. Such hatcheries have been installed all over the Northwest, both to encourage salmon fishing and to compensate for changes in the environment wrought by hydroelectric projects. A **trout hatchery,** on U.S. 12 just south of Ethel, has a similar set-up. For more information, contact the Department of Public Utilities Light Division, P.O. Box 11007, Tacoma 98411.

Below the dams, the Cowlitz River courses through farmland, flowers, and blueberries. Hosts of local farms dot the hillside along the road, many offering U-pick berry bargains during the summer harvest season (late June-Aug.).

Mount St. Helens

On May 18, 1980, sixty-nine years to the day after the death of Gustav Mahler, Mt. St. Helens exploded into space. In the aftermath of the largest natural disaster in recorded American history, a hole 2 miles long and a mile wide opened in the formerly perfect cone. Ash from the crater blackened the sky for hundreds of miles and blanketed the streets of towns as far as Yakima, 80 miles away. Debris spewed from the volcano-flooded Spirit Lake, choked rivers with mud, and descended to the towns via river and glacier. Entire forests were leveled by the blast, leaving a stubble of trunks on the hills and millions of trees pointing like arrows away from the crater. Because the blast was lateral, not vertical, it was more destructive; no energy was dissipated fighting gravity.

Once the jewel of the Cascades, today the Mt. St. Helens National Monument (now administered by the National Forest Service) looks like a disaster area. The vast expanses of downed timber look like nothing more than an immense graveyard, a monument to a blast many times stronger than any man-made detonation to date. The spectacle of disaster is dotted with signs of returning life: saplings push their way up past their fallen brethren, insects flourish near newly formed waterfalls, a beaver has been spotted in Spirit Lake. Nature's power of destruction is matched only by her power of regeneration.

The surrounding area is now the **Gifford Pinchot National Forest.** Much of the monument area, which is shaded on Forest Service maps, is off-limits to the public because of the unpredictability of the volcanic crater and the delicate geological experiments conducted by scientists. Roads inside the restricted zones are undergoing construction, so expect delays or minor mixups.

Practical Information and Orientation

Visitor Information: Mount St. Helens National Volcanic Monument Visitor Center (247-5473), on Hwy. 504, west of Toutle. Take exit 49 off I-5, and follow the signs. The best place to start a trip to the mountain—information on camping and access to the mountain, as well as displays on the eruption and the mountain's regeneration. Interpretive naturalist activities mid-June to Aug. The free 20-min. film *The Eruption of Mt. St. Helens* has fine footage of monstrous steam clouds, muddy ash, and debris choking the Toutle River. Interpretive programs explain the eruption and the state of the mountain. Open daily 9am-7pm. Other visitors centers—Castle Rock, Yale, Iron Creek, and Pine Creek—provide information on the social, economic, and botanic aspects of the eruption.

Gifford Pinchot National Forest Headquarters: 500 W. 12th St., Vancouver, WA (696-7500). Camping and hiking information within the forest. Additional **ranger stations** are located at Randle (497-7565), north of the mountain on U.S. 12, east of the visitors center; Packwood (494-5515), farther east on U.S. 12; Wind River (427-5645), south of the mountain on Forest Service Rd. 30, north of the town of Carson in the Columbia River Gorge; and Mt. Adams (395-2501), at Trout Lake, southeast of the mountain on Hwy. 141, above White Salmon in the Columbia River Gorge.

Buses: Gray Line, 400 NW Broadway, Portland, OR (503-226-6755). Buses from Portland to Mt. St. Helens (round-trip $23, ages under 13 $12).

Current Volcanic Activity: 696-7848. 24-hour recorded information.

Emergency: On the south and east sides of the monument, report emergencies directly to the Pine Creek Information Center or the Iron Creek Information Center, both on Forest Service Rd. 25. 24 hours. On the west side, dial 911.

Area Code: 206.

If you can spend only a short time in the area, visit the **Mt. St. Helens National Volcanic Monument Visitor Center,** on Hwy. 504 near Toutle (take exit 49 off I-5). But if you want a closer view of the volcano, plan to spend the whole day in the monument and visit either the southerly Pine Creek Information Center or the northerly Woods Creek Information Center. While not as large as the center near Toutle, the latter two are each within a mile of excellent viewpoints. From the north, get onto U.S. 12 and turn south on Forest Service Rd. 25 at the town of Randle toward the Woods Creek center. From the south, take Hwy. 503, which turns into Forest Service Rd. 90 in Yale; follow 90 to the Pine Creek center. Those wishing to climb the mountain (see Sights) must enter the monument via Hwy. 503, because all climbers must check in at Yale. Extensive rebuilding efforts have made such a mess of things that only the rangers in each visitors center know exactly what's going on.

Camping

Campsites are scattered throughout the national forest; some are free, some exact a $4-6 fee. For those who want an early start touring the mountain, there are two primitive campgrounds relatively near the scene of the explosion. The closest is the **Iron Creek Campground,** on Forest Service Rd. 25, near the junction with Rd. 76. The other is **Swift Campground,** on Forest Service Rd. 90, just west of the Pine Creek Information Station. Both charge $5 per site and are scenic and uncrowded.

Seaquest State Park (274-8633), on Hwy. 504, east of the town of Castle Rock at exit 49 off I-5. 70 sites, some of which are primitive and reserved for the hiker/biker set. The campground is on Silver Lake, excellent for bass fishing. Sites $7.

Merril Lake, 4 miles north on Rd. 81 from the town of Cougar (Woodland exit 21 off I-5). No fees and few tourists.

Sights

From Road 25, turn east on Road 26, whose one lane (with turn-offs) follows the side of a ridge. This devastated valley did not even receive the brunt of the blow; the explosion vented its principal energy directly north. Viewpoints along the road are listed on handouts at the visitors center.

Road 26 ends at one viewpoint, but you can continue toward the crater over 6 miles of the newly paved, two-lane Road 99. Curves, clouds of ash, and precipices make this stretch a 20- to 30-minute excursion without stops. **Windy Ridge,** at the end of the stretch, is worth the obstacle course. From here you can climb an ash hill that gives a tremendous view of the crater from 3½ miles away. The Forest Service staff conducts nature programs around Road 99.

Road 25 ends to the south at Road 90. Go west here and then north on Road 83 to reach **Ape Cave,** a broken 2½-mile-long lava tube formed in an ancient eruption. Rent a lamp, bring your own flashlight, or shadow a well-lit group. There are fine interpretive tours at noon, 1pm, and 2pm.

On very clear days, you might hire a plane to fly over the crater. **Sunrise Aviation** (496-5510) in Morton, on U.S. 12 east of the visitors center, flies for $40 per person (2-person min.). The ride is thrilling and takes in more than would ever be visible from the ground.

In the last few years, several hiking trails have been reopened. One of these leads to a unique lava canyon exposed by the Muddy River mud flow. Hwy. 504 to Coldwater Lake will be reconstructed, opening up western views of the dome, crater, and newly formed lake. A shuttle bus from there to Johnson Ridge will allow a view directly into the crater, including the spectacle of scientists on the job.

Those with a sense of adventure, the proper equipment, and the foresight to have made reservations (required May 15-Oct. 31) can scale the new, stunted version of the mountain to glimpse the lava dome from the crater's rim. Although not a technically difficult climb, the route up the mountain is steep and often unstable (especially at the rim). Would-be Sir Edmund Hillarys are encouraged to bring the whole package: ice axe, hard hat, sunglasses, sunscreen, crampons, rope, climbing boots, and foul-weather clothing. Between May 14 and November 1, the Forest Service allows only 100 people to hike to the crater each day. Reservations can be made in person at the Mt. St. Helens National Volcanic Monument Visitor Center (see Practical Information), or by writing to the center at 3029 Spirit Lake Hwy., Castle Rock 98611. The **Yale Climbing Center,** a one-room building on Hwy. 503 south of Cougar, reserves 30 of each day's permits for standbys who show up as early as 6pm the day before they plan to climb.

Eastern Washington

In the rainshadow of the Cascades, the hills and vales of the Columbia River Basin once grew little more than sagebrush and tumbleweed. Thanks to irrigation and several strategically placed dams, the basin now yields bumper crops of nearly every imaginable variety of fruit. The same sun that toasts the region's orchards ripens flocks of pale, sun-starved visitors from western Washington who crowd the banks of Lake Chelan and Moses Lake. Farther east, ranching, wheat farming, and mining dominate the economy. Spokane, the largest city east of the Cascades, poses no real threat to the cultural preeminence of the Puget Sound area. Out by the Idaho border, the pickup truck rules life and motion, and many citizens still carry the guns that "won the West."

U.S. 97, stretching north to south on the eastern edge of the Cascades, strings together the main fruit centers and mountain resorts along the Columbia River Basin. **Interstate 90** emerges from the Cascades to cut a route through Ellensburg, Moses Lake, and Spokane, while **Interstate 82** dips south through Yakima and Toppenish.

Greyhound runs on I-90 and makes passes into the Tri-Cities and Yakima. **Empire Lines** runs from Spokane (624-5163) to Grand Coulee (633-2771) and Brewster (689-5541), and along U.S. 97 from Oroville on the Canadian border to Ellensburg (925-1177), with stops in Chelan (682-5541) and Wenatchee (662-2183), among other towns. **Amtrak's "Empire Builder"** serves Spokane, the Tri-Cities, the Columbia River up to Yakima, Ellensburg, and Tacoma.

Okanogan

A soporific little town at the heart of Washington's largest county, Okanogan boasts little more than a sign proclaiming that "Lt. George Washington Goethals, builder of the Panama Canal, slept here." The primary activities of area residents seem to be harvesting cherries and apples, lumbering, and slumbering. Here is the land that agribusiness forgot, where the Thursday cattle auction is still attended by ranchers whose herds number in the hundreds rather than the thousands.

For information about Okanogan and the surrounding area, tourists can turn to the **Chamber of Commerce,** in Okanogan (422-0441) and in nearby Omak (401 Omak Ave., 98841; 826-1180). The emergency number in both towns is 911. Okanogan police are located at the sheriff's office on 149 N. 3rd Ave. (422-2626). The Okanogan **post office** is at 212 N. 2nd Ave., 98840 (422-3830). The **Midvalley Hospital** in Omak is the closest medical facility, 810 Valley Way Rd., Omak (826-1760). The region's **area code** is 509.

Accommodations, Camping, and Food

U and I Motel, 838 2nd St. (422-2920), at the northern end of town. Run by a congenial English couple, the 10-room motel's backyard opens to the slow-moving Okanogan River. Their stories of their travels throughout the world make a stay here enjoyable. Singles $20.

Okanogan County Fairgrounds (422-1621), 1½ miles north of town on the Fairgrounds Access Rd. Isolated and lonely location. Hookups $3.

Apple Valley Inn, 3rd and Queen (422-2405). An excellent place to bring the family; the riotous amalgamation of Americana, from 40s movie posters to a bright orange Gulf gas pump, will entertain kids as well as adults. Pizzas $4-8, hamburgers and fries $2.25. Open Mon.-Thurs. 4-9pm, Fri.-Sat. 4-10pm.

Fletcher's Key, 120 Pine St. (422-1505). Breakfast served all day. 2 sausages and 1 hotcake $2. Open daily 5am-2pm.

Sights and Activities

The **Okanogan County Historical Museum**, 1410 2nd St., (422-4272), presents an ambitious portrait of local history, starting with the Mesozoic Era and ending with the construction of the Grand Coulee Dam. Look for the explanation of how a horseshoe was embedded in a tree and discovered by a logger "whose expletives have been deleted." (Open daily 11am-5pm. Free.) **Okanogan Days,** during the first weekend of June at the County Fairgrounds, combine the usual rodeos and parades with such oddities as the Businessman's Wild Cow Milking Contest. For a list of other annual events, contact the Okanogan Chamber of Commerce, P.O. Box 1125, Okanogan 98840.

The **Okanogan National Forest** amalgamates a variety of landscapes, from rain-soaked peaks to sagebrush-covered valleys. Its hiking trails are equally varied, including trails for wheelchairs as well as tracks for horses and motorcycles. A general list and specific maps (called *Green Trails*) are available at the Supervisor's Office, 1240 S. 2nd St. (422-2704), at the south end of town. (Open Mon.-Fri. 7:45am-5pm.) During winter months, the mile-high **Loup Loup Ski Bowl** sponsors some of the cheapest skiing in the state (lift $10 per day).

The even sleepier, even tinier town of **Omak,** a few miles north of Okanogan on I-97, wakes up during the second weekend in August for the **Stampede and Suicide Race,** in which dozens of horseback riders risk breaking their necks in order to see who can ride down a steep hill into the Okanogan River first. Prices for seats range from $4 to $10. For more information, contact the Omak Chamber of Commerce. Tickets sell out months in advance. Outstanding fishing for croppie and trout can be found nearby, particularly at **Tunk Creek** and **Crawfish Lake.** An excellent guide is the *Fishrapper,* available from the Chamber of Commerce (free).

Lake Chelan

The serpentine body of Lake Chelan (SHE-lan) slithers northwest from the Columbia River into the eastern Cascades. Although the dry, brown lakeshore around the faded resort town of Chelan isn't impressive, the shores farther north are handsome indeed. The lake, at points 1500 feet deep, extends far into Wenatchee National Forest and juts its northwesternmost tip into the Lake Chelan Recreation Area, a part of North Cascades National Park. The town of Stehekin caps the lake, accessible only by foot, boat, or plane.

Practical Information

Visitor Information: Lake Chelan Chamber of Commerce, 208 E. Johnson (682-2022). This modern facility offers plenty of information on the town of Chelan and nearby Manson, but not much on the surrounding wilds (head for the ranger station for that). Doubles as the bus depot. Open daily 8am-5pm.

Chelan Ranger Station: 428 W. Woodin Ave. (682-2576), just south of Chelan on the lakeshore. Joint station for the Forest and Park Services. Staff will explain the intricate regulations for parks, forests, and recreation areas. Open Mon.-Sat. 7:45am-4:30pm; Oct.-May Mon.-Fri. 7:45am-4:30pm.

Laundromat: Chelan Cleaners, 127 E. Johnson (682-2816). Open daily 7am-10pm.

Pharmacy: Green's Drugs, 212 E. Woodin Ave. (682-2566). Open Mon.-Sat. 9am-6pm, Sun. 9am-4pm.

Hospital: Lake Chelan Community, 682-2531. Open 24 hours.

Emergency: 911.

Post Office: 144 E. Johnson (682-2625), at Johnson and Emerson. Open Mon.-Fri. 9am-4:30pm. General Delivery ZIP Code: 98816.

Area Code: 509.

Accommodations, Camping, and Food

Exploiting the sun-deprived citizens of western Washington, Chelan has jacked up the prices on just about everything from egg timers to Ligeti mugs. Most motels and resorts in town are unaffordable during the summer. You can sleep for free on the banks of the Columbia River in Pateros, 21 miles north of Chelan on I-97, although you will be joining a questionable crowd of vagrants in a city park. The cheapest food can be bought at local fruit stands, the farmers' market, or the **Safeway** on 106 Manson Rd. (682-2615; open daily 7am-11pm).

Mom's Montlake Motel,, 823 Wapato (682-5715), at Clifford. Mom takes care of you with well-kept rooms, half with kitchens. Make yourself presentable before checking in, because Mom will turn away "the rowdy-looking elements." Singles $29. Doubles $35.

Travelers Motel, 204 E. Wapato Ave. (682-4215). Kitchens, A/C, cable TV, and BBQs. Singles $20, with bath $35. Doubles $27, with bath $40.

Lakeview Motel, 102 Woodin Ave. (682-5657). An ordinary over-the-tavern type hotel. Call ahead to reserve a room with a view of the lake. Shared bathrooms, no TVs. Singles $30. Doubles $35. $10 per additional person.

Lake Chelan State Park (687-3710), 9 miles from Chelan up the south shore of the lake. Highly developed. Hot showers and facilities for the disabled. Lifeguard on duty at the beach. The 144 sites fill up quickly in summer. Sites $7, with hookup $9.50. Reservations are necessary; write Lake Chelan State Park, Rte. 1, P.O. Box 90, Chelan 98816. Open April-Sept.

Twenty-Five Mile Creek State Park (687-3610), 18 miles up the lake's shore, beyond Lake Chelan State Park. A smaller, concession-operated park with a swimming pool. Sites $9. Open Memorial Day-Labor Day.

Lakeshore RV Park (682-5031), in town. Tents prohibited Memorial Day to Labor Day but permitted the rest of the year. This is a good place for late evening arrivals in the off-season, especially if you're heading up the lake first thing in the morning. Sites $10-18.

Golden Farms Bear Foods, 125 E. Woodin Ave. (682-5535). Natural foods in industrial quantities. All the latest self-help manuals. Open Mon.-Sat. 9am-7pm, Sun. noon-5pm.

Shagnasty's, 109 Woodin Ave. (682-3381). Try a Shagburger (1/6-lb.) or a nastyburger (1/3-lb.) on an egg bun. Pop 51¢. Open daily 8am-10pm.

Judy Lane Bakery, 216 Manson Rd. (682-2151). Delicious baked goods. Chili, hot dog, and soda $2.49. Open Sun.-Thurs. 7am-9pm, Fri.-Sat. 7am-10pm.

Sights and Activities

Stop in Chelan only long enough to see the huge collection of antique apple-labels in the **Lake Chelan Historical Museum** at the corner of Woodin Ave. and Emerson St. (682-2138; open June-Sept. Mon.-Sat. 1-4pm; free).

There are no day hikes out of Chelan itself. Head up to Twenty-Five Mile Creek, or better yet, find your way to **Stehekin**, a town inaccessible by road. The **Lake Chelan Boat Company**, P.O. Box 186, Chelan 98816 (682-2224), runs one round-trip to Stehekin daily April 15 to October 15, leaving at 8:30am. The dock is 1 mile south of Chelan on U.S. 97. No pets are allowed, and regular service is for passengers only, although a barge for vehicles and freight travels to Stehekin once per week. (Boats Oct. 16-May 15 Mon., Wed., Fri., and Sun. $13, round-trip $19; ages 6-11 ½-price; under 6 free.)

A lodge, a ranger station, and a campground cluster around Stehekin. An unpaved road and many trails probe north into the south unit of the **North Cascades National Park.** A shuttle bus ($4) operates along the Stehekin River Rd., linking Stehekin and the lakeshore to the national park. (Buses leave Stehekin Landing at 7:30am, 9am, and 2pm.) All walk-in campgrounds in North Cascades are open May through October (free). An excellent resource for the entire Stehekin area is *The Stehekin Guidebook* (free).

Backcountry use permits are mandatory in the park throughout the year and are available on a first-come, first-serve basis. Pick one up at the Chelan or Stehekin ranger stations. For more information, see North Cascades National Park.

Grand Coulee Area

The drive east on U.S. 2 from the Columbia River south of Chelan plunges you into an area scarred by geological catastrophe. Until the end of the last Ice Age, the Columbia River Basin here was as it was from Wilbur east to Spokane: rolling grasslands grazed by antelope, buffalo, and camels. Eighteen thousand years ago, as the weather warmed, a glacier blocking a lake in Montana gave way. A huge wall of water swept across eastern Washington, gouging out the loess and basalt to expose the granite below. The whole process is believed to have taken one month. The massive canyons that resulted are called "coulees" and the entire region is known as the Chanelled Scab Lands. Geologists, who usually assume that all change takes place gradually, were at first baffled by the Coulees. Today, they see the Coulees as striking evidence that geological transformations can occur as violently and rapidly as social or political change. Consider, for example, the "global warming" of 1988, followed dizzyingly by the "global cooling" of 1989. Anyway; among the largest of the coulees is the appropriately named Grand Coulee, which, now that the Grand Coulee Dam is in place, contains the massive **Franklin D. Roosevelt Lake** and **Banks Lake.**

The area of the Columbia River from Banks Lake north to the Canadian border constitutes the **Coulee Dam National Recreation Area.** The hub of the works is at the Grand Coulee Dam and its surrounding cities—Grand Coulee, Coulee Dam, and Electric City. The **Grand Coulee Dam,** celebrated by Woodie Guthrie and others, was a local cure for Depression—7000 workers were employed for eight years (1934-42) in constructing the engineering marvel. Aside from the pyramids and the Great Wall of China, it's probably the world's biggest man-made structure. Today the dam irrigates the previously parched Columbia River Basin and generates much of the electrical power used in the Northwest.

At the **Visitors Arrival Center** (663-9265), on Hwy. 155 just north of Grand Coulee, you can see a 13-minute film featuring some fascinating 1930s footage of the dam's construction, accompanied by Woody Guthrie himself. The center also provides information on recreational possibilities in the area (including fishing and motorboating on the two enormous lakes), and can start you on a self-guided tour through the power plants. Guided tours of the dam leave from the top of the monolith on the half-hour every day in summer between 10am and 6:30pm. (Open daily 8:30am-10pm; Labor Day-Memorial Day 9am-5pm. Free.) Arrive around 1:20pm to find out what it's like at the base of an avalanche; at 1:30pm the dam's spillway gates open, shooting thousands of gallons of the Columbia down the dam's face. Return to the dam at 9:30pm during the summer to view the multimillion-dollar, multicolor light show.

There is a **Safeway** in Grand Coulee at 101 Midway Ave. (633-2411; open daily 8am-10pm). The **post office** sorts your mail across the street. (Open Mon.-Fri. 8:30am-4:45pm, Sat. 8:30-11:30am. General Delivery ZIP Code: 99133.)

Accommodations, Camping, and Food

Center Lodge Motel, 508 Spokane Way (633-0770), in Grand Coulee. The rooms are big, airy, and built for oompa-loompas—short beds, low showers, and tiny sinks. The manager is an authority on windmills. Singles $17. Doubles $25-27.

Umbrella Motel, 404 Spokane Way (633-1691), in Grand Coulee. Smaller rooms, bigger beds, slightly cheaper. Singles $16. Doubles $18-20.

Campers should head to **Spring Canyon,** 2 miles east of Grand Coulee off Hwy. 174, a gorgeous, scrubby setting on the banks of Franklin D. Roosevelt Lake. Spring

Canyon is with wheelchair-accessible and has flush toilets. Be sure to wake up early; sprinklers begin at 11am. (Sites $6.) Other campsites east of Spring Canyon are accessible only by boat. Eight miles south of the dam on Hwy. 155 by the banks of Banks Lake, **Steamboat Rock State Park** has 100 sites amid striking scenery. Rock walls rise dramatically all around. (Flush toilets, pay showers, and wheelchair access. Sites $6-10.) Numerous **free camping areas** line Hwy. 155 south of Electric City; pull onto any of several unmarked dirt roads that lead to Banks Lake. Keep an ear out for rattlers. Unfortunately, tents cannot be rented anywhere in the area. The **Coulee Playland Resort** (633-2671), in Electric City 4 miles from the Grand Coulee Dam, offers more amenities than the free campsites nearby, but be prepared to pay the price—$7 for tents, $11 for RV hookups. Tours by boat of Banks Lake ($8.50) or Steamboat Rock ($12) depart from the resort three times daily.

You and Me Pizza, 19 Midway (633-2253), in Grand Coulee. The only homemade retail pizza in town. Enjoy the paper flowers, 6-in. pepperoni pizza ($1.90), hefty hoagies ($3), and pitcher of soda pop ($1.75). On Tues., drop in between 6 and 8pm for all the pizza you can swallow (with small soda $5). Open Mon.-Thurs. 3-8pm, Fri.-Sat. 11am-8pm; extra hours in summer.

Tee Pee Drive-In, 211 Midway (633-2111), in Grand Coulee. Cheap burgers ($1-2.60) become even cheaper if you win at Tee Pee Yahtzee—roll the same number on all 5 dice and your meal's free (your chances are 1 in 7776). Unfortunately, they don't give you the dice until after you order. Open Mon.-Fri. 10am-7pm, Sat. 10am-5pm.

Flo's Place, 315 Spokane Way (633-3216), in Grand Coulee. Country cooking served on plastic checkerboard tablecloths. Mel would be proud. Lunch and breakfast specials (including biscuits and gravy) for under $4. Titanic taco salad $3.50. Open Mon.-Sat. 5:30am-8pm; in winter Mon.-Sat. 5:30am-2pm.

Near Grand Coulee

Nespelem, 14 miles north of Coulee Dam, is in the **Colville Indian Reservation.** The town's **Drum and Feathers Club Celebration** brings Native Americans from all over Washington to Nespelem during the first two weeks of July. The celebration ignites dancing, stick games, arts and crafts, and plenty of food. For a place to stay or a good meal, enter the raffle for such prizes as a 16-foot tee pee or a half-side of beef.

South of Grand Coulee, near Coulee City, is **Sun Lakes State Park,** the site of **Dry Falls,** a chasm measureless to man carved by the same waters that shaped the coulees. The falls were once 3½ miles wide. The **Dry Falls Interpretive Center** (632-5583) subjects the area's past to various modes of historical analysis. (Open Wed.-Sun. 9am-6pm; Oct.-April by appointment only.) Camping in the park is plentiful, with facilities for the disabled. (Standard sites $6.)

History buffs and fisherfolk should definitely drive the 70-odd miles northeast from Grand Coulee (along Hwy. 174, 2, and 25) to **Fort Spokane,** near Miles. The fort served as a military outpost in the late 19th century, housing the soldiers who tried to manage affairs between local Native Americans and the white settlers. Self-guided tours begin at the visitors center. (Open daily 9:30am-5pm.) The nearby **campground** features a beach and a fish cleaning station. (Sites $6.)

Ellensburg

Once a candidate to become Washington's state capital, the town was virtually destroyed by fire in 1889. The downtown area has since then been carefully reconstructed to preserve the spirit of the past. Ellensburg is particularly proud of its blue agate gemstones, the largest of which (6 lbs.) is on display at the Kittitas County Museum. Ellensburg is also the home of one of the world's most obese psychedelic bands, the Screaming Trees. Ellensburg celebrates its history as a ranchtown with an annual rodeo, held on Labor Day weekend.

Practical Information and Orientation

Visitor Information: Chamber of Commerce, 436 N. Sprague St. (925-3137). Open Mon.-Fri. 8am-5pm; Oct.-April Mon.-Fri. 9am-5pm.

Greyhound: 801 Okanogan St. (925-1177), at 8th Ave. Six buses per day to Seattle ($14), 2 to Walla Walla ($25), 3 to Spokane ($20), and 2 to Portland ($30). Open Mon.-Fri. 8:30am-5:30pm, Sat. 10:30am-4:45pm, Sun. 10:45-11:15am and 12:15-4:45pm.

Taxi: Kourtesy Kab, 925-2771.

Laundromat: Corner of Walnut and 8th. Open daily 7am-10pm.

Pharmacy: Downtown, 414 N. Pearl St. (925-1514). Senior citizen discount. Open Mon.-Sat. 9am-6pm.

Washington State Patrol: 925-5303.

Hospital: Kittitas Valley Community, 603 S. Chestnut St. (962-9841).

Post Office: Corner of 3rd and Pearl (925-1866). Open Mon.-Fri. 9am-5pm. General Delivery ZIP Code: 98926.

Area Code: 509.

Ellensburg lies 36 miles north of Yakima on I-82, and 100 miles east of Seattle on I-90. The historic district is loosely bounded by 3rd Ave., 8th Ave., Main St., and Poplar St.

Accommodations and Camping

Aside from KOA, the closest campground is in the Wenatchee National Forest, 20 miles north on U.S. 97 (674-4411). During the rodeo, cheap rooms are available at Central Washington University (see Sights).

Regalodge Motel, Motel Square (925-3116), corner of 6th and Water, 2 blocks from the main drag. Spacious rooms include indoor pools. Singles from $26. Doubles from $35. Breakfast included.

Lighthouse Motel, 607 W. Cascade Way (925-9744), off 8th Ave., west of downtown. Dim but clean rooms with cable TV, A/C, and bath. Singles $20. Doubles $28. Kitchen $4.

Rainbow Motel, 1025 Cascade Way (925-3544). Ordinary rooms and outdoor BBQ area. A/C, color TV, and laundromat. Singles from $25. Doubles from $28.

KOA Kampground, 2½ miles west of town down Cascade Way (925-9319), exit 106 off I-90. Only camping in vicinity. Large area with laundry and game room. Sites $13.50, $2 extra per person after two people. Electrical hookup $2; sewer connection $1.50. Open June-Sept. daily 8am-10pm; April-May and Sept.-Oct. 9am-8pm.

Food

All of Ellensburg's restaurants were apparently lost in the fire of 1889; the cuisine has been slow to recover.

Valley Cafe, 105 W. 3rd Ave. (925-3050). The floors and mahogany counters of this art-deco espresso bar have been around since the 30s. The best values on the varied menu are the Mexican specialties (*Chimichungas* $5.35). Superb breakfasts (Fri.-Sun. only) include 2 whole wheat pancakes for $1.65. Delicious salads (avocado-chicken salad $4.35). Lunch menu served all day. The fruit frappé ($2), or "smoothie," makes a trip to Ellensburg worthwhile. Open Mon.-Thurs. 11am-9:30pm, Fri.-Sun. 7:30am-9:30pm.

Casa de Blanca, 1318 S. Canyon Rd. (925-1693). Hefty servings of basic Mexican food ($4-6). Try the $4.50-6.75 combination plates for a dollop of everything. Lunch special $3.75. Open daily 11am-10pm.

Skipper's, 1210 S. Canyon Rd. (925-3474). An island of cheap, efficient mediocrity in an ocean of overpriced, slow mediocrity. Bottomless iced tea (free refills) 65¢. All-you-can-eat fish filets, fries, chowder, and cole slaw $5.09. Open in summer Sun.-Thurs. 11am-10pm, Fri.-Sat. 11am-11pm.

Topper's Drive-In, 608 N. Main (962-1833). Just another cheap drive-in on the interstate of life, but the only one in town. Deluxe burger 89¢, 32-oz. soda 59¢, weekly specials. Go across the street to **Maid O'Clover** for dessert. Ice cream and frozen yogurt in homemade waffle cones for about $1.

Sights

The **Kittitas County Museum,** 114 E. 3rd Ave. (925-3778), at Pine St., is housed in an 1889 building with horseshoe-shaped windows. In addition to Native American artifacts and exhibits on ranching and the area's agricultural history, this veritable Uffizi of the west features an extensive gem and mineral collection. (Open Mon.-Sat. 1-4:30pm. Free.)

Families gather for picnics on weekend afternoons in **Memorial Park.** Located on the east end of 7th St. near the rodeo grounds, the park awakens green thoughts in its green shade. But come Labor Day the park is taken over by one of the nation's ten most popular **rodeos,** as 500 cattlefolk compete for $100,000 worth of prizes in steer-wrestling, bareback bronco-riding, and wild-cow milking. (Seats in the uncovered grandstand $6 per day, in the covered grandstand $8 Fri., $10 Sat.-Mon.) For tickets—hot items indeed—write the Ellensburg Rodeo Ticket Office, P.O. Box 777, Ellensburg 98926. During the rodeo, Central Washington University provides spacious and clean accommodations within 3 blocks of the rodeo grounds. (Singles cost $19, doubles $34.) For information and reservations (strongly recommended), write to the Conference Center, Courson Hall, Ellensburg 98926 (963-1141).

Somehow, the **Kittitas County Fair** manages to compete with the rodeo on the same weekend. The four days of livestock displays, art shows, and goat-milking contests are tamer than the rodeo, and free. The **Annual National Western Art Show and Auction** hot-wires up the town in the third weekend of May with auctions and exhibitions.

Olmstead Place State Park (925-1943) is the site of the area's oldest log cabin and a showplace for early agricultural equipment. Several 19th-century buildings remain, including a dairy barn and a granary. (Open Sat.-Sun. noon-4pm, Mon.-Fri. by appointment only.)

Yakima

An agricultural apotheosis tucked neatly at the foot of the Cascades, Yakima calls itself the "fruit bowl of the nation." Blessed with rich volcanic soil, 300 days of sunshine per year, and a fresh groundwater supply, the area seems to produce more fruit stands than people. Yakima makes an ideal launching pad for a flight into more mountainous atmospheres. But try to resist the mountains long enough to visit Yakima's thriving Native American reservation, and to admire Mt. Rainier and Mt. Adams from a distance.

Practical Information and Orientation

Visitor Information: Yakima Valley Visitors and Convention Bureau, 10 N. 8th St. (575-1300), at E. Yakima. Maps of town and brochures proclaim Yakima's charms. The *Yakima City and County Map* ($1) is useful, but the map in the free *Yakima Valley Visitors Guide* serves just as well. Open Mon.-Fri. 8am-5pm, Sat.-Sun. 9am-5pm.

Greyhound: 602 E. Yakima (457-5131). Buses halt in Yakima on the way from Seattle (3 per day). No service from Yakima to Mt. Rainier. Open Mon.-Fri. 7:45am-5:30pm, 6:30-7:15pm, 9:15-9:45pm; Sat.-Sun. 7:45am-4pm, 6:30-7:15pm, 9:15-9:45pm.

Taxi: Yellow Cab, 122 S. 1st St. (457-6500). Open 24 hours. **Diamond Cab,** 904 S. 3rd St. (453-3113). Open 24 hours.

Car Rental: Economy Auto Rentals, 3811 Main St., Union Gap (452-5555), just outside town, or **U-Save Auto Rental,** Yakima Air Terminal (575-8374). $20 per day if you stay in the state, 100 free miles plus 22¢ per additional mile. $75 deposit. Must be 21 years old. Open Mon.-Sat. 9am-6pm, Sun. 1-6pm.

Camping Supplies: Sunset Sport Center, 2801 W. Nob Hill Blvd. (248-4500). **Svends's Mountain Sports,** 1212 W. Lincoln St. (575-7876). **Rent-A-Tent,** 201 S. 1st (453-1167). Two-person tent $5 per day, 4-person tent $25 per 3-day weekend.

Laundromat: Glenwood, 418-A S. 48th (965-3926). Open Mon.-Sat. 8:30am-9pm, Sun. 10am-6pm.

Recorded Weather Information: 575-1212.

Mountain Pass Conditions: 452-7669.

Crisis Line: 575-4200. 24 hours.

Poison Information: 248-4400.

Pharmacy: Glenwood Drug Co., 432 S. 48th Ave. (966-5330), at Tieton Dr. Open Mon.-Fri. 9am-9pm, Sat. 9am-6pm, Sun. 10am-6pm.

Hospital: Yakima Valley Memorial, 2811 Tieton Dr. (575-8000). Open 24 hours. **St. Elizabeth Medical Center,** 110 S. 9th Ave. (575-5060). Open 24 hours.

Police: 248-1010. 24 hours.

Post Office: 205 W. Washington Ave. (575-5823 or 575-5827). Open Mon.-Sat. 6am-6pm, Sun. noon-5pm. General Delivery ZIP Code: 98903.

Area Code: 509.

Yakima is 36 miles south of Ellensburg on I-82. The downtown area is the northeast portion of the city, by the Yakima River. **Yakima Transit** buses trace ten convenient routes, operating Monday through Friday from 5:45am to 5:45pm, Saturday from 7:45am to 6:15pm. (Fare 35¢, senior citizens 15¢, children 20¢.) For specific route information, call 575-6175 (4:30am-7pm).

Accommodations and Camping

Finding a cheap place to stay in the fruit bowl of the nation is not easy. Affordable places keep clear of downtown. The few campgrounds are overcrowded and noisy. Cheaper, more pleasant campgrounds are on Hwy. 12, west of Yakima on the way to Mt. Rainier. Campgrounds with drinking water are $5; those without are free.

YWCA, 15 N. Naches Ave. (248-7796), downtown. Women over 17 only. Nine single rooms with shared baths $8 per night, $40 per week, $145 per month. No curfew. $15 key deposit. No reservations; odds of getting rooms are best in mid-afternoon.

Log Motel, 1715 S. 1st St. (575-9456). Clean and quiet, largely because of its distance from downtown (a brisk 25-min. walk). Rooms $21.50.

El Corral Motel (865-2365), 18 miles from Yakima on U.S. 97 in Toppenish, on a Native American reservation. A/C, color TV, movie channel. Singles $26. Doubles $32.

Motel 6, 1104 N. 1st St. (454-0080). Everyone's favorite budget chain fastens Yakima to its empire. Singles $23. Doubles $29.

Yakima Sportsman State Park (575-2774), 3 miles east of town at 904 Keys Rd. Exit 34 off I-82. For experienced fishermen and everyone else. Bring insect repellent in spring, though insects may be the least of your troubles—beware of screaming infants, non-stop blaring Bruckner symphonies, and quarreling neighbors. Park open 6:30am-dusk. Sites $7, with hookup $9.50.

Food

There is little reason to set foot in a Yakima restaurant, unless you stay long enough to grow sick of fruit. The *Yakima Valley Farm Products Guide,* distributed at the visitors bureau and at regional hotels and stores, lists local fruit sellers and U-pick farms. Peaches in season cost less per pound in Yakima than per peach in other regions. U.S. 12 heading toward Naches has the best assortment of fruit stands, including the prominent **Cherry Lane Fruit and Gift** (653-2041), near the intersection with I-82.

Brunsbrae, 1813 Naches Heights Rd. (965-0873), and **Johnson Orchards**, 4906 Summitview Ave. (966-7479), are the two U-pick farms closest to town. The former specializes in cherries, the latter in apples. Farms generally stay open in summer from 8am to 5pm. Wear gloves and sturdy shoes, and bring as many empty containers as you can. U-picks are good deals, but you can save just as much by buying directly from the farms (not from roadside stands). **Snokist Warehouse**, 18 W. Mead Ave. (453-5631), sells apples year-round. (Open Mon.-Fri. 8am-4:30 or 5pm.)

Kemper's, 306 S. 1st St. (453-6362). Stands out from the pack of drive-ins with its gaudy purple interior and 75¢ burgers; a 32-oz. soft drink is only 95¢ and refills of regular soft drinks are 27¢. Open Mon.-Thurs. 9am-midnight, Fri. 9am-12:30am, Sat.-Sun. 10am-midnight.

Sport Center Lounge, 214 E. Yakima (453-3300). Look for the larger-than-life rotating skeet shooter as you drive down Yakima's busiest thoroughfare; his red neon muzzle flash is only slightly less tacky than the camouflage carpeting on the walls inside. Bacon, sausage, or ham with eggs and toast $3. Unlimited coffee refills. Open Mon.-Sat. 6:30am-9:30pm, Sun. 6:30am-8pm; buffet at 3pm.

Santiago's, 111 E. Yakima Ave. (453-1644). Named the best Mexican restaurant in the region by *Pacific Northwest* magazine in 1989, Santiago's serves tasty food in an attractive environment. Full dinners $8-9, a la carte $4-5. Open Mon.-Thurs. 11am-2:30pm and 5-10pm, Fri. 11am-2:30pm and 5-11pm, Sat. 5-11pm, Sun. noon-9pm.

Sights and Activities

While many residents suffer from unemployment, the **Yakima Indian Reservation** enriches the history and culture of the region immeasurably. The **Yakima Indian Nation Cultural Center**, 22 miles south on U.S. 97 in Toppenish (865-2800), has a smorgasbord of events and information about the 14 tribes that once inhabited Yakima Valley. The **museum** here concentrates on the oral tradition of the Yakimas. (Admission $1, families $2.50. Open Feb.-Dec. daily 10am-9pm.)

The **Yakima Valley Museum**, 2105 Tieton Dr. (248-0747), presents area history of a different kind. The museum is best known for its collection of 19th-century vehicles and its display of Phil and Steve Mahre's skiing trophies. (Open Wed.-Fri. 10am-5pm, Sat.-Sun. noon-5pm. Admission $2.50, senior citizens and students $1.25, ages under 10 free, families $5.) An electric trolley shuttles between Yakima and Selah for an hour's round-trip; tours leave from the **Trolley Car Barn**, 507 S. 4th Ave. (575-1700; open May-Oct. Sat.-Sun. 11am-3pm; admission $3, ages over 64 and 6-12 $1.50, under 6 free). Unfortunately, **Historic North Front Street** and **Yesterday's Village** have little to do with yesterday's history. Featuring somewhat expensive shops designed expressly for the bored tourist, this area offers the visitor no new information about Yakima—and fewer bargains.

The sagebrush indigenous to Yakima contrasts abruptly with the green fields cultivated by irrigation. In addition to fruit for eating, hillsides around the city support grape crops for the trampling purposes of 17 local wineries. **Covey Run Vintners**, 5 miles out of Zillah on Morris Rd. (829-6235), offers free tours of its cellars and, more importantly, a free tasting room. (Open Mon.-Sat. 10am-5pm, Sun. noon-5pm; Oct.-April Mon.-Sat. noon-5pm, Sun. noon-4:30pm.)

The **Toppenish Powwow Rodeo and Pioneer Fair** (865-3996 or 865-5313) occurs during the first weekend of July on Division Ave. in Toppenish (fair admission $1, rodeo $5). The small town of White Swan hosts the **Tiinowit International Powwow and Treaty Celebration Day and Rodeo** during the first week of June. Both powwows feature games, dancing, live music, a rodeo, and fair food. The **Yakima Valley Air Fair**, held during the last weekend in June at Yakima Municipal Airport, features antique planes. On a larger scale, the **Central Washington State Fair** is held in Yakima in late September. The nine-day event includes agricultural displays, rodeos, big-name entertainers, regional specialties, and horse racing.

Bars like **The Phoenix**, 1219 N. 1st St. (248-8400), feature live country music nightly. The larger motels and hotels in town have live entertainment, with cover charges running $1-3.

Walla Walla

Walla Walla, by any other name, would be somewhat less interesting. From the fake roses languishing in the diners (meticulously dusted daily by middle-aged waitresses with towering beehive wigs) to the serenity of the Seventh Day Adventist College, Walla Walla is an unchanging, sedentary, Pacific Northwest town. "The town's so nice, they had to name it twice," the locals say, transforming idiosyncrasy into pride.

Situated in the center of the state's sweet-onion country, Walla Walla was a hotbed of activity back in the days of the Oregon Trail. Fort Walla Walla, the only military base in the homeland of the Cayuse Indians, provided armed protection for pioneers, while the nearby Whitman Mission offered food and shelter. Today Walla Walla ("many waters," in the local Native American tongue) is a thriving agricultural center.

Practical Information and Orientation

Visitor Information: Chamber of Commerce, 29 E. Sumach St. (525-0850), at Colville. Pick up a copy of their guide to *Food, Fun, and Lodging* in Walla Walla and a street map. Open Mon.-Fri. 8:30am-5pm.

Greyhound: 315 2nd St. (525-9313), at E. Oak St. One bus per day to Boise ($57), 1 to Spokane ($27.45), 3 to Seattle ($28), 2 to Portland ($30). Open Mon.-Fri. 8am-noon and 1:15-5:30pm, Sat. 8-11:45am, Sun. 10-11:45am.

Bassett Transit: 800-342-0210. The cheapest and quickest mass transit to Seattle, Richland, and Yakima. The Seattle-Walla Walla route ($25 one way) takes only 6 hr., as compared to Greyhound's 9 hr.

Valley Transit: 8 W. Poplar St. (525-9140). Five color-coded lines thoroughly cover Walla Walla and beyond. The accommodating drivers will drop you off anywhere along their route. Buses run Mon.-Fri. 6am-7pm, some on Sat. Fare 25¢; students, senior citizens, and disabled 10¢.

Dial-A-Ride: 527-3775. Free transportation for the handicapped and for ages 60 and over. Call the day before you need a ride. Vans run Mon.-Sat. 8am-4pm.

Taxi: A-1 Cab, 7 S. 4th Ave. (529-2525). 24 hours.

Car Rental: Chuck Lightfoot Husky, 2933 Isaacs Ave. (525-1680). A bargain for short hauls only. $19 per day (with 25 free miles) plus 19¢ per mile. $38 for unlimited mileage. Credit card or $250 deposit. Must be 18.

Hospital: St. Mary's Medical Center, 401 W. Poplar St. (525-3320). Open 24 hours.

Senior Citizen Services: The Senior Center (529-2850).

Post Office: 128 N. 2nd St. (522-6337), across from the Chamber of Commerce in a fine old building. Open Mon.-Fri. 9am-5pm. General Delivery ZIP code: 99362.

Area Code: 509.

Walla Walla lies on U.S. 12 in southeastern Washington, at the junction with OR Hwy. 11, a 44-mile connective artery leading to I-84 in Pendleton, OR. Walla Walla is 125 miles east of Yakima and 160 miles south of Spokane. The city is much easier to visit by car than by bus—the only bus from the north arrives at 12:30am.

Accommodations and Camping

Double Walla is a convention center; for some reason, business people love to call meetings at the foot of the Blue Mountains.

Whitman Annex Motel, 204 N. Spokane (529-3400). Have a ready excuse to retreat to the roomy, clean lodgings with A/C, TV, and a small bathtub, because the jolly management can discourse endlessly on the wonders of Walla Walla. Singles $20. Doubles $24.

EconoLodge, 305 N. 2nd Ave. (800-368-4400). This clean, spacious motel is a scant half-block from the Greyhound station. A/C, pool, TV. Singles $25. Doubles $30.

Tapadera Inn, 211 N. 2nd Ave. (800-722-8277), next to EconoLodge. A/C, continental breakfast, and TV with HBO. Singles $25. Doubles $27.

City Center Motel, 627 W. Main (529-2660), 8 blocks from city center. Pleasantly landscaped grounds (including a pool), an exuberant proprietor, and that rare motel phenomenon: matching bedspreads and carpet. Free coffee. Singles $26.50. Doubles $34.50.

Walla Walla College, 204 S. College Ave. (527-2814). Take bus #1W. Nonstudents welcome. Dorm rooms $15 (including linen) at this Seventh Day Adventist College are available June to mid-Sept. Call ahead 9am-5pm.

Fort Walla Walla Campground (527-3770), just southwest of downtown on Dalles Military Rd. A family place with spacious, quiet grounds. Coin-operated showers. Sites $8.50, with electricity and water $11. Open May 1-Oct. 1.

Umatilla National Forest (522-6290), 35 miles southeast of town, off Hwy. 204. Maintains several developed campgrounds. For information, go to the Forest Service Ranger Station, at 1415 W. Rose St., a mile or so west of the city center.

Food

The food in Walla Walla is average at best. Your wisest choice might be the 24 hour **Safeway** at 215 E. Rose St.

Pastime Cafe, 215 W. Main St. (525-0783). The drab, relaxed, homey atmosphere might lull you, but the 12- oz. steak and spaghetti special ($7) is exceptional. Open Mon.-Sat. 6am-midnight.

Ice Burg, 616 W. Birch (529-1793). Mix with the bustling college crowd at this drive-thru. Burgers $1.14, soft drinks 43¢, ice cream 49¢. Try the funky peanut butter shakes ($1.19). Open Mon.-Thurs. 11am-10:30pm, Fri.-Sat. 11am-11pm, Sun. 11:30am-10pm.

Back East Sub Shop, 7 E. Main (525-6408), in the heart of downtown. This high-school hangout serves tasty subs, which vary in length and price from 4 in. ($1.85) to 16 in. ($5.05). Gourmet coffees 65¢. Open Mon.-Fri. 9am-8pm, Sat. 9am-5pm.

Sights

The **Fort Walla Walla Museum Complex,** Dalles Military Rd. and 9th St. (525-7703), in the southwest corner of town, shelters such curiosities as a 19th-century doctor's office and jail. Farm-equipment connoisseurs must not miss the full-scale replica of a 33-mule combine harvester. A complicated harness system allowed one person to control all 33 mules. In mid-July a pioneer-Indian rendezvous is held here. Events include a salmon bake, a mule-packing contest, and a women's rolling-pin throw. (Open June-Sept. Tues.-Sun. 1-5pm; May and Oct. Sat.-Sun. 1-5pm, but may be open during the week for school tours; call ahead. Admission $2, ages 7-12 $1, under 7 free.)

Seven miles west of town on U.S. 12, the **Whitman Mission National Historic Site** (529-2761) presents the more dramatic side of the region's history. In 1837, the missionary Marcus Whitman and his wife Narcissa (the first woman to cross America on the overland route) arrived in the area. Together they ministered to the local Native Americans and to settlers who streamed along the nearby Oregon Trail. The Cayuse were largely unmoved by the missionaries' ideas, and tensions grew. In the Whitman massacre of 1847, Marcus, Narcissa, and 11 others were killed, and 50 people were taken captive at the mission. The **visitors center** at the mission site has a museum and is a good place to start walking the trails to Great Grove and the Whitman Memorial. (Open June-Aug. daily 8am-6pm; Sept.-May 8am-4:30pm. Admission $1, families $3, over 61 and under 17 free.)

The **Sweet Onion Festival** is held in the last week of July in honor of the town's profitable plant. For information and sweet onion recipes, contact the Walla Walla Sweet Onion Commission, P.O. Box 644, Walla Walla 99362.

Pullman

The red brick campus of Washington State University (WSU) sprawls on a hill, its classrooms ringed by bars and frat houses. Below, the people of Pullman go about their business quietly, interrupted only by big football games and commencement. The fields of Whitman County, outside this classic college town, produce more wheat per acre than anywhere else in the U.S.

The Nez Perce tribe inhabited Pullman until a wave of westward immigration in the late 1870s overtook the area. Bolin Farr, founder of the "Three Forks Ranch," around which the original town grew, named the town after his longtime friend George Pullman, the inventor of the famous railroad sleeping cars.

Practical Information and Orientation

Visitor Information: Pullman Chamber of Commerce, N. 415 Grand Ave. (334-3565). Enough brochures on "The Other Washington—The State!" to satisfy even the hungriest fact-seeker. Pick up a copy of *Pullman Dining and Lodging.* Open Mon.-Fri. 8am-5pm. **WSU** has a **Visitor Information Center** in the campus police building on Wilson Rd. (335-3564), to which students are oblivious. Open 24 hours.

Greyhound: NE 115 Olsen (334-1412), at Grand. Buses to Boise (2 per day, $35.25), Spokane (3 per day, $12), Seattle (3 per day, $40), and Walla Walla (1 per day, $20). Open Mon.-Fri. 8am-1pm, 1:30-3pm, and 8:40-9:10pm. No storage lockers available.

Pullman Transit: 725 Guy St. (332-6535). Three lines operate Mon.-Fri. 6:50am-5:50pm. Runs mostly between the WSU campus and downtown. Fare 35¢, ages under 18 20¢.

Taxi: Evergreen Taxi Inc., 332-7433. 24 hours. First ½ mile $1.75, each additional mile $1.40.

Car Rental: Lewiston Hwy. (334-4545). $25 per day, 200 free miles plus 10¢ per extra mile; $100 deposit or credit card required. For local use only. Must be 21.

Bike Rental: Blue Mountain Recreation and Cyclery, N. 131 Grand Ave. (332-1703). Good quality 10-speeds $10 per day, with $25 deposit or credit card. Used bikes only $5 per day, with $10 deposit or credit card. Open Tues.-Sat. 10am-5:30pm.

Laundromat: N. 740 Grand Ave. 24 hours.

Senior Citizen Services: East 502 A, Moscow, ID (208-882-1098).

Rape Crisis Information: Women's Center, 885-6616.

Crisis Line: 332-1505. 24 hours.

Child Care: The Chamber of Commerce (334-3565) keeps a frequently updated list of available babysitters.

Post Office: Lewiston Hwy. (334-3212). Open Mon.-Fri. 8:30am-5pm. General Delivery ZIP code: 99163.

Area Code: 509.

Pullman lies at the junction of Hwy. 27 and 270, fewer than 10 miles west of the Idaho border. U.S. 195, running from Spokane south to Lewiston, bypasses the city to the west. Walla Walla lies 100 miles to the southwest, Spokane 70 miles north, and Moscow, home of the University of Idaho, 9 miles east.

Most of Pullman's enterprises lie along Main Street and Grand Avenue. Grand runs north to south; Main travels west to east, terminating at the WSU campus. The campus has digested the eastern half of town.

Accommodations and Camping

The large number of student travelers who gambol through town draws an encouraging selection of moderately priced, no-frills motels. Rooms are easy to find, except on weekends of home football games and during commencement (first week of May).

Regents Hall (335-3320), on the WSU campus. Call a week or two in advance for the best deal in town, although conventions often make rooms scarce in summer. A student ID and $6.85 buy a dorm room double. Without student ID this package is $14.

Manor Lodge Motel, SE 455 Paradise (334-2511), at Main, 3 blocks from the Greyhound station. A clean and comfortable establishment in a great location. Friendly staff. Live high on the hog with your refrigerator, couch, and bathtub. Singles $21.50. Doubles $23.70.

The Hilltop Motor Inn (334-2555), off U.S. 195 (Colfax Hwy.) at the northwest edge of town. Not very practical for Greyhound travelers. Singles $23.60. Doubles $30.

Cougar Land Motel, W. 120 Main (334-3535), smack dab in the center of town. Where all the visiting WSU parents stay—and the prices reflect it. Pool, rooms with a bathtub and refrigerator. Singles $33. Doubles $43.

Food

There are enough burgers, pizzas, and subs in Pullman to fill the stomachs of thousands of college students for ever and ever and ever. Sanctuaries from student cuisine are few and far between.

Ferdinand's, Troy Hall on WSU campus. Everything made on the premises with milk from WSU's dairy. Sweet basil, smoky cheddar and more prosaic cheeses $8.75 for a 30-oz. tin. Try a cone of peanut butter ice cream (75¢) or a large glass of milk (55¢). Named after the friendly bovine (?). Open daily 9am-4pm; in winter 9:30am-4:30pm.

Cougar Cafe, N. 146 Grand Ave. (332-1132), around the corner from the Greyhound station. Framed pictures of famed Wazzu athletes splatter the walls of this mercifully uncrowded breakfast and lunch stop. Try the heaping stack of French toast for $3. Open Mon.-Sat. 5am-1:30pm, Sun. 7am-1:30pm.

The Pizza Answer, E. 231 Main (334-4417). Mainly delivers to hungry Cougars, but cheesy, filling slices available for $1. 32 oz. pop 50¢. Open daily 11am-4pm.

Couger County Drive-In, N. 760 Grand Ave. (332-7820), a 10-min. walk from downtown. Drive through or slide in a booth at this popular student hang-out. Burgers (from $2) and shakes (lots of flavors, $1.10). Try the CycloneD-soft ice cream mixed with candy (large $1.79). Open 10am-11pm.

Alex's Restaurante, N. 139 Grand Ave. (332-4061). Quiet, well-mannered, and nobly named, with good Mexican dinners ($8-10) and lunches ($3-4). Open Tues.-Thurs. 11:30am-2pm and 5-10pm, Fri. 11:30am-2pm and 4:30pm-1am, Sat. 4:30-11pm, Sun. 5-10pm.

Mandarin Wok Restaurant, N. 115 Grand Ave. (332-5863). Chinese food prepared with care and a minimum of MSG. Dinners are overpriced, but the $4.50 lunch special—main dish, soup, eggroll, fried rice, and tea—is worth the money. The best Chinese food in the area, in an appropriately elegant setting. Open Mon.-Fri. 11:30am-1:30pm and 5-9pm, Sat. 5-9pm, Sun. 5-8pm.

Pizza Haven, E. 420 Main (334-2535). Hearty pizzas (from $2.75) and pastas (from $2.90). Draft 79¢. Wed. 5-9pm is all-you-can-eat pizza and salad night ($3.75). Open Sun.-Thurs. 11am-10pm, Fri.-Sat. 11am-midnight.

Sights and Entertainment

The steeply sloping campus of **Washington State University** in the east of town is Pullman's primary attraction. The second largest university in the state (enrollment 18,000), WSU specializes in agriculture and engineering. WSU's 100th birthday party will take place on March 28, 1990. Call or stop by the **University Relations Office** in the French Administration Building, Room 442 (335-3581), which offers guided tours of the campus every weekday at 1pm during the school year (early Sept. to early May). Pick up a copy of *Museums and Collections at Washington State University.* All campus museums are free and open during the school year only. Johnson Hall houses both the **Entomological Collection**(335-5504) and the **Mycological Herbarium** (335-9541). Enjoy one million insect specimens and seventy thousand living fungi, respectively (open Mon.-Fri. 8am-5pm). The **Anthropology Museum** (335-3441), in College Hall, is a working part of the Anthropology Department, and current research projects are often on display. (Open Mon.-Thurs.

9am-4pm, Fri. 9am-3pm.) The **Museum of Art,** in the Fine Arts Building (335-1910), has a small permanent collection and rotating exhibits of local and international art. (Open Tues. 10am-4pm and 7-10pm, Wed.-Fri. 10am-4pm, Sat.-Sun. 1-5pm.)

The gentle hills and broad views of Washington's Palouse region make the district ideal for exploration by bicycle or automobile. **Kamiak** and **Steptoe Buttes,** north of town off Hwy. 27, make for enjoyable day trips. Pack a picnic lunch and head off into the hills.

For travelers with children, a summer stop into Pullman's **Neill Public Library,** 210 Grand Ave. (334-4555) will work wonders with the grumpy and restless little ones. From 9am-8pm Mon.-Thurs., attentive and helpful librarians will guide kids through a bevy of learning-oriented activities. Out-of-town children are welcome.

For non-children, there are nearly as many bars as Cougar signs in the Palouse. **Pelican Pete's,** SE 1100 Johnson (334-4200), is the unanimous undergrad favorite. Wednesday night is "Happy Wheel Night," based on the gameshow Wheel of Fortune. Rainier Beer is 75¢. Mixed drinks $1.50. (Open 11am to whenever the action dies down, usually around 2am. Happy hour 3:30-6:30pm.) Just down the street from the Regents dorm are two popular university hangouts. At **Cougar Cottage,** NE 900 Colorado (332-1265), true drafts are $1 and burgers and Mexican food range from $2-6. (Open daily 11am-2am.) The **Campus Cavern,** NE 1000 Colorado (334-5151), serves sandwiches and burgers for $3-4.

Spokane

Originally named Spokan Falls after the area's original residents, the Spokan-ee Indians, Spokane was the first pioneer settlement in the Pacific Northwest. After the "great fire of 1889," Spokane quickly reestablished the industries spawned by local natural resources. Today, with an economy still based on lumber, mining, and agriculture, the spunkiest city in Eastern Washington remains one of the Northwest's major trade centers. And its most successful native son, Representative Thomas Foley, is now in the other Washington (DC, that is), where he has a steady job as Speaker of the House, making him the highest-ranking Democratic office-holder in the nation.

In its own unwilling way, Spokane achieves urban sophistication without typical big-city hassles. The downtown thrives, though the pace is slow (not a soul crosses the street until the Walk sign flashes). The Expo '74 legacy includes Riverfront Park's museum and theater, as well as a number of elegant restaurants and hotels. And, in typical Northwest fashion, Spokane gains much from its setting. Arboretums, gardens, abundant outdoor activities, and a spectacular series of bridges spanning the Spokane River and Falls celebrate wonders more ancient than concrete—although bridges perhaps do not "celebrate" the river they cross so much as dispense with them.

Practical Information and Orientation

Visitor Information: Spokane Area Convention and Visitors Bureau, W. 926 Sprague Ave. (747-3230). Overflowing with literature extolling every aspect of Spokane. An exuberant staff gladly answers queries. Open Mon.-Fri. 8:30am-5pm, and most summer weekends 9am-3pm (depending on volunteer availability). **Travelers Aid Service,** W. 1017 1st (456-7169), near the bus depot. Kind staff, accustomed to helping stranded travelers find lodgings. Open Mon.-Fri. 1-5pm.

Amtrak: W. 221 1st St. (624-5144, after business hours 800-872-7245), at Bernard St., downtown. To Chicago (1 per day, $192), Seattle (1 per day, $60), and Portland (1 per day, $60). Depot open Mon.-Fri. 11am-3:30am, Sat.-Sun. 7:15pm-3:30am.

Greyhound: W. 1125 Sprague (624-5251), at 1st Ave. and Jefferson St., downtown. To Seattle (5 per day, $20), Lewiston, ID (1 per day, $20), and Walla Walla (1 per day, $28). **Empire Lines** and **Grey Lines** (624-4116) share the terminal with Greyhound, serving even more of

Eastern Washington, northern Idaho, and British Columbia. Station open daily 6am-8pm and 1-3am.

Spokane Transit System: W. 1229 Boone Ave. (328-7433). Serves all areas of Spokane, including Eastern Washington University in Cheney. Fare 60¢, ages over 64 and disabled travelers 30¢. Free transfers valid for ½ hr. Coupon booklets available at midday, good for discounts in local shops and restaurants. Operates until 12:15am downtown, 9:15pm in the valley along E. Sprague Ave.

Taxi: Checker Cab, 624-4171. 24 hours. **Yellow Cab,** 624-4321. **A-1 Taxi,** 534-7768.

Car Rental: U-Save Auto Rental, W. 918 3rd St. (455-8018), at Monroe. Cars from $19 per day with 100 free miles plus 20¢ per additional mile. $250 deposit or major credit card required. Must be 21. Open Mon.-Fri. 8am-6pm, Sat. 8am-5pm.

AAA Office: W. 1717 4th (455-3400).

Camping Equipment: White Elephant, N. 1730 Division St. (328-3100) and E. 12614 Sprague (924-3006). Open Mon.-Thurs. and Sat. 9am-6pm, Fri. 9am-9pm. **Outdoor Sportsman,** N. 1602 Division St. (328-1556). Open Mon.-Thurs. 9:30am-6:30pm, Fri. 9:30am-7pm, Sat. 9:30am-6pm, Sun. 11am-5pm. **Mountain Gear,** 2002 W. Division (325-9000). High quality and high prices. Open Mon.-Thurs. and Sat. 9am-6pm, Fri. 9am-9pm, Sun. noon-5pm.

Public Library: W. 906 Main St. (838-3361). Reliable source for historical information, bus schedules, and telephone books. Open Mon.-Tues. and Thurs. 10am-8:30pm, Wed. 1-5:30pm, Fri. (and winter Sat.) 10am-5:30pm.

Events Line: 747-2787. 24-hour recorded information on arts happenings in Spokane.

Laundromat: Ye Olde Wash House Laundry and Dry Cleaners, E. 4224 Sprague (534-9859).

Crisis Hotline: 838-4428. 24 hours.

Drug Crisis Line: 326-9550. 24 hours.

AIDS Hotline: 456-3640.

Mental Health Center: 838-4651.

Youth Help: 624-2868. Helps find accommodations. 24 hours.

Senior Center: W. 1124 Sinto (327-2861).

Pharmacy: Hart and Dilatush, W. 501 Sprague (624-2111). 24 hours.

Ambulance: 328-6161. 24 hours.

Police: 456-2233. 24 hours.

Post Office: W. 904 Riverside (459-0230), at Lincoln. Open Mon.-Fri. 8:30am-5pm. General Delivery ZIP Code: 99210.

Area Code: 509.

Spokane lies 280 miles east of Seattle by I-90. The **Spokane International Airport** is off I-90 southwest of town. Downtown is wedged between I-90 and the Spokane River. Exits 279 to 282 serve the area. Avenues run east-west parallel to the river, streets north-south, and both alternate one-way. The city is divided into north and south by **Sprague Avenue,** east and west by **Division Street.** Downtown is the area north of Sprague and west of Division. Street addresses are listed with the compass point first, the number second, and the street name third (e.g., W. 1200 Division). No one knows why.

Riverfront Park adjoins Spokane Falls in the heart of the heart of the city. Two blocks south of here, at Riverside and Howard St., all Spokane Transit System buses start and finish their runs.

Accommodations and Camping

Don't try to sleep in Riverfront Park; the Spokane police will be mortified. A handful of hotels south of downtown are cheap but sleazy. Most camping areas are at least 20 miles away. The hostel is certainly your best option.

Brown Squirrel Hostel (AYH), W. 1807 Pacific Ave. (838-5968), in Browne's Addition. To be safe, walk along Sprague rather than 1st St. to and from the Greyhound station. About 20 beds fill the 2nd story of a classic 3-level house, convenient to a Safeway and a drug store with old-fashioned fountain service (try the egg cream). The rooms are cozy; before long you'll feel like a member of the manager's family. Just don't use his family phone—use the phone 2 blocks away at the Safeway instead. Officially open 8-10am and 5-10pm, but stop in just about anytime. No curfew. Members $8, nonmembers $11. Linens, towels, and (if necessary) transportation to the airport or bus station provided.

Eastern Washington University (359-7022), 18 miles from Spokane in Cheney. Take bus #24 from Howard and Riverside St. downtown. By car, take I-90 southwest 8 miles to exit 270, then Hwy. 904 south; turn right on Elm St. and continue to 10th. Pleasant dorm rooms, rarely full. Program run by helpful students. Inquire at Morrison Hall in the summer, or Anderson Hall during the school year. Singles $9.70. Doubles $19.40. With student ID singles $7, doubles $14. Linen provided. Open year-round.

Otis Hotel, S. 110 Madison (624-3111), ½-block from the bus station. On a very seedy block, but the rooms are relatively safe. No phones, TV in lobby only. Convenient location and low prices are the main reasons to stay here. Rooms $16. $3 key deposit.

Town Centre Motor Inn, W. 901 1st St. (747-1041), at Lincoln St. in the heart of downtown, 4 blocks from the bus depot. Large, comfortable rooms decorated with garish oil paintings. Some rooms have refrigerators at no extra cost. Complimentary coffee served with the morning paper in the motel office. Pay in Canadian currency to save money—they accept it at par. Singles $28. Doubles $35. Call collect for reservations.

El Rancho Motel, W. 3000 Sunset Blvd. (455-9400). On the edge of town, with easy access to freeway. Take 2nd Ave. west to Maple St., where Sunset cuts diagonally across the intersection. Follow Sunset approximately 15 blocks. Rooms have cable, free coffee, and A/C. Equipped with laundromat, pool, and children's play area. Singles $27.50. Doubles $30.50.

Motel 6, S. 1580 Rustle St. (459-6120), at exit 277 on I-90. In other words, far from downtown. TV and pool. Singles $24. Doubles $30. Call 2-3 weeks in advance for reservations; Lemonheads groupies may crowd the place.

Riverside State Park (456-3964), 6 miles northwest of downtown on Rifle Club Rd., off Hwy. 291 or Nine Mile Rd. Take Division north and turn left on Francis. 101 standard sites in an urban setting. Kitchen and small museum in the park. Shower and bath. Facilities for the disabled. Sites $7.

Mt. Spokane State Park (456-4169), 35 miles northeast of the city. Take U.S. 395 5 miles north to U.S. 2, then go 7 miles north to Hwy. 206, which leads into the park. Popular with winter athletes for its cross-country skiing and snowmobiling trails. From the Vista House, views of 4 states and Canada. 12 sites. Flush toilets, no showers, cold water merely. Sites $7.

Smokey Trail (747-9415), 5 miles southwest of the city. Take U.S. 395 to exit 272. Follow Hallett Rd. east to Mallon Rd., then 1 mile south. Warm up with hot showers and free firewood. Sites $9, RV hookups $10. Open May 15-Sept. 20.

Food

Besides supporting a number of small diners and cafes, Spokane works as a trading center for Eastern Washington's fresh produce. On Wednesdays and Saturdays from May to October, the **Spokane County Market** (456-5512) vends fresh fruit, vegetables, baked goods, and arts and crafts in Riverfront Park. The **Green Bluff Growers Cooperative** is an organization of 20-odd fruit and vegetable farms, 16 miles northwest of town off Day-Mountain Spokane Rd. Many of the farms have "U-pick" arrangements, and nearby are free picnic areas with panoramic views. Peak season for most crops is from August to October. Write Green Bluff Growers, E. 9423 Green Bluff Rd., Colbert 99005, or look for a brochure downtown.

For a variety of interesting cuisine downtown, head to **The Atrium,** on Wale St. near 1st. Ave. **Europa Pizzeria,** one of the restaurants in this small brick building, bakes the best pizzas in town.

Dick's, E. 10 3rd Ave. (747-2481), at Division. Look for the pink panda sign near I-90. Receives an honorable mention in the prestigious *Let's Go: Did You Know?* awards. A takeout burger phenomenon whose fame grows as its prices stay the same. Ridiculously low prices; take the panda's advice to buy by the bagful. Burgers 49¢, slice of pie 35¢, sundaes 51¢. You want more? Soft drinks 31¢, fries 37¢, pints of ice cream 67¢. The list goes on and on. Always crowded but the lines move quickly. Open daily 9am-1:30am.

Auntie's Bookstore and Cafe, W. 313 Riverside (838-0206). Browse through a good selection of books, including extensive collections on regional history, gender studies, and religion. Then write your own sandwich for $2.75 and up. Open Mon.-Sat. 9am-9pm, Sun. noon-5pm.

Knight's Diner, N. 2442 Division (327-5365). Take bus #6. A long red-and-black diner in an old train car. Western down-home cooking and hospitality. Hearty breakfasts and lunches ($2-4). Open Tues.-Sun. 6:30am-2pm.

Cyrus O'Leary's, W. 516 Main St. (624-9000), in the Bennetts Block complex at Howard St. A Spokane legend. Devour delicious food from a creative 25-page menu. Dress in proper attire for the 1890s Wild West atmosphere. Costumed waiting staff serves enormous $6-12 meals. Sandwiches $3-5. Happy hour 4-6pm. Open Mon.-Thurs. 11:30am-11pm, Fri.-Sat. 11:30am-midnight, Sun. 11:30am-10pm.

Thai Cafe, W. 410 Sprague (838-4783). This tiny restaurant adds plenty of spice (or a little, depending upon your preference) to Spokane's otherwise Americanized ethnic fare. Traditional dishes like *pad thai* and *gai pahd* cost only $4-6. Open Mon.-Fri. 11:30am-1:30pm and 5-8:30pm, Sat. 5-8:30pm.

Coyote Cafe, W. 702 3rd Ave. (747-8800). This jazzy Mexican joint has *cerveza* (beer) signs on the walls, cacti in the windows, and $2.16 margaritas all day. Specialties include the coyote *chimichanga* ($6) and *fajitas* ($8). Open Sun.-Thurs. 11am-11pm, Fri.-Sat. 11am-midnight.

Benjamins' Burger Inn (455-6771), in the Parkade Plaza. This popular and convenient alternative to Dick's sells larger, juicer—and more expensive—burgers ($1.55). Festoon your beef with curly fries (55¢), carrot cake (95¢), or a bowl of chili ($1.35). Open Mon.-Fri. 7am-6pm, Sat. 8am-5pm.

Señor Froggy, W. 603 3rd Ave. (624-6209) and N. 1918 Division (328-7280). Makes a valiant attempt at authentic Mexican decor and flavor. Although the frog doesn't truly succeed on either count, it comes close enough considering the price and quick service. *Empanadas* (a kind of turnover with a savory filling) 95¢, meaty tacos 59¢. Open Mon.-Thurs. 10:30am-11pm, Fri.-Sat. 10:30am-midnight, Sun. 10:30am-10pm.

The Great Harvest Bread Co., W. 816 Sprague (624-9370). Fresh bread (3kg loaf $2.15) and moist muffins (70¢). Follow your nose. Open Mon.-Fri. 6am-6pm, Sat. 6am-5pm.

Milford's Fish House and Oyster Bar, N. 719 Monroe (326-7251). Don't be fooled by the dingy neighborhood—this is a first-class establishment. And though it may well sink your budget, the freshest seafood in town will certainly buoy your spirits. Choose from a page-long list of fresh specials ($10-14); each includes a bowl of clam chowder that really hits the spot or a dinner salad with bread and vegetables. Truly worth the extra money. Open Mon. 5-9pm, Tues.-Sat. 5-10pm, Sun. 4-9pm.

Sights and Activities

Spokane has few aspirations to flashy art or high-flown architecture. The city's best attractions are those that concentrate on local history and culture. And Jean-François Lyotard reminds us that in the wake of mid-century catastrophe we cannot aspire past the local. The unusually shaped **Museum of Native American Cultures (MONAC),** E. 200 Cataldo St. (326-4550), a few blocks east of Riverfront Park, stands on a hill to the northeast of downtown, off Division St. The four-story museum houses a collection of Native North and South American art and artifacts. Since the museum is financially strapped, few of the pieces are labeled—a frustration to the scholar, but an opportunity for fanciful conjecture to the casual observer. Of particular interest are the war bonnets and prehistoric Peruvian textiles. (Open Tues.-Sat. 10am-5pm, Sun. 11am-5pm. Admission $3, ages over 65 and students $2, families $7.) Each year, in the last part of February, MONAC holds the **Western Art Show and Auction.** The show is highly selective, large, and well attended.

Local Native American organizations have instituted the **Indian Community Center,** E. 801 2nd (535-0886), as both a social resource for Native Americans and a center for preserving their heritage. The center sponsors traditional dances, and is a good source of information on Native American fairs and powwows in the Northwest. These festivals inspire stick games, dancing, and various concessions. The

Cheney Cowles Memorial Museum, W. 2316 1st Ave. (456-3931), also has exhibits on Native American culture and history, in addition to well-explicated displays on the animals and pioneers of Eastern Washington. One gallery of the museum is also given over to contemporary Northwest art. Every Wednesday at 7:30pm, except during the summer, an undead artist lectures and shows her or his work for free. The **Grace Campbell House** (456-3931) next door is affiliated with the museum, and open to the public. Built in Tudor revival style with a fortune extracted from the Coeur D'Alene gold mines in Idaho, this elegant mansion awakens the high-society life of Spokane's 1890s boom era. (Museum open Tues.-Sat. 10am-5pm, Sun. 2-5pm. Admission $2, senior citizens and students $1. House open Tues.-Sat. 10am-4pm, Sun. 2-5pm. Wed. free.) For more on the arts, contact the **Spokane Arts Department,** fourth floor, City Hall, W. 808 Spokane Falls Blvd. (456-3857).

Riverfront Park, N. 507 Howard St. (456-5512), just north of downtown, is clearly Spokane's center of gravity. If the park hadn't been built for the 1974 World's Fair, the populace would have nowhere to stroll on leisurely weekend afternoons. Ride the arrestingly hand-carved **Looff Carrousel** (open daily 11am-9pm; admission 60¢). The **IMAX Theatre** (456-5511) shows 3-D films on a 5½-story screen. (Admission Tues.-Sun. $3.75, ages under 18 $2.75; Mon. $2, ages under 18 $1.) The **Eastern Washington University Science Center** (456-5507) offers hands-on exhibits on computer technology and astronomy. (Open April 10-May 26 daily 9am-3pm; late May-early Sept. 11am-6pm. Admission $3, senior citizens $2.50, children $2.) One section of the park has all the "kiddie" rides at 60¢ a shot. To dizzy yourself over and over again on the Carrousel, the Krazy Kars, the Dragon Coaster, and the rest, invest in a "Single Day Pass" ($8.50, children $7.50). The park offers ice skating in the winter ($2.50) and often hosts special programs and events.

The Day Pass also includes a free trip aboard the park's **Gondola Skyride Over the Falls,** which, as its name implies, travels from one part of the park over Spokane Falls to the north side of the river. (Open in summer daily 11am-9pm. Without Day Pass, admission $2.50, children $1.50.)

Hard-core Bingsters will be drawn to another *Let's Go: Did You Know?* honorable mention, **Crosby Library,** E. 502 Boone St. (328-4220), at Gonzaga University. Here, the faithful display der Bingle's relics: gold records, awards, photographs, and a piece of his right index finger bone. (Open Mon.-Thurs. 8am-midnight, Fri. 8am-5pm, Sat. 9am-5pm, Sun. 1pm-midnight. Free.)

Spokane's collection of two dozen parks includes tranquil, well-groomed **Finch Arboretum,** W. 3404 Woodland Blvd. Over 2000 species of trees, flowers, and shrubs are available for viewing 24 hours. **Manito Park,** on S. Grand Ave. between 17th and 25th Ave. (856-4331), south of downtown, reunites a flower garden, tennis courts, a romantic duck pond, and the Dr. David Graiser Conservatory, which also houses many tropical and local plant species. (Open daily 8am-dusk; in winter 8am-3:30pm. Free.) Adjacent to Manito Park is the **Nishinomiya Garden,** a lush Japanese garden consecrating the friendship of Spokane and her Japanese sister city, Nishinomiya. (Same hours as Manito Park. Free.)

The state runs two parks near Spokane, and both merit a trip. **Riverside State Park** (456-3964 or 456-2499) embroiders the Spokane River with 7655 acres of volcanic outcroppings, hiking trails (especially good in Deep Creek Canyon), and equestrian trails (horse rental $7 per hr. in nearby Trail Town; 456-8249). The park contains a large area for off-road vehicles; it is prime cross-country ski territory in the winter. Also in the park is the **Spokane House Interpretive Center** (325-4692), site of the first structure built by whites in the Northwest, a fur trading post (1810). The center now traces the history of fur trading in the region. (Free.)

Mount Spokane State Park (456-4169) stands 35 miles to the northeast of the city. An improved, toll-free road extends to the summit. Clear days afford views of the Spokane Valley and the distant peaks of the Rockies and Cascades. Mt. Spokane is a skiing center with free cross-country trails and $15-20 downhill ski packages. The area is also good for hiking, horseback riding (no rentals here), and camping (see Accommodations). The **U.S. Forest Service** (456-2574) has more information on the parks.

Turnbull National Wildlife Refuge (235-4723), 21 miles south of Spokane, is a happy breeding ground for bird species of the Pacific flyway. Take the Four Lakes, Cheney exit off I-90, and go left on Badger Rd. Numerous blinds have been set up for photographing, and lucky visitors may catch a glimpse of trumpeter swans. (Open daily until dusk. Free.)

For a less energetic sporting activity, try betting on the horses at **Playfair** (534-0505), at Altamount and Main. From April 30 to October 20, races are every Wednesday and Friday through Sunday at 1:30pm and/or 6pm. Youngsters can get free practice for the big time at **Last Chance Riding Stables** (624-4646) in **Indian Canyon Park**. From Sunset Blvd., turn right at the sign onto Assembly Rd. (Open in summer daily 9am-dusk.)

Don't leave Spokane without tasting a fine Eastern Washington wine. The **Arbor Crest Cliff House**, N. 4705 Fruithill Rd. (927-9894), offers a tour of a national historical house, a view of the city, and free wine. Tours are given daily from noon-5pm. To get there, take I-90 to the Argonne north exit, travel north on Argonne over the Spokane River, turn right on Upriver Dr., proceed 1 mile, and then bear left onto Fruithill Rd. Take a sharp right at the top of the hill and there you are.

Entertainment

Spokane's more traditional tastes are reflected in the large number of bowling alleys and movie theaters gracing the city. A wide spectrum of live music satisfies aesthetic carnivores. The *Spokane Spokesman-Review's* Friday Weekend section and the *Spokane Chronicle's* Friday Empire section have the hoedown on area happenings. During the summer, the city parks present a free **Out-to-Lunch** series at noon on weekdays at various locations around town. Call 624-1393 or check in the Weekend for schedule information.

Spokane supports two minor league professional sports teams. The **Indians** throw the ball, hit the ball, and catch the ball at N. 602 Havana (535-2922) from June through August. (Tickets $2.50.) The **Chiefs** skate and score at the Coliseum (328-0450) from October through March.

The Spokane Coliseum, N. 1101 Howard St. (456-3204 for information, 327-5558 for tickets). Rock concerts, rodeos, and other special events.

The Opera House, W. 334 Spokane Falls Blvd. (456-6006 for ticket information). Home to the Spokane Ballet and the Spokane Symphony Orchestra (624-1200), this riverside complex also opens its stage to special performances, from rock concerts to chamber music.

Civic Theater, N. 1020 Howard St. (325-2507 for reservations, 325-1413 for information), opposite the Coliseum. Tickets Fri.-Sat. $10, Wed.-Thurs. $8, ages over 64 and students $7.

Spokane Interplayers Ensemble, S. 174 Howard (455-7529). Adds drama to Spokane.

Magic Lantern Theatre, S. 123 Wall St. (838-8276). Fantastic films, from American classics to such foreign features as Wim Wenders's *The Airfeet of Desire. Rocky Horror* and Bruce Lee flicks shown frequently as well. Admission $5, senior citizens $3, students $4.

Henry's Pub, W. 230 Riverside Ave. (624-9828). The place for live rock Wed.-Sat. nights. Cover charge varies from $1-3 depending on the band. Local favorites New Language, Young Brians, and the Cruizers belt their 50s and 60s rock here. Draft beer $1. Open Wed.-Sat. 7pm-2am.

Red Lion Inn Tavern, N. 126 Division St. (624-1934). Behind the shabby exterior is some of Washington's best R&B and rock 'n' roll. Ticket prices range from $7-10. Shows start at 9pm. Happy hour 11:30am-6pm. Open Mon.-Fri. 11am-2am, Sat.-Sun. 4pm-2am.

Bradley GT's, N. 1817 Division (326-7668). Near Gonzaga U, this modest bar serves mostly a younger crowd. Arrive between noon and 5pm for free pool and $1 pitchers of beer. Open Mon.-Sat. noon-2am.

The Onion Bar and Grill, W. 302 Riverside (747-3852). A happening bar with a pool room in the back. Different drink special each night of the week. Dinners under $6, frozen margaritas $3.25. Open Sun.-Thurs. 11:15am-1am, Fri.-Sat. 11:15am-2am.

CJ Timothy's Comedy Underground, W. 525 Spokane Falls Blvd. (456-6565). Patio chairs and umbrellas above ground, but you'll have to descend for the laughs. Stand-up acts nightly (admission $5). Dinner and drink prices are out of sight. Shows Sun.-Thurs. 8:30pm, Fri.-Sat. 8 and 10:30pm.

Seasonal Events

On the first Sunday in May, Riverfront Park hosts its premature, annual **Bloomsday Road Race,** the second biggest race on the West Coast and the highlight of the **Lilac Festival,** a week-long hoopla of car shows, arts fairs, house tours, and Special Olympics. The week culminates in a torch-lit parade. For information on these and other events, contact the Chamber of Commerce. In August, downtown salutes the flag in the **Main Street USA** celebration. The annual **Bach Festival** at the end of January is the highlight in a series of Connoisseur Concerts given at W. 310 5th Ave. (call 747-6443). During the Independence Day weekend, friendly citizens of Spokane celebrate a Lehreresque **Neighbors Day** at Riverfront Park. Events include art fairs, an antique car show, and fireworks at sundown.

Colville

One of the last surviving frontier towns in America, Colville (CALL-ville) serves as the last stop for travelers en route to British Columbia on U.S. 395, as the base camp for forays into the **Colville National Forest,** and as the gateway to Nirvana for disenchanted urban refugees from California (American Dream/American Nightmare).

Colville lies 71 miles north of Spokane on U.S. 395, and 135 miles northeast of Grand Coulee via Hwy. 174, 25, and 20. Hwy. 20 runs east-west through Colville and links up with U.S. 395 just west of the city. One bus per day travels to Colville from the Greyhound terminal in Spokane (one way $9.60).

Colville hosts a rodeo the third weekend in June, but to see more exotic animals head into the forest. Rocky Mountain elk and bighorn sheep follow geefels and gonks and migrate in fall and spring to the shores of **Sullivan Lake,** just east of Colville. Camp on the shores of the lake at **Noisy Creek** from late May to early September. To reach the lake from Colville, migrate 36 miles east on Hwy. 20 and then 4 miles north on Hwy. 31; the campground is 1 mile south of Ione on County Rd. 9345. (Sites $6-8.) Closer to town, you can camp for free at **Douglas Falls.** Take Alladin Rd. (off Hwy. 20 just east of town) until it forks, then follow the left fork 3 miles.

Beaver Lodge, a privately owned campground 10 miles east of Colville on the Little Pend Oreille Lakes, offers an alternative to Colville National Forest. The scenic campground provides tent sites ($6.50), hookups ($9), showers, swimming, and fishing. Log cabins that accommodate four are also available ($28.50). Explore the gorgeous lakes aboard rented boats—rowboats $2 per hour, paddleboats $3.50 per hour, and canoes $2.50 per hour.

In the winter, most adventurers head out of the valleys and into the hills. Colville is conveniently equidistant from two ski resorts: **Forty-Nine Degrees North,** in Chewelah, and **Red Mountain,** in Rossland, BC. Red Mountain has more challenging slopes and a more international clientele. Both resorts charge about the same price: $15 per weekday, $18 per weekend day; students $13 weekdays, $15 weekends. Rent skis in Colville at **Clark's All-Sports,** 557 S. Main (684-5069); complete rental package costs $11-12 per day for downhill equipment and $8 per day for cross-country. (Open Mon.-Sat. 8am-5:30pm, Sun. 8am-3pm.) You can also rent at **Ramble's Sport Shop,** 156 N. Main (684-2391) at similar prices. (Open Mon.-Sat. 8:30am-5pm.)

Nearby **Chewelah** hosts the **Chataqua,** held on the second weekend each July. A sort of state fair for the northeast corner of Washington, the Chataqua brings 50,000 visitors to a town of 2000.

If you must eat, try **Ginny's Cafe,** 825 S. Main (684-3459). You'll have trouble finding a cornier corn dog anywhere ($1.20). (Open Mon.-Sat. 7am-7pm.) **Papa's Place,** 526 S. Main (684-5022), serves pizza and sandwiches ($2.10-3) to a young crowd; Papa cooks breakfast, too. (Open Sun.-Thurs. 7am-10pm, Fri.-Sat. 7am-11pm.) The least expensive hotel in town is the **Downtown Motel,** 369 S. Main (684-2565). Painted concrete blocks enclose the rooms while industrial strength air-conditioners keep them cool. Tractor-pull and monster-truck enthusiasts will appreciate the complimentary ESPN.

In an emergency, call the local **police** at 684-2525. The town's **post office** sits at 204 South Oak St. (684-2241; open Mon.-Fri. 9am-5pm, Sat. 11am-noon), and its **General Delivery ZIP Code** is 99114. The **area code** is 509. To get your bearings, drop in at the helpful **Colville Ranger Station,** 775 S. Main (684-3711; open Mon.-Fri. 7:45am-4:30pm), or at the quaint **Panorama Land, Inc.** office, 380 S. Main (684-2910; open daily 9am-5pm).

WESTERN CANADA

US $1 = CDN $1.18
AUS $1 = CDN $.90
UK £1 = CDN $1.96
NZ $1 = CDN $.66

CDN $1 = US $0.85
CDN $1 = AUS $1.12
CDN $1 = UK £ .52
CDN$1 = NZ $1.51

Prices are given in Canadian dollars, unless otherwise specified.

BRITISH COLUMBIA

Larger than California, Oregon, and Washington combined, British Columbia attracts so many visitors that tourism has become the province's second largest industry (after logging). Although Canada's westernmost province does offer excellent skiing year-round, most visitors come to take advantage of the hot summer sun. They are greeted by happy travel infocentres, in essentially every British Columbian town.

The province's southern third, home to populous Vancouver and Victoria as well as the glamorous lakes of the Okanagan Valley, is easily most popular with tourists. The population thins dramatically in the province's central region, where the thick forests, low mountains, and occasional patches of high desert are deranged only by such supply and transit centers as Prince George and Prince Rupert. Farther north, even these outposts of civilization defer to thick spruce forests, every so often tainted by the touch of the voracious logger or blackened by lightning fires.

Originally claimed for Great Britain by Captain James Cook in 1778, British Columbia retains vestiges of its days under the Union Jack without forgetting its Native American roots. Victoria's populace carries on afternoon tea-time in the finest English tradition, while Native Canadians along the Pacific Coast revive handicrafts once feared to be dying arts. Refugees from across the globe mix freely in Vancouver, and such weathered towns as Barkersville pay homage to the miners and loggers of the late 19th century who desperately wrested their livelihood from the wilderness.

And then there is Nature. More than 6000 uninhabited islands shield the province's coastline from the chilly Pacific waters, while oceanic rivers shelter breeding salmon in the Fraser and Skeena Valleys farther inland. Ice fishing and big-game hunting still rage through 5791 square kilometres of untouched forests, glaciers, and lakes—all protected by National Park regulations. Bicyclists might perpend upon exploring Vancouver Island and the many smaller islands on the eastern side of Vancouver Island. For rafting, try the Fraser River. Provincial parks are well maintained and offer secluded campsites supplying the 3 Ws: wood, water, and washrooms (without showers, unfortunately).

Practical Information

Emergency: 911.

Capital: Victoria.

Visitor Information: Ministry of Tourism and Provincial Secretary, Parliament Bldgs., Victoria V8V 1X4, (604-387-1642). Ask especially for the *Accommodations* guide, which lists

243

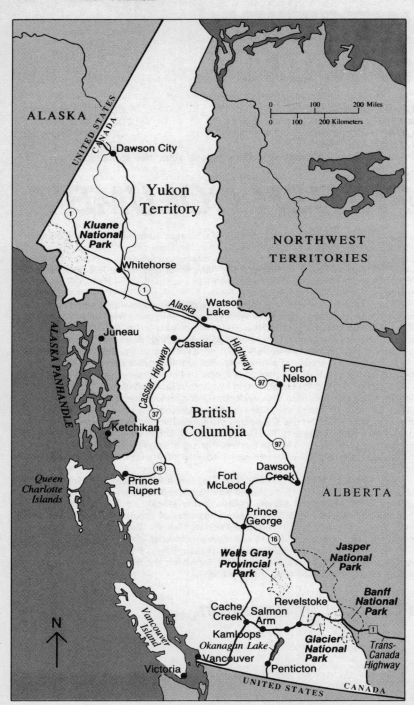

prices and services for virtually every hotel, motel, and campground in the province. Branches in **Seattle,** P.O. Box C-34971, Seattle, WA 98124-1971 (604-387-1642); **Los Angeles,** 2600 Michelson Dr., #1050, Irvine, CA 92715 (714-852-1054); and **San Francisco,** 100 Bush St., #400, San Francisco, CA 94104 (415-981-4780).

Canada Parks Service: Write the Sr. Communications Officer, 220 4th Ave. SE, P.O. Box 2989, Station M, Calgary, AB T2P 3H8, or call **BC Parks** at 604-387-5002.

Time Zone: Mostly Pacific (1 hr. behind Mountain, 2 behind Central, 3 behind Eastern). Small eastern section is Mountain (1 hr. behind Central, 2 behind Eastern).

Traffic Laws: Mandatory seatbelt law.

Postal Abbreviation: BC.

Drinking Age: 19.

Motto: *Splendor sine Occasu* (Splendor without Diminishment).

Year of Royal Naming: 1858, by Queen Victoria.

Area Code: 604.

Travel

British Columbia is Canada's westernmost province, covering over 890,000 square kilometres, bordering four U.S. states (Washington, Idaho, Montana, and Alaska) and three Canadian jurisdictions (Alberta, the Yukon Territory, and the Northwest Territories). Vancouver, on the mainland, can be reached via interstate highway from Seattle; Victoria, on Vancouver Island to the southwest of Vancouver, requires a ferry trip from Anacortes, Port Angeles, Seattle, or the Tsawwassen Terminal near Vancouver. However you travel, get used to thinking in terms of distances with three or four digits.

Road travel throughout the province varies with the immensely diverse terrain. If you decide to take your own vehicle, avoid potential hassles by obtaining a Canadian nonresident interprovince motor vehicle **liability card** from your insurance company before leaving. Border police may turn you away if you are not properly insured. In the south, roads are plentiful and well paved, but farther north, both asphalt and towns seem to have been blown away by the arctic winds. Above Prince George, travel along the two major roads—the Alaska Hwy. and the Cassiar Hwy.—is hindered by stretches of "chip-seal," a cheaper and substantially rougher version of asphalt. Much of British Columbia is served by **Greyhound** (662-3222 in Vancouver).

The new Coquihalla Highway (Hwy. 5, more popularly known as "The Coca-Cola") was completed in 1986 to carry tourists comfortably from Hope, near Vancouver, to Kamloops, a city roughly halfway between Vancouver and Alberta's Banff and Jasper National Parks. The Coquihalla Highway costs $10, eradicating any savings in gas and mileage; enjoy the Fraser River Canyon's scenery via the Trans-Canada Highway instead. The Yellowhead Highway (also Hwy. 5) brings you from Kamloops on to Jasper.

For information about crossing the U.S.-Canada border and for customs regulations, see For International Visitors in the General Introduction.

Vancouver Island

As you go farther north on Vancouver Island, civilization goes elsewhere. This is Canada, after all. Stretching nearly 500km along continental Canada's southwest coast, the island revolves, culturally if not geographically, around the distinctly un-Canadian Victoria, the province's capital since the 1860s. Toasted by frequent sunshine and frosted by Pacific breezes, the city attempts to preserve its popular Victorian charm. Elsewhere, the Native Americans who first walked the northern reaches of the island have left their tradition behind in the locals' respect for nature, love of hiking, and vendetta against fish.

Victoria

The sun may have set on the British empire years ago, but, like a heroic soldier in the Falklands War, Victoria still lives the dream. The 90-minute ferry trip between Vancouver and Victoria imitates an English Channel crossing, and as you step ashore in the Inner Harbour, you will be greeted by double-decker buses, many adorned with British flags. In kilt and sporran, a bagpiper plies his street trade at the corner of the Parliament Buildings, stately stone edifices worthy of Westminster. The ivy-shawled Empress Hotel, also named for the dour queen, gazes regally at its own image in the water. Tea shops are more prevalent than hockey pucks in Victoria—to some, the city practices a sacrilegious subjugation of Canada's number one sport. On warm summer days, the more Anglophilic residents sip their noon teas on the lawns of Tudor-style homes in the suburbs, while downtown, horse-drawn carriages clatter through Bastion Square.

Despite Victoria's refined image, today's citizens are not at all ashamed of the ornery prospectors who swilled beer in front of rowdy brothels on their way to the Cariboo mines during the 1858 gold rush. Hudson's Bay Company moved its western headquarters to the southern tip of Vancouver Island after the site of its former headquarters in Oregon was declared U.S. property. When the Canadian Pacific Railway reached the Pacific Coast, Victoria coaxed an additional stretch across the Strait of Juan de Fuca from Vancouver, and the city stole Vancouver's distinction as Canada's western railroad terminus. In 1869, Victoria was named the capital of British Columbia, partially on the assumption that the promised railroad would cause the city to expand further. The railroad dream was never fully realized, and Victoria did not undergo the adornments of industrialization. Instead of pollution, ugly factory chimneys, and Margaret Thatcher, Victoria has 350,000 well-heeled citizens delighting in the frightfully un-British annual rainfall of only 27 inches.

Practical Information and Orientation

Visitor Information: Tourism Victoria, 812 Wharf St., Victoria V8W 1T3 (382-2127), in the Inner Harbour. Piles of pamphlets that must have decimated entire BC forests. Open daily 9am-8pm; in winter 9am-5pm.

VIA Rail: 450 Pandora St. (383-4324 for departure/arrival info; 800-665-8630 for general info and tickets). Near the Inner Harbour.

Greyhound Depot: 710 Douglas St., at Belleville St., behind the Empress Hotel. **Greyhound** (385-5248), **Pacific Coast Lines (PCL)** (385-4411). PCL buses to Vancouver (every hr. 6am-9pm, $16.50), Seattle (1 per day at 11am, $25), Nanaimo (7 per day 5:15am-7:15pm, $10.50).

BC Ferry: 656-0757 for a recording, 386-3431 for a person. Between Swartz Bay (Victoria) and Tsawwassen (Vancouver) 14 per day 7am-9pm (bike $2.10, car $17, plus $4.75 per person). Between Horseshoe Bay (Vancouver) and Nanaimo 10 per day 7am-9pm, same rates. Take bus #70, fare $1.

Washington State Ferries: 381-1551. From Sidney to Anacortes, WA, via the San Juan Islands: 1 per day in winter, 2 in summer. Buy your ticket straight through to Anacortes and stop over in the San Juans for as long as you like; you can rejoin the ferry at any point as long as you continue traveling eastward. Passengers $7.50; car and driver $35; ages over 64 and 5-11 $4; under 5 free. Take bus #70, fare $1.

BC Stena Line: 390 Belleville St. (386-1124; off-season 388-7397). Round-trip cruises from Pier 48 in Seattle, WA to Victoria aboard the ritzy *Princess Marguerite* or *Vancouver Island Princess* (in summer 2 per day, $29, $39 round-trip; in winter 1 per day for $8 less).

Black Ball Transport: 430 Belleville St. (386-2202). Connects Victoria with Port Angeles, WA. Mid-May to late Sept. 4 per day; early Oct.-late Nov. and mid-March to mid-May 2 per day. Fare $6.80, car and driver $27.80, ages 5-11 $3.40.

Victoria Regional Transit: 382-6161.

Car Rental: A.D.A. Rent-A-Used-Car, 752 Caledonia Ave. (388-6230). $13 per day plus 8¢ per km. Must be 21. $250 deposit for 1 week rental, $150 for 1 day; confirmation of employment requested. Open Mon.-Fri. 8am-5:30pm, Sat. 8am-8pm. **Budget Discount Car Rentals,** 727 Courtney St. (388-7874). Not to be confused with the far more expensive Budget Rent-A-Car on the same block. Must be 21 with a major credit card. Used cars in excellent condition from $13 per day plus 10¢ per km. Open daily 7:30am-7pm.

Canadian Automobile Association: 382-8171. Full benefits for AAA members.

Taxi: Victoria Taxi, 383-7111. **Westwind,** 474-4747.

Bike Rental: Explore Victoria, 1007 Langley St. (381-2453; 382-9928 off-season). 18-speed mountain bikes $5 per hr., $15 for 24 hours. $20 deposit per bike. Open daily 9am-6pm. **Harbour Scooters,** 1223 Wharf St. (385-2314). 18-speed mountain bikes $18 per day. Open daily 9am-6pm.

Scooter Rentals: Harbour Scooters (see above). $25 per day, with credit card or $25 deposit.

Camping Supplies and Rentals: Jeune Brothers, 570 Johnson St. (386-8778). 2-person tent $15 for 3 days, $23 per week. Open Mon.-Sat. 9:30am-5:30pm, Sun. 11am-5pm.

Jazz Hotline: 628-5255.

Laundromat: 812 Wharf St., 1 floor below Tourism Victoria. Also has pay showers.

Lockers: at bus depot, 710 Douglas St. 25¢ for 24 hours.

Crisis Line: 386-6323.

Rape Crisis: 383-3232. Open 24 hours.

Gay and Lesbian Information: 370-1144.

Poison Control: 595-9211. Open 24 hours.

Pharmacy: London Drugs, 900 Yates St. (381-1113), at Vancouver, in the Wilson Centre. Open Mon.-Sat. 9am-10pm, Sun. 10am-6pm.

Police/Fire/Ambulance: 911.

Post Office: E Station, 1230 Government St. (388-3575), at Yates. Open Mon.-Fri. 8:30am-5pm. Postal Code: V8W 2L9.

Area Code: 604.

On Vancouver Island's southern tip, Victoria is connected by ferry and bus to many cities in British Columbia and Washington (see Practical Information above). The city of Victoria surrounds the Inner Harbour; **Government Street** and **Douglas Street** are the main north-south thoroughfares. Traditional tourist attractions crowd this area, and locals are few and far between. Residential neighborhoods form a semicircle around the Inner Harbour, the more popular and wealthy toward the beaches in the east. **Victoria Regional Transit** (382-6161) serves the whole city seven days per week, with major bus connections at the corner of Douglas and Yates St. downtown. Travel in the single-zone area costs 85¢, multi-zone (north to Sidney and the Butchart Gardens) $1. Daily passes for unlimited single-zone travel are available at the visitors center and 7-11s for $3 (ages over 65 and under 12 $2). Transit maps and a riders' guide are available free from Tourism Victoria (see Practical Information).

Accommodations

Victoria Youth Hostel (IYHF), 516 Yates St., Victoria V8W 1K8 (385-4511), at Wharf St. downtown. Big, modern, and spotless. Extensive kitchen facilities. 102 beds. Two family rooms with 4 beds each. Open 7:30-10am and 4pm-midnight. Members $10, nonmembers $15.

University of Victoria (721-8395), 20 min. northeast of the Inner Harbour by bus; take #7 or 14. Private rooms with shared baths. Coin-operated laundry machines. Register in the Housing Office, near the Coffee Gardens entrance that faces Ring Rd. Open 7:30am-midnight. Singles $19.75. Doubles $32. Reservations advisable. Open May-Aug.

Salvation Army Men's Hostel, 525 Johnson St. (384-3396), at Wharf St. Men only. Modern, immaculate, and well run. Dorms open daily at 4pm on a first-come, first-slept basis. Strict 11pm curfew; ask for a late pass. Dorm beds $6, with meals $9.50. Private room $10, with meals $13.50.

YWCA, 880 Courtney St. (386-7511), within easy walking distance of downtown. Women only. Heated pool and private rooms with shared baths. Check-in 11am-6pm. Check-out 6-11am. Singles $21. Doubles $34.

Battery Street Guest House, 670 Battery St. (385-4632), 1 block in from the ocean between Douglas and Government St. Fluent Dutch spoken in this spacious home. Non-smokers only. Singles from $25. Doubles from $40.

Cherry Bank Hotel, 825 Burdett Ave. (385-5380), at Quadra St., 2 blocks from the visitors center. 90-year-old B&B, very traditional. Spotless rooms along winding corridors. *Trivial Pursuit* played incessantly in the lounge—they even advertise it outside. Singles from $34.50. Doubles from $41.

James Bay Inn, 270 Government St. (384-7151), at Toronto St., just 2 blocks south of the Parliament Buildings. Near everything, but quiet and relatively inexpensive nonetheless. The rooms are light and airy. TV, soft beds. Singles $31 with shared bath. Doubles $40, with private bath $52. Reservations necessary July-Sept.

Camping

The few grounds on the city perimeter cater largely to RV drivers who are willing to pay dearly. Be forewarned that many campgrounds fill up in July and August; reservations are wise.

McDonald Park (655-9020), less than 3km south of the Swartz Bay Ferry Terminal, 30km north of downtown on Hwy. 17. Not even slightly rural, no showers, and no beach access. Government-run. 30 tent and RV sites ($6).

Thetis Lake Campground, 1938 Trans-Canada Hwy. (478-3845), 10km north of the city center. Serves traffic entering Victoria from northern Vancouver Island. Sites are peaceful and removed, maybe too removed—it's a long walk to the bathroom. Metered showers and a laundromat. Sites $9, plus 50¢ per person. Full hookups $12.

Fort Victoria Camping, 127 Burnett (479-8112), 7km NW of downtown off the Trans-Canada Hwy. Free hot showers. Laundromat. Sites $12.50, full hookups $15.50.

Goldstream Park, 2930 Trans-Canada Hwy. (387-4363). Government-run, set in a deeply forested area along a river, 20km northwest of Victoria. Great short hiking trails, swimming, and fishing. In November, the river is crowded with salmon heading to their birthplace. Flush toilets and firewood available. 150 gorgeous (albeit gravelly) sites. The nearby **Freeman King Visitor Centre** relates the history of the area from glaciers to the welfare state. Walks are led by naturalists; there is also a self-guided nature trail. (Centre open in summer daily 8:30am-4:30pm; in winter by appointment only.) Sites $10.

Weir's Beach Resort, 5191 William Head Rd. (478-3323), 24km west on Hwy. 14. You pay for the great location on a sandy beach. Metered showers and a swimming pool. Sites $12, full hookups $16.

French Beach, farther west on Hwy. 14, nearly 50km out. Right on the water, the park has 70 sites with pit toilets, swimming, and hiking trails. No showers. Sites $7.

Food

Victoria's predilection for anachronisms is perhaps best evidenced by its eating habits. Victorians actually do take tea—some only on occasion, others every day. Other foods exist, of course, but to indulge in the neo-romanticism of the city, you must participate in the ceremony at least once. Residents of the U.S. should remember not to embarrass themselves by asking for lemon with their tea—milk *only,* please.

Contrasting with the old-world charm of tea shops, a Californian wave of chic sidewalk cafes, bagel delis, and frozen yogurt parlors crashes between Wharf and Government St. If you have kitchen facilities and don't feel like brewing tea, head down to **Fisherman's Wharf,** 4 blocks west at the corner of Harbour and Government St., between Superior and St. Lawrence Streets. On summer mornings, you can buy the day's catch straight off the boats. The **Green Machine,** at Douglas and 4th St. (382-5108), sells fresh produce.

The Blethering Place, 2250 Oak Bay Ave. (598-1413), at Monterey St. in upright Oak Bay. "Blether" is Scottish for "talk volubly and senselessly"—a fact of little relevance for this superb tearoom frequented by sensible, hushed Oak Bay residents. Afternoon tea served with scones, Devonshire cream tarts, English trifle, muffins, and sandwiches all baked on the premises ($5.50). Steak and kidney pie at lunch for $6. Dinners $10. Open daily 8am-10pm.

Floyd and Floyd's Flying Rhino Diner, 1219 Wharf St. (381-5331), just down the street from Tourism BC and Bastion Sq. The vegetarian sandwiches ($5), nut burgers, and homemade soups here are good, and it's the only place in town with as many as 24 freshly brewed herbal teas. Open Mon.-Fri. 8am-8pm, Sat. 10am-6pm, Sun. 10am-4pm.

Goodies, 1005 Broad St., 2nd floor (382-2124), between Broughton and Fort. Build your own omelette for $4.45 plus 65¢ per ingredient, or choose from a list of misleadingly named sandwiches ($5-7). Tex-Mex dinners $8. Breakfast served until 3:30pm, $1 discount on omelettes Mon.-Fri. 7-9:30am. Open daily 7am-9pm.

Lin Heung, 626 Fisgard St. (385-1632), in Chinatown, just across from the police station. Victorians wait in line for pork buns straight from the oven. The seafood is fresh and plentiful. Open Wed.-Mon. 11am-9pm.

Saigon Cafe, 1692 Douglas St., at Fisgard. Try the prawn and pork soup ($4.10) or chicken curry with rice noodles ($4.50) in the fast-food-like setting. Open Mon.-Sat. 11am-8pm.

Eugene's, 1280 Broad St. (381-5456), just up the street. Greek synth-pop and souvlaki. Vegetarian souvlaki $2.50, dinners $5. Eugene claims that you can "call when you leave and it will be ready on your arrival." Ring from a pay phone next door and freak him out. Open Mon.-Fri. 8am-10pm, Sat. 10am-9pm.

Las Flores, 536 Yates St. (386-6313), a steroid-free Olympian's stride from the hostel. Filling burrito/enchilada combos for $8. Loud sound system reveals striking similarities between Mexican top-40 and the stuff they play over at Eugene's.

Scott's Restaurant, 650 Yates St. (382-1289), at Douglas St. Real diner feel; you just *know* they serve a mean chicken à la king. "Breakfast 222" (2 hotcakes, 2 eggs, 2 sausages) for $3.75. Daily dinner specials a good bet ($4.85-6). Open 24 hours.

Sorrento Cafe and Deli, 636 Yates St. (381-3132). Another of the many cheap establishments along Yates St. House-special pizza easily feeds two for $11.25, or acquire a large slice for $2. Open Mon.-Sat. 7:30am-11pm, Sun. 3-10pm.

James Bay Tearoom, 332 Menzies St. (382-8282), just behind the Parliament Buildings at Superior St. Crowded with silly pictures of the royal family and memorabilia from Charles and Diana's wedding. Excellent afternoon tea Mon.-Sat. 1-5pm. Sunday high tea 2-5pm. Reservations recommended but not essential. For lunch—if you're daring—there's a $4.75 Welsh rarebit, for dinner a $9 roast beef and Yorkshire pudding. Open Mon.-Sat. 7am-9pm, Sun. 8am-9pm.

Willow's Galley, 2559 Estevan St. (598-2711), at Willow's Beach in Oak Bay, 6km east of the Inner Harbour. Take bus #1. Best $3 burger in town with "chips" ($1.25) wrapped in newspaper. Blueberry yogurt and vanilla ice cream combo cone $1. Eat on the lovely beach nearby. Open Tues.-Sat. 11am-7pm, Sun. noon-7pm.

Sights and Activities

Victoria is a small city; you can wander the Inner Harbour, watch the boats come in, and take in many of the city's main attractions—on foot! The elegant residential neighborhoods and the city's parks and beaches, farther out, are accessible by both car and public transportation.

The first stop for every visitor should be the **Royal British Columbian Museum,** 675 Belleville St. (387-3014 for a tape, 387-3701 for a person). Considered by most to be the best museum in Canada, it chronicles the geological, biological, and cultural histories of the province and displays detailed exhibits on logging, mining, and fishing. The extensive exhibits of Native American art, culture, and history include full-scale replicas of various forms of shelter used centuries ago. (Open daily 9:30am-7pm; Oct.-April 10am-5:30pm. Admission $5; senior citizens, disabled people, students with ID, and ages 13-18 $3; ages 6-12 $1. Free Mon. Oct.-April.) Fascinating free films about British Columbia's heritage run in the summer from 11am to 3:30pm in the museum's Newcombe Theatre. Behind the museum, **Thunderbird Park** is a striking bevy of totems and longhouses, backed by the intricate towers of the Empress Hotel.

Also on the grounds of the museum is **Helmcken House,** a Heritage Conservation building, part of which dates from 1852. Originally the home of Dr. John Helmcken, the medic for Fort Victoria, the house still contains many of the family's furnishings and displays some of the doctor's medical instruments. Needlework and paintings in the house were done by members of the family's first Canadian generation. (Open Wed.-Sun. 10am-4pm. Free.)

Across the street from the front of the museum are the imposing **Parliament Buildings,** 501 Belleville St. (387-6121), home to the province's government since 1859. The delightfully gaudy rococo ornamentation inside is plated with gold and aluminum. It seems the architect who won the competition for the buildings' design prevaricated on his entry form, claiming to be a partner in a prestigious firm. Free tours leave from the main steps daily 9am-5pm, departing every 20 minutes in summer, every hour in winter. If you ask your guide to explain the *exact* relationship between Canada and the British monarchy, she will become visibly flustered and slip out of her ever-so-slight English accent.

Avoid the tourist-trap attractions around the Inner Harbour unless you want to pay $5 to view our trapped, scaled friends at the **Undersea Gardens,** or to see adults swoon at the sight of a fascimile of the Prince of Wales at the **Royal London Wax Museum.** The **Classic Car Museum** with crown jewel replicas and fine china, **Miniature World,** and **Sealand** are also best left for those who have money to burn.

Four blocks north along Wharf St. lies **Bastion Square,** where the much-touted 19th-century buildings exhibit a rather uninteresting gray stolidity. The back alleys and walkways make excellent exploring territory, however. In summer, street musicians perform in the square. The **Maritime Museum,** 28 Bastion Sq. (385-4222), houses ship models, nautical instruments, and a 13m Native American canoe that left from Victoria in 1901 for a daring (but ultimately unsuccessful) trip around the world. (Open Mon.-Sat. 10am-4pm, Sun. noon-4pm. Admission $4, senior citizens $3, students $1, ages under 6 free.)

Around the corner on Wharf St. is the **Emily Carr Gallery,** 1107 Wharf St. (387-3080). Carr was a respected BC artist who painted at the beginning of the century. Her originality lay in her synthesis of British landscape conventions and Native American style. This collection includes many of her paintings of Native totems and lifestyles, conscious attempts to preserve what she saw as "art treasures of a passing race." Also on display are photographs and manuscripts. Free films on her life and work show at 2:30pm. (Open Mon.-Sat. 10am-5pm. Free.)

North on Fisgard St., the Government St. entrance to the now-tiny **Chinatown** is marked by the large "Gate of Harmonious Interest." A hundred years ago, Victoria's Chinatown covered a great deal of this region. Today, the area is just as tailored as the rest of the city. Still, the great restaurants and inexpensive trinket shops make Chinatown a rewarding place to spend an hour or so.

South of the Inner Harbour, **Beacon Hill Park** has arresting views over the Strait of Juan de Fuca. Take bus #5. The park's flower gardens, 350-year-old garry oaks, and network of paths, make for a perfect picnic spot.

East of the Inner Harbour, **Craigdarroch Castle,** 1050 Joan Crescent (592-5323), embodies Victoria's wealth. Take bus #11 or 14. The house was built in 1890 by Robert Dunsmuir, a BC coal and railroad tycoon, in order to tempt his wife away from their native Scotland. His former home is packed with Victoriana, and the interior detail is impressive. The tower has a mosaic floor and the dining room a built-in oak sideboard. (Open daily 9am-7:30pm; in winter 10am-5pm. Admission $3, senior citizens and students $2.50.)

Nearby, the **Art Gallery of Greater Victoria,** 1040 Moss St. (384-4101), has a fine contemporary collection, including the works of many Asian-Canadian artists. Take bus #10, 11, or 14. (Open Mon.-Sat. 10am-5pm, Thurs. until 9pm, Sun. 1-5pm. Admission $3, senior citizens and students $1.50, ages under 12 free.) Stay on bus #11 out to Oak Bay Ave. and stop at Blethering Place for tea (see Food), or continue out to **Willow's Beach,** along Beach Dr., a somewhat rocky spot to sit in the sunshine. Windsurfing is popular in the protected bay; equipment can usually be rented from trucks along the beach for about $10 per hour.

Heading in the opposite direction from the Inner Harbour, take Bay St. west off Government and stop just before crossing the Point Ellice Bridge at the **Point Ellice House,** 2616 Pleasant St. (385-5923). Take bus #14. Understood? Tall trees shelter the house from the depressed industrial area around it. Another Heritage House, the 1861 Point Ellice is decorated exactly as if the elitist oppressor residents had just stepped out for a spot of croquet. The dining table is set, the chess set is laid out in the drawing room, and cast-iron pots and period kitchen utensils are strewn about the kitchen. Guided tours are provided. (Open July-Sept. 5 Thurs.-Mon. 10am-5pm. Free.)

Across the bridge, you'll find **Craigflower Heritage Site,** at the corner of Craigflower and Admirals Rd. (387-3067), a complex of historical buildings on a farm built by Hudson's Bay Company in the 1850s. Take bus #14. Craigflower is more rustic than Point Ellice, though the kitchen is equipped with all the Cuisinart equivalents of its day. (Open Wed.-Sun. 10am-3:45pm. Free.) At **Fort Rodd Hill National Historic Park,** on Ocean Blvd. (388-1601), off Hwy. 1A, old defense batteries and **Fisgard Lighthouse,** the first of Canada's west-coast beacons, compete for attention with excellent views of the strait. Take bus #50 or 61 to Western Exchange, transfer to #60, get off at the end of Belmont St., and walk along the path to the park. There's no service on evenings, Sundays, or holidays. (Park open daily 8am-sunset.)

Almost worth the exorbitant entrance fee are the stunning **Butchart Gardens,** 800 Benvennto, 22km north of Victoria (652-5256 for a recording, 652-4422 for a person Mon.-Fri. 9am-5pm). Begun by Jennie Butchart in 1904 in an attempt to reclaim the wasteland that was her husband's quarry and cement plant, the gardens are a maze of pools and fountains. Rose, Japanese, and Italian gardens cover 50 acres in a blaze of colors. From mid-May through September, the whole area is lit at dusk, and the gardens, still administered by the Butchart family, host variety shows and cartoons. Saturday nights in July and August, the skies shimmer with fireworks displays. Seventy thousand Christmas lights compensate for the lack of vegetation in December. Take bus #74. Motorists should consider an approach to Butchart Gardens via the **Scenic Marine Drive,** following the coastline along Dalles and other roads for a 45-minute ride. The route passes through sedate suburban neighborhoods and offers a memorable view of the Olympic Mountains across the Strait of Juan de Fuca. (Gardens open May-June and Sept. 9am-9pm; July-Aug. 9am-11pm; March-April and Oct. 9am-5pm; Jan.-Feb. and Nov. 9am-4pm; Dec. daily 9am-8pm. Admission in summer $8.50, ages 13-17 $4, ages 5-12 $1; otherwise, prices vary with the number of flowers in bloom.)

Entertainment and Seasonal Events

Several professional theaters and clubs in Victoria offer live entertainment, mostly on weekends. Pick up a copy of *Monday Magazine,* the free news and entertainment weekly, for a complete listing of evening activities. Jazz, blues, country, rock, and folk are all heard from.

The **Victoria Symphony Society,** 846 Broughton St. (385-6515), performs regularly under conductor Peter McCoppin, and the **University of Victoria Auditorium,** Finnerty Rd. (721-8480), plays home stage to a variety of student productions. The

Pacific Opera performs at the McPherson Playhouse, 3 Centennial Sq. (386-6121), at the corner of Pandora and Government St. During the summer, they undertake a popular musical comedy series. Keep in mind, as well, that on Tuesdays movies throughout Victoria cost a mere $3.50 (rather than the usual $7).

> **Harpo's Cabaret,** 15 Bastion Sq. (385-5333), at Wharf St. Specializes in garage rock and reggae but occasionally sells out to classic rock 'n' roll. Open Mon.-Sat. 9pm-2am; cover around $5.

> **The Forge,** 919 Douglas St. (383-7137), at Courtney, in the Strathcona Hotel. "Don't admit anyone over 25" is the rule here. Hardcore and speed metal bands. Our dear Queen would have been shocked. Open Mon. and Fri.-Sat. 7:30pm-2am, Tues.-Thurs. 8pm-2am.

> **Rumors,** 1325 Government St. (385-0566). Gay and lesbian clientele; drinking and dancing. Open Mon.-Sat. 9pm-3am.

The **Folkfest** in late June celebrates Canada's birthday (July 1) and the country's "unity in diversity" with performances by politically correct and culturally diverse musicians. The **JazzFest,** sponsored by the Victoria Jazz Society (381-4042), also occurs around this date. The **Classic Boat Festival** is held Labor Day weekend and displays pre-1955 wooden boats in the Inner Harbour. Free entertainment accompanies the show. Contact the visitor and convention bureau (382-2127) for more information on all Inner Harbour events.

Near Victoria

Victoria is the staging area for any number of excursions into the undeveloped areas of Vancouver Island. Roads on the southeastern part of the island are the most heavily trafficked, and are therefore the best hitching areas; public transportation is restricted to the larger towns and cities. Vancouver Island's population clusters near Victoria and along the eastern coast, facing the Georgia Strait and the mainland. The island's scalloped fringe was gouged out by glaciers moving down from the mountains. Mining once attracted many settlers but has since been replaced by logging. The fishing industry thrives; some of the world's largest salmon have been caught here.

Excellent beaches line the southwestern corner of the island. Farther north on the west coast, ancient fjords and mountains make this side inaccessible. West of Victoria on Hwy. 14 lies the town of **Sooke,** whose famous **All Sooke Day,** held in mid-July, draws loggers from the whole island to compete in logging events. The **Sooke Region Museum,** on Hwy. 14 (642-6351), just beyond the Sooke River Bridge, delivers an excellent history of the area. A film is shown regularly on the salmon fish traps that were an important part of the island's culture and economy until the 1950s. Take bus #50 to the Western Exchange and transfer to #61. (Open daily 10am-6pm; Oct.-April 10am-5pm. Free.)

North of Sooke are some of the handsomest beaches on the southern island. Hwy. 14 continues along the coast to **Port Renfrew,** at the southeastern end of the **West Coast Trail.**

Pacific Rim National Park

The eclectic mixture of terrain comprising Pacific Rim National Park seems united by name only. The three units of land and sea that form the park are each separated from the others by several kilometres. Taken as a whole these three regions present an astonishing variety of wilderness. **Long Beach** offers broad vistas of Sitka spruce and Western red cedar near a beach over 20km long. Its gentle trails contrast sharply with those found on the **West Coast Trail,** hewn into the wilderness back in 1907 for the sake of shipwrecked sailors; today, Gortex-clad hikers struggle across its craggy length in six to eight days. Separating the landlubbers from the old salts are the **Broken Group Islands** in Barkley Sound, accessible only to boaters and kayakers.

Gray whales commute past the park each spring; at that time, you should manage to see at least one of the 20,000 processing offshore. Behold also the less imposing forms of wildlife: sea lions, black-tailed deer, black bears. Bring a poncho, however; even the mosquitoes here wear raincoats.

Practical Information

Visitor Information: Park Information Centre (726-4212), 3km into the Long Beach unit on Hwy. 4. Offers trail maps, interpretive information, and helpful hints of all kinds. Detailed information on the West Coast Trail is available and should certainly be read by would-be hikers. Also available by writing The Superintendent, Pacific Rim National Park, P.O. Box 280, Ucluelet, BC V0R 3A0. Open mid-March to mid-Oct. daily 8am-6pm. **West Coast Trail Information Centre** (728-3234), in Pachena Bay, 5km SE of Bamfield, at the NW terminus of the West Coast Trail. Offers information on current trail conditions. Open mid-May to Sept. daily 9am-5pm. **Port Renfrew Information Centre** (647-5434), at the southeast terminus of the West Coast Trail. Open mid-May to Sept. daily 9am-5pm. **Travel Infocentre**, 351 Campbell St., Tofino (725-3414).

Ferry: Alberni Marine Transportation, Inc., P.O. Box 188, Port Alberni, V9Y 7M7 (723-8313). Operates the *M.V. Lady Rose* year-round to Bamfield (3 per week, $13, round-trip $25) and Ucluelet (3 per week, $16, round-trip $32).

Hospital: 261 Neill St., Tofino (725-3212).

Coast Guard: 725-3231.

Emergency: RCMP (725-3242), in Tofino.

Area Code: 604.

The small but increasingly touristic communities of **Tofino** and **Ucluelet** act as bookends for the Long Beach unit, just as **Bamfield** and **Port Renfrew** bracket the West Coast Trail unit. Highway 4 connects Long Beach with **Port Alberni,** sometimes thought of as the used-car dealership capital of Canada. A humble dirt road ties Port Alberni to Bamfield; your vehicle would prefer that you billet it somewhere, and take the passenger-only ferry instead. An indispensable addition to any park user's equipment is *The Pacific Rim Explorer* by Bruce Obee (Whitecap Books, $10); you should at least glance at the copy in the park information centre (see Practical Information) before exploring the wilds.

Accommodations and Camping

Tin Wis Guest House (725-3402), on MacKenzie Beach, 2km south of Tofino (725-3402). Small but clean rooms with bunk beds. $15 for a room with two beds without bedding, $20 with bedding. Reservations necessary in July.

Park Place Bed and Breakfast, 341 Park St. (725-3477). Friendly proprietor offers doubles for $35 and $45, with little apparent difference between them. Reservations absolutely necessary.

Green Point Campground (726-4245), 10km north of the park information centre. The 94 sites, equipped with hot water, flush toilets, and fireplaces, swarm with campers and mosquitoes in July and Aug. Ranger-led programs nightly. Lines form at 7am. Sites mid-June to Aug. $10.50, Sept.-March $5, April to mid-June $8.50.

Schooner Campground, at the northern end of Long Beach. A kilometre-long trail drastically reduces demand for this backpacker's Valhalla, supplied with cold water and outhouses. Unfortunately, high tides threaten the grounds every other week during the winter. Sites $5.

Ucluelet Campground, at Ucluelet Harbor (726-4355). Showers and toilets, with prices to show for it. $14 per site, electricity $2, water $1, sewer $1.

Food

Long Beach Fish 'n' Chowder, 921 Campbell St. (725-3244), outside Tofino. No aspirations to elegance, but plenty of mariners' paraphernalia on the wall to keep you entertained while you wait for the clam chowder ($2.25). Three pieces of French toast $4.20. Open Mon.-Thurs. 8am-3pm, Fri.-Sun. 8am-7pm.

Alleyway Cafe, at Campbell and 1st (725-3105), in Tofino. Small, clean, and colorful. Consume a clamburger ($5) or the unique taco-in-a-bowl ($4) while marveling at the inflatable cacti that line the windows. Open Sun.-Thurs. 10am-8pm, Fri.-Sat. 10am-9pm.

Common Loaf Bake Shop, 131 1st St. (725-3915), in Tofino. Raise your consciousness with a chocolate chunk cookie (60¢) or the ever-radicalizing coffee date-nut bread (70¢) and help the locals plan their next anti-logging protest. Open Mon.-Sat. 8am-8pm, Sun. 8am-7pm.

The Gray Whale, 1596 Peninsula St. (726-7336), in Ucluelet. Polish off a pizza sub ($2.49) with a blue bubble gum milkshake ($2). Open daily 11am-8pm.

Sights and Activities

Whale watching is the premier outdoor activity on Long Beach from mid-March to mid-April. Local mariners will gladly take you on a three-hour ride to observe the grays closely (about $30). Smooth rides in large boats are available, but the real thrill-seekers venture out in **zodiacs,** hard-bottomed inflatable rafts with massive outboard motors that ride the swells at 30 knots.

Educational programs run every night at **Green Point Campground** (726-4245), 15km south of Tofino. Park officials often lead morning beach-exploration trips, pointing out all sorts of bizarre tide pool life forms. **Radar Hill,** a few km north of Green Point, is connected to the highway by a short paved road and is an excellent lookout point. Learn about the indigenous wildlife at the newly opened **Wickaninnish Centre** (726-4212), 3km off Hwy. 4 just past the park entrance. (Open daily mid-May to Labor Day. Free.)

Most visitors take advantage of the park's magnificent **hiking trails.** Pick up a *Hiker's Guide* for the Long Beach unit at the visitors center for a list of nine hikes ranging from 100m to 5km in length. When the rain finally overwhelms you, seek refuge in the Native American art galleries in Ucluelet and Tofino. Ucluelet's **Du Quah Gallery,** 1971 Peninsula Rd. (726-7223) is more modest than Tofino's **Eagle Aerie Gallery,** 350 Campbell St. (725-4412), which protects unusual and striking paintings behind $17,000 carved wooden doors. **Second Circle Native Arts and Museum,** Campbell St at 3rd St., contains a small but varied collection of artifacts and handicrafts. (Open daily 10am-6pm. Free.)

Nanaimo

Nanaimo's 50,000 inhabitants are perhaps the most amiable folk on Vancouver Island. When the coal industry floundered after WWII, BC's first settlement quickly shifted its focus to logging and fishing. As logging turned to pulp throughout the province, Nanaimo shifted to tourism as its prime source of revenue. The combination of affable, outgoing people, easy access by car or ferry, and a slow-paced, relaxing atmosphere has drawn vacationers (especially anglers) from all parts of the continent. The community's citizens have immigrated from lands as varied as England, China, Finland, and Poland, but they are now bound together by their willingness to flash welcoming smiles and show off their city to anyone who drives, hikes, or sails by.

Practical Information and Orientation

Visitor Information: Travel Infocentre, 266 Bryden St. (754-8474), on the Trans-Canada Hwy., just northwest of downtown. Plenty of information on all of Vancouver Island. Call ahead for accommodation referrals. Open daily 8am-7pm.

BC Ferry: 680 Trans-Canada Hwy., Nanaimo V9S 5R1 (753-6626 for recorded info, 753-1261 for a person). To Vancouver 10 per day 7am-9pm (passenger $4.75, car and driver $21.75). Ferries leave from terminal at the northern end of Stewart Ave. (Take bus #2.) Check-in 15 min. before departure.

Island Coach Lines: Comox and Terminal (753-4371), behind Tally Ho Island Inns. To Victoria (6 per day, one way $10.50), Port Hardy (2 per day, one way $45), and Port Alberni (3 per day, one way $7.50, with connecting service to Tofino and Ucluelet).

Car Rental: Rent-A-Wreck, 41 Nicol St. (753-6461). Used cars start at $20 per day plus 11¢ per km. 50 free km per day. Must be 21 with a major credit card. Open Mon.-Sat. 8am-6pm, Sun. 10am-4pm.

Bus Information: 390-4531.

Crisis: 754-4447.

Youth Crisis: 754-4448.

Hospital: 1200 Dufferin Crescent (754-2141). Open 24 hours.

Emergency: Police, 753-2212. **Ambulance,** 758-8181.

Post Office: 60 Front St., at Church St. Open Mon.-Fri. 8:30am-5pm. Postal Code: V9R 5J9.

Area Code: 604.

Nanaimo lies on the eastern coast of Vancouver Island, 111km north of Victoria on the Trans-Canada Hwy., 391km south of Port Hardy via Hwy. 19. Both highways meet downtown at the waterfront and become the major roads in town. The ferry terminal is 2km north of the junction on Stewart Ave.

Ten bus routes serve the area, although almost everything is within walking distance of downtown. Fare is 65¢ (exact change) or $1.80 for a day pass.

Accommodations

Nicol St. Mini-Hostel (IYHF), 65 Nicol St. (753-1188), 7 blocks SE of the bus depot. Take bus #7. Ten comfy beds. Friendly management, friendly cat, and a friendly world map with pins showing hometowns of guests. Registration 4-11pm. Members $10, nonmembers $12. Laundry facilities $1.50. Open May-Sept. 15.

Thomson Hostel (IYHF), 1660 Cedar Hwy. (722-2251), 10km south of Nanaimo. Take bus #11, or free pickup at bus depot at 9pm. Accommodates 12 in 4 bedrooms, plus camping space. Kitchen facilities. Ping-pong table, billiards, and piano. Register between 9am and 11pm. Members $10, nonmembers $12. Laundry facilities $1.50. Open year-round.

May House Bed & Breakfast, 2415 Cosgrove Crescent (758-1423). The cheerful folks who live here will pick up all guests from the ferry, bus, or train terminals and take them to the fantastic location overlooking Departure Bay. Laundry facilities are available, and coffee brews 24 hours. Singles $28. Doubles $38.

Colonial Motel, 950 Terminal Ave. (754-4415), on the Trans-Canada Hwy. Immaculate rooms. A popular nook for fishermen; the management will happily schedule you on a charter. Singles $27. Doubles $31.

Big 7 Motel, 736 Nicol St. (754-2328), downtown. Typical loud, cheap motel decor, but the rooms are in good shape. Waterbed units available for those who don't want to give up that seasick feeling after a hard day of open-ocean fishing. Singles $30. Doubles $32.

Camping

No commercial campgrounds are within walking distance of downtown, but plenty line the highway to the north and south.

Beban Park Campground, 2300 Bowen Rd. (758-1177). Take Bowen Rd. 1½km west of Hwy. 19, or bus #4. Closest location to town. Flush toilets and hot showers. No hookups. Sites $7.

Brannen Lake Campsite, 4228 Biggs Rd. (756-0404), 6km north of ferry terminal. Follow the signs from Hwy. 19. Definitely worth the trip. Clean bathrooms with hot showers (25¢). Remote, quiet sites layered with a lush cushion of green grass. Helpful staff. Sites $9, hookups $11.

Triple E Tent and Trailer Park, 2029 S. Wellington (754-3611), 8km south of Nanaimo on the Trans-Canada Hwy. Not rustic per se, but an extremely well-run affair with a convenient location. Free hot showers. Small playground. Sites $8, full hookups $12.

Food

Watch out Ring Dings and Susie Q's, here comes the **Nanaimo Bar,** three layers of sinfully delicious graham crackers, butter, and chocolate. Residents take great pride in their home-town concoction; a 1986 contest uncovered nearly 100 separate recipes for this dentist's nightmare. Most of the neighborhood restaurants and bakeries offer their own special rendition. Locals claim that leaving the city without trying a Nanaimo Bar is like belting a home run and forgetting to touch third.

Up Stewart Ave., hungry travelers waiting to grab a boat to Vancouver can stop in at the **Nanaimo Public Market,** where food stands serve the finest in British cuisine: fish and chips. (Open daily 9am-9pm; Sept.-June 9am-6pm.)

The Scotch Bakery, 87 Commercial St. (753-3521). The acknowledged headquarters of Nanaimo Bar aficionados (65¢). Also consider the chocolate macaroons (60¢) and sausage rolls (90¢). Open Mon.-Fri. 8:30am-5:30pm, Sat. 8:30am-5pm.

New York Style Pizza, 426 Fitzwilliam (754-0111), at Richards. Classy framed posters of Gotham and Louis Armstrong, and pizza that doesn't taste anything like Ray's. Live jazz Sun. nights. Lunch specials $4, pizza for 2 $11. Open Mon.-Thurs. 11:30am-9pm, Fri. 11:30am-10pm, Sat.-Sun. 5am-10pm.

Doobee's, Church and Commercial St. (753-5044). Delicious sandwiches $3-4. Sidewalk tables, sunshine, harried pedestrians, 75¢ espresso, and $1.25 cappuccino will keep you humming. Open Mon.-Fri. 7am-9pm, Sat. 9am-5pm.

Nanaimo Harbour Lights Restaurant, 1518 Stewart Ave. (753-6614). The owner, ex-NHL referee Lloyd Gilmour, is more than willing to "talk puck" with any interested party. Surf and turf entrees also let you face off with the salad bar ($9-12). Lunches a more sporting $6. Open Mon.-Thurs. 11:30am-3pm and 5-9pm, Fri.-Sat. 11:30am-3pm and 5-10pm.

Sights

The **Nanaimo Centennial Museum,** 100 Cameron St. (753-1821), has a collection of Coastal Salish masks and totems, and a series of full-scale walk-through models patterned after those in Victoria's museum. (Open Mon.-Fri. 9am-6pm, Sat.-Sun. 10am-6pm.) The informed staff can tell you all about other Nanaimo sights. Nearby on Front St. is the **Bastion,** an old tower built to thwart Native American attacks. Unused as a defensive fortress, the Bastion has found its calling as a shelter for historical knick-knacks. (Open daily 10am-5pm. Free.)

More can be found a kilometre or two south of town. The **Madrona Exposition Centre,** 900 5th St. (755-8790), at Malaspina College, has a gallery featuring local artists and changing exhibits. Take bus #6 from the terminal at Wharf and Cameron downtown. (Open Mon.-Sat. 10am-5pm, Sun. noon-5pm.) While you're up on the hill, visit the **Morrell Nature Sanctuary** at the corner of Nanaimo Lakes and Dogwood Rd. The 278-acre area surrounds Morrell Lake and includes 4km of *pianissimo* walking trails. The archaeologically inclined will enjoy the 2000-year old petroglyphs (carvings in stone) at **Petroglyph Park,** on Hwy. 19.

Recreation in Nanaimo means sun, so head for **Departure Bay,** off Stewart Ave. **Kona Buds** (758-2911), right on the beach, rents sailboards, canoes, bicycles, jet skis, and wet suits for under $10 per hour. They also run a shop downtown at the corner of Commercial and Albert. (Open Mon.-Sat. 10:30am-5:30pm.)

The annual **Nanaimo Festival** (formerly Shakespeare Plus) presents plays about the city's history in late June and early July. All plays are held at Malaspina College; ticket prices range from $6-12. For reservations, contact the festival at P.O. Box 626, Nanaimo V9R 5L9 (754-7587), or stop by the office above the Travel Infocentre.

The week-long **Marine Festival** is held during the second week of July. Highlights include the Silly Boat Race and the renowned **Bathtub Race.** Bathers from all over the continent race porcelain tubs with monstrous outboards across the 55km Georgia Strait, from Nanaimo to Vancouver. The organizer of this bizarre but beloved event is the **Loyal Nanaimo Bathtub Society**, P.O. Box 656, Nanaimo V9R 5L5 (753-7223). They hand out prizes to everyone who makes it across, and ceremoniously present the "Silver Plunger" trophy to the first tub that sinks.

North Vancouver Island

Traveling up into the northern third of Vancouver Island, known to the residents as "North Island," one notices an abrupt shift from Peugeots to pickups, Bacardi to Budweiser, crumpets to clamburgers. Fishing and logging dominate the economy, and rivers and mountains mark the land.

Campbell River

Although 67km south of the acknowledged boundary of North Island, Campbell River is close enough in spirit to be included among its northern neighbors. Its visitor economy is geared toward fishing, skiing, kayaking, scuba diving, and mountain climbing.

The promise of a "Northwest Passage," the fabled northern waterway connecting the Atlantic and Pacific Oceans, brought Captain George Vancouver up the Discovery Passage in 1792. News of the enormous salmon regularly wrested from the river by Cape Mudge Natives sparked a tremendous influx of sport fishermen at the turn of the century. Today every pamphlet, billboard, and menu shouts "Salmon Capital of the World" in obtrusively large print.

Practical Information and Orientation

Visitor Information: Travel Infocentre, 923 Island Hwy. (286-0764). One of the island's best-stocked Infocentres. Open daily 8am-8pm; in winter Mon.-Fri. 9am-5pm, Sat. 10am-5pm.

Buses: Island Coach Lines (287-7151), corner of 13th and Cedar. To Port Hardy (1 per day, $28.35) and Victoria (4 per day, $22.40).

Car Rental: Rent-A-Wreck, 1437 N. Island Hwy. (287-8353), in Lakeland Auto and Marine. Must be 19 with major credit card. Chevettes $17 per day plus 11¢ per km. Open Mon.-Fri. 8am-5:30pm, Sat. 8am-5pm.

Crisis Line: 287-7743.

Emergency: Police, 286-6221. **Ambulance,** 286-1155.

Post Office: on Beech, at Alder. Open Mon.-Fri. 8:30am-5:30pm. Postal Code: V9W 4Z8.

Area Code: 604.

Campbell River is a crossroads in the middle of Vancouver Island's eastern coast, 240km equidistant from Victoria at the southern tip and Port Hardy at the northern end. Highway 19, the town's principal artery, runs along the waterfront.

Accommodations and Camping

You may be hard pressed to find a room under $30 during the height of the July fishing season. The few campgrounds in town are overpriced and aesthetically bleak. Stop at any one of the cheaper spots a few km west on Hwy. 28 or north and south on Hwy. 19.

Willow Point Bed & Breakfast, 2460 S. Island Hwy. (923-1086). Conservative atmosphere. Immaculate rooms. Singles from $30. Doubles from $40. Reservations necessary.

Vista Del Mar, 920 S. Island Hwy. (923-4271). Overlooks the briny waters of Georgin Stait. Well-maintained, with plenty of amenities for fisherfolk—boat ramp, fishing guides, and a freezer for the day's catch. Singles $32. Doubles $36.

Parkside Campground (287-3113), 5km west of Campbell River on Hwy. 28. Appealing wooded sites in private, quiet surroundings. Free hot showers in clean bathrooms; laundromat. Sites $8, full hookups $12.

Friendship Inn Motel and RV Park, 3900 N. Island Hwy. (287-9591). An adequately appointed amalgam of hotel and campground. Rooms include full bath and telephone. Singles $32. Doubles $36. Campground with hot showers (25¢ per 9 min.); RVs only. 28 sites with full hookup $13.

Food

For a town of its size, Campbell River has disappointingly few innovative eateries, and fast-food joints cha-cha drunkenly along the highway. Look for a place that serves the area's obvious specialty: **fresh-baked salmon.**

Susi's Seafood, 560 11th Ave. (287-2457), off Hwy. 19. Rest assured that your seafood will be fresh—you can watch your shellfish crawl around in the salt-water tanks before their corpses are laid to banquet at your behest. Take-out only; grab a crab ($3.75 per lb.) or clasp some clams ($2.25 per lb.) and have a cookout elsewhere. Open daily 10am-6pm.

Del's Burgers, 1423 N. Island Hwy. 31 varieties of milkshake ($1.50) liven up an otherwise unexceptional burger shack right out of *Happy Days.* Open daily 8am-midnight; in winter 9am-10pm.

Cafe California, 969 Alder St. (287-7999). Specializes in commodified but filling Mexican food, but its varied menu includes the "catch of the day." Lunch entrees around $6. Open daily 9am-11pm.

Sights and Activities

Plenty of 15-kilo Tyee salmon hop off the hooks annually in Campbell's waters. You can shell out a small fortune paying for guides and charters, but amateur fishermen reap deep-sea prizes from the new **Discovery Pier** (fishing charge $1) in Campbell Harbor. The pier has 200m of boardwalk planks and an artificial, underwater reef built to attract astigmatic fish. Attendant fishermen rent full outfits for under $15.

National Geographic once praised Campbell River's **scuba diving** as "second only to the Red Sea." Experienced divers should not miss out on the aquatic delights, especially the octopi that turn up frequently during night dives. A few hideously expensive stores along the waterfront offer rentals.

Nearby **Strathcona Provincial Park** is a veritable varicose vein network of hiking trails, ranging from short strolls to challenging overnight routes. These are all described in a free Strathcona pamplet available at the Travel Infocentre. The most convenient place to embark on a hike is the Ironwood Mall, origin of **Nunns Creek Park Trail**, a short, serene walk not connected to Strathcona Park.

No visit to the self-proclaimed "Salmon Capital of the World" would be complete without the requisite **Salmon Hatchery Tour** (287-9564), on the Quinsam River. An audio-visual display and live viewing introduce you to happy little fish that one day will be bloated dead trophies. (Open daily 8am-4pm.) Escape to the **Campbell River District Museum** (287-3103), in the same building as the Travel Infocentre. The small array of Native American artifacts includes tidbits from "cowboy history." (Open daily 10am-4pm; in winter 1-4pm.)

About an hour north of Campbell River up Hwy. 19 is the **Valley of 1000 Faces** (282-3303), in Sayward. A five-acre enclosure displays a logger's nightmare: 1000 neatly cut logs, each one with a unique face carved on its butt end. Actually conceived by a local artist, the odd valley impresses most with an awe for the ecstatic indefatigability of the post-modern mind. (Open May 15-Aug. 10am-5pm. Admission $2, children $1.)

Port Hardy

Port Hardy is in a certain sense the modern Canadian equivalent of Liverpool. Originally, the unassuming town was completely content to be a quiet logging and fishing community. Then the BC ferry established the city as the drop-off point for visitors heading south from upper BC and Alaska. Virtually overnight, Port Hardy etched a name for itself as a major transportation port, evidenced by the city welcome sign, carved out with a chainsaw. Unlike Liverpool, it remains a mild coastal town, an excellent place for ferry passengers to spend the night.

Practical Information and Orientation

Visitor Information: Travel Infocentre, 7250 Market St. (949-7622). Take Hardy Bay Rd. off Hwy. 19 to Market St. Pick up a restaurant menu guide and tour maps. Open daily 9am-6pm.

Buses: Island Coach Lines, Market St. (949-7532), across from the Travel Infocentre. To Victoria 1 per day, one way $50.75.

Ferry: BC Ferry (949-6722), 3km south at Bear Creek. Service between Prince Rupert and Port Hardy every other day (one way $56).

Taxi: North Island Taxi, 949-8800.

Crisis: 949-6033.

Coast Guard: 974-5413.

Hospital: 949-6161.

Emergency: Police, 949-6335. **Ambulance,** 949-7225.

Postal Code: V09 2P0.

Area Code: 604.

On the northern tip of Vancouver Island, Port Hardy serves as the southern terminus for ferries carrying passengers down from Prince Rupert and Alaska. Highway 19 runs south from the center of downtown.

Accommodations and Camping

Because many of the people arriving via ferry bring along RVs, the demand for hotel rooms is not as high as you would expect in a port town.

Airport Inn (949-9424). Take Byng Rd. off Hwy. 19 toward the airport. Once the cheapest rooms in town. Cable TV. Restaurant downstairs. Singles $40. Doubles $45. Kitchen units $6.

Pioneer Inn (949-7271), off Hwy. 19 on Old Island Hwy., 2km south of town. Next to a salmon hatchery. Laundry facilities and a dining room. Singles $38. Doubles $42.

Quatse River Campground, Hardy Bay Rd. (949-2395), across from the Pioneer Inn. Quiet, wooded setting with private sites. Toilets come in the flush and pit varieties. Showers and laundromat. Sites $8, full hookups $11.

Wildwoods Campsite (949-6753), on the road from the ferry, within walking distance of the terminal. Comfortable sites lined with pine needles. Plenty of spaces crammed into a relatively small forest area, but well-designed to afford maximum privacy. Hot showers, but expect a line in the morning. Sites $7, with car $9, with hookup $10.

Food

Port Hardy maintains its excellent cuisine in the face of growing ferry traffic. A brigade of superb budget restaurants serve dinners for under $10.

Brigg Seafood House (949-6532), at Market and Granville St. Seafood served in a large old house. The "you catch it, we'll cook it" service can get you dinner with all the trimmings for $5. Children's menu available. Bistro dinners from $7. Open Sun.-Wed. 11:30am-3pm and 5-10pm, Thurs.-Sat. 11:30am-3pm and 5:30-11pm.

Sportsman's Steak & Seafood House (949-7811), on Market St. across from the Infocentre. Lunch sandwiches stuffed with meat from $4. Stocked salad bar. Surf-and-turf entrees under $9. Open daily 11:30am-2pm and 5pm-"whenever."

Carrot's (949-8525), at the Best Western on Granville St. Tons of pasta dishes in the $6 range. Spicy dijon chicken $9. Open daily 8am-10:30pm.

Snuggles (949-7575), at the Pioneer Inn on Old Island Hwy. Must be 19. A good place to bring a date without blowing your junk-bond buffer account. Live entertainment and live cooking; watch the chef whip up your meal. Salads $4-6, entrees from $11. Open Mon.-Thurs. 5:30-10pm, Fri.-Sun. 5-11pm.

Sights

For a peek at vignettes of city history, head to the **Port Hardy Museum,** 7110 Market St. (949-8143), near the Infocentre. The small library/museum holds early native artifacts and some yellowed photographs; not very heady stuff, but it's free. Port Hardy's most prized possession is a paragon of signification-becoming-situation: the **"Welcome to Port Hardy"** sign on Market St. It was carved with the sculptor's ultimate chisel: a chainsaw. After you've snapped a picture of yourself in front of this bewilderingly overrated post, stroll along the seawall to absorb the town's coastal beauty.

Port McNeill, 65km south of Port Hardy on Hwy. 19, runs fishing charters booked through the Travel Infocentre along the highway or at the ferry dock booth. **Bud's Charters** (956-4781) has a half-day, four-person excursion for relatively low prices, not including a Bud. The **BC Ferry** (956-4533) sells rides to nearby **Alert Bay** (40 min.), a renowned area for spotting pods of orcas (killer whales). One of the world's largest totem poles (58km) overshadows the nearby Nimpkish Natives' reserve. For more information on the small village, stop by the **Travel Infocentre** on Fir St. (974-5213).

Vancouver

Canada's third largest city (after Toronto and Montreal) comes as a pleasant surprise to the jaded metropolis-hopping traveler. Its 1.4 million residents display big-city sophistication, but they escape most conventional urban traumas. Tune out the language, and Vancouver could be a North American Sweden or Switzerland: the transit system is immaculately efficient, the sidewalks are largely spotless, and even the seediest areas are basically safe. Although you will find some fantastically dingy back alleys, the streets are broad, clearly laid out, and well marked. Vancouver's citizens display a rare humility, at times approaching naïvete—traits rare in a city of this size.

Vancouver is fast joining the post-industrial age: the unemployment rate has fallen by half in recent years, and electronics and international finance have largely replaced timber and mining as the city's economic base. A growing wave of Chinese immigration, largely from Hong Kong, is turning Vancouver increasingly towards the Far East. To many, Vancouver is the very model of a modern multi-ethnic metropolis; others fear that racial tensions will soon begin to rise. Mayor Gordon Campbell promises that his city will meet this challenge and "not become like a city in the United States." (Well!)

Practical Information

Visitor Information: Travel Infocentre, 1055 Dunsmuir (683-2000), near Burrard, in the West End. Help with tickets, reservations, and tours. Currency exchange available. Open daily 8:30am-6:30pm.

BC Transit Information Centre: 261-5100.

Parks and Recreation Board: 681-1141.

The Gray Line: 900 W. Georgia St. (681-8687), in Hotel Vancouver. Expensive but worthwhile city tours with a number of package options. Basic tours leave daily and last 3½ hr. ($27.50, children $14). Reservations required.

Taxis: Yellow Cab, 681-3311. **Vancouver Taxi,** 255-5111.

Car Rental: Rent-A-Wreck, 1015 Burrard (688-0001), in the West End, and 1085 Kingsway (876-5629), at Glen. From $17 per day plus 10¢ per km. Must be 25 with credit card. Open Mon.-Fri. 8am-9pm, Sat. 8am-6pm, Sun. 9am-5pm. Kingsway location open Mon.-Fri. 8am-7pm, Sat. 9am-5pm.

Road Conditions: 660-9775. 24 hours.

Bicycling Association of BC: 1367 W. Broadway, #332, Vancouver V6H 4H9 (731-7433 events line, 737-3034 office). One-page cycling map of city; more detailed maps available through the mail. Open Mon.-Fri. 9am-5pm.

Camping Equipment Rentals: Sports Rent, 2560 Arbutus St. (733-1605), at Broadway. Take bus #10 or 14 from Granville Mall. Backpacks ($8 per day, $20 per week), 2-person tents ($15 per day, $40 per week), and every other kind of camping or sports equipment imaginable. Open Mon.-Wed. 8am-7pm, Thurs.-Sun. 8am-9pm.

Scuba Rentals: The Diving Locker, 2745 W. 4th St. (736-2681). Complete outfit $50 first day, $25 every day thereafter. Open Mon.-Thurs. 9:30am-6pm, Fri. 9:30am-8pm, Sat. 9:30am-6pm.

Public Library: 750 Burrard (665-2280 or 665-2276 for a recording), at Robson St., downtown. Open Mon.-Thurs. 9:30am-9:30pm, Fri.-Sat. 9:30am-6pm; Oct.-March also Sun. 1-5pm.

Arts Hotline: 684-2787.

Weather: 666-1087.

Distress Line: Vancouver Crisis Center, 733-4111. 24 hours.

Women's Services: Rape Crisis Center, 875-6011. **Rape Relief Center,** 872-8212. Both 24 hours. **Battered Women's Support Services,** 2515 Burrard (734-1574). Open Mon. and Fri. 10am-2pm, Tues.-Thurs. 10am-4pm. 24 hour **emergency** line: 872-7774. **Women's Resource Center,** 1144 Robson (685-3934), in the West End between Thurlow and Bute. Open Mon.-Fri. 10am-2pm; in winter Mon.-Fri. 10am-4pm, Sat. 1-4pm.

Senior citizens Information and Support Network: 531-2320 or 531-2425.

Gay and Lesbian Switchboard: 1-1170 Bute St., 684-6869. Counseling and information. Open Mon.-Fri. 7-10pm, Sat.-Sun. 4-10pm.

AIDS Vancouver: 687-2437.

Poison Control: 682-5050.

Police/Fire/Ambulance: 911.

Post Office: Main branch, 349 W. Georgia St. (662-5725). Open Mon.-Fri. 8am-5:30pm. Postal Code: V6B 3P7.

Area Code: 604.

Getting There

Vancouver is located in the southwestern corner of the British Columbia mainland, across the Georgia Strait from Vancouver Island and the city of Victoria. **Vancouver International Airport,** on Sea Island 11km south of the city center, makes connections to major cities on the West Coast and around the world. To reach downtown from the airport, take Metro Transit bus #100 to 70th Ave. Transfer there to bus #20, which arrives downtown heading north on the Granville Mall. The private **Airport Express** bus leaves from airport level 2 every 15 minutes between 6:15am and 12:30am and heads for downtown hotels and the Greyhound station ($6.75 per person; 266-0376 for info).

Greyhound makes several connecting runs daily between Seattle and Vancouver. The downtown Greyhound station offers easy access to the city's transit system. Catch bus #11 heading north on Nanaimo St.; it travels through Vancouver's Chinatown, arriving downtown along Pender St. heading west. **VIA Rail** runs one train per day on the famed Trans-Canada Railway, bound for the eastern part of the con-

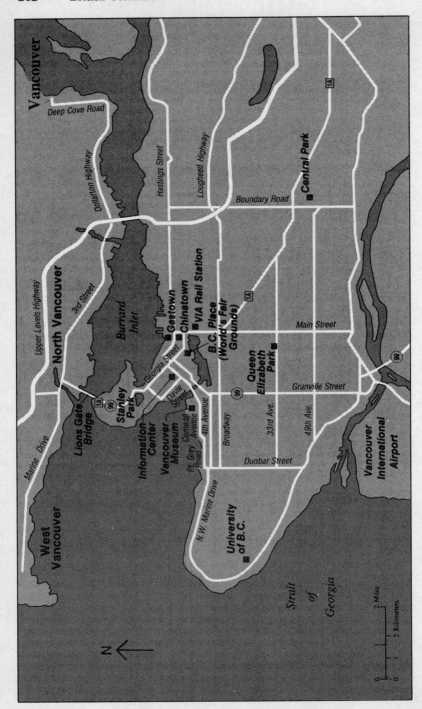

tinent. **BC Rail's** station in North Vancouver launches trains toward northern British Columbia. **BC Ferries** regularly connect the city of Vancouver to Vancouver Island and the Gulf Islands. Ferries leave from the Tsawwassen terminal, 25km south of the city center. To reach downtown from the ferry terminal, take bus #640 to the Ladner Exchange and transfer there to bus #601. The bus arrives downtown on Seymour St.

> **Greyhound:** 150 Dunsmuir (662-3222), downtown at Beatty St. Service to the south and across Canada. Open daily 5:30am-midnight. To Calgary (4 per day, one way $65), Banff (4 per day, one way $62), Jasper (3 per day, one way $61), and Seattle (7 per day, one way $24.33).

> **Pacific Coach Lines:** 150 Dunsmuir (662-3222). Serves southern BC, including Vancouver Island, in conjunction with Greyhound. To Victoria $16.50, including ferry.

> **VIA Rail Canada:** 1150 Station St. (800-665-8630), off Hwy. 99 (Main St.) at 1st Ave. To Banff (1 per day, $75), Calgary (1 per day, $86), and Jasper (1 per day, $70). Open daily 9am-6pm.

> **BC Rail:** 1311 W. 1st St. (984-5246), just over the Lions Gate Bridge in North Vancouver. Take the SeaBus downtown to North Vancouver, then bus #239 west. To Garibaldi (one way $9), Williams Lake (one way $44.50), Prince George (one way $61), Whistler (one way $11), and Squamish and points north daily. Open daily 7am-9pm.

> **BC Ferries:** To Victoria, the Gulf Islands, Sunshine Coast, Inside Passage, Prince Rupert, and the Queen Charlotte Islands. General information 669-1211, recorded information 685-1021, Tsawwassen ferry terminal 943-9331. Mainland to Vancouver Island ($4.75, car and driver $21.75, motorcycle and driver $12.75, bicycle and rider $6.85; ages 5-11 ½-price). The terminal serving Victoria is actually located in Swartz Bay, north of Victoria. (See Victoria Getting There for more information.)

Bicyclists will find many excellent routes both in the city itself and outside it—in the Fraser River Canyon, along the shore of Georgia Bay, on the Gulf Islands, and on Vancouver Island. The Bicycling Association of BC (see Practical Information) can recommend specific trips, and Tourism BC publishes a thorough pamphlet on bicycling. Note that the George Massey Tunnel on Hwy. 99, under the Fraser River, is closed to bicycles.

Getting Around

Vancouver's various neighborhoods are better fused than in the past, when marsh waters connecting False Creek with Burrard Inlet would detach the downtown peninsula at high tide. Landfill has brought residents closer together, but the profusion of waterways can still confuse even the most diligent map reader. Most of the city's attractions are concentrated on the city center peninsula and the larger rhino snout to the south. Many neighborhoods are not labeled as their residents refer to them on the city maps issued by Tourism BC. The residential area of the city center peninsula, bounded by downtown to the east and Stanley Park to the west, is referred to as the **West End.** The western portion of the southern peninsula from around Alma Ave. west to the University of British Columbia campus is **Point Grey,** while the central area on the same peninsula from the Granville Bridge to Alma Ave. is "The Kitsilano," familiarly known as "Kits".

Don't try to make any distinction between streets and avenues in Vancouver—there is no apparent standard, and even maps usually omit the surname. The one exception to this madness is the numbered streets, which are always *avenues* in Vancouver proper (running east-west), and always *streets* in North Vancouver (running every which way but loose). Downtown, private vehicles are not allowed on Granville between Nelson and West Pender, which is referred to as the **Granville Mall.** Both **Chinatown,** running east-west between Hastings and East Pender from Garrel Ave. to Gore Ave., and **Gastown,** on Alexander as it runs into Water St., are easily reached on foot from the Granville Mall.

Vancouver's **Metro Transit** covers most of the city and suburbs, with direct transport or easy connecting transit to the city's points of departure: Tsawwassen, Horseshoe Bay, and the airport (see Getting There for specific lines). Often one bus will run along a route in one direction while a bus of a different number will run in the other direction; ask a local resident or bus driver for assistance.

If you have a car, consider using **Park 'n' Ride** from New Westminster to circumvent the city's perpetual rush hour. Exit Hwy. 1 at New Westminster and follow signs for the Pattullo Bridge. Just over the bridge, you'll see signs for the Park 'n' Ride lot to your right, between Scott Rd. and 110th Ave. A fare bus will be waiting where you can purchase one-way tickets for the bus, SkyTrain, and SeaBus, or one-day passes for $3.50. Parking here is free, and taking the SkyTrain downtown is faster than driving.

You can ride in Metro Transit's central zone one way for $1.25 (senior citizens and ages 5-11 65¢) at all times. During peak hours (6:30-9:30am and 3-6:30pm), it costs $1.75 (senior citizens and ages 5-11 90¢) to travel two zones. During off-peak hours, passengers pay only the one-zone price. Day-passes are $3.50, and transfers are free. Single fares, passes, and transfers are also good for the SeaBus and SkyTrain (running southeast from downtown to New Westminster). Timetables are available at 7-11 stores, public libraries, city halls, community centers, and the Vancouver Travel Infocentre (see Practical Information). To retrieve **lost property** in Metro Transit's possession, call 682-7887 (Mon.-Fri. 9am-5pm); otherwise stop by the lost property office at 611 W. Hastings, in the Harbour Centre Building.

Metro Transit's **SeaBus** operates from the Granville Waterfront Station, at the foot of Granville St. in downtown Vancouver, to the Lonsdale Quay at the foot of Lonsdale Ave. in North Vancouver. The fares are the same as one-zone bus fares, and all transfers and passes are accepted. While waiting, study *The Buzzer,* Metro Transit's weekly pamphlet on transit updates and community events, available wherever transit timetables are distributed.

Driving in car-mad Vancouver is a serious hassle. Rush hour begins at dawn and ends at dusk. Beware of the 3-6pm restrictions on left turns and street parking. If you can find no parking at street level, look for underground lots and be prepared to pay exorbitant prices. Try the lot below Pacific Centre at Howe and W. Georgia, sometimes called "Garageland" by those unfortunates who lose their cars in the maze. One-way streets are a curse throughout the city, but many maps have arrows indicating directions. The free Tourism BC maps don't cover the area outside the city center in detail; purchase the larger-scale street map, available from the Infocentre for $2.

Accommodations

Greater Vancouver has a robust network of bed and breakfast accommodations. Cheaper than their American equivalents (but still not as affordable as English B&Bs), these private homes are usually comfortable and have personable proprietors. Rates average about $25 for singles and $35 for doubles. The visitors bureau has a four-page list of B&Bs in Vancouver. Several private agencies also match travelers with B&Bs, usually for a fee; get in touch with **Town and Country Bed and Breakfast** (731-5942) or **Best Canadian** (738-7207). Always call for reservations at least two days in advance.

Vancouver International Hostel (IYHF), 1515 Discovery St. (224-3208), in Point Grey on Jericho Beach. Turn north off 4th Ave., following the signs for Marine Dr., or take bus #4 from Granville St. downtown. Comely location on beach and park, with a superlative view of the city from False Creek. Over 350 beds, massive dorm rooms, good cooking facilities, and occasional opportunities to spend a few hours cleaning in exchange for a room. TV room inside, and plenty of grassy space outside to discuss Lao Tzu or practice *tai chi.* Three-day limit enforced in summer, but flexible otherwise. Eight family rooms. Midnight curfew strictly enforced, as is the lights-out rule for the entire building. Lockout 10am-4pm. Members $10, nonmembers $12. Bedding $10.

Vincent's Backpackers Hostel, 927 Main (682-2441 or 254-7462), right next to the VIA station, 2 blocks from the Science World dome and the Main St. SkyTrain station. Not quite as clean or as structured as the IYHF hostel, but more colorful, cheaper, and within walking distance of downtown. Kitchen, fridge, TV, stereo, and the music of Greyhounds gleefully revving their engines until late at night. Office open 8am-midnight. Check in before noon for best chance at a bed. Shared rooms $8. Singles with shared bath $16. Doubles with shared bath $20.

YWCA, 580 Burrard St. (662-8188), downtown at Dunsmuir, 7 blocks from the bus depot. Women, male-female couples, and families only. Recently remodeled and clean, but expensive. High-quality sports facilities for female guests over 15 (free). Kitchens on every other floor, and cafeteria in basement. Staff on duty 24 hours, but building locked at midnight—buzz for entry. No male visitors allowed upstairs. Some singles smaller than others, so ask to see a few before choosing. Four-week max. stay. Singles $31. Doubles $46. Extra bed $10. 10% discount for YWCA members, senior citizens, and groups. Weekly and monthly rates available Sept.-June.

YMCA, 955 Burrard (681-0221), between Smithe and Nelson, 4 blocks south of the YWCA. Newly renovated. Concerned staff on duty 24 hours. Pool, gymnasiums, ball courts, and weight rooms (free). All rooms have shared washrooms and showers. Cafeteria open Mon.-Fri. 7am-4pm, Sat. 8am-2pm. Singles $27. Doubles $46. Weekly and monthly rates available Oct.-April.

Dufferin Hotel, 900 Seymour (683-4251), at Smithe. Clean rooms, color TV. Safer than many other hotels in the area. No visitors after 11:30pm. Check-out 1pm. Singles $45. Doubles $50. Prices reduced $5 in winter.

Nelson Place, 1006 Granville (681-6341), at Nelson St., 1 block from the Dufferin. Borders on Vancouver's small and tame red-light district. Great access to downtown. Small but tame rooms with TV and bath. Singles $35. Doubles $40. Prices reduced $5 in winter.

Sylvia Hotel, 1154 Gilford St. (681-9321), 2 blocks from Stanley Park in a quiet residential neighborhood. Magnificent singles $40. Doubles $48. Additional cots $8. Reservations recommended.

University of British Columbia Conference Centre, 5959 Student Union Mall, Walter Gage Residence (228-2963), at the end of Vancouver's largest peninsula. Take bus #4 or 10 from the Granville Mall. Draws swarms of conventioneers in summer. Check-in after 2pm. Singles $28. Doubles $45. $5 per additional person.

Simon Fraser University, in Burnaby (291-4503 or 291-4201), 20km east of the city center. 190 singles and 9 twins available May.-Aug. Shared bath. Call Mon.-Fri. 8:30am-4:30pm. Check-in 2-4:30pm. Check-out 11am. Singles $15. Twins $25. With linen and towels: singles $26, twins $37. No reservations necessary.

Horseshoe Bay Motel, 6396 Bruce St., in N. Vancouver/Horseshoe Bay (921-7454). Perfect location for people using the BC Ferry. Combination baths. Singles $55. Doubles $60. In winter singles $42, doubles $50. Kitchen units $10.

Camping

Greater Vancouver is unlittered with public campgrounds; one must resort to expensive, private campgrounds. The visitors bureau has a complete list of campgrounds outside Vancouver; many are for RVs only. **Sports Rent** offers tents (see Practical Information), but the prohibitive cost makes it more sensible to spend the money on a bed at Vincent's or the hostel. The town of **White Rock,** 30 minutes southeast of Vancouver, has campgrounds that allow tents. Take bus #351 from Howe St. downtown.

Richmond RV Park, 6200 River Rd. (270-7878), near Holly Bridge in Richmond. Take Hwy. 99 to Westminster Hwy., then follow the signs. Unquestionably the best deal within 15km of downtown. Sites offer little privacy, but the great showers and soothing staff are sure to wash your cares away. Sites $13, RV hookups $13-20. Open April-Oct.

Hazelmere RV Park and Campground, 18843 8th Ave. (538-1167), in Surrey. Off Hwy. 99A, head east on 8th Ave. Quiet sites on the Campbell River with beach access. Sites $12, RV hookups $16. Each additional adult $2. Showers 25¢.

ParkCanada, 4799 Hwy. 17 (943-5811), in Delta, about 30km south of downtown Vancouver. Take Hwy. 99 south to Tsawwassen Ferry Terminal Rd., then go east for 2.5km. The campground, located next to a giant waterslide park, has flush toilets and free showers, though the lines may be long. Sites $11.50.

Dogwood Campground, 15151 112th St. (588-1412), 31km east on Hwy. 1 in Surrey. Flush toilets and pay showers. Sites $14.

Food

Steer clear of restaurants hawking "Canadian cuisine"—nobody really knows what Canadian cuisine is. The city's best offerings are the diverse ethnic gastrocentres and the older natural-foods culinaria. The East Indian neighborhoods along Main, Fraser, and 49th St. synthesize the spicy dishes of the subcontinent. Vancouver's **Chinatown** is second in size only to San Francisco's in North America. Here groceries, shops, and restaurants cluster around E. Pender and Gore St.

Eateries in the **West End** and **Gastown** compete to extract the highest prices in the city; the former caters to executives with expense accounts, while the latter attracts gullible tourists fresh off the cruise ships. Many of the greasy spoons along Davie and Denman St. stay open late or around the clock.

The **Granville Island Market,** under the Granville Bridge, off W. 4th Ave. across False Creek from downtown, intersperses trendy shops, art galleries, and restaurants with countless produce stands selling local and imported fruits and vegetables. Take one of the many buses that run south on Granville and cross the Granville Bridge; get off at W. 4th St. and walk 6 blocks back down the hill. Otherwise, stay on the bus to Broadway and Granville Exchange and change to bus #51; it will take you directly to the island. The bakeries also sell day-old bread and bagels at half-price. The range of delicacies offered by the stalls at the north end of the island will blow your mind. Slurp cherry-papaya yogurt soup (in an edible sugar waffle bowl, of course), indulge in almost-kosher cheese blintzes and potato knishes, or pick up some duck or shrimp stock to take back to the hostel's stew pot. Picnicking spontaneously erupts from the parks, patios, and walkways that surround the market. (Market complex open daily 9am-6pm; Labor Day-Victoria Day Tues.-Sun. 9am-6pm.)

The Naam, 2724 W. 4th Ave. (738-7151), in the Kits area. Take bus #4 or 7 from Granville. Vancouver's oldest natural-foods restaurant, the Naam is a delight for the fanatic and the indifferent alike. Fireplace and patio. Yumsy tofu-nut-beet burgers ($4.25), spinach enchiladas ($8), and salad bar ($1.10 per 100g). Open 24 hours.

Dos Amigos Tapas, 3189 W. Broadway (731-5444), at Trutch. Not much Spanish ambience (it used to be a Swensen's), but the food is unadulterated. Go with a friend and order 3 or 4 dishes, following tapa tradition. Melon and smoked ham $3.75, marinated mushrooms $2.75, deep-fried squid $4. Open Tues.-Thurs. 11:30am-10:30pm, Fri.-Sat. 11:30am-11pm.

Dar Lebanon Palace, 678 W. Broadway (873-9511). Take bus #10 or 14 from Granville. Dinners can be pricy (beef or lamb shish kabob with rice and veggies for $12), but lunches are more reasonable ($5 pita sandwiches, $4.50 stuffed grape leaves). Anything can be made for take-out. Open daily 10am-midnight.

The Sitar, 564 W. Broadway (879-4333). Take bus #10 or 14 from Granville. Indian food in a standard Iindian setting often enhanced by Bryan Adams's presence. *Tandoori* chicken $8, *mulligatawny* $2.50, full dinners $11. Open Mon.-Fri. 11:30am-10pm, Sat. noon-10pm, Sun. 4-10pm.

Singapore Restaurant, 546 W. Broadway (874-6161). Take bus #10 or 14 from Granville. The mix of Malaysian, Chinese, and Indian cuisine corresponds to the tangled demography of Singapore. The spartan surroundings are also redolent of Singapore. The restaurant is therefore aptly named. Fried noodles $5.50, chicken curry $8, beef or chicken *satays* $1 each. Open Mon.-Fri. 11am-2:30pm and 5-10pm, Sat. 11am-10pm, Sun. noon-10pm.

Bill Kee Restaurant, 8 W. Broadway (874-8522 or 879-3222). Take any bus to the Broadway and Granville Exchange, then bus #9 east on Broadway. Cleaner and more pleasant than most of the city's Chinese joints. Fantastic Cantonese food (transplanted from Hong Kong).

Most dishes $5-8.50. The wonton soup is a meal in itself ($2.25). Take-out and free delivery. Open Sun.-Thurs. 10:30am-2am, Fri.-Sat. 10:30am-3am.

Isadora's Cooperative Restaurant, 1540 Old Bridge Rd. (681-8816), on Granville Island, 1 block on your right immediately after entering the shopping area. This natural-food restaurant sends its profits to community service organizations. Sandwiches $7, dinner entrees $10, Bamfield burger made with filet of rock sole $6.25. Open Mon.-Thurs. 7am-10pm, Fri. 7am-11pm, Sat. 9am-11pm, Sun. 9am-10pm. Closed Mon. evenings in winter.

Frannie's Deli, 325 Cambie (685-2928), at W. Cordova St. In the heart of downtown, near Gastown. Doesn't look like much from outside (or inside), but your stomach is the better judge. A variety of sandwiches, including a $3 vegetarian sandwich. A gathering place for casually dressed Canadian capitalists. Open Mon.-Sat. 6:30am-6:30pm.

The Souvlaki Place, 1807 Morton (689-3064), at Denman, near Stanley Park. A Greek establishment with an inspiring view of English Bay. *Souvlaki* $4.25; yogurt, honey, and pita $2.75. Open daily 11:30am-11pm.

The Green Door, 111 E. Pender (685-4194), in central Chinatown. Follow the garbage trucks down the alley off Columbia St. to find the hidden entrance. This legendary, wildly green establishment plays a prominent role in the copious annals of Vancouver hippie lore. Huge, slightly greasy servings of Chinese seafood quiver around $5.50. Open daily noon-10:30pm; Oct.-May Wed.-Mon. noon-10pm.

The Only Seafood Cafe, 20 E. Hastings St. (681-6546), at Carrall St. on the edge of Chinatown, within walking distance of downtown. Large portions of great seafood at decent prices, and a reputation that has spread throughout the Northwest. They've been around since 1912, and they *still* don't have a rest room. Fried halibut steak $8. Open Mon.-Thurs. 11am-9:30pm, Fri.-Sat. 11am-10pm.

A Taste of Jamaica, 941 Davie St. (683-3464), downtown. Reggae, Jamaica posters, and red, green, and yellow seat covers. Food's just like you'd find it in Kingston. Ox-tail stew $6, goat or lamb curry $6, blended banana/carrot drink $2.50. Open Mon.-Sat. 11am-11pm, Sun. 5-11pm.

Stephos, 1124 Davie St. (683-2555). Much more elegant than The Souvlaki Place, but prices are only slightly higher. Full *souvlaki* meal $6-10, hummus and pita $3.50, baklava $2.50. Open Mon.-Thurs. 11:30am-11:30pm, Fri.-Sat. 11am-1am, Sun. 4-11:30pm.

Fresgo Inn, 1138 Davie St. (689-1332), in the West End between Bute and Thurlow St. Cafeteria-style food subjected to multiple heat lamps. Joshua Goldstine might be disappointed, but it's relatively cheap. Subs $5; 2 eggs, 2 pancakes, 2 sausages and 2 strips of bacon $2.75. Open Mon.-Sat. 8am-3am, Sun. and holidays 9am-midnight.

Did's Pizza, 622 Davie St. (681-7368), near Seymour. The clintele is as tame as the graffiti and loud music are wild. The pizza is excellent—thin crust, with just the right amount of semi-coagulated grease. $2.75 per slice regardless of toppings. Open Mon.-Sat. 11am-3:30am, Sun. 5pm-1am.

Nick's Spaghetti House, 631 Commercial Dr. (254-5633), on the main drag of the Italian district. Take bus #20. An old restaurant under new management. Standard Italian food in a traditional atmosphere. How you dare ignore the great spaghetti ($8.50)? Open Mon.-Thurs. 11:30am-11pm, Fri. 11:30am-midnight, Sat. 4pm-midnight, Sun. 4-10pm.

Joe's Cafe, 1150 Commercial Dr. A unique cross between cappuccino bar and pool hall, Joe's is something of a nexus for students and artists living in the area. You will find absolutely nothing with nutritional value here. Usual array of coffee drinks $1-2. Open daily 10am-midnight.

Arriva Ristorante, 1537 Commercial Dr. (251-1177), up the hill from Nick's, on the same bus line. Gourmet Italian food for a special night out. The interior is elegant but unpretentious, the service impeccable. Full range of vegetarian, meat, and seafood sauces for the $8 pasta. Dinners $10-15. Open Mon.-Fri. 11:30am-3pm and 5-10:30pm, Sat.-Sun. 5-10:30pm.

Cafe Madeleine, 3763 W. 10th (224-5558), out toward UBC. Take bus #10 or 14. Enjoy the pleasant, nuclear-free northern environment. The sandwiches, burgers, and big breakfasts (all $6) are overpriced but filling. Open daily 8am-midnight.

Sights and Activities

Although it's not difficult to understand why residents amble in droves to their many parks, beaches, and museums, only an Erwin Schrödinger or a Danny Nevins could understand how they go about choosing a favorite spot—there are so many possibilities. Expect company wherever you go.

World's Fair Grounds and Downtown

Expo '86 was the first world's fair to be held in two different locations. The **main grounds,** between Granville and Main St., are now devolving into office space, housing for senior citizens, and a cultural center. The Canada Pavilion, now called **Canada Place,** is about ½ km away and can be reached by SkyTrain from the main Expo site. Visitors who make this four-minute journey are treated to Canadian arts and crafts along with films in the CN IMAX Theatre (682-4629). The 5-story flat screen doesn't compare to the domed screens of other IMAX theatres. (Tickets $5.50-8. Open daily noon-9pm.)

The landmark of Expo '86 is a 17-story, metallic, geodesic sphere in the former main Expo grounds. The sphere now houses **Science World,** 1455 Quebec St. (687-7832), at Terminal Ave. next to the Main St. SkyTrain stop. Science World features hands-on exhibits for children and the **Omnimax Theatre,** a high-tech hemispheric screenhouse. Film subjects range from dinosaurs to asteroids. (Admission to the museum *or* to Omnimax movies $6, senior citizens and ages under 18 $4.50. Open daily 10am-6pm. Call 875-6664 for Omnimax show times.)

Several points of interest cluster in and around the downtown area. The **BC Place Stadium,** 777 S. Pacific Blvd. (669-2300), popularly referred to as a "mushroom in bondage," houses the Canadian Football League's Lions and is also a popular space for rock concerts. Take Main St. 1 block south from Chinatown to the stadium.

The **Harbour Centre Observation Deck,** 555 W. Hastings St. (683-5684), is actually worth the admission price for the 360° views of the city and surrounding areas. Plaques point out the world's narrowest building (2m thin) and other wonders. To reach the tower, take Hastings St. 2 blocks west from Gastown. (Admission $3, senior citizens and students $2.50. Open daily 9am-10pm.)

The **Vancouver Art Gallery,** 750 Hornby St. (682-5621), in Robson Sq., has a small but well-presented collection of art (classical, contemporary) and photography. British Columbian Emily Carr's paintings of surreal trees and totem poles are displayed in abundance, along with an entire floor devoted to the works of Canadian artists. The Gallery compensates for its small collection with innovative exhibitions. Free tours are frequently given for large groups; just tag along. (Open Mon.-Wed. and Fri.-Sat. 10am-5pm, Thurs. 10am-9pm, Sun. noon-5pm. Admission $2.75, senior citizens and students $1.25. Free Thurs. 5-9pm.)

A few smaller, wackier museums are fun to visit. The **BC Sugar Museum,** 123 Rogers St. (253-1131), 1 block west of Clark Dr., at the foot of Rogers on Burrard Inlet, traces the zany history of one company's development since its inception in 1890. The museum is full of old sugar-making equipment, plus goofy letters and photographs related to the industry and those involved in it. Phone ahead for groups larger than 5 people. (Open daily 9:30am-3:30pm. Free.) The **Beatles Museum,** 456 Seymour St. (685-8841), in RPM records at Pender is a Fab Four fanatic's fantasia. Since all the stuff's for sale, the place doesn't qualify as a real museum, but browsers are welcome and the manager has great stories to tell. (Open Mon., Wed., and Sat. 10am-6pm, Thurs.-Fri. 10am-9pm, Sun. noon-5pm.)

Gastown and Chinatown

Gastown is a revitalized turn-of-the-century district viewed with disdain by most locals as an expensive tourist trap. The area is named for "Gassy Jack" Deighton, the glib con man who opened Vancouver's first saloon here in 1867. His statue now stands at the intersection of Water, Powell, and Alexander St. In 1886, a fire flattened 1000 buildings in 45 minutes, including the infamous saloon. But the name thrived on Gastown's subsequent plunge to infamy and poverty. In the 1960s, community groups led the fight for restoration. Today the area is bouncing with craft shops and nightclubs, restaurants and boutiques. Many cater exclusively to tourists, but the area can still be rewarding, especially along **Water Street.** Listen for the continent's only steam-powered clock on the corner of Cambie and Water St.—it chimes every 15 minutes.

Gastown is a fair walk from downtown or a short ride on bus #22 along Burrard St. to Carrall St. It is bordered by Richards St. to the west, Columbia St. to the east, Hastings St. to the south, and the waterfront to the north.

Just east of Gastown, **Chinatown** is within walking distance of downtown. You can also take bus #22 on Burrard St. northbound to Pender and Carrall St., and return by bus #22 westbound on Pender St. The area is rundown and some consider it unsafe. At night, women traveling alone should exercise caution. A safer (albeit expensive) way to see this huge Chinatown is through Gray Line Tours (see Practical Information).

Parks

Stanley Park

Probably the most popular of the city's attractions is Stanley Park (681-1141), on the westernmost end of the city center peninsula. Take bus #19. The massive park is still forested, with running and cycling trails and paved roads crisscrossing under the trees. A **seawall promenade** hugs the watery perimeter. Stanley Park is not an ordinary park with ordinary park facilities. Within the boundaries are odd restaurants, extraordinary tennis courts, the Malkin Bowl (an outdoor theater), and fully equipped beaches that swim. The **Brockton Oval,** located on the park's small eastern peninsula of Brockton Point, is a cinder running track—notice the hot showers and changing rooms. Nature walks are given May-Sept. Tues. at 10am and July-Aug. at 7pm. They start from the Lost Lagoon bus loop (in the morning in May, June, and Sept.) or from Lumberman's Arch Water Park (all other times). **Bike rentals** are possible at the park entrance across from the bus stop (676 Chilco St.; 661-5581). 5-speeds cost $5 per hour or $20 per day, while mountain bikes cost $6 per hour or $25 per day. (ID and $20-30 deposit required.) The shop also distributes a free map of the park. **Lost Lagoon,** a marshy lake next to the Georgia St. entrance, bristles with a number of fish and bird varieties, including the rare trumpeter swan. Stranger aquatic species practice for their Red Cross tests at the **Vancouver Aquarium** (682-1118), on the eastern side of the park, not far from the entrance. The British Columbian, Tropical, and Amazonian Halls are named for the environments they skillfully replicate. The marine mammal complex forces orca and beluga whales to perform in sideshows. The aquarium stages performances several times per day; you'll have to settle for fish flicks on rainy days. (Open daily 9:30am-8pm; in winter 10am-5:30pm. Admission $5.75, senior citizens and ages 13-18 $4.75, under 12 $3.25.) Stanley Park's small, free **zoo** next door is worth visiting just to see the green monkeys pelt the neighboring harbor seals with apple cores. (Open daily 10am-5pm.) The best views in town strike your rods and cones from the middle of the towering, lengthy **Lion's Gate Bridge,** which connects Stanley Park to North Vancouver. Chirping benches in the middle are perched hundreds of metres above the churning green water.

Vanier Park

During the summer, a tiny **ferry** (684-7781) carries passengers from the Aquatic Centre across False Creek to Vanier (VAN-yay) Park and the museum complex located there. (Ferries daily, every 15 min. 10am-8pm. Fare $1.) Another ferry runs from the Maritime Museum in Vanier Park to Granville Island. (Fare $2.) Vanier Park can also be reached by bus #22, heading south on Burrard from downtown.

Once you reach the park, visit the round **Vancouver Museum,** 1100 Chestnut St. (736-7736), guarded by an abstract crab fountain. The museum displays artifacts from Pacific Northwest Native American cultures and several rotating exhibits. Down in the basement lurks Glenn Gould's piano, now considered a national treasure. (Open Mon.-Fri. 10am-9pm, Sat.-Sun. 10am-5pm. Admission $4, senior citizens, students, and ages under 13 $1.50, families $10.) The museum also sponsors a number of free outdoor concerts, dance performances, and workshops during the summer. Contact the museum for details.

Housed in the same building, the **H. R. MacMillan Planetarium** (736-3656) sometimes runs four different star shows per day. Laser shows set to rock music illuminate the roof Tues.-Sun. at 8:30pm. (Star shows $4.25, laser shows $5.25.) The adjacent **Gordon Southam Observatory** is also open to the public, weather permitting. (Open Fri. 7-11pm, Sat.-Sun. noon-5pm and 7-11pm—but call ahead at 738-2855 to make sure. Free.)

The **Maritime Museum** (737-2211) is also part of the complex in Vanier Park. Mercifully non-military in its emphasis, the museum's exhibits exploit photographs and models to trace the growth of Vancouver's harbor and port. An exception to the pacifist atmosphere is the well-restored *St. Roch.* This 1928 Royal Canadian Mounted Police Arctic Patrol Service Vessel gained its fame during World War II, when it became the first ship to negotiate the Northwest Passage. The boat is displayed in its towering entirety, and guided tours are given daily. (Open daily 10am-5pm. Admission $3, senior citizens, students, and ages under 13 $1.50, families $6. Wed. 5-9pm free. Combination tickets to both the Maritime Museum and the Vancouver Museum available.) The Maritime Museum displays more wooden boats in the **Museum Harbour,** on the water. You can wander free of charge at all times of the day and night. The museum holds a "shanty sing" on the dock every Wednesday evening in the summer.

More Parks

Another adored city park is the **Van Dusen Botanical Garden,** 37th Ave. and Oak St. (266-7194). Take bus #17 from Granville Mall. Floral collections of this 55½-acre beauty range from a Sino-Himalayan garden to a growth of heather to an indoor exhibit of Japanese bonsai trees. Summer concerts and craft shows take place in the garden, and special days are planned for senior citizens and the disabled. (Open daily 10am-dusk; in winter 10am-4pm. Admission $3.75, senior citizens and children $2, families $11.)

A quarry transformed into an ornamental sunken garden, **Queen Elizabeth Park,** at 33rd Ave. and Cambie St. (872-5513), overlooks the city center. Take bus #15 from Burrard. Atop the hill, the **Bloedel Conservatory** shoves a collection of tropical plants and birds into a geodesic dome. (Open in summer daily 10am-9pm; otherwise 10am-5:30pm. Admission $2.30, senior citizens and ages 6-18 $1.15.)

The **Dr. Sun Yat-Sen Classical Chinese Garden,** 578 Carrall St. (662-3207), is yet another quiet place to escape from the city. Designed and built by artists brought to Vancouver from China, the garden brandishes many imported plantings and carvings. (Open daily 10am-8pm; Oct.-Apr. 10am-4:30pm. Admission $3, senior citizens, students, and children $2, families $6.)

Beaches

Follow the western side of the seawall south to **Sunset Beach Park** (738-8535), a strip of grass and beach that extends south all the way to the Burrard Bridge. All of Vancouver's beaches have lifeguards from Victoria Day to Labor Day daily from 11:30am to 9pm. At the southern end of Sunset Beach is the **Aquatic Centre,** 1050 Beach Ave. (689-7156), a public facility with a 50m indoor saltwater pool, sauna, gymnasium, and diving tank. (Open Mon.-Thurs. 6:30am-10pm, Sat. 8am-9pm, Sun. 10am-9pm; pool opens Mon.-Thurs. at 7am. Gym use $3, pool use $2.15.)

Kitsilano Beach, known to locals as "Kits," on the other side of Arbutus Ave. from Vanier, is a local favorite beach. It is equipped with a heated saltwater outdoor pool (731-0011; open in summer only). The pool has changing rooms, lockers, and a snack bar. (Beach open daily 7am-8:45pm; Oct.-May Mon.-Fri. noon-8:45pm, Sat.-Sun. and holidays 10am-8:45pm. Admission to the pool $1.35, senior citizens and children 70¢, families $2.70.)

Jericho Beach, to the west, harbors the massive youth hostel (see Accommodations); it tends to be less heavily used than Kits Beach. Jericho begins a border of beaches and park lands that hems Point Grey and the University of British Columbia. Old-growth forest covers much of the extensive UBC campus in a delightfully untailored fashion. Bike and hiking trails cut through the campus and around its edges. The university rests on a hill, granting Lycabettan views of the city and the surrounding mountains.

A scramble down the cliffs to the southwest of the campus will take you to **Wreck Beach,** an unofficial, unsanctioned, unlifeguarded beach for those who will stop at nothing to achieve that all-over tan. In other words, be bare or be square. Any UBC student can point you toward one of the semi-hidden access paths.

Universities

The high point of a visit to the **University of British Columbia (UBC)** is the university's **Museum of Anthropology,** 6393 NW Marine Dr. (228-3825). To reach the campus, take bus #4 or 10 from Granville. The museum's collection is housed in a dramatic glass-and-concrete building whose high ceilings and powerful lines provide an appropriate environment for totems and other massive sculptures by the Native peoples of the Pacific Northwest coast. *Raven and the First Men,* a contemporary carving by Haida artist Bill Reid, strikingly integrates traditional mythologies and modern forms. The $1 *Guide to the UBC Museum of Anthropology,* available at the entrance desk, deepens your understanding of the cultural differences among the various nations that produced these works; much of this information does not appear on exhibit labels. The museum also displays artifacts of other global cultures. Hour-long guided walks will help you sort out the maze of ancient and contemporary works. (Open Tues. 11am-9pm, Wed.-Sun. 11am-5pm. Admission $3, senior citizens and students $1.50, ages 6-12 $1. Tues. free.)

Behind the museum in a weedy courtyard designed to simulate the Pacific coastal islands, the **Outdoor Exhibit** displays a mortuary house and memorial totems of the Haida nation. Each carved figure represents one aspect of the ancestral heritage of the honored dead. Even if you can't afford admission to the museum itself, don't miss this proud, silent soliloquy from a unique and little-known culture.

Curators of the **Nitobe Memorial Garden** (228-3928), to the south of the museum across Marine Dr., keep the small garden immaculate, in traditional Japanese fashion. (Open daily 10am-8pm; Sept.-June 10am-5pm. Admission $1.25, students 50¢. Free in winter Mon.-Fri. 10am-3pm.) The **Asian Centre,** 1871 West Mall (228-2746), near the gardens, often has free exhibits of Asian-Canadian art. The Asian Centre Library contains the largest collection of Asian materials in Canada. (Open Mon.-Fri. 9am-5pm. Call for a schedule of events.)

All of UBC's gardens fall under the official rubric of the **Botanical Garden** (228-4208). The **Main Garden** is in the southwest corner of the campus at 16th Ave. and SW Marine Dr. (note that the entrance and visitor parking area are on Stadium Rd., north of the West Mall). The Main Garden may not be worth the bother, especially to the non-horticulturist. Although pebbles outnumber pistils, the **Physick Gardens** are fascinating; signs alert you to the poisonous nature of some of the plants therein. In the 30-acre **Asian Garden,** through the tunnel and across the street, quiet paths lead past blue Himalayan poppies and rhododendrons. For general and tour information on all the gardens, call the Botanical Garden office weekdays 8:30am-4:30pm. (Open daily 10am-8pm. Admission $2 per garden, free Wed.)

Large maps at entrances to UBC's campus indicate other points of interest and bus stops. In addition to its gardens, UBC also has a public swimming pool in the **Aquatic Centre** (228-4521), a free **Fine Arts Gallery** (228-2759), free daytime and evening concerts (228-3113), and a museum of geology (228-5586). (Museums and pool open Mon.-Fri. 8:30am-4:30pm.) To arrange a walking tour of the campus May through August, call 228-3131.

Vancouver's other major academy is **Simon Fraser University (SFU),** located at the top of Burnaby Mountain, off Hwy. 7A east of the city center. Take bus #10 or 14 to Kootenay Loop, then #135-SFU. The views are splendid, and student activities are plentiful. Call the Student Union at 291-3181 for more information.

Shopping

Granville Mall, on Granville Ave. between Smithe and Hastings St., is one of the few open-air pedestrian malls in Vancouver. Vehicles other than buses are not allowed here. From Hastings St. to the Orpheum Theatre, most shops and restaurants on the mall capitulate to young professionals and business executives on their lunch hours. Beyond W. Georgia St., the mall takes an adolescent twist as expensive department stores defer to theaters, leather shops, and raucous record stores.

A few blocks to the west, the **Harbour Centre,** 555 W. Hastings St., lands a snazzy mall with distinctly non-budget restaurants and a **skylift** for panoramae. (See Sights and Activities: Downtown.) If you are dying to fill your suitcase with chic purchases, head to the ritziest mall west of New York: the **Park Royal Shopping Centre** on Marine Dr. in West Vancouver. Take bus #250, 251, or 252 on Georgia downtown. Graced with pseudo-European delicatessens and shops, the **Robsonstrasse** shopping district, on Robson St. between Howe and Broughton St., invites its patrons to spend their money under kaleidoscopic awnings. **Pacific Centre,** 700 W. Georgia, is proud to be one of Vancouver's newest malls. It is located at the Granville SkyTrain station.

Entertainment

To keep abreast of the entertainment scene, pick up a copy of the weekly *Georgia Straight* (an allusion to the body of water between mainland BC and Vancouver Island), free at newsstands and record stores. The 25¢ *Westender* lists entertainment in that lively neighborhood and also reports on community issues, while the free *Angles* serves the city's gay community. Believers in the New Age and other kinds of upcoming entertainment should peruse the free *Common Ground,* a quarterly with listings and advertisements for restaurants, services, events, bookstores, and workshops. Music of all genres can be found in Vancouver's pubs and clubs; both *Georgia Straight* and the *Westender* have the full rundown.

Blarney Stone Inn, 216 Carrall St. (687-4322). Live Irish music, restaurant, and dance floor. Lunch $5, dinner around $12. Cover $3. Open Mon. 11:30am-5pm, Tues.-Fri. 11:30am-2am, Sat. 5pm-2am.

Town Pump, 66 Water St. (683-6695), a few blocks away from the Blarney Stone in the center of Gastown. Live music nightly from jazz to reggae. Clientele ranges from college students to business people. Snack menu available all day, burgers $6. Open Mon.-Sat. 11:30am-2am, Sun. 11:30am-midnight.

Darby D. Dawes, 2001 MacDonald St. (731-0617), at W. 4th Ave. near Kits Beach. A neighborhood pub with famous Sat. afternoon rock jam sessions. Bring your tuba (or ukelele). Full meals served daily 11:30am-7pm, snacks until 10pm. Entertainment Fri.-Sat. 8pm-1am, Sun. 8pm-midnight.

The Railway Club, 579 Dunsmuir St. (681-1625). Lively jazz sessions Sat. 3-7pm. Get there before the band in the evening and duck the cover charge. Open Mon.-Sat. noon-2am, Sun. 7pm-midnight.

The Gandy Dancer, 1222 Hamilton St. (684-7321), in the warehouse district. Enter on the side facing Pacific Blvd. Most innovative of the dozen gay and lesbian clubs in the city. Tues. and Wed. occasionally feature amusing contests; Fri. for men only. Open daily 7:30am-2am.

Castle Pub, 750 Granville St. (682-2661). Quieter than many of the other gay and lesbian pubs. Frequently sponsors benefit receptions for local charities. Open Mon.-Sat. 10am-midnight.

The **Vancouver Symphony Orchestra (VSO)** plays in the refurbished **Orpheum Theater,** 884 Granville St. (280-4444). The VSO ticketline is 280-3311. The 51-year-old **Vancouver Bach Choir** (921-8012) sometimes performs with the VSO in the Orpheum. Smaller groups appeal to a variety of musical tastes—check the *Westender* for listings.

Robson Square Media Centre, 800 Robson St. (660-2487), sponsors events almost daily during the summer and weekly the rest of the year, either on the plaza at the square or in the centre itself. Their concerts, theater productions, exhibits, lectures, symposia, and films are all free or nearly so. The centre's monthly brochure *What's Happening at Robson Square* is available from the visitors bureau or businesses in the square.

Vancouver also has an active theater community. The **Arts Club Theatre,** Granville Island (687-1644), hosts big-name theater and musicals, and the **Theatre in the Park program,** in Stanley Park's Malkin Bowl, puts on a summer season of musical comedy. Call 687-0174 for ticket information. The annual **Vancouver Shakespeare Festival** (June-Aug. in Vanier Park) often needs volunteer ticket-takers and program-sellers, who may then watch the critically acclaimed shows for free. Call 734-0194 for details. **UBC Summer Stock** (228-2678) puts on four plays during the summer at the Frederick Wood Theatre.

For movie lovers, the **Ridge Theatre,** 16th Ave. and Arbutus (738-6311), often shows European and non-mainstream films. (Tues. free; other nights $6.) The **Hollywood Theatre,** 3123 W. Broadway (738-3211), also runs artsy films, but mixes a heavy dose of Joel Silver into their schedule. (Tickets $3. Doors open at 7pm.) **Vancouver East Cinema,** 2290 Commercial Dr. (253-5455), at E. 7th Ave., screens documentaries and art films for $5.50. **Cinema Simon Fraser,** Images Theatre, SFU (291-4869), charges $2.50 for a variety of films, both Joel Silver and otherwise. (Open Sept.-May.) The **Paradise,** 919 Granville (681-1732), shows double features of first-run movies (triple features on weekends) for $2.50.

Vancouver's universities never cease from cultural activity. The **SFU Centre for the Arts** (291-3514) offers both student and guest-professional theater, primarily from September to May. For UBC's activities, call Public Events Information at 228-3131 or pick up a free copy of *Ubissey.* UBC's film series screens high-quality movies Thursday and Friday nights for $1.50.

Seasonal Events

Attend one of Vancouver's annual fairs, festivals, or celebrations to confirm rumors of the city's cosmopolitan nature. The famed **Vancouver Folk Music Festival** is held in mid-July in Jericho Park. For three days the best acoustic performers in North America give concerts and workshops. The poster for the 1989 festival depicted a muscular woman from a 1920s Soviet propaganda poster offering "real music in a sea of shit." Tickets can be purchased for each event or for the whole weekend. Buy a whole-weekend ticket before June 1 to receive a $5 discount. For more details, contact the festival at 3271 Main St., Vancouver V6V 3M6 (879-2931).

Experience the area's original culture at the **First People's Cultural Festival,** held each June at a different area reserve. A full day of traditional dance and crafts is capped with a salmon barbecue. (Admission $10.) Proceeds benefit the Urban Native Education Centre, 285 E. 5th St. (873-3761). Call the centre for information on the date and location of the festival.

Vancouver's Chinese community fêtes its heritage on **Chinese New Year** (usually in early to mid-Feb.). Fireworks, music, parades, and dragons highlight the celebration. The **Folkfest** (736-1512) in early June features two weeks of multicultural celebrations in Gastown and Robson Sq. All the festivities are free. The Italian and Greek communities both reserve their days of festivities (July and the last week of June, respectively). Food stands, musical performances, food stands, carnivals, and more food stands cluster around each community's center.

Vancouver objectifies its relationship with the sea several times per year. The Maritime Museum in Vanier Park (see Sights and Activities) hosts the annual **Captain Vancouver Day** (736-4431) in mid-June to commemorate the 1792 exploration of Canada's west coast by Captain George Vancouver. Thrills include free boat tours of the harbor, a miniature boat battle, boat model building, hot air balloon rides, and performances by the Shanty Singers. In mid-July, the **Vancouver Sea Festival** (684-3378) schedules four days of parades, concerts, sporting events, fireworks, and salmon barbecues. All events take place in English Bay for free, but you have to pay for the salmon. The headline attraction is the notorious **Nanaimo to Vancouver Bathtub Race,** a journey across the rough waters of the Strait of Georgia for Gilgameshes with rubber duckies.

Near Vancouver

Puff along on the **Royal Hudson Steam Locomotive** (688-7246), operated by 1st Tours. After a two-hour journey along the coast from Vancouver to Squamish (the gateway to Garibaldi Provincial Park), passengers are freed for 90 minutes to browse in town before they head back. (Excursions May 21-July 16 Wed.-Sun.; July 19-Sept. 4 daily; Sept. 6-24 Wed.-Sun. Fare $24, senior citizens and youths $20, children $14.) The train departs from the BC Rail terminal, 1311 W. 1st St., across the Lions Gate Bridge in North Vancouver. Reservations are required.

To the east, the town of **Deep Cove** maintains the salty atmosphere of a fishing village. Sea otters and seals gather on the pleasant Indian Arm beaches. Take bus #210 from Pender to the Phibbs Exchange on the north side of Second Narrows Bridge. From there, take bus #211 or 212. **Cates Park,** at the end of Dollarton Hwy. on the way to Deep Cove, has popular swimming and scuba waters and is a good destination for a day bike trip out of Vancouver. Bus #211 also leads to **Mount Seymour Provincial Park.** Trails leave from Mt. Seymour Rd., and a paved road winds the 8km to the top. One hundred campsites ($7 per site) are available, and the skiing is superb.

For a less vigorous hike that still offers fantastic views of the city, head for **Lynn Canyon Park.** The suspension bridge here is free and uncrowded, unlike its more publicized look-alike in Capilano Canyon. Often called a rip-off by Vancouverites, Capilano charges the gullible tourist $4.50 to walk across its bridge. Try Lynn instead; besides, it's 6m longer. Take bus #228 from the North Vancouver SeaBus terminal and walk the ½km to the bridge. While there, take in the concise exhibits of the **Lynn Canyon Ecology Centre** (987-5922; open daily 10am-5pm; free).

Grouse Mountain, very crowded in winter, is the ski resort closest to downtown Vancouver. Take bus #246 from the North Vancouver SeaBus terminal; at Edgemont and Ridgewood transfer to bus #232, then the "supersky ride." The $10 aerial tramway runs from 9am to 10pm. The slopes are lit until 10:30pm from November to May, and the tram ride is popular with sightseers in summer. On sunny days, helicopter tours leave from the top of the mountain, starting at $25 per person. For more information contact Grouse Mountain Resorts, 6400 Nancy Greene Way, North Vancouver V7R 4N4 (984-0661, ski report 986-6292). Ski rental is available for $16.50 per day; no deposit is required. Full day adult lift tickets are $22.

West of Lions Gate Bridge lies your chance for a closer look at **Georgia Bay.** Cruise down **Marine Drive** or take bus #250 from downtown. Ask to be let out at **Lighthouse Park,** the site of many lovely walking trails. Scuba divers explore the clear waters of **Howe Sound,** just to the west.

The **Reifel Bird Sanctuary** on Westham Island, 16km south of Vancouver, is just northwest of the Tsawwassen ferry terminal. Bus #601 from Vancouver will take you to the town of **Ladner,** 1½km east of the sanctuary. Two hundred and thirty species of birds live in the 850 acres of marshlands, and spotting towers are set up for long-term birdwatching. (Open daily 9am-4pm.) For information contact the **BC Waterfowl Society** at 946-6980.

A classic trip farther outside Vancouver is the two-hour drive up Hwy. 99 to the town of **Whistler** and nearby **Garibaldi Provincial Park.** Follow Hwy. 99 north from Horseshoe Bay, or take local **Maverick Coach Lines** (255-1171). **BC Rail** (see Getting There) also serves Whistler from Vancouver; their run stops directly behind the local youth hostel (see below). Check the ride board at the International Youth Hostel in Vancouver, as trekkers frequently travel between the two. Whistler Mountain is considered top skiing, with the highest accessible vertical drop in North America. Slopes for the beginner and intermediate are also available. For more information contact Whistler Resort Association, Whistler V0N 1B0 (932-4222, or toll-free from Vancouver 685-3650). The park also has some fine wilderness trails, but vehicle access is out of the question. On Alta Lake in Whistler is a pleasant **IYHF youth hostel** (932-5492), which has 35 beds, a living room, cafeteria, but unfortunately no kitchen for personal use. (Members $8, nonmembers $10.50; in winter members $10.50, nonmembers $25.) There is also a **backpacker's hostel** (connected to Vincent's in Vancouver) at 2124 Lake Placid Rd. (932-1177), near the train station. Shared rooms start at $15 per person, and the hostel offers a kitchen, laundry facilities, TV, and a sauna.

On the way to Whistler, stop at the **BC Museum of Mining** in Britannia Beach (688-8735, or 896-2233), 50km north of Vancouver. An electric mine train pumps passengers through an old copper artery into the mountain that produced the largest amount of copper in the British empire: 1.3 billion pounds. (Open mid-May to June Wed.-Sun. 10am-5pm; July-Labor Day daily 10am-5pm; Sept. Sat.-Sun. 10am-5pm. Admission $6, senior citizens and students $3.50.)

Golden Ears Provincial Park is less exciting terrain than Garibaldi, but closer to Vancouver. Drive, cycle, or hitch 50km east to the town of Haney. Turn north on 224th St. and follow it 4km until it ends, then turn right and proceed for 8km. The roads are not well marked, but all roads lead to Golden Ears. Inside the park, the **Cultus Lake Campground** operates 346 tentsites ($10 per site). The park itself has numerous hiking trails, including some short ones to waterfalls.

Fraser River Canyon

Simon Fraser, Canada's solo equivalent of Lewis and Clark, braved 1300km of turbulent water to reach Vancouver from Mt. Robson in 1808. Today a far easier path (the Trans-Canada Hwy.) snakes down the Fraser River between the towns of Hope and Cache Creek. The 200km of snaking rapids are tamer than the Infocentre pamphlets would have you believe, but the sheer size of the steeply sloping, pine-scented Fraser River Canyon qualifies it as the most striking patch of mountains in the province.

In the original "Rambo" movie, *First Blood,* Sylvester Stallone singlehandedly destroyed the town of **Hope**—shooting up cars, blowing up buildings, and maiming a dozen policemen. After a few major repairs and some new draftees to the sheriff's office, the metropolis of 2500 residents remains the most populous stop along the Fraser Canyon, 150km east of Vancouver and 190km south of Cache Creek.

Hope's **Travel Infocentre,** 919 Water Ave. (869-2021), on the main thoroughfare, disseminates exhaustive information on the town and the entire Fraser River Canyon region. (Open daily 8am-8pm; Labor Day-June 25 Tues.-Thurs. 9am-5pm, Fri.-Mon. 8am-8pm.) Try the **Flamingo Hotel** (869-9610), east of town, where singles are $25, doubles $30, and kitchens $5 extra. The town operates a large campground, **Coquihalla River Park,** at 800 Kawkawa Lake Rd. (869-5671), off Hwy. 3 via 7th Ave. Many sites have full hookups, and metered showers make every drop count. (Sites $10.) Hope has its share of fast-food joints, but **Ryan's,** at the junction of the Trans-Canada Hwy. and Hwy. 3 (869-5716), puts great chicken pot pies on your table with more deliberation for $6. (Open daily 6am-10:30pm.)

For a closer look at the Fraser River, set out on the moderate **hiking trails** that lead from trailheads near Hope. The 20-minute **Rotary Trail,** which starts off Wardle St., runs into the confluence of the Fraser and Coquihalla Rivers. If you are looking for something a bit more challenging, climb to the summit of **Thacker Mountain.** To reach the foot of the path, cross Coquihalla River Bridge, make two quick lefts across the creek, then a right onto the road leading to a housing development. The car park at the road's end marks the beginning of a 5km gravel path to the peak, which features clear views of Hope and the Fraser River.

The Gold Rush town of **Yale** boasted a population of 20,000 in 1858, the largest west of Chicago and north of San Francisco; today, the population has dwindled below 250. Yale's inexpensive hotels are conveniently close to Hell's Gate and the town itself is just 30km north of Hope on the Trans-Canada Hwy. Find out every last bit there is to know about the town at the **Yale Historical Society** (863-2324), next to the church at Park and Fraser (open daily June-Sept.). Overnight guests should try the **Fort Yale Motel,** on the Trans-Canada Hwy. (863-2216), an air-conditioned abode with disabled access, near several budget restaurants. (Singles $26. Doubles $30.) **Snowhite Campsite** (863-2252), 5km south on the highway, provides shady sites with coin-operated showers and rakish plaster dwarves. RV facilities. (Sites $9, with hookups $12. Open April-Sept.) Noise from the nearby railroad tracks will plague you no matter where you stay in Yale—be thankful that the trains are short.

Simon Fraser's pioneering jaunt down his namesake river bypassed Yale altogether, but he likened one particularly tumultuous stretch of rapids to the "Gates of Hell." A resort area 25km north of Yale on the Trans-Canada Hwy., **Hell's Gate,** even as viewed from afar, makes Fraser's successful trip seem miraculous, indeed. When melting snow floods the river in spring, the 60m-deep water rushes through the narrow gorge with such force that the air around it vibrates and sizzles. Rockslides, resulting from construction of the Canadian Northern Railway, halted salmon runs here temporarily in 1914. **Airtram,** a gondola straddling the raging waters, offers an eagle's eye view of a 1944 fishery built to give salmon a sexual outlet. (Airtram $6.50; open daily 9am-7pm.) Hitchhikers will find it difficult to leave Hell's Gate.

Hardcore campers will enjoy **Gold Pan River Campground,** 16km west of **Spences Bridge.** The 12 sites ($6) offer no privacy but are only metres away from the rushing **Thompson River.** The less intrepid should opt for **Skihist Provincial Park Campground,** 12km east of **Lytton.** The 50 sites ($8) are protected by gates which are locked 11pm-7am; water and flush toilets are provided (leave yours at home).

According to a popular local legend, two ornery bandits robbed a freight wagon during the 19th-century Cariboo Gold Rush, but were not quick enough to escape the long arm of the Canadian mounties. One of the two was so badly wounded, he barely had time to cache his treasure near a small creek. Residents have yet to find the treasure, but **Cache Creek,** 80km west of Kamloops, grew up around the legend. Visitors can learn more about the town through the **Travel Infocentre** (457-9118), but there is little to do there besides sleep and refuel. Impossible to overlook, the **Castle Inn** (457-9547) is the garish gray medieval castle perched incongruously alongside the highway. The hotel's large, impeccably air-conditioned singles start at $25; the **Dairy Queen** next door is one of the few cheap-eats in town. The closest campground is **Brookside Campsite** (457-6633), just east on Hwy. 1; showers are free, and there is an adjacent store. (Sites $8, with hookups $11. Open May-Oct.)

Okanagan Valley

Brandishing the opulence of its fruit harvests, the somnolence of its towns, and the tranquility of its lakes, the Okanagan Valley plays Herod to Salome-like hordes of tourists. Although some visitors may find only ennui in the long swaths of empty road and the dreamy pace of events, the valley drapes itself in subtler pleasures—camping in an orchard that bursts with newly ripened cherries, romping along lake-adorned Hwy. 97, munching fruit at a family stand, or lapping up the wines at a local winery. In larger Okanagan towns such as Penticton and Kelowna, heated pools, waterslides, and luxury hotels are flaunted; yet these seem drowned out by the deafening silence of the surrounding countryside.

Penticton

Native American settlers named the area wedged between the Okanagan and Skaha Lakes *Pen-tak-tin,* "a place to stay forever." Today those same settlers would spin in their graves if they knew the extent to which their eternal paradise has been usurped by weekend tourists. Hot weather, sandy beaches, and proximity to Vancouver, Seattle, and Spokane have ushered in the inevitable ascension of commercialization and the decline of Penticton's natural serenity. Budget travelers may find it a strain to spend a weekend here, let alone forever. Prices, however, seem not to hinder the zealous sun-worshipers who visit in summer; the beaches bulge with scantily clad men and women, smelling of coconut oil and sporting golden tans. The warm, clean water and sprawling beaches of the Okanagan and Skaha Lakes make for ideal sailing and fishing conditions.

Practical Information and Orientation

Visitor Information: Chamber of Commerce, 185 Lakeshore Dr. (492-4103). Take Riverside Dr. north off Hwy. 97, then right on Lakeshore. A copious supply of travel brochures and an attentive staff. Open daily 8am-8pm; Sept. to mid-June Mon.-Fri. 9am-5pm, Sat.-Sun. 10am-4pm. In summer, the city also sets up **Information Centres** along Hwy. 97 N. and S. While not as expansive as the main office, the information centres carry an ample supply of literature. Open mid-June to Sept. daily 8am-8pm.

Greyhound: 307 Ellis (493-4101). To Vancouver (5 per day, $26.90), Vernon (5 per day, $9.15), and Kelowna (6 per day, $5.25). Open Mon.-Fri. 5:45am-12:45am.

Buses: Penticton Transit Service, 301 E. Warren Ave. (492-5602). Bus service around the city for 65¢ per ride. The Chamber of Commerce carries complete schedules. Service also available to nearby Naramata.

Taxi: Rainbow Taxi, 492-6700.

Car Rental: Budget Rent-A-Car, 1597 Main St. (493-0212). From $10 per day plus 16¢ per km. Must be 21 with major credit card.

Bike Rental: Riverside Bike Rental, 75 Riverside Dr. (493-1188), at Lakeshore Dr. Mountain bikes $6 for 1st hr., $4 per additional hr. Tandems $9 per hr. Open May-Sept. daily 8am-dusk.

Weather: 492-0539.

Women's Shelter: 493-7233.

Hospital: 492-4000. **Ambulance:** 493-1020.

Police: 492-4300.

Post Office: 492-5717. Postal Code: V2A 6J8.

Area Code: 604.

Penticton lies in southcentral British Columbia, 400km east of Vancouver on Hwy. 97. Lake Okanagan borders the north end of downtown. Penticton Airport and the smaller Skaha Lake lie to the south. Main Street (Hwy. 97) bisects the city from north to south.

Accommodations

Because they occupy a major resort city, hotels in Penticton charge more than those in the surrounding towns. Singles do not come much cheaper than $35, especially after Canada Day. Campgrounds convenient to town are scarce.

Ti-ki Shores, 914 Lakeshore Dr. (492-8769). Take advantage of the Okanagan Lake Beach across the street or the hotel's heated pool. Units are clean and fairly large. Singles and doubles $32. In summer $49 (may be cheaper when it rains).

Three Gables Hotel, 353 Main St. (492-3933), in the heart of Penticton, only 5 min. from the depot and the beach. The newly renovated rooms are spaciously appealing. Showers, cable TV, and A/C. Singles $30. Doubles $32. Triples $35. $5 per additional person.

Kozy Guest House, 1000 Lakeshore Dr. (493-8400). Great location on Okanagan Lake Beach. The prices are low for Penticton. Each room features a revolutionary revolving television invented by the owner; you can watch TV even from the bathroom. Showers, but no bathtubs, in every room. Singles $25. Doubles $35. In summer singles $35, doubles $45. Kitchens $10.

Peach Bowl Motel, 1078 Burnaby Ave. (492-8946). Decent rooms in a decent location (2 blocks from the beach) at a splendid price. Singles $25. Doubles $30. In summer singles $30, doubles $35. Kitchens $5.

The Pines Motel, 1896 Main St. (492-3115). The friendly manager is prepared to haggle. The location on Hwy. 97 is convenient for passers-through, not for beach bums. Traffic noise does not die down until 11pm. Singles $40. Doubles $45. Kitchens $6.

Camping

Since you will be paying through the nose anyway, you might as well try to find a campground on the shores of Okanagan Lake. Make reservations well in advance; open sites are a rare find in July and August.

Wright's Beach Camp, Site 40, Comp. 4, R.R. 2 (492-7120). Directly off Hwy. 97 on the shores of Skaha Lake at the south end of town. Nearby traffic is often noisy. Adequate washrooms and showers. Sites $16, hookups $2. Make reservations at least 1 week in advance.

South Beach Gardens, 3815 Skaha Lake Rd. (492-0628), across the street from the beach, east of the Channel Parkway. Fully equipped sites $12.

Park Royal RV Park, 240 Riverside Dr. (492-7051), off Hwy. 97. 25 shaded tenting sites ($15) with extensive facilities.

Food

Although intransigent budget travelers may have to swallow their pride and sell out to McDonalds or Burger King, there are a few local sandwich shops that provide workable alternatives.

Sunshine Sandwich Shop, 410 Main St. (493-2400). This alliterative hole-in-the-wall serves soups, salads, and sandwiches in a variety of combinations for $3. Simple muffin and coffee 95¢. Open Mon.-Fri. 8:30am-4:30pm.

Judy's Deli, 129 W. Nanaimo (492-7029). Healthy beachgoers stop here for thick homemade soups ($1.25-1.50) and butter-laden sandwiches ($2-2.50). Open Mon.-Sat. 9am-5:30pm.

Taco Grande, 452 Main St. (492-7440). Average fast-food Mexican dishes ($1.75-4), but a superior breakfast special—2 eggs, 3 sausages, hash browns, toast, and coffee ($3). Plain gringoburger $2. Open Mon.-Sat. 9am-9pm.

Sights and Seasonal Events

Not surprisingly, much of the Penticton tourist trade revolves around the Okanagan Lake. Sandy, guano-covered beaches and an arid summer make Penticton a popular tanning hangout for a chic young crowd. Try to get off the sand and into the water. **Sail Inland** (492-2628 or 493-8221) arranges cruises, charters, and lessons. **The Marina,** 293 Front St. (492-2628), offers rentals of ski boats and fishing equipment. **Roli's** (493-0244), on the beach next to the Penticton Lodge (the mammoth hotel on the hill), offers windsurfing rentals and lessons. Rentals start at $11 for the first hour. The *Casabella Princess,* 45 E. Lakeshore Dr. (493-5551), gives pleasant paddlewheel cruises on the Okanagan for less active water-worshipers ($8.50, senior citizens and students $6.50).

For a sample of local culture (and a free sample at that) take a trip to the **Art Gallery of the South Okanagan,** 11 Ellis St. (493-2928), at Front St. This lovely beachfront gallery deploys exhibitions on the local and international levels; it firmly stands by its claim to be the world's first solar art gallery. (Open Tues.-Fri. 11am-5pm, Sat.-Sun. 1-5pm.) The **Penticton Museum** (a.k.a. the **R.N. Atkinson Museum**) at 785 Main St. (492-6025) presents a potpourri of Western Canadiana, tracing the history of the region with Native artifacts and wildlife displays. (Open Mon., Wed., and Fri.-Sat. 10am-5pm, Tues. and Thurs. 10am-8:30pm; in winter Mon.-Sat. 10am-5pm.)

Resembling an East African wildlife preserve, the **Okanagan Game Farm,** (497-5405) on Hwy. 97 just south of Penticton, covers 560 acres and protects 130 animal species from the boisterous summer visitors on the lake. All creatures roam free from fences and bars. Cars can drive throughout the park, and animal checklists should keep the children amused. (Admission $6, ages 5-15 $4. Open 8am-dusk.)

During spring (the best season to visit), the colorful **Blossom Festival,** held in April, welcomes the fresh flowers blooming in hundreds of apple, peach, and cherry orchards. The city shifts into full gear with the **Peach Festival** at the end of July and the torturous **Ironman Canada Triathlon** in August. The Peach Festival offers recreational and aquatic activities for all ages, while the nonstop triathlon commits true athletes to 4km of swimming, 180km of bicycling, and 45km of running. The mists and mellow fruitfulness of fall mark the ripening of the wine season. There are five wineries within easy driving distance of Penticton; the closest one, **Casabello Wines,** 2210 Main St. (492-0621), offers regular tours and free tasting. Nearby, **Apex Alpine,** 185 Lakeshore Dr. (collect 492-4181), provides winter diversion with six ski lifts, 35 runs, and a 670m vertical drop.

Kelowna

Gravitating towards Ogopogo, Kelowna's cordial riposte to the Loch Ness monster, summer events in this pleasant resort cluster about the lake. However, the renowned 81-year-old Kelowna Regatta, traditionally the summer's centerpiece, came to a screeching halt in 1988 after two riots deranged the extravaganzas. That summer, events from watersports to air shows quickly evolved into something quite different from family-oriented fun; tear gas was even called into play. The second, Adorno-incited riot was, in fact, better organized than the regatta itself. Signs as far away as Vancouver advertised the event and trucks filled with rocks drove in just for the "festivities." The city of Kelowna has since discontinued its annual celebration. Despite this somewhat unexpected setback, Kelowna still tempts tourists with a diverse dining scene, dozens of reasonable motels, miles of smashing beaches, and enough free wine to make you forget there ever was a regatta.

Practical Information and Orientation

Visitor Information: Travel Infocentre, 544 Harvey Ave. (861-1515). Large office plastered with brochures on local tours and events. The staff smiles. Open daily 8am-8pm; Labor Day-late June 9am-5pm. **Infocentre II,** 500m north of the airport (765-0338). More brochures and beaming smiles. Same hours as the mothership.

Greyhound: 2366 Leckie Rd. (860-3835). To Calgary (2 per day, $47), Banff (2 per day, $37.30), Cache Creek (2 per day, $18.45), and Kamloops (2 per day, $13).

Buses: Kelowna City Bus Transit (860-8121). Limited service to the beach, downtown, shopping centers, and Greyhound. You can catch all the buses downtown at the intersection of Ellis St. and Bernard Ave. Fares start at 65¢, senior citizens and students 50¢. A Day Pass costs $1.75 (senior citizens and students $1.25).

Car Rental: Budget Rent-A-Car, 1553 Harvey Ave. (860-2464). From $36 per day plus 17¢ per km on weekdays. 3-day weekend specials from $20 plus 16¢ per km. Must be 21 with credit card. Open Mon.-Fri. 7am-6pm, Sat. 7am-4pm, Sun. and holidays 9am-4pm. **Rent-A-**

Wreck, 2702 Hwy. 97 N. (763-6632). From $19 per day plus 14¢ per km. Must be 21 with credit card.

Bike Rental: Scott's Rent-A-Bike (762-9463), on Rotary Beach off Lakeshore Rd. From BMX bikes ($4 per hr., $18 per day) to tandems ($7 per hr., $30 per day). Also sponsors guided 3½-hr. tours of Kelowna during July and Aug., picnic lunch included, for $16.50. Open June Sat.-Sun. 11am-6pm; July-Aug. daily 11am-6pm.

Crisis Hotlines: Adults 763-9191; teens 763-3366.

Weather: 765-4027.

Emergency: 911.

Police: 762-3300.

Post Office: 471 Queensway Ave. (762-2118 or 763-4095). Open Mon.-Fri. 8:30am-5pm. Postal Code: V1Y 7N2.

Area Code: 604.

Downtown Kelowna crams against the eastern side of Lake Okanagan. **Highway 97,** which becomes Harvey Avenue downtown, runs directly through the city and crosses the lake on a 620m floating bridge, the largest of its ilk in Canada. The highway leads directly north to Salmon Arm and south to Penticton. Streets in the downtown area are plotted according to an ordered grid system.

Accommodations and Camping

Rooms in Kelowna can be as elusive and as commodified as Ogopogo. Call well in advance for reservations in both the summer and winter, when many hotels fill up with monthly renters. Rates often take a dive during the off-season.

Rainbow Motel, 1810 Gordon Dr. (763-3544), 2 blocks off Hwy. 97. Some of the lowest prices in town. All rooms have A/C and cable TV; some have refrigerators. Singles $32. Doubles $34.

Ponderosa Motel, 1864 Harvey Ave. (860-2218). About as homey and secluded as a roadside motel can be—friendly rooms and tidy management. Only 16 units, so call ahead. Singles $33. Doubles $36. Kitchens available.

Kenogan Motel, 1750 Gordon Dr. (762-3222) at Harvey Ave. Peeling paint and abused furniture, but everything functions. Singles $24. Doubles $26.

The Meadows, 4193 Gordon Dr. (764-4296), 5km south of the city. One of many nearby bed and breakfasts, this delightful old farmhouse is only a short drive from the city center. A great escape. Singles $20. Doubles $30. Open May-Sept.

Quo Vadis Motel, 3199 Lakeshore Rd. (763-4022). Too expensive for the single traveler, but king-sized beds in singles can sleep 2 easily, 3 if you're all close chums. Suites accommodate up to 6. Gargantuan TV in room. Heated swimming pool. Singles $45. Doubles $50. Kitchenettes available.

Kelowna has two major camping areas, one on the east side of the river and one on the west. For some unknown reason, the western campgrounds are less expensive than their eastern neighbors. Traveling west along Hwy. 97 across the floating bridge, take a left on Boucherie Ave. and continue for a few kilometres to campground country. **Happy Valley** on Pritchard St. (768-7703; $14), **Billabong Beach** on Boucherie Ave. (768-5913; $11), and **Green Bay** on Green Bay Rd. (768-5913; $15) all offer sandy services and sophisticated beaches. Happy Valley tends a cherry orchard where happy visitors are happily welcome to pick as many cherries as they wish (remember *The Witches of Eastwick,* though). Green Bay operates cabins where four can sleep for $40 per night.

Food

Although beef still reigns supreme in Kelowna (seafood runs a distant second), the town is beginning to discover the delights of lighter fare. Try cruising the backstreets for mouth-watering bakeries and ice cream shops. There is a **Safeway** super-market on Richter and Bernard (open daily 8am-10pm).

Jonathan L. Segals, 262 Bernard Ave. (860-8449). Stay cool on the roof overlooking the lake while pecking at some of Kelowna's best food. An original menu features everything trendy from tofu burgers ($4) to pizza bagels ($2). Sandwiches and burgers quietly soar at $4-6. "Open 11:30am-Late!" it says—at least 1am, 2am on weekends.

Roxy's Cafe, 1630 Ellis St. (763-1000). High ceilings, tall drinks, and a lunatic menu ensure popularity with locals. Moderately priced burgers ($4-6) and salads ($3-6). Open Mon.-Thurs. 11:30am-9pm, Fri.-Sat. 11:30am-midnight, Sun. 5-9pm.

Earl's Hollywood on Top, 211 Bernard Ave. (763-2777). Turn north on Bernard just east of Okanagan Lake off Hwy. 97. This area favorite serves up Hollywood Ribs ($11) as well as other beef and fresh seafood dishes. Outdoor dining. Open Sun.-Thurs. 11:30am-11pm, Fri.-Sat. 11:30am-midnight.

The Little Affair Soup and Sandwich, 325 Bernard Ave. (860-1955). This aptly named sand-wich shop shies away from the big meals, serving superb sandwiches instead. You can get anything you want between two slices—from peanut butter and banana to shrimp and avo-cado. Delicious carrot muffins. Open Mon.-Fri. 8am-8pm, Sat. 10am-2pm.

Poor Boys, 450 Bernard. Hums 7 days a week. Your choice of liver and onions, meatloaf, Cornish game hen, or halibut and chips $5, $4.45 for senior citizens. Draft beer $1.25. Soup and sandwich lunch special $3. Open Mon.-Sat. 8am-10pm, Sun. 10am-8pm.

Sights

In Kelowna, the term "vineyards" translates into "four wineries and four free wine-tasting rooms." **Calona Wines,** 1125 Richter St. (762-9144), 6 blocks directly off Hwy. 97, is the second largest winery in all of Canada and offers free guided tours on the half-hour, between 9am and 4pm in the summer. Sample as many wines as you wish, then stumble into the gift shop and buy 35 rhinestone *Batman* jackets. (Open daily 9am-6pm; in winter Mon.-Sat. 10am-5pm, Sun. 11am-5pm.) Other win-eries near the city include **Grey Monk Estate Cellars,** 5450 Lakeshore Dr. (766-3168), north of Kelowna (tours given daily noon-3pm on the hour; free), the **Cedar Creek Estate Winery** (764-8866) south of town; and **Mission Hill Vineyards,** corner of Boucherie Rd. and Mission Hill (768-5125), to the west (tours given daily 10am-7pm on the hour; free). True connoisseurs should arrive in early October for the annual **Okanagan Wine Festival,** which features fashion shows, craft fairs, and, of course, an evening of serious wine tasting.

Sippers who like free samples but prefer their grapes somewhat younger should visit the **Sun-Rype Fruit Juice Factory,** at 1165 Ethel St. in Kelowna (762-2604). This Canadian company has been harvesting plants for its plant since 1889, and from June through September they'll show you how it's done at no charge. (Open Mon.-Fri. 9am-3pm.) Hardcore drinkers should sprint for some spirits to the **Hiram Walker Okanagan Distillery** in nearby Winfield on Jim Bailey Rd. The producers of over 50 potables, including Canadian Club whisky, offer free tours and tastings five times per day (Mon.-Fri.) during the summer. Call ahead (763-4922) to arrange a tour.

With the loss of the regatta, summertime visitors searching for seasonal entertain-ment will have to settle for the less rowdy theatrical tradition of the **Sunshine The-atre.** The established ensemble presents professional dramas from late June to late August in the air-conditioned **Kelowna Community Theatre.** For more information write to Sunshine Theatre, P.O. Box 443, or call 763-4025.

Water buffs who want to risk an appearance by Ogopogo can rent canoes from **Lee Outfitters,** S1-C6 R.R. #1, Glenmore Rd. (762-8156). Waterskiers, fishermen, and families wishing to cruise on the Okanagan will find everything they need at **Kelowna Marina,** P.O. Box 1167 (762-3128). Bring your bathing suit and gobs of the white stuff lifeguards wear on their noses.

Kelowna definitely focuses on the outdoorsy crowd, but rained-in geologists can visit the **Kelowna Museum,** 470 Queensway (763-2417), for a view of the city's natu-ral history; the **Kelowna Art Gallery** (762-2226) is in the same building. Free **walk-**

ing tours of Kelowna's art galleries leave from the Chamber of Commerce; call 763-9803 to arrange a tour.

Southeastern British Columbia

Revelstoke

Named after the British banker who supplied the money to build a much-needed railroad into the wilderness, 19th-century Revelstoke was once a town straight out of a Peckinpah film, with dust-encrusted maniacs maiming each other amid the gold-infested Selkirk Mountains. Nestled between the impressive snow-capped peaks of the Selkirk and Monashee Mountains, the town now seems best suited for an older, Winnebago-ensconced crowd. The city is, however, striving to entice a younger set of skiers and hikers.

Practical Information and Orientation

Visitor Information: Travel Information Centre, junction of Hwy. 1 and Hwy. 23 (837-3522). **Chamber of Commerce,** 205 E. 1st St. (837-5345), downtown. Useful and convenient. For more information write to the Chamber, P.O. Box 490, Revelstoke V0E 2S0.

Greyhound: 1899 Fraser Dr. (837-5874), just off Hwy. 1. To Calgary ($31.80), Vancouver ($40), and Salmon Arm ($7.70). Open Mon.-Fri. 5:30am-7pm and 10pm-midnight.

Taxi: Johnnie's, 314 Townley St. (837-3000).

Car Rental: Tilden Car Rental, 301 W. 1st St. (837-2158). New cars at decent rates. $32 per day with 100 free km plus 10¢ per additional km. Must be 21 with credit card.

Bicycle Rental: Revelstoke Cycle Shop, 120 Mackenzie Ave. (837-2648). Rents mostly mountain bikes ($6 per hr. or $24 per day) and an occasional 10-speed. Also offers guided tours through town and, in July, tours of Glacier National Park. Open Mon.-Thurs. and Sat. 9am-5:30pm, Fri. 9am-8pm.

Ambulance: 374-5937.

Police: 837-5255.

Post Office: 307 W. 3rd St. (837-3228). Open Mon.-Fri. 8am-5pm. Postal Code: V0E 2S0.

Area Code: 604.

Revelstoke borders the Trans-Canada Hwy., 410km west of Calgary and 575km east of Vancouver. The town itself is relatively small and can be easily covered on foot or by bicycle.

Accommodations and Camping

Numerous inexpensive hotels line Revelstoke's rim along the Trans-Canada Hwy. A quick detour into the town, however, will give you a bed for the same low price. Local campgrounds tend to favor the RV driver over the backpacker.

L & R Nelles Bed & Breakfast, Hwy. 23 (837-3800), 2km from the Trans-Canada Hwy. A bit more expensive than most bargain hotels, but the atmosphere will cure your homesickness. One night's lodging in this large family ranch includes a parental breakfast of bacon, eggs, hash browns, and coffee. Singles $25. Doubles $35. Twin beds $40. Each additional adult $15, child $10. No reservations necessary.

Hidden Motel, 1855 Big Eddy Rd. (837-4240). Take Hwy. 23 south from Trans-Canada Hwy., turn left on Big Eddy Rd. Cozy, comfortable family-operated hotel. Every room comes with its own stove, refrigerator, kitchen sink, and cable TV. Great for groups of up to 6; families and children welcome. Singles and doubles $33. Each additional person $5. Senior citizen discount $2.

Frontier Motel, corner of Trans-Canada Hwy. and Hwy. 23 (837-5119). 28 small but adequate rooms. Exuberant staff. Popular restaurant run by the same management next door. 24-hour store. Singles $34. Doubles $37. Quads $40. Prices drop $3 in winter.

Smokey Bear Campground, Hwy. 1, 5km west of Revelstoke. Convenient location, but so close to the highway that logging trucks rumbling by at 2am may awaken light sleepers. Clean bathrooms, metered showers, laundromat, and amply stocked store. Both RVs and tents are welcome. Sites $7, each additional person 75¢. Electricity $2, sewer $1, fresh water 50¢. Open May-Oct.

Canyon Hot Springs, Hwy. 1 (837-2420), 35km east of Revelstoke on the border of Mt. Revelstoke National Park. The staff is pleasant, and the scenic location—near both Mt. Revelstoke and Glacier National Parks—is convenient for exploring the mountains. Caters more to RVs than to backpackers. Sites $12. Group rates available on request. Open May-Sept.

Food

The downtown dining scene is dominated by a variety of Chinese and Italian restaurants. You would have to head many kilometres to the west along Hwy. 1 for a Whopper or a box of McDonaldland Cookies.

Annie's Kitchen, 1401 Victoria Rd. (837-2042). Baseball caps and plaid shirts pack in for the large portions. The $3 breakfast special includes a cup of good, strong coffee. Soup and sandwich $3.50. Open daily 6am-9pm.

Manning's Restaurant, 302 MacKenzie Ave. (837-3253). The best Chinese food in town; a wide array of continental dishes, also. Reasonably priced. Beef and broccoli $5.75, sweet and sour spareribs $6, 8- or 12-oz. steaks $1 per oz.

Frontier Restaurant, at the junction of Hwy. 1 and Hwy. 23 (837-5119). The Frontier dishes out large helpings of the "Ranchard," ½-lb. of beef with the works ($6). Tenderfoots may prefer the simpler "bareback" ($3.25). Open daily 6am-9pm.

Brenda's, 104 Connaught (837-3030), in the Macleod's Bldg. This is where the locals serve themselves homemade food. Self-service lunch and breakfast specials $2-4. Try the belgian waffles made by **Gerard's Belgian Waffle Store** down the street.

A.B.C. Family Restaurant, Victoria St. (837-5491). Part of a chain of "family" restaurants, but maintains an original atmosphere nonetheless. Huge menu ranges from $6-9 for dinner entrees. Try the croissant lunch ($4.75), and how you dare pass up a homemade slice of pie ($2-3). Open daily 6am-10pm.

Burger Junction, 1601 Victoria Rd. (837-2724). Better-than-average fast-food burgers ($2-3) satisfy many. Follow your meal with a chocolate banana delight ($2). Open daily 10am-10pm; in winter Mon.-Sat. 10:30am-7:30pm.

Sights

All tourism in town revolves around the **Revelstoke Dam,** 5km north of Hwy. 1 on Hwy. 23 (837-6515 and 837-6211). Don't think that if you've seen one dam, you've seen them all. The dam's **visitor centre** underscores the dam's mechanical marvels by means of a free tour directed via shortwave radio receiver. Take the elevator to the top of the dam for an impressive view. (Open daily mid-March to mid-June 9am-5pm; mid-June to mid-Sept. 8am-8pm; mid-Sept. to Oct. 29 9am-5pm. Disabled access.) Dedicated tourists trekking downtown should poke their heads into the **Revelstoke Museum and Archives** (837-3067), 315 1st St. W. Like most other small town museums, this one resides in an old government building (the post office) and features a modest ensemble of local turn-of-the-century artifacts. Note the extensive collection of early 20th-century photography. (Open June-Aug. Mon.-Sat. noon-9pm; May, Sept., and Oct. Mon.-Fri. 1-5pm; Nov.-April Mon., Wed., and Fri. 1-4pm.)

Mt. Revelstoke National Park has many of the scenic attractions one expects from the Canadian national parks. Despite its relatively small size (260 sq. km), the park produces enough different flora and fauna to keep biologists and nature lovers eternally confused. Thirty-five kilometres of established trails lead to many excellent **fishing** lakes—apply at the park information centre for a permit. Those not wishing to climb to the summit of Mt. Revelstoke can take a winding scenic road all the way to the peak. **Summit Road** leaves the Trans-Canada Hwy. 1.5km east of Revelstoke and takes about an hour to drive. Ask the **park superintendent,** 313 3rd St. W. (837-5155), about the park's other pleasures.

Two special **boardwalks** just off Hwy. 1 on the eastern border of the park allow visitors to explore the local flora in depth. One trail leads through "acres of stinking perfection"—a vast expanse of skunk cabbage plants which grow to heights of over 1.5m. The other wanders into a forest full of giant cedar trees, some over 1000 years old.

Revelstoke has tried some curious variations on the downhill theme to spice up its winter ski season. **Mount Mackenzie, P.O.** Box 1000 (collect 837-9489), 5km outside of town, gives you a chance to climb deep bowls of powdered snow in motorized Snow Cats. Experts may want to try **Helicopter Skiing, P.O.** Box 1409, Golden (344-5016), in the Selkirks, while **cross-country** skiers can find more than enough snow and trails in the nearby national parks to keep them busy all winter long. Contact **Ski Revelstoke, P.O.** Box 1479 (837-9489), for more information. Summer vacationers might wish to contact **Monashee Outfitting, P.O.** Box 2958 (837-3588), which sponsors just about every outdoor activity possible, including horse rides, fishing trips, hunting trips, and gold panning.

Glacier National Park

For a $5000 salary bonus and immortality on the map, Major A.B. Rogers discovered a route through the Selkirk Mountains which finally allowed East to meet West in Canada's first transcontinental railway. Completed in 1885, the railway was a dangerous enterprise; over 200 lives were lost to avalanches during its first 30 years of operation. Today, **Rogers Pass** lies in the center of Glacier National Park, 1350 square kilometres that commemorate the efforts of Rogers and other hardy frontiersmen toward uniting British Columbia with the rest of Canada.

Avalanches, grizzly bears, and harsh winters conspire to render Glacier National Park a beloved stomping ground for rugged outdoor enthusiasts. With over 140km of challenging trails, Glacier provides plentiful hiking and camping for those who wish to rough it in the Selkirks. For the hiker on wheels, the Trans-Canada Highway bisects the park into a pleasant 45-minute drive, complete with spectacular views of over 400 glaciers. The best time to visit Glacier is from mid-June to late September, when the climate is relatively mild; unfortunately, during the summer months rain falls one out of every two days.

Hikers not directly descended from Sir Edmund Hillary should avoid the park in winter, as near-daily snowfalls and the constant threat of avalanches often restrict travel to the Trans-Canada Hwy. Preemptive snowslides, often induced by the Canadian Armed Forces and their 105mm howitzers, can block the highway itself.

Practical Information and Orientation

Visitor Information: Park Administration Office, 313 3rd St. W. (837-5155), west of the park in Revelstoke. Knowledgeable staff ready to answer any questions about the Canadian National Parks. Open Mon.-Fri. 8am-4pm. Write the Superintendent, P.O. Box 350, Revelstoke V0E 2S0. **Rogers Pass Centre,** located along the Trans-Canada Hwy. in Glacier National Park, has enough computerized information, large scale models, and photographs on the history of Glacier to warrant a visit. Do not miss the free 25-min. movie *Snow War,* which is shown on the hour and includes a chilling scene from an actual avalanche rescue. Open daily 8am-9pm; in winter 9am-5pm.

Greyhound: 837-5874.

Emergency: 837-6274.

Area Code: 604.

Glacier lies right in the path of the Trans-Canada Hwy., 262km west of Calgary and 723km east of Vancouver.

Accommodations, Camping, and Food

The pickings for indoor lodging in the park are mighty slim. The **Best Western Glacier Park Lodge,** Trans-Canada Hwy., The Summit, Rogers Pass (837-2126), has the only beds in town. Rooms are nice, with comfortable beds and clean bathrooms. Not surprisingly, these amenities make the lodge too expensive for the average budget traveler: singles $75, doubles $80 during peak summer months, with children under 12 free and a 10% discount for senior citizens.

Glacier National Park has three campgrounds: **Loop Brook, Mountain Creek,** and **Illecillewaet** (ILL-uh-SILL-uh-watt). Backcountry camping is also permitted, but be sure to register beforehand with the warden service and pitch your tent at least 3km from the highway. All three open in mid-June and close by the end of September, though Illecillewaet stays open in winter without plumbing. Winter guests must register at the **Administration Office** at Rogers Pass. Be forewarned, however, that 10-foot snow drifts in November make camping a survival sport. Unserviced sites at Mountain Creek, the largest of the three campgrounds, cost $6.50. Similar sites at the other two run $8.50 per night. The brochure *You Are In Bear Country* at Rogers Pass will be of use if you prefer not to become a late-night snack for a Smoky-become-Freddy. During the summer the camps have bathrooms with fresh cold water, but no showers. Park passes are $20 per year, with a daily rate of $3 per car (4 days $6). The only restaurant in the area is at the Best Western, where prices are certainly not budget and proper attire is required.

Sights

The Trans-Canada Hwy.'s numerous scenic turn-offs are embellished by picnic facilities, bathrooms, and historical plaques. For a more detailed description of the various hiking trails, contact the Park Administration Office or pick up a copy of *Footloose in the Columbias* at the Rogers Pass Information Centre. The highest concentration of hiking trails can be found near the Illecillewaet campground, 3.4km west of Rogers Pass. Seven well-marked trails provide spectacular views of the area's mountains and glaciers. From early July to late August, the Rogers Pass Information Centre runs daily interpretive tours through the region beginning at 10am. Come prepared for one of these 4-6 hour hikes with a picnic lunch, a rain jacket, and a sturdy pair of walking shoes. The park also promotes skiing, snowshoeing, and, on a trial basis, mountain biking. Talk to a park official, however, before propelling yourself in such fashion.

Northern British Columbia and the Yukon

The sheer physical beauty of the Yukon and Northern British Columbia amply rewards those willing to put up with the nasty weather, poor road conditions, and the loneliness of a land that averages one person per 15 square kilometres. Native Canadians gave this area its name when they called the Yukon River "Yuchoo," or Big River. The first region of North America to be settled, some 20,000 years ago, the Yukon and Northern British Columbia have remained largely untouched.

The Cariboo Highway

The portion of Hwy. 97 known as the Cariboo Hwy. runs approximately 500km north-south between Cache Creek and Prince George. So uninteresting is most of the route that stops carry official names such as "100 Mile House" and "108 Mile Ranch." Fortunately, two towns went out on a limb with their names. **Williams Lake,** at Mile 155, has several motels with rooms under $30. **Valley View Motel** (392-4655) is right off the highway, with a restaurant and air-conditioned singles for $25. Just next door is the **Lakeside Motel** (392-4181), with singles for $25, campsites for $7.50, and full hookups for $13.50. The town of **Quesnel,** precisely halfway between Williams Lake and Prince George, is home to the **Wheel Inn Motel,** 146 Carson Ave. (992-8975), which has the cheapest rooms in town (singles from $24). **Roberts Roost Campground,** 3121 Gook Rd. (747-2015), is in **Dragon Lake,** 16km south of Quesnel. Open April to October, the campground has showers, flush toilets, laundry facilities, and a swimming beach. (Sites $10, full hookup $13.)

Williams Lake places a **Travel Infocentre** right on the highway, and Quesnel hides one in Le Bourdais Park, 703 Carson Ave. Williams Lake carries on the Western rodeo tradition, jumping and carousing to the **Williams Lake Stampede,** held for four days starting the first weekend of July. For further information, contact the Infocentre at 1148 Broadway, V2G 1A2 (392-5025). Eighty kilometres east of Quesnel, the hollers of a restored gold-mining town echo in **Barkerville.** The town survives solely by luring tourists with wild-west costumes, period buildings, and gold-panning. Check with the Visitor Services Officer, Barkerville V0K 1B0 (994-3332), for a schedule of the town's events. For reasonably complete coverage of the entire Cariboo region, pick up a free copy of *Cariboo Calling,* published by the 100 Mile Free Press each year.

Prince George

Named for the British Prince whom Shelley described as "mud from a muddy spring," Prince George was not incorporated until its infusion with railway workers in 1915. Today, the town prides itself on its spontaneity and originality; during February's Mardi Gras festival, elaborately costumed locals compete in a golf tournament—in the snow. In between festivals, however, the town has a strange, almost eerie, feel to it. The 50-square-block downtown is made up mostly of one-story buildings in various states of disrepair. A few modern, 15-story office buildings perch around the edge of the area, confusing the picture. The streets are broad and virtually devoid of cars or people, and yet the city proudly publicizes the fact that it has installed parking structures supplying 5000 spaces. It seems as if the town grew rapidly, only to have its citizens quickly and mysteriously pack up and head out. Perhaps Prince George's 68,000 residents simply spend all their time in the suburbs, enjoying the city's 100 parks and 60 baseball diamonds.

Practical Information and Orientation

Visitor Information: Travel Infocentre, 1198 Victoria St. (562-3700), at 15th Ave. Pick up a free, detailed map of the city. Open Mon.-Fri. 8am-5pm. Another location at the junction of Hwy. 16 and 97 (563-5493), open May-Sept. daily 9am-8pm. Pick up a free, detailed map of the city.

BC Rail: 561-4033, at the end of Terminal Blvd., 2km south on Hwy. 97. To Vancouver (1 per day in summer, 3 per week in winter, $61) along one of British Columbia's most eye-popping routes. Reservations recommended. **VIA Rail,** 1300 1st Ave. (564-5233), at the foot of Quebec St. To Edmonton, AB (3 per week, $75), Jasper, AB (3 per week, $43), and Prince Rupert (3 per week, $59). Senior citizen and student 1/3 off. Terminal open Mon., Wed., Fri. 3-6pm and 7pm-midnight; Tues. and Thurs. midnight-6:30am and 8am-9:30pm; Sat. 1-6:30am.

Greyhound: 1566 12th (563-4508), across from the Infocentre. Buses to Whitehorse, YT (1 per day, $141.55), Edmonton, AB (2 per day, $58.25), Vancouver (3 per day, $52.80), Prince Rupert (2 per day, $53.25), and Dawson Creek (2 per day, $31.65). Open Mon.-Sat. 5:30am-midnight, Sun. 5:30-10:15am, 3:15-6pm, and 8:30pm-midnight.

Public Transportation: Prince George Transit, 1039 Great St. (563-0011). Limited service around the downtown area, but everything's within walking distance anyway. Fare 75¢, senior citizens 50¢, students 60¢. Runs Mon.-Sat. 8:30am-5pm.

Taxi: 564-4444.

Car Rental: Rent-A-Wreck, 1956 3rd Ave. (563-7336). $17 per day, plus 11¢ per km. Must be 21 with credit card. Open Mon.-Fri. 8:30am-5:30pm, Sat. 9am-5pm. **Tilden,** 1155 1st Ave. (564-4847). $35 per day, plus 12¢ per km. Weekend special $15 per day with 100 free km. Must be 21 with credit card. Open Mon.-Fri. 7:30am-5:30pm, Sat. 8am-5pm, Sun. 8am-4pm.

Library: 887 Dominion (563-5528 for a machine, 563-9251 for a person). Open Mon.-Thurs. 10am-9pm, Fri.-Sat. 10am-5:30pm.

Highway Conditions: 564-2524.

Crisis Center: 563-1214.

Ambulance: 564-4558.

Police: 563-1111.

Post Office: 1323 5th Ave. (561-5184). Open Mon.-Fri. 8:30am-5pm. Postal Code: V2L 4R8.

Area Code: 604.

Prince George lies roughly equidistant from four major Canadian cities: 780km northeast of Vancouver, 720km southeast of Prince Rupert, 735km west of Edmonton, and 790km northwest of Calgary. The airport is at the eastern end of town, a $5 cab ride from downtown. Both the VIA Rail and Greyhound stations are centrally located, within walking distance of hotels and restaurants.

Accommodations and Camping

Queensway Court Motel, 1616 Queensway St. (562-5068), near downtown. Take Queensway north off Hwy. 97. Standard hotel fare, but reasonably inexpensive. Singles $29. Doubles $33.

Spruceland Inn Ltd., 1391 Central St. (563-0102), at the junction of Hwy. 97 and 15th Ave. near the Infocentre. Costs a bit more than the run-of-the-mill budget hotel, but the indoor pool, excellent large rooms, and central location make it worth the extra money. Singles $36. Doubles $40. Make reservations well in advance.

The National Hotel, across from VIA station. Pulsating music from the bar below and the loud voices of the semi-permanent residents might keep you awake. The only redeeming quality of this hotel is the price. Singles with shared bath $18. Doubles $32.

South Park Trailer Park, on Hwy. 97 (963-7577), 5km south of Prince George. Somewhat bare sites, but removed from the highway. The bathrooms are clean but woefully inadequate, with only one toilet and one shower—expect a shower line in the morning. Sites with full hookup $8.

Red Cedar Inn, on Bear Rd. (964-4427), 5km west off Hwy. 16. Low prices, but the sites are so close to the highway that you can see the whites of the eyes of drivers passing by. Sites $9, with full hookup $13.

Spruceland KOA, on Hwy. 16 (964-7272), immediately across from Red Cedar Inn. The high quality expected from a KOA: heated pool, free showers, laundry room, and store. Sites $12, with full hookup $16.

Food

Prince George serves middle-of-the-road cuisine: average plates for average prices. Two days out of town you will not remember when, where, or how much you ate. The hyperkinetic eateries lined up along Central St., west of downtown, are not a bad option considering the bleak culinary landscape.

Earl's, 15th Ave. and Central St. (562-1527). Part of a Canadian chain, but well worth a visit. On your way in, dodge droppings from the countless *papier mâché* parrots overhead. To stand out from the crowd, wear something that *isn't* Day-Glo. Burgers, fish, creative sandwiches (all around $6), and steaks ($10-12). Open Mon.-Thurs. 11:30am-midnight, Fri.-Sat. 11:30am-1am, Sun. 11:30am-10pm.

Nick's Place, 363 George St. (562-2523). Bare bulbs on the walls make it difficult to see what you're eating. Large dish of surprisingly good spaghetti $5.50. Open Mon.-Sat. 11am-3:30pm, Sun. 4-11pm.

Royal Jade Restaurant, at 3rd and Dominion (562-8888). Standard breakfast with eggs, bacon, and toast $2. Lunch and dinner are strictly Chinese ($5 per dish). Open Mon.-Sat. 8am-7pm, Sun. 8am-2pm.

Pastry Chef Bakery (564-7034), across from Nick's. 30% off day-old goodies. Open Mon. 10am-5pm, Tues.-Thurs. and Sat. 9am-5:30pm, Fri. 9am-6pm.

Sights and Seasonal Events

Cottonwood Island Nature Park, a 3km walk from downtown along Patricia Blvd., has plenty of comfortable walking trails. For a bird's eye view of the rich landscape, climb to **Connaught Hill Park,** off Queensway on Connaught Dr. **Fort George Park,** at the eastern end of 20th Ave., houses the **Fort George Regional Museum,** which includes a wooden life preserver, a collection of primitive chain saws, and $1.25 rides on an original steam-engine train. (Open Wed.-Mon. 10am-5pm, Tues. 10am-8pm; Sept. 16-May 14 Mon.-Fri. 10am-3pm. Admission $1.25, senior citizens and children 75¢.)

A half-hour drive from downtown will bring visitors well into the British Columbian wilderness, full of excellent fishing and hunting opportunites. **Bobsports,** 680 Victoria St. (562-2222), sells a complete line of equipment for both pursuits. (Open Mon.-Thurs. and Sat. 9am-6pm, Fri. 9am-9pm.)

The **Native Art Gallery,** 144 George St. (564-3003), in the Native Friendship Centre, exhibits pricy but genuine works from the Kwagiutl, Cree, and Carrier tribes. (Open Sun.-Fri. 10am-6pm, Sat. 10am-5pm.) Craft markets and special cultural events center around **Studio 2880,** 15th Ave. (562-4526), and the free **Prince George Art Gallery** next door.

As the travel brochure proudly claims, Prince George's Napoleonic events and festivities "range from the sublime to the ridiculous and beyond." A perfect example is the February **Mardi Gras,** which lasts 10 days and features such totally wacko events as Snogolf, softball in the snow, and the ultimate test of physical agility—knurdling (jousting with padded poles). Summer events include a rodeo and triathlon. Prince George's **Oktoberfest** is the biggest event of the fall, and includes exactly what you'd expect it to: beer, bands, and braided blondes.

Prince Rupert

Wealthy entrepreneur Charles Hays dreamt of completing a second trans-Canada railroad, ending at then-uninhabited Kaien Island. This Fitzcarraldo of the north bought himself a ticket to England to drum up the money—a one-way ticket aboard the S.S. *Titanic.* Although Hays's fundraising and design plans lie peacefully with him on the Atlantic floor, the Grand Trunk Pacific Railway eventually established a company city, on the island. They named it Prince Rupert, after the second cousin of Charles II.

Although it offers neither mind-blowing sights nor a high-powered tourist industry, Prince Rupert is graced with genuine Canadian amiability. Let your friends at the Travel Infocentre give you a walking tour map spanning the 15 downtown blocks. The tour includes all that can be considered sights—namely the Infocentre's free museum, a tiresome wealth of totem poles, the carefully manicured Sunken Gardens, and a Native American carving shed.

A few minutes from downtown, a **gondola** (624-2236) carries the vista-seeking visitor up Mt. Hayes in the summer months. Walk or drive to the end of Wantage Rd., off Hwy. 16. (Open Wed.-Thurs. and Sun. noon-6pm; Fri.-Sat. noon-10pm. Admission $4, senior citizens and children $3.) Sixteen kilometres farther east along Hwy. 16 sits **Diana Lake Park,** a picnic area set against an enticing lake—especially alluring in the lazy oven of summer. **Prudhomme Lake Provincial Park** offers overnight camping next door to Diana Lake.

Practical Information and Orientation

Visitor Information: Travel Infocentre, 1st Ave. and McBride St. (624-5637). Hwy. 16 turns into McBride at the edge of town. Brochures a plenty, including extensive information on Alaska for visitors heading north up the Marine Hwy. Free museum displays relics of ancient Native American tribes. Open Mon.-Sat. 9am-9pm, Sun. 9am-5pm; mid-Sept. to mid-May Mon.-Sat. 10am-5pm.

Flights: Air BC, 700 2nd Ave. W. (624-4554). Three flights per day to Vancouver (one way $230). **Canadian Air** (624-9181), on the bottom floor of the mall on 2nd Ave., offers the same service at the same price.

Greyhound: on 3rd Ave. near 8th St. (624-8090), across from Overwaitea. Two buses per day to Prince George ($53.25). Open Mon.-Fri. 8am-8pm, Sat. 8am-noon and 4-8pm, Sun. 9:30-11am and 6:30-7:45pm.

Alaska Marine Highway: Ferries north from Prince Rupert into the Alaskan Panhandle. To Ketchikan (US$26, with car US$56), Wrangell (US$42, with car US$89), Petersburg (US$52, with car US$111), Juneau (US$84, with car US$178), and Haines (US$96, with car US$203).

BC Ferry: 1045 Howe St. (624-9627). Take Hwy. 16 west until it ends at the ferry terminal. Service to the Queen Charlotte Islands (5 per week, $14, with car $69), Vancouver, and Port Hardy (4 per week, $68, with car $210). Reservations required for vehicles.

Local Transportation: Prince Rupert Bus Service, 624-3343. Limited service around downtown. Operates Mon.-Sat. Fare 75¢, senior citizens 45¢, students 55¢.

Library: On McBride at 6th St. Open Mon.-Thurs. 10am-9pm, Fri. 10am-5pm, Sat. 9:30am-5:30pm; in winter Sun. 2-5pm.

Police/Ambulance: 911.

Post Office: 2nd Ave. and 3rd St. (627-3085). Open Mon.-Fri. 9am-5:30pm. Postal Code: V8J 3P3.

Area Code: 604.

The only major road into town is **Highway 16,** which becomes McBride at the city limits and then curves left to become 2nd Ave. downtown. Prince George is 720km east.

Accommodations, Camping, and Food

Ferry riders fresh from Alaska will rejoice when they see Prince Rupert's overstock of rooms, many of which are remaindered for $40. Nearly all the hotels are located within the 6-block-square area circumscribed by 1st Ave., 3rd Ave., 6th St., and 9th St.

Oceanview Hotel, 950 1st Ave. W. (624-6259). Recently renovated chambers justify its good reputation among locals, despite the occasional brouhaha from the railway tracks below. Singles $22. Doubles $25, with bath $35.

Commercial Hotel, 901 1st Ave. W. (624-6142). The spartan rooms are generally clean, although it's often hard to tell in the dim light. Singles $18.

Aleeda Hotel, 900 3rd Ave. W. (627-1367). Cheapest of the ritzier places in town. All the standard amenities. Singles $40. Doubles $50.

Park Ave. Campground, 1750 Park Ave. (624-5861), less than 2km east of the ferry terminal via Hwy. 16. The only campground actually in town. The sites are by no means private, but the hot showers and short walk to the ferry terminal make this a welcome stopover for weary ferry passengers. Tentsites $9. RVs $12.

Prudhomme Lake Campground, 16km east on Hwy. 16. A province-managed spot with toilets and drinking water. 24 sites at $8 each.

Pizza Stop, 830 2nd Ave. W. (624-3101). Better-than-average pizza for this neck of the cosmic woods. One person pizzas $6.45-8.50. Open Mon.-Sat. 4pm-4am, Sun. 4pm-2am.

New Moon, 630 3rd Ave. (627-7001). One of the better Chinese restaurants on the Alaska Marine Highway. Daily lunch specials ($6) include soup, tea, and dessert. All-you-can-eat smorgasbord with BBQ ribs (served Mon.-Fri. noon-1:30pm, Fri.-Sun. 4:30-8pm) $7.75. Open Mon.-Thurs. 11am-midnight, Fri.-Sat. 11am-3am, Sun. 11am-11pm.

Green Apple, 301 McBride St. (627-1666). Huge servings of fish and chips $6. Open Mon.-Sat. 11am-9:30pm, Sun. noon-8pm.

Cu's Steak and Seafood, 816 3rd Ave. (624-3111). You guessed it. Burgers $3.50-5, steaks from $12, seafood around $11. Open Mon.-Thurs. 11am-10pm, Fri.-Sat. 11am-11pm, Sun. 4-10pm.

Queen Charlotte Islands

Over 150 islands are convened just 130km west of Prince Rupert, Graham Island to the north and Moresby Island to the south being the largest and most heavily populated. In comparative isolation, the "Canadian Galapagos" have enjoyed a botanical history slightly different from that of normal places. The islands' 6000 residents (over half of whom live in Masset and Queen Charlotte City on Graham Island) coexist with the world's only known Golden Spruce tree, a yellow-flowering perennial daisy, and a quarter of Canada's Pacific coast birds. Sailor Juan Perez first discovered the islands in 1774, but not until four years later did Captain George Dixon put them on the map under the name of his beloved ship. Little has changed since the first encroachments by European settlers over 200 years ago.

The islands' Natives, the Haida (HIGH-duh), make up a large percentage of the population, and an even larger proportion of the islands' many artists. The land itself is heavily forested and largely mountainous. The beaches tend to be rocky and the water cold, but kayakers and anglers heap unending praise on the archipelago. Keep in mind the great distances between cities on Graham and Moresby Islands, and remember that there is no public transportation at all. Try to find fellow travelers willing to form a popular front to share the astronomical car rental fees, or be prepared to bike the 110km between Queen Charlotte City on the south shore of Graham Island and Masset on the north.

Queen Charlotte City

Registered in 1908, Queen Charlotte City grew up around a sawmill and still relies on logging as its major industry. Only now teetering on the brink of modernity, the town has so far been immune to the pesky virus of development. Some residents feel that they are being held back by lack of government funds, while others are satisfied with simply preserving their slow-paced lifestyle.

Practical Information and Orientation

Visitor Information: Travel Infocentre, 559-4742. Follow 3rd Ave. east out of town 1km. Buy the $3 *Guide to the Queen Charlotte Islands* and let the unusually perspicacious staff highlight, annotate, and amplify the already comprehensive book.

BC Ferry: Terminal in Skidegate Landing (559-4485), 5km east. To Prince Rupert (5 per week, $14, with car $69).

Interisland Ferry: Runs between Skidegate Landing on Graham Island and Alliford Bay on Moresby Island (12 trips per day, $1.60, with car $6.80).

Budget Car Rental: 559-4675, in the same building as Sears and Dutch Oven. $49 per day plus 18¢ per km. Must be 21 with credit card. Open Mon.-Fri. 9am-4pm, Sat. 10am-4pm, Sun. 10am-2pm.

Bike Rental: 559-4559, just east of town. Look for the black bicycle climbing up the edge of the sign. Mountain bikes $19 per day, $70 per week. Open daily 8am-5pm.

Kallahin Travel Service: 559-8455 or 559-4746, upstairs from Rainbows. Arranges all sorts of boat charters and special trips to the islands.

Laundromat: 121 3rd Ave. (559-4444). Open Mon.-Sat. 9:30am-6pm, Sun. 11am-5pm.

Hospital: 3rd Ave. (559-8466).

Emergency: Police, 559-4421. **Ambulance,** 559-4506. **Fire,** 559-4488.

Post Office: in the City Centre Bldg. on 2nd Ave. (559-8349). Open Mon.-Fri. 8:30am-5:30pm, Sat. 8:30am-12:30pm. Postal Code: V0T 1S0.

Area Code: 604.

Queen Charlotte City juts inward from the water at the southern end of **Graham Island.** The city stretches for 2km along 3rd Ave., which turns into Hwy. 16 to the east, leading to Tlell, Port Clements, and Masset.

Accommodations and Camping

Spruce Point Lodging, (559-8234), on the little peninsula across from the Chevron station at the west end of town. Brand-new hostel beds for $12.50. Laundry and cooking facilities. Also operates a bed and breakfast next door (singles $40, doubles $45).

Premier Hotel, 3101 3rd Ave. (559-8401). Friendly staff and eclectic decor. Singles with shared bath from $20. Doubles with balconies from $40.

Bellis Lodge (557-4434), in Tlell, 40km north of the ferry terminal. Hostel beds and kitchen facilities, but the nearest supplies are 19km to the north. Members $12, nonmembers $17.

Haydn Turner Park Campsite, at the west end of 4th Ave. $8 sites with toilets and water.

Joy's Island Jewellers, 3rd Ave. at the east end of town. Makes a few tentsites available in the yard next door ($3.50). Showers are a whopping $5, but a private well provides some of the best drinking water on the islands.

Food

Lucy's Place, 233 3rd Ave. (559-4684), just west of the town center. Outstanding breakfasts a mere $3.50. Seafood lovers will appreciate the fish 'n' chips ($7.25) and halibut dinner ($13). Open daily 8am-10pm.

Margaret's, 3223 Wharf (559-4204). The popular $5.50 sandwich specials, with soup and fries, are usually a good bet. Open Mon.-Sat. 6:30am-3pm, Sun. 9am-3pm.

Dutch Oven Bakery and Deli, on Wharf St. (559-4645), next to Margaret's. Light snacks, including meatpies ($2.45) and carrot muffins (75¢). Open Tues.-Wed. and Fri.-Sat. 10am-5pm.

Kathy's (559-4231), in Skidegate Mission. This converted RV in the center of town is applauded for its octopus burger ($4). Open Wed.-Mon. noon-6pm.

Sights

Contemporary Haida artwork sparkles on display at **Rainbows Art Gallery and Gift Shop,** on 3rd Ave. at Alder (559-8420), a gallery of silver, gold, and argillite (black shale) carvings. (Open Mon.-Sat. 9am-6pm.) Botanical pilgrims can trek 65km north up the gravel road to Juskatla, about 5km south of Port Clements, and follow signs toward a teasing 10-minute stroll to the world's only **Golden Spruce tree,** a freak of nature whose needles are actually bleached by sunlight. **Skidegate Landing** (SKID-uh-git), where the ferry docks, is 5km east of Queen Charlotte City. There is no public transportation on the islands, so try to share a taxi into town.

Skidegate Mission, known as "the village," is a cluster of small houses with big TV satellite dishes 2km east of the landing. In summer, head down to the village on Thursday nights for the **seafood feast** at Old Skidegate Hall, a $20 extravaganza (ages under 13 $10) featuring the biggest and best of the week's catch. Dinner starts at 6pm, but locals recommend arriving 30 minutes early. Halfway between Skidegate Landing and Skidegate Mission is the **Queen Charlotte Islands Museum** (559-4643), presenting a large collection of argillite carvings and other relics of Haida history. (Open Tues.-Sat. 9am-5pm. Admission $2.)

Masset

Surrounded by a wildlife sanctuary to the north, an ancient village to the west, and ebbing tides to the south, Masset is the largest metropolis on the islands by virtue of its whopping population of 1600. In 1909, the Graham Steamship, Coal, and Lumber Company built "Graham City" at the north end of Graham Island, but the city later became "Masset," in honor of the Native Massett Haida who laid first dibs on the area.

Old Massett Village, 2km west of town at the terminus of Hwy. 16, bustles with 600 descendants of the original tribe. The alleys are lined with Haida housefront/storefronts selling an array of carvings. Be sure to walk all the way to the peninsula's tip for some of the island's finest ocean views. Old photographs and Native artwork now fill what was once a two-room schoolhouse for Haida children, at the jumbled **Ed Jones Haida Museum.**

Red-breasted sapsuckers, orange-crowned warblers, glaucous-winged gulls, great blue herons, and binocular-toting naturalists converge on the **Delkatla Wildlife Sanctuary,** off Tow Hill Rd. The best paths from which to sight the 113 airborne species leave from the junction of Trumpeter Dr. and Cemetery Rd. The **Golden Spruce** itself can be reached more easily via paved Hwy. 16, running south from Masset. (See Queen Charlotte City.)

Practical Information and Orientation

Visitor Information: Travel Infocentre, Old Beach Rd. (626-3982), at Hwy. 16. Plenty of local history and trail maps for choice birdwatching. Open July-Aug. The **Masset Village Office** on Main St. will give you further information, as can the **Chamber of Commerce,** Box 38, Masset V0T 1M0 (626-5211).

Car Rental: Budget Rent-A-Car, Collison Ave. (626-5571). Must be 21 with credit card. $49 per day plus 18¢ per km.

Taxi: Island Taxi, 557-4230.

Ambulance: 626-3636.

Police: 626-3991.

Postal Code: V0T 1M0.

Area Code: 604.

Masset is at the north end of Graham Island along Hwy. 16. Collison Ave. is the main drag. **Old Massett Village** lies 2km farther down the road.

Accommodations, Camping, and Food

It's something of an understatement to say your options in Masset are limited. **Naikoon Park Motel,** on Tow Hill Rd. (626-5187), close to the beach and Naikoon Provincial Park, charges $35 for singles and doubles. **Masset-Haida Lions RV Site and Campground,** on Tow Hill Rd. next to the Wildlife Sanctuary, is the town's only campground and has metered showers, flush toilets, and (unfortunately) gravel sites. (Sites $8, electricity $2; open late May-late Sept.) **Naikoon Provincial Park** dominates the eastern half of Masset's peninsula, and maintains two campgrounds. **Agate Beach** is 20km east of Masset on the northern edge of the park, and **Misty Meadows** is just outside of Tlell in the southeast corner of the park. (Both charge $8 for sites with toilets and water.)

The **Pizza Place,** on Orr St. (626-5493), comes closest to offering a local specialty in the form of "Pizza with Pizzazz." (Open Mon.-Sat. 11:30am-midnight.) Break the diet next door at the city's only dough outlet, the **Dutch Oven Bakery** (626-3283; open Tues.-Sat. 9am-5:30pm).

The Cassiar Highway

Most travelers journey between British Columbia and Alaska via the Alaska Hwy. or aboard Alaska Marine Hwy. ferries. But a third and largely ignored route traces 750km of **Highway 37,** commonly known as the Cassiar Highway. This lonely road slices through spectacular extremes of burnt forest, logged wasteland, and virgin wilderness from Hwy. 16 (between Prince George and Prince Rupert) to Mile 655 of the Alaska Hwy. (near the Yukon border). Long stretches of unpaved road, swirling dust, and flying rocks can chip windshields, crack headlights, and generally gum up the car's works. Nevertheless, the Cassiar is a good way to cut hundreds of kilometres off the Alaska Hwy. Gas stations are few and far between, so bring along a spare tire and an emergency gas supply.

The road is divided into three sections. From Hwy. 16, the intrepid motorist follows 172km of paved road to **Meziadin Junction.** The **Rest and Be Thankful Cafe** allows the dazed driver to do just that, featuring dinner specials and fresh berry pies. The cabins next door run the gamut from about $25 for a single bunkhouse bed to $57 for two single beds and a double bed in one room.

A 340km trek across hard-packed dirt will take you on to **Dease Lake.** Here the **Boulder Cafe** serves impossibly expensive breakfasts but reasonable dinners. (Open Mon.-Sat. 6am-10pm, Sun. 7am-10pm.) **The Grayling** has well-kept singles for about $32.

The final leg of the trip is the most scenic, each turn of the paved road to the Alaska Hwy. revealing a new lake or mountain. These last 237km reward the adventurer with one of the best restaurants on the Cassiar: **Yukon Ma's Cafe.** Try the salisbury steaks and huge burgers.

A Complete Guide for Highway 37, available at the **Terrace Infocentre,** offers a partial list of the many facilities and campgrounds on the route. Hitchhikers on the Cassiar, as usual, will find locals and truckers friendly and RV drivers unfriendly.

Skeena Valley

The Gitksan tribe once used the Skeena River as a convenient route from the coast into the mainland mountains. Dubbed *K-shian* (water of the clouds) by the trading Natives, the river flows west from Hazelton and empties into the Pacific at Prince Rupert, all the way carving out the foggy Skeena Valley.

Gitksan villages dot Hwy. 37, which follows the river through the valley to Prince Rupert. "Gitksanomics" (the tribal economy) depends on the trickle-down theory of handicraft sales to passing motorists. Craft shops and totem poles grow quicker than dandelions on the roadsides of **K'san** and **Kitwanga.**

In the heart of the Skeena Valley at the intersection of Hwy. 16 and 37, **Terrace** is a perfect stopover on the way to or from Prince Rupert ferries. The **Travel Infocentre,** 4511 Keith Ave. (635-2063), provides ample background on the Skeena's colorful history, as well as information on the nearby Native villages. (Open daily 9am-8pm.) If you plan to spend the night, the **Cedars Motel,** 4830 Hwy. 16 (635-2258), has some of the cheapest rooms in town (singles from $29) and an adjoining restaurant. Campers can sleep under the stars at **Ferry Island Campground** (638-1174), 3km east of Terrace on Eby St., off Hwy. 16. Its pit toilets, drinking water, and electrical hookups make a night in the wilderness just that much cozier. (Open Victoria Day-Labor Day. Sites $7, electricity $2.)

Dawson Creek

Do not confuse dull Dawson Creek, BC with Disneyesque Dawson City, former capital of the Yukon. While the latter is worth seeing to relive the gold-mining era, the former should be used only as an emergency rest stop on your way to bigger and better things. Dawson Creek's major distinction is the cairn marking Mile Zero on the Alaska Highway, the major access road to the Land of the Midnight Sun. Nonetheless, Dawson Creek is the only real city within a hundred-kilometre radius.

A 408km drive between Prince George and Dawson Creek on Hwy. 97 (John Hart Hwy.) offers little apart from a few snowcapped mountains and a number of pretty lakes. **McLeod Lake,** about 100km into the trip, has a campground, a few hotels, and little else. Unless the monotony of the drive has weighted your eyelids to the point where you need to rest, plunge forward in the manner of Jack Nicholson in Antonioni's *The Passenger* and knock off the next 160km to **Chetwynd**—home of the **Country Squire Motor Inn** (788-2276) and the **Pinecone Motor Inn** (788-3311). Both hotels lie directly on the highway as you enter from the south, and both offer the same basic necessities: rooms with bathrooms and a restaurant downstairs that serves decent food. Singles run about $35. The **Chetwynd Court Motel** (788-2271) is in the city center and has singles from $26.

Overnight guests in Dawson Creek looking for econorama lodgings should try the **Cedar Lodge Motel,** 801 110th Ave. (782-8531; singles $25). Another option is the **Peace Villa Motel,** 1641 Alaska Ave. (782-8175). Behind the neo-Victorian exterior you'll find large, clean rooms, nice bathrooms, and a friendly staff toting free coffee. (Singles from $32.) RV drivers should head for **Tubby's RV Park,** 20th St. and Hwy. 97 (782-2584); tenters should try **Mile 0 City Campground,** 1km west of the Alaska Hwy.'s starting point (782-2590). Tubby's has an industrial, RV feel, with its 71 sites (open May-Oct.), while Mile 0 manages a generally greener atmosphere. Both have showers and rent sites for $7.

The best place for nourishment in Dawson Creek is the **Stagecoach Restaurant,** 1725 Alaska Ave. (782-8419), at Mile 0 of the Alaska Hwy. McDonald's, at 11628 8th St., is just down Hwy. 2.

Greyhound in Dawson Creek runs buses to Whitehorse, YT (1 per day, $109.90), Prince George (2 per day, $31.65), and Edmonton, AB (2 per day, $46.20). In an emergency, contact the **police** (782-5211), or call the **ambulance** (782-2211). The **tourist information centre,** 900 Alaska Ave. (782-9595), in the old train station just off Hwy. 97, brandishes brochures that promote the few areas of interest in Dawson Creek. The **post office** is at 11622 7th St. (782-2322), and the **postal code** is V1G 4J8.

The Alaska Highway

Built during World War II, the unpredictable Alaska Highway maps out an astonishing 2647km route between Dawson Creek, BC, and Fairbanks, AK. One probably apocryphal story maintains that all the bends and dips in the road were created intentionally to prevent Japanese fighter pilots from landing during the war. The route is barren of any trace of civilization, just as it was when 19th-century prospectors first planted mileposts arbitrarily amid the arctic winds. Do not use the mileposts as official calibration standards, but rather as a general guide; the new kilometre posts, though not as frequent, are more accurate. **Fort Nelson,** 480km north of Dawson Creek, is the last city of any note before Whitehorse. The **Pioneer Motel Ltd.,** at Mile 300 (774-6459), convenient to the highway, rents singles for $28, doubles for $30, and kitchenettes for $4 extra. Campers should continue another kilometre to **Westend Campground** (774-2340), a veritable oasis in the middle of the Yukon with hot showers, a laundromat, and a free car wash. Sites are $9. Fort Nelson cuisine consists of nothing more than standard hotel restaurant fare.

Just past Fort Nelson, road conditions take a turn for the worse. Pavement gives way to "chip-seal," a layer of packed gravel held in place by hardened oil. In the dry summer, dust and rocks fly freely, virtually guaranteeing shattered headlights and a chipped windshield. All drivers should fit their headlights with plastic or wire-mesh covers. Most locals protect their radiators from bug splatter with large screens mounted in front of the grille. As if to compensate for the deteriorating road conditions, the scenery picks up considerably after Fort Nelson. The stone mountains shooting up every few kilometres are especially dramatic. The spruce timberlines are low in altitude and razor sharp, leaving only cold gray rock to meet the sky above. Near the BC-Yukon border, the road winds through vast areas of land scorched by forest fires; gray arboreal skeletons stretch as far as the eye can see in all directions. Watch for jackrabbits along this stretch of road. They have become so bold of late that they barely bat an eye as *Hrududus* hurtle by. At night, this area offers prime viewing of the northern lights, since there are no city lights to clutter the sky.

Small hotels, plain but expensive, pockmark the remainder of the highway every 80 to 160km. Campers' needs are pampered by the provincial parks that spring up constantly along the road. **Stone Mountain Campground,** about 160km past Fort Nelson, is a park campsite set in the scenic paradise beside Summit Lake. Each park makes sites with toilets and fresh water available for $5 per night. Great views conjure themselves now and again along the remainder of the drive to Whitehorse; the long journey is nonetheless quite taxing.

Pick up the exhaustive listing of *Emergency Medical Services* in a visitors bureau, or write the Department of Health and Social Services, P.O. Box H-06C, Juneau, AK 99811 (907-465-3027). The free pamphlet *Help Along the Way* lists emergency numbers along the road from Whitehorse to Fairbanks.

Whitehorse

Whitehorse's population exploded to 13,000—nearly half of the Yukon's total population—when in 1942 the U.S. Army built the Alaska Highway to defend against the Japanese. The Yukon's capital maintains its century-old gold-rush architecture and continues to exude the self-reliant individualism of that time. Today, the descendants of the original gold miners coexist with Native Canadians who have lived in this region for 20,000 years.

Practical Information and Orientation

Visitor Information: Visitor Reception Centre, 302 Steele St. (667-2915), in the T.C. Richards Bldg. at Steele and 3rd Ave. Since there are only 7 official reception centres in the entire Yukon, each one comes stocked with an astounding amount of literature. The centre also offers free audiovisual shows downstairs. Open May-Sept. daily 8am-8pm. The **Parks Canada Building,** South Access Rd. and 2nd Ave. (667-4511), next to the S.S. *Klondike,* stores information on the history of the Yukon's sternwheeler river boats. Free boat tours are given daily. Open May-Sept. daily 9am-7:30pm.

Flights: Canadian Airlines (668-4466, for reservations 668-3535). To Calgary (2 per day, $398), Edmonton (2 per day, $342), and Vancouver (3 per day, $342).

Greyhound: 3211 3rd Ave. (667-2223). To Vancouver (1 per day, $142), Edmonton (1 per day, $142), and Dawson Creek (1 per day $110). There is *no* Greyhound service to Alaska. Open Mon.-Fri. 8am-noon and 1-5:30pm, Sat. 9am-noon, Sun. 5:30-9am.

Alaskan Express: in the Greyhound depot (667-2223). Buses run late May to mid-Sept. To Anchorage (2 per week, US$140), Haines (2 per week, US$71), and Fairbanks (2 per week, US$129).

Norline: in the Greyhound depot (668-3355). Operates bus service to Dawson City (3 per week in summer, 2 per week in winter; $66).

Local Transportation: Whitehorse Transit, 668-2831. Limited service downtown 6am-7pm. Fare $1, senior citizens 50¢, children and students 75¢.

Taxi: Yellow Taxi, 668-4811. **Yukon Taxi Service,** 668-6830.

Car Rental: Economy Rentals, 4th and Strickland (668-2355). From $30 per day plus 20¢ per km. A limited number of cars are available for use within city limits only for $10 per day plus 25¢ per km. Must be 21 with credit card.

Library: 2nd Ave. at Hawkins. Open Mon.-Fri. 10am-9pm, Sat. 10am-6pm, Sun. 1-9pm.

Crisis Line: 668-9111.

Ambulance: 668-9333.

Police: 667-5555.

Post Office: 3rd and Wood, in the Yukon News Bldg. General Delivery postal code for last names A-L is Y1A 3S9, M-Z Y1A 3S8.

Area Code: 403.

To reach Whitehorse by car, take the downtown exit off the Alaska Highway. Once there, park the car and use your feet; downtown is relatively compact. The airport is to the west, a short cab ride away, and the bus station is on the northeastern edge of town, a few minutes' walk from downtown.

Accommodations and Camping

Call the **Yukon Bed and Breakfast Association** (633-4609) to reserve a room in a Klondike household. Singles average $30 and doubles $40, plus $15 per extra person. Hotels often exploit their guests' joy at finding a town with more than 100 residents and pets—singles average $50. Camping in Whitehorse can be a problem since there is only one RV campground and one tenting park near the downtown area. Tenters praying for a hot shower should venture to the group of campgrounds clustered 10-20km south of town on the Alaska Highway.

Fourth Avenue Residence (IYHF), 4051 4th Ave, (667-4471). Offering long- and short-term housing, the residence boasts cooking and laundry facilities, good security, and free use of the city pool next door. Extremely well run. Hostel beds $13.50, nonmembers $15. Private singles $30. Doubles $40.

Chilkoot Trail Inn, 4190 4th Ave. (668-4190). Clean rooms graced with TV, private bath, and lots of highway noise. Singles $40. Doubles $45, with kitchenette $58.

Fort Yukon Hotel, 2163 2nd Ave. (667-2594), near shopping malls and Greyhound. Rooms are a little past their prime, but kept clean by the friendly management. Singles $38. Doubles $45.

Pioneer Trailer Park, at Mile 911 on the Alaska Highway (668-5944). Food store, laundromat, RV repair shop, isolated tentsites, showers, and a car wash. Not bad in the middle of the wilderness, though the tent sites are an inconvenient 3-min. walk from the washrooms. This is the closest campground to Whitehorse that has showers for tenters, but they cost 25¢ per min. Sites $7, with hookups $13. Open May-Sept.

Robert Service Campground, 1km out South Access Rd. A convenient stop for tenting folk, but provides almost as few amenities as it did when Robert Service (the poet of the Yukon) visited here in the 19th century; there are toilets, but water must be boiled 10 min. before consumption. No showers. Sites $4.

Sourdough City RV Park, 2240 2nd Ave. (668-7938), across from Greyhound. All the earmarks of a post-romantic Utopia, with RVs stretching as far as the eye can see. 104 full hookup sites, laundromat, showers, and a courteous staff. Complete hookups $16. Open May-Sept.

Food

Do not be disillusioned by the dilapidated exteriors of many Whitehorse gastrocentres; the insides are usually well-worn but cozy. The high prices are reasonable by Yukon standards.

No Pop Sandwich Shop, 312 Steele (668-3227). Very popular with Whitehorse's small suit-and-tie crowd. The beltch (BLT and cheese, $4) and vegie burger ($3.75) are worth trying. Open Mon.-Sat. 9am-9pm.

Talisman Cafe, 2112 2nd Ave. (667-2736). Good food in a totally nondescript environment. Get all 4 food groups in the Russian *peroshki* ($6). Burritos $6 and breakfasts $5.50. Open Mon.-Sat. 6am-9pm.

Mom's Kitchen and Donut Shop, 2157 2nd Ave. (668-6620), at Alexander. Serves all meals, but breakfast is a specialty. "Mom" whips up pretty good omelettes for $4.75-8. Lunch on a "Burger Supreme" with *everything* ($8.45). Open Mon.-Fri. 6:30am-7pm, Sat.-Sun. 6:30am-4pm.

The Bistro, 205 Main St. (668-7013), at 2nd Ave. Expensive Canadian cuisine and a finale of delectable desserts. The Canuck croissant sandwich (sliced smoked salmon and onion) is $8 and the carrot cake $2.50. Rather dressy atmosphere. Open Mon.-Thurs. 7am-7pm, Fri. 7am-9pm, Sat. 7am-5pm.

Sights

Considering the size of its city, the Whitehorse welcoming committee has put together an astonishing array of scheduled tours and visitor activities. The **Yukon Museum Association,** 3126 3rd Ave. (667-4704), sponsors "Heritage Walks"—free daily tours of downtown Whitehorse, which leave from the office next to the visitors centre. The **Yukon Conservation Society,** 302 Hawkins St. (668-5678), arranges hikes Monday through Friday during July and August to explore the Yukon's natural beauty. **Yukon Native Products,** 4230 4th Ave. (668-5935), sells traditional goods; tour the garment factory to see how far Klondikes will go to keep warm in the frigid winters. (Open Mon.-Sat. 7:30am-8pm, Sun. 10am-4pm; tours given Mon.-Sat. at 10:30am and 3:30pm.)

The restored *S.S. Klondike,* on the South Access Rd. (667-4511), is a permanently dry-docked sternwheeler recalling the days when the Yukon River was the city's sole artery of survival. (Free guided tours May-Sept. daily 9am-6pm.) The **Whitehorse Rapids Dam and Fish Ladder,** at the end of Nisutlin Drive (667-2235), 2km southeast of town, allows salmon to bypass the dam and continue upstream on the world's longest salmon migration. (Open mid-July to Aug. daily 8am-10pm. Free.)

Visitors missing local culture will find it at the **MacBride Museum,** 1st Ave. and Wood St. (667-2709). The exhibit features memorabilia from the early days of the Yukon, including photographs of Whitehorse as a tent city. (Open mid-May to early Oct. daily. Admission $3, senior citizens and students $2, families $6.) The **Old Log Church Museum,** 303 Elliot St. (668-2555), at 3rd, has converted its pews into a museum that fully explicates the history of missionary work in the territories. Built by its pastor, the church required only three months of labor; cold has a way of motivating people. (Open late May to mid-June Mon.-Fri. 9am-5pm; mid-June to late Aug. Mon.-Sat. 9am-8pm, Sun. noon-4pm. Admission $2, children $1.) On stage, the big attraction is the annual summer showing of the **Frantic Follies Vaudeville Revue,** produced by Atlas Tours at the Westmark Whitehorse Hotel, 2nd Ave. and Wood St. (668-3161). The nightly show runs June to Sept. and highlights the Yukon's early history in poetry, Gold Rush songs, skits, and cancanning by long-legged dancers. (Admission $14, ages under 12 $7.) The **Eldorado Show,** nightly at 8pm in the Gold Rush Inn, 411 Main St. (668-6472), also tries to enlighten its audience about the history of the gold rush. Tickets are available at the shack at 1st Ave. and Steele ($12.50, children $6.25). Music comes to Whitehorse via the **Frostbite Music Society** (668-4921), which puts together a summer concert series featuring local entertainers. Vacationing scholars are welcome to browse and research at the **Yukon Archives,** in the Yukon Government Administration Building, 2140 2nd Ave. (667-5321).

Two-hour river sightseeing trips are offered by **Youcon Voyage** (668-2927) from June to Sept. Boats leave daily at 1 and 3pm from the ramshackle pier at 1st and Steele. ($14, senior citizens $11, children $7.) The **Yukon Gardens** (668-7972), 3km southwest of town at the junction of the Alaska Hwy. and South Access Rd., blossoms with 22 acres of indigenous northern wild flowers and plants. (Open early June to mid-Sept. daily 9am-9pm. Admission $4.75, students $2.75.)

ALBERTA

The icy peaks and turquoise lakes of Banff and Jasper National Parks preside as Alberta's most sought-after landscapes. The vast Columbia Icefield, straddling the parks as well as the Alberta/British Columbia border, feeds three of the world's largest bodies of water. As the Athabasca, Saskatchewan, and Columbia Glaciers melt, their waters flow into three river systems: The Mackenzie flows to the Arctic Ocean, the Saskatchewan reaches the Atlantic Ocean through Hudson Bay, and the Columbia empties into the Pacific.

But there is more to Alberta than Banff and Jasper—plenty more farmland, prairie, and oil fields, that is. Rural Alberta features kilometre after kilometre of untraveled roads, thousands of prime fishing holes, world-renowned dinosaur fossil fields, and intriguing remnants of Native American culture.

Petrodollars have brought gleaming, modern cities to the prairie. Calgary caught the world's eye when it hosted the XV Winter Olympics, and is perennially host to the wild and wooly Stampede. Edmonton, slightly larger than its southern rival, is home to the world's largest shopping mall, and, until recently, Wayne Gretzky.

More than half of the province lies to the north of Edmonton. This is the uninhabited land of the midnight twilight. Since the north is void of any substantial cities, the ethereal charm of rural towns must support you as you venture farther toward the pole.

Travel

Highway 16 connects Jasper with Edmonton, while the **Trans-Canada Highway** (Hwy. 1) runs right through Banff and then continues 120km east to Calgary. **Highway 3** connects Medicine Hat with Vancouver, BC, passing a plethora of historical signposts along the way. The extensive highway system makes possible many bus connections between the major points of interest. Use Calgary as a travel hub. **Greyhound** and **VIA Rail** run from Calgary to Edmonton to Jasper, as well as from Calgary to Banff. **Brewster** runs an express bus between Banff and Jasper. Calgary and Edmonton have the two major airports in Alberta.

You must leave the Trans-Canada Hwy. to explore rural Alberta—a feat easier said than done. Writing-On-Stone Provincial Park and Elk Island National Park, two of the province's most intriguing destinations, lie off of the usual tourist trail. **Hitching** in such areas is a hit-or-miss proposition. If you can get a ride, it'll probably last a long time, but you might have to wait an eternity between lifts. To reach out-of-the-way (but highly worthwhile) sights, consider renting a car from **Rent-A-Wreck**, a Canadian-based company that rents cars that aren't really wrecks for very reasonable rates.

Another option is **Exitreks** (403-269-1464), a new company run by enthusiastic Albertans eager to show off the isolated campgrounds and forestry trunk roads of their province. Exitreks conducts six-day tours and occasional shorter tours. For information and tour itineraries, write Exitreks Ltd., #208, 604 1st St. SW, Calgary T2P 1M7.

More adventurous and independent travelers should have no problem discovering alternative methods of transportation in Alberta. From the glaciers of Jasper National Park to the huge northern lakes, the Ice Age designed the province with the hiker, ice climber, canoeist, and bicyclist firmly in mind. Virtually every region of Alberta can accommodate any outdoor activity; however, there are some "hot spots" for each. **Hikers, mountaineers,** and **ice climbers** will find the most, and the best, terrain in Banff's Canadian Rockies, Jasper National Park, and Kananaskis Country. **Canoeing centers** frequent the lakes of northern Alberta and the Milk River in the south. Bicyclists love the Icefields Parkway, but they can travel easily on the wide shoulders of other Alberta highways as well. Some highway segments,

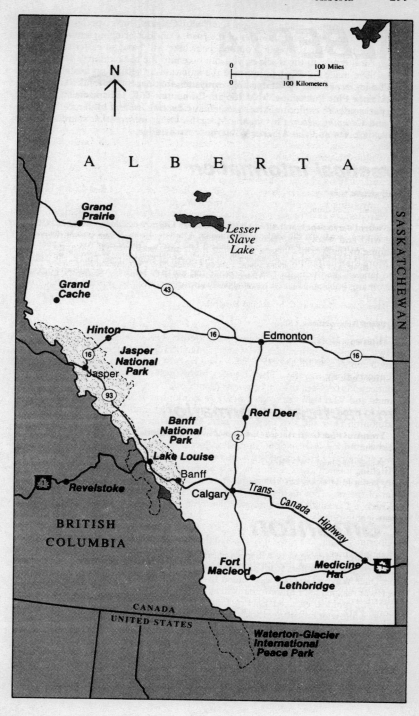

such as the Trans-Canada between Banff and Calgary, have special bike routes marked on the right-hand shoulder of the road. Consider bringing a mountain bike instead of the usual 10-speed. You and your bike will have an easier time on the rough rural roads; in the Rockies, you can bike into the backcountry. The national parks have made an effort to improve the situation by setting up **hostels** between Banff and Jasper and by establishing **campsites** that accept only hikers and bicyclists. Lone Pine Publishing, 9704 106 St., Edmonton T5K 1B6, prints an extensive array of guides to exploring Alberta (such as *Canoeing Alberta* by Janice MacDonald and *Camping Alberta* by Joanne Morgan). Other information sources include **Travel Alberta** and the **Alberta Wilderness Association.**

Practical Information

Emergency: 911.

Capital: Edmonton.

Visitor Information: Travel Alberta, 15th floor, 10025 Jasper Ave., Edmonton T5J 3Z3 (800-661-8888, in AB 800-222-6501). Information on Alberta's provincial parks can be obtained from **Recreation and Parks,** #1660, Standard Life Centre, 10405 Jasper Ave., Edmonton T5J 3N4 (427-9429). For information on the province's national parks (Waterton Lakes, Jasper, Banff, and Wood Buffalo), contact **Parks Canada,** Box 2989, Station M, Calgary T2P 3H8 (292-4440). The **Alberta Wilderness Association,** P.O. Box 6389, Station D, Calgary T2P 2E1, carries information on off-highway adventures.

Time Zone: Mountain (2 hr. behind Eastern).

Postal Abbreviation: AB.

Drinking Age: 18.

Traffic Laws: Mandatory seatbelt law.

Area Code: 403.

Impractical Information

Provincial Bird: Great Horned Owl. Chosen in 1977 by Alberta schoolchildren in a province-wide vote.

Provincial Flower: Wild Rose.

Provincial Tree: Lodgepole Pine.

Edmonton

Although Edmonton is Alberta's capital city and is indeed more populous than Calgary, the city suffers from an urban inferiority complex. And since star Edmonton Oiler Wayne Gretzky was traded to the Los Angeles Kings, there may indeed be fewer reasons for Edmontonians to appreciate their hometown. Gretzky's departure still rankles: enraged hockey fans boycott companies owned by the Oiler's owner while economists nervously estimate the trade's effect on the Canadian economy.

Trumpeting its West Edmonton Mall as "The World's Largest Indoor Mall" and constructing Towers of Babel to rival Calgary's skyscape, Alberta's other petropolis is nonetheless determined to prove its worth. Unfortunately, Edmontonians rarely brag of handsome Fort Edmonton Park, the Provincial Museum, or the Muttart Conservatory. Instead, "The Mall" is all you'll hear from man-on-the-street inter-

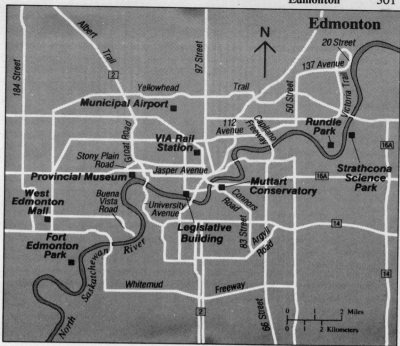

views, and The Mall may be all you see of Edmonton unless you orient yourself toward the city's hidden, less crass attractions.

Raised by the Klondike gold rush and the railroad, Edmonton was born in 1795 as the site of a Hudson's Bay Company trading post. Fur trapping and trading accounted for most of Edmonton's early industry until 1905, when the Canadian National Railway decided to lay its tracks through Alberta's soon-to-be-capital city. Leduc, just south of the city, hit black gold (oil, that is) in 1947, and Edmonton has felt the pleasures and pangs of the fluctuating industry ever since. While the huge cash influx from the 60s and 70s paved the way for Edmonton's monolithic office buildings, clean subway system, and "Mall from Hell," it also set the stage for the rapid development of an unusually variegated cultural community. Edmonton quietly boasts a broad range of museums, galleries, and musical events. The city also claims the world's most theaters per capita.

Practical Information and Orientation

Visitor Information: Edmonton Tourism, 9797 Jasper Ave. (422-5505). Information, maps, brochures, and directions. Helpful staff. Open daily 8:30am-4:30pm; in winter Mon.-Fri. 8:30am-4:30pm. Also at **Gateway Park,** on Hwy. 2 south of the city. Open daily 8am-9pm; in winter Mon.-Fri. 8:30am-4:30pm, Sat.-Sun. 9:30am-5pm. Edmonton also operates two smaller offices on Hwy. 16 during the summer. One is in the western section of the city near 190 St., and the other is in the east by 23 Ave. Both open daily 10am-6pm. For paraphernalia on the rest of the province, head to **Travel Alberta,** 10025 Jasper Ave. (427-4321), on the 15th floor.

VIA Rail: 10004 104 Ave. (422-6032, for reservations 800-665-8630), in the CN Tower, easily identified by the huge red letters on the building. A little more expensive than the bus: $34 to Jasper and $85 to Vancouver. Open Mon.-Fri. 9am-5:30pm, Sat.-Sun. 9:30am-5:30pm.

Edmonton Transit: 423-4636 for schedule information. Buses and light rail transit (LRT) run frequently and all over the sprawling city. As in Calgary and Portland, you can ride free on the LRT if you stay in the downtown area (between Corona Station, at 107 St. and Jasper Ave., and Churchill Station, at 99 St. and 102 Ave.) Mon.-Fri. 9am-3pm and Sat. 9am-6pm.

Otherwise the fare for bus and LRT is $1.25, ages over 65 and under 15 60¢. No bikes allowed on the transit system. For more information, stop by the **Downtown Information Centre**, 100 A St. and Jasper Ave. (open Mon.-Fri. 9am-5pm, Sat. 8am-5pm, Sun. and holidays 9am-5pm).

Greyhound: 10324 103 St. (421-4211). A bus leaves for Calgary nearly every hour 8am-8pm (one way $19). Buses to Jasper (3 per day, $24.80) and Vancouver (3 per day, $65). The daring can take the bus to Yellowknife, capital of the Northwest Territories, for a mere $112. Open daily 5:30am-12:30am.

Car Rental: Rent-a-Wreck, 10140 109 St. (423-1755). Rates start at $13 per day plus 10¢ per km, or $20 per day with 100 free km plus 11¢ per additional km. Must be 21. Credit card or cash deposit required ($250, ages under 25 $500). Visitors from overseas must show a passport. Open Mon.-Fri. 7am-8pm, Sat.-Sun. 9am-5pm. A little more money will rent a sprightlier auto at **Thrifty**, 10036 102 St. (428-8555). Rates start at $33 per day with 100 free km plus 12¢ per km. Must be 21 with credit card.

Bike Rental: Campus Outdoor Centre, at the University of Alberta, 116 St. and 87 Ave. (492-2767). Mountain bikes only, $19 per day. Camping equipment also available.

Weather Information: 468-4940.

Hospital: 482-8111.

Emergency: 911.

Police: 423-4567.

Post Office: 9808 103A Ave. (495-3100), adjacent to the CN Tower. Open Mon.-Fri. 8am-5:45pm. Postal Code: T5J 2G8.

Area Code: 403.

Although Edmonton holds the dubious distinction of being the northernmost major city in North America, it's actually in the southern half of Alberta, making it an easy 3½-hour drive from Calgary on Hwy. 2 and a 4-hour jaunt from Jasper on Hwy. 16. The city is well-served by bus, train, and plane. But while Greyhound and VIA Rail let you off downtown, the **airport** sits far south of town, a prohibitive cab fare away. You might be able to find an airport shuttle bus taking travelers to downtown hotels; try to hop on.

While Calgary conveniently divides itself into directional quadrants, Edmonton figures adults should be able to figure out such trivialities unaided. The system sounds simple enough: **Avenues** run east-west, numbers increasing as you travel farther north, and **streets** run north-south, with the higher numbers at the west end of town. But the meandering North Saskatchewan River complicates matters. While 99 Ave. and 109 St. are on the north bank of the river, 99 Ave. and 71 St. are well into the south bank. Your best bet is to get a transit map, available all over town.

When speaking of streets, remember the cardinal rule. There are no typos on the street signs: 104 St. means "one-oh-four street," not "one-hundred-and-fourth street." Jasper Ave., the city's central thoroughfare, is just another name for 101 Ave.

Accommodations

Your smartest choice in Edmonton is to stay at the hostel, and even in summer there's usually space available. You'll have more privacy at St. Joseph's College or the University of Alberta, however.

Edmonton International Youth Hostel (IYHF), 10422 91 St. (429-0140), off Jasper Ave. The laid-back staff will play poker or canasta with you right up to the midnight curfew—and often beyond. They also provide a wealth of information on Edmonton and the rest of Alberta (especially the wild North). The conspicuous absence of a living room television results in livelier meals, conversations, and friendships. Everyone is required to do some kind of chore, like vacuuming or cleaning the stove. The area surrounding the hostel is not the finest; to be safe, walk via Jasper Ave., which is always busy and well-lit. Lockout 10am-5pm. Beware: the curfew is strictly enforced—if you stay out past midnight, you will spend the night at one of the exciting 24-hour convenience stores on Jasper Ave. Members $8.50, nonmembers $12. Call ahead during the winter.

St. Joseph's College, 114 St. at 89 Ave. (492-7681), in the University of Alberta neighborhood. Office on 2nd floor, #223. Several buses, including bus #43, blow through the area. The rooms here are smaller, less institutional, and cheaper than those at the nearby university. Shaded lawn out front. In summer, make reservations—rooms tend to fill up fast. Singles $15. Doubles $20 (limited number of them). Breakfast $3.

University of Alberta, 87 Ave., between 112 and 114 St. (492-4281), on the ground floor of Lister Hall. The university is crowded in the summer, but they always seem to have a free room somewhere. Classic institutional rooming units with beds and desks permanently fastened to the wall. Three sterile and quiet high-rise dormitories. Singles $16. Doubles $20. For nonstudents singles $21, doubles $32.

YWCA, 10305 100 Ave. (492-8707). Men not allowed on the residential floors. Women sleep in quiet rooms, many with balconies. Free use of pool and unlimited local calls for $1 per day. Dorm-style bunks $7. Singles $20. Key deposit $5. Elevator card deposit $15.

YMCA, 10030 102A Ave. (421-9622). Close enough to the bus and VIA Rail stations to produce convenience without paranoia. A lively, clean building with rooms availing both men and women. There are deluxe rooms on the newly renovated 4th floor. Singles $18.50, deluxe $21.50. Doubles $21.50, with bath $25, deluxe $28.50. Bunk beds $9 per night (2-night max. stay).

Mayfair Hotel, 10815 Jasper Ave. (423-1650). If you're in the money, treat yourself to an evening in this elegant, recently renovated downtown bed and breakfast. Expensive for the budget traveler, but worth every penny. Singles $40, $5.25 per additional person. Corner rooms $45. Suites $50.

Hotel Cecil, 10406 Jasper Ave. (428-7001). Kindler, gentler, and in a safer location than most rooms-above-a-tavern. Singles $18, with bath $21. Key deposit $5.

Food

One might guess that citizens of Edmonton—the self-labeled "City of Champions"—might begin their day by consuming bowl after bowl of Wheaties, the "Breakfast of Champions." Little evidence can be found to support this theory, however; Edmontonians prefer a more eclectic morning meal. In fact, should Edmonton redesign the culinary culture of the West, it would probably reduce everything to a delicious pancakes, bacon, and eggs breakfast. The city's restaurants just don't seem to do a great job with more substantial repasts. Both **downtown** and **Old Strathcona,** a region along 82 (Whyte) Ave. between 102 and 105 St., ooze with an unusually high number of restaurants.

For a quick and inexpensive meal, zip into one of Edmonton's numerous cafeterias. Lunch with gourmet pages and politicians in the main cafeteria of the **Alberta Legislature Building** (open Mon.-Fri. 7am-4pm). Or, for a less bombastic meal, try the cafeterias at the **YWCA** (men allowed; open Mon.-Thurs. 7am-7pm, Fri. 7am-6pm, Sat.-Sun. 8am-4pm) and the **YMCA** (open Mon.-Fri. 7am-6:30pm). The YMCA offers the cheapest breakfast special—eggs, sausage, toast, and hash browns for $2—while the YWCA allows you to create your own menu at the sandwich bar for $3.

Real Pizza & Steaks, 9449 Jasper Ave. (428-1989). Real great pizza and steaks. Superb blueberry pancakes (no wimpy soft berries—just good, thick ones) for $3.25. Go low budget with the breakfast special (2 eggs, toast, bacon, and hash browns) for $3. Open 24 hours.

Uncle Albert's Pancake House, 10370 82 (Whyte) Ave. (439-6609). One of 5 Edmonton locations. Again, breakfasts—and pancakes in particular—are the specialty here. Come in any Tues. in July during the Klondike days for free pancakes and ham—as much as you can eat, served all day. Even if you can't make it on a Tues. in July, you can still get good, cheap pancakes ($3 for a stack of 5). Open daily 7am-8pm.

Tivoli Gardens, 10423 Jasper Ave. (429-0867). Fills the hungry local clientele with daily lunch specials (e.g. corned beef sandwich and soup for $3) and cheers them up with the Have a Happy Day sign on the sidewalk. Open Mon.-Fri. 7:30am-5:30pm, Sat. 8:30am-3:30pm.

Dave's Place, 10217 97 St. (422-6754). No frills here, just fast cheap food. For $2 dine on 2 eggs, bacon, hash browns, toast, and coffee, or a hamburger and fries. Not the safest location, but the law courts are just across the street. Open daily 6:30am-5:30pm.

The Silk Hat, 10251 Jasper Ave. (428-1551). One of Edmonton's classic original restaurants, the Silk Hat still provides jukeboxes at each dimly lit booth. The daily sandwich special (about $4.50) even comes with dessert. Wash it all down with a mug of Molson ($1.25). Open Mon.-Fri. 6:30am-8pm, Sat. 6am-8pm, Sun. 11am-7pm.

Hot Pastrami Delicatessen, 8405 112 St. (432-1371). Frequented by U. of A. students and such traveling academic superstars as Morris Zapp. Try the Korean favorite *jab-chai* (cellophane noodles, beef, and vegetables, $5). Open daily 7am-10pm.

9th St. Bistro, 9910 109 St. (424-7219). Hearty soups and creative sandwiches $5-7. The burger with cream cheese and kiwi should not be missed. Wayne Gretzky might have eaten here. Open daily 11am-midnight.

New York Bagel Cafe, 8209 104 St. Part of a continental trend towards subjecting the bagel to all kinds of unnecessary and humiliating encumbrances—for instance, chicken liver pâté. 007 fanatics can contemplate a James Bond favorite—bagel with malasol Beluga caviar ($22.60). Wash it all down with a tasty pineapple or raspberry milk cocktail ($3), then choose from the 9 types of coffee.

Sights

The "oh-my-god-that's-*obscenely*-huge" **West Edmonton Mall** (444-5200 or 800-661-8890), stalking the general area of 170 St. and 87 Ave., is still the talk of the town. The cosmos' largest conglomeration of retail stores under one roof, the Mall shelters shivering Edmontonians during −4°F (−30°C) winters, but it leaves most tourists with a cold impression of the town. The Mall seized 30% of Edmonton's retail business, effectively destroying downtown shopping. Encompassing a water park, an amusement park, and dozens of hopelessly caged exotic animals, the world's biggest Mall appears even bigger thanks to mirrors plastered on nearly every wall. Among its highly touted achievements, the Mall boasts twice as many submarines as the Canadian Navy, a full-scale replica of Columbus' *Santa Maria,* and **Lazermaze,** the world's first walk-thru video game. Go to the Mall if you're out of clothes, toothpaste, and dozens of other essentials, but don't waste a day there. You can get to the Mall via bus #10. (Hours vary from store to store, so call ahead if you plan to go late in the day.)

For an almost refreshing change, head downtown to **Eaton's Mall,** 102 St. and 102 Ave. Owned and operated by the 555 Corporation, the same company that owns the "West Ed." Mall, Eaton's Mall is smaller, keeps no caged animals and is far superior in architecture and design. Lined by colorful plants, Eaton's is a much more pleasant place to walk through than its monstrous uncle.

After sampling the "pleasures" of the late 20th century at the malls, the late 19th century will seem a welcome relief as you head for **Fort Edmonton Park,** off the Whitemud Freeway near the Quesnell Bridge. At the end of the park (farthest from the entrance) sits the fort, a 19th-century "office building" for Alberta's first entrepreneurs, the ruthless whiskey traders. Between the fort on 1846 St. and the park entrance are three long streets (1875 St., 1905 St., and 1920 St.), each bedecked with period buildings—apothecaries, blacksmith shops, and barns—from the streets' respective years. Like figures out of a genre painting, appropriately clothed park volunteers greet visitors with the inquisitiveness of a 19th-century schoolmarm or the warmth of a general-store owner. Watch these vicars of things past conduct their daily business, or pick their brains with questions about stagecoaches or 19th-century loos. Be warned that the quaint stores and restaurant charge up-to-date prices. Hungry souls can get back to the entrance via a miniature train, which choochoos the length of the park. (Open Victoria Day-Labor Day daily 10am-6pm; May-June 9:30am-4pm; Labor Day-Thanksgiving Sun., Mon., and holidays 10am-6pm. Admission $4.75, senior citizens and ages 13-17 $3.50.) The park is accessible by bus #123 or 32.

While visiting the fort, stop in at the **John Janzen Nature Centre** and pet the salamanders. Then, sprint across Hwy. 2 to the **Valley Zoo,** at 134 St. and Buena Vista Rd. (483-5511). The zoo may not compare with Calgary's, but it does flaunt more species than the Mall. The zoo originally followed a storybook theme but has since burst the strictures of narrative to offer a more intercontinental selection of species. (May-Sept. 5 open daily 10am-6pm; admission $3, senior citizens and youths $2.25. Sept. 8-March 27 open Sat.-Sun. noon-4pm; admission $2, senior citizens and youths $1.50.)

Lest you think Edmonton has gone overboard with re-created history, fear not: the four Giza-like, glass pyramids across the river are merely the hi-tech greenhouses covering the **Muttart Conservatory,** 9626 96A St. (428-5226 for a recording). In summer and winter, this botanical garden's choose-your-own weather chamber can comfort you with the heat, humidity, and aromas of its Tropical Pavilion. Migrate to the more soothing climates of the Temperate and Arid Pavilions, lush with flowers, bushes, and trees. (Open daily 11am-9pm; Sept.-May Sun.-Wed. 11am-9pm, Thurs.-Sat. 11am-6pm. Admission $3, senior citizens and ages under 18 $1.75.) Bus #51 whisks you to Muttart.

The **Alberta Legislature Building,** 97 Ave. and 109 St. (427-7362), is as stately and ornate as any capitol building in Alberta. Indeed, there is a point on the top floor where water sounds as if it's pouring down torrentially from above (an echo from the fountain 3 floors below). You can sample this "Ripley's Believe It or Not" effect yourself on the free, thorough tour of the building, given every half hour. (Open Mon.-Fri. 9am-8:30pm, Sat.-Sun. 9am-4:30pm; Labor Day-Victoria Day Mon.-Fri. 9-11:30am and 1-4pm, Sat.-Sun. noon-4pm.) The legislature is in session from early March to late May and again during October.

On a sunny summer day, as the Legislature Building's negentropic carillon rings in the lunch hour, join most of the city in front of this grand political palace. A spectacular network of fountains and pools stretches before the building's steps. To escape the sun and the carnivorous crowd, enter the Government Centre Pedway, an underground walkway that connects the Legislature Building with other government offices. The **Alberta Pedway Display,** 9804 107 St. (427-7362), features exhibits on Alberta's history, inhabitants, technology, and wildlife. (Open daily 10am-4pm; Labor Day-Victoria Day Mon.-Fri. 10am-4pm. Free.) If you'd prefer to observe Edmonton from *above* the city, check out the **AGT Vista 33** on the 33rd floor of the Alberta Telephone Tower, 10020 100 St. (493-3333). Although the Vista 33 lacks the height and majestic mountain view of the Calgary Tower, this lookout spot costs much less and also includes a small **telephone museum.** The homesick can dial up their local area code and light a bulb in their hometown (oh wow). A number of other hands-on displays might make this elevator trip well worth the nominal admission fee. (Open daily 10am-8pm. Admission 50¢, senior citizens and pre-schoolers free.)

A walking tour of the city at street level might behoove those who fear heights (or depths). You can retrace the steps of Alberta's pioneers along **Heritage Trail.** The self-guided tour begins at 100 St. and 99 Ave. and saunters past the Legislature Building, Edmonton's first schoolhouse, and other historic landmarks. Just follow the red brick road. Follow, follow, follow, follow, follow the red brick road. Another self-guided tour, the **Walking Tour of Old Strathcona,** starts at 8331 104 St. (433-5866) in the Old Strathcona Foundation Building. (Open Mon.-Fri. 8:30am-4:30pm.) Trace the history of this area from its incorporation as a town in 1899 through its union with Edmonton in 1912. **Royal Tours of Edmonton** (425-5342) and **U-C Tours** (921-2104) will show lazy people the sights aboard buses.

Both of these tours stop at the **Provincial Museum of Alberta,** 12845 102 Ave. (427-1730), which stashes all kinds of Albertan artifacts, from threshers and old plows to Native American clothing and primitive stone tools. Despite the impressive collection, the museum fails to create a very convincing impression of either pioneer or Native life. The museum does, however, contain one of the only photographs of Edmonton's downtown taken before modernization festooned the area with skyscrapers. (Open daily 9am-8pm. Free.) Take bus #1 or 2. The museum recently opened up another exhibit entitled **Traces of the Past,** which features dinosaur fossils. (Open daily 9am-8pm; Labor Day-Victoria Day Tues. and Thurs.-Sun. 9am-5pm, Wed. 9am-8pm.)

Pick up your nightstick and throw on your badge at the **Police Museum,** 9620 103A Ave. (421-2274), on the third floor of the police station. While real cops track nefarious no-gooders downstairs, the museum explains the history of law enforcement in the province, from the Royal Canadian Mounted Police to the Alberta Provincial Police to Edmonton's finest. See uniforms and radar sets used in the pursuit of criminals and the preservation of justice. (When staffed, open Tues.-Sat. 10am-3pm. Free.)

Strathcona Science Park, at the city's eastern edge 1km south of Hwy. 16, features the **Strathcona Archaeological Centre** (427-2022), established near the site of a recently unearthed Native American settlement. Cluttered with tepee rings and buried stone tools, the site was discovered by construction workers preparing to raze the area. The small archaeological center and its alert staff explain the Native Americans' periodic peregrinations through the area. Outside the museum, a hiking trail leads to the site of the archaeological excavation in progress. (Open Victoria Day-Labor Day 10am-6pm. Free.) Bus #20 or 28 will take you from the center of Edmonton to Rundle Park, a ½-hour walk across the river from Strathcona Science Park.

Entertainment and Activities

Led by the late Wayne Gretzky, the **Edmonton Oilers** skated off with four of five consecutive Stanley Cups. They play from October through April in the **Northlands Coliseum,** 115 Ave. and 79 St. (471-2191). The "City of Champions" also holds its **Edmonton Eskimos** in high regard. The Eskimos, winners of the Canadian Football League's 1988 Grey Cup, tackle their competition at **Commonwealth Stadium,** 11000 Stadium Rd. (429-2881).

Edmonton caters to the sports *participant* as well: kilometre after kilometre of paved bike trails and unpaved hiking/skiing trails weave through the river valley within the city limits. **Milk Creek Ravine Park,** on the river's south bank bounded by 82 (Whyte) Ave. and 91 and 98 St., has an extensive network of running trails. For a real splash, the **Mill Woods Recreation Centre,** 7207 28 Ave. (428-2888), offers a wave pool as well as a number of calmer outdoor activities.

If you want to get smashed, you might consider frequenting bars in the downtown area. Homesick Brits should perceive **Sherlock Holmes,** at 10012 101A Ave. (426-7784). This English-style pub features sing-along songfests and a passel of staple British ales on tap. There's also a new Sherlock Holmes (with sing-alongs, of course) in The Mall, on Bourbon St. For real bands, check the listings in *The Edmonton Bullet,* the city's free monthly guide to entertainment, which includes theater, film, and music listings. For live music, check out the blues clubs **Sidetrack Cafe** at 10333 112 St. (421-1326) and **Blues on Whyte** at the **Commercial Hotel,** 10329 82 Ave. (439-3981). Country fans should saddle up and mosey on over to **Cook County Saloon,** 8010 103 St. (432-0177), while jazz aficionados will dig **Yardbird Suite** at 10203 86 Ave. (432-0428).

Save at least one night for a visual fest at the **Space Sciences Centre,** 11211 142 St. (452-9100 for a real person, 451-7722 for a recording). Spectacular shows air either on the IMAX giant wraparound screen or in the Margaret Ziedler Star Theatre. The IMAX theatre screens thrillingly realistic films such as "Seasons," which yokes Vivaldi's *Four Seasons* to enormous images of nature's transformations. Rock laser shows, inflicting music ranging from Elton John to U2, blaze through the Star Theatre. (Open daily. IMAX movies $4.50, senior citizens and children $2. Laser shows in Star Theatre $5.50, senior citizens and children $3.50.) Buses #11, 22, and 37 rocket past the Space Sciences Centre.

For a more cerebral evening, buy tickets to the **Princess Theatre,** 10337 82 (Whyte) Ave. (433-0979, for a recording 433-5785). The movies here change every night, concentrating on popular reruns such as *The African Queen* and *The Gods Must Be Crazy*. Watch for the Princess's film festival in June. Schedules are available at the theatre and at dozens of stands around town. (Tickets $4.50, senior citizens $1.50.) The **National Film Theatre** screens everything from *Nanook of the North* to *Scott of the Antarctic* in the Edmonton Art Gallery Theatre, 2 Winston Churchill Square. (Admission $4.)

Seasonal Events

Edmonton, presumably jealous of Calgary's success with the Stampede, conjured up its own summertime carnival a few years back. Held for 10 days in mid-July, **Klondike Days,** like the Stampede, occasions the painting of cartoon figures on storefront windows and causes an epidemic of free (or nearly free) breakfasts. Edmonton even tries to rival Calgary's chuckwagon race with its very own pig races. But while Calgary is showing off the sunnier sides of Alberta's heritage, Edmonton's Klondike Days recalls what can only be called an inglorious sham (heritage of a sort, perhaps). During the Yukon gold rush around the turn of the century, Edmontonians lured treasure seekers through their city, claiming a specious "Klondike Trail" from Edmonton to Dawson City. Prospectors found the trail a much more difficult path than the traditional Alaska route, and to some it proved impassable. Stymied gold-hunters turned back to settle in Edmonton, boosting the population from 2000 to 50,000. Despite its shameful namesake, the festival has gained heartfelt local support, thanks to a barrage of stimulating events such as the Fun Tub Race and the Hairiest Chest Competition. Write to Edmonton's Klondike Days Exposition, P.O. Box 1480, Edmonton T5J 2N5, or call 471-7210 for information.

Each August, alternative entertainment happenings dominate the Old Strathcona District along 82 (Whyte) Ave. The **Fringe Theatre Event** (432-1553) features 150 alternative theater productions in area parks, theaters, and streets. During an earlier August weekend, the **Edmonton Folk Music Festival** brings country and bluegrass banjo-pickin' to the city. In late June and early July, take in the **Jazz City International Festival,** which jams together ten days of club dates and free performances by some of Canada's (and the rest of the world's) most noted jazz musicians. This musical extravaganza often coincides with a visual arts celebration called **The Works.**

Near Edmonton

For those without the means or desire to trek west or north, wilderness cries out a mere 35km east of Edmonton at **Elk Island National Park.** In 1906, civic concern prompted the establishment of the park in order to protect endangered herds of elk. Since then, all sorts of exotic mammals (plains bison, wood bison, moose, and hikers) have moved in, but some might consider the park "for the birds": 240 species share the airspace over Lake Astotin. While black bears and grizzlies may terrify tourists in Banff and Jasper, you'll have to deal with a different natural threat at Elk Island—bison. Pick up your copy of *You Are in Bison Country* at the Park Information Centre, just off Hwy. 16. Bison are dangerous; they're faster than horses and five times bigger than Andre the Giant. The lakeshore is the center of civilized activity in the park. The **Astotin Interpretive Centre** (922-5790) answers questions, screens films, and schedules activities daily. It also explains that Elk Island is not one of the many water-bound forests in Lake Astotin, but rather "an island of forest amidst a landscape of man." (Open Thurs.-Tues. 11am-6pm; in winter Sat.-Sun. 11am-6pm.) Soviet defectors can feel at home in a replica of a thatched-roof Ukranian pioneer home. (Open mid-May to Labor Day Fri.-Tues. 10am-6pm.)

Backcountry camping is allowed in certain areas with a free permit, obtainable at the information centre. If you want a shower and the prospect of 100-plus neighbors leaves you sanguine, set up camp at the **Sandy Beach Campground,** off Hwy.

16 (992-6387; no reservations accepted). Swimming is not recommended at the beach, because if the leeches don't get you, the "swimmer's itch" probably will. The snack bar near the campground flings buffalo burgers at those who forgot to pack a lunch. The park also features 12 well-marked hiking trails, most from 3-17km in length, which double as cross-country and snowshoeing trails in the winter.

Continue east on Hwy. 16 all the way to the Soviet Ukraine—not quite the land of *glasnost* itself, but the **Ukranian Cultural Heritage Village,** a living tribute to one of Alberta's strongest ethnic groups. Like Fort Edmonton Park, it features the requisite historic buildings (including a hardware store), and its staff of "interpreters" carries on early 20th-century chores and guided tours. (Open Victoria Day-Labor Day daily 10am-6pm. Free.)

Red Deer

When the Edmonton Oilers and the Calgary Flames clashed in the second round of the 1988 NHL playoffs, sportswriters from both cities flocked to Red Deer. Red Deer? Yes, Red Deer, a quiet town of nearly 55,000 residents which happens to lie equidistant from the two oil (and hockey) superpowers along Hwy. 2. While reporters deconstruct the town's allegiance, however, most citizens of Red Deer simply avoid choosing sides in the feud and go about their own agribusiness.

Practical Information and Orientation

Red Deer lies 145km north of Calgary and 149km south of Edmonton at the junction of Hwy. 2 and 2A. Gaetz Ave. (Hwy. 2A) runs north-south through the city, while the Red Deer River flows southwest to northeast through the center of town. Red Deer is a frequent stop for Greyhound buses traveling to Calgary, Edmonton, or points east and west. The small, hectic **Greyhound terminal** at 4303 Gaetz Ave. (343-8866) sees dozens of buses every day, launching four express trips per day to Calgary and Edmonton (each $9.50 one way).

For tourist information and maps of the city, drop by the **Chamber of Commerce,** 3017 50 Ave. (347-4491). Though most of the brochures lining the walls advertise other vacation spots, the staff here can suggest how you might spend a day or two in Red Deer. (Open Mon.-Fri. 8:30am-6pm, Sat 9am-5pm.) In an **emergency** dial 911, or the local **hospital** at 343-4422. To buy stamps or send letters, stop by the Red Deer **post office** at the corner of Ross St. and 49 Ave. (340-4209). (Open Mon.-Wed. and Thurs. 9am-5pm, Tues and Fri. 9am-5:30pm.) Its **postal code** is T4N 1XO.

Accommodations and Food

The **Arlington Hotel** at 4905 51 Ave. (346-2509) is the cheapest place to crash in town (singles from $17). If the Arlington's full, the **Buffalo Hotel,** right around the corner at 5331 Ross St. (346-2061), should have space available (singles $13-22). Campers can settle down at the **Lions Campground,** Riverside Dr. and 49 Ave. (342-8183), which offers plenty of modern amenities (semi-serviced sites $9, fully serviced $11).

You can wander indecisively among a multitude of fast-food restaurants which line Gaetz Ave., or sample some good local grease at **Clancy's Soup and Sandwich,** 50005a Gaetz Ave. (342-0380). A Clancyburger with the works costs $2; for breakfast, try the $3.50 "Clancy's Classic." (Open Mon.-Fri. 7:30am-5pm, Sat. 10am-4:30pm.) For a slightly healthier meal try **David's Soup 'n' Greens,** 4901 48 St. (347-1826), in the lower mall of Parkland Sq., for . . . soup and greens! (Open Mon.-Fri. 7am-4pm.) Sample the homemade taste of a thicker and more expensive soup at **Pumpernickel Deli,** 5010 43 St. (343-1272; open Mon.-Fri. 7am-4pm). When dinner time rolls around, many local restaurants expire. Order a pizza from **Red Onion Pizza,** 5020 Ross St. (340-1221), and find out why this local chain has such a following. The 10-inch vegetarian pie costs $10. (Open Mon.-Wed. 11am-8pm, Thurs.-Sat.

11am-midnight.) For a high quality meal without high prices, the best place in town is the **Good Food Company,** 5001 Ross St. (343-8185), at Gaetz. Enjoy a sandwich on freshly baked bread or a gourmet salad as Vivaldi pollutes the clean, airy café.

Activities and Seasonal Events

Waskasoo Park, snaking its way through town in the Red Deer River Valley, witnesses year-round activity. The clean, convenient park includes lazy rivers for canoeing and biking, hiking trails, a golf course, campgrounds, cross-country ski trails, picnic facilities, and to top it all off, **Heritage Ranch.** The equestrian center for the park and the city, Heritage Ranch offers riding lessons and family Western-style events, from rodeos to barbecues. Folks from all around are invited to bring, rent, or pet their favorite pony (call 340-0755 for further ranch information).

For even more Wild West thrills, head to **Westerner Park** on 4900 Delburne Rd., at the southern junction of Hwy. 2 and 2A. Besides frequent dog shows and rodeos, the park also hosts the Shrine Circus in May, horse shows and races starting in April, and the annual **Highland Games,** the largest festival of its kind in Western Canada. Lads and lassies take over the town for one day in June as Scottish clans battle it out in traditional field events like the tug-o'-war and caber toss. The town also chooses a clan to honor with piping, drumming, and a nip of ale.

From the town of **Rocky Mountain House,** 82km east of Red Deer, you can drive the obscure **David Thompson Highway** (Hwy. 11) into the northern half of Banff National Park. Named for the early 19th-century explorer who mapped this area, the highway is valued by Albertans as an undiscovered national treasure. En route to Banff, stay at the renowned **Shunda Creek Hostel** (721-2140), 3km north of Nordegg. (Members $6, nonmembers $9. Open Thurs.-Mon.)

Western Alberta

Jasper National Park

Jasper claims natural wonders and outdoor opportunities comparable to Banff's, yet it lacks the trendy demeanor of its southern neighbor. The town is small, the attitude casual, and the locals affable. Surrounding the tiny townsite are 10,000 square kilometres of breathtaking wilderness. Your gaze will wander from fragrant alpine wildflowers to jagged mountain peaks. Reserve a couple of days for a backcountry trek, which requires a free permit available at the Park Information Centre. At the very least, shut off your car's engine for a few hours and take a day hike.

Practical Information and Orientation

Visitor Information: Park Information Centre, 500 Connaught Dr. (852-6176). Trail maps and information on all aspects of the park. Open June 14-Labor Day daily 8am-8pm; in spring and fall 9am-5pm. **Travel Alberta,** 632 Connaught Dr. (in AB 800-222-6501). Open May-Oct. daily 8am-7:30pm. **Jasper Chamber of Commerce,** 634 Connaught Dr. (852-3858). Open Mon.-Fri. 9am-5pm. **Park Headquarters,** Superintendent, Jasper National Park, Box 10, Jasper T0E 1E0 (852-6161).

VIA Rail: 314 Connaught Dr. (800-665-8630 or 852-4102). To Vancouver (1 per day, 16 hr., $70), Edmonton ($39), and Winnipeg ($141). Prices 1/3-off for senior citizens and students. Coin-operated lockers 75¢ for 24 hours. Open daily 8am-10:30pm, shorter hours in off-season.

Greyhound: 314 Connaught Dr. (852-3926), in the VIA station. To Edmonton (3 per day, $24.80 one way) and Kamloops ($34.90 one way).

Brewster Transportation and Tours: 852-3901, in the VIA station. To Banff (full-day tour $42, daily 5½-hr. express $24) and Calgary (1 per day, 8 hr., $31).

Car Rental: Jasper Car Rental, 626 Connaught Dr. (852-3373). $50 per day with 100 free km and 19¢ per additional km or $30 with no free km. Senior citizen and student rate $40 with 100 free km. Must be 21 with credit card. Reduced rates for multi-day rental.

Scooter Rental: Jasper Scooter Rental (852-5603), across tracks from Texaco above Dick's Auto. Rentals $6.50 per hr., $39 per day. Open daily 9am-9pm.

Bike Rental: Free Wheel Cycle, 600 Patricia St. (852-5380). Enter through the alley behind Patricia St. 10- and 15-speeds $3 per hr., $8 per half-day, $15 per day. Mountain bikes (better suited to the terrain) $4 per hr., $10 per half-day, $17 per day. Must have valid ID for deposit. Open Mon.-Sat. 9am-8pm, Sun. 10am-8pm; April-July 1 and Labor Day-Oct. 9am-6pm. **Whistler's Youth Hostel** also rents mountain bikes. IYHF members $8 per half-day, $14 per day. Nonmembers $10 per half-day, $16 per day.

Hospital: 852-3344.

Ambulance: 852-3100.

Emergency: 852-4848.

Post Office: 502 Patricia St. (852-3041), across from the townsite green. Open Mon.-Fri. 9am-5pm, Sat. 9am-3pm; Sept.-June Mon.-Fri. 9am-5pm. Postal Code: T0E 1E0.

Area Code: 403.

All of the above addresses are in Jasper Townsite, which sits near the middle of the park, 362km southwest of Edmonton and 287km north of Banff. **Highway 16** shuttles travelers through the park north of the townsite, while the **Icefields Parkway** (Hwy. 93) connects to Banff National Park in the south. Buses run to the townsite daily from Edmonton, Calgary, Vancouver, and Banff. Trains arrive from Edmonton and Vancouver. Arrange a ride between Banff and Jasper if you've been hitching, since most cars traveling between the two parks are jammed with tourists and backpacks. Renting a bike is the most practical option for short jaunts within the park.

Accommodations

Hotels in Jasper Townsite are too expensive to recommend as budget options. You may, however, be able to stay cheaply (singles $20-30, doubles $25-35, triples $35-40, quads $30-55) in a bed and breakfast; ask for the *Approved Accommodations List* at the Park Information Centre. Since few visitors know of the list, space is often available on short notice. Four of the three dozen homes on the list appear below. If you prefer mingling with the youthful set, head to a hostel (listed below from north to south). Reservations, as well as information on closing days and on the winter "key system," are channeled through the Edmonton-based Southern Alberta Hostel Association (439-3089).

Lena Hollenbeck, 716 Connaught Dr., P.O. Box 1052 (852-4563). Close to town. Two rooms with double bed in each; one room with twin beds. Courtesy coffee/tea, use of BBQ, living room with color TV. Expect to find heated international conversations between guests. Ms. Hollenbeck will make you feel at home. Doubles $25 ($20 for one person). Twins $35.

Betty Ens and Ed Simpson, 718 Connaught Dr., Box 816 (852-3640). Three rooms with private or semi-private entrances (the Simpsons will give you a key to come and go as you please). Single $20. Doubles $25-30. Each additional person $5.

Gordon and Darlene Middleton, 732 Patricia St., P.O. Box 921 (852-3783). Three blocks from bus and train. The immobile Middletons have been in Jasper for 30 years. TV room for common use. Each of the 2 bedrooms converts between double and single. Singles $20. Doubles $20-25. Each additional person $5. Kitchen $5. Complete suite $50. Year-round accommodations.

Brenda and Dennis Onyschuk, 1230 Cabin Creek Dr., P.O. Box 368 (852-5964). The Onyschuks offer a large room with a private entrance, two double beds, and color TV. Nonsmokers only. Double $35. Each additional person $5.

Maligne Canyon Hostel (IYHF), on Maligne Canyon Rd., 15km northeast of the townsite. Space for 24 people. Members $4, nonmembers $6. Closed Wed.

Whistlers Mountain Hostel (IYHF), on Sky Tram Rd. (852-3215), 7km south of the townsite. Closest to the townsite, this is the park's most modern (and crowded) hostel. A hike from town, mostly uphill. You may have to sweep out the fireplace before you leave in the morning, but at least you'll know it's working. Accommodates 50. Members $6, nonmembers $9.

Mt. Edith Cavell Hostel (IYHF), on Edith Cavell Rd., off Hwy. 93A. Accommodates any 32 visitors. The road is closed in winter, but the hostel welcomes anyone willing to ski the 11km from Hwy. 93A. They mean what they say. Members $4, nonmembers $6. Open June 15 to mid-Sept. Fri.-Wed.; Dec. 15 to mid-April Fri.-Tues.

Athabasca Falls Hostel (IYHF), on Hwy. 93, 30km south of Jasper Townsite, near the churning Athabasca Falls. Members $4.50, nonmembers $7. Closed Tues.

Beauty Creek Hostel (IYHF), on Hwy. 93, 78km south of Jasper Townsite. Next to the handsome Sunwapta River. Accommodates 20. Accessible through a "key system" in winter. Members $4, nonmembers $6. Open May to mid-Sept. Thurs.-Tues.

Camping

The campsites below are listed from north to south. For campground updates, listen to AM1450 on your radio near Jasper Townsite.

Pocahontas, on Hwy. 16, at the northern edge of the park. 140 sites. Sites $8.50. Open May 15-Sept. 8.

Snaring River, on Hwy. 16, 20km north of the townsite. 60 sites, 10 of which are walk-in tentsites. Sites $6. Open May 15-Sept. 7.

Whistlers, on Whistlers Rd., just south of the townsite. If you're intimidated by the wilderness, the humans occupying 781 neighboring sites will keep you company. Sites $9-14. Showers.

Wapiti, on Hwy. 93, close to Whistlers. A magnet for RV visitors, with 345 sites. Sites $9-10.75. Showers. Open June 19-Sept. 8.

Wabasso, on Hwy. 93A, about 20km south of the townsite. 238 sites, 6 of which are walk-in tentsites. Sites $6.50. Open May 15-18 and June 26-Sept. 7.

Mount Kerkeslin, on Hwy. 93, about 35km south of Jasper Townsite. 42 sites. Sites $6. Open May 15-Sept. 7.

Honeymoon Lake, on Hwy. 93, about 50km south of the townsite. 36 sites. Sites $6. Open June 12-Sept. 14.

Jonas Creek, on Hwy. 93, about 70km south of the townsite. 25 sites, 12 of which are reserved for tents. Sites $6. Open May 15 to mid-Oct.

Columbia Icefield, on Hwy. 93, 103km south of the townsite, at the southern border of the park. Not on the Athabasca Glacier, but near enough to receive an ice-cold breeze on the warmest summer nights. 22 tentsites. Sites $6. Open May 15 to mid-Oct.

Wilcox Creek, on Hwy. 93, at the southern park boundary. 46 sites. Best spot for RVs. Sites $6-8. Open June 12-Sept. 14.

Food

Your best bet for cheap meals is to stock up at a local market or bulk foods store and head for the backcountry. For around-the-clock grocery supplies, stop at the **Red Rooster Food Store,** 605 Patricia St. **Nutter's,** also on Patricia St., offers grains, nuts, dried fruits, and (if you're sick of healthy food) candy, all in bulk form. They also sell deli meats, canned goods, and freshly ground coffee. (Open Mon.-Sat. 9am-10pm, Sun. 10am-9pm.)

Mountain Foods and Cafe, 606 Connaught Dr. (852-4050). Claim a table before you order at this popular streetside cafe. The menu has both hot and cold sandwiches, soups and desserts—all of them healthy. Cold sandwiches $3, pita melt with avocado, turkey, and tomato $5, hearty bowl of lentil soup $1.75. Prepare for the millenium by stocking up on bulk grains, holistic books, and frozen yogurt ($1.35). Open daily 8am-10pm.

Scoops and Loops, 504 Patricia St. (852-4333). Average food at great prices. Croissant sandwiches ($2.50) and bran muffins (50¢) are fine for lunch, but be sure to save room for dessert. A huge selection of hard and soft ice cream, pies, and pastries. Open daily 10am-10pm.

Tricia's Ice Cream, Patricia St. (852-4945). Home of the 99¢ hotdog as well as more delicious and expensive fresh-fruit ice creams and yogurts. Open May-Oct. daily 10am-11pm. In winter, Tricia's is transubstantiated into **Edge Control Ski Shop.**

The Red Dragon, (852-3171), in the Athabasca Hotel. The cheapest Chinese cuisine in Jasper. Eat in or take out an order of "egg foo young" ($6) or shrimp chow mein ($6). Offers breakfast, lunch, and dinner. Open daily 7am-midnight; in winter 8am-10pm.

Sights and Activities

An extensive trail network connects most parts of Jasper, many paths starting at the townsite. Information centres distribute free copies of *Day Hikes in Jasper National Park* and a summary of the longer hikes. Three ecological zones are represented in the park. Lodgepole Pine, Douglas fir, White Spruce, and Trembling Aspen characterize the **montane zone** in the valley bottoms. Subalpine Fir and Engelmann Spruce inhabit the **subalpine zone** that comprises 40% of the park. Small, fragile plants and wildflowers struggle for existence in the **alpine zone,** which makes up another 40% of Jasper. Hikers should always remain on the trail in the alpine area to avoid trampling endangered plant species.

Kick off any foray into the wilderness with a fun-filled conversation at the Park Information Centre in the townsite. Friendly experts will direct you to appropriate hiking and mountain-biking trails. If Jasper Townsite is not in your path, the Icefield Centre, on Hwy. 93 at the southern entrance to the park (see Icefields Parkway), provides similar services.

Mt. Edith Cavell, named after a WWI hero, shakes skeptics with the thunderous sound of avalanches off the Angel Glacier. Take the 1½ km loop trail or the 8km return **Path of the Glacier.** Mt. Edith Cavell rears its enormous head 30km south of the townsite on Cavell Rd. **Maligne Lake,** the largest glacier-fed lake in the Canadian Rockies, has vivid turquoise water and every conceivable water sport. Trails leave from the chalet and warden station. Drive 50km southeast from the townsite on Maligne Lake Rd. One special feature of Jasper National Park is **Medicine Lake,** 30km east of Jasper Townsite. Water flows into the lake, but there is no visible outlet. The trick? The water flows out through a series of underground caves, emerging in such areas as **Maligne Canyon,** 11km east of the townsite on Maligne Canyon Rd. Squirrels can jump across the narrow 46m-deep gorge. Humans cannot, though; several have fallen to their deaths. At the far end of **Medicine Lake** is a trail leading to **Beaver Lake** (about 2km). Here even novice fishermen can catch a bucket full of brook trout. Because of the walk, the lake is uncrowded. Rent equipment at **Curry's,** 622 Connaught Dr. (852-5650); rod and reel with worms $10.

Not to be outdone by Banff, Jasper has a gondola of its own. Rising 2½ km up the side of Whistlers Mountain, the **Jasper Tramway** (852-3093) grants a panoramic view of the park and an opportunity to spend money at its gift shop and restaurant. (Fare $7, ages under 14 $3.50. Open March 24-May 18 daily 9:30am-4:30pm; May 19-June 15 8:30am-7:30pm; June 16-Sept. 4 8am-9:30pm; Sept. 5-Oct. 9 9am-4:30pm.) A steep 10km trail starting from the Whistlers Mountain Hostel also leads up the slope; to spare your quadriceps you'll want to take the tram ride down ($3.50). No matter which way you go, be sure to bring along a warm coat and sunglasses to withstand the rapidly changing climate at the peak.

Guided trail rides are available for high prices. One-and-a-half-hour rides cost $20 at the Jasper Park Lodge (852-5794), 5km north of the townsite on Hwy. 16. Guided rides at Pyramid Lake are $9 per hour (852-3562).

Whitewater Rafting (Jasper) Ltd. runs several rafting trips from $32-50 (less expensive with bigger groups). If the whitewater doesn't tickle you, the guides' jokes will. Register at the Texaco station or phone 852-7238. **Boat rental** is available at Pyramid Lake (852-3536; canoes and rowboats $6 per hr., $10 per 2 hr., $15 per day; $20 deposit or a valid ID), and Maligne Lake (852-3370; canoes $7 per hr.,

$3 per additional hour; rowboats $30 per day; ID required for deposit). For a less exhausting tour of Maligne Lake, narrated cruises in enclosed and heated tour boats are available. **Maligne Lake Scenic Cruises** recommends reservations. (Write P.O. Box 280, or visit them at 626 Connaught Dr.)

After dipping in Jasper's glacier-fed waters, salvage your numbed body at **Miette Hot Springs,** north off Hwy. 16 along the clearly marked, 15km Miette Hotsprings Rd. The 1986-vintage building houses lockers and two pools (one of which is wheelchair accessible). Devoid of nutrient-filled additives and rotten-egg reek, the pools are heated via external pipes through which the spring water is pumped. Unfortunately, the 40°C (102°F) water is off-limits in winter. (Open June 19-Sept. 7 8:30am-10:30pm. Admission $1.75. Suits $1, towels 75¢, lockers 25¢.) Rotten-egg-lovers can wallow in the sulphur-soused spring itself. A short trail leads south from a picnic area near the modern pool complex to one of the steamy outlets. Don't drink the water—it's 55°C (131°F) and full of unnamed and untamed microscopic organisms.

More curious hikers should attempt the three-faced **Mystery Lake Trail,** leading east and uphill from the pools. The trail changes from paved path to dirt road to serious trek along the 11km to Mystery Lake.

Winter may keep you away from the springs, but you can always generate heat on the slopes of **Marmot Basin,** near Jasper Townsite. A full-day lift ticket costs $25, half-day $18. For information, write "A Marmot Experience," Box 1570, Jasper T0E 1E0 (800-661-1931 or 852-4242). Ski rental is available at **Totem's Ski Shop,** 408 Connaught Dr. (852-3078). The full package (skis, boots, and poles) runs $12 per day. (Open daily 9:30am-10pm; Labor Day-Victoria Day 8am-6pm.) There is also cross-country skiing at Maligne Lake from November through May.

Icefields Parkway

A glacier-lined, 230km road connecting Jasper townsite with Lake Louise, the Icefields Parkway (Hwy. 93) snakes past dozens of ominous peaks and glacial lakes. Wise drivers and cyclists set aside at least three days for the parkway. The challenging hikes and endless vistas are never monotonous. Thanks to the extensive campground and hostel networks which line the parkway, drawn-out trips down the entire length of Jasper and Banff National Parks are convenient and affordable. (See Accommodations and Camping under each park.) All points on the parkway are within 30km of at least one place where you can roll out your sleeping bag.

Before setting your wheels (2 or 4) on the road, pick up a free map of Icefields Parkway, available at park information centres in Jasper and Banff. The pamphlet is also available at the **Icefield Centre,** at the boundary between the two parks. The centre sits in sight of the **Athabasca Glacier,** the most prominent of the eight glaciers which flow into the 325-square-kilometre Columbia Icefield. Summer crowds hold snowball fights on the vast, empty icefields to the side of the road. **Brewster Transportation and Tours** (762-2241) carries visitors right onto the glacier in futuristic tanks called "Snocoaches." You pay $13 (ages 6-15 $6) for the slippery, 75-minute ride. (Tours given May 20-Sept. 26 daily 9am-5pm.)

If you have the time—and a burning curiosity about the geological history of the glaciers—sign up for a guided interpretive hike on the Athabasca. A three-hour hike called "Ice Cubed" costs $12 (ages 8-17 $6), and the five-hour "Icewalk Deluxe" is $16 (children $8). Hikes are conducted from June 29 to Labor Day. Write **Athabasca Glacier Icewalks,** Attention: Peter Lemieux, Box 2067, Banff T0L 0C0.

When the frozen layers of ice make a trip onto the glacier too dangerous, settle for the 13-minute explanatory film inside the cozy **Icefield Centre.** (Open mid-June to Aug. daily 9am-7pm; mid-May to mid-June and Sept. 9am-5pm.) Although the centre shuts down in winter, the parkway closes only after heavy snowfalls, and then only until the plows clear the way.

If you only have time for a quick hike, try the **Parker Ridge Trail.** The 2.4km hike (one way) guides you away from the parkway, past the treeline, and over Parker

Ridge. At the end of the trail awaits a postcard view of the Saskatchewan Glacier. The trailhead is located 1km south of the Hilda Creek Hostel, at the northern edge of the Banff section of the parkway. Bring a windbreaker, since snow is common even in summer.

Hinton

Don't follow the road signs to Hinton; just roll down your window and follow the smell. A large pulp mill in Hinton hurls a most vicious odor miles around. In spite of this, Hinton, 29km east of Jasper's eastern gate, is an excellent place to stop over on your way to or from the national park. It is also a good place to stock up on groceries; many Jasperites do their weekly shopping here.

In summer, Hinton presents a few attractions of its own. See what it's like for a bishop *really* to take a queen when, three times during the summer months, citizens of Hinton act out the roles of chessboard warriors during **Live Chess Theatre.** On Tuesday afternoons at 12:30pm, the **Obed Mountain Coal Company** gives tours of its mine. The **Alberta Forest Technology School** (865-8211) also maintains a post in Hinton and arranges tours through the Tourist Information Booth. The museum here explores the work of early forest rangers. (Open daily 8:30am-4:30pm. Free.) The town's modern **Recreation Complex** (865-4412) contains two indoor ice rinks, indoor pool, sauna, jacuzzi, squash and racquetball courts, and a cafeteria. For a late-night nordic expedition, check out the **Athabasca Look-out Nordic Center,** which boasts one of the few lighted cross-country ski trails in Alberta. Call the visitors centre for information.

You can choose from a catalog of a dozen local inns and lodges. The **Timberland Hotel** (865-2231), conveniently next door to the Tourist Booth, is the cheapest of the bunch, offering singles starting at $25 and doubles from $35. The floorboards may creak, but the rooms are clean and well-tended. The Timberland also features a country-style restaurant (steak and eggs breakfast special $5). (Open Mon.-Sat. 5am-10pm, Sun. 8am-5pm.) Avoid the fast-food chains that have capitalized on Hinton's lucrative position along Hwy. 16, and dig into a pizza at **Vegas Pizza** (small cheese $3) at the Hill Shopping Mall (865-4116; open Mon.-Wed. 11am-midnight, Thurs.-Sat. 11am-2am, Sun. 4pm-midnight).

Those desparate to put their tents and RVs to use can find a (temporary) home at the **Hinton Campground** on Switzer Dr. The 65 sites here offer modern amenities for a reasonable $7, and you'll be right next door to **Moose Hall,** a convention center and site of some of Hinton's most heated bingo games. For a more complete escape from civilization, drive 20km north to **William Switzer Provincial Park** (865-5600). Open year-round, this secluded adventure area contains seven campgrounds with a total of 196 sites ($7 per night). The streams in the area provide excellent trout fishing and canoers will enjoy floating down Jarvis Creek, which links the park's five major lakes. (For more information write to William A. Switzer Provincial Park, P.O. Box 1038, Hinton, T0E 1B0.)

The **Tourist Information Centre** (865-2777), on the south side of Hwy. 16 in Green Sq., has a cordial and enthusiastic staff eager to sell you on Hinton as they pass out brochures on Jasper, Edmonton, and Banff. Open Mon.-Fri. 9am-5pm, Sat.-Sun. 10am-6pm.

Banff National Park

Yellowstone and Yosemite rolled into one, Banff is Canada's most sublime and well-loved national park. Its snowcapped peaks and turquoise lakes are among the grandest sights in the entire Rockies. Free-roaming wildlife is plentiful; moose rule the marshes of Bow River Valley and bighorn sheep reign on the rocky slopes. Be aware that Banff's wildlife is protected by Canadian law, which states that it is illegal to feed, entice, or molest any animal.

The townsites of Banff and Lake Louise re-create the atmosphere and prices of a European resort. A deluxe suite at the Banff Springs Hotel costs $735 per night plus $15 per pet. Visitors can relax in an old-fashioned hot sulphur pool while wearing 1914-style bathing suits or ride a gondola to one of Banff's peaks.

Bicyclists from around the world come to enjoy the park's facilities. The Trans-Canada Hwy. has a large shoulder built as a bike path, while the older Hwy. 1A draws less traffic and allows better access to campgrounds and hostels. The profusion of hostels enables cyclists to leave their tents behind and better enjoy the open road. Banff is equally well set-up for hiking and camping.

Practical Information and Orientation

Visitor Information: Banff Information Centre, 224 Banff Ave. (762-4256). Open daily 8am-10pm; Oct.-May 10am-6pm. **Lake Louise Information Centre** (522-3833). Open mid-May to mid-June daily 10am-6pm; mid-June to Aug. 8am-10pm; Sept.-Oct. 10am-6pm.

Park Headquarters: Superintendent, Banff National Park, Box 900, Banff T0L 0C0 (762-3324).

VIA Rail: at the intersection of Lynx and Elk St. (800-665-8630 or 762-3255), in the northwest corner of Banff Townsite. To Lake Louise (4:25pm, 45 min., $8), following the old Hwy. 1A, and Calgary (12:15pm, 2 hr., $14). Also to Vancouver (20½ hr., $65) and Montreal (2 days, $238). Trains no longer run to Jasper but buses do traverse the Icefields Parkway.

Greyhound: operates out of the Brewster terminal. To Lake Louise (5 per day, $6.15) and Calgary (6 per day, $9.20). The Lake Louise buses continue to Vancouver ($55).

Brewster Transportation: 100 Gopher St. (762-2286), near the train depot. Monopoly on tours of the area, and runs 1 express daily to Jasper ($24). Depot open daily 7am-midnight.

Car Rental: Banff Used Car Rentals, junction of Wolf and Lynx (762-3352). $34 per day with 100 free km plus 10¢ per additional km. Must be 21 with major credit card. **Avis,** 209 Bear St. (762-3222). $50 per day with 100 free km plus 19¢ per additional km. Ask about IYHF member discount.

Moped Rental: Mountain Mopeds, in the Sundance Mall (762-5611). $8.50 per hr., $30 per ½-day, $45 per day. Must have ID. No deposit required. Open daily 10am-8pm.

Bike Rental: Spoke 'n' Edge, 315 Banff Ave. (762-2854). 3-, 5-, and 10-speeds. $2.50 per hr., $10 per day; mountain bikes $4 per hr., $16 per day.

Hospital: 762-4333.

Emergency: In Banff 762-2226, at Lake Louise 522-3811.

Police: 762-2226.

Post Office: Corner of Buffalo and Bear St. (762-2586). Open Mon.-Fri. 9am-5:30pm. Postal Code: T0L 0C0.

Area Code: 403.

Banff National Park hugs the Alberta-British Columbia border, 120km west of Calgary. The **Trans-Canada Highway** (Hwy. 1) runs east-west through the park. Both Greyhound and VIA Rail connect the park with major points in British Columbia and Alberta. Civilization in the park centers around the townsites of Lake Louise and Banff. Lake Louise is 55km northwest of Banff on Hwy. 1. Buses and the daily train are expensive. If you're hitching, expect plenty of competition.

Accommodations

Although the budget traveler may have difficulty finding an affordable restaurant in town, inexpensive lodging is abundant. Over 20 residents of the townsite offer rooms in their own homes—many year-round, and the majority in the $20-40 range. Ask for the *Banff Private Home Accommodation* list at the Banff Townsite Information Centre. The local **YWCA** (762-3560) also opens its doors to travelers, both male and female. Although not well-decorated, their rooms are spacious and affordable with singles $25, doubles $33, and bunk beds $12. Crowded in summer. You can backpack in the woods with a free permit, obtainable at the Information Centre.

Banff International Hostel (IYHF), Box 1358, Banff T0L 0C0 (762-4122), 3km from Banff Townsite on Tunnel Mountain Rd., among a nest of condominiums and lodges. The look and setting of a chalet, but, when full, the feel of an overstuffed warehouse. In winter, a large fireplace warms the lounge area for cross-country and downhill skiers. A hike from the center of the townsite, but the modern amenities and friendly staff make the trek worthwhile. Ski and cycle workshop. Laundry facilities. Wheelchair-accessible. Clean quads with 2 bunk beds. Registration 6-10am and 4pm-midnight. Members $9, nonmembers $14. Linen provided.

Hilda Creek Hostel (IYHF), 8.5km south of the Icefield Centre on the Icefields Parkway. Features a primitive sauna that holds about 4 people—uncomfortably. In the morning, guests must replenish the water supply with a shoulder-bucket contraption. Accommodates 21. Members $5, nonmembers $6. Closed Thurs. night.

Rampart Creek Hostel (IYHF), 34km south of the Icefield Centre. Has a wood-heated sauna, larger than Hilda Creek's. Accommodates 30. Members $5, nonmembers $6. Closed Wed. night.

Mosquito Creek Hostel (IYHF), 103km south of the Icefield Centre and 26km north of Lake Louise. Fireplace and sauna. Accommodates 38. Members $5.50, nonmembers $6.50. Closed Tues. night.

Corral Creek Hostel (IYHF), 5km east of Lake Louise on Hwy. 1A. The hostel nearest Lake Louise. Accommodates 50. Members $5, nonmembers $6. Closed Mon. night.

Castle Mountain Hostel (IYHF), on Hwy. 1A (762-2637), 1.5km east of the junction of Hwy. 1 and Hwy. 93. Recently renovated. Accommodates 36. Members $6, nonmembers $8. Closed Wed. night.

Cascade Inn, 124 Banff Ave. (762-3311), in the heart of the townsite. Prices are usually high, but there are sometimes ½-price specials mid-week. Senior citizens stay 2 nights for the price of 1.

Camping

Campgrounds at Banff lead a happy life. Human visitors fill them daily throughout the summer and an occasional black bear meanders by to create a little excitement. One-night timeshares in these popular pieces of real estate are inexpensive and easy to procure if you enter the market early. Some of these campgrounds raise their prices during the "premium period" (late June-Labor Day). None will take reservations, so arrive early. Mosquito Creek, Lake Louise, Johnston Canyon, and Tunnel Mountain Village have the best facilities and are located closest to a townsite. The following are listed from north to south.

Cirrus Mountain, 24km south of the Icefield Centre. 16 sites, $8. Open June 26-Sept. 8.

Waterfowl Lake, 57km north of Hwy. 1 on Hwy. 93. 116 sites, $8. Open mid-June to mid-Sept.

Mosquito Creek, 103km south of the Icefield Centre and 26km north of Lake Louise. Near the Mosquito Creek hostel. 32 sites, $8. Open June 19-Sept. 14.

Lake Louise. Not on the lake, but 221 sites for tents (and 163 for RVs). Sites $8.50, "premium period" $10.50. Open mid-May to mid-Sept.

Protection Mountain, 11.5km east of Castle Junction on Hwy. 1A. 89 sites, $8.50. Open June 23-Sept. 1.

Castle Mountain, midway between Banff and Lake Louise along Hwy. 1A. 44 sites, $7.50.

Johnston Canyon, 26km northwest of Banff on Hwy. 1A. The only campground besides Tunnel Mountain with showers. Excellent trail access. Sites $9, "premium period" $11. Open mid-May to mid-Sept.

Two Jack Main, 13km northeast of Banff. 381 tentsites and flush toilets. Sites $6.50. Open mid-May to Aug.

Two Jack Lakeside, just south of Two Jack Main. 80 sites on a lake that tempts the polar bear in you. Sites $8.50. Open mid-June to Sept 7.

Tunnel Mountain Village, 1km past the International Hostel, closest to Banff townsite. A village indeed, with showers and 622 tentsites. Sites $9.50. Two other campgrounds at Tunnel Mountain reserved for RVs.

Food

For many, the wilderness calls to mind campfires, roasted marshmallows, and pork and beans. Bring along your favorite recipes, and you'll eat well here. On your way to your favorite hiking trail or campground, make a quick stop at Banff's largest and cheapest supermarket, **Safeway**, 318 Marten St., at Elk St. Banff's restaurants generally charge high prices for mediocre food. Even fast food restaurants are expensive and slow. But the Banff International Hostel and the Banff YWCA do serve affordable meals. The hostel's cafeteria serves up great breakfast specials for $2-4 from 7-9am. It also cooks dinners from 5-7pm. The **Spray Cafe,** at the Y, boasts an even bigger breakfast deal: two eggs, bacon, hashbrowns, and toast for $2.75. Burgers for lunch. Open Thurs.-Tues. 8am-3pm. The other restaurants below also promise cheap meals, a rarity in a town so strongly supported by international tourists.

Banff Townsite

Coriander Nature Food, Banff Ave. (762-2878), in the Sundance Mall, upper level. This place even smells healthy thanks to the freshly cut lilacs at each table. Take a break from that burger diet with Mexican beans and rice in a pita ($3, with tofu $4.50) or a sandwich on thick 7-grain bread. For dessert, try a fruit shake made from apple juice, blueberries, and strawberries ($3). Pick up vitamins and trail mix on your way out. Open Mon.-Sat. 10am-6pm, Sun. 11:30am-5:30pm.

Craig's Way Station, 124 Banff Ave., in the lobby of the Cascade Inn. Those in quest of the ordinary coffee shop can rest here. Though the menu is unexciting, the food is good and the crowd local. Burgers and sandwiches $3-5, veal cutlet $7, other full meals $5-7.

Mr. J. Jolly's Sandwich and Coffee House (762-4788), hidden in the back of the Clock Tower Village Mall on Banff Ave. Serves cappuccino ($1.75), but the cellophane-wrapped sandwiches (from $3) more accurately represent the nature of this hole-in-the-wall. Open daily 9:30am-5pm.

Joe Btfsplk's Diner, 221 Banff Ave. (762-5529). Named after a *L'il Abner* character, its moniker may be hard to pronounce (bi-TIF-spliks), but you'll be speechless anyway when you see this imitation 50s diner in the Rockies. Burgers and specialty salads $6-7. Open daily 8am-11pm.

Sights and Activities

Hike to the **backcountry** for privacy, beauty, over 1600km of trails, and trout that bite anything. The pamphlet *Drives and Walks* covers both the Lake Louise and Banff areas, describing day and overnight hikes. You need a permit to stay overnight in the backcountry, and you can get one free of charge from park information centres and park warden offices. All litter must be taken out of the backcountry with you; in addition, no wood may be chopped in the parks. Both the International Hostel and the Park Information Centre have copies of the *Canadian Rockies Trail Guide,* an excellent, in-depth source of information and maps.

Canada's first national park (and the world's third) began in 1885 as Hot Springs Reserve, featuring the **Cave and Basin Hot Springs** nearby. In 1914, a resort was built at the springs. Refurbished as the **Cave and Basin Centennial Centre** (762-4900), the resort now screens documentaries and stages exhibits. Explore the original cave or relax in the hot springs pool where lifeguards wear pre-World War I bathing costumes. The centre is southwest of the city on Cave Ave. (Centre open daily 10am-8pm; Sept. 1-early June 10am-5pm. Pool open early June-Sept. 1 only. Admission to pool $2, ages under 12 $1.25.) If you find Cave and Basin's 32°C (90°F) water too cool, follow the hard-boiled eggs into the **Upper Hot Springs pool,** a 40°C

(104°F) cauldron up the hill on Mountain Ave. (Open June-Sept. daily 8:30am-11pm. Admission $2, ages 3-16 $1.25. Bathing suit rental at either spring $1, towel rental 75¢, and locker rental 25¢.)

Taking a gondola to the top of a peak is an expensive way to see the park, but saves your legs for hiking at the summit. The **Sulphur Mountain Gondola** (762-2523), located right next to the Upper Hot Springs pool, dangles you over Banff Townsite. (Open Nov. 15-Dec. 15 and in summer daily 9am-8pm. Fare $8, ages under 12 $4.) The **Summit Restaurant** perched atop Sulphur Mountain serves good but expensive meals and an "Early Bird" breakfast special for $3. The **Sunshine Village Gondola** (762-6555) climbs to the 2215m-high resort village. The village is a good base for high alpine hiking. (Open June 27-Sept. 7 Mon.-Thurs. 8:30am-7:30pm, Fri.-Sun. 8:30am-10:30pm. Fare $6, ages under 12 $3.) If that's not high enough for you, jump on the Standish chairlift, which will carry you to the peak, almost 2430m up.

Brewster Tours (a subsidiary of Greyhound) offers an extensive array of guided bus tours in the park. If you have no car, these tours may be the only way to see some of the main attractions, such as the Valley of the Ten Peaks, the Great Divide, the Athabasca Glacier, Johnston Canyon, and the spiral railroad tunnel cut into a mountain (the trains are so long, you can see them entering and exiting the mountain at the same time). The tour-guide/drivers are professional, knowledgeable, and entertaining. If you were planning on taking the regular Brewster bus from Banff to Jasper ($24), you might want to spend $20 more and see the sights in between. A walk on the Columbia Icefields costs $12 extra. Tickets can be purchased at the bus depot. Call 762-2241 for more information.

If you'd prefer to look up at the mountains rather than down from them, all the nearby lakes will provide a serene vantage point. **Two Jack Lake** (near Banff) and **Moraine Lake** (near Lake Louise) can be explored by boat and canoe. On Two Jack Lake, rowboats cost $8.50 per hour, $42.50 per day; canoes $8 per hour, $40 per day; there's a $20 deposit. (Open July-Aug. daily; June Sat.-Sun. only.) On Moraine Lake, canoes can be paddled for $10 per hour with a $20 deposit (522-3733; open daily in summer 9am-sundown). **Fishing** is legal virtually anywhere you can find water, but you must hold a National Parks fishing permit, available at the information centre ($5 for a 7-day permit, $10 for an annual permit). Superb trout fishing awaits those willing to hike the 7km to **Bourgeau Lake.** Closer to the road, try **Herbert Lake,** off the Icefields Parkway between Lake Louise and the Columbia Icefield. **Lake Minnewanka,** adjacent to Two Jack Lake, provides excellent fishing in its infamous waters, rumored to be the home of an Indian spirit—half human, half fish. You can find out about this ancient myth during a 2-hour guided tour sponsored by **Minnewanka Tours Ltd.** (762-3473; $12, children $6), but rest assured—the 33-pound lake trout caught here in 1987 is no fish story.

The hilly road leading to Lake Minnewanka provides cyclists with an exhilarating trip, as do many other small paths throughout the park. Bicycling is also allowed on most trails in the Banff Townsite area. Remember, however, to dismount your bike and stand to the downhill side if a horse approaches. Also be forewarned that the quick and quiet nature of trail bicycling is more prone to surprise a bear than the tromping of hikers.

The palatial **Banff Springs Hotel,** Spray Ave. (762-2848), dominates the townsite. This enormous 825-room castle recently celebrated its 100th birthday with a series of posh parties and its own special brand of beer. You probably won't have enough money to spend the evening here, or even order dinner, but the hotel does offer free tours of the grounds daily at 3pm. The tour reveals fascinating secrets about the hotel and offers a grand opportunity to view lavish architecture against an indifferently spectacular background. The hotel also offers horseback riding (daily 9am-5pm; $10 for 1 hr., $22 for 3 hrs.; reservations recommended).

For those who have exhausted their bodies, Banff Townsite has several small but illuminating museums. The **Whyte Museum of the Canadian Rockies,** 111 Bear St. (762-2291), traces the mountain chain from its discovery and exploration through its metamorphosis into a world-famous tourist attraction. You'll learn that the sights in Banff have changed little in the last century; they have simply become more crowded. A gallery downstairs shows paintings of the mountains and their inhabitants. (Open daily 10am-6pm. Admission $2, senior citizens and students $1.) The nearby **Park Museum,** on Banff Ave. near the bridge, provides two floors of taxidermists' delight: all species indigenous to the park (and even some that aren't) stuffed and placed in glass cases. Come face-to-face with a grizzly and look a gray wolf square in the eye. Built in 1903, the museum also contains a well-stocked reading room where you can locate the differences between buffalo and bison, or caribou and moose. (Open daily 10am-6pm. Free.) Less than a block away, on the second floor of the Clock Tower Village Mall (112 Banff Ave.), the **Natural History Museum** rounds out Banff's archival troika. The complete tour includes a 20-minute video documentary focusing on volcanoes, namely Mt. St. Helens, and 10 minutes to explore the tiny fossil and lumber collections. On the way out be sure to appreciate the legend of Bigfoot by snickering at an eight-foot-tall "authentic" model of the spurious Sasquatch. (Open daily 10am-8pm; in winter 10am-6pm. Admission $2, senior citizens and children $1.)

Banff's bartenders contend that "the real wildlife is at the bars." Just to make sure, each night one bar features a "Locals Night" with $1.75 drinks. Watch for long lines of up to two hours, especially on Mondays, when "Locals Night" is at **Tommy's Bar and Grill.**

The culture industry moves into Banff every year for the summer-long **Banff Festival of the Arts,** producing drama, ballet, jazz, opera, and other aesthetic commodities. Pick up a brochure at the Visitor Information Centre or call 762-6300 for details.

Lake Louise

The crystal waters of Lake Louise, framed by snow-capped peaks, often serve North American filmmakers' need for Swiss alpine scenery. On a clear day, the view from the palatial lakeside chateau evokes images of St. Moritz. Unfortunately most visitors spend only enough time at the lake to snap a couple photos; few spend the time to experience the area as explorer Tom Wilson did in the 1880s, who wrote of its majesty, "I never in all my explorations...saw such a matchless scene."

To gain a deeper appreciation of the turquoise-blue lake and the surrounding glacier, consult the **Lake Louise Information Centre** (522-3833). (Open May 19-June 18 10am-6pm; June 19-Sept. 4 8am-10pm; Sept. 5-Oct. 9 10am-6pm.) Renting a canoe from the **Chateau Lake Louise Boat House** (522-3511) will give you the closest look at the lake. Canoes rent for $12 per hour, and binoculars to scan the hills for wildlife cost $3. Several hiking trails begin at the lake. As incentive, aim for one of the two teahouses, at the end of the 3.4km Lake Agnes Trail and the 5.3km Plain of Six Glaciers Trail. Be prepared to pay dearly for this mountainous meal—all the food must be brought up on horseback. (Teahouses open in summer daily 9am-6pm.) **Timberline Tours** (522-3743) offers guided horseback rides through the area. The 1½-hour tour costs $13, and the daytrip $50 (lunch included). The **Lake Louise Gondola** (522-3555), which runs up Mt. Whitehorn, across the Trans-Canada Hwy. from the lake, provides another chance to gape at the landscape. (Open mid-June to late Sept. daily 9am-6pm. Fare $6.50, ages 5-11 $3.25. "One way hiker's special" $4.) Like its counterpart at Sulphur Mountain, Lake Louise's gondola offers a $3 breakfast deal; just make sure to purchase your lift ticket by 9:30am.

Calgary

When the North West Mounted Police set up shop here in the 1860s, Commander-in-Chief Ephrem Brisebois named the town after himself. He was subsequently ousted from power for abusing his authority, and Col. James MacLeod renamed the settlement "Calgary"—Scottish for "clear running water." The city now thrives on a less transparent liquid. Since the discovery of oil in 1947, Calgary has become a wealthy and cosmopolitan city—the oil may be crude, but the people are refined. Office buildings rise higher than the oil derricks, businessmen scurry about in three-piece suits toting leather briefcases, and a newly built transport system soundlessly threads through the immaculate downtown streets.

Calgarians take pride in their petroleum-subsidized city. They cling to memories of hosting the XVth Winter Olympic Games. They are quick to brag that their Flames captured the 1989 Stanley Cup (remember, this is hockey country). And everyone puts on their cowboy hats, Wranglers, and western accents when the Stampede rolls around in July.

Practical Information and Orientation

Visitor Information: Calgary Tourist and Convention Bureau, 237 8th Ave. SE (263-8510). Call or write for help finding accommodations, especially around Stampede time. Open daily 8:30am-4:30pm. **Information booth** at the same address open daily 8:30am-7pm; Sept.-June Mon.-Fri. 8:30am-4:30pm. Staff eager to assist you. **Trans-Canada Highway office,** 6220 16th St. NE. Open daily 8am-9pm; Sept.-June 10am-5pm. **Airport office** open daily 7am-11pm. **Travel Alberta,** 455 6th St. SW (297-6574, in AB 800-661-8888), on the main floor. Oozes with information about the entire province. Open Mon.-Fri. 8:15am-4:30pm.

VIA Rail: 131 9th Ave. SW (265-8033, in AB 800-665-8630), at Centre St. Trains to Banff (1 per day, $16) and Vancouver (1 per day, $86). Tickets sold daily 9am-5pm. Full-time students receive 1/3 off fares. Some restrictions apply.

Greyhound: 850 16th St. SW (260-0877 or 800-332-1016; reservations 265-9111). To Edmonton (8 per day, $20); frequent service to Banff ($9.25). Free shuttle bus from C-Train at 7th Ave. and 10th St. to bus depot. 10% senior citizen discount.

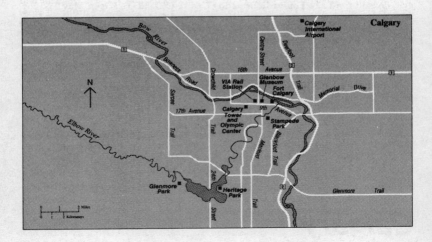

Calgary Transit: Information and Downtown Sales Centre, 206 7th Ave. SW. Bus schedules, passes, and maps. Open Mon.-Fri. 8:30am-5pm. Fare $1.25, ages 6-14 75¢, under 6 free. Exact change required. Day pass $3.50, children $2. Book of 10 tickets $10, children $6.50. **Information line** (276-7801) open Mon.-Fri. 6am-11pm, Sat.-Sun. 8am-9:30pm.

Taxi: Checker Cab, 272-1111. **Red Top Taxi,** 250-9222. **Yellow Cab,** 250-8311.

Car Rental: Rent-a-Wreck, 2339 Macleod Trail (237-7093). Cars start at $30 per day with 100 free km, plus 11¢ per additional km. Must be 21 with major credit card. Open Mon.-Fri. 8am-7:30pm, Sat. 9am-5:30pm, Sun. 10am-5:30pm. **Thrifty,** 117 5th Ave. SE (262-4400), airport (250-7233). Rates start at $44 per day with 150 free km, plus 12¢ per additional km. Must be 21 with major credit card. **Tilden,** 114 5th Ave. SE (263-6386), airport (250-0770).

Bike Rental: Sports Rent, 7218 Macleod Trail SW (252-2055). 12-speeds $12 per day; mountain bikes $20 per day. **Abominable Sports,** 640 11th Ave. SW (266-0899). Mountain bikes $15 per day; mopeds $20 per day.

Gay Lines Calgary: 223 12th Ave. SW (234-8973), on the 3rd floor. Recorded phone message provides gay community information; peer counseling available at the office. Phone and office open Mon.-Sat. 7am-10pm.

Women's Resource Center: 320 5th Ave. SE (263-1550), at the YWCA. For women of all ages seeking any kind of assistance. Open 24 hours.

Time and Weather: 263-3333.

Hospital: Calgary General, 841 Centre Ave. E. (268-9111).

Emergency: 911.

Police: 316 7th Ave. SE (266-1234).

Post Office: 220 4th Ave. SE (292-5512). Open Mon.-Fri. 8am-5:45pm. Postal Code: T2P 2G8.

Area Code: 403.

Calgary is accessible by several highways, including the Trans-Canada Highway. Planes fly into **Calgary International Airport** (292-8400), about 5km from the city center. It's a hefty $19 for a cab into the city, but free shuttle buses service downtown hotels. Public transportation to the city is infrequent. The simplest way to get into the city from the airport is the **Airporter Bus,** which offers frequent and friendly service for $6. Dropoff points may be flexible. **Greyhound** drops off close to the city center (about ½-hr. walk from downtown) and has free shuttle buses to the C-Train. **VIA Rail** unloads passengers next door to the Calgary Tower, in the heart of downtown. At the VIA Rail station, large lockers can be rented for 75¢.

Calgary is an extremely well-planned city and a cinch for back-seat navigators. The city is divided into quadrants: **Centre Street** provides the east-west division, and the **Bow River** (with the adjacent Memorial Drive, where the Bow starts bowing) divides the north from the south. Address numbers increase as you move away from these thoroughfares. You can always determine the street from an avenue address by disregarding the last 2 digits: thus 206 7th Ave. is at 2nd St, and 2339 Macleod Trail is at 23rd St. Avenues run east-west, streets north-south. Pay careful attention to the quadrant designation (e.g. NW or SE) at the end of each address.

Public transportation throughout the city is excellent and inexpensive. **Calgary Transit** operates both buses and streetcars ("C-Trains"). Buses run all over the city and cost $1.25. C-Trains cover less territory, but you can ride them free in the downtown area (along 7th Ave. S.; between 10th St. SW and City Hall). The $1.25 fare returns if you go outside of downtown on a C-Train. Though you can get on the trains without buying a ticket, beware of spot checks by policemen. If caught without a valid ticket on the train or platform, you pay a $25 fine. Honesty is the best policy here. Most of what you'll need—lodging, food, and sights—is within the C-Train's free zone anyway.

Hitchhiking is illegal within the Calgary city limits. And don't tempt fate—the law is enforced and punished with a cruel $500 fine.

Accommodations

Cheap rooms in Calgary are rare only during the Stampede. While most of the places listed below don't raise their prices seasonally, reserve ahead for July.

Calgary International Hostel (IYHF), 520 7th Ave. SE (269-8239). Conveniently located several blocks south of downtown with access to C-train and public buses. Complete with snack bar, meeting rooms, cooking and barbeque facilities, laundry, and a cycle workshop. Disabled access. Discount tickets for the Calgary Tower can be purchased at the hostel with a hostel card. Lockout 10am-5pm. Curfew midnight. Members $9, nonmembers $12. Sept.-April members $7, nonmembers $10.

University of Calgary, 3330 24th Ave. (220-3203), in the NW quadrant of the city. A little out of the way, but easily accessible via bus #9 or the C-Train. If you can't make an Olympic squad, at least you can sleep in their beds—U of C was the Olympic Village home to 1988 competitors. Olympian-sized rooms for competitive prices. There's also a cafeteria and a pub on this serene campus. Room rental office, in the Kananaskis Building, open 24 hours. Virtually unlimited supply of rooms in the summer, fewer rooms available in winter (but do inquire). With student ID singles $15.75, shared rooms $10.50. Without student ID singles $22, doubles $30; breakfast included.

YWCA, 320 5th Ave. SE (263-1550). A deluxe place, for women only, in a fine, quiet neighborhood. A range of rooms. The security makes for a somewhat lifeless lodging. Cafeteria open all day. Singles $22, with bath $29.50. Dorm beds $10. Sleeping bag space (summer only) $7.

St. Louis Hotel, 430 8th Ave. SE (262-6341), above the St. Louis Tavern. Depending on your point of view, the location means either excitement or danger. Not suggested for women. The few grim-looking long-term residents generally keep to themselves. Friendly management. Singles $15.75, with TV and bath $21. Doubles with bath and TV $26.25.

York Hotel, 636 Centre St. SE (262-5581). More central location and larger rooms than the St. Louis. Bath and cable TV included. Singles and doubles regularly cost over $40, but with a Greyhound ticket or receipt your first night's lodging is only $26. 20% discount for senior citizens.

Food

Finding a good, inexpensive place to eat is relatively easy in Calgary. Ethnic and cafeteria-style dining spots line the **Stephen Ave. Mall,** 8th Ave. S. between 1st St. SE and 3rd St. SW, and the indoor mini-malls nearby. Good, cheap food is also readily available in the **"Plus 15" Skyway System.** Designed to provide indoor passageways during bitter winter days, this bizarre mall connects the second floors of dozens of buildings throughout the city. You can join the system at any "participating" building; just look for the blue and white "Plus 15" signs on street level.

For more expensive, trendy restaurants, go to the **Kensington District,** along Kensington Rd., between 10th and 11th St. NW. Take the C-train to Sunnyside or use the Louise Bridge to reach this area. Other good and lively café-restaurants are on 4th St. SW. The area can be reached most easily by taking the #3 or 53 bus.

City Hall Cafeteria, in the City Hall Municipal Building at the intersection of 7th Ave. SE and Macleod Trail (2nd St.). Backpackers and briefcasers guzzle cheap coffee (40¢) and consume muffins (65¢). Early birds with time for a more balanced morning meal can feast on the breakfast buffet ($3, 7-8am). Open Mon.-Fri. 7am-4pm.

Hang Fung Foods Ltd., 119 3rd Ave. SE (269-5853), located in the rear of a Chinese market with the same name. Enormous bowl of plain *congee* (rice broth) $1, with abalone and chicken $3. A heaping plateful of BBQ duck and steamed chicken on rice is $4. Bring your own silverware if you haven't mastered chopsticks. Open daily 8:30am-9pm.

4th Street Rose, 2116 4th St. SW (228-5377). California cool pervades this fashionable restaurant on the outskirts of town: high ceilings, tile floors, and waitrons sporting jeans and short-sleeved shirts. Gourmet pizzas, homemade pasta, and fresh salads ($2.75-8). Take bus #3 or 53 and avoid the hike. Open Mon.-Thurs. 8am-midnight, Fri.-Sat. 10am-1am, Sun. 10am-8pm.

Pasta Frenzy, 2120 4th St. SW (245-1888). If 4th St. Rose is either too loud or too crowded, go to Pasta Frenzy next door. Open-air seating and relaxed pace. A sophisticated Italian assortment includes pizza ($6-8), pasta, and salads ($2-5); good deserts too. Open Mon.-Sat. 11:30am-midnight, Sun. 11am-midnight.

Take Ten Cafe, 304 10th St. NW (270-7010). Light dining in Kensington with a German accent. Everything under $4.50. The wiener schnitzel ($4.45) includes gravy, vegetable, and fries. ½-lb. basket of curly fries with gravy $1. Hungarian ghoulash $4, homemade cakes and muffins. Open Mon.-Wed. 8am-5:30pm, Thurs.-Fri. 8am-7pm, Sat. 10am-4pm.

Bohemia Bistro, 124 10th St. NW (270-3116), near Kensington Rd. (tucked away on 2nd floor). Bohemia in the original sense of the word—the region around Prague. Perhaps the most unusual of the Kensington district restaurants. An eclectic menu features unkosher kosher sandwiches ($6-7) and pastas with original combinations ($7-8.50). Lunch is a good buy at $4-6. Pick up a chocolate truffle on the way out ($1). Open Tues.-Thurs. 11:30am-midnight, Fri.-Sat. 11:30am-1am.

The Roasterie, down the street from the Bohemia Bistro, near Hungary. No meals here, just cookies, muffins, and about 20 kinds of coffee, ranging from Rioberry ($1.75) to HiTest ($1) to Vietnamese Iced Coffee ($2)—all served in giant cups. *NY Times* sold for $4.25. Before you leave, play the "tip game"—pelting coins into the tip cup from behind the counter (a 10-ft. jumper).

Under the Sunbrella Cafeteria, 610 8th Ave. SE (262-6342), on the 2nd floor of the Golden Age Club. Very convenient to the hostel, this center for the retired welcomes the hungry of all ages. Patio furniture and bright lights create a cheerful, relaxing atmosphere. Daily hot lunch and dinner specials ($3-5) include potato, vegetable, and roll plus coffee or tea, reminding many of their grade school days. Open Mon.-Fri. 8am-6pm; last hot meal before 5pm.

Sights

The **Calgary Tower** (266-7171), 101 9th Ave. SW, presides over the city. Rather than simply gaze up at the spire, ride an elevator to the top ($2.75, children $1) for a spectacular view of the Rockies on clear days. The 190m tower also affords a 360° view of the city. Xybots, Pacmania, and other video games will keep vidiots amused. The revolving **Panorama Dining Room** atop the tower can be expensive, but the "Breakfast in the Sky" special, a full morning meal for $9.75 (children $4.50), includes a free elevator ride in the price. (Rides Mon.-Sat. 7:30am-11:30pm, Sun. 7:30am-10:30pm.)

The **Glenbow Museum,** 130 9th Ave. SE (264-8300), just across the street from the Tower, is a nexus of cultural pride in this boomtown. The odd mix of modern art, military artifacts, and mineral samples attempts to reconfigure cultural and institutional space. The impressive pastiche has something for everyone, including an assortment of edifying exhibits for schoolchildren, who often ruthlessly stampede through the museum on weekday mornings. At the entrance are five cases of Olympic pins, the most extensive collection in town. (Open daily 10am-6pm. Admission $2, senior citizens 50¢, students and children $1; free on Sat.) Less than a block northeast of the museum, the **Olympic Plaza** still attracts crowds on sunny days. The site of the medal presentations during the Winter Games, this open-air park now hosts a variety of special events, from the Kids' Fest to the Calgary Jazz Festival (both in June). For an update on Olympic Plaza programming, call 268-4776 during business hours. One of the park's most interesting features, the **walkway,** was constructed out of more than 20,000 bricks, each purchased for $20-30 and engraved with the name or personal message of the patron. Try to decipher such cryptic, possibly Satanic messages as "NGF 1959 BN B IN YYC."

A short walk down 8th Ave. to the west will bring you to the home of **Devonian Gardens.** Located on the fourth floor of Toronto Dominion Sq. (8th Ave. between 2nd and 3rd St. SW), this 2.5-acre indoor garden contains fountains, waterfalls, bridges, and over 20,000 plants, including 138 different local and tropical varieties. After a few hours of wading through shopping oceans in the downtown malls, make yourself dizzy watching a school of goldfish swim in circles. If you require absolute privacy, Devonian Gardens can be rented for four hours for a mere $1130. (Open daily 9am-9pm. Free.)

A few blocks to the northwest, the **Energeum**, 640 5th Av. SW (297-4293), in the lobby of the Energy Resources Building, is Calgary's shrine to fossil fuel. A film in the upstairs theater of this small but informative oil museum recreates the mania of Alberta's first oil find. Displays and short video segments downstairs subject oil drilling to the latest technologies of representation. You can put the tar-like substance right up to your nose, and run your hand (gloved, of course) through a pile of the oozing glop. (Open Sun.-Fri. 10:30am-4:30pm; Sept.-May Mon.-Fri. 10:30am-4:30pm. Free.)

Farther west, about 4.3 light-years from Alpha Centauri, is the **Alberta Science Centre and Centennial Planetarium** (11 St. and 7th Ave. SW in earthspeak, near the Greyhound Bus Terminal). Hands-on experiments here test the laws of physics, while a simple pendulum and a few descriptive plaques explain how the elder Foucault determined that the earth rotates on its own axis. Planetarium shows disclose that Jupiter's Great Red Spot could swallow three Earths and still have room for dessert. (Science Centre open Wed.-Sun. 1-9pm. Most planetarium shows after 6pm. Laser shows on weekend evenings. Admission to both planetarium and Science Centre $4, children $2; Science Centre only $2, children $1.)

Just a stroll away from the Science Centre is **Prince's Island Park,** which can be reached by footbridges from either side of the Bow River. The park contains biking and fitness trails, playground equipment, and a snack bar. Although usually quiet, the park sometimes hosts loud events such as the Caribbean Cultural Festival in June.

Calgary's other island park, **St. George's Island,** is accessible by the river walkway to the east. The island is home to the **Calgary Zoo.** Try to visit in the late spring when many of the animals give birth to new attractions—the Australian mothers seem to be especially prolific. After you've observed all the animals and learned why the giraffe has the highest blood pressure of any animal, take a relaxing walk through the **botanical garden.** The zoo also features a **prehistoric park,** which takes you back in time some 65 million years, and a **children's zoo.** (Open daily at 9am; closing time is seasonally adjusted. For more information, call Zooline, 262-8144. Admission $5.50, senior citizens and ages 12-17 $3, under 12 $2. "Tuesdays are special:" adults $2.75, senior citizens free.)

The nearby **Fort Calgary Interpretive Centre** (290-1875) utilizes an exhibit hall and a comprehensive film to map out Calgary's evolution from cowtown to oiltown. Take a scenic walk on one of the riverside interpretive trails that begin from the center and explore the remains of a 19th-century fortress set up by the Royal Canadian Mounted Police and torn down by callous developers. (Open daily 9am-5pm. Free.) The center is on 9th Ave. SE, just east of downtown; grab bus #1 ("Forest Lawn") eastbound.

Although the actual Olympic flame has long since extinguished in Calgary, retailers still carry the torch, offering hundreds of different forms of official Olympic merchandise, many at sale prices. The more substantial and important legacies of the Games are several newly built, world-class athletic facilities—not only great arenas for recreation but also fascinating architectural sights. The two most impressive are the **Olympic Oval,** an indoor speed-skating track on the University of Calgary campus (hours vary from season to season; call 220-7890 for more information), and **Canada Olympic Park,** the site of the bobsled, luge, and ski jumping competitions. A guided tour of Olympic Park will cost you $5 (senior citizens and children $2), but take the plunge—the one-hour trip around the facilities includes a chance to stand in the bobsled track and to glance down the slope from atop the 90m ski jump tower. The **Olympic Hall of Fame** (268-2632), also located at Olympic Park, reinforces the Olympic ideology with displays, films, and videos. (Open daily 10am-5pm. Admission $6; senior citizens, students, and children $3.)

For non-vicarious downhill excitement, turn to the slopes of **Nakiska at Mount Allan** (591-7777), a newly carved ski area on Hwy. 40 in Kananaskis Country (see Near Calgary). Lift tickets cost $25 per day (children $12) and $18 per half-day (children $8). Senior citizens and the disabled pay only $8 for the whole day, and children under 8 ski free. Nordic skiers receive an even better deal—they can tread where Olympians once trod for free at the **Canmore Nordic Centre** (678-2400), in Kananaskis Country just outside the town of Canmore. The 56km of trails are designed for all skill levels. If you have brought along your biathlon association membership card and a rifle, you are cordially invited to use the shooting range and, in summer, the roller-ski course.

The Stampede

Even people who think that rodeo is grotesque and silly have trouble saying "Calgary" without letting a quick "Stampede" slip out. Somehow, it seems as though everyone envisions the city as wedded to "The Greatest Outdoor Show on Earth." Calgarians themselves are perhaps the most guilty of perpetuating this relationship. Every year around Stampede time, the locals throw free pancake breakfasts and paint every ground-level window downtown with cartoon cowboy figures offering misspelled greetings ("Welcum, y'all"). Capped by ten-gallons, locals command tour groups to yell "Yahoo" in the least likely of circumstances. Simply put, at Stampede time the entire city of Calgary wigs out.

And why not? Any event that draws millions from across the province, the country, and the world deserves the hoopla—and your attention. Make the short trip out to **Stampede Park,** just southeast of downtown. Those smart enough to arrive in July will get a glimpse of steer wrestling, bull riding, wild cow milking, and the famous chuckwagon races, where canvas-covered, box-shaped buggies whiz by in a chariot race that defies the laws of aerodynamics. (Tickets $9-31.) The Stampede also features a **midway,** where you can perch yourself atop the wild, thrashing back of a roller coaster.

Parking is ample, but the crowd is always more than ample in July—take the C-Train from downtown to the Stampede stop. In 1990, the Stampede will run from July 6-15 and in 1991 from July 5-14. For official information and ticket order forms, write Calgary Exhibition and Stampede, Box 1060, Station M, Calgary T2P 2K8, or call 800-661-1260. If you're in Calgary, call 261-0101 or visit Stampede Headquarters, 1410 Olympic Way.

If you are visiting Calgary any time other than mid-July, Stampede Park still has sights to amuse and educate. The **Olympic Saddledome** (261-0405) startles the area with its unique architecture. Site of hockey and figure skating events for the Winter Olympics, the Saddledome now hosts concerts, Calgary 88s basketball, horse racing, and Calgary Flames NHL hockey. Come here to catch a game or a one-hour tour of the Saddledome, available Mon.-Fri. (on non-event days). Check out Alberta Wheat Pool's **Grain Academy** (263-4594) on the second floor of the Roundup Centre in Stampede Park. A classroom for amateur agronomists, the academy uses a metre-tall model of a grain elevator as its mobile textbook. An intricate model train display traces the route that the harvested grain takes from Alberta's prairie to Vancouver's international ports. (Open Mon.-Fri. 10am-4pm, Sat. noon-4pm. Free.)

Those who prefer doing sports to watching them should visit **Lindsay Park Sports Centre,** 2225 Macleod Trail S. (233-8393), across from Stampede Park. This athletic salmagundi offers four swimming pools, an indoor track, numerous basketball and volleyball courts, a weight room, and aerobics. Call ahead to be sure the facilities in this immense, dome-like structure are open to the public on a particular day. (Admission $4.50, children $1.)

Entertainment

After a long, hard day counting barrels of crude, many Calgarians like to knock down bottles of local brew along **"Electric Avenue,"** the stretch of 11th Ave. SW between 5th and 6th St. SW. Here, several look-alike clubs swim in neon, all spinning the same electrifying Top-40 music. Last call in Calgary is at 1:45am.

Bandito's, 620 11th Ave. SW (266-6441). A current favorite, but any of the joints along 11th Ave. will do. Drinks $3-4. Most open for lunch around 11am and stay open until somewhere past 2am.

Ranchman's Steak House, 9615 Macleod Trail S. (253-1100). One of Canada's greatest honkytonks. Experience Calgary's Wild West tradition firsthand, on the dance floor to the tune of live C&W tunes or in the not-so-subtle flavor of Calgary Stampede beer. Open Mon.-Sat. 7pm-2am.

St. Louis Tavern, 430 8th Ave. SE (262-6341). Cheaper drinks and more character than most places on 11th Ave. Open Mon.-Tues. 10am-midnight, Wed.-Thurs. 10am-1am, Fri. 10am-2am, Sat. 10am-1am.

O'Brien's Pub & Restaurant, 636 Centre St. S (262-5581). Located in the core of downtown, this bar serves great drinks and cheap food. Billiards in the back room, dancing out front. Open Mon.-Sat. 11am-2am.

Dinero's, 310 Stephen Ave. Mall (264-6400). Popular as a place for drinks after work, this Tex-Mex outpost serves up plenty of *cerveza* (beer). No Corona on tap, but keg upon keg of Molson and Coors ($2), not to mention Heineken ($3). Bar open daily 11am-2am.

The Stadium Keg, 1923 Uxbridge Dr. NW (282-0020). Where the "Dinos" from the nearby University of Calgary eat, drink, and be merry. On Thurs. nights from 6-10pm, devour chicken wings (25¢ each) and wash them down with a mug of Big Rock ($1.25), the dark, delicious local brew. Students love the loud modern music and cozy chairs by the fireplace. Open daily 4:30pm-1am or 2am (depending on business).

Calgary has many movie theaters, including one in the Stephen Ave. Mall. The **Centre for Performing Arts,** 9th Ave. and 1st St. SW (294-7444), hosts part of the Calgary Jazz Festival, dance concerts (ballet), and the Calgary Philharmonic Orchestra. Most tickets $10-20. Call to see if senior citizen and student discounts apply.

Near Calgary

You won't lose the crowds by going to the **Tyrrell Museum of Palaeontology** (TEER-ill), near Drumheller (823-7707), but you will lose all sense of self-importance. The world's largest display of dinosaur specimens reminds you that humanity is a mere crouton in the Caesar salad of Earth's history. Primitive reptiles of all types have been reconstructed and placed in eerie models of subtropical marshlands that rival *Land of the Lost.* Unless you have about four hours (or a son named Joseph) you'll have to skip some exhibits, but regardless of time constraints, do not pass up the once-in-a-lifetime chance to play God. In keeping with the museum's hands-on approach, conspicuous computers throughout the museum let you Create-A-Dinosaur from head to hind legs. Judgment Day arrives quickly when the computer analyzes whether your "sillysaurus" has any chance of surviving.

The museum is on Secondary Hwy. 838, a.k.a North Dinosaur Trail, 6km from Drumheller. From Calgary, it's a 90-minute drive via Hwy. 2 N. to Hwy. 72 and 9 E. As with many tourist attractions in Alberta, Tyrrell is not directly served by public transportation, but you can ride **Greyhound** from Calgary to Drumheller (2 per day, one way $10.45) and hoof it out to the museum. The museum's cafeteria will provide sustenance to tourists, especially those who made the hike from Drumheller. The food is surprisingly inexpensive and tasty. Grab a seat beneath an umbrella on the patio and beat the heat (but not the flies) with a breakfast or lunch special (about $4). (Open daily 9am-9pm; Labor Day-Victoria Day Tues.-Sun. 10am-5pm. Donations $2, senior citizens and young adults $1.50, families $5.)

Those yearning for a stroll in the Badlands will enjoy Tyrell's free 90-minute **interpretive walks** through Dinosaur Country. Midland Provincial Park staffers lead these tours two or three times per day during the spring and summer. Check the information desk at Tyrell (where the tours start) for exact times. For the serious wildlife connoisseur, **Prairie Hawk Encounters** (823-3880) invites visitors to spend a day exploring the Red Deer River Valley with a wildlife scientist aboard a 14-passenger bus. Tours leave from Tyrell Museum or Drumheller Inn and last two or five hours ($12-35 per person).

Tyrell lies within **Midland Provincial Park,** one of the newest and most underdeveloped parks of its kind in Canada. Only about 10% of the park's 1500 acres have been developed, and the park's facilities are still only open for day use. Nonetheless, tourists on their way to Tyrell should not be deterred from making a stop at **McMullen Island** for a quick picnic, or at the site of the **Old Midland Mine Office** (823-8086), 2km east of the museum. This renovated coal miner's credit union now dispenses a map of the park and ideas on how to explore the area. Most of the park facilities are open only in summer. For camping in town, two options are available: **Shady Grove Campground** (823-2576), located in Drumheller on Hwy. 9 N. just off the north side of the bridge, and **Dinosaur Trailer Court** (823-3291) at the intersection of Hwy. 9 N. and Dinosaur Trail North.

Those who prefer to observe non-extinct scaly vertebrates should visit **Reptile World** (823-8623) on Hwy. 9, a 10-minute walk from Drumheller. A converted flea market that looks more like a store than a museum, Reptile World is the self-touted "largest collection of live reptiles in Canada." Hands-on displays (hold a boa) accompany interesting facts (a snake can swallow prey twice as wide as its head). (Open daily 10am-10pm; in winter 10am-6pm. Admission $3.75, senior citizens and children $2.50.)

Drumheller itself is certainly an unenticing tourist destination, but if you spend too much time at Tyrrell you should consider spending the night at either the newly renovated **Alexandra Hotel** (823-2642) or the **Waldorf Hotel** (823-2623), both on Railway Ave. in the center of town. There are pleasant rooms inside both establishments. Singles at the Alexandra cost $25, doubles $30. The Waldorf charges similar rates: singles $20, doubles $30. Make sure your room's air conditioner functions. Those planning to spend an evening or two in Dinosaur Country should consider the more comfortable charm of a local B&B. For more information write to **Big Country Bed and Breakfast,** P.O. Box 714, Rosebud T0J 2T0, or call 677-3333 (days) or 677-2269 (evenings). Singles are from $20, doubles from $30. The **Trave-Lodge,** farther down Railway, is more expensive (singles start at around $40) but has cable TV and free movies. While in Drumheller, chow down at the **Corner Grill** (823-3214), at the corner of 3rd Ave. and Centre St. (Open Sun.-Thurs. 6am-1am, Fri.-Sat. 6am-2am.) If you're short on time and money, visit the **Burger Barn** (823-8866) at 305 4 St. W. for a quick ¼-pounder ($2). The drive-thru window at this barn-turned-burger joint is reminiscent of a million other fast food restaurants, but nothing the Golden Arches offers could match the Barn's Super Backbacon Burger (with fries and a small soda $4). (Open Mon.-Sat. 10am-9pm, Sun. 11am-8pm.) For the friendliest service in town, head to the poorly named **The Old Grouch's** (823-5755), 175 3 Ave. W. Everything in this mom-and-pop establishment is of the highest quality. Stop in for a hot sausage roll ($1.50) or gorge yourself on a super sub ($7.50), enough meat, cheese, and hot peppers to satisfy even the hungriest Stegosaurus. Beware of long lunch lines in the summer; but when they're not busy, Mr. and Mrs. Grouch will chat with you over coffee and a homemade cookie. (Open Mon.-Sat. 10am-10pm, Sun. noon-10pm.)

The area's dinosaur fetish persists at **Dinosaur Provincial Park,** 118km southeast of Drumheller. Actually the main field station for the Tyrrell Museum, the park sits amid the Canadian Badlands of eastern Alberta near **Brooks.** The **Field Station** (378-4342) contains a small museum that complements Tyrrell, but the main attraction is certainly the **Badlands Bus Tour,** which runs four to 10 times per day between Victoria Day and Labor Day. For $1.50, you get chauffeured into the restricted archaeological hot spot for dinosaur discoveries. Many fossils still lie within the ever-eroding rock; you might make some kind of discovery yourself at one of the stops on the tour (Dick Cavett, perhaps). Unfortunately, all you can take home are your memories and your Polaroids. If you point out your discovery to the knowledgeable guide, you can also take home the coveted "Fossil Finder Certificate." The

campground in the park is shaded from the summer heat (unlike the rest of the park), and grassy plots cushion most campsites. The campground stays open year-round but is fully serviced only in summer. (Sites $5. Park open Victoria Day-Labor Day daily 9am-9pm. After Labor Day, you must make an appointment for a tour.) Call or write the Field Station, Dinosaur Provincial Park, Box 60, Patricia T0J 2K0. From Drumheller, follow Hwy. 56 S. for 65km, then take Hwy. 1 about 70km to Brooks. Once in Brooks, go east along the well-marked Hwy. 873 and 544. To get to Dinosaur Provincial Park, travel with wheels; the 48km from Brooks to the park are a little much for the feet. Bikers should be especially cautious since much of the route from Brooks is paved only in loose gravel.

Kananaskis Country

Tucked away between two of Alberta's most conspicuous tourist magnets, Kananaskis Country recently celebrated its tenth anniversary. South of the Trans-Canada Highway and midway between Calgary and Banff, K-Country is a 4000-square-kilometre conglomeration of three provincial parks—**Bow Valley, Peter Lougheed,** and **Bragg Creek**—and several recreational areas (**Spray Lakes** and **Highwood/Cataract Creek** are two of the largest). Preservation and development of K-Country began in 1978, yet even in high season, tourists are sure to find this wilderness tranquil and unspoiled.

For outdoor types, Kananaskis Country offers skiing, snowmobiling, windsurfing, golfing, biking, and hiking. Eager staff members at the five park information centers can help design itineraries for park visitors. Expect to be showered with topographical maps, elaborate brochures, and thick non-fiction books on your activity of choice. A **Park Visitor Centre** lies within or nearby each of the three provincial parks. The Alberta parks system operates out of a center in **Bow Valley,** just north of Hwy. 1 between Seebe and Exshaw (673-3663; open daily 8am-7pm); another in **Gooseberry** on Hwy. 66 near **Bragg Creek** (949-4261); and a cozy, chalet-style office, complete with a fireplace and a wooden deck overlooking Pocaterra Creek, in **Peter Lougheed Park,** on the Kananaskis Lakes Trail (591-7222; hours vary from season to season). The parks system also runs a more central office on **Barrier Lake,** near the junction of Hwy. 40 and 68 (673-3985; open daily 9am-5pm, with extended hours during peak season). **Travel Alberta** maintains an especially helpful office in **Canmore,** just off Hwy. 1A near the northwest border of K-Country (678-5277; open Sun.-Thurs. 9am-6pm, Fri.-Sat. 8am-7:30pm).

Kananaskis' hiking trails accommodate many different kinds of nature lovers. Those with limited time or endurance will enjoy the interpretive hour-long hikes. The Canadian Mt. Everest Expedition Trail (2.4km), for example, provides a majestic view of both Upper and Lower Kananaskis Lakes. More serious hikers will find Gillean Dafferns' *Kananaskis Country Trail Guide* the definitive source on area trails, detailing 337 hikes (published by Rocky Mountain Books). For additional hints and trail updates, ask a staff member at an Information Centre. Bikers will also find the park staff helpful for planning treks along the untraveled highways and trails.

Public transportation does not service Kananaskis Country. However, frequent buses to Banff will drop you within 20km of the region's northwestern boundary at **Canmore** (see Calgary Practical Information). Once in Kananaskis, **hitchhiking** is a realistic option for the vehicle-less.

No less than 3000 campsites are accessible via K-Country roads, and camping is unlimited in the backcountry as long as you set up camp at least 1km from a trail. Established campsites in Kananaskis cost $5 per night. The **Ribbon Creek Hostel** (591-7333), near the Nakiska Ski Area, 24km south of the Trans-Canada Hwy. on Hwy. 40, accommodates 40 people. The hostel's private family rooms hold four beds each, and its living room has a fireplace. (Members $6, nonmembers $10. Closed 9am-5pm and all day Tues.) **William Watson Lodge** (591-7227), a few kilometres north of the Information Centre in Peter Lougheed Park, accommodates disabled people, as well as their friends and families. Although only eligible disabled people and Alberta citizens may make reservations to stay in the cabins, the main lodge is open year-round and anyone may drop by to enjoy the highly accessible local trails.

Southern Alberta

While central Alberta churns relentlessly toward post-modernity, propelled by the rivalry between oil-rich Calgary and Edmonton, southern Alberta remains a revolution or two behind the times. Bereft of oil, southern Albertans farm and ranch. Some of North America's best-preserved Native archaeological sites are in the parks of this region, sporting such unseemly names as Head-Smashed-In and Writing-On-Stone. If endless fields of wheat and the unrelenting chinook winds do not soothe you, nothing shall.

Medicine Hat

The curious name Medicine Hat comes from an Indian legend about a young brave who sacrificed his wife in exchange for a holy bonnet. Today this type of barter is frowned upon.

Riverside Park in downtown Medicine Hat greets visitors with fountains, chirping magpies, and plush lawns perfect for picnickers. City Hall's glass wall provides a heavenly view of the South Saskatchewan River on sunny days. On those same days, however, the mercury may reach upwards of 35°C (95°F). In a scenario redolent of *The Two Jakes,* the ground beneath the quiet city of 42,000 contains countless gallons of natural gas—Rudyard Kipling christened Medicine Hat "the City with All Hell for a Basement."

Practical Information and Orientation

Visitor Information: Medicine Hat Tourist Information Centre, 8 Gehring Rd. (527-6422), just off Trans-Canada Hwy. at Southridge Dr. Scads of information on the past, present, and future of Medicine Hat. Open daily 8am-8pm; Labor Day-Victoria Day Mon.-Fri. 9am-5pm.

Greyhound: 557 2 St. SE (527-4418). Five buses per day to Calgary ($20.10 one way) and 2 per day to Lethbridge ($12.10 one way). Open Mon.-Fri. 5:30am-11:30pm, similar hours Sat.-Sun.

Buses: Medicine Hat Transit (529-8214) runs 6 routes throughout the city; pick up a schedule at City Hall. Catch all the buses in the downtown terminal, at the corner of 4 St. and 6 Ave. SE. Fare $1, senior citizens and children 75¢.

Taxi: Care Cabs, 529-2211.

Car Rental: Rent-A-Wreck, 740 Gershaw Dr. SW (526-5400). Must be 21 with credit card. From $9 per day, plus 9¢ per km.

Women's Shelter: 529-1091.

Sexual Assault Crisis Line: 800-552-8023.

Emergency: 527-4111.

Police: 527-2251.

Post Office: 406 2 St. SE (526-3998). Open Mon.-Fri. 8:30am-5pm. Postal Code: T1A 7E4.

Area Code: 403.

Medicine Hat lies along the Trans-Canada Hwy., 293km southeast of Calgary. Highway 3, the Crowsnest Highway, originates in the city and winds its way 164km west to Lethbridge. In the city, avenues run north-south and streets east-west. The South Saskatchewan River flows through the center of the city, dividing it into north and south sections, while Division Ave. separates east from west.

Accommodations

The youth hostel is still unknown in Medicine Hat, but the motels along the highway and the hotels downtown manage to offer inexpensive rates and above-average rooms.

Trans-Canada Motel, 780 8 St. SW (526-5981). Comfortable rooms at comfortable prices and confortably located (you guessed it) just off the Trans-Canada Hwy. Singles $18. Doubles $24.

The Hat Motel, 560 9 St. SW (527-5445). A bit run-down, but this friendly family-run motel offers units with kitchenettes and color cable TV. $26.25 for 1 person. $31.50 for 2 people.

Assiniboia Inn, 680 3 St. SE (526-2801). Although rooms are above a rowdy tavern, the central downtown location makes them especially convenient. The restaurant in the basement serves up good, cheap breakfast and lunch specials. Singles $15, with bath $20. Doubles with bath $22.

Gas City Campground, 7 St. SW (529-8300), 1km west of the highway. Gas City offers 97 camping sites, a few trees, and a locust-storm of amenities. Tenting sites $7, serviced sites $10-14.

Medicine Hat Inn, 530 4th St. SE (526-1313), 2 blocks from the Greyhound Station. Trade in your spouse and kids to sleep in these tasteful, large rooms endowed with air conditioning, bath, color TV, and, most importantly, thick bathrobes! One night will cost you about $45, but what else is there to buy in Medicine Hat?

Food

Just off the Trans-Canada Hwy. is a veritable Versailles Conference of multinational fast-food restaurants. For more local cuisine, head downtown.

H & R Delicatessen, 519 2 St. SE (527-4511). Hefty sandwiches and homemade soups ($1). Try the delicious Dogwood ($2.25). Open Mon.-Fri. 8am-6pm, Sat. 8am-5:30pm.

The Diner, 108 266 4 St. SW (529-9415). This cozy restaurant just outside the downtown area serves neither marinated mongoose nor puréed periwinkle. Feast on the $2 breakfast special (eggs, bacon, toast, and hash browns) or the featured burger of the day. Open Mon.-Fri. 8am-8pm, Sat.-Sun. 9am-7pm.

Pink Lantern, 639 3 St. SE (527-4141). Remarkably indistinguishable Canadian and Chinese cuisine. Daily lunch and dinner specials, like almond chicken with chicken-fried rice, include soup and dessert and usually run less than $7.

B & B Submarines 'n' Stuff, 570 3 St. SE (527-8833). Decent subs ($3-4.50) and sandwiches ($2-3.50), but a great place for coffee and dessert. Pop in for a Nanaimo bar and coffee, just 95¢ in June. Open Mon.-Sat. 8am-9pm.

Sights and Seasonal Events

While in the area, pick up a complimentary **Historic Walking Tour** pamphlet at the Tourist Information Centre. The guide highlights ten downtown landmarks, from the impressive Gothic towers of **St. Patrick's Church** to the demure Corinthian columns of the **Canadian Bank of Commerce.** On your tour of these turn-of-the-century buildings, make a stop at the ultra-modern **Medicine Hat City Hall,** 580 1 St. SE (529-8100). This $20 million glass-and-brick colossus makes possible a spectacular view of the South Saskatchewan River and cuddles a collection of local art. Pick up a self-guided tour booklet at the information desk, or arrange for a group tour by phoning 529-8220. (Open Mon.-Fri. 8:30am-4:30pm.)

Historical contextualists will love the **Medicine Hat Museum and Art Gallery** (527-6266 for the museum, 526-0486 for the gallery) located at 1302 Bomford Crescent SW, next door to the Tourist Information Centre. The museum paints a nifty picture of local life near the turn of the century with a palette of artifacts and displays, some demanding the exegetical skills of costumed guides. (Museum and gallery open Mon.-Fri. 9am-5pm, Sat.-Sun. 1-5pm; in winter Mon.-Fri 10:30am-noon and 1-5pm, Sat.-Sun. 1-5pm. Admission $1, students free.)

Now that you have thoroughly explored downtown Medicine Hat, why not head in just about any direction to one of the city's parks? The three most prominent of these lie in the South Saskatchewan River Valley. **Echo Dale Regional Park,** located almost 10km west of downtown, features a man-made swimming lake and Echo Dale Farm, where you can visit the restored **Ajax Coal Mine.** The farm (529-6225) operates daily from 9am-9pm. The boathouse (527-8318; open in summer daily 10am-8:30pm; Aug. 15-Sept. 1 10am-8pm) rents paddleboats and canoes for $3.50 per ½-hour, aquabikes for $4.50 per ½-hour. You can also rent mountain bikes here ($3.50 per ½-hour). The other two River Valley Parks—**Police Point** and **Strathcona Island**—lie about 3km east of downtown. Police Point (529-6225) provides ample opportunity to view a variety of wildlife, while Strathcona Island (529-5724) features such family-oriented facilities as a super-sized water playground. For more information on Medicine Hat's park system, write City of Medicine Hat, Community Services Division, City Hall, 580 1st St. SE, Medicine Hat T1A 8E6, or call 529-8300.

During the third week of July, rodeo fans not sated by Calgary can head for the annual **Medicine Hat Exhibition and Stampede** at the aptly named Medicine Hat Exhibition and Stampede Grounds, 5km southeast of downtown. For information about upcoming events, call 526-3979.

Near Medicine Hat: Cypress Hills Provincial Park

The south Albertan landscape strikes a sharp dichotomy: while the west is dominated by enormous peaks and commanding lakes, the east often offers little more than a vast expanse of grain fields seemingly lifted out of Terence Malick's *Badlands.* But a short drive from Medicine Hat along the Trans-Canada Highway will bring you to the enchanting green hills of an Oz on earth—**Cypress Hills Provincial Park.** The name Cypress Hills is actually a misnomer; European voyagers who discovered the area misidentified the park's lodgepole pines as jackpines, or "cypress" in the arboreal jargon of the age.

Cypress Hills lies along Hwy. 41, 34km south of its junction with Hwy. 1. No public transportation runs the 65km from Medicine Hat to the park. In summer, Canadians on holiday crowd the park, but the nine campgrounds can accommodate everyone, their uncle, and aliens from Saturn. The campgrounds run the gamut from the popular **Firerock "A"** campsite (serviced sites $9-11) to the seemingly undiscovered (and frequently uninhabited) **Nichol Springs** and **Battle Creek** campsites. Despite its seclusion and its hostility to motorhomes, Nichol Springs is a mere Batleap from **Elkwater Townsite,** the park's nerve center. You can drive to Battle Creek, but you should know that if it rains only four-wheel drive vehicles will survive the unpaved ground. As unserviced campsites without flush toilets, these two are the cheapest at Cypress Hills (sites $7). What's more, each has several kilometres of readily accessible hiking trails to keep you in shape. In a pinch, you might be able to rent a tent at **Elkwater Service** (893-3844) at the entrance to the townsite. They charge only $5 per night but have a limited supply, so try to bring your own.

If you prefer water travel, rent virtually any kind of boat at the well-advertised **Elkwater Boat and Bike** (893-3877), a little shack on the banks of Elkwater Lake, 72km outside of Medicine Hat. Canoes and rowboats go for $6 per hour and $30 per day, and windsurfers for $10 per hour and $50 per day. Take your rented canoe up to peaceful **Reesor Lake,** some 20km from Elkwater. Elkwater Boat and Bike, of course, also rents bicycles ($4 per hr., $20 per day) and tandem bicycles ($5 per ½-hr., $45 per day). Motor boats ($10 per hr., $60 per day) and jet skis ($20 per hour, $120 per day) are also available. (Open June 1-Sept. 15 daily 9am-9pm.)

When the cold and snow hits, this summertime oasis becomes prime territory for **cross-country skiing, ice fishing,** and **downhill skiing. Hidden Valley Ski Hill** allows you to ride the slope on the very same lift used by the '88 Olympians!! ($15 per day.) Trails for skiers of all levels are widely publicized, and easily accessible.

March around **Cypress Hills Provincial Park** any time of year; there are three lakes and 220 square kilometres covered by trails. The **Cypress Hill Visitors Centre** offers a kaleidoscope of interpretive programs and an outdoor theatre on weekends between Victoria Day and Labor Day. Contact the center at 893-3833 to find out each weekend's schedule. (Open July-Aug. daily 9am-9pm; May-June 9am-5pm.) After Labor Day, take your questions to the **Cypress Hills Provincial Park Administration Office** (893-3777), at the entrance to the townsite. (Open Mon.-Fri. 8:30am-4pm.)

Writing-On-Stone Provincial Park

An archaeological marvel almost lost in a sea of wheat, Writing-On-Stone Provincial Park guards the 200-year old drawings that Native Americans carved into the area's sandstone cliffs. Unfortunately the Native Americans are not the only people who have displayed their artistic talents on the windswept rocks. More contemporary messages, such as "Tania J, 1967" are inscribed everywhere on the cliffs in the park, at times right on top of the archaeologically priceless Native carvings. This idiocy has caused the park to restrict visitors to one walking trail, heralded in the park's brochures as a chance to glimpse the most extensive of the writings-on-stone, "The Battle Scene." You do get a glimpse—but that's all. Because this faded drawing has been so vandalized, a barbed-wire fence keeps today's visitors a safe 5m away. To see some less spectacular but nonetheless impressive carvings, arrive at 2pm for the free guided tour (May-Labor Day). This tour takes you into the otherwise off-limits archaeological preserve, which contains the majority of the carvings in the park. Here, too, the hand of modern man is readily visible, but many Native American carvings have survived unscathed—and unfenced. Walk up and stare the "pointed-shoulder man" right in his eroded eye.

Writing-On-Stone features a winsome **campground** (May-Labor Day $7 per site; off-season free), and a small beach on the murky but clean Milk River. The town sits about 150km southeast of Lethbridge. Rent a car in Lethbridge (there's no public transport to the park) and go south on Hwy. 4 to **Milk River,** then east on Secondary Rte. 501 to the cliffs.

Lethbridge

Lethbridge seems out of place in southern Alberta—and not only because its main tourist attraction is a lush, green Japanese garden. Amidst the miniscule prairie towns that dot the region, the city of 60,000 is home to two universities and one of Canada's most interesting historical and recreational parks. The expanding urban development and the frequent gusty winds that plague the city may make Lethbridge seem like a sort of light-weight Chicago. Nonetheless, Alberta's third largest city manages to retain the tempered rustic pride characteristic of the surrounding villages.

Practical Information and Orientation

Visitor Information: Chinook Country Tourist Association, 2805 Scenic Dr. (329-6777), at the intersection of Scenic and Mayor Magrath Dr. Staff will gladly help you plan a tour of southern Alberta. Maps, brochures, and guides to the city and the entire region. Open May-Labor Day daily 8am-9pm; Labor Day-Oct. 15 9am-5pm; Oct. 16-April 8:30am-4:30pm. A newer **Information Centre,** located on Brewery Hill, on 1 Ave. S. off Hwy. 3 (320-1222), provides the same maps and pamphlets and features a voluptuous vista of Brewery Gardens. Open May-Labor Day daily 8am-9pm; Labor Day-Sept. 9am-5pm.

Greyhound: 411 5th St. S. (327-1551). Several buses daily to Calgary ($17.15) and Edmonton ($38.15). Open Mon.-Sat. 8am-7pm, Sun. 8-11:30am and 1-7pm.

Buses: Lethbridge City Transit runs 9 routes that will take you anywhere within the city. You can catch all of the buses at the intersection of 4th Ave. S. and 6th St. S. Fare $1, students (to grade 12) 75¢, senior citizens and children 60¢. For more information call 320-3885.

Taxi: Lethbridge Cabs, 327-4005. $1.85 plus $1 per km thereafter. Senior citizen discount 10%. 24 hours.

Car Rental: Rent-A-Wreck, 3230 24th Ave. S. (328-9484). Must be 21 with credit card—or a steady job. $19 per day plus 10¢ per km. Open Mon.-Sat. 8am-5:30pm.

Weather: 320-7623.

Women's Shelter: Harbour House, 604 8th St. S., run by the YWCA (320-1881, phone staffed 24 hours).

Sexual Assault Crisis Line: 327-4545 or 800-552-8023.

Police: 328-4444.

Post Office: 704 4th Ave. S. (382-3132). Open Mon.-Fri. 8:30am-5pm. Postal Code: T1J 3Y2.

Area Code: 403.

Lethbridge lies along Highway 3, the Crowsnest Highway. Highways 4 and 5 run into the city from the south. From Calgary or Edmonton, drive south on Hwy. 2 until it intersects Hwy. 3, then go about 50km east. In the city, avenues run east-west and streets north-south. The Canadian Pacific Railroad passes through the center of the city, dividing it into north and south sections.

Accommodations

Cheap rooms? No problem. The reputable motels along Mayor Magrath Dr. cost only $35, and in summer hotels invariably flash vacancy signs. Unless your coffers are hollow, stay away from the sleazy, ultra-cheap hotels in the city center.

University of Lethbridge (329-2584), across the Oldman River from the city but easily reached by bus #7 and 8. In summer, the residence office—Room C-442 in University Hall—rents rooms to virtually anyone. Spartan dorm rooms and shared bathrooms but clean sheets, good security, friendly neighbors, and a convenient location. Singles $17. Shared rooms $13. With student ID singles $15.80, shared rooms $11.60, large singles $17.80.

YWCA, 604 8th St. S. (329-0088). Very safe for women traveling alone. Comfortable, homey place complete with shared kitchenette. Singles $20. Shared rooms $18.

Parkside Inn, 1009 Mayor Magrath Dr. (328-2366), next to the Japanese Gardens, Heritage Lake, and the golf course. Take bus #1 from downtown. At the high end of the totem pole. The recently remodeled rooms are big and plush; each includes A/C, cable TV, and bathroom. Singles $40. Doubles $44.

Henderson Lake Campgrounds (328-5452), at Henderson Lake in the southeast corner of the city. Shaded and peaceful sites for tenters, virtual driveways for RVs. The RVs have the last laugh, though—the lower tenting area floods in biblical deluges. Tent sites $10, with hookups $11.50-15.50.

Food

Those travelers who become addicted to the common Canadian $2.99-or-less breakfast special might find Lethbridge is unable to satisfy their early-morning habit. Lethbridgians are careful choosing words to describe the cost of local cuisine—it's always "moderate" or "reasonable," rarely "cheap." Budget travelers can either spend the extra few dollars and enjoy local meals or experience their fair share of McDonaldses, A&Ws, Bonanzas, and Kentucky Frieds along Mayor Magrath Dr. or near the City Centre. There are also several inexpensive and good eateries in the Lethbridge Centre Mall, across the street from the bus depot. Try Grandma Lee's for some grandmotherly cooking.

Mary's Place, 411 5 St. S. (327-9330). So what if Mary shares the building with the Grey-hound depot? She serves one of Lethbridge's only true bargain breakfasts: 2 eggs, sausage, hash browns, toast, and coffee or tea for $3. Delicious lunch and dinner specials cost less than $5, and include soup and dessert. Open Mon.-Fri. 7am-7pm, Sat. 8am-7pm, Sun. 8am-2pm.

The Shasta, 329 5 St. S. (329-3434). Ignore the gaudy lamps and wallpaper and explore the long list of luncheon specials. Get a grilled cheese and mushroom sandwich with salad and fries for $3. Great Caesar's Ghost—the steak and Caesar salad dinner special includes garlic toast and potato for only $5. Open Mon.-Thurs. 11am-10pm, Fri.-Sat. 11am-11pm.

Top Pizza and Spaghetti House, 11 St. and 4 Ave. S. (327-1952). Good pizza at good prices. A medium pie with pepperoni and mushroom costs $8; large dish of spaghetti with meatballs $6.25. Open Mon.-Thurs. 11am-1am, Fri.-Sat. 11am-3am, Sun. noon-midnight.

The Duke of Wellington, 132 Columbia Blvd. W. (381-1455), in the West Village Mall. Stu-dents and visiting nobility dine here infrequently; it's close to the university but somewhat expensive. Daily sandwich specials (under $5) include soup and fries. Open Mon.-Sat. 11am-10pm.

Sights

Fort Whoop-Up (329-0444), located in **Indian Battle Park** on the east bank of the Oldman River, is but a replica of the notorious whiskey trading outpost which originally stood some 10km from present-day Lethbridge. Nonetheless, this place feels like the real thing. Dressed in period costumes, the guides working out of the **Interpretive Centre** explain the history of the whiskey and fur trade from the days of the fort's construction. Europeans introduced the Native Americans to make-shift whiskey—pure grain firewater flavored with tobacco, lye, dirt, or whatever else was handy at the time—and in the process took advantage of the local tribes-men. Numerous incidents of violence and disorder occurred between the two trad-ing partners until 1874, when the Mounties galloped into the fort. A well-balanced slide show is projected regularly; a film shown by request. (Interpretive Centre open daily 10am-8pm; Labor Day-May 15 10am-4pm.) For an additional 50¢ hop aboard the **Whoop-Up Wagon Train,** a motorized modern-day stagecoach which will take you on a 20-minute tour of the park and the Oldman River valley.

A stop that young children and naturalists alike will appreciate is the **Helen Schuler Coulee Centre and Nature Reserve** (320-3064), a section of Indian Battle Park consecrated to for the protection of local vegetation, prairie animals, and the occasional porcupine. (Open Sun.-Thurs. 1-8pm, Fri.-Sat. 10am-6pm; Labor Day-Victoria Day Tues.-Sun. 1-4pm.) Here you can learn about creepy crawly creatures and the tremendously talented toad. One of the trails leads outside the Reserve to the **Coal Kiosk,** an information-packed outpost that quickly traces the coal mining industry in Lethbridge from the first excavation in 1881 through Lethbridge's incor-poration as a city in 1906. The kiosk lies beneath the spectacular **High-Level Bridge,** the longest and highest of its kind in the world. The black steel skeleton began ac-cepting trains in 1909 and is still in use today, handling traffic many times heavier than its designers imagined.

Those still hankering for local history after a day at Indian Battle Park should climb the hill to downtown Lethbridge for a quick tour of the **Sir Alexander Galt Museum** (320-3898), located on 5 Ave. S. at 1 St. The museum's main gallery fol-lows Lethbridge through 100 lethargic years of industrial change—from whiskey to coal to agriculture and irrigation. (Open Mon.-Thurs. 9am-8pm, Fri. 9am-4pm, Sat.-Sun. 1-8pm; Sept.-June Mon.-Tues. and Thurs.-Fri. 10am-4pm, Wed. 10am-8pm, Sat.-Sun. 1-4pm. Free.)

The **Nikka Yuko Japanese Garden** in the southeast corner of town is the most trumpeted of the city's attractions. Constructed and reconstructed (to be safe) in Japan, then dismantled and shipped to Lethbridge for another reconstruction, the main pavilion blends well into the Albertan placidity. An informative Japanese host-ess appears at each point of interest to guide you through the garden. Don't forget to ring the Japan-Canada peace bell, or to remove your shoes upon entering the pavilion. (Open May 15-June 20 daily 9am-5pm; June 21-August 9am-8pm; Sept.-

Oct. 4 9am-5pm. Admission $2, senior citizens and ages under 17 $1.) Adjacent to the Japanese Garden is **Henderson Lake;** this manmade reservoir is the nucleus of a city park in the southeast corner of Lethbridge. The park offers boat rentals (rowboats $6, canoes $7) and a trail around the lake perfect for a morning run or an evening stroll. Take bus #1 to both the garden and the lake. For more information call 322-7545. Boat rental available May-Aug. (Open Mon.-Fri. noon-10pm, Sat.-Sun. 10am-10pm.)

The University of Lethbridge displays $14 million of **art** (329-2690) downtown in an old Eaton's department store. The exhibition ranges from 20th-century Canadian painters to the brand-name pop artists of the 50s. Since the art is looking for a permanent home, call ahead. (Open Fri.-Wed. noon-7pm, Thurs. noon-9pm. Admission $2, senior citizens and students $1, ages 6-12 50¢, families $5. Wed. free.)

Near Lethbridge: Fort Macleod

Fort Macleod witnessed a rare instance of European benevolence toward Native Americans. In 1873, alarmed by the lawlessness, violence, and exploitation incited by the whiskey trade, the Northwest Mounted Police (NWMP) dispatched 300 of its men to clean up this den of debauchery. In a performance worthy of the Keystone Cops, the Mounties got lost en route, giving Fort Whoop-Up's whiskey traders time to escape south of the border down Montana way. When the force finally arrived, it was greeted not by a hail of gunshots but by the sole remaining whiskey trader. Unable to purchase the fort from the conniving moonshiner, the mounted police moved on to found Fort Macleod and to keep whiskey traders out of Native American territory.

The Fort Macleod Museum (553-4703) at 219 25 St., in a 1957 replica of the 1874 fort, exhibits typical NWMP uniforms, guns, tools, and furniture; stop by only if you're a real Mounties fan. The Interpretive Centre at Fort Whoop-Up in Lethbridge presents a much better synopsis of the area's history for no charge. (Fort and museum open May-June 14 daily 9am-5pm; June 15-Sept. 7 9am-7pm; Sept. 8-Oct. 15 9am-5pm. Off-season tours by appointment only. Admission $2.50, ages 13-18 50¢, under 13 25¢.) Try to visit in July or August when the real spectacle unfolds. Four times daily during these peak tourist months, the Fort Museum's **Mounted Patrol Musical Ride** takes its song-and-dance to the streets. If you cannot photograph the real thing, photocopy the picture of the Mounties on the back of the $50 bill.

For nighttime fun in Fort Macleod, the **Great West Summer Theatre** (553-4151) puts on a summer-long production at the **Empress Theatre,** on Main St. If you like bad jokes, plotlessness, zany madcap antics, and off-key singing, you'll just love this show. Even if you don't, it's the only thing to do at night anyway. (Tickets $6, ages 11-17 $4, under 11 $3.) If you are compelled to spend the night in Fort Macleod, the **DJ Motel,** 416 24 St., has 15 comfortable rooms with bath and cable TV. Singles start at $26, doubles at $30. You can pick up a $2 coupon for a room at the Head-Smashed-In Interpretive Centre.

Greyhound (800-332-1016) runs to Fort Macleod from Lethbridge (3 per day, $3.60 one way). Step into the bus station for a bite to eat at the **Java Shop** (533-3063). A subdued crowd of townsfolk congregates here for the quick and filling breakfast special—sausage, two eggs, hash browns, and coffee ($4). The cinnamon rolls are as big as a house. (Open daily 6am-8pm; sometimes open until 1am if there's a late bus getting in.) Just around the corner you can order up a more sophisticated morning meal at the **Continental Bake Shoppe and Lunch Counter** (553-4124). An omelette with coffee, hash browns, and toast costs $3.75. Those with more petite appetites will enjoy a hot sausage roll ($1.05) or a homemade muffin. (Open Mon.-Sat. 7:30am-5:30pm.) For supper, head on over to **Luigi's Pizza and Steak House,** on Main St., 1km east of the Greyhound depot. (Small specialty pizza $5.50, medium $8.)

Head-Smashed-In Buffalo Jump

The buffalo was once a sacred supermarket to the Blackfoot Nation tribes of southern Alberta. Coveted as a source of fresh meat, winter sustenance, tools, and shelter, the buffalo became the victim of one of the most innovative forms of mass slaughter in history: the buffalo jump. Agile Blackfoot tribesmen wearing coyote skins would slither behind a herd, skillfully force it into a "gathering basin," and then wildly spook the 500-odd bison into a fatal stampede over a 10m cliff. For over 5500 years, the buffalo jump technique was practiced by Native American tribes throughout the plains region of North America. But no buffalo jump site is as well-preserved as the Head-Smashed-In Buffalo Jump, named about 150 years ago after a young thrill-seeking warrior was drowned by a waterfall of buffaloes as he watched the event from front row seats at the base of the cliff.

Although UNESCO will fine you $50,000 if you forage for souvenirs in the 10-metre-deep beds of bone, you can learn about buffalo jumps and local Native American culture at the **Interpretive Centre** (553-2731), a $10-million, 7-story, brand-new facility built into the cliff itself. The centre also shows films of a reenactment of the fatal plunge, which, to the relief of the SPCA, used frozen buffalo to hurl off the cliff. Two kilometres of walking trails, both above and below the cliff, serve as venues for the fascinating and free guided tours. (Open daily 9am-8pm; Labor Day-Victoria Day 9am-5pm. Free.)

There is not yet any public transportation to this unique North American hunting ground. Rent a car or hitch from Lethbridge or from Fort Macleod, which is 18km southeast of the buffalo jump along Secondary Rte. 785.

Crowsnest Pass

Crowsnest Pass is an easy daytrip from Lethbridge and an alluring stopover for travelers en route to southern Alberta via British Columbia or Montana. Named for Crowsnest Mountain, the mesa-like peak that dominates the valley, Crowsnest Pass is actually comprised of five tiny towns: **Coleman, Blairmore, Frank, Hillcrest,** and **Bellevue.** In its days of glory nearly a century ago, the Pass was heralded as the promising "Pittsburgh of Canada." Entrepreneurs and immigrants flocked to the mountains with dreams of mining a fortune—or simply a month's good pay—from the abundant coal deposits of the Pass. As disasters struck the area and underground coal mining became obsolete, the putative Pittsburgh perished. The mining communities have disappeared, but their legacy remains hewn in the unforgiving hills of the Pass.

Accommodations, Camping, and Food

You might have to spend the night in the Pass, particularly if you're coming from central British Columbia. However, the settlements wilt quickly once the sun has plunged from sight.

Turtle Mountain Motor Inn, on Hwy. 3 just west of Frank (562-2412). The rooms are a bit worn, but it's the cheapest place in the Pass. Singles $24. Doubles $26.

Stop Inn Motel, on Hwy. 3 in Coleman (562-7381). Your classic non-franchised motel: drive-up rooms and kitchenettes ($3 extra). Singles $30. Doubles $33.

Chinook-Allison Campground. Follow Hwy. 3 west from Coleman for 9km, then follow the signs up Allison Creek Rd. Free camping virtually inaccessible to the foot traveler. Bring a sleeping pad to counteract stones strewn over most of the 70-odd sites.

Crowsnest Campground (562-2932), just off Hwy. 3A in Blairmore. More commercial than most in the Pass, this campground offers hot showers, a heated pool, and 110 sites for RVs or tenters.

Rocky Mountain Burger and Pizza, 8505 20 Ave. (563-5232), just off Hwy. 3 in Coleman. Sure, they sell pizzas ($5-14), but only a vegetarian would pass up the enormous Rocky Mountain Burger ($4.50, with a mountain of homemade fries $6.25). Try the hefty breakfast special ($2.50). Open daily 8am-11pm.

Chris and Irvin's Cafe, 7802 17 Ave. (563-3093), in downtown Coleman. Serves up a chicken burger ($2.25) and, for the unsuperstitious, the miner's deluxe ($4). Delicious homemade fries $1.50. Open Mon.-Fri. 6am-10pm, Sat. 7am-10pm, Sun. 8am-7pm.

Sights and Activities

Start your day at the **Leitch Collieries** (562-7388), on Hwy. 3 at the east end of the Pass. Nineteenth-century miners put their picks to the wall inside the hills about 2km from the road, but the coal was later processed in a complex of buildings right where Hwy. 3 passes today. Most of the company's remaining buildings are weed-covered ruins, but the power house and mine manager's house are well preserved. Ask one of the casually clad guides who roam the area to decipher the coal miner's lingo on the signs. (Open May 15-Sept. 15 daily 9am-5pm; off-season tours can be arranged. Free.)

Heavy mining turned Crowsnest Pass into a modern Pompeii in 1903. When one-too-many tunnels made Turtle Mountain a giant sandcastle on April 29 of that year, 90 million cubic feet of rock spilled into the town of Frank, burying 70 people and their houses in less than 100 seconds. A few kilometres west of the collieries on Hwy. 3, the metre-high rock garden is in much the same condition as it was after the accident. The **Frank Slide Interpretive Centre,** also on Hwy. 3 (562-7388), gives you a notion of what Frank was like before Turtle tumbled; its award-winning multimedia presentation details the lives, origins, and attitudes of the miners. For a close look at a mining ghost town, inquire about guided hiking tours to **Lille,** inaccessible by auto. (Centre open daily 9am-8pm; Labor Day-Victoria Day 10am-4pm. Free.)

An equally tragic disaster befell **Hillcrest** in 1914 when methane in the mine shafts ignited, killing 189 miners. According to the interpretive film, these miners learned that "you're only as safe as the stupidest guy in the mine." Their memorial cemetery is hard to find but worth the effort. Many of the gravestones within the mass burial area are inscribed in Slavic tongues—testimony to the popularity of the risky mining career to new immigrants at the turn of the century. There is no charge to see the gravesite. Follow the Hillcrest access road off Hwy. 3 until the road forks; take the right fork and immediately make a sharp right down a gravel road to the fence-enclosed cemetery.

For a historical overview of the entire Crowsnest Pass region, pack your lunchbox and go to school—to Coleman High School, that is, in downtown Coleman. The high school was transformed into the **Crowsnest Museum** after the Crowsnest Historical Society purchased it for $1 in 1983 (talk about budget-minded). Exhibits highlight the Pass community near the turn of the century with displays depicting traditional school rooms and barber shops. (Open daily 10am-5pm; Labor Day-Victoria Day Mon.-Thurs. 9am-noon. Free.) In winter, the **Allison Lake Recreation Area** operates an extensive network of cross-country ski trails in the shadow of Crowsnest Mountain. Take Hwy. 3 west from Coleman for 9km, then follow the signs up Allison Creek Rd.

ALASKA

Called "Alashka" or "The Great Land" by the Aleuts and "The Last Frontier" by European adventurers, Alaska is large enough to devour one-fifth of the continental United States. Misty fjords, mountain lakes, willow forests, giant glaciers, and alpine tundra complement a population as varied as the Great Land itself. It is hard to say exactly what being "Alaskan" means because the term encompasses everything from Native American to *cheechako* (outsider). But Alaskans of all spots pride themselves on their determination, and from this has emerged a strong sense of community.

On Good Friday, 1989, the Exxon *Valdez* ran aground on Naked Island, spilling 1.5 million gallons of crude oil into the Prince William Sound. Thousands of sea otters, seals, and birds were killed. The spill immediately caused the cancellation of the summer's fishing in the Sound and on the eastern Kenai Peninsula. Many fishermen took to the more lucrative enterprises of reimbursement litigation and assisting in the ineffectual cleanup efforts. Predictions of the long-term effects of the spill on fishing and wildlife range from prophecies of complete catastrophe to expectations of a one-year bounce back. (One enduring effect of the spill will be the common media-enforced mispronunciation of Valdez to rhyme with "Cortez." The correct pronunciation rhymes with "goat cheese" or "Maltese.")

Alaska, and the Sound in particular, is a land of booms and busts, of prosperity rising from and returning to adversity. Exactly 25 years to the day before the *Valdez* spill, the same area was rocked by the biggest earthquake ever recorded in North America. The town of Valdez was leveled. Kodiak and Anchorage were declared national emergencies. Largely due to a massive infusion of Federal funds, the state

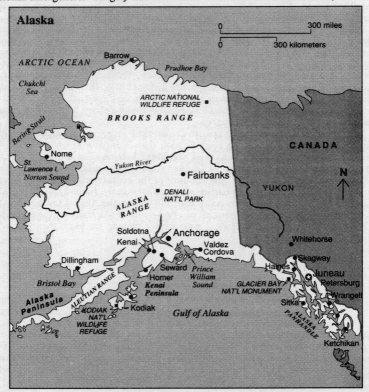

recovered in little over a year. (Valdez itself was rebuilt, house for house, 5 miles from its former site.) Seen in the context of Alaskan history, the spill is just another entry in the catalogue of natural catastrophes. This attitude reflects the Alaskan character: rugged and relaxed people prospering in a harsh and furious environment, taking in stride the extremes of earthquake and oil spill, volcanic eruption (1912) and Japanese invasion (1940), winters 100° below and summers 100° above.

If the spill seems less cataclysmic in the context of Alaskan history than it does in the daily papers, it becomes almost infinitesimal in light of Alaska's geography. "O.K., the spill was the size of Rhode Island," said the Coast Guard commander of the spill cleanup efforts. "We have *glaciers* here the size of Rhode Island." Although the oil soiled a string of beaches that would stretch from San Diego to Portland, it still only coated 10% of the Prince William Sound, and perhaps 2% of the Alaskan coastline all told. "The outsiders," said one resident, "are just milking this for political hay." The metaphor may be mixed, but the message is clear—the vast majority of this vast state is as untouched and pristine as it was before the spill. Moreover, many areas remain as they were before the Europeans, with their knack for reducing forests and ice floes to garages and highways, even arrived.

Vitus Bering, a Dane in the service of the Russian czar, began the pillaging process, sailing in the early 18th century from Kamchatka to the Kenai Peninsula. Bering died in the effort, but his crew brought home so many valuable furs that Russian traders soon overran Kodiak Island with traps in hand (and rubles in mind). But otter pelts don't grow on trees, and the fur harvest ended in less than a century, leaving the otter population decimated and the Native peoples nearly destroyed by slavery. (Today, Alaskan law allows the possession of marijuana but prosecutes a felony for the possession of a sea otter pelt.) Dead broke from the Crimean War, the Russians decided to sell what they considered to be a territory sucked dry of its natural resources. In 1867 the U.S. bought the immense wasteland for less than 2¢ per acre. Alaska soon became known as "Seward's Icebox," a jab at Secretary of State William Seward, who negotiated the $7,200,000 purchase. But within 20 years, Yankee prospectors unearthed enough gold to turn Seward's Folly into a billion-dollar profit. Greed depleted most gold reserves by World War I, and Alaska once again became a quiet frontier. To halt the Japanese advance during World War II, the U.S. Corps of Army Engineers built an astonishing 1500-mile road from British Columbia to Fairbanks. Alaska's strategic military value has appreciated since the idle threats of 1942; Little Diomede Island on the Aleutian chain lies less than 2½ miles from Soviet territory. In 1974, Alaskans voted to move their capital away from Juneau. A commission picked out a perfect site for the new capital (between Anchorage and Fairbanks) but the voters changed their minds. Juneau remains the center of state business.

True to the spirit of the last frontier, civilization has scratched out only tiny enclaves for itself in the Alaskan wilderness. Despite the 800-mile Alaska Pipeline, the Alaska Highway, and the still-secret Nuclear Access Roads, only one-fifth of the land is accessible—the float plane is the primary mode of transportation. Natives still live with something approaching the privacy and dominion their ancestors enjoyed before the larceny of the Europeans; Athabaskans, Aleuts, Eskimos, Tlingits, and Haidas still subsist on the land's abundant resources. The rivers teem with salmon; the rocky shores harbor water fowl and seals, while whales yodel offshore. Black, brown, grizzly, polar, and Kodiak bears compete with wolves, lynx, and other carnivores for food and territory. Such magnificent northern species as the caribou and the walrus roam unfettered. Moose, bighorn sheep, and bald eagles carouse in numbers unparalleled anywhere.

Stunning natural wonders blanket the largest state of the Union. Mountaineers can choose from a variety of rugged trails traversing primordial scenery—from the glacial slopes of the Panhandle's Coastal Mountains and the serene, detergent-white summits of the Wrangell and Chugach Mountains in the southcentral area, to the tundra terrain and towering peaks of the Alaska Range and the refrigerating polar isolation of the Brooks Range beyond the Arctic Circle. Less rugged outdoor explorers can also reach much of Alaska's scenic beauty, including the verdant archipelago of Tongass National Forest, the bizarre volcanic landscape of Katmai National Monument, the misty fjords of the Kenai Peninsula, and the unbelievable Glacier Bay National Park and Preserve—a dazzling display of mammoth glacial formations policed by an armada of floating icebergs.

Practical Information

Emergency: 911.

Capital: Juneau.

United States Customs Service: 202-566-8195. This Washington, DC office will connect you with the Canadian Customs and Excise office for information regarding the rules and regulations of traveling through Canada.

Avalanche and Mountain Weather Report: 271-4500.

State Troopers: 269-5511 in Anchorage, 452-2114 in Fairbanks.

Time Zones: Alaska (most of the state; 4 hr. behind Eastern); Aleutian-Hawaii (Aleutian Islands; 5 hr. behind Eastern).

Drinking Age: 21.

Postal Abbreviation: AK.

Area Code: 907.

Impractical Information

Nicknames: The Last Frontier and Land of the Midnight Sun.

Population: 523,048.

Motto: North to the Future.

Flower: Forget-Me-Not.

Bird: White Ptarmigan.

Year of Incorporation: Jan. 3, 1959 (49th state).

Majority Party: Republican.

Area: 586,412 square miles (1,507,215 square kilometres).

Tourist Information

Alaska Division of Tourism, Pouch E-101, Juneau 99811 (465-2010). Open Mon.-Fri. 8am-4:30pm.

Alaska Public Lands Information Center, Old Federal Bldg., Anchorage 99510 (271-2737). Help in traversing any and all wilderness areas. Open daily 9am-8pm. Branch office in Fairbanks; others under construction in Ketchikan and Tok.

Alaska State Division of Parks, Pouch 7-001, Anchorage 99510 (561-2020). Open Mon.-Fri. 8am-4:30pm.

United States Forest Service, P.O. Box 1628-ATD, Juneau 99802 (586-7282). General information regarding national parks and reserves. Open Mon.-Fri. 8am-4:30pm.

National Park Service, Parks and Forests Information Center, 2525 Gampbell, Anchorage 99503 (261-2643). Open Mon.-Fri. 8am-5pm.

Alaska Department of Fish and Game, P.O. Box 3-2000, Juneau 99802. Get your hunting and fishing regulations here.

State Employment Service, P.O. Box 3-7000, Juneau 99802. For those hunting for jobs, instead of game. Branch offices in Anchorage, Ketchikan, and Petersburg.

Legislative Information Office, 1024 W. 6th Ave., Anchorage 99501. For those who'd like to delve into Alaska's ever-juicy political debates. Or call the Alaska State Government General Information service at 465-2111.

Anyone venturing onto Alaska's roads should buy a copy of the *Milepost,* published by the Alaska Northwest Publishing Company, 130 2nd Ave. S., Edmond, WA 98020 (for information, call 907-563-1141, Mon.-Fri. 8:30am-4:30pm). The *Milepost* ($15) is packed with information about Alaskan and Canadian communities as well as up-to-date ferry schedules and maps of the highways and roads.

Getting There and Getting Around

The **Alaska Highway** is a rocky inroad from British Columbia; friendly RV drivers are the distinct majority on the largely unpaved route. The **Alaska Marine Highway** navigates an extensive ferry system from Seattle up through the scenic islands of the Panhandle and alongside the glaciers of the central coast. No matter how you come to Alaska, make your travel plans well in advance because of the exorbitant cost of travel both to and within the state. You might swim from Siberia, for example. One excellent way to compensate for money lost in transportation is to make full use of Alaska's free state campgrounds.

Air Travel

Flying to Alaska is the quickest and often the cheapest way to escape northward. Winging directly to Anchorage from the Lower 48 is the most common route. As of August 1989, round-trip fares from Boston to Anchorage ran $636 (with 30-day advance purchase). Check with the major domestic carriers serving Alaska: **Western, Northwest, United,** and **Alaska Airlines** (800-426-0333, in WA 800-654-5669). In Anchorage, try **Travel Center** (266-6300) or **Polaris Travel Service** (272-8476).

One in 36 Alaskans has a pilot's license, and for a good reason: Alaska lacks an extensive road or rail network. Given Alaska's size, air travel is often a necessity. Several intrastate airlines transport passengers and cargo to virtually every village in Alaska: **Alaska Airlines** (to larger Bush towns and Cordova); **Mark Air** (to larger Bush towns, Kodiak, and the Aleutians; 800-426-6784); **ERA Aviation** (southcentral; 243-3300); **Southcentral Air** (southcentral; 243-8791); **Reeve Aleutian Airways** (Aleutians; 243-4700); and **Ryan Air Service** (practically anywhere in the Bush; 248-0695). Many other charters and flight-seeing services are available. Check the *Milepost* (see Tourist Information), or write **Ketchum Air Service Inc.,** North Shore Lake Hood, Anchorage 99503 (243-5525), to ask about their charters. One-day flights and overnight or weekend trips to uninhabited lakes, mountains, and tundra range upwards from $165. Although expensive, they are a great way to get away from the tourist centers, see wildlife, and perhaps catch some of Alaska's famous fish.

Railroad Travel

In 1984 the **Alaska Railroad** became one of the last nationally owned railroads in the country to be sold. This frontier railroad, the northernmost in North America, covers 470 miles of land, much of it inaccessible by road or boat. For some folks in isolated cabins, the train is the only link to civilization. The train connects Seward and Whittier in the south with Anchorage, Fairbanks, and Denali National Park.

Service runs from Anchorage to Fairbanks ($88) daily in the summer, once per week in the winter. Given advance notice in the winter, the engineer will drop cargo or passengers along the way. On the way to Fairbanks, trains stop at Denali National Park. Southbound from Anchorage, the train is the only land route to Whittier (one way $36). The short 30-minute ride ducks under two tunnels and runs from Portage several times per day to coincide with the schedule of the M.V. *Bartlett*. Passenger service to Seward was recently reintroduced for summer visitors. Advance reservations are required for all except Whittier trips. Write **Alaska Railroad Corporation,** Passenger Services, P.O. Box 7-2111, Anchorage 99510-7069. (Call 265-2623 for schedules, fares, and reservations.)

On the Panhandle, the 90-year-old **White Pass and Yukon Route** carries passengers over an old Klondike Gold Rush trail from Skagway to Bennet, BC. Motorcoach service continues on from there to Whitehorse. For more information, contact the White Pass and Yukon Route, P.O. Box 435, Skagway 99840 (983-2217 or 800-343-7373).

Bus Travel

Although Greyhound doesn't run beyond Whitehorse, YT, scheduled bus services connect British Columbia, Whitehorse, and Haines with central Alaska, including Anchorage. **Whitepass-Yukon Motorcoaches,** P.O. Box 100479, Anchorage 99510 (279-0761), runs two buses per week in summer from Whitehorse to Anchorage. The one-way fare is about $140; you'll also need to pay for overnight accommodations (about $85). Service from Haines is also available twice per week. One-way fare is $135, plus overnight accommodations. Several enterprising van owners run small operations from Haines to Anchorage, synchronized with the ferry. Fares can be as low as $105, but service is often unreliable.

Charters and tours often appear expensive, but many include meals, lodging, and sights otherwise difficult to reach. **Gray Line Tours,** 547 W. 4th Ave., Anchorage 99501 (277-5581), offers a two-day excursion from Whitehorse to Anchorage that includes a sail across the Prince William Sound, a train ride from Whittier, and one night's accommodations, all for $309.

Driving in Alaska

Juneau is the only state capital in the nation that cannot be reached by automobile. In fact, roads reach only a quarter of the state's area. The highways that traverse the southern part of the state are narrow, often gravely ribbons extending from point to point with few services.

The Alaska Highway, built in eight months by the Army Corps of Engineers during 1942, runs from Dawson Creek, BC, to Fairbanks. Anchorage can be reached via the Tok Cut-off. The interminable Canadian stretch of the road is poorly maintained, dragging out the entire drive to three to five days. Only hardsiders should attempt this; lodgings en route are hard to come by. Winter and summer travelers alike are advised to let a friend or relative know of their position along the highway several times in the course of a trip.

To the embarrassment of most residents, many major roads in Alaska are still in deplorable condition. Dust and flying rocks are a major hazard in the summer, as are the road construction crews who seem to interrupt long-distance trips with miserable 10- to 30-mile patches of gravel. Radiators and headlights should be protected from flying rocks with a wire screen, and a fully functioning spare tire is absolutely essential. Winter can actually offer a smoother ride. Active snow crews keep roads as clear as possible, and the packed surface and thinned traffic permit easy driving without summer's mechanical troubles. At the same time, the danger of avalanches and ice are cause for major concern. Check the road conditions before traveling; in Anchorage call 333-1013, or simply tune in to local radio stations.

Hitchhiking

Many people hitchhike instead of depending on buses in Alaska. Hitching is generally safer than in the Lower 48, but beware of being stranded on lightly traveled stretches of road. A wait of a day or two is not unusual on certain stretches of the Alaska Hwy. Luckily, Alaskans are a friendly and cooperative group, and most rides last at least a day. Campgrounds and service stations make the best bases for hitching, providing an opportunity for mutual inspection before a long journey.

Catching a ride into Alaska on the Alaska Hwy. involves passing the Alaska-Yukon "border" check, which is a series of routine questions about citizenship, residency, insurance, contraband, and finances, followed by an auto inspection. In the event that a hitchhiker is turned back, it is the driver's responsibility to return the hitchhiker to the "border." Hitchers should walk across the border to avoid hassles.

A popular alternative to hitching the entire length of the Alaska Hwy. is to take the Marine Hwy. to Haines and hitch a ride from there with cars off the ferry. Often the competition in summer is heavy; it may be easier to remain on the ferry to Skagway, take a bus or train to Whitehorse in the Yukon, and hitch the Alaska Hwy. from there. Always carry extra money, food, and warm sleeping gear. The next town or ride could be days away.

Alaska Marine Highway

The Alaska Marine Highway consists of two *unconnected* ferry systems administered by one bureaucracy. The southeast system runs from Seattle up the coast to Skagway, stopping in Juneau, Ketchikan, Haines, and other towns. The southwest network serves Kodiak Island, Seward, Homer, and the Prince William Sound. Practically none of southeast Alaska (the Panhandle) is accessible by road; these areas can be reached only by plane or on the Marine Highway.

The full trip from Seattle to Skagway takes three days and costs $241 (ages 6-12 near ½-price, under 6 free). The route is vision-quenching, peppered with whales, bald eagles, and the majesty of the Inside Passage. (The *Love Boat's* Alaskan voyages took this trip.) All southeast ferries have free showers, cafes, lectures on history and ecology, and a heated top-deck "solarium" where cabinless passengers can sleep (bring a sleeping bag!). These ferries are a great way to travel. **Cabins** costs at least $175 from Seattle to Skagway, and are unnecessary—everyone, young and old, sleeps in the solarium. **Vehicles** up to 40 feet can be taken aboard (van from Juneau to Ketchikan costs $85). Spaces for vehicles are very limited; reservations are crucial and often necessary months in advance in summer. Cabinless passengers rarely need reservations, however.

The ferries in the southwest are more expensive and less plush than those in the southeast. They lack showers, the food is worse, and the solariums are smaller. They also ride the open sea, where navies of seasickness bugs love to rock your vessel to and fro.

The ferry schedule, a function of tides and other navigational exigencies, is a byzantine maze. Write ahead; for all schedules, rates, and information, contact Alaska Marine Highway, P.O. Box R, Juneau 99811 (907-465-3941 or 800-642-0066). On all ferries, senior citizens sail free if they travel standby (space is usually available). Disabled travelers can do so as well (permits are issued by mail).

Employment

Finding work in Alaska depends largely on being there, being energetic, and being persistent. Alaska's booms in construction, fishing, and lumber are not wholly fictitious. As more people head to the state each year in search of employment, however, jobs become harder to find. Summer is the best season for job hunting, as the state makes the most of good weather before winter closes many industries down. It is best to come with a return ticket in hand.

Cannery and fish processing jobs are currently the most popular forms of summer employment. Many processing plants in the southeast, on Kodiak Island, and in the Aleutians have long waiting lists. Nearly two-thirds of their employees are hired through company offices in Washington, Oregon, or California, but canneries that need help often have jobs on short notice. You can obtain a list of processors from the **Alaska Department of Fish and Game**, Division of Commercial Fisheries, P.O.

Box 3-200, Juneau 99802 (465-4210; open Mon.-Fri. 8am-4:30pm). Inquiries about the current employment outlook should be addressed to the **Alaska Department of Labor,** P.O. Box 1149, Juneau 99811 (465-4839; open Mon.-Fri. 8am-4:30pm).

To some, the continued popularity of cannery work is baffling. The work (gutting fish by hand) is difficult, boring, and unpleasant. Pay in July 1989 averaged $5.75 per hour, with time-and-a-half for overtime. Most workers do a great deal of over-time, thereby making better than average wages.

The job market for Fairbanks and the Interior differs greatly from the rest of the state. However, seasonal jobs are available. For more information, call and sign up with the **Private Industry Council** (456-5189; open Mon.-Thurs. 8am-noon and 1-4:30pm). Also, keep in mind Forestry Service jobs. Though usually low-paying, they are often easy to acquire, and the chance to see Alaska's wilderness makes them truly worthwhile.

Camping

The **U.S. Forest Service** maintains more than 178 **wilderness** log cabins for public use: 142 in **Tongass National Forest** in Southeastern Alaska, and 36 in **Chugach National Forest** in Southcentral Alaska. The cabins are scenic and well maintained. User permits are required along with a fee of $10 per party (no limit in size) per night. Reserve several months in advance. Most cabins have seven-day use limits, except hike-in cabins (3-day limit May-Aug.). Cabins sleep six, and are usually ac-cessible only by air, boat, or hiking trail. Facilities at these sites rarely include more than a wood stove and pit toilets. Some cabins provide skiffs (small boats). For maps or further information write to the U.S. Forest Service (see Tourist Information). For information about free cabins within wildlife ranges, contact the **U.S. Fish and Wildlife Service,** 1011 E. Tudor Rd., Anchorage 99504.

State-run campgrounds are always free. They usually offer toilets and drinking water, but no showers. For information on state campgrounds and waysides, contact the Alaska State Division of Parks (see Tourist Information).

Four **federal agencies** control and manage park lands in Alaska: the U.S. Forest Service (USFS), the Bureau of Land Management (BLM), the National Park Serv-ice, and the U.S. Fish and Wildlife Service. The USFS maintains numerous camp-grounds within the Chugach and Tongass National Forests (sites $4-5), and strictly enforces a 14-day maximum stay. The BLM runs about 20 campgrounds through-out the state, all free except the Delta BLM campground on the Alaska Highway. The National Park Service maintains campgrounds in Denali National Park, Gla-cier Bay National Park, and Katmai National Park and Preserve. Camping fees usually range from $4 to $6. The several campgrounds managed by the U.S. Fish and Wildlife Service are confined to the Kenai National Wildlife Refuge, P.O. Box 2139, Soldotna 99669. Government campgrounds in Alaska rarely have dump sta-tions or electrical hookups.

Remember to leave an itinerary at the offices of parks, hotels, state troopers, and guides. It is an important safety measure that takes little time to prepare.

For additional information about hiking and camping in Alaska, consult *Adven-turing in Alaska,* written by Peggy Wayburn and published by the Sierra Club. Suc-cessful hiking and camping adventures require advance planning. After reading about the area you plan to visit, stop by the Forest Service office in Anchorage (2525 Gampbell, #107) or chat with the local Forest Service employees.

Southcentral Alaska

The regions of southcentral Alaska—Anchorage, the Prince William Sound, the Kenai Peninsula, and Kodiak Island—are each separate and self-contained. What ties them together is a network of well-maintained roads, a rare convenience not to be taken lightly in the northland. The roads transform the area into one big market, keeping prices reasonably close to those in the Lower 48, and providing inexpensive travel for the adventurer.

The smooth roads do not (yet) steal from the area's rough beauty—towering snow-coated peaks, rivers teeming with fish, and a full bestiary of wildlife are all visible from just off the highway. After a spell in the great outdoors, Anchorage, Alaska's largest city by a factor of ten, provides all the usual satisfactions of American civilization.

In the tumultuous aftermath of the Exxon *Valdez* spill, the usually sleepy towns of Valdez and Cordova became 24-hour carnivals, rendering any coverage *Let's Go* could provide useless. Those interested in visiting the Prince William Sound should contact tourist offices beforehand, lest they be disposed of by errant cleanup crews.

Anchorage

Perhaps the most remarkable fact about Anchorage is that everything—the glass and steel of the buildings, the food and merchandise of the supermarkets and department stores—arrives here the same way people do: via 1500 miles of tortuous road, on an expensive air journey, or by barge or container ship across one of the roughest seas in the world. The city has an aroma of prefabrication—John McPhee has called it "condensed, instant Albequerque." "Los Anchorage," as some rural residents prefer to call it, is "big city" Alaska. Approximately half the state's population—some 250,000 people—live here. A decentered jumble of fast-food joints and discount liquor stores, Anchorage also boasts semi-professional baseball and basketball teams, frequent performances by internationally known orchestras and pop stars, dramatic theater, and opera. The *Anchorage Daily News* recently won a Pulitzer Prize for its reporting on suicide and alcoholism in the region.

Anchorage's history is something of an anomaly for Alaska: no one ever struck gold here, Baranof and the Russians didn't stop by, its location is not a natural travel hub. But the Federally-run Alaska Railroad's decision in 1914 to move its headquarters to a small rail camp turned Anchorage into the state's Grand Central Station. While Juneau remained the state's capital, Anchorage became the organizational hub and staging area for the massive buildup in Alaska by the national authorities during and after WWII. Today Anchorage's international airport is among the world's busiest, serving passengers en route to the Far East.

Downtown Anchorage, centered on 4th Avenue, was until recently a shady, red neon, adult bookstore district. But the state has hosed down the filth with a quick spray from the petrodollar hydrant. New Federal and state buildings pass aesthetic muster before even the most fastidious tourist. While the area between A St. and Fairbanks is still strewn with bars and pull-tab joints, it's difficult to maintain a nocturnal netherworld in a city where the night may last for as little as one hour.

Practical Information and Orientation

Visitor Information: Anchorage Convention and Visitors Bureau, 201 E. 3rd Ave. (276-4118). **Log Cabin Visitor Information Center,** W. 4th Ave. at F St. (274-3531). Open daily 7:30am-7pm; Oct.-April 8:30am-6pm. The Log Cabin is generally crammed with visitors and a staff of volunteers. Plenty of maps and brochures. The **All About Anchorage Line** (276-3200) runs a recorded listing of each day's events. For information on fine arts and dramatic performances, call the **Artsline** (276-2787). Smaller visitor information outlets are located in the airport's domestic terminal near the baggage claim, in the overseas terminal in the central atrium, and in the Valley River Mall, first level.

Alaska Public Lands Information Center, Old Federal Bldg. (271-2737), 4th Ave. between F and G. An astounding conglomeration of 8 state and Federal offices (including the **National Park Service, U.S. Forest Service, Division of State Parks,** and the **U.S. Fish and Wildlife Service**) under one roof provides the latest information on the entire state. Animal displays,

Anchorage

N ←

Orca St.
Nelchina St.
Latouche St.
Medfra St.
Karluk St.
Juneau St.
Ingra St.
Hyder St.
Gambell St.
Fairbanks St.
Eagle St.
Denali St.
Cordova St.
A St.
B St.
C St.
D St.
E St.
F St.
G St.
H St.
I St.
K St.
L St.
M St.
N St.
O St.
P St.

11th Ave.
12th Ave.
13th Ave.
14th Ave.
15th Ave.
16th Ave.

7th Ave.
8th Ave.
9th Ave.
10th Ave.

3rd Ave.
4th Ave.
5th Ave.
6th Ave.

Ship Creek Salmon Viewing Platform
Alaska Railroad Depot
Post Office
Log Cabin Visitor Center
YMCA
AYH Hostel
Bus Accommodation Center
Anchorage Museum of History and Art
Delaney Park Strip

computerized sportfish map, and an interactive trip-planning video unit. Films daily at 12:15 and 3:30pm or upon request. Open daily 9am-8pm.

Alaska Railroad: 2nd Ave. (265-2494), at the head of town. To Denali ($62), Fairbanks ($88), Seward ($35), and Whittier ($27.50). Ten-day unlimited mileage railpass $209. For more information write to Passenger Service, P.O. Box 107500, Anchorage 99510. Office open daily 8am-8pm; may be closed if no trains are arriving.

Alaska Marine Highway: 333 W. 4th St. (272-4482), in the Post Office Mall. No terminal, but ferry tickets and reservations. Open Mon.-Fri. 8am-5pm.

People Mover Bus: 343-6543, in the Transit Center, on 6th St. between G and H. Buses leave from here to all points in the Anchorage Bowl 5am-midnight. Cash fare 85¢, tokens 75¢ (the hostel sells them for 60¢). The Transit Center office is open Mon.-Fri. 9am-5pm.

Taxi: Yellow Cab, 272-2422. **Checker Cab,** 276-1234.

Airport Limousine: ACE Limo Bus Service, 694-6484. Service from the airport to downtown $5.

Car Rentals: Rent-a-Dent, 512 W. International Airport Rd. (561-0350), at the airport. $25 per day with 50 free miles, 20¢ each additional mile. Open daily 7am-11pm.

Road Conditions: 243-7675.

Bicycle Rental: at the **Clarion Hotel** (243-2300), on Spenard just east of Minnesota. Close to the Coastal Bike Trail. $5 for 2 hr., $10 for 4 hr., $15 for 8 hr. **Scooters** are available in front of the Federal Bldg. $10 per hr. 8-11am and 1-7pm, $7 per hr. 11am-1pm.

Weather: 936-2525. **Motorists Forecast:** 936-2626. **Marine Weather Forecast:** 936-2727.

Camping Equipment: Recreational Equipment, Inc. (REI), 2710 Spenard (272-4565), at Minnesota. Bus #60. High-quality equipment including packs, clothing, tents, stores, and dried food. Open Mon.-Fri. 10am-9pm, Sat. 9:30am-6pm, Sun. noon-5pm. The **Army-Navy Store,** on 4th Ave. across from the Post Office Mall, offers even lower prices. Open daily 10am-7pm.

Laundromat: K-Speed Wash, 600 E. 6th St. (264-2631). Take bus #60 or 3. Open Mon.-Sat. 9am-10pm.

Crisis Line: 276-1600. 24-hour hotline with referral services. **Rape Crisis:** 276-7273.

Visitor Language Assistance: 276-4118 or 274-3531. Preprogrammed assistance in languages from Laotian to Finnish. Anchorage also shelters **consulates** from most Western European countries and Japan.

Handicap Access Line: Challenge Alaska, 563-2658. The Log Cabin (see above) is equipped with a TTY for the communicatively disabled.

Hospital: Humana, 2801 De Darr (276-1131).

Emergency: 911.

Post Office: W. 4th Ave. and C St. (277-6568), on the lower level in the mall. Open Mon.-Fri. 10:30am-5pm, Sat. 9am-3pm. General Delivery ZIP Code: 99510. The state's central post office is located next to the international airport. It does not handle general delivery mail, but is open 24 hours.

Area Code: 907.

Anchorage dominates the southcentral region of Alaska from its perch 114 miles north of Seward on the Seward Hwy., 304 miles west of Valdez on the Glenn and Richardson Hwy., and 358 miles south of Fairbanks on the George Parks Hwy. It is due north of Honolulu, and equidistant from Atlanta and Tokyo.

Anchorage can be reached by road, rail, or air. **Anchorage International Airport,** a few miles southwest of downtown off International Airport Rd., is served by all the Alaska airlines, as well as by major American and international airlines. The People Mover Bus runs only three times per day from the airport to downtown, but the visitors center near the baggage claim can direct you a short distance from the terminal to more frequent routes. Airporter vans run incessantly to downtown ($5); a cab ride will set you back about $13.

The downtown area of Anchorage is laid out in a regular grid pattern. Numbered avenues run east-west, and addresses are designated East or West from **C Street.** North-south streets are lettered alphabetically west of **A Street,** and named alphabetically east of A Street. The rest of Anchorage is spread out along the major highways. The **University of Alaska-Anchorage** campus lies on 36th Ave. off Northern Lights Blvd.

Accommodations

Although Anchorage is blessed many times over with affordable lodgings, few Good Samaritans built their inns downtown. The best bet is, as usual, the hostel. Several bed and breakfast referral agencies operate out of Anchorage. Try **Alaska Private Lodgings,** 1236 W. 10th Ave., Anchorage 99511 (258-1717), or **Stay With a Friend,** P.O. Box 173, 3605 Arctic Blvd., Anchorage 99503 (344-4006). Both can refer you to singles from $45 and doubles from $55.

Anchorage Youth Hostel (AYH), 700 H St. (276-3635), 1 block south of the Transit Center downtown. Excellent location, clean rooms, common areas, kitchens, showers, and laundry. Large enough to offer family rooms and hardly ever be full. Lockout 9am-5pm. Members $10, nonmembers $13. Not to be confused with the Alyeska Youth Hostel, and certainly not to be confused *or* associated with the Dog Patch Hostel.

Alyeska Youth Hostel, P.O. Box 10-4099, Anchorage 99510 (783-2099 or 277-7388). Rustic 6-bed hostel near a ski slope. Members $8, nonmembers $11. Reservations required.

Green Bough Bed and Breakfast, 3832 Young St. (562-4636). Take bus #93 from the airport. The only independent B&B in Anchorage, Green Bough has clean rooms and a casual, family atmosphere. Three rooms share 2 baths. Singles $40, with king-sized bed $50.

Heart of Anchorage Bed and Breakfast, 725 K St. (279-7066 or 279-7703), at 8th. Intimate house with amusing decor. Dorm beds $15. Singles $35. Doubles $40. Call ahead for reservations.

Midtown Hotel, 604 W. 26th (258-7778), off Arctic Blvd. Cheap prices attract long-term residents. All rooms share baths. Singles $24-28. Doubles $32.

Samovar Inn, 720 Gambell (277-1511), at 7th. Plush rooms equipped with jacuzzi-style bathtubs. King-sized doubles only $67.50.

Northern Lights Thrift Apartments, 606 Northern Lights (561-3005). The clean rooms are not much bigger than the queen-sized beds. Singles and doubles $27.90.

Arctic Inn Motel, 842 W. International Airport Rd. (561-1328), at Arctic Ave. Not particularly exciting, but a free taxi runs the mile between motel and airport. Family-run, with a home-style restaurant and bar. Singles $40. Doubles $48. Two-room family suites with kitchen $54.

Anchor Arms Motel, 433 Eagle St. (272-9619), near the 4th Ave. strip (the bad part of downtown). Gray exterior heralds comfortable rooms, all with kitchen and bath. Singles $55.

Camping

The two camping areas within the city are both suitable for tents and RVs. Many free campgrounds lie just outside the city limits, maintained by the State Division of Parks and Outdoor Recreation. These campgrounds have some of the state's best sites, including water and toilets. Most sites lie off the highway along dirt roads, but the rough ride is rewarded by untouched scenery. Bring your own food and supplies. Among the best of the state campgrounds are **Eagle River** and **Eklutna** (EE-cloot-nah), which are (respectively) 12.6 miles and 26.5 miles south of Anchorage along Glenn Hwy. For more information on these and other campsites, contact the Alaska Division of Parks, 3601 C St., 10th Floor, Pouch 7-001, Anchorage 99510 (561-2020), or the Anchorage Parks and Recreation Dept., 2525 Gambell St., #404 (271-2500).

Centennial Park, 8300 Glenn Hwy. (333-9711), north of town off Muldoon Rd.; look for the park sign. Take People Mover Bus #3 or 75 from downtown. Facilities for tents and

RVs. Showers, dumpsters, fireplaces, pay phones, and water. 7-day max. stay. Check-in before 6pm in peak summer season. Sites $12, senior citizens $8.

Lions' Camper Park, 5800 Boniface Pkwy. (333-1495), south of the Glenn Hwy. In Russian Jack Springs Park next to the Municipal Greenhouse; 4 blocks from the Boniface Mall. Take People Mover Bus #12 or 45 to the mall and walk. Connected to the city's bike trail system. 10 primitive campsites with water station, fire rings, and showers. Self-contained vehicles only. 7-day max. stay. Sites $12. Open May-Sept. daily 10am-10pm.

John's RV Park, 3543 Mt. View Dr. (277-4332). Only 2 miles from downtown. Full hookups $16.75.

Food

By virtue of its size and largely imported population, Anchorage is a culinary coat of many colors. Within blocks of each other stand greasy spoons, Chinese restaurants, and classy hotel-top French eateries. Alaskan sourdough and seafood—halibut, salmon, clams, crab, and snapper—are often served in huge portions. The city's finer restaurants line the hills overlooking Cook Inlet and the Alaska Range. The closest grocery to the hostel is the **Family Market,** 1301 I St., at 13th Ave. (272-4722; open Mon.-Sat. 7am-10pm, Sun. 8am-6pm).

The White Spot, A St. and 4th Ave. Lenore has been singlehandedly slinging the hash and burgers since '59. Eggs, hashbrowns, toast, and coffee $2.25. Open daily 7am-7pm.

Blondie's Cafe (279-0898), on D between 4th and 5th. Jazzy atmosphere with poor ventilation. Reuben sandwich more successful than Debbie Harry's solo career (and at $6.50, cheaper than an album). Open daily 11am-8pm.

Skipper's, at 5 locations: 3960 W. Dimond Blvd. (248-3165), 702 E. Benson Blvd. (276-1181), 5668 DeBarr Rd. (333-4832), 601 E. Dimond Blvd. (349-8214), and 3611 Minnesota Dr. (563-3656). Skipper's all-you-can-eat specials guaranteed to stuff the hungriest of sailors. Only $5.29 for all the fishfries, chowder, and cole slaw you can ram down your gullet (with shrimp $8). Open daily 11am-11pm.

Burger Jim's, 704 4th St. (277-4386), at Gampbell. Jim takes his work seriously. Burger, fries, and a coke $3. Open Mon.-Sat. 10am-8:30pm.

Wing and Things, 529 I St. (277-9464), at 5th. Unbelievably delicious BBQ chicken wings. Decorated with wing memorabilia and inspirational poetry. Nobody should pass through Anchorage without an airfoot. Ten wings, celery, sauce $6. Open daily 10am-9pm.

Sack's Cafe, 625 *5th Ave.* (274-3546). Best vegetarian food in the state sold for designer prices. Avocado, marinated Swiss, and red onion sandwich with soup $8.

Cyrano's Book Store and Cafe (274-2599), on D between 4th and 5th. Come here to ghostwrite love letters and rest your nose. Classical music, a current *Wall Street Journal*, tall glass of lemonade, and an excellent cup of chicken gumbo $5. Sat. night is open mike nite. The best book store in the state proves that Anchorage has come a long way since the days remembered by author John McPhee when books were sold for 47¢ per lb. Open Sun.-Thurs. 11am-9pm, Sat. 11am-2am.

Downtown Deli, 525 W. 4th Ave. (274-0027), across the street from the Log Cabin visitors center. Slightly more elegant and expensive (entrees $5-9) than your basic Lower 48 deli. Owned by Anchorage's former mayor, Tony Knowles. Open daily 6am-10pm.

Old Anchorage Salmon Bake, 251 K St. (279-8790), in the Bluff at 3rd and K. $17 buys an all-you-can-eat dinner of salmon, halibut, reindeer sausage, and crab legs, plus salad, beans, and sourdough rolls. Smaller, *cheechako* meals also available. Salmon and all-you-can-eat salad $13. Lunch includes salad bar and beans with such orders as the salmon burger ($6.25) or reindeer dog ($5.50). Open May-Sept. daily 11am-2pm and 4-10pm.

Simon and Seafort's Salon and Grill, 420 L St. (274-3502). Down a few beers and a bowl of great clam chowder ($3.50) in the salon. Prices are steep (dinner $12-20), but the incredible view of Cook Inlet and delectable seafood and pasta keep people flocking in. Open Mon.-Fri. 11:15am-2:30pm and 5-10:30pm, Sat. noon-2:30pm and 5-10:30pm, Sun. 5-10:30pm. Salon open daily 11:30am-11:30pm. Reservations recommended.

Kumagoro Restaurant, 531 4th St. (272-9005). The combination of Alaskan fish and Japanese efficiency results in an excellent, reasonably priced sushi restaurant. *Sashimi* combo $14.80. Open daily 9am-10pm.

Thai Cuisine, 444 H St. (277-8424). Typical Thai fare in a cozy environment. Huge bowl of soup $4. Open Mon.-Sat. 11am-10pm, Sun. 5-10pm.

Sights and Seasonal Events

Watching over Anchorage from Cook Inlet is **Mount Susitna,** known to locals as the "Sleeping Lady." For a fabulous view of Susitna, as well as of the other mountains that tower over Anchorage's ever-growing skyline, drive out to **Earthquake Park** at the end of Northern Lights Blvd. Once a fashionable neighborhood, the park now memorializes the disastrous effects of the Good Friday earthquake in 1964, a day Alaskans refer to as "Black Friday." Registering at 8.6 on the old Richter scale (9.2 on the current scale), it was the strongest earthquake ever recorded in North America. On a clear day, you'll even be able to see **Mt. McKinley** far to the north. Or just take a walk downtown—head toward the water on 9th Ave., cross the railroad tracks, and stroll along the gray sand. Glacial silt feeds into Cook Inlet from the **Matanuska Glacier** north of Anchorage, turning the water a murky gray.

A four-hour walking tour of downtown begins at the visitors center. Interesting street-corner signs describe the history of the locale, and the tour can be followed in smaller segments as one wanders about downtown. For guided walking tours, contact **Historic Anchorage Inc.,** 542 W. 4th Ave. (562-6100, ext. 338), on the second floor of the Old City Hall. Tours leave Monday through Friday at 10am ($2, senior citizens $1). The People Mover sponsors less strenuous jaunts. Hop on one of the double-decker buses downtown for a $1 ride through the area. **Alaska City Tours** (276-7431) offers more complete bus tours of the Anchorage Bowl, leaving daily at 9am, 1pm, and 4pm. (3-hr. tours $14.50, senior citizens $14, children—4pm tour only—$7.) Look for the booth next to the visitors center.

Downtown Anchorage swarms with public and private museums. The best is the **Anchorage Museum of History and Art,** 121 W. 7th Ave. (264-4326), on the corner of 7th Ave. and A St. The museum features permanent exhibits of Alaskan Native artifacts and art, as well as a Thursday night Alaska wilderness film series (7pm). (Open Mon.-Sat. 10am-6pm, Sun. 1-5pm; Sept.-May Tues.-Sat. 10am-6pm, Sun. 1-5pm. Admission $3.) The **Office of Public Lands** (see Practical Information) has many displays on the use and abuse of Alaska's land, and screens free wildlife films every two hours starting at 10am. The **Alaska Wildlife Museum,** 844 W. 5th St. (274-1600), has informative if uninnovative displays on the wildlife of Alaska and charges a steep $5. (Open daily 9am-9pm.) Your museum dollar may be better spent at the **Imaginarium,** 725 5th Ave. (276-3179), a hands-on "science-discovery center" recreating aurora borealis, glacier formation, and other scientific oddities of the north. (Open Mon.-Sat. 10am-6pm. Admission $4, ages under 12 $3.) The more visually minded can check out the **Visual Arts Center,** 5th and G St. (274-9641), which showcases the best Alaskan artists residing north of Homer. (Open Mon.-Sat. 10am-6pm. Admission $1.) The menacing black-glass **Arco Tower** (263-4545), on G between 6th and 7th, the tallest building in Alaska, is a metaphor for our time, showing oppressively propagandist films on Alaskan industry in the lobby and maintaining a quiet art gallery in the tower. Artists present their work on weekdays at 2 and 3pm. (Free.) The **Heritage Library** (276-1132), in the National Bank of Alaska Office Bldg. at Northern Lights Blvd. and C St., contains a display of rare books and Native artifacts. (Open Mon.-Fri. 1-4pm. Free.)

If you wish to see real Alaskan wildlife in the comfort of an urban setting, visit the **Alaska Zoo,** Mile 2 on O'Malley Rd. (346-3242) where you can say hi to Binky the Bear and other orphaned Alaskan beasts. (Open daily 10am-6pm. Admission $3.50, senior citizens and ages 13-18 $2.50, under 13 $1.50.) **Star the Reindeer** lives in a fenced-in courtyard closer to downtown on 10th and I. He has paced this tiny plot for 25 years, becoming something of an Anchorage celebrity in the process. You can feed him carrots if you so wish.

Shopping

If you want to shop where the air literally reeks of authenticity, head to the close confines of the nonprofit gift shop at the **Alaska Native Medical Center,** 3rd and Gampbell. Because many Natives pay for medical services with their own arts and handicrafts, the Alaska State Museum in Juneau sent its buyers here last year to improve its exhibitions. Walrus bone *ulus* (knives used by Natives; $15-60), fur moccasins, Eskimo parkas, and dolls highlight the selection. (Open Mon.-Fri. 10am-2pm.) There are also several somewhat tamer shops downtown. **David Green Master Furrier,** 130 W. 4th Ave. or 423 W. 5th Ave. (277-9595), features parkas and other fur garments stripped from the backs of Alaskan animals. The merchandise is expensive but tours are free; call ahead. (Open daily 9am-6pm.) The **Fur Factory,** 120 E. 5th Ave. (277-8414), just across the street, offers to make small garments while you wait. Pick out the smoothest fur and best colors you can find, stroll downtown for an hour, then come back to claim the softest, warmest, least expensive slippers on the block ($35).

Craftworks from Alaska's Bush country, similar to those on display at the Museum of History and Art, are sold at the **Alaska Native Arts and Crafts Showroom,** 333 W. 4th Ave. (274-2932). Birch baskets start at $10, beadwork and other jewelry at $20, ivory carvings at $30. (Open Mon.-Fri. 10am-6pm, Sat. 10am-5pm.) Many Native Alaskan handicrafts are born at the **Gingham House,** corner of K St. and 6th Ave., where local craftsmen carve ivory, weave baskets, and work on animal skins. (Open Mon.-Sat. 10am-4pm.) **Bering Sea Originals,** in Dimond Mall, 800 E. Dimond Blvd. (349-3322), and in Northway Mall, 3101 Penland Pkwy. (274-7126), features all sorts of Native Alaskan handicrafts. *Ulus* start at $10 and ivory carvings at $25. (Both locations open daily 10am-9pm.)

Entertainment and Seasonal Events

Alaska's best-known show is also its most touristy: frantic **Larry Beck** acts out and reads the poems of Robert Service every night in the summer at 5:30 and 8pm in the Egan Court, 555 5th Ave. (278-3831 for reservations; 8pm show $12; 5:30pm show $25, includes dinner). More exciting and less expensive is the **Alaska Experience Theater,** 705 W. 6th Ave. (276-3730), where brown bears and Native dances come alive on the inner surface of a hemispherical dome. (The 40-min. film shows hourly Sun.-Thurs. noon-8pm, Fri.-Sat. noon-9pm. Admission $6, children $4.) Yearning for a touch of Arctic Broadway? The **4th Avenue Theatre,** 628 4th Ave., 1 block west of the Log Cabin visitors center and 5000 miles west of New York City, offers summer shows such as *West Side Story.*

Anchorageans of all shapes and incomes party at **Chilkoot Charlie's,** 2435 Spenard Rd. (272-1010), at Fireweed. The bar has a rocking dance floor and a quiet lounge. Ask about the nightly drink specials; otherwise you'll end up paying an outrageous amount to subsidize those who *do* ask. That's why Chilkoot Charlie's motto is "We screw the other guy and pass the savings on to you!" Take bus #7 or 60. Less crowded and more interesting is **Mr. Whitekey's Fly-by-Night Club,** 3300 Spenard Rd. (279-7726), a "sleazy bar serving everything from the world's finest champagnes to a damn fine plate of Spam." The Pythonesque house special gives you anything with Spam at half-price when you order champagne (free with Dom Perignon). Try Spam nachos or Spam and cream cheese on a bagel ($2-6). Nightly entertainment ranges from rock to jazz to blues. (Open 3pm-2:30am.) The Midnight Express, 2612 Spenard Rd. (279-1861), hosts rock-and-roll bands Tuesday though Saturday; music starts at 9pm. (Open Sun.-Thurs. 10am-2:30am, Fri.-Sat. 10am-3am.) Downtown bars get nastier around C St., but the **Frontier Club** on 4th and H St. is quiet, inexpensive, and filled with talkative, cribbage-playing Alaskans.

For more spontaneous entertainment, watch for annual events celebrated Alaska-style. Call the **event hotline** (276-3200) to see what's coming up. The **Campbell Creek Classic** in early June is, according to the visitors bureau, a "zany race covering approximately 4 miles . . . on almost anything that floats." The longest day of the year (June 21) brings dancing to the streets and runners from all over the world to the inspirational **Mayor's Marathon.** The **Iditarod Race,** a grueling 1049-mile sled dog competition traversing two mountain ranges, 150 miles of the Yukon River, and the ice pack of the Norton Sound, begins in Anchorage on the first weekend in March. Twelve to 18 days later, the winner arrives in Nome. The tortuous route commemorates the heroic journey of mushers who carried serum to halt Nome's diptheria epidemic in Anchorage's early days. The **Fur Rendezvous,** held the second week of February, is a reminder of the days when fur trappers gathered to whoop it up. Today, affectionately referred to as "Fur Rondy," it includes the world sled dog championship races, a grand prix, and snowshoe softball games.

Near Anchorage: South

Driving south on the Seward Hwy. one follows the **Turnagain Arm** of the Cook Inlet. Miles of the arm are uncovered at low tide only to be buried under 10-ft. high "bores," waves created by the 15mph riptide. Fifteen miles down the arm sits the **Potter Section House Historical Site** (345-2631), the last standing original road-house for the Alaska Railroad. The site now houses a ranger station for Chugach National Forest and a small railroad museum. (Open daily 9am-6pm.) Off of Seward Hwy. (follow the ubiquitous signs) lies the **Alyeska Ski Resort,** site (the faithful fervently hope) of the 1994 or 1998 Winter Olympics. The resort is open November to April for skiing, and June 14 to September 14 from 10:30am to 5pm for sight-seeing chairlift rides ($10, children $5, 4-person family ticket $25). While in Al-yeska, stay at the **Alyeska International Youth Hostel (AYH)** (see Anchorage Acco-modations). Turn left onto Alyeska Blvd. off Seward Hwy., right on Timberline, then right on Alpina.

Just up Crow Creek Rd. is **Erickson's Mine,** a national historic site with eight original buildings and an active gold mine run by New Yorker Cynthia Toohey and her children. (Admission $4 for goldpanners, $2 for sight-seers.) The strike here predates even the Klondike and Fairbanks strikes, and the site is not a reconstruc-tion. Campsites are available for $5. As you leave Crow Creek Rd., stop in at the **Double Muskie** (783-2822), set back from the road in the trees. The "Muskie" has gained a reputation as the best restaurant in Alaska. If you can't swing dinner ($14-25), just treat yourself to a dessert or a drink. Try the Muskie Pie. (Open Tues.-Thurs. 5-11pm, Fri.-Sun. 4-11pm.)

Portage Valley

Four roadside glaciers lounge over the Portage Valley, grinding channels through the earth in an ice-age-old tradition. As the glaciers gradually recede, frozen chunks fall into Portage Lake, leaving huge blue icebergs within a stone's throw of shore. Perched on the lakeside, the **Begich, Boggs Visitors Center** boasts the strangest name and most modern displays of any Alaskan information outlet. The center's exhaustive glacial exhibitions and historical movie ($1) attract plenty of visitors. (Open daily 9am-6pm.) Take the 5-mile (10-min.) detour off Seward Hwy., south of Alyeska along the well-paved Portage Highway.

Three state-run campgrounds on Portage Hwy. have excellent sites with pan-oramic glacial views (sites $5). **Beaver Pond, Black Bear,** and **Williwaw** all provide water and toilets; Williwaw also features a short hiking trail and a viewing ledge overlooking salmon-spawning areas (salmon season late July-Aug.). Beside the visi-tors center is the **Portage Lodge,** a gift shop/restaurant that breaks no new ground for originality or bargains (open until 6pm); bring your own food into the valley. Trained naturalists introduce travelers to the few easy hiking trails that begin from the visitors center. For more information on the hikes and trails, call the **Anchorage Ranger District Office** (345-5700), or write to Chugach National Forest, Anchorage Ranger District, 201 E. 9th Ave., #206, Anchorage 99501 (271-2500).

Portage is 45 minutes from downtown Anchorage by car along Seward Hwy. Hitchhiking is easy (see Kenai Peninsula for tips). Every tour group and its mother runs day trips to Portage. The cheapest may be the one given by Alaska Intercity Lines ($45), headquartered in the Alaska Wildlife Museum (see Anchorage Sights).

Whittier

Whittier plays Piraeus to Anchorage's Athens. In other words, Whittier is a place Anchorageans go only in order to go somewhere else, usually the Prince William Sound. Whittier's main attraction is **Begich Tower,** a building unremarkable save for the fact that 95% of Whittier's populace lives, eats, works, shops, criticizes, and otherwise exists therein. Whittier musters a **visitors center** (472-2379) in the railcar next to the ferry terminal. The slight **museum** in Begich Tower features a collection of bottles. The **post office** is also in Begich Tower, as is the expensive **grocery store.**

Whittier has two hotels. The **Sportsman Inn** offers a four-person room *sans* floorboards for only $45. The **Anchor Inn** provides smaller, just as ramshackle rooms for the same price. The Anchor has a better restaurant, however.

Anchorage is accessible from Whittier via the **Alaska Railroad** (472-2379) to Portage. There is no terminal—just get on and pay on board ($7.50 to Portage). A bus to Anchorage meets the Portage train ($17.50). The train leaves Whittier Thurs.-Mon. every three hours from 6:30am until 6:30pm. Tues. and Wed. the train leaves at noon, 3, 6, and 9pm. The **ferry terminal** in Whittier is unmanned except for just before departures. Check times and buy tickets in Anchorage (see Anchorage Practical Information).

Easily accessible from Whittier, the 5-mile-wide **Columbia Glacier** rises hundreds of feet above the waters of the Prince William Sound, jutting into 440 square miles of ocean. Because the glacier is observable only by boat, glorious yachts frequently cruise by the glacier's face, their passengers sipping champagne. But more proletarian cruises can be just as enjoyable; giant icebergs still calve the ice wall and seals still frolic on the glacier's icy bed.

The least expensive way to navigate the treacherous waters for a view comes from the decks of the M.V. *Bartlett* (in Valdez 835-4436). The state ferry takes time off from its run between Valdez and Whittier ($24 each way) for an impromptu tour of the glacier's face. Closer trips to the glacier are offered by numerous sight-seeing tour companies; none is much cheaper than $50. **Glacier Charter Service,** on Kobuk St. in Valdez (835-5141), has six-hour tours, lunch included, for $45 per person with a two person minimum. (Free RV parking.) For those who want the luxury yacht with all the trimmings, contact **Alaska Sightseeing Tours,** 349 Wrangell Ave., Anchorage 99501 (276-1305). Round-trip from Anchorage to Valdez aboard the M.V. *Glacier Seas* with food, champagne, and an overnight stay in Valdez runs about $250; a daytrip goes for over $65.

Near Anchorage: North

To counteract urban claustrophobia, head for the summit of **Flattop Mountain** in the Chugach Range near Anchorage. The excellent view of the city and (if it's clear) sunsoaked Mt. McKinley is well worth the hour-long hike. When climbing, watch out for bears—they're after the same luscious blueberries you are. If Flattop can't satisfy your craving for wilderness, head for **Chugach State Park,** which covers 495,000 acres east and south of the city. The **Eagle River Visitors Center** (694-2108) is at Mile 12.7 on Eagle River Rd., off Glenn Hwy. The wildlife displays, hiking trails, and other facilities are spellbinding. (Open Fri.-Mon. 11am-7pm; in winter Fri.-Sun. 10am-6pm.)

Due north is **Matanuska Valley,** an area settled by Scandinavian farmers in 1935 as part of a New Deal program. President Roosevelt wanted to transplant families from the depressed Midwest to experiment with agriculture in Alaska. The idea was never popular enough to create the exodus that Roosevelt hoped for, but the experimentation did result in something the President never dreamed of—the birth of 75-pound cabbages. Long summer daylight turns garden-variety vegetables into mastadon-sized meals. Fist-sized strawberries are popular as snacks. In summer, fresh produce is available from roadside stands along Glenn Hwy. between its junction with George Parks Hwy. and the town of Wasilla.

Perhaps the valley's biggest event is the **Alaska State Fair,** on the fairgrounds at Mile 40.2 on Glenn Hwy. This 11-day event, ending on Labor Day, includes parades, rodeos, livestock, and agricultural exhibits starring the aforementioned cabbages. (Open daily 10am-10pm. Admission $6, senior citizens $2, ages under 13 $1.)

But wait—there's more to the Matanuska than cabbages borrowed from the set of *Sleeper.* The **Knik Museum and Mushers Hall of Fame,** at Mile 14 on Knik Rd., features mushing memorabilia and famous dog sleds in its Canine Hall of Fame. Remember the pleasant days when dog sleds carried medical supplies across miles of subfrozen ($-40°F$) tundra. (Open June 15-Sept. 15 Wed.-Sat. 11am-5pm, Sun. 1-6pm. Call Vi Reddington at 376-5562 for visits at other times.) Twenty-two miles from downtown Wasilla, **Independence Mine State Historic Park** (745-5897), in Hatcher Pass, features hiking, hang gliding, fishing, restored mine buildings, and a lodge. Take either Glenn Hwy. to Mile 50 and the Fishhook-Willow Rd. to the park, or Parks Hwy. to Mile 71, Fishhook-Willow Rd.'s other end.

Camping, lodging, canoeing, fishing, and more can be found at **Big Lake** (Mile 52 on Parks Hwy.) and **Nancy Lake** (Mile 67.5 on Parks Hwy.). Or try a whitewater adventure on the lower **Matanuska River** for as little as $40. (Call collect 745-5753, or write NOVA, P.O. Box 1129, Chickaloon 99674.) Check *The Milepost* for an extensive list of hunting and fishing lodges and campgrounds in the area.

Torrents of brochures will entreat you to join hunting expeditions, river floats, sea-plane excursions, or combinations of all three. **Ketchum Air** (243-5525), the most persistently advertised, charges $120-1000 for custom-tailored adventures. But NOVA (745-5753) and other companies can toss you about in the whitewater for $50.

Palmer

Palmer has long been the major educational and commercial center south of Anchorage—extraordinary, considering that it is actually located to the north of Anchorage. Learn more about its history at the **visitors center** (745-2880), a log cabin downtown, across the railroad tracks on South Valley Way at E. Fireweed Ave. (Open May-Sept. daily 9am-6pm.) The **Alaska Historical and Transportation Museum,** at Mile 40.2 on Glenn Hwy. (745-4493), is only a mile from the town center. The museum features implements from the loggers, miners, fishermen, and farmers of Alaska's past. (Open daily 8am-4pm. Admission $3, ages under 12 $1.50.) For a closer gander at Alaska's modern agriculture, tour the dairy facilities and gardens of the **University of Alaska Experiment Station** (745-3257), on Trunk Rd., ½ mile north of the junction of Glenn and Parks Hwy. (Tours June-Aug. daily.)

A few miles off Parks Hwy. on Hatcher Pass Rd. lies the world's only domesticated **Musk-Ox Farm.** Neither relatives of oxen nor reservoirs of musk, these beasts are very hairy nephews of the buffalo. Natives weave their hair into scarves and hats. Huzzahs the Wasilla visitors center: "Musk-oxen love to have fun. They even play soccer." You be the judge.

Sleep to the distant moans of roaming musk-oxen at the **Denali Park Campground,** on Denali St. off Arctic Ave. near the visitors center. The state-run park has 100 spots, sewage disposal facilities, and showers for a nominal fee.

Wasilla

Taste a chunk of "real Alaska" down the road in Susitna Valley, between Wasilla and Lucille Lakes. Wasilla, which means "breath of air," shares Palmer's agricultural heritage. Despite its location only 42 miles north of Anchorage on the Parks Hwy., the town lives in the wild outback of rough frontier days—recalled by the nearby Dog Musher's Hall of Fame. If you want to mush for real, call **Mush Alaska,** P.O. Box 871752, Wasilla 99687 (376-4743). Half-hour excursions start at $15 per person.

Take in the **Wasilla Museum** (376-2005) and the town's **visitors center,** on Main St. off the Parks Hwy. Behind the museum is **Frontier Village,** complete with Wasilla's first school, sauna, and ferris wheel. (Open daily 10am-6pm. Admission $1, ages under 13 free.)

Anchorage's **Stay-With-A-Friend B&B** (344-4006) projects its sphere of influence north to Wasilla. Singles start at $40, doubles $50. Campers should continue south toward Anchorage for another 13 miles to **Eklutna Campground,** a state-run spot with free water and toilets. For more information on the area, contact the **Wasilla Chamber of Commerce,** P.O. Box 871826, 1801 Parks Hwy., #A-8, Wasilla 99687 (376-1299).

Kenai Peninsula

Life on the Kenai Peninsula has always been as rough as the Alaskan terrain. For centuries, the Kenaitze tribe fed off the land for fish and wild game. In the late 1700s, seeing a chance to profit from the sources of Kenaitze subsistence, Russian fur trappers established some of Alaska's first white settlements here. Their zest for capturing the coveted sea otters nearly drove the animal to extinction by the mid-19th century, depleting the area's wildlife population and decreasing the peninsula's value as a trapper's paradise. The United States arrived in 1867, and salmon fishermen rapidly replaced the fur traders. Today the peninsula's fabulous fishing remains—nearly 40% of Alaska's sport fishing is done in the Kenai's lakes and rivers. Energetic stocking programs conducted by the U.S. Fish and Wildlife Service ensure that the Kenai's waterways will teem with salmon for years to come. The Kenai Peninsula still shows vestiges of its colorful history. Many of the original Native American and Russian names remain, as well as old Russian Orthodox log churches. And the Kenai Peninsula's residents still depend on the region's natural resources for their livelihood.

The **Seward-Anchorage Highway** to the Kenai Peninsula winds south from Anchorage along the Turnagain Arm and the Chugach Mountains, which rise 12,000 feet straight up from Cook Inlet. The two forks of the highway terminate at Seward and Homer, small fishing communities of exceptional beauty. On the way to Homer the road passes Kenai (site of one of Alaska's first oil discoveries), and the small towns of Soldotna, Clam Gulch, and Ninilchik. Across Kachemak Bay from Homer sits Seldovia, site of an old Russian church. **Hitching** from Anchorage is no problem in summer, especially on weekends. Take bus #9 from Anchorage as far south as it will go and ask the driver to point you the ¼-mile to the Seward-Anchorage Hwy.; from there, motorists are often willing to help. The peninsula's rivers and inlets afford fabulous fishing opportunities. If you plan to fish, make sure to ask locals for tips—everyone's an expert. They know where the fish are and how to catch them.

The Kenai is where Alaskans vacation, especially those from Anchorage and the Interior. They avoid all the towns save Homer. You'll find a state park or USFS campground—such as those at Bird and Quartz Creeks—about every 8 miles along the highway. Freshwater streams are also common along the highway and throughout the peninsula, but in summer most are crowded. Good camping can be found outside designated areas. There are great spots hidden in the brush near every town. **Showers** are available near most harbors for a minimal fee; check with the harbormaster. For more information on hiking, hunting, fishing, camping, and other recreational opportunities, as well as regulations, contact the following: **Kenai Fjords National Park** (see Seward); **Alaska Maritime National Wildlife Refuge** (see Homer); **Kenai National Wildlife Refuge** (see Soldotna); **Chugach National Forest,** 201 E. 9th Ave., #206, Anchorage 99501 (261-2500); **State of Alaska, Division of Parks and Outdoor Recreation,** P.O. Box 1247, Soldotna 99669 (262-5581); and **State of Alaska, Department of Fish and Game,** P.O. Box 3150, Soldotna 99669 (262-9368).

Kenai

Kenai (KEE-ny), the second oldest white settlement in Alaska, is the largest and oldest such settlement on the peninsula. First a Native community, it became a Russian village with the builiding of Fort St. Nicholas in 1791, and then an American garrison when the U.S. Army built Fort Kenay in 1889. Kenai finally became known as the "Oil Capital of Alaska" with the 1957 discovery of oil in Cook Inlet. Vestiges of each era are scattered throughout town: native artifacts, a Russian Orthodox church, an American military installation, and oil rigs stationed in the inlet.

Practical Information and Orientation

Visitor Information: Chamber of Commerce and **Visitors Center** (283-7989), in "Moosemeat John" Hedburg's Cabin at the corner of Main St. and Kenai Spur Rd., behind the grizzly bear. Open Mon.-Fri. 9am-5pm. Write to P.O. Box 497, Kenai 99611. **Nikiski,** an unincorporated area just north of Kenai, has its own visitors center at the Nikishka Shopping Mall (776-8369), P.O. Box 8053, Nikiski 99635. Open Mon.-Fri. 8am-5pm.

National Park Service: 502 Overland St. (262-7021). Open Mon.-Fri. 9am-5pm.

Flights: Southcentral Air, 135 Grant Point Court (283-7343).

Taxi: City Cab, 283-7101.

Car Rental: National, 305 Willow St. (283-9566). **Avis** (283-7900), at the airport.

Tours: Kahtu Tours (283-7152). $15 for a good 3-hr. tour.

Crisis Line: 283-7257.

Women's Resource Center: 325 S. Spruce St. (283-7257).

General Delivery ZIP Code: 99611.

Area Code: 907.

Kenai, on the western Kenai Peninsula, is about 160 miles from Anchorage and 144 miles north of Homer. It can be reached via Kalifornsky Beach Rd., which joins Sterling Hwy. from Anchorage just south of Soldotna, or Kenai Spur Rd., which runs north through the Nikishka area and east to Soldotna. Both roads boast superb views of the peninsula's lakes and snow-capped peaks.

Accommodations and Camping

Remember that all along the highway are **recreational campgrounds. Kenai city campground** is mosquito infested, loud, and a bit of a haul from the center of town—but free for three days. Take Kenai Spur Rd. to Forest Dr. and turn towards the ocean. Grab a spot as close to the water as possible—the view can be great.

There are also three fine bed and breakfasts. **Irene's Lodge,** 702 Lawton Dr., Kenai 99611 (283-4501), charges $49 for singles and $60 for doubles, while **Daniel's Lake Lodge,** P.O. Box 1444, Kenai 99611 (776-5578), offers singles for $53 and doubles for $64.50. **Chinulna Point Lodge,** 36725 Chinulna Dr., Kenai 99611 (283-7799), has a fantastic view and hot tubs. Write for reservations and rates.

Katmai Hotel, 10800 Kenai Spur Hwy. (283-6101), 1 block from downtown. Spartan rooms. Singles $40. Doubles $50.

Kenai Merit Inn, 260 S. Willow (283-7566, outside AK 800-544-0970), near the center of town and visible from Kenai Spur Hwy. Each of the large rooms has a full bath and small refrigerator. Fancy dining downstairs, airport courtesy car, and fishing guide service. $50 flat rate for groups of up to 4 people.

Kenai Riverbend Campground, Porter Rd. (283-9489, 262-5715, or 262-1068). Take Kalifornsky Beach Rd. off Spur Hwy. Rooms as well as full hookup camping sites. In summer fishermen descend to the Kenai Riverbend, one of the best salmon fishing holes in the world. The 1985 world record King salmon (97 lbs.) was caught just a few minutes upstream. Riverbend has everything you need: boat launching and rentals, rods and tackle, bait, laundry, and showers. Singles $60. Doubles $65. Camping sites $12; RVs $18, with hookups $20. Reservations often necessary, though not required.

Overland RV Park, P.O. Box 326, Kenai 99611 (283-4227), and **Kenai RV Park,** P.O. Box 1913, Kenai 99611 (283-4646), both in Old Kenai. Full hookups $6.

Food

Carr's Grocery (283-7829), in the Kenai Mall on Kenai Spur Rd., has a great deli and sandwich bar. (Open 24 hours; deli closes at 8pm.)

Bookey's Drive Inn (283-4172), next to the visitors center. The 89¢ ¼-lb. burger is the cheapest in town. Open daily 10am-10pm.

Pizza Paradisio, on Kenai Spur Rd. (283-7008), across from the Kenai Mall. Thick pizza with plenty of toppings ($11 and up for a large) as well as other Italian food. Spaghetti dinners run $8. Open daily 11am-11pm. Free delivery.

Windmill Restaurant, 145 Willow (283-4662), just off Kenai Spur Hwy. Inexpensive family fare, with beef a specialty. Their claim to serve the "best steak in Alaska" may be a bit presumptuous, but you will be sated. Beer and wine served. Dinner $8-12. Open Mon.-Sat. 7am-9pm.

Harry Gaines Bar-B-Q Express (283-3018), in the Kenai Mall. Southwestern specialties. Try "the cowpoke" (sandwich, beans, and drink) $4, with ribs and bread $6. Open Mon.-Thurs. 9am-7pm, Fri.-Sat. 9am-8pm, Sun. noon-5pm.

Sights and Activities

The grandest sight in Kenai is **Cook Inlet,** where miles of white sand, two mountain ranges, and volcanic Mt. Augustine are all visible. See all this as well as beluga whales, salmon, and gulls from the overlook at the end of Forest Dr., or from the bluff at Alaska and Mission Ave.

In what passes for a town, **Ft. Kenay** and the **Kenai Historical Museum** do their best to lure tourists. The museum is threadbare, and the fort a cheap replica of the original 1868 structure. Both are on Overland Dr. and Mission St. (283-7294; open Mon.-Sat. 10am-5pm). Across the RV park from the fort is the **Holy Assumption Russian Orthodox Church,** the oldest building in Kenai. Originally built in 1846 and rebuilt in 1896, this national historic landmark contains a 200-year-old Bible. Call the priest at the rectory (283-4122) for a tour. The **Kenai Library** on Main St. Loop, next to the courthouse, shows free films on the area at 2pm. (Open Mon.-Sat. 8:30am-8pm.)

Recreational opportunities in the Kenai area abound. Check at the Chamber of Commerce for fishing charter information (prices are comparable to those in Soldotna), or with the Forest Service for canoeing and hiking opportunities. The **Captain Cook State Recreation Area,** 30 miles north of Nikiski at the end of Kenai Spur Rd., offers swimming, canoe landing points on the Swanson River, fishing, and free camping. Contact the Kenai Chamber of Commerce for rules and regulations.

Soldotna

Soldotna, once merely a fork in the road on the way to Homer, Kenai, or Seward, has become the center of government and recreation in the Kenai Peninsula. Soldotna, which means "soldier" in Russian, is the peninsula's premier fishing spot. World-record salmon are regularly caught in the Kenai River, a few minutes from downtown. Kenai Riverbend Campground, halfway between Soldotna and Kenai (see Kenai Accommodations) is offering a $10,000 reward to the person who catches a salmon weighing more than the current record of 97 pounds. Even in Alaska, ten thousand dollars may go a long way toward paying for a budget vacation.

Practical Information and Orientation

Visitor Information: Visitors Center (262-1337), between Miles 95 and 96 on Sterling Hwy., just across the river from downtown. Modern facility with photo displays and stairs down to the river. Open mid-May to Labor Day daily 10am-6pm. **Chamber of Commerce,** P.O. Box 236, Soldotna 99669 (262-9814), next door to the visitors center. Open Mon.-Fri. 9am-5pm.

Division of Parks and Outdoor Recreation: on Morgans Rd. at Mile 85, Sterling Hwy. P.O. Box 1247, Soldotna 99669. Information on campgrounds and fishing.

Car Rental: Avis (283-7900). $49 per day, with 100 free miles. 30¢ each additional mile.

Crisis Line: 283-7257.

Ambulance: 262-4500.

Hospital: Central Peninsula General, Marydale Dr. (262-4404).

General Delivery ZIP Code: 99669.

Area Code: 907.

Soldotna is 140 miles southwest of Anchorage on Sterling Hwy., at its junction with Kenai Spur Rd. Take the Seward Hwy. south from Anchorage and turn right onto Sterling at the only fork in the road.

Accommodations and Camping

Soldotna caters to both ends of the bed market: backpackers with tents and anglers with cash. The former can stay at nearby campgrounds and shell out $2 for hot, clean showers at the **River Terrace RV Park** on the river, while the latter can stay directly across the highway at the **Kenai River Lodge,** 393 Riverside Dr., Soldotna 99669 (262-4792), for $78 per night (fishing guides extra).

Skip's Idle Hour Inn, Mile 3 on Kalifornsky Beach Rd. (262-5041). P.O. Box 3634, Soldotna 99669. Probably the best prices on the entire peninsula. All rooms with private bath. Singles $30.75. Doubles $35.75. No reservations.

Soldotna Inn, 35041 Kenai Spur Hwy. (262-9169), just north of downtown. P.O. Box 565, Soldotna 99669. Luxurious high-priced rooms, with a snazzy restaurant downstairs. Singles $58. Doubles from $67.

Lake Country Bed and Breakfast (283-9432), 2 miles out of town. HC-2 Box 584, Soldotna 99669. Large home with sun deck, library, and recreation room. Rooms $39-69.

Swiftwater Park Municipal Campground, south on Sterling Hwy. at mile 94, and **Centennial Park Municipal Campground,** off Kalifornsky Beach Rd. near the visitors center, are both in the woods and have boat launches. Conveniently located on the river, the campgrounds have excellent fishing. There are even tables set aside for cleaning fish. One-week maximum stay. Sites $6. The woods between Centennial Campground and the Visitors Center are unowned and have "unofficial" tentsites for free.

Food

Soldotna arose as a highway crossroads, and fast food (along the road downtown) came snapping in its wake. Burger-chain prices are slightly higher than in the Lower 48, but visitors may still have to opt for the Big Mac over sit-down dining. There is a **Safeway** in the middle of town on the highway (open 24 hours).

Sal's Klondike Diner, 44619 Sterling Hwy. (262-2220), ½ mile from the river and several hundred miles from the Klondike. Best diner in town. Menu is full of gold rush trivia. "Local Yocals" specials include the $4 Sourdough special (French toast, 2 eggs, bacon). Burgers from $3.25. Coffee $1 per hr. Open Mon.-Sat. 7am-9pm, Sun. 9am-6pm.

Four Seasons, 43960 Sterling Hwy. (262-5006), just north of the Soldotna Y. Lunches start at $5.25 and feature homemade soup and bread. Immense dinners $11-19. Great sausage lasagna and vegetable skewers. Open Tues.-Sun. 11am-3pm and 5:30-10pm.

China Sea Restaurant (262-5033), on the upper level of the Blazy Mall, ¼ mile from the river. Chinese and American food. All-you-can-eat buffet (served daily 11:30am-1:30pm and 5-8pm, $7). Open daily 11am-9pm.

J.B. Supper Club (262-9887), 5 miles south on Sterling Hwy. Meat and potatoes at excellent prices. Friday-night dinner special with steak, soup, fries, and garlic bread $9. Live music on weekends. Open Tues.-Sat. noon-midnight.

Bunk House Inn, 44701 Sterling Hwy. (262-4584). Restaurant belongs to hotel of the same name in the heart of downtown. Expensive, but the portions are large. Chicken dishes start at $10, steaks $15. Open 24 hours.

Sights and Activities

The **Damon Memorial Historical Museum,** at Mile 3 on Kalifornsky Beach Rd., holds artifacts from native burial grounds and a large diorama. (Open Mon.-Fri. 9am-5pm. Admission $1.) The **Kenai National Wildlife Refuge Visitors Center** (262-7021), off Funny River Rd. at the top of Ski Hill Rd., directly across from the Soldotna visitors center, is a great source of information on this 197-million-acre refuge for moose, Dall sheep, and other wild animals. It also shows dioramas and victims of taxidermy. A ½-mile nature trail is nearby. (Open Mon.-Fri. 8am-6pm, Sat.-Sun. 10am-6pm; Labor Day-Memorial Day Mon.-Fri. 8am-4pm, Sat.-Sun. 10am-5:30pm.)

The **Kenai River** teems with wildlife of a slippery kind. Pink and silver salmon glide through at various times during the summer, and steelhead and dolly varden multiply all summer long. Numerous **fishing charters** run the river, usually charging $100-125 for a half-day of halibut or salmon fishing, or $150 for both (contact the visitors center for more information). There is no reason to spend so much, however. The downtown area is loaded with equipment rental shops that will fully outfit you with everything from bait to licenses for under $25 per day. Just stand in the Kenai and plunk in your line.

Fast-paced river sports weave into the **Kenai National Wildlife Refuge** and dozens of one- to four-day long **canoe routes** wind their way through the forest. A few places in town, including the Riverbend Campground, will rent you boats. Boats are also available on the highway: more than one resident puts his vessel in the front yard and hangs a "for rent" sign on it. Boat rentals are far from inexpensive, but the experience of gliding through some of the nation's most remote waterways is well worth any bounty. For free canoe route maps, write the Refuge Manager, Kenai National Wildlife Refuge, P.O. Box 2139, Soldotna 99669 (262-7021).

The end of July brings **Soldotna Progress Days,** in celebration of the completion of a natural gas line in 1961. Activities include a parade, a rodeo, and an airshow. The **Peninsula Winter Games** at the end of January attempt to expel the winter doldrums. Finally, the **Alaska State Championship Sled Dog Races** and **Dog Weight Pull Contest** take place in February in conjunction with Anchorage's Fur Rendezvous. Pick up a copy of the *Cheechako News,* Soldotna's weekly newspaper, for more information.

Ninilchik and Clam Gulch

Ninilchik is yet another small town (pop. 845) with spectacular fishing and fantastic scenery. Its strong Russian heritage, however, distinguishes it from other small peninsula towns. The only real sight-seeing attractions are the old **Russian fishing village** on Village Rd. north of town, and the **Holy Transfiguration of Our Lord Orthodox Church** (built in 1901). Both overlook Cook Inlet. The church and cemetery are still in use, but the Russian village is overshadowed by the huge wolverine mascot staring at the highway from the high school's facade.

The **Deep Creek Recreation Area,** nearby, is one of the most popular on the peninsula. Locals say it has the world's best salt-water King salmon fishing. Silver and pink salmon, dolly varden, and steelhead trout often swim by. Ninilchik's "Biggest Little Fair in Alaska," the **Kenai Peninsula State Fair,** is held each August. It's similar to a county fair in the Midwest—horse show, 4-H exhibits, livestock competition, arts and crafts, and entertainment. (For more information, contact the Fair Association, Box 39210, Ninilchik 99639.)

Groceries can be bought at the **General Store** on Sterling Hwy. (567-3378). **R&R's Burger Bar,** next door, has great cajun chicken ($6). Open daily, hours vary.

If you decide to stay in town for the night, the **Beachcomber Motel and RV Park,** on Village Rd. (567-3417), offers the cheapest rooms. Each room has a shower, full kitchenette, TV, and a great location on the beach. (Singles $45. Doubles $58. Full hookups for RVs $15.) For campers the choice is obvious: stay at one of the **state campgrounds** near town—each with water and toilets ($5). Superb sites in **Ninilchik State Recreation Area** are less than 1 mile north of the library. There are RV hookups closer to town at **Hylea's Camper Park,** Mile 135.4 on Sterling Hwy. (567-3393).

The library's **Visitor Information** section is more informative than the local visitors center. The library also shows free films on Alaska every Wed. at 7pm (567-3333; open Mon.-Sat. 11am-4pm).

Travel to nearby **Clam Gulch** (pop. 141) to see what all the clamor over clams is about. Clamming requires a sports fishing license and there is a daily limit of 60 clams per person. Rubber gloves and waterproof footgear are highly recommended. Clam Gulch claims only one cot-cluttered corner store, the **Clam Shell Lodge,** Mile 118.3 (262-9926). The lodge has clean hotel rooms, RV parking with electricity, a bar/restaurant, and showers. The restaurant specialty? Clam chowder, of course. Other good places for madcap clammers are Deep Creek, Ninilchik, and Homer Spit.

Homer

Ah, Homer. Blind to the encroaching highway, Homer is a bucolic artists' enclave with a deep sense of community. Homer is the kind of place where the natural food store is the town hearth and the movie theater shows provocative foreign films.

Surrounded by 400 million tons of coal, Homer rests on Kachemak (smoky) Bay, named after the mysteriously burning coal deposits that the first settlers came upon. Homer is split into two parts: the town and the Spit, a 3.5-mile sandbar jutting into Kachemak Bay. The two are connected by Spit Road. The Homer shuttle ($2) runs along this road; hitching, however, is extremely common and easy.

Practical Information and Orientation

Visitor Information, half-way down the Spit (235-7740 or 235-5300). Offers the epic work *250 Ways to Enjoy Homer.* Open daily 7am-10pm. In town, go to the **Pratt Museum,** 3779 Bartlett St. (235-8365), for brochures. Open daily 10am-5pm.

Park Information: Kachemak Bay Visitor and Convention Association, P.O. Box 1001, Homer 99603 (235-6030). **Alaska Maritime National Wildlife Office,** 202 Pioneer Ave. Wildlife exhibits, marine photography, and helpful advice on backcountry adventures in Kachemak Bay. Open Mon.-Fri. 8am-5pm.

Intercity Bus: Alaska Intercity Line (800-478-2877). From Anchorage $37.50.

Local Bus: Homer Shuttle runs the 6 miles between downtown and the Spit (one way $2). May 28-Sept. 5 daily 10am-8pm. Check at the tourist office for a schedule.

Alaska Marine Highway: P.O. Box 355, Homer 99603 (235-8449), terminal at the end of the Spit. The M.V. *Tustumena* sails into Homer several times per week from Valdez or Cordova ($104), from Seward ($74), and from Kodiak ($36).

Taxis: A-Smile Taxi, 235-6995.

Bike Rental: Shorepeddler, on the Seabreeze Boardwalk (235-2575), on the Spit. 10-speed mountain bikes $14 per day.

Camping Equipment: Quiet Sports, 144 W. Pioneer (235-8620). The best selection. **South Central Sports,** 1411 Lakeshore Dr. (235-5403). Rents everything from hip boots ($8) and camp stoves ($10) to 20-ft. motorboats ($175).

Laundromat: Homer Cleaning Center, Main St. (235-5152), downtown. Open Mon.-Sat. 8am-10pm, Sun. 9am-8pm.

Women's Crisis Line: 235-8101.

Pharmacy: Homer Rexall, 125 Pioneer Ave. (235-8757), at Main St. Open Mon.-Sat. 9am-5pm.

Ambulance: 235-8300.

Police: 235-8113.

Harbormaster: 235-8959.

Post Office: 235-6125. On Homer Bypass near Kachemak Way. Open Mon.-Fri. 9am-5pm. General Delivery ZIP Code: 99603.

Area Code: 907.

Homer sits cozily on the southwestern Kenai Peninsula on the north shore of Kachemak Bay. The Sterling Hwy. links it with Anchorage (226 miles away) and the rest of the Kenai Peninsula.

Accommodations and Camping

Of Homer's two **municipal campgrounds,** one is in town and one is on the Spit. To get to the former, take Pioneer to Bartlett St., go uphill, and take a left at the hospital entrance on Fairview St. The campground on the Spit covers most of the Spit's edges out two miles. Both sites are $5, usually uncollected. Spit sites can be windy.

The tourist office has a list of B&Bs, from $45 per night up.

Heritage Hotel, 147 W. Pioneer (235-7787), in the middle of downtown. A large, log cabin building with three types of accommodations: rooms with shared baths, rooms with private baths, and suites. Rooms are spacious and sterile. Prices start at $45 and rise to $67.

Driftwood Inn, 135 W. Bunnell (235-8019), a short walk from downtown. Take the Homer Bypass, turn right on Main St., then right again on Bunnell. Rustic, family-run place. Barbecues on the large porch. Originally Homer's first schoolhouse. Courtesy van. Rooms $45-60.

Ocean Shores Motel, 300-TAB Crittendon (235-7775), off Sterling Hwy. 1 block from downtown. Excellent views of mountain and ocean. Singles from $39.

Seaside Farm Bed and Breakfast, 58335 East End Rd. (235-7850), off Pioneer Ave. One of the best. Private cottages with kitchens, showers, and courtesy phones. The great beach location is ideal for fishing and cookouts, though the water is a mite too brisk for swimming. Trail rides, including ponies for children, are available. Doubles $40, each additional person $10.

Brass Ring Bed and Breakfast, 987 Hillfair Court (235-5450). Take the Homer Bypass to Lake St., then turn right on Hillfair Court. Five bedrooms share 2 bathrooms, but laundry facilities, nice decor, and friendly owners combine to make a very attractive B&B. No smoking. Rooms $40-50, depending on the number of people and choice of breakfast.

City Camping, Parks and Recreation Dept., 600 Fairview Ave.

Spit Camping, Harbormaster's Office, 4350 Spit Rd. (255-3160).

Homer Spit Campground (235-8206), at the end of the Spit. Tent sites $6, RV hookups $13. Free showers.

Homer Cabins, 3601 Main St. (235-6768). All units with double beds, cable TV, kitchens. Funky little log cabins cost $55 per night.

Food

Of course you'll get your groceries at **Homer Natural Foods,** 248 Pioneer Ave. (235-7242; usually open daily 7am-9pm). Those desiring less subversive fare can shop **Kachemak Food Cache** (235-8618), on the corner of Pioneer and Lake.

On the Spit, you can buy fresh seafood for campfire cookouts directly from fishermen or at one of the large retail outlets: **Icicle Seafood Market,** 842 Fish Dock Rd. (235-3486), near the mouth of the harbor; or **The Exchange** (235-6241), just up the road.

Sourdough Express Bakery and Coffee Shop, 1316 Ocean Dr. (235-7571), on the main drag to the Spit. The name says it all, except for the "delicious" added by the clientele. Comfortable granola atmosphere. Open Tues.-Sun. 6:30am-10pm. **The Sourdough Connection** (253-8701), its affiliate on the Spit next to the Salty Dawg, serves sandwiches and coffee and specializes in charter lunches (from $5.50).

Boardwalk Fish 'n' Chips (235-7749), at the end of Cannery Row Boardwalk across from the harbormaster's office. A local favorite. Big hunk of halibut with chips $5.25. Open daily 11:30am-6pm.

Sights and Seasonal Events

The **Pratt Museum**, 3779 Bartlett St. (235-8635), is probably the best museum on the peninsula. Historical exhibits and an excellent gallery of local art will soon be joined by a permanent exhibit on the Exxon *Valdez* oil spill. If you're at the Pratt on a Friday afternoon, be sure to help feed the resident octopus. (Admission $3, senior citizens $2. Open daily 10am-5pm).

Everyone who comes to Homer spends some time on the **Homer Spit**. Here one can merely admire the view and wonder how in the world geology created and preserved the 3.5-mile strip of land jutting into the unruly Pacific. The Spit is lined with fishing charter services and typical boardwalk candy and ice-cream stores.

Homer has any number of **art galleries**, such as **Homer Artists** at 564 Pioneer, and two good **theaters**: the **Family Theater** (235-6728), on Main and Pioneer, and the **Pier One** (235-7333), halfway down the Spit. The Pier One features concerts as well as plays (admission $7).

Homer never nods; nightlife ranges from beachcombing at low tide in the midnight sun to discovering whether the sawdust- and sourdough-filled **Salty Dawg Saloon** under the log lighthouse at the end of the Spit ever really closes (open 11am-whenever, as the sign says). The bar at **Land's End Resort**, at the very end of the Spit, has an expansive if expensive view of Kachemak Bay; for cheaper country fare head to **Alice's Champagne Palace**, 196 Pioneer Ave. (235-7650), a wooden barn with honkytonk music as well as nickel beers and dollar tacos on Monday nights.

Since Homer is often billed as the halibut capital of the world, it should perhaps come as no surprise that a pair of halibut derbies are the town's most popular annual events. The **Homer Jackpot Halibut Derby** offers prizes from $500 to $10,000 for the biggest fish and the tagged fish. The **Rescue 21 Derby** is held in July. But Homer celebrates more than just halibut: the annual **Winter Carnival**, the first week in February, features sled dog races and snow machine competitions. In March, Homer's small population of artists exhibits at the **Art Rondy**.

Near Homer

For a closer look at the bay and its wildlife, hike or boat into **Kachemak Bay State Park**. Within the park, trails are rough and visitors facilities limited. (For park regulations and precautions call 262-5581 in Soldotna, or write the State of Alaska Department of Natural Resources, Pouch 7-0001, Anchorage 99510.) **Charter boats** are another great way to tour (and fish in) the bay. Over 80 charter companies operate out of Homer, offering sightseeing, salmon fishing, halibut fishing, and clam digging excursions. Check along the Spit boardwalks. For $15-30 sightseeing adventures, contact **Rainbow Tours**, Box 1526, Homer 99603 (235-7272), located on the Cannery Row Boardwalk. **Central Charters Booking Agency**, 4241 Homer Spit Rd., Homer 99603 (235-7847), offers $30-78 sightseeing runs, $60-105 salmon runs, and $105 halibut runs. (Open daily 10am-6pm.) **South Central Sports**, 1411 Lakeshore Dr. (235-5403), runs a shuttle service convenient for backpackers, with non-scheduled stops across Kachemak Bay. (Round-trip fares $35-40.)

Halibut Cove, an artists' community and fishing village, is accessible from Homer only by boat or plane. The cove has some of the best bird watching in the region. Check out the octopus-ink paintings at **Diana Tillion's Cove Gallery** (open until 8pm). The **Saltery** (296-2223) is the cove's only restaurant. Specialties include chowder and sushi rolls. (Open daily 2-9pm. $5-12 per person; reservations recommended.) Make this a daytrip—the only places to stay in town are **Halibut Cove Cabins**, Box 1990, Homer 99603 (296-2214), which charges $55 for singles and $65 for doubles (bring your own bedding and food), and the **Quiet Lodge Bed and Breakfast** (296-2212), which charges $100 for doubles in separate cabins.

The easiest way to see the sloping bluffs that rise behind Homer is to cruise **Skyline Drive**, which runs along the rim of the bluffs. The wildflowers (mostly fireweed, accompanied by scattered bunches of geranium, paintbrush, rose, and others) bloom from June to September.

Proudly billing itself as the most westerly point on the U.S. Highway System, the tiny village of **Anchor Point** lies 16 miles northwest of Homer on the Sterling Hwy. The town is quickly becoming a suburb to Homer. Like the next town, it has its **Salmon Derby,** in mid-May. If you decide to spend the night, go to the **Anchor River Inn** (235-8531), just off Sterling Hwy. in front of the bridge (mile 157). Rooms from $30; groceries 24 hours. The town's **visitors center** is in **Kyllonen's RV Park** (235-6435), on River Rd. (P.O. Box 610, Anchor Point 99556).

Visitor-shy but extremely interesting is **Nikolaeusk,** maybe the only village in the U.S. where Russian is the primary language. Nikolaeusk's Old Believers are Russian Orthodox schismatics who in the past 200 years have lived variously in China, Brazil, Oregon, and Kenai, venturing ever farther from decadent, *pagoni* influences. Today, the town is dirt poor and rife with schism over whether to accept a priest trained in Rumania. The economy survives on fishing and a shop selling the handmade traditional Russian clothing that the village's inhabitants regularly wear. To find Nikolaeusk, take North Fork Rd (in the center of Anchor Point) east to the Nikolaeusk post office. Go down the gravel road at the post office until you get to the village. *Don't* hitchhike, because you'll never get out, and *don't* act like a tourist—the Believers have other things on their mind besides serving visitors.

Seldovia

Right across Kachemak Bay from Homer, this small town has been virtually untouched by the ideology of progress prevailing on the rest of the peninsula. The Russians named Seldovia for its herring, but today the year-round king crab industry keeps the town afloat. Stop by the small **museum,** 206 Main St. (234-7625), sponsored by the Seldovia Native Association (open Mon.-Fri. 8am-5pm). The **Pacific Pearl Fish Processing Plant** (234-7680) will let visitors tour the facility, something unheard of on the rest of Kenai. On a hill overlooking the water, the **St. Nicholas Orthodox Church** was built in 1891 (open daily 1-2pm).

Nearly everything in town can be covered on foot, but taxis are available (234-7859). **Rainbow Tours** (235-7272) offers a daily tour of Seldovia ($30). Twice per week, the ferry M.V. *Tustumena* runs between Homer and Seldovia ($24 roundtrip). Enjoy the midnight sun on the Tues. 2:45am ferry, or book a saner crossing; the Wednesday morning ferry departs at 11:45am and returns three hours later, leaving time to see the town. If you miss the ferry, you can sleep on **Outside Beach,** 2 miles out of town. Public rest rooms, water, and showers can all be found at the harbormaster's office. To avoid roughing it in the sand, make reservations before you leave Homer at the **Bayview Lodge** (234-7633; singles $40, doubles $60) or the **Boardwalk Hotel** (234-7816; singles $44, doubles $48).

Seldovia triples in size on Independence Day. The old-fashioned celebration draws visitors from all over the peninsula and includes parades, log-rolling, and greased pole climbing, as well as a potluck picnic.

Seward

History-hungry Seward traces its origins to a Russian shipyard built somewhere nearby by the ubiquitous Russian explorer Alexander Baranof in the 1830s. The present town was built in 1904 as the southern terminus of the Alaska railroad, and is now enshrined in Alaskan consciousness as the beginning of the toughest race on the earth, the Iditarod dogsled race.

Like Homer, Seward is divided into two parts of interest to outsiders, one near the ferry dock and one near the small-boat harbor. The streets in Seward are named after the U.S. Presidents from Washington to Van Buren. A, B, C, and D Streets usurp, however, the rightful places of John Quincy Adams and Andrew Jackson.

Practical Information

Visitor Information: Chamber of Commerce, 3rd and Jefferson St. (224-3094), in the railroad car *Seward.* Pick up a map with a self-guided walking tour on it, and (yawn) mark your own hometown on the Chamber's world map. Open Memorial Day-Labor Day daily 9am-5pm.

National Park Service Visitor Center: 1212 4th Ave. (224-3375), at the small-boat harbor. Information on and maps of the spectacular Kenai fjords. Listings of tours and kayak rentals. Open Mon.-Thurs. 8am-5pm, Fri.-Sun. 8am-7pm; Labor Day-Memorial Day Mon.-Fri. 8am-noon and 1-5pm. **Seward Ranger Station, Chugach National Forest (USFS),** 334 4th Ave., at Jefferson. Extensive trail information, maps, and advice on trails close to town, as well as the complete Iditarod route. Cabin reservations. Open Mon.-Fri. 8am-7pm.

Harbor Air: Seward Airport (224-3133 in Seward, 243-1167 in Anchorage), 2 miles north of town on the Seward-Anchorage Hwy. Flights to and from Anchorage daily (one way $52). 45-min. flight tours $50 per person.

Alaska National Railroad: 265-2494. Depot at northern edge of town. Train Thurs.-Mon. to Anchorage ($35).

Seward Bus Line: 550 Railway Ave. (224-3608, in Anchorage 278-0800), in the red music store. To Anchorage daily at 9am (one way $25).

Alaska Marine Highway: The M.V. *Tustumena* serves Kodiak (one way $44), Seldovia (one way $78), Homer (one way $74), and Valdez (one way $52). Call 224-5485 for schedule information.

Trolley: 224-8075, ext. 03210. Just wave it down and it will go anywhere for $1.

Taxi: Seward Taxi, 224-5508. **Yellow Cab,** 224-8788.

Car Rental: National, 217 5th Ave. (224-5211), at New Seward Hotel. From $52 per day with 100 free miles, each additional mile 31¢. Must be 21 with major credit card.

Laundromat: Seward Laundry, 4th and C St. Showers $2. Open Mon.-Sat. 10am-9pm, Sun. 11am-6pm.

Hospital: Seward General, at 1st Ave. and Jefferson St. (224-5205).

Emergency: 911.

Post Office: 5th and Madison. Open Mon.-Fri. 9:30am-4:30pm, Sat. 10am-2pm. General Delivery ZIP Code: 99664.

Area Code: 907.

Accommodations

Strangely, Seward has some nice, cheap rooms. This is a good place to sleep in a bed and dry out your tent.

Van Gilder Hotel, 308 Adams St. (224-3525), just off 3rd. A well-preserved National Historic Site that could be the setting of any frontier Western. Elegant bar. Clean rooms. Rooms $40, with bath $60. Bunks in dorms $30. Definitely call for reservations.

The Korner House Bed and Breakfast, 501 Ash St. (224-3231). Turn west at Mile 2.1 off Seward Hwy. onto Ash. It's tough to find a better-kept room in Seward. Singles $38. Doubles $55. Breakfast included.

The New Seward Hotel and Saloon, 219 5th Ave. (224-8001). Ask to stay in the original hotel, not the addition. Singles $56, with bath $74. Fantastic bar downstairs.

Tony's Hotel, Bar, and Liquor Store (224-3045), on Railway and 4th. Surprisingly clean, safe rooms considering it's on top of a gin joint. Singles $25. Weekly: singles $100.

Camping

Seward's municipal campgrounds charge $4.25 and are nothing to write home about, yet they are the best deal for tenters who do not truly want to rough it. Several private campgrounds offer RVers more services at higher prices.

Municipal Campgrounds: City Greenbelt Camping Area, off 7th Ave. along the beach north of Jefferson. Grassy tenting area with water, fireplaces, clean toilets. Strategically located on

Resurrection Bay. **City RV Parking,** on 4th Ave. at Van Buren, by the small-boat harbor and beyond the ball park. Toilets and water. **City Campground,** Mile 2 of Seward Hwy., by Forest Acres. 22 sites. 14-day max. stay. All sites $4.25.

Kenai Fjords RV Park, 4th Ave. and D St. (224-8779). Gravel parking near the boat harbor. Sites $9, full hookups $4.50.

Bear Creek Mobile Home Park (224-5725). Turn off Seward Hwy. at Mile 6.6 and take Bear Leg Rd. ½ mile. Slightly off the beaten path. Laundry and hookups. No tents. RVs $12. Hot showers $2.

Food

Downtown Seward has seafood restaurants, hamburger joints, and pizza parlors galore. Pick up groceries at **Bob's Market,** 207 4th Ave. (Open Mon.-Sat. 9am-7pm, Sun. noon-6pm.)

The Depot, Mile 1 on Seward Hwy. (224-5500), near the railroad depot (hence the name—silly). So what if the "drive-thru" concept seems out of place in a small Alaskan port. Big burgers with the works cost only $3, as do chicken sandwiches. Eight flavors of shakes $1.50. Open daily 11am-9pm.

Alaska Custom Seafood, next to the harbormaster near the small-boat harbor. No sit down, but great salmon, halibut, and other fresh fish. Salmon jerky $1.75. Open Mon.-Fri. 10am-7pm, Sat.-Sun. 9am-8pm.

Breeze Inn, in the small-boat harbor (224-5237). Not your average hotel restaurant. Breeze in for the huge all-you-can-eat buffet ($8). Breakfasts include the "2-2-2" (two each of eggs, bacon, and pancakes, $5). Great view of harbor and bay. Open Mon.-Fri. 7am-10pm, Sat.-Sun. 8am-10pm. Live music (country and rock) on weekend nights.

Fairweather Cafe, 106 4th Ave. (224-3907). Croissants for breakfast, homemade soups and sandwiches for lunch, and mushroom schnitzel and chicken *cordon bleu,* along with other dishes that don't appear in Alaska every day, for dinner. Lunches $4-7. The $12-17 dinner might be your Seward's Folly. Open daily 7am-2pm and 5-10pm.

Salmon Cache, in the small-boat harbor (224-3676). Great for dessert. Try "Alaskan-size" (larger than "Texan-size") ice cream cones, the biggest you'll see for $1.25. Open May-Sept. 7am-10pm.

Sights and Seasonal Events

The walking tour of Seward printed on the map available at the Chamber of Commerce passes many homes and businesses that date back to the early 1900s. A complete tour takes two to three hours. The **Resurrection Bay Historical Society Museum,** in the basement of City Hall (corner of 5th and Adams), exhibits Native artifacts and implements used by pioneers. (Open June 15-Labor Day daily 11am-4pm. Admission 50¢, children 25¢.) From June 15 to Labor Day you can see *Seward's Burning* (the "Earthquake Movie," as residents call it) at the **Seward Community Library,** 5th Ave. and Adams St. (224-3646). No, it doesn't star Charlton Heston or Ava Gardner; rather, this movie shows actual footage of the 1964 Good Friday earthquake (supported by fires and tidal waves), which destroyed much of Seward when it hit southcentral Alaska. (Library open Mon.-Fri. 1-8pm, Sat. 1-6pm. Screenings Mon.-Sat. at 2pm. Donations $1.) The **K.M. Rae Educational Building,** on 3rd Ave. between Washington and Railway, part of the Seward Marine Science Institute, contains marine life displays and the results of institute research. (Open May 25-Aug. Mon.-Fri. 1-5pm, Sat. 9am-5pm. Movie daily at 4pm. Free.)

Seward is a great place for **day hikes.** Nearby **Mt. Marathon,** scaled by locals in a race every July 4, offers a great view of the city and ocean. From the corner of 1st and Jefferson, take Lowell St. to its very end to reach the trail. **Exit Glacier,** billed as Alaska's most accessible glacier, is 9 miles west on the road that starts at Seward Hwy. Mile 3.7. From the ranger station, take the steep and slippery 4-mile trail to the magnificent Harding Ice Field above the glacier. This hike is only for the intrepid. Check the ranger station (see Practical Information) for other trails if you are not intrepid.

Known as the gateway to Alaska because of its position as the southern terminus of the railroad, Seward is also the point of entry to the **Kenai Fjords National Park.** Much of the park consists of a coastal mountain system marinated with wildlife. The best way to see this area is from boats in the bay; pick up the list of charters at the Park Service visitors center or from shops along the boardwalk next to the harbormaster's office. Most run $70-100 per day, $45-50 per half-day. For more information, contact **Kenai Fjord Tours** (224-8068 or 224-8069), **Mariah Charters** (243-1238), or **Quest Charters** (224-3025; open in summer 6am-10pm).

Fishing is heavenly in the Seward area. Salmon and halibut can be caught in the bay, grayling and dolly varden right outside of town. Some people just fish off the docks. For better odds, try a fishing charter. Charters are available for both halibut and salmon throughout the summer; prices run from $90-100, with all gear provided. Call Quest Charters or Mariah Charters (see above).

One of the best times to go fishing is during one of Seward's biggest events—the **Silver Salmon Derby.** The derby opens each year on the second Saturday in August and closes eight days later. Prizes go for the largest fish (up to $5000) and the tagged fish (up to $10,000 for the fish specifically marked by officials prior to the event). Seward's other big event is the **Mountain Marathon** on the 4th of July. Alaska's oldest footrace began when one sourdough challenged a fellow sourdough to make it up and down the 3022-foot peak in less than an hour. That was in 1915, and that sourdough couldn't do it. Last year, the winners of the men's race (45 min.) and the women's (55 min.) demonstrated that humankind is on the move. The race has been joined by a parade, the governor, and hundreds of enthusiasts running, sliding, falling, and bleeding down the steep mountain to the shores of Resurrection Bay. Thousands of sadistic spectators set up lawnchairs anywhere in town and watch the race through binoculars.

Near Seward: Moose Pass

Known, barely, for Ed Estes' waterwheel (an alleged "internationally known landmark"), tiny Moose Pass began as a flag-stop for the Alaska Railroad and now isn't much of anything. Moose Pass offers a **Solstice Festival** on the weekend nearest every solstice with lots of beer, a carnival, and fun for kids and adults. Located at Mile 29 on Seward Hwy., the town has four campgrounds with excellent fishing: Primrose at Mile 18, Ptarmigan Creek at Mile 23, Trail River at Mile 24, and Wye at Mile 36. All are run by the Chugach National Forest; write **Alaska Public Lands Information,** 605 W. 4th, Anchorage 99501 (271-2737). There is a hotel, the **Moose Pass Inn** (288-3110), at Mile 30. Rooms are expensive ($65 and up) and reservations often necessary.

Kodiak Island

Nearly one hundred miles off the Kenai Peninsula stands Kodiak Island, perhaps the harshest and most majestic area of southern Alaska. Rain falls on Kodiak about half the days in the year. In this century, the island has been rocked by earthquakes, washed over by *tsunamis,* and covered in two feet of volcanic ash. Kodiak gives its name to the fiercest creature of the Alaskan wild, the Kodiak brown bear, which weighs up to 1500 lbs. and can outrun horses.

The magnitude of Kodiak's roughness is equalled by its beauty and the wealth of its resources. The island is ringed by glacially sculpted fjords. Rugged mountains and lush flora cover its 3670 square miles. The fishing port is the third most productive in the U.S.

Kodiak

Kodiak was the first capital of Russian Alaska (1792-1804), before Alexander Baranof moved the Russian-American Company headquarters to Sitka. It was here the Russians carried out their worst atrocities, enslaving Aleut natives to hunt the sea otters to near extinction.

The city's setting is absolutely spectacular, but the mountains that form Kodiak's backdrop have not always been so quiet. In 1912 Mt. Katmai erupted, covering Kodiak Island with 18 inches of ash and destroying much of the area's wildlife; plots of ash remain in the forests today. Then in 1964 the biggest earthquake ever recorded in North America shook the area, creating a tidal wave that destroyed much of downtown Kodiak, including 158 homes. There was $24 million worth of damage in total. The Army Corps of Engineers and local resourcefulness turned Kodiak back into a thriving fishing port—one wrecked 200-foot vessel, *The Star of Kodiak,* was cemented into the ferry dock and turned into a cannery.

Practical Information and Orientation

Visitor Information: Information Center (486-4070), at Center St. and Marine Way, right in front of the ferry dock. Hunting and fishing information, charter arrangements, and a self-guided walking tour map. Open Mon.-Fri. 8am-5pm. **Chamber of Commerce, P.O.** Box 1485, Kodiak 99615 (486-5557), in the same building.

Sport Fishing Division: Alaska Department of Fish and Game, Box 686, Kodiak 99615 (486-4791). Information on fishing regulations and seasons.

Flights: Mark Air, 487-2424 or 487-4080. Flights from Anchorage daily. Round-trip $185 if booked 2 weeks in advance, otherwise one way $123.

Municipal Bus: Kodiak Driver Express passes through town once every hr. and goes as far as the airport (near Buskin State Recreation Site) and all the way to Fort Abercrombie. Pick up a schedule at the tourist office. Fare $1. Runs daily 6am-11:40pm.

Alaska Marine Highway: The M.V. *Tustumena* (486-3800) sails to Kodiak May-Sept. 3 times per week; Oct.-April less frequently. To Homer ($36), Seward ($44), Valdez or Cordova ($96), and Whittier ($102). Week-long run to Dutch Harbor once every 3 weeks.

Car Rental: Rent-a-Heap, at the airport (486-5200). $33 per day. **Hertz,** at the airport (487-5200).

Taxis: Kodiak Cab Co., 486-3100. **Ace Mecca,** 486-3211.

Camping Equipment: Mac's Sports Shop, 117 Lower Mill Bay (486-4276), at the end of Center Ave. Open Mon.-Sat. 9am-6pm, Sun. 10am-3pm.

Laundromat: Ernie's, 218 Shelikof (486-4119), across from the harbor. Drop-off available. Shower $2. Open Mon.-Sat. 7am-10pm, Sun. 8am-8pm.

Weather: 486-4338.

Hospital: Kodiak Island, 1915 E. Rezanof Dr. (486-3281).

Post Office: on Lower Mill Bay Rd. Open Mon.-Fri. 9am-5:30pm, Sat. 10am-4pm. General Delivery ZIP Code: 99615. Substation in **Kraft's Grocery,** 111 Rezanof. Open Mon.-Sat. 10am-6pm.

Area Code: 907.

The city of Kodiak is on the eastern tip of Kodiak Island, roughly 200 miles south of Homer. The airport is 4 miles south of town, while the ferry terminal is downtown. If you are traveling to and from the Kenai by ferry, study the schedule carefully or you might find yourself stranded on Kodiak for longer than you would like.

Accommodations and Camping

If you want to stay in a hotel in Kodiak, *make a reservation.* The hotels are generally filled, and finding a room becomes almost impossible when the airport shuts down due to bad weather, which is often.

Kodiak has just built a tent city 2 miles west on Rezanof Hwy. to accommodate cannery workers. Called **Sandy Beach Park,** the place looks and feels like a gravel parking lot, and smells like fish. It's only $3, and has free, hot showers. Two miles farther up Rezanof is the prettier **Buskin River Recreation Area.** Contact Mary

Monroe at **Kodiak Bed and Breakfast,** P.O. Box 1729, Kodiak 99615 (486-5367) for a local referral. Rooms start at $40.

Shelikof Lodge, 211 Thorsheim Ave. (486-4141), behind the McDonalds at the end of Center Ave. Comfortable rooms with cable TV. Singles $55. Doubles $60.

Star Motel, 119 Brooklyn Terrace (486-5657). Dreary exterior hides equally dreary rooms. Singles $51.40.

Northland Ranch/Resort, P.O. Box 2376 (486-5578). Far from downtown. Northland can set you up horseback riding, hunting, or fishing on the ranch. The attached restaurant is excellent. Rooms $35-75. Horseback riding $15 per hr.

Sandy Beach Campground (Tent City), 2 miles from ferry terminal. From terminal take Center St. to Rezanof, and turn left. After two miles turn left on Sandy Beach Rd.

Fort Abercrombie State Park Campground, 4 miles northeast of town on Rezanof-Monashka Rd. Water, shelters, and outhouses. No RV hookups; designed for campers. WWII ruins, a trout fishing lake, and spectacular sunsets. 7-night max. stay. Sites $5.

Buskin River State Recreation Site, 4½ miles southwest of the city. Water, toilets, and sewage dumping. Over 50% of Kodiak's sport fishing is done on the river. 7-night max. stay. Sites $5.

Pasagshak State Recreation Site, 40 miles from the city at the mouth of the Pasagshak river. Water and toilets. Noted for King salmon fishing. 14-day max. stay. 7 sites. Free.

Food

Kodiak has an odd dearth of restaurants. **Kraft's Grocery,** 111 Rezanof, is a big, everything-you-might-ever-need kind of place. **City Market,** on Lower Mill Bay Rd. (also called Rezanof East St.), is very low-budget and stocks inscrutable frozen goods. Try a *Daing na galung-gong* for 65¢.

Kodiak Café, 203 Marine Way (486-5470), between the boat ramp and the "Star of Kodiak." A fishermen's diner with fare to match. Enormous burgers with fries $5.25-7.50. Hot cakes from $2.75. Open Mon.-Sat. 6am-3pm, Sun. 7am-2pm.

Fox Inn, 211 Thorsheim (486-4141), in the Shelikof Lodge. Straightforward country specials from burgers to chicken. Halibut dinner $10.75. Open Mon.-Sat. 5am-2pm and 5-9pm, Sun. 9am-3pm.

Out to Lunch (486-4868), in Bakery Mall on Rezanof and Center. Trying to be an upscale deli. Excellent avocado and sprouts croissant $5.25. Open Mon.-Sat. 9am-7pm.

Captain Keg's Peking Cuisine (486-5469), at Center and Rezanof. Typical Kodiak Chinese fare. Dinners from $7.50. Open Mon.-Sat. 11:30am-midnight.

Sights and Seasonal Events

Built in 1793 as a storehouse for sea otter pelts, the **Baranof Museum,** 101 Maine Way (486-5920), is the oldest Russian structure standing in Alaska, as well as the oldest wooden structure on the entire West Coast. The museum displays Russian and native artifacts. Check out their small library of period photos and literature ranging from the Russian colony to the 1964 earthquake. (Open Mon.-Fri. 10am-3pm, Sat.-Sun. noon-4pm. Admission $1, ages under 12 free.) The **Russian Orthodox Church,** not far from the museum, houses the oldest parish in Alaska (1794). Its elaborate icons date back to the early 19th century, and its old church bells are still rung by hand. (Tours given by appointment. Call 486-3854.) Alaska's only outdoor theater, **The Frank Brink Amphitheater** on Minashka Bay, presents the historical play *Cry of the Wild Ram* every year on August weekends. The play covers 30 years of the life of Alexander Baranof, the Russian settler who established the first colonies on Kodiak and the Kenai Peninsula. Dress warmly. (Admission $10, senior citizens and children $5. Contact Land 5 Travel Service, P.O. Box 221, Kodiak 99615, or call 486-3232 for reservations.)

Beautiful **Fort Abercrombie State Park,** 3½ miles north of town, was the site of the first beautiful secret radar installation in Alaska. The fort is also the site of a WWII defense installation; some bunkers and other reminders of the Alaskan campaign remain. Six and a half miles southwest of Kodiak is an old naval station, now the base for the Coast Guard's North Pacific operations.

Home to the largest commercial fishing fleet in Alaska, Kodiak Island also has very popular **sport fishing.** Try Cascade Lake for trout, Buskin River or Saltery Creek for dolly varden, crab, and salmon. For information on regulations and seasons, contact the Sport Fishing Division (see Practical Information).

Fifty-four miles north of Kodiak is **Shuyak Island State Park,** an undeveloped area with ample hunting, fishing, and kayaking. There are four public-use **cabins** available for $15 per night. Reserve ahead at the Division of Parks and Outdoor Recreation, SR Box 3800, Kodiak 99615, or call 486-6339 for more information.

The **Kodiak Crab Festival,** held for one week in late May, celebrates the area's major industry with parades, a seal skinning contest, races—including kayak and crab—and a blessing of the fleet. **St. Herman's Day,** August 9, celebrates the first saint of the Russian Orthodox Church in North America (canonized in 1970). The **Great Buskin River Raft Race,** in June, is a rousing affair—five beer breaks are part of the rules. The **State Fair and Rodeo,** in mid-August, includes crafts and livestock.

Kodiak National Wildlife Refuge

The Wildlife Refuge, on the western half of Kodiak Island, was inaugurated in 1941 and has grown to nearly two million acres. An estimated 2400 Kodiak bears live on the island along with a variety of other mammals and several hundred bald eagles. The bears are usually seen in July and August, when they fish in streams. They hibernate from December to April, bearing cubs in February and March. Though the bears are half-vegetarian and usually avoid contact with humans, be careful. The largest and most powerful carnivore in North America, Kodiaks can easily kill humans with one claw tied behind their back.

Other mammals native to the area are red foxes, land otters, weasels, tundra moles, and little brown bats. These are found in many other parts of Alaska as well. Deer, snowshoe hares, beavers, muskrats, Dall sheep, mountain goats, and red squirrels have been transplanted from other parts of the state to Kodiak. The 800 miles of coastline in the refuge are home to thousands of waterfowl and about 20 seabird species. Off the coast, whales, porpoises, seals, sea otters, and sea lions frolic.

For those who want to get close to the animals, the refuge has 12 **cabins.** Unfortunately, it is difficult to reach the refuge without paying a lot of money. Air charters should be booked in advance and cost upwards of $275. Boats can also take you to the refuge; inquire at the information center in Kodiak. The cabins are free, but they are invariably full. Make advance reservations, then cross your fingers and hope that you are one of the lucky few selected in the drawing held every three months. For information about the park as well as cabin reservations, contact the Kodiak National Wildlife Refuge Managers, 1390 Buskin River Rd., Kodiak 99615 (487-2600). If you're in town, drop by the **U.S. Fish and Wildlife Headquarters and Visitor Center,** just outside Buskin State Recreation Site, 4 miles southwest of town, for wildlife displays and more information. (Open Mon.-Fri. 8am-4pm.)

Southeastern Alaska (The Panhandle)

The Panhandle is flung 500 miles from the Gulf of Alaska to Prince Rupert, BC. The Tlingit (KLING-kit) and Haida (HI-duh) tribes have left a deep mark on the region, which forms a loose network of islands, inlets, and deep saltwater fjords, surrounded by deep valleys and rugged mountains. Temperate rain forest conditions, 60-odd major glaciers, and 15,000 bald eagles distinguish the Panhandle.

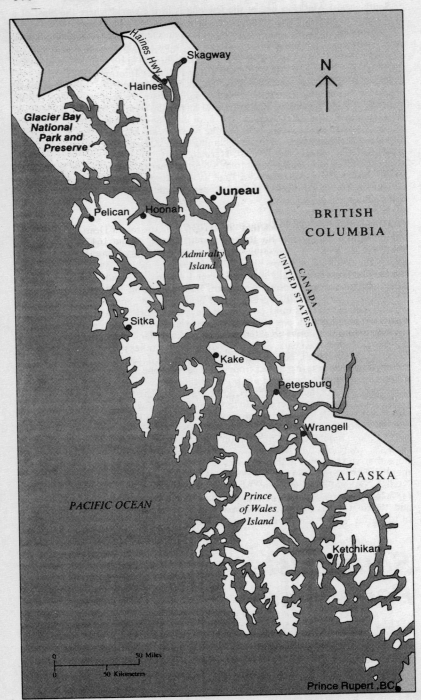

Southeastern Alaska is one of the few places in the world where the blast of a ferry boat heralds the day's important event. The 1000 islands and 10,000 miles of coastline in the Alexander Archipelago are connected to each other and to Seattle by ferries run by the Alaska Marine Highway. While the Interior and the Southcentral regions of Alaska have experienced great urban sprawl (by Alaskan standards), the communities of Southeastern Alaska cling to the coast. While Gold Rush days haunt such towns as Juneau and Skagway, others, like Sitka and Wrangell, hearken back to the era of the Russian occupation. Petersburg, on the other hand, is a busy fishing depot with strong ties to its Norwegian heritage; Ketchikan is a charming mill town.

The cheapest, most exciting way to explore Southeastern Alaska is on the Alaska Marine Highway system. The state-run ferries connect Seattle, Ketchikan, Petersburg, Wrangell, Sitka, Juneau, Haines, and Skagway, as well as some smaller Native and fishing communities. You can avoid the high price of accommodations in smaller communities by planning your ferry trip at night and sleeping on the deck.

Ketchikan

A Ketchikan proverb holds that "if you can't see the top of Deer Mountain, it's raining, and if you *can* see the top, it's about to rain." About 164 inches per year marinate this good-sized working community of 14,600, cradled at the watery base of the mountain; locals have to ignore the rain, or nothing would ever get done. The southernmost city in Alaska, Ketchikan is also the first port for ferries and cruise ships visiting the state. Elevated walkways and numerous staircases between multi-leveled streets keep tourists—the most important source of the town's income—high and dry.

Practical Information and Orientation

Visitor Information: Ketchikan Visitors Bureau, 131 Front St. (225-6166), across from the cruise ship docks downtown. Offers map of a good walking tour, along with friendly advice. Open daily 9am-6pm.

United States Forest Service: Ranger District Office, Federal Building, Ketchikan 99901 (747-6671 or 225-2148), on Stedman at Mill. Information on cabins and trails, as well as films and displays of the Ketchikan area.

Airport: A small ferry from the town dock next to the cruise ship terminal transports people to the airport, which lies across the bay from Ketchikan ($1). **Alaska Airlines** (225-2141), in the Ingersoll Hotel, at the corner of Mission and Dock St. Office open daily 8am-5pm. Daily flights to Juneau $65.

Alaska Marine Highway: At the far end of town on N. Tongass Hwy. (225-6181). Buses run into town, but if you arrive late you might want to hitch to avoid a $5 fare.

Buses: Fare $1, senior citizens and ages under 11 75¢. Buses stop frequently: about every 3 blocks and about every ½-hr. Buses run Mon.-Sat. 6:45am-6:45pm.

Taxis: Sourdough Cab, 225-6651. **Alaska Cab,** 225-2133. **Yellow Cab,** 225-5555.

Car Rental: Rent-A-Dent, 2828 Tongass Ave. (225-5123), at 3rd. Courtesy van picks up anywhere in town. $24 per day plus 20¢ per mile. All major credit cards accepted. Must be 21.

Alaska State Employment Office: 225-3181, corner of Dock and Main St. Open Mon.-Fri. 8am-4:30pm.

Laundromat: Suds and Duds, 325 Bawden (225-9274), near the hostel. Open daily 8am-8pm.

Sexual Assault/Rape Crisis Line: W.I.S.H. (225-9474).

Pharmacy: Rare Ketchikan Pharmacies, 300 Front St. (225-3144). Open Mon.-Fri. 9am-5pm.

Post Office: Main office next to the ferry terminal. Open Mon.-Fri. 9am-5pm. General Delivery ZIP Code: 99901. Substation in the back of Tongass Trading Company, on the corner of Main and Mission St.

Area Code: 907.

Ketchikan sits on an island 235 miles south of Juneau, 90 miles north of Prince Rupert, BC, and 600 miles north of Seattle, WA. The Parks and Recreation Center, 345 Main St., will store your backpack free Mon.-Fri. 9am-5pm.

Accommodations

If you want something more glamorous than the hostel, Anne Rothrock at the **Ketchikan Bed and Breakfast Network,** Box 3213, Ketchikan 99901 (225-8550), can find you rooms ranging from $30 to $65.

Ketchikan Youth Hostel (AYH), P.O. Box 8515, Ketchikan 99901 (225-3319). On the corner of Main and Grant St. in the United Methodist Church. Very nice houseparents. No beds, just mats on the floor, a common area, and a kitchen. Only two showers. Lockout 8:30am-6pm. Lights off at 11pm, on at 7:15am. Members $4, nonmembers $7. No reservations. Open June 1-Sept. 1.

Rain Forest Inn, 2311 Hemlock St., Ketchikan 99901 (225-9500). Take Tongass Ave. about 6 blocks into town from the ferry terminal, then follow Jefferson St. left for ½ block. Dorm rooms. Kitchen and laundromat available. Your fellow dormmates most likely work in the canneries and smell like fish. Beware. Bunks $17. Singles $39.

Union Rooms Hotel, 319 Mill St., Ketchikan 99901 (225-3580). Quiet, nicely located, and reasonably clean. Rooms $26.50 and up.

Pioneer Hotel and Bar, 118 Front St., Box 8535, Ketchikan 99901 (225-2336). Bartender is also hotel manager. Singles with bath $40. $10 key deposit.

Camping

Signal Creek Campground, 6 miles north on Tongass Hwy. from the ferry terminal. A U.S. Forest Service campground on the shores of Ward Lake. Water and pit toilets. 25 units. Sites $5. Open in summer.

Last Chance Campground, 2.2 miles from Signal Creek Campground down Ward Lake. Privately run. Caters mostly to RVs. 23 sites, water, pit toilets. Sites $5. Open in summer.

Three C's Campground, ½-mile north of Signal Creek. Four units for backpackers. Water, pit toilets, firewood.

Ketchikan RV Park. Parking for 14 RVs in town, next to Sea Mart supermarket. No hookups, but water and trash facilities.

Clover Pass Resort, P.O. Box 7322-U, Ketchikan 99901 (247-2234), 14 miles north of Ketchikan. 35 complete RV hookups with dump station.

Food

The supermarket most convenient to downtown is **Tatsuda's,** 633 Stedman at Deermount St., just beyond the Thomas Basin. (Open daily 7am-11pm.) **Bayside Grocery,** on Stedman near the docks, has a smaller selection but is open 24 hours.

Harbor Inn, 316 Mission St. (225-2850). Good food, friendly atmosphere. Three eggs, gravy, hashbrowns, and all the trimmings $4.75. Open daily 7am-10:30pm.

Chico's, Dock and Edmond St. (225-2833). Mexican and Italian food. $4.50 for lots of spaghetti. Interesting Mexican/Italian decor, music. Open daily 10am-11pm.

Pioneer Pantry, 124 Front St. (225-3337), across from the visitors bureau. Clean-cut decor with few tables and a long bar. Sandwiches come with salad, fries, or soup ($4.25-7). Breakfast specials $5. Open daily 8am-6pm.

Kay's Kitchen, 2813 Tongass Ave. (225-5860), 600m toward town from the ferry terminal. A busy little cafe with homemade everything. Always filled with locals. Open June-Sept. Tues.-Sat. 11am-4pm.

Jimbo's Corner Kafe, 307 Mill St. (225-2240), across from the cruise ship docks. Try a 1-lb. Alaskan burger for $8. Open 24 hours.

Pete's Sourdough Inn, 834 Water St., a few hundred meters past the tunnel from downtown. Frequented by fishermen from the docks across the road. Huge breakfast portions: eggs, hash browns, bacon, and toast $6. Soup and sandwich lunches $5.

Gilmore Garden Restaurant and Lounge, 326 Front St. (225-9423), in the Gilmore Hotel. European-style food at Alaskan-style prices. Salmon around $16. Open daily 7am-10pm.

Sights

The best way to see the sights in Ketchikan is to follow the excellent walking tour map offered by the visitors bureau. Ketchikan's history as a mining boomtown settled by fortune-hunting prospectors is preserved on **Creek Street,** which thrived as a Red Light District until 1954. They say that Creek St. was the only place where both sailors and salmon went upstream to spawn. At #24 you can revel in the nebulous history of **Dolly's House** (225-6329), a former brothel turned museum by its enterprising madam. Hours vary, so call ahead if you want to visit. (Admission $2.)

Also on the walking tour is the **Totem Heritage Center,** 601 Deermount St., which houses 33 well-preserved totem poles from Tlingit and Haida villages. (Open Mon.-Sat. 8am-5pm, Sun. 9am-5pm. Admission $1.50, ages under 18 free; Sun. afternoon free.) The **Tongass Historical Society Museum,** on Dock St., explains the strange interaction of Natives, rain, salmon, and prostitutes. (Open mid-May to Sept. Mon.-Sat. 8:30am-5pm, Sun. 1-5pm. Admission $1, ages under 18 free; free Sun.) Next door to the museum, the scenic chairs of the **Ketchikan Library** are the best place to pass a rainy day. (Open Mon. and Wed. 10am-8pm, Tues. and Thurs.-Fri. 10am-6pm, Sat. noon-5pm.) All those obsessed with the love-lives of fish will be enamored of the **Deer Mountain Hatchery,** in the city park off Fair St. The hatchery is free and open sporadically; just poke your head in.

The largest and best totem park in the world is 2½ miles southwest of Ketchikan on Tongass Hwy. in the **Saxman Native Village.** The native village has a tribal house, native dances, and an open artisans' studio where new totems are made. (Open daily 9am-5pm and on weekends when a cruise ship is in.) Thirteen-and-a-half miles north of Ketchikan on Tongass Hwy. is **Totem Bight,** with 13 totems. Entry to both parks is free.

A good day-hike from Ketchikan is up **Deer Mountain.** Walk past the city park on Fair St. until it becomes a gravel road. Follow this up to the trailhead. In 2½ hours you'll have a spectacular view of Ketchikan and Prince of Wales Island.

The magical **Misty Fjords National Monument** lies 30 miles east of Ketchikan and is accessible by boat or float plane. This 2.2-million-acre park offers excellent camping, guided tours in summer, and workshops year-round. Call the Ketchikan Visitors Bureau or the Misty Fjords Visitor Center, on Mill St., for information about tours to the park (over $100). In town, the **Frontier Saloon** (225-4407), at 127 Main St., has live music Tuesday though Sunday in summer. (Open daily 10am-2am.) The **Arctic Bar** (225-4709), on the other side of the tunnel, is a more earthy fishermen's haunt. (Open Sun.-Wed. 9am-midnight, Thurs.-Sat. 9am-2am.)

Wrangell

An isolated fishing and logging town on the Alaska Marine Highway, Wrangell (RANG-uhl) thrives upon its own small-town atmosphere. In 1986, the hamlet defeated a U.S. Postal Service attempt to install rural delivery—townspeople didn't want to lose the communal endeavor of picking up their own mail. Surrounded by forests and snow-capped mountains, the small city was founded by miners seeking gold on the Stikine River. Their descendants host Alaska's largest Independence Day celebration; the $30,000 blowout includes speedboat racing, log rolling, and fireworks.

Practical Information

Visitor Information: Wrangell Visitors Bureau, Box 1078-IP, Wrangell 99929 (874-3901 or 874-3770), in the A-frame building at Outer Dr. and Brueger St. next to the large totem pole. Open May-Sept. Mon.-Fri. 10am-4pm, Sat.-Sun. if a cruise ship is in port.

United States Forest Service: Ranger District Station, 525 Bennet St. (874-2323), past 2nd Ave. about 10 min. from downtown. Helpful advice on wilderness expeditions to the Stikine River and the LeConte Glacier. Open Mon.-Fri. 8am-5pm.

Alaska Marine Highway: Terminal in town (874-2021 or 874-3711). Usually 1 northbound or southbound ferry per day. To Ketchikan ($18), Sitka ($30), and Juneau ($46).

Taxi: Star Cab, 874-3622.

Car Rental: Rent-A-Dent, Box 1349, Wrangell 99835 (800-426-5243 or 874-3322), in the Thunderbird Hotel on Front St. Used cars from $25 per day plus 10¢ per mile. Must be 21. Save $2 on the car rental if you stay at the hotel.

Laundromat: Cassair Cleaners, 218 Front St. (874-3649).

Pharmacy: Wrangell Drug, 202 Front St. (874-3422). Open Mon.-Sat. 9am-5pm.

Emergency: 874-2000.

Police: Public Safety Building, Zimovia Hwy. (874-3304).

Post Office and Customs House: On Church St., 3 blocks from ferry terminal. Open Mon.-Fri. 9am-5:30pm, Sat. 11am-1pm. General Delivery ZIP Code: 99929.

Area Code: 907.

Accommodations and Camping

Backpackers can sleep for free in **city park,** 2 miles from the ferry. From the terminal, take 2nd St. until it becomes Zimovia Hwy.; keep going until the cemetery. The park is behind the cemetery, next to the ballpark. Bathrooms and picnic tables available. (Unenforced 24-hour limit.)

Harding's Old Sourdough Lodge, P.O. Box 1062, Wrangell 99929 (874-3613). On the other side of town from the ferry terminal. Follow Case Ave. until it ends, then go down the dirt road about 50 yards. A quiet, family-run hotel. Laundry facilities. Singles $40. Doubles $65. Full pension $75 per person. Inquire once you arrive, as rates may vary in your favor. Charters, skiff rentals available.

Thunderbird Hotel, P.O. Box 110, Wrangell 99929 (874-3322). In the center of town, 3 blocks down Front St. The hotel owns the good-sized laundromat next door. Outlet for Rent-A-Dent. Spaciously sterile rooms. Singles $50.70. Doubles (with 1 bed) $58.12.

Stikine Inn, P.O. Box 990, Wrangell 99929 (874-3388). Centrally located on one end of Front St., on the way into town from the ferry terminal. Wrangell's oldest and largest inn, with great rooms overlooking the ocean. Sun.-Thurs. singles $66.60, doubles $72; Fri.-Sat. singles $45.40, doubles $50.

Clark Bed and Breakfast, 732 Case Ave., P.O. Box 1020, Wrangell 99929 (Mon.-Fri. 10am-5pm, tel. 874-2125; Mon.-Fri. 7-9pm and Sat.-Sun. 10am-9pm, tel. 874-3863). Only 2 rooms. Singles $35. Doubles $45. $25 deposit required.

RV Camping: Shoemaker Bay, 5 miles south of downtown on Zimovia Hwy. Water tap; holding tank dump but no electrical hookups.

Food

Get groceries at **Benjamin's** (874-2341), between Front St. and the town harbor. A big turkey sandwich is just $2.79 in the deli section. (Open Mon.-Sat. 8am-6pm.)

The Dockside (874-3388), in the Stikine Inn (see Accommodations). Although dinners complete with salad, rolls, and potato run $10.50-17.50, you can still fill your belly cheaply and enjoy the best view in town with the fishburger and fries ($3.55). Two eggs, bacon, hot cakes, and coffee $5.50. Open Mon.-Sat. 6am-10pm, Sun. 7am-10pm.

The Wharf, across from the Thunderbird Hotel on Front St. Nautical and sheet-rock decor. Soup-and-sandwich special (served Mon.-Fri. $4.30). Burgers $3.25-5.25. Open Mon.-Sat. 6am-3pm, Sun. 9am-1pm.

J & W's, 1 block down Front St. A burger stand with Alaskan prices. Burgers from $3. In stiff competition with the **Snack Shack,** 3 buildings farther down Front St., a similar stand with the same fare and prices.

Maggie's and Son Pizza, 108 Lynch St. (874-3205). $1.50 per slice. Packed with locals. Open daily 11am-8pm.

Sights

Wrangell's **waterfront** supports a steady trickle of fishing trawlers and log booms plying through the large channel. A walk down **Front Street** passes by a few false-fronted buildings and will give you the flavor of the harbor. Ancient **petroglyphs,** the wall drawings of Bering Strait immigrants, can be seen just outside town. Take a left from the ferry terminal on the old Airport Rd., walk 15 minutes along the road, and then follow the signs to the beach. Taking rubbings is permitted. The **Wrangell Museum** (874-3770) contains the history of the local Tlingit tribes and of the city's development. (Open in summer Mon.-Sat. 1-4pm and when a cruise ship is in town. Admission $1, ages 16 and under free.)

Chief Shakes Island and Bear Tribal House (874-3505), on the harbor, draws most of Wrangell's few visitors. If the tribal house is closed, you can always walk around the island and view the seven outstanding totems. (Open Tues. 3:30-6:30pm, Wed. 10am-1pm and 3:30-6:30pm, Sat. 1-2:30pm and 3:30-6:30pm.)

Motorists should explore some of the logging roads outside town. (Rental car agencies do not allow you to drive on these roads.) Bears, moose, mink, and beavers are as plentiful alongside logging roads as billboards are on the highways of the Lower 48. Wrangell's immense **salmon bake** in early June raises money for the July 4th celebration but is a party in itself. The **Tent City Festival,** held in February, frenzily commemorates logging.

Ten float-plane minutes from Wrangell is **LeConte Glacier,** the southernmost active tidewater glacier in North America. A trip to the glacier can cost as little as $35, but usually costs much more. Try **Diamond Aviation** (874-2319) for good, cheap tours.

Petersburg

Proud port of the largest halibut fleet in the world, Petersburg became a boom-town in the late 70s, when someone discovered an insatiable Japanese appetite for salt-soaked halibut eggs. Everyone in town claims to be descended from Peter Buschmann, a Norwegian immigrant who built the first cannery here. The residents of Petersburg are proud of their Scandanavian heritage: *rosemaling* (a Norwegian form of decorative painting) adorns many buildings.

Practical Information

Chamber of Commerce/Visitor Information: P.O. Box 649, Petersburg 99833 (772-3646), in the Harbormaster Bldg. Helpful staff. Open Mon.-Fri. 8am-5pm. Take any problem to the **harbormaster's office** next door (772-3355).

U.S. Forest Service: Petersburg Ranger District Office, P.O. Box 309, Petersburg 99833 (722-3871), upstairs in the Post Office Bldg. on Nordic Dr. at Haugen. Supervises the Stikine Area of the Tongass Forest (write for information on wilderness cabins in the area). Information on trails. Open Mon.-Fri. 8am-5pm.

Airport: Alaska Airlines (772-4255), 1 mile from the Federal Bldg. on Haugen Drive. Helicopter and float planes available for sight-seeing. $60 per person.

Alaska Marine Highway Terminal (772-3858), mile 0.9 Mitkof Hwy., 1 mile from the center of town. To Ketchikan ($28), Sitka ($20), Wrangell ($14), and Juneau ($36).

Taxi: Petersburg Cab (772-3003). Aggressive drivers handle Petersburg traffic with ease. $4 from ferry to Tent City.

Car Rental: Rent-A-Dent (772-4424), at the Scandia House Hotel. $25 per day plus 10¢ per mile.

Employment: Petersburg Job Service (772-3791), on Haugen at 1st. All 3 canneries hire through this agency. Cannery or deckhand openings posted in the window. Line for day labor forms at 8:15am. Open Mon.-Fri. 8am-noon and 1-4:30pm.

Laundromat: Glacier Laundry, downtown on Nordic and Dolphin. Will clean sleeping bags. Open daily 8am-8pm.

Emergency: City Police (772-3838). **State Troopers** (772-3100).

Post Office (772-3121), on Haugen and Nordic Dr. Open Mon.-Fri. 9am-5:30pm, Sat. 9am-noon. General Delivery ZIP Code: 99833.

Area Code: 907.

Accommodations

The only place for backpackers is Tent City, an amiable community of student cannery workers. Stagnant muskeg makes camping closer to Petersburg impossible, and the next nearest campground is miles away.

Tent City, on Haugen past the airport, 2.1 miles from the ferry. Operated, oddly enough, by the cab company (772-3003). If it is full, as it may be in late July and early Aug., ask someone to double up. Toilets, platforms, community fire. $3 per night, $20 per week. 7 days' credit available.

The Narrows (772-3434), across from the ferry. Extremely thin, clean rooms. 10 units with two beds (in a bunk) each, $38. Call for reservations.

Jewels By the Sea, 1106 Nordic Dr. (772-3620), ½ mile north of the ferry terminal. Small B&B with a great view. Bicycles available. Airport or ferry pickup. Singles about $40. Doubles about $45. Try bargaining.

Scandia House, 110 Nordic Dr. (772-4281), between Fram and Gjoa St. Exceptionally clean rooms. Boat and car rental offices based here. Anyone can reserve the hot tub and spa for $7.50 per hour, $6 per person for two or more. Suites $55, plus $5 per additional person.

LeConte RV Park, P.O. Box 1548, Petersburg 99833 (772-4680), at 4th and Haugen. One mile from ferry, 3 blocks from downtown. Full hookup. Rates vary.

Ohmer Creek Campground, Mile 22 Mitkof Hwy. 15 sites. 14- day max. stay.

Food

Grab the seafood here while you can—many local restaurants get their catches from area fishermen. **Hammer and Wikan,** Nordic Dr. (772-4246), has a huge selection of groceries and also sells camping gear, insect repellent, etc. (Open daily 10am-6pm.)

Homestead Cafe (772-3900), Nordic Dr. at Excel, across from the general store. Overwhelming burgers (with potato salad) $3.50-6.25. Dinners (served after 4pm) include fresh seafood, salad, potatoes, and bread ($11.25-14.25). Open Mon.-Sat. 24 hours.

Greens and Grains Deli and Bakery (772-4433), in the center of town on Nordic Dr. 49¢ coffee! Homemade pastries! Salad bar ($3 per lb.)! Open Mon.-Sat. 7am-6pm.

Helse-Health Foods and Deli (772-3444), on Sing Lee Alley off Nordic Dr. Great cinnamon rolls for $1.85. Large pita sandwiches (with havarti, boursin, and other cheeses) $4.75-5.50. Open Mon.-Fri. 9am-5:30pm, Sat. 10am-3pm.

Harbor Lights Pizza, Sing Lee Alley (772-3424), overlooking the harbor. Come here for the incredible view of the dock and the $6-7.50 pitchers of beer. Open daily 11am-11pm.

Pellerito's Pizza (772-3727), across from the ferry. 85¢ per scoop of ice cream. "Louisiana Torpedo" sandwich $2.45. Open daily 11am-8pm.

Sights

This is the best place in the Panhandle to see a fishing town at work. Although none of the town's three canneries is open to the public, you can walk up Nordic Dr. to the boat docks for a close view of longliners, trollers, and trawlers as they unload.

To understand the development of this pristine Norwegian village, head to the **Clausen Memorial Museum,** on 2nd Ave. and Fram St., which shows Native artifacts and a history of fishing techniques. The highlight of the hall is the world-record 126½-lb. king salmon. Outside the museum is the stunning **Fisk Fountain**, dedicated to the fish on which Petersburg thrives. (Museum open daily noon-4pm; Oct.-April Wed.-Thurs. and Sun. noon-4pm. Admission $1.) A **boardwalk** creaks through the muskeg from Tent City to the beach amid a stretch of opulent rain forest.

On the weekend closest to May 17, Petersburg joins the entire world in joyous celebration of Norwegian independence from Sweden. During the **Little Norway Festival,** mock Vikings are as plentiful as halibut eggs.

On the opposite side of Kupreanof Island from Petersburg the weather clears for the tiny and peaceful settlement of **Kake,** home of the world's largest totem pole (132' 6"). Kake is a permanent village of the Tlingit (KLING-kit), who comprise 85% of the population of 600. Across the channel a large population of brown bears roams the outskirts of **Angoon,** another Native village. The economy of this village is still subsistence level, despite the coming of the commercial fishery. The old Native customs survive more strongly here than in other nearby settlements. There are no campgrounds in Angoon, but two hotels provide 18 units of housing for visitors. **Tenakee Springs** on Chichagof Island is a community of wooden houses erected on stilts and connected by plank walkways. The hot springs here have been attracting bathers since the *fin-de-siècle*.

Sitka

Dominated by the snow-capped volcano of Mt. Edgecumbe, Sitka was the center of Alaskan history until the early 20th century. Alexander Baranof, the manager of the Russian-American Company, quelled the bloody uprisings of the native Tlingits by establishing "New Archangel" as the capital of Russian Alaska in 1804. The settlement was Russia's "Paris of the Pacific" for the next 63 years, larger than either San Francisco or Seattle. Visitors from all nations came here to profit from the trade in sea otter pelts and to enjoy the trappings of a glittering society life. After the transfer of Alaska to American hands in 1867, Sitka became the territory's capital from 1884 until 1906.

Practical Information and Orientation

Chamber of Commerce/Visitors Bureau, Centennial Bldg., 330 Harbor Dr. (747-8601 or 747-5940). Open Mon.-Sat. 9am-5pm. No backpacks allowed in building. New Archangel Dancers and Isabel Miller Museum located here as well.

Event Hotline: 747-3739. 24 hours.

U.S. Forest Service: Sitka Ranger District, Tongass National Forest, 204 Siqinaka Way, Sitka 99835 (747-6671), off Katlian St. Open Mon.-Fri. 8am-5pm. Pick up a copy of *Sitka Trails* at the **information booth** in front of the Centennial Bldg. at Lincoln St. Open May-Sept. daily 8am-5pm.

Airport: Alaska Airlines (966-2266). Regular service to Seattle, Anchorage, Juneau, Ketchikan, Wrangell, and Petersburg. To Juneau or Ketchikan $65.

Alaska Marine Highway: 7 Halibut Rd. (747-8737), 7 miles from town. To Ketchikan ($44), Petersburg ($20), and Juneau ($20).

Buses: Sitka Tours runs a shuttle bus and tour guide service from the ferry terminal. Ride into town $2.50; tours $8.

Taxis: Island Taxi, 747-8657. **Haida Cab,** 747-6621. **Sitka Taxi,** 747-5001.

Car Rental: Rent-A-Dent (966-2552), in airport. $34 per day with unlimited mileage, or $6 per hour. Open 24 hours. **Avis** (966-2404), in airport as well. Similar rates.

Laundromats: Homestead Laundromat, 619 Katlian St. (747-6995), near the Ranger bldg. $2 for a shower. Open daily 8am-8pm. **Duds 'n' Suds Laundry,** 908 Halibut (747-5050), near hostel. $1.25 shower. Open Mon.-Fri. 7am-9pm, Sat.-Sun. 7am-10pm.

Pharmacy: Harry Race Pharmacy, 102 Lincoln St. (747-8666), by Castle Hill. Open Mon.-Sat. 9am-6pm, Sun. 10am-3pm.

Post Office: 1207 Sawmill Creek Rd., far from downtown. General Delivery ZIP Code: 99835. In town, try the **substation,** 407 Lincoln (747-6286), in the back of Bayview Trading Co. on Harbor Dr. Both open Mon.-Fri. 9am-5pm.

Area Code: 907.

Sitka inhabits the western side of Baranof Island, 95 miles southwest of Juneau and 185 miles northwest of Ketchikan. The O'Connell Bridge connects downtown to Japonski Island and the airport.

Accommodations and Camping

AYH is having a hard time setting up a hostel in Sitka; it has moved three times in two years. The current edition is in the basement of the Methodist Church. Sitka also has eight **bed and breakfasts** from $30 a night up. The Centennial Building Chamber of Commerce office has rates and phone numbers for all.

Sitka Youth Hostel (AYH), Box 2645, Sitka 99835 (747-8356). In the United Methodist Church on Edgecumbe and Kimsham St. Find the McDonald's, a mile out of town on Halibut Point Rd., and walk 25m up Peterson St. to Kimsham. A small hostel with army cots. No kitchen facilities. One chore required. Lockout 8am-6pm. Curfew 11pm. Members $5, non-members $8.

Potlatch House, 713 Katlian St., Box 58, Sitka 99835 (747-8611). Clean and modern. Singles $52.30. Doubles $64.50.

Sitka Hotel, 118 Lincoln, Sitka 99835 (747-3288). Cheap; clean, quiet rooms. The building itself is a little dingy. 60 units. Singles $35, with bath $40. Doubles $40, with bath $45. Senior citizen discounts available.

Super 8 Motel, 404 Sawmill Creek Blvd. (747-8804). Poor location, but allows pets and has wheelchair-accessible rooms. Singles $60. Doubles $64.

Starrigaven Creek Campground, at the end of Halibut Point Rd., 1 mile from the ferry terminal, 8 miles from town. A USFS campground. 23 sites, pit toilets. 14-day max. stay. Sites $5.

Sealing Cove. From ferry go south on Halibut Point Rd. to Lake St. Follow Lake St. across the bridge to Sealing Cove. 26 RV spots. Water but no electricity. Sites $5.

Food

Pick up your groceries at the **Market Center Grocery,** Sawmill Creek and Baranof St., uphill from the Bishop's House (open Mon.-Sat. 10am-8pm, Sun. noon-6pm), or close to the hostel at **Lakeside Grocery,** 705 Halibut Point Rd. (Open Mon.-Sat. 9am-9pm, Sun. 11am-7pm.) You can also pick up fresh seafood from fishermen along the docks or at **Sitka Sound Seafood** on Katlian St., which occasionally offers fish for retail sale.

The Bayview Restaurant, 407 Lincoln St. (747-5440), upstairs in the Bayview Trading Company. Everything from *russkia ribnia blyood* ($6.50) to a Mousetrap sandwich (grilled cheese, $3.25). Great burgers. A spectacular view of the harbor. Open Mon.-Sat. 11am-7pm.

Sitka Cafe, 116 Lincoln St., next to Sitka Hotel. Mexican, American, and Oriental fare. Beef teriyaki $5, nachos $3.50. Filled when it opens for breakfast at 6am. Open daily 6am-9pm.

Channel Club, 2906 Halibut Point Rd. (747-9916), 3 miles from downtown. The restaurant every native will recommend. Fantastic salad bar with over 30 toppings. Open Sun.-Thurs. 6-11pm, Fri.-Sat. 6pm-midnight.

Sights

The one thing not to miss in Sitka is the onion-domed **St. Michael's Cathedral.** The original was destroyed by fire in 1964, but the present structure was built with the same plans, materials, and tools as the original. Everything inside the church was saved from the fire by locals, including haunting icons by Russian masters and silver and gold vestments. The services are open to the public. (Open daily noon-4pm; 9am-4pm if a cruise ship is in. $1 donation.)

Next, check out the home of the cathedral's builder, the **Bishop's House,** two blocks farther down Lincoln. The Park Service has turned the ground floor into a museum of Sitka's Russian past and restored the upstairs to its 1842 condition. (Open daily 8am-5pm; tours of the upstairs 8am-noon and 2-4pm.) For more of Slavic Sitka, head over to the **Centennial Building** on Harbor Dr. The **Isabel Miller Museum** inside might be skipped, even though Ms. Miller herself is often around to show off her collection of Sitka artifacts. (Open Mon.-Fri. 9am-5pm, Sun. 1-5pm if a cruise ship is in.) Do catch the **New Archangel Russian Dancers,** who perform Russian folk dances every night at 9:30pm, or in the afternoon if (you guessed it) a cruise ship is in. Admission $12.50. The **Sheldon-Jackson Museum** (747-5228), on the Sheldon Jackson College campus, focuses on the transfer of Alaska from Russian to American ownership, a small transaction concluded in Sitka in 1867. It also contains a fine collection of native crafts and Russian relics. (Open daily 8am-5pm; Sept. 15-May 15 Tues.-Fri. and Sun. 1-4pm. Admission $1, free with student ID.)

The other side of town from the college is where history was forged. Historic **Castle Hill,** site of Baranof's Castle and Tlingit forts, grants an incredible view of Mt. Edgecumbe, an inactive volcano known as the "Mt. Fuji of Alaska." It was on Castle Hill that Alaska was sold to the United States in 1867. Stroll down the enchanting, manicured trails of the **Sitka National Historic Park** (Totem Park, as locals call it), at the end of Lincoln St. (747-6281), 1 mile east of St. Michael's. The trails pass by many restored totems on the way to the site of the **Tlingit fort,** where hammer-wielding chieftain Katlian almost held off the Russians in the battle for Alaska in 1804. The park **visitors center** offers audiovisual presentations and the opportunity to watch native artists work at the Native American Cultural Center. (Open daily 8am-5pm.)

Sitka's economy today is built upon its commercial **fisheries.** Wander up Katlian St. to view the processing, or clamber down to the docks at Crescent or Thomsen Harbors. A better taste of local life can be found at the **Pioneer Bar** on Katlian St. (747-3456), whose walls are covered with planks left over from local boats and southeast shipwrecks.

There are excellent **hiking** opportunities in the Sitka area—make sure to pick up the thick booklet *Sitka Trails* at the USFS information booth or office (free). The outstanding trails include the Indian River Trail, an easy 5.5-mile trek up the valley to the base of **Indian River Falls,** and the 3-mile uphill trail to the top of **Gavan Hill.** A fine 3-mile trek from downtown crosses the runway at the Japonski Island airport to the old WWII causeway that heads past abandoned fortifications all the way to **Makhanati Island.**

The June **Sitka Summer Music Festival** ranks as one of the state's most popular events and draws world-renowned musicians to play chamber music. The concerts, held in the Centennial Building on Tuesday, Friday, and some Saturday evenings, can be crowded—reservations are a good idea (prices vary). Contact the visitors bureau for information (747-8601). The **All-Alaska Logging Championships** are held the weekend before Independence Day.

Juneau

Built on a tiny strip of land at the base of noble Mt. Juneau, Alaska's capital city is the only one in the nation inaccessible by highway. This "little San Francisco" mixes and matches Victorian mansions, log cabins, Russian Orthodox churches, "Federal" style *quonset* huts, and simple frame houses with shutters painted in the Norwegian *rosemaling* style. The potpourri of styles only hints at the richness of Juneau's history.

Tlingit Chief Kowee led Joe Juneau and Richard Harris to the "mother lode" of gold in the hills up Gold Creek in October, 1880. By the next summer, boatloads of would-be prospectors had found themselves at work in the already claimed mines. Twenty-five years later Juneau superseded Sitka as capital of the territory of Alaska.

Mining ended in Juneau in 1941, but by then fishing, lumber, and the government had filled in to support Juneau's economy. Today, Juneau exists for the government and tourists. It remains a city of energy and beauty.

Practical Information and Orientation

Juneau Visitors Information Centers: Davis Log Cabin, 134 3rd St. (586-2284), at Seward St. Excellent source for pamphlets on walking tours, sights, and the natural wonders in the vicinity, although you'll have to probe hard for information on accommodations and hiking trails. Open Mon.-Fri. 8:30am-5pm, Sat.-Sun. 10am-4pm; Oct.-May Mon.-Fri. 8:30am-4pm. **Marine Park Kiosk,** Marine Way at Ferry Way (no phone), right by the cruise ship unloading dock. Manned by enthusiastic volunteers armed with pamphlets and information. Open May-Sept. daily 9am-6pm.

U.S. Forest and National Park Services: 101 Egan Dr. (586-8751), in Centennial Hall. Excellent place to watch movies on rainy days. Helpful staff provides free maps for local trails, fishing tips, and reservations for USFS cabins in Tongass Forest. Write for application packet (see Ketchikan Camping). Open daily 9am-6pm; Labor Day-Memorial Day Mon.-Fri. 9am-6pm.

Juneau International Airport: 9 miles north of Juneau on Glacier Hwy. Serviced by Alaska Air, Mark Air, and local charters. **Alaska Air** (789-0600 or 800-926-0333), on Franklin St. at 2nd St., in the same building as the Baranof Hotel. One way to Anchorage ($122), Sitka ($65), Ketchikan ($65). Flights every morning. Check Log Cabin Visitors Center for schedules and routes of all airlines.

Alaska Marine Highway: P.O. Box R, Juneau 99811 (465-3941 or 800-642-0066). Ferries dock at the Auke Bay terminal at Mile 13.8 Glacier Hwy. To Seattle, WA ($190, car and driver $464), Ketchikan ($60, car and driver $150), and Sitka ($20, car and driver $44).

Buses: Capital Transit (789-6901). Runs from downtown to Douglas, the airport, and Mendenhall Glacier. Leaves Marine Park for airport and glacier 5 min. after the hr. every hr. 7am-3pm. From 3-10pm, leaves Marine Park 35 min. after the hr. The fare is 75¢ to all points. **Mendenhall Glacier Transport** (789-5460) runs vans to the airport ($3) and has an excellent, cheap tour of Juneau and Mendenhall Glacier (2½ hr., $7). Departs 10:30am and 2:30pm from the Marine Park.

Taxis: Capital Cab (586-2772) and **Taku Taxi** (586-2121). Both conduct city tours as well as runs to Mendenhall ($50 per 1½ hr.).

Car Rental: Ugly Duckling, 287 S. Franklin St. (586-3825), across from the parking garage. $25 per day, 10¢ per mile. **Rent-a-Dent** (789-9000), at the airport, with free courtesy van pickup. $30 per day plus 100 free miles.

Bike Rental: Alaska Discovery, S. Franklin St. (586-1911), in a booth across from the Marine Park Garage. Mountain bikes $20 per day, $15 per half-day, and $5 per hr. Open daily 9am-5pm.

Camping Equipment: Foggy Mountain Shop, 134 Franklin St. (586-6780), at 2nd. High-quality but expensive gear. Open daily 10am-5pm.

Fishing Hot Line: 465-4116. For more information, call the **Department of Fish and Game** at 465-4100.

Weather: 586-3997.

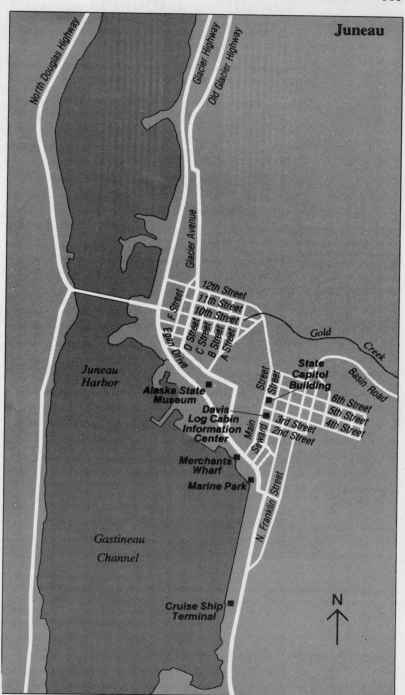

Juneau

North Douglas Highway

Glacier Highway

Old Glacier Highway

Glacier Avenue

12th Street
11th Street
10th Street

F Street

D Street
C Street
B Street
A Street

Egan Drive

Gold   *Creek*

Basin Road

*Juneau
Harbor*

State
Capitol
Building

Street

6th Street
5th Street
4th Street

**Alaska State
Museum**

**Davis
Log Cabin
Information
Center**

Main

Seward

3rd Street
2nd Street

**Merchants
Wharf**

Marine Park

N Franklin Street

*Gastineau
Channel*

**Cruise Ship
Terminal**

N

Laundromat: The Dungeon Laundrette, 4th and Franklin St. Open daily 8am-8pm. Hostel also has facilities.

Pharmacy: Juneau Drug Co., 202 Front St. (586-1233). Open Mon.-Sat. 9am-9pm, Sun. 10am-7pm.

Crisis Line: 586-HELP (586-4337). 7-11pm.

Gay-Lesbian Switchboard: 586-4297.

Ambulance: Juneau/Douglas, 586-1414. **Glacier Valley,** 789-9512.

Hospital: Bartlett Memorial, 3½ miles off Glacier Hwy. (586-2611), north of downtown.

Emergency: 911.

Police: 210 Admiralty Way (586-1414), near Marine Park. Visitors can pick up a permit here to allow 48 hr. parking in a 1-hr. zone.

Post Office: 709 W. 9th St. (586-7138). Open Mon.-Fri. 9am-5:30pm. General Delivery ZIP Code: 99801.

Area Code: 907.

Juneau stands on the Gastineau Channel opposite Douglas Island, 650 miles southeast of Anchorage and 900 miles north of Seattle. **Glacier Highway** connects downtown, the airport, the residential area of the Mendenhall Valley, and the ferry terminal.

Accommodations

If you can't get into Juneau's wonderful hostel, the **Alaska Bed and Breakfast Association,** P.O. Box 3/6500 #169, Juneau 99802 (586-2959), will provide information on rooms in local homes year-round. Most Juneau B&Bs are uphill, beyond 6th St., and offer singles from $40 and doubles from $45. Reservations recommended.

Juneau Youth Hostel, 614 Harris St. (586-9559), corner of 6th and Harris. A glorious hostel: clean, friendly, and well-managed. Make reservations well in advance. 24 bunk beds. Showers, laundry, and kitchen facilities available. Lockout 9am-5pm. Members $7.50, nonmembers $9.50.

Alaska Hotel, 167 Franklin St. (586-1000). A handsome hotel made all of dark wood, right in the center of downtown. Has been restored to its original 1913 Victorian decor. Singles $40, with bath $50. Doubles $45, with bath $55. Hot tubs 8am-4pm $10.40, after 4pm $20.80.

Driftwood Lodge, 435 Willoughby Ave., Juneau 99801 (586-2280). Behind the State Office Building. Courtesy van will whisk you to and from the airport, and sometimes out to Mendenhall Glacier. Singles $49. Doubles $56. Kitchen units $56-63.

Camping

Both campsites within Juneau's vicinity are carefully groomed by the Forest Service (see Practical Information). Both have a 14-day limit.

Mendenhall Lake Campground, Montana Creek Rd. Take Glacier Hwy. north 9 miles to Mendenhall Loop Rd.; continue 3½ miles and take the right fork. A nice view of the glacier, with trails that can take you even closer. 61 sites. Fireplaces, water, pit toilets. Sites $5.

Auke Village Campground, on Glacier Hwy., 15 miles from Juneau. 11 sites. Fireplaces, water, pit toilets. Sites $5.

Food

Juneau tries to accommodate those seeking everything from fresh salmon to processed Big Macs. Travelers on a shoestring should head to the **Foodland Supermarket,** 631 Willoughby Ave., past the Federal Building and near Gold Creek. (Open Mon.-Sat. 9am-7pm, Sun. 10am-6pm.) There you might pack a picnic lunch and head up to the observation platform on the eighth floor of the **State Office Building** (affectionately called the S.O.B. by locals) for an expansive view of downtown, Douglas Island, and the Channel. Seafood lovers should haunt **Merchants Wharf**, next to Marine Park.

Fiddlehead Restaurant and Bakery, 429 W. Willoughby Ave. (586-3150), ½-block from the State Museum. Caters to the sprouts set. Lures mobs with its beef, salads, seafood, exquisite desserts, and fresh Alaskan sourdough. Great sandwiches and burgers on Fiddlehead buns ($3-6). Dinner $7-18. Open Mon.-Sat. 7am-9pm, Sun. 9am-9pm.

Heritage Cafe and Coffee Co., Franklin St. (586-1088), across from the Senate Bldg. An upscale espresso bar, complete with ferns and formica. Best place in town for vegetarians. Excellent coffee $1. Soup du jour and ½-a-deli sandwich $5.25. Open daily 7:30am-6pm.

Vito 'n' Nicks, 299 N. Franklin (463-5051), at 3rd. Surprisingly good pizza, Italian fare. 16" pizza with 8 toppings $24, 1 cheese slice $2. Open Mon.-Thurs. 11:30am-8pm, Fri.-Sat. 11:30am-10pm.

Silverbow Inn, 120 2nd St. (586-4146), downtown. This is the place to bust your budget. French and American cuisine served on antique oak tables in a country-inn atmosphere. Rotating menu. Lunch $7-13, dinner $12-24. Reservations recommended. Open daily 9am-9pm; in winter Mon.-Fri. 9am-9pm, Sat. 5:30-9pm.

Gold Creek Salmon Bake, on Basin Rd. (586-1424), 10 min. from downtown in the historic Last Chance Basin. Beside crystal-clear Gold Creek and the ruins of the original A-J Gold Mine. All the salmon you can eat with all the fixings for $17. Live local musicians nightly. A free bus leaves the Baranof on N. Franklin daily at 6pm. Open daily June 1-Sept. 7 5:30-9 pm.

Sights

Juneau's greatest attraction is undoubtedly the **Mendenhall Glacier,** about 10 miles north of downtown. The glacier, descending from the thousands of square miles of the Juneau Ice Field to the east, glowers over the valley where most downtown workers reside. At the glacier visitors center, rangers explain the relation of the glacier to the ice field, how the moving ice carves out a valley, and why the glacier is now retreating. (Open daily 9am-6:30pm.) The rangers give a good ecology walk everyday at 10:30am. The best view of the glacier without a helicopter is from the 3-mile-long East Trail. To reach the glacier, you can either hitchhike or take the local public bus down Glacier Hwy. and up Mendenhall Loop Rd. until it connects with Glacier Spur Rd. From here it's less than a half-hour walk to the visitors center. **Mendenhall Glacier Transport's** two-and-a-half-hour Juneau tour spends almost an hour at the glacier—a bargain at $7 (see Practical Information and Orientation). Call for arrangements at 789-5460, or meet MGT's representative at Marine Park when the cruise ships are unloading.

Seven miles north of the glacier on Glacier Hwy. is the **Shrine of St. Terese** (mile 23). Although inaccessible by public transportation, travelers with cars can enjoy a startling view of the ocean and a touching shrine far from the madding crowd of tourists.

In Juneau itself, the **Alaska State Museum,** 395 Whittier St. (495-2901), is a good introduction to the history, ecology, and native cultures of "The Great Land." The museum's exhibits are unusually informative on the differences among Alaska's four main native groups: Tlingit, Athabaskan, Eskimo, and Aleut. (Open May 15-Sept. 15 Mon.-Fri. 9am-6pm, Sat.-Sun. 10am-6pm; off-season Tues.-Sat. 10am-4pm. Admission $1, students free.)

The unimpressive **state capitol** building is located at 4th and Main. Tours are offered daily from 9am to 5pm in the summer, but your time is better spent wandering uphill to check out the **St. Nicholas Russian Orthodox Church** on 5th St. between N. Franklin and Gold St. Built in 1894, the church is the oldest of its kind in southeastern Alaska. Services, conducted in English, Slavonic, and Tlingit, are open to the public. One block farther uphill on 6th St. is a 45-foot **totem pole** carved in 1940.

Farther downhill along N. Franklin, the **Historic Senate Building** shelters an atrium with specialty gift shops. The atrium is an excellent place to watch the quotidian antics of Juneau's residents. In nearby **Marine Park,** you can observe the shipping traffic in the channel or, from mid-June to September, listen to free concerts on Friday nights from 7 to 8:30pm.

Finding the best view of downtown is simply a matter of walking to the end of 6th St. and then up the trail to the summit of **Mt. Roberts** (3576 ft.)—a steep 4-mile climb. Miners flocked to "them thar hills" in the 1880s after Joe Juneau and Dick Harris found treasure in Gold Creek. Mining is no longer an active industry in Juneau, but the mines are active tourist sights and frequently host salmon bakes. The **Alaska-Juneau Mine** was the largest in its heyday. **Last Chance Basin,** at the end of Basin Rd., is now Gold Creek's mining museum.

Juneau is one of the best hiking centers in the southeast. In addition to the ascent of Mt. Roberts, a popular daytrek is along the first section of the **Perseverance Trail,** which leads past the ruins of the historic **Silverbowl Basin Mine** behind Mt. Roberts. For more details on this as well as several other area hikes, drop by the state museum bookstore, the park service center, or any local bookstore to pick up *Juneau Trails,* published by the Alaska Natural History Association ($2). The rangers will provide copies of particular maps in this book at the park service center. (See U.S. Forest and National Park Service under Practical Information.)

During winter the slopes of the **Eaglecrest Ski Area** on Douglas Island (contact 155 S. Seward St., Juneau 99801, 586-5284), offer good skiing. ($19 per day, children up to 6th grade $10, grades 7-12 $14. Rental of skis, poles, and boots $17-18, children $14. Call about possible tourist discounts.) In summer, the Eaglecrest "Alpine Summer" self-guided nature trail is a good way to soak in the mountain scenery.

At night, tourists head to the **Red Dog Saloon** (463-3777) on S. Franklin. This bar, with imported sawdust on the floor and folksy frontier sayings on the wall, tries hard to be authentic but winds up as kitsch. It does have live music on weekends, though. Locals hang out farther up Franklin: the **Triangle Club** (586-3140), at Front St., attracts the more hard-drinking set, while young people (as well as the cruise ship crowd) congregate at the **Penthouse,** on the fourth floor of the Senate Building. The **Lady Lou Revue** (586-3686), a revival of Gold Rush days, plays multiple shows daily at the Elks Lodge on Franklin. (Admission $8.)

Near Juneau: Glacier Bay National Park and Preserve

In 1879, when naturalist John Muir became the first white man to see what nature had uncovered in Glacier Bay, he wrote, "These were the highest and whitest mountains, and the greatest of all the glaciers I had yet seen." Crystal boulders float in the 65-mile-long fjords of Glacier Bay, while humpback whales glide smoothly past. **Glacier Bay National Park** currently encloses 16 tidewater glaciers, as well as Mt. Fairweather of the Saint Elias Range. Here you can see with your own eyes what you've probably only glimpsed on *Mutual of Omaha's Wild Kingdom:* gigantic icebergs caving off glaciers and crashing dramatically into ice blue water. Charter flights, tours, and cruise ships all make the spectacular voyage into Muir Inlet, offering close-up views of glaciers, rookeries, whales, and seals.

Because of the sensitive wildlife in the area, the number of people allowed into the park is limited. Visitors should contact the Superintendent, Glacier Bay National Park and Preserve, Gustavus 99826 (697-2230). An **information center** is maintained in Bartlett Cove by the park service. (Open June-Sept. daily 8am-7pm. In winter, call 697-2232 Mon.-Fri. 8am-4:30pm.) Wilderness camping and hiking is permitted throughout the park, and tour-boat skippers will drop passengers off at points designated by the Park Service; you'll have to make arrangements to be picked up later.

Any visit to this park will be expensive. Transportation is the highest cost, but indoor lodging is expensive, too. Plan to stay at one of the **USFS cabins** in the Tongass National Forest; contact the Forest Service Offices in Ketchikan or Juneau.

Backpackers will want to make their way to Glacier Bay through the small town of **Gustavus,** 10 miles from the national park. Round-trip fare from Juneau on **Alaskan Airlines** (800-426-0333) is $60. Surrounded by Glacier Bay, the **Gustavus Inn,** P.O. Box 31, Gustavus, 99826 (697-2255) is only 50 miles by air from Juneau. The inn provides lodging, three meals, transportation from the Gustavus airport, and free use of bikes and fishing gear, all for $100 per night per person (open year-round).

From Gustavus it's a short hitch to **Bartlett Cove** (697-2230), the park headquarters. The campground here has 25 free sites and is rarely full. Limited and expensive accommodations are available at the **Glacier Bay Lodge** (800-622-2042) next to Bartlett Cove. The tourboat *Spirit of Adventure* departs from the lodge for tours of the park's West Arm. (May 27-Sept. 18, 9½ hr., $136; will drop kayakers off for $96.)

Northern Panhandle

North of Juneau, the inside passage grows in magnificence: the mountains become bigger and snowier, the whales and eagles friendlier and more plentiful. The **Alaska Marine Highway** can take you up to Haines ($14 from Juneau, ages 6-11 $8; vehicle up to 15 ft. $35). Sleep on the ferry or stay up all night traveling through this land of many glaciers and soaring peaks.

Haines

In the early 1890s, adventurer Jack Dalton improved an old Indian Trail from Pyramid Harbor up to the Yukon. During the Gold Rush from 1897 to 1899, thousands of stampeders paid outlandish rates for a quick trip into the Klondike. Thanks to the army's improvements on the road during World War II, the **Haines Highway** is now the most traveled overland route into the Yukon and the Interior from southeastern Alaska.

The area's main attraction is the convergence of over 3000 bald eagles (almost double the town's population) on the Chilkat Peninsula's "Council Grounds" from November to January each year. Haines is perhaps the most attractive of the southeast fishing villages. A magnificent granite coastal range offsets the graceful white walls of Victorian Ft. Seward. While Haines lacks the energy of Juneau and Ketchikan or the history of Sitka, it is worth a trip for the scenery alone.

Practical Information

Visitor Information Center: 2nd Ave. near Willard St. (766-2234). Information on accommodations, hiking around town, and the surrounding parks. Make sure to pick up the free pamphlet *Haines is for Hikers.* Free coffee and a place to stash your pack inside. Open June-Sept. daily 8am-8pm.

State Park Information Office: 259 Main St. (766-2292), above Helen's Shop. Ranger Bill Zack can tell you all you need to know about camping in the area, the dangers of bears, and the Chilkat Bald Eagle Preserve. Open Thurs.-Mon. 8-8:30am and 4-4:30pm.

Buses: White Pass & Yukon Motorcoaches, on 2nd Ave. (766-2030), across from the information center in the Wings of Alaska office. Buses leave Haines along the Haines Hwy. on Tues. and Fri. To Anchorage ($173), Fairbanks ($149), and Whitehorse ($71). Open Mon.-Sat. 7am-7pm.

Alaska Marine Highway Terminal: 5 Mile Lutak Rd. (766-2111), 3½ miles from downtown. You can either hitch into town or take the Haines Street Car ($5).

Laundromat: Susie Q's, Main St., just up from the harbor and across from the museum. Open Mon.-Fri. 8am-8pm, Sat.-Sun. 8am-5pm.

Emergency: 911.

Police: 766-2121.

Area Code: 907.

Both the U.S. and Canada have **customs offices** at 42 Mile Haines Hwy. (767-5511 and 767-5540, open daily 7am-11pm). Travelers must have at least $50 or a credit card to cross into Canada, although it is up to the discretion of border officials to decide when this requirement should be enforced.

Accommodations and Camping

Rather than wander 3 miles out of town to the hostel, campers should crash in **Port Chilkoot Camper Park** down 2nd Ave. in front of Ft. Seward.

Port Chilkoot Camper Park, Box 473, Haines 99827 (766-2755). 60 neat campsites for tents ($5.50) and RVs (full hookup $9). Laundromat, showers, telephone available.

Hotel Halsingland, Box 1589MD, Haines 99827 (766-2000 or 800-542-6363). Dollar-for-dollar the best hotel in Haines. Located in the old Ft. Seward officers' quarters. 60 rooms. Singles $30, with bath $54. Doubles without bath (few available) $35, with bath (many) $79. Some rooms have fireplaces or claw-footed bathtubs. Avis car rental located here.

Officer's Inn Bed and Breakfast (766-2000 or 800-542-6363), in Ft. Seward. Similar to Halsingland, but much smaller and just a B&B. Rooms from $55.

Bear Creek Camp & Hostel (AYH), Box 1158, Haines 99827 (907-766-2259), on Small Tract Rd. almost 3 miles outside of town. From downtown, follow 3rd Ave. out Mud Bay Rd. to Small Tract Rd. 22 beds. Kitchen facilities. No curfew. Call ahead for ferry pickup. Members $8, nonmembers $12. Cabins $30. Showers $2.

Campgrounds: Chilkat State Park, 7 Mile Mud Bay Rd. (32 sites), **Chilkoot Lake,** 10 Mile Lutak Rd. (32 sites), and **Mosquito Lake,** 27 Mile Haines Hwy. (10 sites). All sites $5 with water and toilets.

Haines RV Park, P.O. Box 383, Haines 99827 (766-2882). ½ mile west of town on Main St. 92 full-hookup units, $14.

Food

Those wishing to forgo restaurant fare can hit **Howser's Supermarket** on Main St. (open Mon.-Sat. 9am-8pm, Sun. 10am-7pm). The store has a great salad bar with a large pasta selection ($2.49 per lb.).

Porcupine Pete's, Main and 2nd Ave. (766-9199). Great sandwiches from $2.90. The pita pockets ($6.90) make a decent meal. Open daily 10am-7pm.

Bamboo Room (776-9109), 2nd Ave. near Main St., next to the Pioneer Bar. Great breakfast spot, always crowded with fishermen on their way out to the nets. Hot cakes and coffee $3.75, omelettes from $4. Hours vary. Opens at 6am.

Port Chilkoot Potlatch, at the Tribal House of Ft. Seward (766-2000). All-you-can-eat salmon bake with all the trimmings ($17.50). Reservations recommended since tickets are pre-sold to cruise ships. Served nightly 5-8pm.

Fogcutters, 2nd and Main (776-9109). $7.25 all-you-can-eat chili and chicken. Great chili. Open daily 2pm to 7 or 8pm, whenever they run out.

Sights

You will be astonished to learn that **Fort William Seward,** on the west side of town, was once the only army barracks in Alaska. In the middle of the fairgrounds there is a **Totem Village** with a tribal house. On selected nights, the **Port Chilkoot Dancers** do native dance. (766-2160; Mon., Wed., Sat. at 7:30pm. Admission $7, children $4. Tribal House open Mon.-Fri. 9am-5pm, weekends if a cruise ship is in.) In town, the **Sheldon Museum,** 25 Main St., houses Native art and artifacts downstairs and exhibits on the history of Haines upstairs. Movies are shown at 2pm. (Open daily 1-5pm. Admission $2.) The museum serves free Russian tea. Haines is also something of an **artists' colony.** Check out the works of local artists like Jenny Lyn Smith and Tresham Gregg in galleries near the visitor center.

The **Haines Highway,** one of the grandest in the state, winds 40 miles from Haines through the **Chilkat Range** and up through the Yukon Territory in Canada. **Chilkat**

State Park, a 19-mile drive up the highway, protects the largest population of bald eagles in North America—3500 all told. From November through January, travelers can see great numbers of eagles perched on birchwoods in the rivers or flying overhead. **Chilkat Guides** (766-2409), P.O. Box 170, leads four-hour raft trips in eagle season down the Chilkat River. ($55, rubber boots and ponchos provided.) Haines is also home to the **Southeast Alaska State Fair** and the **King Salmon Derby** in late August. The **Winter Carnival** and **Alcan 200 Snowmobile Races** liven up February considerably for those in the area.

Skagway

The *Excelsior* docked in San Francisco on July 15, 1897, bearing gold from the Klondike fields in Canada's Yukon Territory, and Skagway exploded. In less than three months, a one-cabin town had become a port of 30,000, an instant city of gold-seekers eager to plunge 600 miles upland through either the Chilkoot Trail or Skagway's White Pass. The mounted police viewed this mass collection of greed as "little better than a hell on earth . . . about the roughest place there ever was." The stampeders of the winter of 1898 reached the Klondike only in time to work as hired hands—all the claims had already been staked. Today, the population has plunged to 500 and Skagway is as much a gold rush theme-park as someone's hometown. Most of the main street, Broadway, is a National Historic Park, restored to its 1898 condition, and even townsfolk occasionally wear fin-de-siècle garments on tourship days.

Practical Information and Orientation

Visitor Information: Klondike Gold Rush National Historical Park Visitor Center, 2nd and Broadway (983-2921). Walking tours daily at 11am and 3pm. Ranger talks daily at 10am. Special trail information lecture daily at 4pm. Also shows on the hour a film on the gold rush, an excellent introduction to Skagway's history. Open June-Aug. daily 8am-8pm; May and Sept. 8am-6pm. **Skagway Convention and Visitors Bureau** (983-2854), in the City Building, 1 block off Broadway on 7th. P.O. Box 415, Skagway 99840. Open Mon.-Fri. 9am-5pm.

Alaska Marine Highway: 983-2941. Ferries daily to Haines ($12) and Juneau ($22).

Flights: Skagway Air Service (983-2218). Four flights per day to Juneau ($65).

Trains: White Pass and Yukon Route (983-2217), 1 block off Broadway on 2nd. Service to White Pass Summit (round-trip $67), Fraser, and Lake Bennet, on one of the steepest railroad grades in North America. Motorcoach service from Lake Bennet to Whitehorse (train and coach $89).

Buses: Alaskan Express, in the lobby of the Westmark Inn. Two per week to Haines, Anchorage ($185), and Fairbanks ($159).

Taxi: Pioneer Taxi (983-2623). Tour of town $10. Ferry to Broadway $2.

Tours: Frontier Tours (983-2512). Takes backpackers to Dyea for $5 per person (3-person min.). **Skagway Sourdough Tours** (983-2521). White Pass Summit Tour $12.

Laundromat: Klothes Rush Laundry, Broadway and 5th (983-2370). Open Mon.-Sat. 9am-10pm, Sun. 10am-10pm.

Post Office: Broadway and 6th, next to the bank. Open Mon.-Fri. 8:30am-noon and 1-5pm. General Delivery ZIP Code: 99840.

Area Code: 907.

On the same latitude as Stockholm, Skagway is the terminus of the Alaska Marine Hwy. From here, travelers can connect to the Alaska Hwy. by bus or car via Yellowhead Hwy. 2 to Whitehorse via Carcross. Haines is located only 12 miles away by water, but 359 miles away by road. Hitchers would do best to spend $12 on the ferry to Haines and try the more heavily traveled Haines Hwy. to the Interior.

Accommodations

The bunkhouse in Skagway has been usurped by an art gallery. Campers can either shell out $6.25 for sites at **Hanousek Park** on 14th at Broadway (drinking water, toilets, fireplaces; no showers), or head out for the Chilkoot Trail in Dyea, 9 miles from Skagway, to stay at the free ranger-staffed campground there (pit toilets, no drinking water). You should call ahead for reservations at all four of Skagway's hotels.

Golden North Hotel, P.O. Box 343, Skagway 99840 (983-2294), on 3rd Ave. and State St. A splendid hotel, the oldest operating in the state. Each room restored differently to period style, some with canopy beds, claw-footed bathtubs, and the like. Singles $35, with bath $60.

Skagway Inn, P.O. Box 500, Skagway 99840 (983-2289), on Broadway at 7th. Built in 1897 as a brothel, the inn is now thoroughly refurbished and thoroughly respectable. All rooms with shared baths. Singles $48. Doubles $55. Breakfast included.

Sergeant Preston's Lodge, P.O. Box 538, Skagway 99840 (983-2521), at 6th and State. Barracks-like exterior belies such interior luxuries as comfortable rooms and cable TV. Singles $45, with bath $55. Doubles $55, with bath $65.

Irene's Inn, 6th and Broadway (983-2500). Small, clean, unremarkable rooms with shared baths. Singles $31.80, with bath $50. Each additional person $5. Check-in at Sgt. Preston's.

Skagway RV Parks, P.O. Box 304, Skagway 99804 (983-2374), on 4th Ave. at State St. Full hookups, showers.

Food

Campers can pick up last-minute groceries for the Chilkoot trail at the **Fairway Supermarket** at 4th and State. (Open Mon.-Sat. 9am-8pm, Sun. 9am-6pm.)

Northern Lights Cafe (983-2225), on Broadway in the Historic District. The best prices on the block—try the "Mermaid Burger" (halibut sandwich with fries, $5.25) or the monstrous stack of sourdough pancakes ($2.50). Open daily 7am-8pm; May-Sept. 6am-10pm.

Sourdough Cafe, on Broadway between 1st and 2nd. Cafeteria atmosphere vastly improved by the delectable all-you-can-eat spaghetti dinner with meatballs, salad, and garlic bread (served daily 4-8pm $7). Open daily 11am-8pm.

Sweet Tooth Salon (983-2405), on Broadway across from the Sourdough. Sandwiches $3-4. Open daily 6am-6pm.

Pack Train Inn, on Broadway at 4th Ave. Big, fresh sandwiches ($5.25) and occasional health food (fresh carrot juice $3). Open daily 10am-9pm.

Sights

Most of Broadway, which is most of town, is preserved in pristine 1898 form as the **Klondike Gold Rush National Historic Park.** Check out the hourly film *Days of Adventure, Dreams of Gold* at the Park's **Visitor Center** (see Practical Information). Then wander down Broadway to peep at the facade of the **Red Onion Saloon,** on 2nd Ave., Skagway's first bordello. In the good ol' days, each lady marked her availability by placing one of the dolls on a rack downstairs in the appropriate position—prone or erect. Twenty thousand pieces of driftwood cover the facade of the 1899 **Arctic Brotherhood Hall,** an excellent example of Victorian rustic architecture, next door to the saloon.

True gold rush buffs can foxtrot in ecstasy at the **Trail of '98 Museum,** on the second floor of City Hall, at 7th Ave. and Spring St. (Open June-Sept. daily 8am-8pm; May 9am-5pm. Admission $2, students $1.) The new **Corrington Museum,** on 5th and Broadway (983-2580), is more interesting than the city's, but tempts visitors with the ivory store that houses the collection. (Open daily 8:30am-7:30pm. Free.)

At night, go to the Red Onion to hear live jazz (no cover) and then to the *Skagway Days of '98* show in the Eagles Dance Hall at 6th and Broadway. The show, in its 64th year, features song and dance, play money gambling by the audience, and audience-actor interaction. Definitely worth your $7 (983-2234; shows mid-May to mid-Sept. daily at 8pm, during the day if cruiseship is in).

Resurrected from the locomotive graveyards of the West, the renovated **railroad cars** of the White Pass & Yukon Route, built in 1900 at the end of the gold craze, run from Skagway to the summit of White Pass and back. The scenery of this narrow passage is overwhelming. (Trains run May 24-Sept. 27 daily at 9am. Irregular service before May 24. Fare $67, ages under 13 $32.50.) On the way out of town, the tracks pass by the **Gold Rush Cemetery,** where Frank Reid is honored for giving his life to cleanse the streets of local crimelord "Soapy" Smith. Beyond the cemetery and farther out of town stands **Reid Falls,** a gentle waterfall that cascades 300 feet down the mountainside.

Near Skagway: The Chilkoot Trail

In the winter of 1898, nine out of every ten stampeders to the Klondike passed through Skagway, each one somehow moving one ton of gear in the harsh weather. Formerly an Indian footpath, the Chilkoot Trail extends 33 miles from the ghost town of Dyea to the shores of Lake Bennett over the precipitous Chilkoot Pass. The three-to-five-day hike is littered with wagon wheels, horse skeletons, and relics the prospectors left behind, as well as commemorative plaques placed by the National Park Service.

The Chilkoot is considered the best hiking trail in Alaska, but it is extremely demanding. Weather conditions change rapidly, especially in the Summit area; even well into June, avalanches are not uncommon. Be sure to check with the ranger at the visitors center in Skagway for current trail conditions before you leave. Rangers are also usually at the trailhead in Dyea daily from 5-7pm. If you are planning to continue into the Yukon Territory, be sure to call Canadian customs (403-821-4111) before leaving Skagway (Dyea has no phones), and have proof of solvency ($50 or a credit card) before crossing the border.

To return to Skagway, leave the trail between Lake Bennett and Bare Loon Lake and follow the White Pass railroad tracks back to the Klondike Hwy., where hitching is fairly easy in summer.

The Interior

Between the Alaska Range to the south and the arctic Brooks Ranges to the north sprawls Alaska's vast interior, blanketing 166,000 square miles with the nation's most wild and startling terrain. Most of the Interior alternates between low, flat patchworks of forest and marshy, treeless tundra. The drainage of four great rivers has created the sloughs, inlets, lakes, bogs, and swamps that sustain the world's largest waterfowl population. Moose, grizzlies, wolves, caribou, white Dall (bighorn) sheep, lynx, beavers, and hares would all together defeat any human in a plebiscite. The unofficial state bird, the mosquito, outnumbers all other animals in the summer by over 1000:1. (Natives love to joke that there is not a single mosquito in the state of Alaska—they are all married and have kids.) The region is sparsely inhabited, excepting Fairbanks, the state's second-largest city.

Interior Alaska is the home of Athabaskan Native Americans, many of whom still trap, hunt, and fish along the Interior's network of waterways. These nomadic hunters traditionally covered an area much larger than the Eskimos did, following the migration of caribou and the spawning cycles of salmon. Unlike Native Americans in the Lower 48, Athabaskans have not been forced to live on reservations; instead, as a result of the Alaska Native Land Claims Settlement Act, they own their own land. Although many have left their remote villages and traditional lifestyle for Fairbanks and Anchorage, their pride in their physical endurance lives on in their stories and games. Today Athabaskans still compete in dog-sled races and the annual World Eskimo-Indian Olympics, where thousands of spectators thrill to such traditional Native sports of pain and endurance as races involving 10-pound weights tied to participants' earlobes.

Like the rest of Alaska, the Interior is not cheap; high prices are a fact of life up North. On the other hand, transportation to Mt. Denali, Fairbanks, and its environs is relatively easy. Moreover, the region plays hi-lo with natural beauty, from the pinnacle of Mt. McKinley, the highest mountain in North America, down to the wildflowers of the low-lying tundra. Nature, at least, can be enjoyed for free.

Denali National Park

Established in 1917 to protect wildlife, Denali National Park just happened to include within its boundaries the highest mountain in North America. Athabaskan Native Americans have long called this mountain Denali, or "The Great One." One can only hope the Princeton-educated prospector who renamed the peak after Republican presidential nominee William McKinley in 1896 was not trying to translate its original name. From base to summit the greatest vertical relief in the world, Denali stands 20,320 feet above sea level and 18,000 feet above the meadows below. Denali is so big it manufactures its own weather—it is visible for only about 20% of the summer. You can experience the glories of Denali without seeing it, though—the park's tundra, taiga, wildlife, and lesser mountains make any trip worthwhile.

Practical Information and Orientation

Visitor Information: Riley Creek Information Center, Mile 237 on the Parks Hwy. (683-2686 recording, 683-2294 park headquarters), 3 miles past park entrance. The terminus of the shuttle bus service; pick up your bus tokens ($3) up to 24 hours in advance. Maps, free shuttle-bus schedules, free backcountry permits for overnight hiking, and information on campsites, wildlife tours, sled dog demonstrations, and campfire talks. All travelers are asked to stop here for orientation. Denali Park's indispensable publication, the *Alpenglow,* is also available (free). Open in summer for information and bus tokens daily 5:45am-7pm, for campground registration and backcountry permits daily 8am-7pm. Outside the building is a recorded weather forecast and an interactive video information display for the park and nearby services. **Eielson Visitors Center,** another shuttle-bus stop 30 miles into the park, is staffed by helpful rangers who post a valuable calendar on day-to-day sightings of the mountain. Open in summer daily 9am-8pm. **Denali National Park and Preserve,** P.O. Box 9, Denali Park 99755 (683-2686), is the place to write for information on the park. Or consult the **Public Lands Information Center** (see Anchorage Practical Information).

Alaska Railroad: Traffic Division, Pouch 7-2111, Anchorage 99501 (683-2233). Stops at Denali daily in summer on its way to Fairbanks (one way $33; 4 hr.) and to Anchorage (one way $62; 7 hr.).

Bus Service: Denali Express Van, in Alaska Glacier Tours, 405 L St., Anchorage (274-3234). Bus leaves from Anchorage office Tues., Thurs., and Sat. in summer at 6am. Fare $35. **Eagle Custom Tours** (349-6710) stops in front of the hostel in Anchorage daily at 6:30am and reaches the park for $38.50.

Denali Shuttle Bus: leaves from Riley Creek daily 6am-4pm. Tokens ($3) available 24 hours in advance. Annual pass $15.

Medical Clinic: 683-2211, in Healy. Open Mon.-Fri. 9am-5pm.

Emergency: 683-2295.

Post Office: next to Denali National Park Hotel. Open Mon.-Fri. 8:30am-noon and 1-5pm, Sat. 9:30-11:30am; Oct.-May Mon.-Fri. 9:30-11:30am. General Delivery ZIP Code: 99755.

Area Code: 907.

Denali Park is accessible by road, railroad, and aircraft. **Denali Highway,** a 90-mile gravel road leading east from McKinley to Paxson, is your box seat for some of the most striking views of the Alaska Range, and can make you an expert fisherman wherever you cast a line. (Open summer only.) The park entrance is 237 miles

north of Anchorage and 121 miles south of Fairbanks via **George Parks Highway.**
Alaska Airlines (800-942-9911) runs $99 flights to and from Anchorage.

Accommodations and Camping

Any hotel room in or near the park will be expensive. **ARA Outdoor World, Ltd.,**
825 W. 8th Ave., #240, Anchorage 99501 (276-7234), runs the park's tourist services, including the **Denali National Park Hotel** (683-2215), which more resembles
Grand Central Station than it does a wilderness outpost. Nearby are the railroad
station, airstrip, nature trails, sled dog demonstrations, park headquarters, campfire
talks, grocery store, and gas station (all of which, of course, are ridiculously expensive). You pay for the railroad station theme and accessibility to tourist services.
(Open May 20-Sept. 10. Singles $93. Doubles $105. Reserve early.) More rustic accommodations deep inside the park near Wonder Lake are somewhat less expensive.
The best is **Kantishna Roadhouse** (radio phone 345-1160 WQH 23; $70 per night).

Hardsiders are going to have a hard time in Denali. There are few hookups or
dump stations, and driving is allowed on only 12 miles of Denali Park Rd. RVs
can pay $10 per night to park at **Riley Creek Campground** in the middle of it
all—the hotel, the visitors center, the train depot—or park on **Denali Road** outside
the park behind the yellow trash cans for free.

Backpackers are assured a space for free in **Morino Campground,** next to the
hotel, while they wait to get an inside-the-park site or a backcountry permit. Sites
inside the park are distributed on a first-come, first-serve basis, so arrive at the visitors center as early as possible in the morning.

Denali Grizzly Bear Cabins and Campground, Mile 23 Parks Hwy. (683-2696), 6 miles south
of Riley Creek. Wide range of immaculate, restored wood cabins from Fairbanks gold mines
of the 20s and 30s. For more information, write P.O. Box 7, Denali National Park 99755,
or call 488-3932. In winter, write to 5845 Old Valdez Trail, Salcha 99714, or call 488-3932.
Doubles from $49. Triples from $60. Quads from $67. Sites $12, tent cabins $16, electrical
and water hookups $5.

Denali Cabins, P.O. Box 229, Denali National Park 99755 (683-2643), 1 mile south of Denali
Grizzly Bear Cabins and Campground. More rustic cabins, though hot tubs are included.
No baths. Check-out 11am. Cabins sleeping 1-4 people $72. Reservations required.

Lynx Creek Campground, 2 miles north of the entrance (276-7234). The closest private campground. RV sites $14.50, with hookups $18.75. Open May 20-Sept. 17.

Morino Creek, Mile 2.4 on Denali Park Rd., a ¼-mile trail from Riley Creek. The backpackers' staging area. Bear-resistant food locker. Closest water at Chevron station ¼ mile away.
Pit toilets. No vehicles. Just walk in and pitch a tent. As many sites as needed. Free.

Wonder Lake, Mile 85 on Denali Park Rd. You are a happy camper indeed if you reach
the park and Wonder Lake is not full. Spectacular views of Mt. McKinley. Piped water, flush
toilets. No vehicles allowed. Tents only. Sites $10.

Riley Creek, Mile ¼ on Denali Park Rd. Often has the only open sites by mid-morning.
Piped water, flush toilets, and a sewage dump. Sites $10. Open year-round.

Savage River, Mile 12 on Denali Park Rd. Flush toilets and water. Accessible only by shuttle
bus or by a vehicle with a permit. Sites $10.

Sanctuary River, Mile 22 on Denali Park Rd. River water and pit toilets. Accessible only
by shuttle or by a vehicle with a permit. Sites $10.

Teklanika River, Mile 29 on Denali Park Rd. Piped water and pit toilets. Accessible only
by shuttle or by a vehicle with a permit. Sites $10.

Igloo Creek, Mile 34 on Denali Park Rd. River water and pit toilets. Accessible only by shuttle. No vehicles allowed. Tents only. Sites $10.

Food

Groceries in Denali are available at the **Mercantile,** next to the Chevron, for
shamefully high prices—a small jar of peanut butter costs $4.50. *Bring your groceries*

into the park with you. The hotel has an expensive restaurant and an unappealing snack shop. The only eats worth the price are at **Lynx Creek,** 1 mile north of the park entrance (excellent Mexican food runs $6 and up; open daily 11am-midnight), and, of course, the local **salmon bake** at Denali Chalets near the park entrance. (All-you-can-eat salmon, ribs, and beans for $18.)

Sights and Activities

Denali accommodates hardcore and softcore hikers alike. **Shuttle buses** from Riley Creek visitors center leave every ½-hour to various points in the park, including all campsites, Eielson visitors center, and Wonder Lake at the end of the line. Tokens ($3) are available at Riley Creek 24 hours in advance. (A shuttle bus for wheelchair users leaves the center Tues.-Sun. at 9:30am.) Although the 10-hour, 170-mile round-trip bus tour is an excellent way to see the wilds, it's nonetheless an awfully long time to ride along a bumpy road in a crowded school bus. Visitors, especially those with small children, would be wise to opt for either the seven- or five-hour trips leaving from the same point. Once the tour begins, do not remain glued to your seat. The shuttles make frequent stops; live life to the fullest. The first shuttles leave Riley Creek at 6am. The earlier one departs, the better one's chances of seeing wildlife.

Those wishing to get off the roads can take the shuttle anywhere for a day hike. If you plan to spend the night in the park, you must either obtain a **campsite** for $10 or a free **backcountry permit** from the visitors center at Riley Creek. Only two to 12 hikers can camp in each of the 43 zones, so select a few different areas in the park in case your first choice is booked. Many zones require you to carry a black, cylindrical bear-resistant food container, available for free at Riley Creek. You can also obtain topographic maps ($2.50) at Riley Creek.

Catching a glimpse of both the majestic peak and its many creatures takes perfect timing and better luck. You can increase your chances of seeing Denali's denizens by watching for them in their specific habitats. Dall sheep generally cluster near the Igloo and Cathedral Mountains as well as along Primrose Ridge near Savage River in the summer; look for them near Polychrome Pass in the fall. Caribou congregate in alpine meadows in summer, and move to the hills between the Eielson visitors center and Wonder Lake in the fall. Moose can be found almost everywhere, but are especially common during early mornings and late evenings near the Riley Creek Campground, in Savage River, and between Teklanika and Igloo campgrounds. Grizzly bears are everywhere; 200 to 300 live in Denali Park. Though no one has ever been killed by a bear in Denali, you know what they say. If you meet a bear, rangers advise *slowly* backing up and talking slowly and loudly to the bear. Avoid politics—most bears' views are signficantly outside the bourgeois mainstream. Recite Durkheim backwards instead. Running is a recipe for disaster. Rangers also advise hikers to travel in small groups and to talk while hiking to alert bears to your presence. They advise solitary campers to wear bells or play Penderecki recordings for the same purpose. Bells are available at Riley Creek for 50¢.

The best times to see Mt. McKinley, which emerges only about once every three days, are evenings in the late fall (Sept.-Oct.); during the summer, fog usually shrouds "the Weathermaker." In any season, your best chance to view the mountain is to stick to the Wonder Lake Campground. Otherwise, take a shuttle to the Stony Hill Overlook, the Eielson visitors center, or the overlook near the Savage River Campground (at the rise in Sable Pass). The most impressive views of the mountain materialize in the morning and late in the evening. A climb to the summit takes 30 days round-trip and costs thousands of dollars. Bush plane operators from Anchorage, Fairbanks, and Talkeetna can get you close to the summit faster and cheaper, though the price is still steep (about $100 per person). Denali Park Hotel will set you up with a pilot. Scheduled flights from the hotel leave at 4 and 7pm daily, last an hour, and cost $105.

Several rafting companies run the rapids of the Nenana River. **Owl Rafting** (683-2215) runs both a fast-action canyon run and a scenic float. (Both 2 hr. $32. Must be 12. Departures at 9am, 3pm, and 7pm.) They also run a special raft at 5:45pm to the McKinley Resort. The $40 ticket includes a dinner of salmon and ribs as well as a show at the end. (Tickets available at hotel front desks.)

The Park's **Ranger Headquarters,** 1 mile down Denali Park Rd. from Riley Creek, schedules nature hikes and lectures. Lectures take place in the auditorium of the Denali Park Hotel most nights at 7pm. Check the *Alpenglow* for information.

Fairbanks

When Captain E.T. Barnette was stranded on the banks of the Chena (CHEE-nuh) River in 1901, his friend, the Italian miner Felix Pedro, convinced him to settle there. Pedro helped the merchant unload his goods, rounded up clientele, and as an extra precaution, discovered gold one year later. Fairbanks, "The Golden Heart" of Alaska, thus became a boomtown of the utmost magnitude. Incorporated in 1903, the city remained under the control of Captain-*cum*-Mayor Barnette, who named it after his era's Dan Quayle, Indiana senator and future vice-president Charles Fairbanks.

Today, the Trans-Alaska Pipeline carries far more riches through Fairbanks than the gold-inlaid pebbles of mountain streams. The city is now—as it was at the century's turn—largely a service and supply center for the surrounding Bush. To the north, the lonely highway escorts the pipeline to Prudhoe Bay. And to the south, needles of black spruce and carpets of permafrost roll out a green and gold carpet for breathtaking Mt. Denali and the Alaska Range.

Practical Information

Visitor Information: Convention and Visitors Bureau Log Cabin, 550-Q 1st Ave., Fairbanks 99701 (456-5774). Free 1-hr. walking tours of the city with friendly and knowledgeable guides. Pick up their free pamphlet *Fairbanks: Extremely Alaska,* listing tourist offices, transportation services, maps, annual events, activities, and shops. Open daily 8:30am-6:30pm; Oct.-April Mon.-Fri. 8:30am-5pm.

Alaska Public Lands Information Center: 3rd and Cushman St. (451-7352). Exhibits and recreation information. Free daily films. Staff welcomes requests for information about hiking; write to 250 Cushman St., #1A, Fairbanks 99701. Open daily 8:30am-9pm; in winter Tues.-Sat. 10am-6pm. Come after 5pm to avoid the tourist busloads.

Fairbanks Information Hotline: 456-4636. 24-hour recording of festivals and events.

Airlines: Delta (474-0238) flies to the Lower 48. **Alaska Air** (452-1661) goes to Anchorage ($128) and Juneau ($185). **Mark Air** (474-9166) flies to larger Bush towns. Round-trip to Barrow $564.

Alaska Railroad, 280 N. Cushman (456-4155), next to the *Daily News-Miner* building. An excellent way to see the wilderness. One per day May-Sept. to Nenana ($17), Anchorage ($88), and Denali National Park ($33). Ages 5-11 ½-price.

Buses: Alaska Sightseeing Tours (276-7141). $269 to Prudhoe Bay. **Gray Line of Alaska,** 1980 Cushman (456-7742). Similar rates to Bush towns.

City Bus: MACS, 6th and Cushman (456-3279). Three routes through downtown Fairbanks and the surrounding area, as well as one to the North Pole area. Fare $1.50, senior citizens, ages 5-18, and disabled people 75¢, under 5 free. Day pass $3. Pick up a schedule at the convention and visitors bureau.

Taxi: Yellow Cab, Co., 308 Noble St. (452-2121). **Independent Cab Co.,** 452-3375.

Car Rental: Rent-A-Wreck, 2105 Cushman St. (452-1606). $25 per day with 50 free miles, each additional mile 15¢. Must be 21 with credit card. Open Mon.-Fri. 8am-5:30pm, Sat. 9am-4:30pm. You cannot return cars Sun. **Avis** (474-0900) and **Budget** (474-0855) are located at the airport and charge higher rates.

Road Conditions: 456-7623.

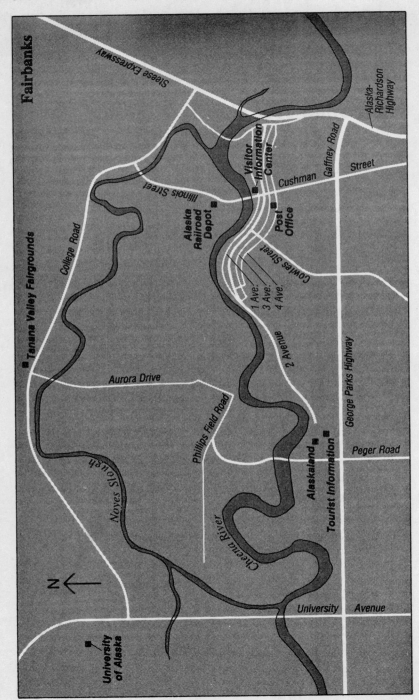

Fairbanks

Camping Equipment: Clem's Backpacking Sports, 315 Wendell (456-6314), near the visitors bureau. **Rocket Surplus,** 1401 Cushman (456-7078). The latest in camouflage fashions. **Apocalypse Design, Inc.,** 101 College Rd. (451-7555), at Illinois. Fast repairs on zippers and straps.

Library: Noel Wein, 1215 Cowles St. (452-5177).

Laundromats: B & C, at University and College (479-2696), in Campus Mall. Open Mon.-Sat. 8am-midnight, Sun. 9am-midnight. Also at 3rd and New Steese (452-1355), in Eagle Mall. Open Mon.-Sat. 8am-10pm, Sun. 9am-noon. Both have shower facilities ($2, with towel $2.50).

Weather: 452-3553.

Help Lines: Rape Emergency, 452-7273. **Poison Control Center,** 456-7182. **North Star Council on Aging,** 452-1735. **VD Hotline,** 474-6000. **Traveler Rescue Service,** 451-0544.

Crisis Line: 452-4357. Also provides contacts with gay and lesbian support groups.

Senior Citizens Center: 1424 Moore St. (452-1735).

Hospital: Fairbanks Memorial, 1650 Cowles St. (452-8181).

Alaska State Troopers: 452-1313.

Post Office: 315 Barnette St. (472-0722). Open Mon.-Fri. 9:30am-5:30pm, Sat. 10am-2pm. General Delivery ZIP Code: 99707.

Area Code: 907.

Accommodations

Cheap accommodations limp in the far reaches of town and are often unsavory. Stick to the hostel or the hotels listed below and avoid flophouses in the outskirts. For referrals to private homestays, track down the **Fairbanks Bed and Breakfast,** P.O. Box 74573, Fairbanks 99707 (452-4967), which provides singles for $36, doubles for $48. Write ahead for reservations.

Fairbanks Youth Hostel (AYH), at College and Aurora, behind the farmer's market. Call operator for new telephone number. A white and green quonset hut with 16 beds. The proprietor has a wealth of information about the area and sets up occasional free raft trips. No lockout. Members $5.25, nonmembers $7.25. Open May-Sept.

Fairbanks Hotel, 517 3rd Ave. (456-6440). Rooms are musty but clean. Ignore the list of prohibited persons in the office. Singles $27. Doubles $33.

Gaffney Hotel, 741 Gaffney Rd. (452-3534). The side of the hotel facing Cushman is a windowless cinderblock wall—the other side is paneled with wood and has sliding glass doors and balconies. Singles $58. Doubles $65.

Cripple Creek Resort Hotel, P.O. Box 101, Ester 99725 (479-2500), 8 miles south of Fairbanks off Parks Hwy. Pleasant atmosphere with an old-style saloon next door. Management takes pride in the fact that the rooms are cleaner than in the old days, but not much fancier. Singles $33. Doubles $38. Triples $43.

Camping

Tanana Valley Campground (456-7956), next to the hostel. Tanana has the least expensive commercial sites in town, but some of them resound with noise from the fairground and busy street nearby. Free showers, laundromat, and grocery store down the street. Sites $9.

Norlite Campground, 1660 Peger Rd. (474-0206). Take Airport Way west off the Richardson Hwy. 2.8 miles; then left on Peger across from Alaskaland. Very expensive. Space usually available. Restaurant, groceries, laundromat, and hot showers. Sites $13, with full hookups $18.

Chena Lake Recreation Area, University Ave. Take Airport Way west from the Richardson Hwy., right on University. The most popular place in town, and invariably full. Arrive early—no reservations. Water, toilets, and picnic tables provided. Sites $5.

Food

Fairbanks throbs with fast-food joints and pleasant, expensive, outdoor bistros. There is little in between. Groceries are available at **Safeway,** University and Airport Way, and at **Pay 'n' Save,** on the other side of town at Cushman and Airport. (Both open 24 hours.) **Green Gopher Produce,** at College and Antoinette, sells the cheapest fresh fruit in town during the summer. (Open Mon.-Sat. 8am-8pm, Sun. 8am-7pm.)

A Moveable Feast, Minnie and Old Steese (456-4701), downtown in Northgate Sq. Great menu for vegetarians; delicious homemade soups and salads, croissant sandwiches, and hot pasta. Small pasta specials are big enough to fill even Hemingway's stomach ($5). Exquisite pastries and desserts (try the Chocolate Rhapsody or Amaretto Almond Cake). Pasta to Go (8 flavors) is a godsend for campers living off hot dogs. Lines form furiously at lunchtime. Open Mon.-Fri. 7am-9pm, Sat. 9am-9pm.

Souvlaki (452-3672), across the bridge from the visitors center. Excellent grape leaves 3 per $1. Lamb casserole and soup lunch specials $3.50. Open Mon.-Sat. 10am-8pm.

Alaska Salmon Bake, Airport Way and Peger Rd. (452-7274), inside Alaskaland. One of the best salmon bakes in town. $14 buys more than enough salmon, halibut, ribs, and fixin's to satisfy a pioneering appetite. Tues. $3 off on halibut. Open May-Sept. daily 5-9pm.

Cafe de Paris, 244 Illinois St. (456-2800). A delightful outdoor café for lunch and breakfast. Pretty expensive: chicken Kiev $9. Open Mon.-Sat. 9am-2pm.

Speedy Submarine Sandwich Shop, 542 3rd Ave. (451-8305). Speedy is straight from Chicago and makes the best subs in Fairbanks. Tuna sub $4. Open daily 10am-6pm.

Food Factory, 36 College Rd. (452-3313), and at 18th and Cushman (452-6348), both downtown. Caters to the Alaskan appetite ("Food just like Mom used to send out for!"). Cheesesteaks $5.75-7. Their *forte* is beer (106 varieties from around the globe). Open Mon.-Thurs. 10:30am-11pm, Fri.-Sat. 10:30am-1am, Sun. noon-10pm.

Royal Fork Buffet, 414 3rd St. (452-5655), at Steese Expressway. One in a national chain of all-you-can-eat restaurants dedicated to stuffing its patrons with tasty cafeteria food. Different menu each day. Dinner $8, Sunday breakfast $6. Open Mon.-Thurs. 11am-8pm, Fri.-Sat. 11am-9pm, Sun. 9am-8pm.

Foodland Deli, Gaffney St. (452-1121), downtown in the Foodland Market. Deli sandwiches ($3.50), hamburgers ($2), and bagels. The cheapest deli around. Open 24 hours.

Cripple Creek Resort, 8 miles south of Fairbanks, in Ester. The restaurant offers a $9 buffet-style, all-you-can-eat halibut and caribou stew meal. Open daily 5-9pm.

Sights

One of Fairbanks's proudest institutions is the **University of Alaska-Fairbanks,** at the top of a hill overlooking the flat city. The **University of Alaska Museum,** 907 Yukon Dr. (474-7505), on West Ridge Hill, presents an excellent jumble of exhibits on subjects ranging from the formation of coal to Russian Orthodox vestments to Native baskets—all in the same room. (Open daily 9am-7pm; May and Sept. 9am-5pm; Oct.-April noon-5pm. Admission $3, senior citizens and students $2.50, families $10. Oct.-April Fri. free.) Another interesting stop at the university is the **Agriculture Experimental Station** where, with the aid of the long summer days, cabbages grow to the size of large subwoofers. Also at the university, the **Large Animal Research Station** offers tours on Tuesdays and Saturdays at 1:30 and 2:30pm ($2). The Student Activities Office in the **Wood Campus Center** posts listing of movies ($3-5), outdoor activities, and occasional music fests.

Alaskaland, P.O. Box 1267, Fairbanks 99707, on Airport Way, is a poor man's arctic Disneyland. What it lacks in rides, it makes up for with gift shops, fake cancan shows, pioneer homes relocated from old Fairbanks, gunfights, a sternwheel riverboat, and a pioneer museum. Fortunately, the park is free. Although it may please kids, Alaskaland is essentially a tourist trap.

View a technological wonder of the world, the **Trans-Alaska Pipeline,** on the Steese Hwy. heading out of Fairbanks. The pipeline was elevated to protect the tundra's ecological system. (Overcome by his new-found passion for the environment, George Bush noted that caribou love the pipeline so much they even rub themselves up against it.) Or take the **Riverboat Discovery** (479-6673) on a four-hour tour down the magnificent Chena River to the Tanana River past Athabaskan summer fish camps. During the trip, the captain and his crew unleash a relentless torrent of history. The riverboat leaves the docks on Dale Rd. (off Airport Way) at 8:45am and 2pm daily (June-Aug.). (Fare $25, ages 12-18 $22.50, under 12 $17.)

Fairbanks harbors many art galleries but few artists. **Artworks,** 3677 College Rd. (479-2563), **Fine Arts Center,** Art Dept., #307 (456-7015), and **New Horizons Gallery,** 815 2nd Ave. (456-2063), all rise above the Elvis-on-velvet genre, but only by degrees. None charges admission.

Outside town lie all sorts of trivialities. The **Dog Mushers Museum,** at Mile 4 Farmer Coop Rd. (457-6528), is the canonic statement on the subject. **Pedro's Monument** marks the original site of Pedro Felix's 1902 gold discovery at Mile 16 Steese Hwy.

Entertainment

With nothing but black spruce to keep them company in the surrounding tundra, Fairbanksans head to the bars at night. Expect stiff drinks and boisterous rugged types fresh from the North Slope oil fields. UAF students head for the **Howling Dog Saloon,** 11½ miles down Steese Hwy. (457-8780), for the live rock 'n' roll scene. (Open Tues.-Sun. 5pm-5am.) At some of the downtown bars, rowdiness flirts with violence.

Sunset Inn, 345 Old Richardson Hwy. (456-4754). Looks like a warehouse, but since Fairbanksans need only the bare necessities (drinks, dance floor, pool tables), it's usually jampacked. Live top-40 dance music. Open Wed.-Thurs. and Sun. 10pm-3:30am, Fri.-Sat. 9:30pm-4am.

Senator's Saloon, Mile 1.3 on Chena Pump Rd. (479-8452), in the Pump House Restaurant. Boasts the only oyster bar in Fairbanks. Take drinks out to the deck and watch float planes land and river boats whiz by. Open Sun.-Thurs. 11am-1am, Fri.-Sat. 11am-2am.

The Roof, Airport Way (479-3800), in the Center. A private comedy club with a formal ambience. Open to the public Fri.-Sat. only.

Uncles, at Terminal and Illinois. $1 drafts and cheesy cover bands on weekend nights. Open daily 11am-1am.

Seasonal Events

The best time to visit the city is in July—citizens don Gold Rush costumes for **Golden Days,** a celebration of Felix Pedro's discovery of gold in July 1902. Parades, sales, and many other gala events highlight the festivities. Watch out for the traveling jail; if you haven't purchased a button commemorating the event, you may be taken prisoner, and sometimes you pay a steep price to get out. Buttons can be purchased at most stores and businesses in town. But the adventurer might as well stay on board the jail—it's a free ride and it goes all over Fairbanks. For details, write the Fairbanks Chamber of Commerce, P.O. Box 74446, Fairbanks 99707 (452-1105).

The **Tanana Valley Fair** (452-3750), in the second week of August, features many shows and competitions. Follow the line of cars down College Rd. to the fairgrounds. (Admission $4, senior citizens $3, ages under 12 $2; $25 family pass covers all family members each day of the fair.)

For a sports spectacular with a local topspin, see the **World Eskimo-Indian Olympics,** P.O. Box 2433, Fairbanks (452-6646). At the end of July, Natives from all over Alaska compete in shows of strength and endurance, all the while entertaining one another with ancient stories and traditional dances.

In June the **Yukon 800 Marathon Riverboat Race** sends 20 lunatics in 16-foot trawlers 800 miles up and down the mighty Yukon, beginning and ending in Fairbanks. Contact Fairbanks Outboard Association, P.O. Box 340, Fairbanks 99707

(452-6347). A few days later comes the **Nuchalawogya Festival,** three days of fascinating Athabaskan culture. Contact Tanana Native Council, P.O. Box 93, Tanana 99777 (366-7160) for exact dates.

Near Fairbanks

Fairbanks is, culturally speaking, a C-major triad amid the atonality of the deep Interior wilderness. If you seek a break from city life and have conquered Mt. McKinley, dangle your feet in the plentiful lakes and hot springs nearby. Since many of the recreational lakes are continually stocked with fish, casting lines can be a fully predictable sport.

Two major roads lead south of Fairbanks. George Parks Highway heads southwest by Denali National Park, and Richardson Highway runs to Valdez in the Prince William Sound. Take George Parks Hwy. south 60 miles to the state's **agricultural areas.** Grain crops planted on land bought from the state for next to nothing thrive on the healthy soil and long summer sun.

Lakes

The **Chena River Recreation Area,** at Mile 26-51 on Chena Hot Springs Rd., covers 254,080 acres of fishing, hiking, canoeing, and camping around the Upper Chena River and Chena Lakes. Rentals can be found right on the lake: canoes $6 per hour, rowboats $8 per hour, sailboats $10 per hour, fishing rods $2 per day. The 78 campsites, some of which offer disabled access (off Laurence Rd.), are free. Hiking trails include: **Granite Tors** (trailhead at Mile 39 campground), a 12-16 mile round-trip hike to granite rocks—great for overnight campouts; **Angel Rocks** (starting at Mile 48.9 campground), an easy 3½-mile trek through breathtaking wilderness; and **Chena Dome Trail** (beginning at Mile 15.5), a more remote 29-mile adventure overlooking the river valleys. There is also a shooting range at Mile 36.5. (Admission $1 per person, $3 per vehicle.)

Harding Lake (Mile 42 on Richardson Hwy.), **Birch Lake** (Mile 48 on Richardson Hwy.), and **Quartz Lake** (Mile 86.2 on Richardson Hwy.) are each an unlucky fisherman's dream. The state stocks the lakes with salmon and trout. Boat ramps are provided at each lake, and small boats can be rented at Quartz and Harding ($7 per hr.). Campsites are available only at Harding and Quartz Lakes (free).

Hot Springs

Fifty-seven miles northeast of Fairbanks on Chena Hot Springs Rd., the **Chena Hot Springs Resort** allows you the chance to go soak your head—or body. Expect fine fishing near this inn once the water temperature drops after the spring snows melt. Handsome hiking trails are nearby. The chalet accommodations are a bit steep (singles with half-bath $48, with full bath $58; doubles $68-78), although pool admission is included. Non-patrons may use the pool for $5.50, ages under 13 $4.50. There are also tent and RV campsites in the area. (Sites $5. For reservations, write 110 Antoinette St., Fairbanks 99701, or call 452-7867. Open Mon.-Fri. 10am-3pm.) On the way to the hot springs stands the **Two Rivers Lodge and Restaurant,** Mile 16 Chena Hot Springs Rd. (488-6815). In a rustic cove of pine trees near a scenic pond, this restaurant is a great place for succulent ribs (cooked on a big grill) and Alaskan specialties. (Open Wed.-Sun. 6-11pm.)

The **Arctic Circle Hot Springs** (520-5113), discovered in 1893, are three hours north of Fairbanks on Steese Hwy. The **hostel** on the fourth floor charges $15 for bunk accommodations, $35 for a room. Several **campgrounds** line Steese Hwy. nearby, where the scenery is brain-shattering. Gaze up at **Eagle Summit** while diving into the Olympic-sized swimming pool or indulging yourself at the ice cream parlor. On June 21 and 22, those on the peak can watch the midnight sun cha-cha across the horizon without ever setting.

Cripple Creek Resort

Seven miles south of Fairbanks (Mile 351.7 on the George Parks Hwy.) lies the drunkard's dream of Cripple Creek Resort, a reconstructed turn-of-the-century village built with all the creature comforts of the 1990s. This quiet little town with reasonable prices and a measure of authenticity (the general store sells fresh reindeer meat) comes as welcome relief from the overpriced gift shops of Alaskaland.

A bus makes the circuit of 10 Fairbanks hotels before heading south to the resort. To make the necessary reservations (round-trip $4), call 479-2500. The all-you-can-eat buffet ($12, with crab $18) lines up such local delicacies as reindeer stew (sorry, Rudolf) and Alaska Dungeness Crab. Dinner is served under the roof of a charming hotel designed to resemble an old miners' bunkhouse. (Singles $33. Doubles $38. Triples $43. Continental breakfast included.) After-dinner entertainment takes two forms. The *Crown of Light,* a film shown twice per night in the Firehouse Theatre, spectacles the aurora borealis on a giant 30-foot screen while symphonic music plays over the speakers. After the film, sidle through the swinging doors onto the sawdust floor of the **Malemute Saloon,** and watch the can-can dancers strut their stuff stuff. The cost of buffet dinner and show, including drinks, gratuity, and transportation, is $24 per person.

Campers can park their RVs a minute's walk from the saloon for $5 per night. A sewage dump and water are available.

While rowdy young travelers looking for a rocking party gravitate toward the UAF saloons in town, families and older couples will find Cripple Creek just their speed. Call or write for reservations at least a few days in advance (Cripple Creek Resort, P.O. Box 109, Ester 99725; 479-2500).

North Pole

Yes, Paula, there is a town called North Pole. It's just 13 miles south of Fairbanks on Richardson Hwy., and its post office receives thousands of letters each Christmas. Unfortunately for Santa and the elves, the town's population has doubled in the last four years. Four shopping malls now dot the landscape, and a monstrous overpass guards Badger Road from the perils of the highway.

The only place of any interest to most tourists is **Santa Claus House** (488-2200), just off (inevitably) Santa Claus Lane. The world's largest Santa Claus statue guards the door. The house is packed with expensive trinkets and souvenirs, so stay outside and marvel at the colorful Christmas murals. (Open May-Dec. daily 8am-7pm.)

At Mile 11 on Richardson Hwy., **Apple Joe's Supper Club,** P.O. Box 186, Fairbanks 99707 (488-6611), offers unbeatable prime rib and lobster (it's anybody's guess how they swam that far). Joe's entrees start at $10.50.

Nenana

Nenana (nee-NAN-nuh) lies 53 miles south of Fairbanks on George Parks Hwy. Once the end of the Alaska Railroad, and situated at the confluence of the Tanana and Nenana Rivers, the town is now famous for the **Nenana Ice Pool.** Alaskans and residents of the Yukon Territory, bored out of their skulls during the long winter months, bet on the exact minute when the ice will give out, thereby dislodging a large tripod ceremoniously stuck into the ice. The pot regularly amounts to over $115,000. Today this tradition is just one of the events at the **Nenana Ice Classic,** a festival that attracts people from far and wide. Even in the off-season you can see the famous tripod that houses the timing device for the big event. Beware of locals who try to sell you a ticket or a trip in advance. For more reliable information on the event, write P.O. Box 272, Nenana 99760 (832-5446). The town's nightlife revolves around the two ornery-looking corner bars next to the train station. No hotels are of note, and the nearest campgrounds are another 20 miles south on George Parks Hwy. The **Alaska Railroad** stops here on its way to Anchorage.

Delta Junction

Farmers and buffalos duke it out at Delta Junction, 97 miles south on Richardson Hwy. The scuffle has been settled as a draw; the farmers' barley and the buffalo (brought here in the early part of the century) have been relegated to opposite sides of the central road. Planting programs, studies of bison chips, and continuous work by the government and farmers have worked toward keeping the bison on their side of the street. The **Delta Agriculture Project,** well over 50,000 acres now, will harvest its ninth major crop in 1989. The **Delta Youth Hostel (AYH)** is located 3 miles off the road from Mile 272. (Open May-Sept. For information, call 895-5074 Mon.-Fri. 9am-5pm. Members $5. Nonmembers $7.) **Big Delta Historic Park,** near Delta Junction, is the home of **Rika's Roadhouse,** a restored roadhouse full of genuine pioneer spirit.

Eagle

Eagle started as a telegraph post, and today survives as a petroleum restaurant for the few boats taking their chances on the Yukon. The history and socio-religious chemistry of this miniscule town are described with great sensitivity and detail in John McPhee's *Coming Into the Country.* The author devoted over 200 pages to Eagle's 150-odd residents. **Eagle Trading** offers $50 rooms, all looking out over the river. The Bureau of Land Management maintains laundry facilities, showers, campsites, and, surprisingly, full RV hookups on the banks of the Yukon. The town is 250 miles northwest of Fairbanks, and 12 river-miles from the Canadian border. More information is available at the **Village Store** (547-2270), or from the ranger station for the **Yukon-Charley Rivers National Preserve** (P.O. Box 64, Eagle 99738; 547-2233).

Tok

At Delta Junction, the Alaska Hwy. breaks off from Richardson Hwy. on its way toward the Yukon and British Columbia. One hundred miles southeast of Delta, the town of Tok (TOKE) puffs away at Alaska Hwy.'s Anchorage turn-off. Historically a trading center for Athabaskans, today Tok is primarily of interest to travelers on the Alaska Hwy. who are deciding whether to head for Fairbanks or Anchorage. Make your decision at the **Tok Youth Hostel (AYH),** 1 mile south along Pringle Dr. from Mile 1322 of the Alaska Hwy. (Members $5.50, nonmembers $8.50. Open May-Sept.) The hostel is in fact just a big canvas tent. The **Stage Stop Bed and Breakfast** rents a great cabin and a free stable for your horse for $35. (Write P.O. Box 69, Tok 99780, or call 883-5338.) **Fast Eddy's Pizza** warms decent pizza (from $13) but better showers and washing machines. (Mile 1313; 883-2382). **Christochina's Trading Post** (822-3366), Mile 32.7 Tok Cut-off, has full RV hookups, *free* tenting, and great sourdough. (Post open daily 6am-11pm.) While in Tok, you can walk the **Eagle Trail,** a great short hike just 2 miles from downtown, or pay homage to the mighty **Tanana River** only 1 mile away. Tok's **visitors center** is on the highway; it shares the 883-5667 line with the hostel.

The Bush

Nome, Bristol Bay, Kotzebue, Bethel—all Alaskans know of these places, few have glimpsed them. This is the Alaska where polar bears still ride the icefloes. This is the Alaska where cannery workers and oil drillers flock to earn money, and then have nowhere to spend it. Known variously as the Country, the Wilderness Rim, and the Bush, this vast expanse of harsh tundra and jagged coastline is only occasionally disturbed by small Native settlements, narrow landing strips, and other insignificant signs of human presence. These many millions of acres fill the northeast, northwest, and southwest quadrants of the state.

Each area of the Bush has its own distinctive features. The Southwest is characterized by its many lakes, ponds, and sloughs, and by amazing Bristol Bay, where the breeding salmon draw brown bears in droves. Nome, on the Bering Sea, is a gold town on the tundra. Arctic Alaska is frozen with permafrost, supporting polar bears, walrus, caribou, bowhead whales, and "bird-sized" mosquitoes. Wherever you go, be prepared for rough and inhospitable country, and always give the right-of-way to bears.

Transportation through these regions is expensive. Tour outfitters flourish, ready and willing (for a steep price, of course) to lead you into the wilds to fish, hunt, canoe, kayak, camp, photograph, and explore. "Fly-in" fishing trips (usually $100-300) include round-trip airfare, accommodations, meals, fishing license, and equipment. A one-day tour to Barrow from Anchorage runs $381; a two-day tour to Nome and Kotzebue $442. Contact **Mark Air**, P.O. Box 196769, Anchorage 99519 (243-6275) or **Gray Line of Alaska**, 547 W. 4th Ave., Anchorage 99501 (277-5581). Regular air service is more expensive and entails planning your own itinerary and finding lodgings. Always reserve in advance to get supersaver fares. In addition to Mark Air, **Alaska Airlines** (243-3300 in Anchorage) and **Reeve Aleutian** (243-4700) fly into most of the larger Bush communities; **Ryan Air Service** (248-0695) serves a number of the smaller towns. Hanging around small airports such as Merrill Field in Anchorage is another possibility for finding a flight.

Some of the best places for making big Alaskan money are in the Bush; Bristol Bay canneries, Unmak Island trawlers, and Barrow's oil base among them. It is common practice for employers (except small-time commerical fishermen) to fly employees to these areas once they have hired them in Anchorage or Fairbanks. Anyone who offers you a job in the Bush without transportation is probably a charlatan.

Southwest Alaska

Southwestern Alaska's Bering Sea coast, inaccessible by road, comes to life in a few small, coastal Native villages. The immense flatland is the home of the Aleut and Eskimos, who live off the land as their ancestors did. The area's thousands of lakes, ponds, and sloughs, and the great **Bristol Bay,** provide most of the world's sockeye salmon. Thousands of commercial fishermen from around the world come here in June and stay until the salmon run ends in early August. The villages offer many opportunities for working in canneries.

Dillingham, on the northern shore of Bristol Bay, and **King Salmon** are good bases for exploration. King Salmon is the gateway to **Katmai National Monument,** an area scarred by the second greatest volcanic eruption in recorded history. Surrounded by spectacular ocean bays, fjords, and volcanic crater lakes, the ash-covered valley still jets columns of steam into the air, earning the sobriquet "Valley of Ten Thousand Smokes." Mark Air flies to King Salmon, the staging area for Katmai treks, twice weekly (round-trip from Anchorage $241 with 30-day advance purchase). **Bethel,** farther north on the Yukon Delta, is the commercial center of the area. Once among the largest Native villages in Alaska, Bethel is now home to more non-Natives than Natives. Mark Air flies to Bethel (round-trip from Anchorage $241 with 30-day advance purchase).

Nome

One of the largest Bush towns, Nome boomed during the 1897-98 gold rush, and folks still dig ore today. Visit the **Carrie McLain Museum** on Front St. (443-2566) when it's too cold to venture into the Bush. There are exhibits on the Bering Land Bridge, Eskimo culture, and the Gold Rush, as well as a fine collection of photographs of northwestern Alaska dating from the beginning of the century. (Open Tues.-Sat. 11am-3pm and 6-8:30pm.)

The 1000-mile **Iditarod Trail** from Anchorage is not the easiest way to reach Nome, but in February, the traffic thickens for the arduous Iditarod Trail Dog Sled Race. Following the trail of a musher who once carried life-saving serum to combat an epidemic in Nome, the race currently attracts participants from all over the world. The **Midnight Sun Festival** in June includes Eskimo dancing, baby contests, a waterskipping competition, and the daffy Nome River Raft Race. For more information, contact the **Nome Convention and Visitors Bureau**, P.O. Box 251, Nome 99762 (443-5535; open Mon. 8:30am-5pm, Tues.-Fri. 8:30am-6:30pm, Sat. 10:15am-6:30pm). Alaska Airlines flies to Nome (round-trip from Anchorage $310 with 30-day advance purchase).

Arctic Alaska

Arctic Alaska coldly embraces everything north of 67°30'. This inhospitable environment rests gingerly on a layer of permafrost. Numerous lakes dapple the land, the result of snowmelt unable to penetrate the permafrost. The region's sand dunes, deserts, and tundra-bred wild flowers may shatter your preconceptions about the Arctic.

The population of Arctic Alaska is almost entirely Native. Contemporary society has made its mark in the powerful Native-owned corporations (at least one has made the Fortune 500), formed in 1971 by the statewide Alaska Native Land Claims Settlement Act. Membership in a corporation has allowed many Natives to maintain their way of life without the economic pressures that have affected Native Americans elsewhere.

Barrow is the world's largest Eskimo village and a focal point for Native-rights action. It may be a modern city in the Alaskan sense of the word, but the Eskimos have not forgotten their customs. In April and May, villagers carry on the tradition of the whale hunt, both to preserve the culture and to eat. The entire community participates, some hunting, some hauling, others carving up the whale (a bowhead whale can feed entire villages, even today).

East of Barrow lies **Prudhoe Bay,** where the crude oil from the north slope begins its 800-mile journey down the pipeline to Valdez. South and east of Prudhoe Bay is the huge **Arctic National Wildlife Refuge,** home of grizzly, black, and polar bears, along with caribou, moose, and other citizens of the ice republic.

While **Dalton Highway** runs along the pipeline from Fairbanks to Barrow and Prudhoe Bay, it is only open to Disaster Creek (Milepost 211) for the general public. Permits are needed to travel farther. They are available from the Dept. of Transportation, 2301 Peger Rd., Fairbanks 99701 (451-2209). Those who need to say they've entered the Arctic can drive 8 hours from Fairbanks to **Coldfoot** (678-9301), Mile 175, the only hotel on the Dalton and 60 miles past the Circle. Rooms and full RV hookups are predicably expensive. Guests do, however, get the chance to meet Dick Mackey, hotel proprietor and winner of the 1987 Iditarod by one minute. The lifting and falling course of the Dalton periodically brings into sight phantasmagoric configurations of river, pipeline, and pump station.

Kotzebue is the commercial center of a 43,000-square-mile area in western Alaska. It is also the home of the **Kotzebue National Forest** (consisting of one tree). The **Ootukahkuktuvik Museum** ("place having old things") presents old whaling guns, old Russian beads from trading history, and other old things.

. . . Now days are dragon-ridden,
The nightmare rides upon sleep . . .

INDEX